DOMESDAY BOOK

Dorset

History from the Sources

DOMESDAY BOOK

A Survey of the Counties of England

LIBER DE WINTONIA

Compiled by direction of

KING WILLIAM I

Winchester
1086

DOMESDAY BOOK

general editor

JOHN MORRIS

7

Dorset

edited by

Caroline and Frank Thorn

from a draft translation prepared by

Margaret Newman

PHILLIMORE
Chichester
1983

1983
Published by
PHILLIMORE & CO. LTD.
London and Chichester
Head Office: Shopwyke Hall,
Chichester, Sussex, England

ISBN 0 85033 489 6 (case)
ISBN 0 85033 490 X (limp)

Printed in Great Britain by
Titus Wilson & Son Ltd.,
Kendal

DORSET

Introduction
The Exeter Domesday (Introduction)
Exon. Sample

The Domesday Survey of Dorset

Introductory Notes
General Notes
Exon. Notes and Table 'D'
Appendix
Persons Index
Places Indices
Maps and Map Keys
Systems of Reference
Technical Terms

History from the Sources
General Editor: John Morris

The series aims to publish history
written directly from the sources
for all interested readers, both
specialists and others. The first
priority is to publish important
texts which should be widely
available, but are not.

DOMESDAY BOOK

The contents, with the folio on which each county begins, are:

Supplementary volume (35) BOLDON BOOK

Domesday Book is termed *Liber de Wintonia* (The Book of Winchester) in column 332c

INTRODUCTION

The Domesday Survey

In 1066 Duke William of Normandy conquered England. He was
crowned King, and most of the lands of the English nobility were soon
granted to his followers. Domesday Book was compiled 20 years later.
The Saxon Chronicle records that in 1085

> at Gloucester at midwinter ... the King had deep speech with his counsellors
> ... and sent men all over England to each shire ... to find out ... what or how
> much each landholder held ... in land and livestock, and what it was worth ...
> The returns were brought to him.[1]

William was thorough. One of his Counsellors reports that he also sent a
second set of Commissioners 'to shires they did not know, where they
were themselves unknown, to check their predecessors' survey, and
report culprits to the King.'[2]

The information was collected at Winchester, corrected, abridged,
chiefly by omission of livestock and the 1066 population, and fair-
copied by one writer into a single volume. Norfolk, Suffolk and Essex
were copied, by several writers, into a second volume, unabridged, which
states that 'the Survey was made in 1086'. The surveys of Durham and
Northumberland, and of several towns, including London, were not
transcribed, and most of Cumberland and Westmorland, not yet in
England, was not surveyed. The whole undertaking was completed
at speed, in less than 12 months, though the fair-copying of the
main volume may have taken a little longer. Both volumes are now
preserved at the Public Record Office. Some versions of regional
returns also survive. One of them, from Ely Abbey,[3] copies out the
Commissioners' brief. They were to ask

> The name of the place. Who held it, before 1066, and now?
> How many *hides*?[4] How many ploughs, both those in lordship and the men's?
> How many villagers, cottagers and slaves, how many free men and Freemen?[5]
> How much woodland, meadow and pasture? How many mills and fishponds?
> How much has been added or taken away? What the total value was and is?
> How much each free man or Freeman had or has? All threefold, before 1066,
>   when King William gave it, and now; and if more can be had than at present?

The Ely volume also describes the procedure. The Commissioners took
evidence on oath 'from the Sheriff; from all the barons and their
Frenchmen; and from the whole Hundred, the priests, the reeves and
six villagers from each village'. It also names four Frenchmen and four
Englishmen from each Hundred, who were sworn to verify the detail.

The King wanted to know what he had, and who held it. The
Commissioners therefore listed lands in dispute, for Domesday Book
was not only a tax-assessment. To the King's grandson, Bishop Henry of
Winchester, its purpose was that every 'man should know his right and
not usurp another's'; and because it was the final authoritative register
of rightful possession 'the natives called it Domesday Book, by analogy

---

[1] Before he left England for the last time, late in 1086.   [2] Robert Losinga, Bishop of Hereford
1079-1095 (see *E.H.R.* 22, 1907, 74).   [3] *Inquisitio Eliensis,* first paragraph.   [4] A land unit,
reckoned as 120 acres.   [5] *Quot Sochemani.*

from the Day of Judgement'; that was why it was carefully arranged by Counties, and by landholders within Counties, 'numbered consecutively ... for easy reference'.[6]

Domesday Book describes Old English society under new management, in minute statistical detail. Foreign lords had taken over, but little else had yet changed. The chief landholders and those who held from them are named, and the rest of the population was counted. Most of them lived in villages, whose houses might be clustered together, or dispersed among their fields. Villages were grouped in administrative districts called Hundreds, which formed regions within Shires, or Counties, which survive today with minor boundary changes; the recent deformation of some ancient county identities is here disregarded, as are various short-lived modern changes. The local assemblies, though overshadowed by lords great and small, gave men a voice, which the Commissioners heeded. Very many holdings were described by the Norman term *manerium* (manor), greatly varied in size and structure, from tiny farmsteads to vast holdings; and many lords exercised their own jurisdiction and other rights, termed *soca*, whose meaning still eludes exact definition.

The Survey was unmatched in Europe for many centuries, the product of a sophisticated and experienced English administration, fully exploited by the Conqueror's commanding energy. But its unique assemblage of facts and figures has been hard to study, because the text has not been easily available, and abounds in technicalities. Investigation has therefore been chiefly confined to specialists; many questions cannot be tackled adequately without a cheap text and uniform translation available to a wider range of students, including local historians.

Previous Editions

The text has been printed once, in 1783, in an edition by Abraham Farley, probably of 1250 copies, at Government expense, said to have been £38,000; its preparation took 16 years. It was set in a specially designed type, here reproduced photographically, which was destroyed by fire in 1808. In 1811 and 1816 the Records Commissioners added an introduction, indices, and associated texts, edited by Sir Henry Ellis; and in 1861-1863 the Ordnance Survey issued zincograph facsimiles of the whole. Texts of individual counties have appeared since 1673, separate translations in the Victoria County Histories and elsewhere.

This Edition

Farley's text is used, because of its excellence, and because any worthy alternative would prove astronomically expensive. His text has been checked against the facsimile, and discrepancies observed have been verified against the manuscript, by the kindness of Miss Daphne Gifford of the Public Record Office. Farley's few errors are indicated in the notes.

[6] *Dialogus de Scaccario* 1,16.

The editor is responsible for the translation and lay-out. It aims at what the compiler would have written if his language had been modern English; though no translation can be exact, for even a simple word like 'free' nowadays means freedom from different restrictions. Bishop Henry emphasized that his grandfather preferred 'ordinary words'; the nearest ordinary modern English is therefore chosen whenever possible. Words that are now obsolete, or have changed their meaning, are avoided, but measurements have to be transliterated, since their extent is often unknown or arguable, and varied regionally. The terse inventory form of the original has been retained, as have the ambiguities of the Latin.

Modern English commands two main devices unknown to 11th century Latin, standardised punctuation and paragraphs; in the Latin, *ibi* ('there are') often does duty for a modern full stop, *et* ('and') for a comma or semi-colon. The entries normally answer the Commissioners' questions, arranged in five main groups, (i) the place and its holder, its hides, ploughs and lordship; (ii) people; (iii) resources; (iv) value; and (v) additional notes. The groups are usually given as separate paragraphs.

King William numbered chapters 'for easy reference', and sections within chapters are commonly marked, usually by initial capitals, often edged in red. They are here numbered. Maps, indices and an explanation of technical terms are also given. Later, it is hoped to publish analytical and explanatory volumes, and associated texts.

The editor is deeply indebted to the advice of many scholars, too numerous to name, and especially to the Public Record Office, and to the publisher's patience. The draft translations are the work of a team; they have been co-ordinated and corrected by the editor, and each has been checked by several people. It is therefore hoped that mistakes may be fewer than in versions published by single fallible individuals. But it would be Utopian to hope that the translation is altogether free from error; the editor would like to be informed of mistakes observed.

The maps are the work of Frank Thorn and Jim Hardy.

The preparation of this volume has been greatly assisted by a generous grant from the Leverhulme Trust Fund.

This support, originally given to the late Dr. J. R. Morris, has been kindly extended to his successors. At the time of Dr. Morris's death in June 1977, he had completed volumes 2, 3, 11, 12, 19, 23, 24. He had more or less finished the preparation of volumes 13, 14, 20, 28. These and subsequent volumes in the series were brought out under the supervision of John Dodgson and Alison Hawkins, who have endeavoured to follow, as far as possible, the editorial principles established by John Morris.

Conventions

★   refers to note on discrepancy between MS and Farley text

[ ]   enclose words omitted in the MS   ( )   enclose editorial explanation

THE EXETER DOMESDAY

For the south western counties there exists the Exeter Book (*Liber Exoniensis*; abbreviated Exon. in this edition), the bulk of which appears to be a preliminary draft of the Exchequer DB, though differently arranged and worded and containing much information not in its successor, such as details of villagers' land, numerous bynames, livestock and often more precise dating of the values of manors and how they were held. It seems very likely, however, that the Exchequer Domesday was taken directly from the Exeter Book; see the Introduction to the Exon. Notes below. Comparison with the Exchequer version shows that certain folios in Exon. have clearly not survived, such as all those dealing with Wiltshire except for one entry, more than half Dorset and four fiefs and a few entries for Devon. In Exon. the overriding principle of arrangement is the individual fief, not the county; the county's lands appear as subdivisions within the fiefs and, generally speaking, Devon, Cornwall and Somerset appear in this order within the fief. The returns for Dorset, with the one Wiltshire entry, form a separate group, placed near the beginning of the Exeter Book as it is now paginated and bound. Within each county places are often grouped in Hundreds, although without the Hundred name given, and frequently (especially for Devon) the Hundreds occur in the same order under different holders. This provides important evidence for the identification of places and in part offsets the lack of Hundred headings in the text of Exchequer DB here (see Introductory Note 1 below). Information is sometimes duplicated in Exon., as for example in Cornwall where the same 11 hides are listed under the King's manor of Winnianton (folios 99-100) and among the Count of Mortain's holdings (folios 224-227) as he had seized them.

Apart from the Exon. Domesday proper, the *Liber Exoniensis* contains the Tax Returns or geld accounts (entitled *Inquisitio Gheldi* on folio 532a) for all five counties, compiled c. 1084-1086, which the present editors hope to publish in a separate volume; see the Appendix below. Also included are details for Devon, Cornwall and Somerset of 'Appropriated Lands' (*Terrae Occupatae*), folios 495-525. These contain condensed entries of certain manors, which had had land taken from, or added to, them, or which had not paid their customary dues, or which had been held as two or more manors before 1066 by one or more holders, or which were unusual in some other way; see the Introduction to the Exon. Notes for Somerset and Devon. The information given in the *Terrae Occupatae* almost always repeats what is in the main Exeter Domesday, but occasionally new information is given; see the Exon. Notes for the counties concerned. A few lists of Hundreds and some summaries complete the *Liber Exoniensis*. A convenient contents table of the whole is printed in V. H. Galbraith *Domesday Book* (Oxford 1974) pp. 184-188.

The extant Exon. folios dealing with Dorset, including the odd blank folio and the one Wiltshire entry in the middle, are: 11a-12b (= B 4,1-3 in DB); 17a-24a (Tax Returns); 25a-62b (= in order, DB Ch. 1 with Ch. 18 and part of Ch. 24 and an odd Winterborne entry included, Chs. 58, 11, 13, 15-16, 12, 36, 47-48, 55, 41). Summaries of the holdings of Glastonbury Abbey in Dorset, of Robert son of Gerald and of the Count of Mortain are to be found in the imperfect folios 527b; 530b-531a.

The Exon. MS is preserved in the library of Exeter Cathedral and was printed in 1816 by Sir Henry Ellis in the third volume (fourth in certain bindings) of the Record Commission's edition of DB, from a transcript made by Ralph Barnes (1731-1820), Chapter Clerk. No facsimile, such as the Ordnance Survey made for Exchequer DB, exists for Exon. The MS consists of 532 folios of parchment, the majority of them measuring about 6½ by 9¾ inches (16½ by 25 cms.); folios 1-3 and 526-528 are smaller. Each folio contains a single column on each side, most with about 20 lines. These folios fall into a series of quires, or gatherings, varying in number between one and twenty folios. Generally a new quire was started for each major landholder, and a new side for most tenants. This led to many blanks, the number of which was increased by spaces sometimes left for information not to hand. There is no indication of the original sequence of quires, and the present order and system of reference date from the last rebinding in 1816; alas, these are not perfect: folios 519-525 were bound after folio 494 and folio 400 should have been numbered 401 and folios 401-402 should be 402, 400. The MS is the work of about a dozen scribes and the hand changes often between entries and even within them (e.g. 3 times in 98 a 3, = Devon 1,50); see R. Welldon Finn 'The Exeter Domesday and its Construction' in BJRL vol. 41 no. 2 (1959).

The text cannot be economically reproduced in this edition; nine-tenths of it is repeated in the DB survey, with discrepancies of a fraction of one per cent in many tens of thousands of figures. Ellis' edition has here been used in the main, though the MS has been checked where Exon. and DB differ and in a number of other places. The principal corresponding Exon. reference, where it survives, is given beside each entry in the translation, with other references in the Exon. Notes; the last number refers to the order of the entry on each side, as indicated in the MS generally by gallows marks. All additional information and all discrepancies for Dorset are given either in small type in the translation (when the former can easily be inserted without disturbing the meaning of Exchequer DB) or in the Exon. Notes or in the table of details of holdings not given in DB, signalled in the right margin of the translation by E and D respectively. A specimen entry, with the DB equivalent, showing the differences in formulae, is given below. The substance, though not the wording, of the whole of the Exeter Domesday returns for Dorset is therefore here reproduced.

For a detailed description and evaluation of Exon., see R. Welldon Finn *The Liber Exoniensis*, London 1964; N. R. Ker *Medieval Manuscripts in British Libraries* vol. ii pp. 800-807, Oxford, 1977; Sir Henry Ellis *DB3*, Introduction p. ix ff. See also the Introduction to the Exon. Notes in this edition.

EXTRACTS TO SHOW COMPARISON BETWEEN
EXON. AND EXCHEQUER DB ENTRIES

DORSET Exchequer DB 12,14, folio 78 b

Ipſa æccɫa ten *ERTACOMESTOCHE*.7 Herueus de abɓe.T.R.E.geldɓ ᵱ.x.

hiđ.Ťra.ē.xvi.caɼ.De ea ſt in dñio.iiii.hidæ.7 ibi.ii.caɼ.7 iiii.ſerui.

7 xl.uiɫɫi hñt.xx.caɼ.Ibi.iii.molini redđ xxxvii.deñ.7 xx.iii.ắc ᵱti.

Silua.xiii.q́ɀ lg̅.7 xii.lat̄.Valet.ix.liɓ

Hoc m̅ fuit sēp de dñio ꝳonachoɀ ad uiᶜtū 7 ueſtitū eoɀ.

The Church [of Milton Abbas] holds STOCKLAND itself, and Hervey from the Abbot. Before 1066 it paid tax for 10 hides. Land for 16 ploughs, of which 4 hides are in lordship; 2 ploughs there; 4 slaves.
   40 villagers have 20 ploughs.
   3 mills which pay 37d; meadow, 23 acres; woodland 13 furlongs long and 12
      wide.
Value £9.
   This manor was always (part) of the monks' lordship for their supplies and clothing.

Exon. 44 b 3

⟨V⟩ Abɓ ht́.i.mañs q̃ uocat ertacomeſtoca.

hec reddiđ gilđ ᵱ.x.h̃ tᵽr regis.e.qs poſſt arare.xvi.caɼ.de

his ht́ abɓ in dñio.iiii.h̃.&.ii.caɼ.&.uiɫɫ.vi.h̃.&.xx.caɼ.ibi

ht́ abɓ xl.uiɫɫ.&.iiii.feru.&.iiii.animł.&.vii.porᶜ.&.xx.caps̀

& iii.molenđ q reddt́ p anñ.xxx.&.vii.đ.&.xiii.qdrag nemor

i̇ log̀ & xii.i̇ lat̀.&.xxiii.agros ṕti.& ual& p anñ.viiii.liɓ.

hanc manfionē ten& de abɓ heruei⁹ fili⁹ anfgerii & hẹc mañs fuit

ſēp ad uiᶜtū & ad ueſtimtu monacoɀ. & dñia fuit tᵽr regis.e

de firma abɓ.

The Abbot [of St Peter's Church, Milton] has a manor called STOCKLAND. Before 1066* it paid tax for 10 hides, which 16 ploughs can plough. Of these the Abbot has in lordship 4 hides and 2 ploughs and the villagers (have) 6 hides and 20 ploughs. The Abbot has there 40 villagers, 4 slaves, 4 cattle, 7 pigs, 20 goats, 3 mills which pay 37d a year, 13 furlongs of woodland in length and 12 in width, 23 acres of meadow. Value £9 a year. Hervey son of Ansger† holds this manor from the Abbot. This manor was always for the monks' supplies and clothing and it was always before 1066* (part) of the Abbot's lordship‡ revenue.

---

* Unusually for Exon. *tempore regis eduuardi*; see Introduction to the Exon. Notes below.
† The 1086 sub-tenant normally appears earlier in an Exon. entry, after the plough estimate.
‡ In the Exon MS *dñiᶜa*, not as Ellis prints.

IN DoreCestre TĒPORE REGIS EDWARDI. Erant
.c.lxxii.dom. Hæ ꝓ oĩi feruitio regis fe defendeb 7 geldb
ꝓ.x.hid. Scilicet ad opus Hufcarliũ unā Mark argti.
exceptis cĩuetudinib₂ quæ ꝓtiñ ad firmā noctis.
Ibi erant.ii.Monetarij.q́fq̃ eoꝝ redd ɫunā Mark argti.
7 xx.folid quando moneta uertebatur.
Modo ſt ibi q̃t.xx 7 viii.dom.7 c.penit deftructæ
a tēpore Hugonis uicecomit ufq̃. nunc.

IN BRIDEPORT TꝒR REGIS EDW̃ erant.cxx.domus.
7 ad oĩe feruitiũ regis defendeb fe 7 geldab ꝓ.v.hid.
Scilicet ad opus Hufcarliũ regis dimid Mark argti.
exceptis confuetudinib₂ quæ ꝓtiñ ad firmā uni noctis.
Ibi erat uñ monetari redd regi.i.Mark argti.7 xx.fol q̃do
moneta uertebat́. ⌐ maneꝗ geld foluere ñ ualeꝗ.
Modo ſt ibi.c.dom.7 xx.funt ita deftitutæ.́qd q̃ in eis
IN WARHAM TꝒR REGIS EDW̃ erant.cxliii.dom.
in dñio regis. Hæc uilla ad oĩe feruitiũ regis fe defdb
7 geldb ꝓ.x.hid. Scilicet.i.Mark argti Hufcarlis regis.
exceptis cĩuetudinib₂ quæ ꝓtiñ ad firmā uni noctis.
Ibi erant.ii.monetarij.quifq̃ redd.i.Mark argti regi.
7 xx.folid q̃do moneta uertebatur. ⌐ hugonis uicecom.
Modo ſt ibi.lxx.dom.7 lxxiii.ſt penit deftructe a tꝒr
De parte S̃ Wandregifili ſt ibi.xl.v.dom.7 xvii ɪuaftæ.
De partib₂ alioꝝ baroñ ſt ibi.xx.dom.7 lx.ſt deftructæ.
IN BVRGO SCEPTESBERIE T.R.E.erant.c.7 iiii.dom.
in dñio regis. H uilla ad oĩe feruitiũ regis fe defdb
7 geldb ꝓ.xx.hid.Scilicet.ii.Mark argti Hufcarl regis.
Ibi erant.iii.monetarij quifq̃ reddeb.i.Mark argenti.
7 xx.folid q̃do moneta uertebatur.
Modo ſt ibi.lxvi.dom.7 xxxviii.dom ſt deftructæ.
a tꝒr Hugonis uicecomitis ufq̃ nc̃.
In parte abbatiffæ erant T.R.E.dom.cliii.Modo ſt
ibi.cxi.dom.7 xlii.funt oĩino deftructæ.
Ibi ht̃ abbiffa.cl.7 uñ burgs.7 xx.manſ uacuas.7 i.hortũ.
Valet.lxv.folid.

B [BOROUGHS]

1 IN DORCHESTER before 1066 there were 172 houses. They answered   E 75 a
for every service of the King and paid tax for 10 hides; that is,
1 silver mark for the use of the guards, apart from the customary
dues which belong to the night's revenue. There were 2 moneyers,   11
each of them paying to the King 1 silver mark and 20s whenever   b 1
the coinage was changed. Now there are 88 houses there; 100   E
have been completely destroyed from the time of Hugh the
Sheriff until now.

2 IN BRIDPORT before 1066 there were 120 houses. They answered   E
for every service of the King and paid tax for 5 hides; that is,   12
½ silver mark for the use of the King's guards, apart from the   a 1
customary dues which belong to one night's revenue. There was   E
1 moneyer who paid to the King 1 silver mark and 20s whenever
the coinage was changed. Now there are 100 houses there; 20   E
have been so neglected that those who live in them are not able   E
to pay tax.

3 IN WAREHAM before 1066 there were 143 houses in the King's   E
lordship. This town answered for every service of the King and   E
paid tax for 10 hides; that is, 1 silver mark for the King's guards,
apart from the customary dues which belong to one night's   E
revenue. There were 2 moneyers, each paying to the King 1   12
silver mark and 20s whenever the coinage was changed. Now   b 1
there are 70 houses there; 73 have been completely destroyed   E
from the time of Hugh the Sheriff. In the part (belonging to)   E
St. Wandrille's there are 45 houses standing and 17 are derelict;   E
in the parts (belonging to) the other barons there are 20 houses   E
standing and 60 have been destroyed.

4 IN THE BOROUGH OF SHAFTESBURY before 1066 there were 104   E
houses in the King's lordship. This town answered for every   E
service of the King and paid tax for 20 hides; that is, 2 silver   11
marks for the King's guards. There were 3 moneyers; each paid 1   a 1
silver mark and 20s whenever the coinage was changed. Now   - 2
there are 66 houses there; 38 houses have been destroyed from   E
the time of Hugh the Sheriff until now. In the part (belonging
to) the Abbess there were 153 houses before 1066; now there
are 111 houses there; 42 have been utterly destroyed. The   E
Abbess has 151 burgesses and 20 empty dwellings and 1 garden.   E
Value 65s.

HIC ANNOTANT TENENTES TRAS IN DORSETE.

.I. REX WILLELMVS.

.II. Eps Sarifberienfis.

.III. 7 Monachi Scireburn

.IIII. Eps Baiocenfis.

.V. Eps Conftantienfis.

.VI. Eps Lifiacenfis.

.VII. Eps Lundonienfis.

.VIII Abbatia Glaftingbez.

.IX. Abbatia Wintoniens.

.X. Abbatia Creneburnens.

.XI. Abbatia de Cernel

.XII Abbatia de Middeltune

.XIII Abbatia de Abedefberie

.XIIII Abbatia de Hortune

.XV. Abbatia de Adelingi.

.XVI Abbatia de Taueftoch.

.XVII Abbatia de Cadomis.

.XVII Abbatia S Wandregifili.

.XIX Abbatiffa de Sceftefberie.

.XX. Abbatiffa de Wiltune.

.XXI. Abbatiffa de Cadom.

.XXII Abbatiffa de Monaft uillar.

.XXII Canonici Conftantienfes

.XXII Reinbald 7 alij clerici

.XXV. Comes Alanus.

.XXVI. Comes Moritonienfis.

.XXVII Comes Hugo.

.XXVIII Rogerius de belmont.

.XXIX. Rogerius de Curcelle.

.XXX. Robertus filius Girold.

.XXXI. Eduuard de Sarisberie.

.XXXII. Ernulfus de Hefding.

.XXXIII. Turftinus filius Rolf.

.XXXII. Willelmus de Ou.

.XXXV. Wilts de Faleife.

.XXXVI. Wilts de Moiun.

.XXXVII Wilts de Braiofe.

.XXXVII Wilts de Scohies.

.XXXIX Walfcin de Douuai.

.XL. Waleran uenator.

.XLI. Walterius de Clauile.

.XLII. Balduin de Execeftre.

.XLIII Berenger Gifard.

.XLIIII Osbernus Gifard.

.XLV. Maci de Moretanie.

.XLVI. Rogerius Arundel.

.XLVII Serlo de Burci.

.XLVII Aiulf uicecomes.

.XLIX. Hunfrid camerarius.

.L. Hugo de Porth.

.LI. Hugo de S Quintino. ☞

☞ .LII. Hugo de boscherbti. LIII. Hugo de Luri .7 alij Franc.

LIIII. Vxor Hugonis. LV. Ifeldis. LVI. Gudmund 7 alij taini

.LVII. Wilts 7 alij feruient regis.

.LVIII. Comitiffa Bolonienf.

75 a

LIST OF LANDHOLDERS IN DORSET

1 King William
2 The Bishop of Salisbury
3 & the Monks of Sherborne
4 The Bishop of Bayeux
5 The Bishop of Coutances
6 The Bishop of Lisieux
7 The Bishop of London
8 Glastonbury Abbey
9 Winchester Abbey
10 Cranborne Abbey
11 Cerne Abbey
12 Milton Abbey
13 Abbotsbury Abbey
14 Horton Abbey
15 Athelney Abbey
16 Tavistock Abbey
17 Caen Abbey
18 St. Wandrille's Abbey
19 The Abbess of Shaftesbury
20 The Abbess of Wilton
21 The Abbess of Caen
22 The Abbess of Montivilliers
23 The Canons of Coutances
24 Reinbald the priest
   and other clergy

25 Count Alan
26 The Count of Mortain
27 Earl Hugh
28 Roger of Beaumont
29 Roger of Courseulles
30 Robert son of Gerald
31 Edward of Salisbury
32 Arnulf of Hesdin
33 Thurstan son of Rolf
34 William of Eu
35 William of Falaise
36 William of Mohun
37 William of Braose
38 William of Écouis
39 Walscin of Douai
40 Waleran Hunter
41 Walter of Claville
42 Baldwin of Exeter
43 Berengar Giffard
44 Osbern Giffard
45 Matthew of Mortagne
46 Roger Arundel
47 Serlo of Burcy
48 Aiulf the Sheriff
49 Humphrey the Chamberlain
50 Hugh of Port
51 Hugh of St. Quentin

52 Hugh of Boscherbert 53 Hugh of Ivry and other Frenchmen
54 The wife of Hugh son of Grip 55 Isolde 56 Godmund and
other thanes 57 William Bellett and others of the King's Servants
58 The Countess of Boulogne

TERRA REGIS.

Rex tenet infulā quæ uocat̃ *PORLAND*. Eduuard̃ tenuit in uita fua.

ibi h̃t rex . III . car̃ in dñio . 7 v . feruos . 7 un uitts 7 c . bord̃ . x . min̄ h̄nt . XXIII . car̃ . Ibi . VIII . ac̃ p̃ti . Paftura . VIII . q̃ lg̃ . 7 VIII . lat̃. Hoc ꝏ cũ fibi p̃tintib̃ redd̃ . LXV . lib albas.

Rex ten̄ *BRIDETONE* . 7 *BERE* . 7 Colesberie . 7 Sepetone 7 Brate polle 7 Cidihoc . H̃ tenuit Rex . E . in dñio . Nefcit̃ quot hidæ s̃t ibi. nec geld̃b T.R.E. Tra . ē . LV . car̃ . In dñio s̃t . VIII . car̃ . 7 xx. ferui . 7 XLI . uitts 7 xxx . bord̃ 7 VII . colib̃ti . 7 LXXIIII . cotarii. Int om̄s h̄nt . XXVII . car̃ . Ibi . VIII . molini red̃d . IIII . lib 7 xxxv. denar̃ . 7 cxi . ac̃ p̃ti . Paftura . IIII . leu lg̃ . 7 tn̄td lat̃. Silua . III . leũ lg̃ . 7 una leũ lat̃.

Hoc ꝏ cũ fuis appendic̃ 7 c̃fuetudinib̃ redd̃ firmā uni̅ noctis.

★ Bofcus ten̄ *HAVOCVBE* p̃tin ad *BRIDETONE* . ita q̃d T.R.E. duæ partes ej erant in firma regis . tcia ũ pars t̃ tcia quercus erat Eduini. quæ m̃ p̃tin ad *FRANTONE* ꝏ S̃ Stefani cadom̄fis.

Rex ten̄ *WINBORNE* . 7 Scapeuuic . 7 Chirce 7 Opewinburne. Rex tenuit . E . in dñio . Nefcitur q̃t hidæ s̃t ibi . q̃a ñ reddid̃ geld̃ . T.R.E. Tra . ē . XLV . car̃ . In dñio s̃t . v . car̃ . 7 xv . ferui. 7 LXIII . uitti . 7 LXVIII . bord̃ 7 VII . cotar̃ h̄nt . XXII . car̃. Ibi . VIII . molini redd̃ . c . x . folid̃ . 7 CL . ac̃ p̃ti . Paftura . VI. leũ lg̃ . 7 III . leũ lat̃ . Silua . v . leũ lg̃ . 7 una leũ lat̃. Hoc ꝏ cũ append | redd̃ firmā unius noctis.

Rex ten̄ *DORECESTRE* . 7 Fortitone . 7 Sutone . 7 Gelingehā 7 Frome. Rex . E . tenuit . Nefcit̃ q̃t hidæ fint ibi . q̃a ñ geld̃b T.R.E.

LAND OF THE KING

The King holds   E

1 the island called PORTLAND. King Edward held it during his
life. ... The King has 3 ploughs in lordship; 5 slaves.
1 villager and 100 smallholders, less 10, have 23 ploughs.   26
Meadow, 8 acres; pasture 8 furlongs long and 8 wide.   a 1
3 cobs; 14 cattle; 27 pigs; 900 sheep.
This manor with what belongs to it pays £65, blanched.   E

2 BURTON (Bradstock), BERE (Regis), COLBER, SHIPTON (Gorge),   E
BRADPOLE and CHIDEOCK. King Edward held them in lordship.   E
It is not known how many hides are there and they did not
pay tax before 1066. Land for 55 ploughs. In lordship 8
ploughs; 20 slaves;
41 villagers, 30 smallholders, 7 freedmen and 74 cottagers;
between them they have 27 ploughs.
8 mills which pay £4 35d; meadow, 111 acres; pasture 4   27
leagues long and as wide; woodland 3 leagues long and   a 1
1 league wide. 6 cobs; 9 cattle; 108 pigs; 800 sheep.
This manor with its dependencies and customary dues pays
one night's revenue.
Scrubland at 'HAWCOMBE' belongs to Burton (Bradstock) (and   E
belonged) in such a way that before 1066 two parts of it were
in the King's revenue and the third part, or the third oak, was
Earl Edwin's; it now belongs to Frampton, a manor of St.
Stephen's of Caen.

3 WIMBORNE (Minster), SHAPWICK, (Moor) CRICHEL and WIMBORNE
(St. Giles). King Edward held them in lordship. It is not
known how many hides are there because they did not pay tax
before 1066. Land for 45 ploughs. In lordship 5 ploughs;
15 slaves.
63 villagers, 68 smallholders and 7 cottagers have 22 ploughs.   27
8 mills which pay 110s; meadow, 150 acres; pasture 6   a 2
leagues long and 3 leagues wide; woodland 5 leagues long
and 1 league wide. 3 cobs; 30 pigs; 250 sheep; 44 goats.
This manor with its dependencies pays one night's revenue.   E

4 DORCHESTER, FORDINGTON, SUTTON (Poyntz), GILLINGHAM and
'FROME'. King Edward held them. It is not known how many
hides are there because they did not pay tax before 1066.

Tra.̄e.LVI.car̄.In dn̄io s̄t.VII.car̄.7 xx.ſerui.7 XII.colibi.7 CXIIII.

uilli 7 q̃t xx.7 IX.bord.hn̄tes.XLIX.car̄.Ibi.XII.molini redd̄

VI.lib̄.7 v.ſolid̄.7 CLX.ãc p̃ti.Paſtura.II.leũ lḡ.7 una leũ lat̄.

Silua.IIII.leũ lḡ.7 una leũ lat̄.

H̄ m̃ cũ appendic̄ ſuis redd̄ firmã unius noƈtis.

Rex ten̄ PINPRE.7 Cerletone.Rex.E.tenuit in dn̄io.Neſcit̄ q̃t

hidæ ſint ibi.d̃a n̄ geldb̄ T.R.E.Tra.̄e.xx.car̄.In dn̄io s̄t.IIII.car̄

7 v.ſerui.7 I.colibt̄.7 xvIII.uilli.7 LX.vIII.bord.cũ.XIIII.car̄.

Ibi.II.molini redd̄.XL.ſol 7 vI.den.7 q̃t xx.7 xIIII.ãc p̃ti.

Paſtura.II.leũ lḡ.7 II.leũ lat̄.Silua.I.leũ lḡ.7 dimid̄ leũ lat̄.

Hooc m̃ cũ append̄ ſuis redd̄ dimid̄ firmã unius noƈtis.

Rex ten̄ WINFRODE.7 Luluorde 7 Wintreborne.7 Chenoltone.

Rex.E.tenuit in dn̄io.Neſcit̄ q̃t hidæ ſint ibi.d̃a n̄ geldb̄ T.R.E.

Tra.̄e.xxIIII.car̄.In dn̄io s̄t.IIII.car̄.7 vIII.ſerui.7 xxx.uilli 7 xxx.

bord cũ.I.cotar̄ hn̄tes.xvI.car̄.Ibi.IIII.molini redd̄.L.ſolid̄.

7 q̃t xx.ãc p̃ti.Paſtura.III.leũ lḡ.7 tn̄td̄ lat̄.Silua tn̄td̄ in lḡ 7 lat̄.

H̄ m̃ cũ append̄ ſuis 7 c̄ſuetudinib̄.redd̄ dim̄ firmã uni̇ noƈtis.

Ista Maner̄ quæ Secvnt̄ Tenvit heraldvs comes T.R.E.

Rex ten̄ ACFORD.T.R.E.geldb̄ ꝑ.v.hid̄ Tra.̄e.vI.car̄.De ea

s̄t in dn̄io.III.hidæ.7 ibi.II.car̄.cũ.I.ſeruo.7 vI.uilli 7 vIII.bord

cũ.II.car̄.Ibi.II.molini redd̄.xx.ſol 7 xL.ãc p̃ti.7 II.q̃rent̄

paſturæ.Silua.IIII.q̃ʒ lḡ.7 una q̃ʒ 7 dim̄ lat̄.Valuit 7 ual̄.x.lib̄

Rex ten̄ PIRETONE.T.R.E.geldb̄ ꝑ dim̄ hida.Tra.̄e.xv.car̄.

In dn̄io s̄t.IIII.car̄.7 xII.ſerui.7 xIIII.uilli 7 xxIx.coſcez cũ.x.

car̄.Ibi.II.molini redd̄.xxxII.ſol.7 cxxvI.ãc p̃ti.Paſtura

.I.leũ 7 dim̄ lḡ.7 una lat̄.Silua.II.q̃ʒ lḡ.7 tn̄td̄ lat̄.

Land for 56 ploughs. In lordship 7 ploughs; 20 slaves;
12 freedmen;
  114 villagers and 89 smallholders who have 49 ploughs.
  12 mills which pay £6 5s; meadow, 160 acres; pasture 2
    leagues long and 1 league wide; woodland 4 leagues long
    and 1 league wide. 5 cobs; 20 cattle; 72 pigs; 800 sheep; 40 goats.
This manor with its dependencies pays one night's revenue.

27
b 1

E

5 PIMPERNE and CHARLTON (Marshall). King Edward held them
in lordship. It is not known how many hides are there
because they did not pay tax before 1066. Land for 20 ploughs.
In lordship 4 ploughs; 5 slaves; 1 freedman;
  18 villagers and 68 smallholders with 14 ploughs.
  2 mills which pay 40s 6d; meadow, 94 acres; pasture 2
    leagues long and 2 leagues wide; woodland 1 league long
    and ½ league wide. 2 cobs; 16 cattle; 25 pigs; 400 sheep; 36 goats.
This manor with its dependencies pays half of one night's revenue.

27
b 3

E

6 WINFRITH (Newburgh), LULWORTH, 'WINTERBORNE' and KNOWLTON.
King Edward held them in lordship. It is not known how many
hides are there because they did not pay tax before 1066.
Land for 24 ploughs. In lordship 4 ploughs; 8 slaves;
  30 villagers and 30 smallholders with 1 cottager who have
  16 ploughs.
  4 mills which pay 50s; meadow, 80 acres; pasture 3 leagues
    long and as wide; as much woodland in length and width.
    2 cobs; 50 pigs; 300 sheep; 6 goats.
This manor with its dependencies and customary dues pays a
half of one night's revenue.

28
a 1

E

BEFORE 1066 EARL HAROLD HELD THE MANORS WHICH FOLLOW

7 (Child) OKEFORD. Before 1066 it paid tax for 5 hides.
Land for 6 ploughs, of which 3 hides are in lordship; 2
ploughs there, with 1 slave;
  6 villagers and 8 smallholders with 2 ploughs and 2 hides.
  2 mills which pay 20s; meadow, 40 acres; pasture, 2
    furlongs, woodland 4 furlongs long and 1½ furlongs
    wide. 1 cob; 7 cattle; 10 pigs; 48 sheep.
The value was and is £10.

E 25
E a 1

E

8 PUDDLETOWN. Before 1066 it paid tax for ½ hide. Land for
15 ploughs. In lordship 4 ploughs; 12 slaves;
  14 villagers and 29 Cottagers with 10 ploughs.
  2 mills which pay 32s; meadow, 126 acres; pasture 1½
    leagues long and 1 wide; woodland 2 furlongs long
    and as wide. 4 cobs; 17 cattle; 60 pigs; 1,600 sheep; 60 goats.

25
a 2

E

Huic ꝯ ptin . I . hida 7 dimid in *PORBI*.7 in *MAPERTVNE* dimid hida . Tra . ē . I . car 7 dimid.
Huic etiā ꝯ piretone adjacet tcius denar de tota scira *DORSETE*.
Redd cū omib; appendic . LXXIII . lib.
REX ten *CEREBERIE* . T.R.E. geldb p . V . hid . Tra . ē III . car 7 dimid . De ea st in dnio . III . hidæ 7 dim.7 ibi . I . car.7 IIII . serui. 7 V . uilli 7 IIII . bord cū . I . car 7 dimid . Ibi Silua . II . qrent lg. 7 una lat . Valuit 7 ual . IX . lib.

75 c
REX ten *ABRISTETONE* . T.R.E. geldb p . V . hid . Tra . ē . V . car. De ea st in dnio . II . hidæ 7 dimid.7 ibi . II . car.7 II . serui.7 X . uilli 7 VII . bord cū . III . car . Ibi . XI . ac pti.7 Pastura . VII . q lg. 7 III . q lat . Silua . IIII . q lg.7 II . q lat . Valuit 7 ual . X . lib.
REX ten *FLETE* . T.R.E. geldb p . V . hid . Tra . ē . V . car . De ea st in dnio . III . hidæ 7 dim.7 ibi . II . car.7 II . serui.7 IIII . uilli 7 VII . bord cū . III . car . Ibi . VI . qrent pasturæ . Valuit 7 ual . VII . lib.
REX ten *CALVEDONE* . T.R.E. geldb p XIII . hid . Tra . ē . X . car. De ea st in dnio . VI . hidæ.7 ibi . I . car .7 IIII . serui.7 XVI . uilli 7 XV . cotar cū . VI . car . Ibi molin redd . X . sol.7 XX . ac pti . Pastura una leu lg.7 dim leu lat . Valuit 7 ual . XIII . lib.
REX ten *LODRES* . T.R.E. geldb p . XVIII . hid . Tra . ē totid car. De ea st in dnio . VIII . hidæ .7 ibi . III . car.7 IX . serui.7 XXVIII . uilli 7 XXIIII . bord . cū . VI . car . Ibi . II . molini redd . XXIII . sol.7 IIII . den. Ibi . XL . ac pti . Silua minuta . III . q lg.7 una q lat.
Valuit 7 ual . XXXIII . lib. Valent . XXX . solid.
In hoc ꝯ st . II . hidæ Tainland q ñ ibi ptin . T.R.E. teneb eas . II . taini.

To this manor belong 1½ hides in 'PURBECK' and ½ hide in
MAPPOWDER. Land for 1½ ploughs.   E
Also to this manor of Puddletown is attached the third
penny of the whole shire of Dorset.   E
It pays with all (its) dependencies £73; when Aiulf (acquired) it,
it paid as much.

9 CHARBOROUGH. Before 1066 it paid tax for 5 hides. Land for
3½ ploughs, of which 3½ hides are in lordship; 1 plough   E
there; 4 slaves;   25
    5 villagers and 4 smallholders with 1½ ploughs and 1½ hides.   b 2
Woodland 2 furlongs long and 1 wide. 1 cob; 13 pigs; 105 sheep.
The value was and is £9.   E

10 IBBERTON. Before 1066 it paid tax for 5 hides. Land for   75 c
5 ploughs, of which 2½ hides are in lordship; 2 ploughs
there; 2 slaves;
    10 villagers and 7 smallholders with 3 ploughs and 2½ hides. 25
Meadow, 11 acres; pasture 7 furlongs long and 3 furlongs   b 3
  wide; woodland 4 furlongs long and 2 furlongs wide.
2 cobs; 4 cows; 10 pigs; 50 sheep; 50 goats.
The value was and is £10.   E

11 FLEET. Before 1066 it paid tax for 5 hides. Land for 5 ploughs,
of which 3½ hides are in lordship; 2 ploughs there; 2 slaves;
    4 villagers and 7 smallholders with 3 ploughs and 1½ hides.   26
Pasture, 6 furlongs. 1 cob; 3 cattle; 4 pigs; 144 sheep.   a 2
The value was and is £7.

12 CHALDON. Before 1066 it paid tax for 13 hides. Land for 10
ploughs, of which 6 hides are in lordship; 1 plough there;
4 slaves;
    16 villagers and 15 cottagers with 6 ploughs and 7 hides.   26
A mill which pays 10s; meadow, 20 acres; pasture 1 league   b 1
  long and ½ league wide. 2 cobs; 3 cattle; 500 sheep; 13 goats.
The value was and is £13.

13 LODERS. Before 1066 it paid tax for 18 hides. Land for as
many ploughs, of which 8 hides are in lordship; 3 ploughs
there; 9 slaves;
    28 villagers and 24 smallholders with 6 ploughs and 10 hides. 26
2 mills which pay 23s 4d. Meadow, 40 acres; underwood   b 2
  3 furlongs long and 1 furlong wide. 2 cobs; 16 pigs; 100 sheep, less 7.
The value was and is £33.   E
In this manor are 2 hides (of) thaneland which do not belong
there; before 1066 two thanes held them. Value 30s.

Rex ten̄ *Litelpidele* . Mat̄ Heraldi comit' tenuit T.R.E.7 geldb̄ ᵱ.v.hid.T̄ra.ē.iii.car̄ De ea st̄ i͏n dn̄io.ii.hidæ 7 dim̄.7 ibi.ii. car̄.7 viii.ſerui.7 ii.uiłłi 7 iii.bord cū dim̄ car̄.Ibi.viii.āc p̄ti.7 x.q̄rent̄ paſturæ.Valuit.c.ſolid.Modo.vii.lib̄.

Has Svbier Scriptas terras tenvit Mathildis Regina
Rex ten̄ *Litelfrome*.T.R.E.geldb̄ ᵱ.xiii.hid.T̄ra.ē.viii.car̄. De ea st̄ in dn̄io.x.hide 7 dim̄.7 ibi.iii.car̄.7 vi.ſerui.7 x.uiłłi 7 iii.bord cū.iii.car̄.Ibi molin̄ redd.iiii.ſoł.7 x.āc p̄ti.Paſtura xx.q̄ʒ l̄g.7 ii.q̄ʒ lat̄.Silua.viii.q̄ʒ l̄g.7 vi.q̄ʒ lat̄. Valuit.xii.lib̄.Modo.xvi̇ꞮꞮ·lib̄.

Rex ten̄ *Creneburne*.T.R.E.geldb̄ ᵱ.x.hid.T̄ra.ē.x.car̄. De ea st̄ i͏n dn̄io.iii.hidæ 7 dim̄.7 ibi.ii.car̄.7 x.ſerui.7 viii.uiłłi 7 xii.bord.7 vii.cotar̄ cū.viii.car̄.Ibi.iiii.molini redd.xviii. ſolid.7 xx.āc p̄ti.Paſtura.ii.leū l̄g.7 una q̄ʒ 7 una leū lat̄. Silua.ii.leū l̄g.7 ii.lat̄.Valuit.xxiiii.lib̄.Modo redd.xxx.lib̄ De ead̄ t̄ra ten̄.iii.taini.iii.hid̄.7 redd.iii.lib̄ excepto ſeruitio.
Rex ten̄ *Aisemare*.T.R.E.geldb̄ ᵱ.viii.hid.T̄ra.ē.vii.car̄. De ea st̄ in dn̄io.iiii.hidæ.7 ibi.iii.car̄.7 viii.ſerui.7 x̄.uiłłi. 7 vi.bord cū.iiii.car̄.Ibi.x.āc p̄ti.Paſtura.x.q̄ʒ l̄g.7 una q̄ʒ lat̄.Silua.ii.leū l̄g.7 una leū lat̄.Valuit 7 uał xv.lib̄. Ḧ.iii.Man tenuit Brictric T.R.E.
Rex ten̄ *Medesha*.Dodo tenuit T.R.E.7 geldb̄ ᵱ.ii.hid.T̄ra.ē iii.car̄.De ea.ē in dn̄io.i.hida 7 ibi.i.car̄.cū.i.ſeruo.7 viii.bord. Ibi molin̄ redd.v.ſoł.7 ii.āc p̄ti.Paſtura.iii.q̄ʒ l̄g.7 una q̄ʒ lat̄. Silua.v.q̄ʒ l̄g.7 una q̄ʒ 7 dimid̄ lat̄.Valuit 7 uał.iii.lib̄.

[1]

14 LITTLE PUDDLE. Earl Harold's mother held it before 1066.
It paid tax for 5 hides. Land for 3 ploughs, of which 2½
hides are in lordship; 2 ploughs there; 8 slaves;
2 villagers and 3 smallholders with ½ plough and 2½ hides.
Meadow, 8 acres; pasture, 10 furlongs. 1 cob; 100 sheep.
The value was 100s; now £7.

25
b 1

E

QUEEN MATILDA HELD THE LANDS WRITTEN BELOW   E

15 FROME (St. Quintin). Before 1066 it paid tax for 13 hides.
Land for 8 ploughs, of which 10½ hides are in lordship;
3 ploughs there; 6 slaves;
10 villagers and 3 smallholders with 3 ploughs and 2½ hides.
A mill which pays 4s; meadow, 10 acres; pasture 20
furlongs long and 2 furlongs wide; woodland 8 furlongs
long and 6 furlongs wide. 2 cobs; 19 cattle; 400 sheep; 50 goats.
The value was £12; now £18.

E 29
a 1

E

16 CRANBORNE. Before 1066 it paid tax for 10 hides. Land for 10
ploughs, of which 3½ hides are in lordship; 2 ploughs there;
10 slaves;
8 villagers, 12 smallholders and 7 cottagers with 8 ploughs
and 3½ hides.
4 mills which pay 18s; meadow, 20 acres; pasture 2 leagues
long and 1 furlong and 1 league wide; woodland 2 leagues
long and 2 wide. 4 cobs; 10 cows; 51 pigs; 1,037 sheep; 40 goats.
The value was £24; now it pays £30.
Three thanes hold 3 hides of this land; they pay £3 apart
from service.

29
a 2

E
E

E
E

17 ASHMORE. Before 1066 it paid tax for 8 hides. Land for 7
ploughs, of which 4 hides are in lordship; 3 ploughs there;
8 slaves;
10 villagers and 6 smallholders with 4 ploughs and 4 hides.
Meadow, 10 acres; pasture 10 furlongs long and 1 furlong wide;
woodland 2 leagues long and 1 league wide. 3 cobs; 10 cattle;
27 pigs; 826 sheep; 50 goats.
The value was and is £15.

29
b 1

Brictric held these three manors before 1066.

18 EDMONDSHAM. Doda held it before 1066. It paid tax for 2 hides.
Land for 3 ploughs, of which 1 hide is in lordship; 1 plough
there, with 1 slave;
8 smallholders.
A mill which pays 5s; meadow, 2 acres; pasture 3 furlongs long
and 1 furlong wide; woodland 5 furlongs long and 1½
furlongs wide. 8 cattle; 22 sheep.
The value was and is £3.

E

29
b 2

E

75 c

Rex ten̄ *HAME* . Saul tenuit T.R.E. 7 geldb̄ ,p . 11 . hid̄ 7 una v̄ træ.
T̄ra . ē . 11 . car̄ . De ea . ē in dn̄io . 1 . hida 7 ibi . 1 . car̄ 7 11 . ſerui . 7 v . uilli
7 1111 . bord̄ . cū . 1 . car̄ . Ibi . xl . ac̄ p̄ti . 7 paſtura . 1 . leu lḡ . 7 v . q̄ʒ̄ lat̄ .
7 11 . ac̄ filuæ . Redd̄ . l . folid̄ .
Rex ten̄ *WICHEMETVNE* . Duo taini tenuer̄ T.R.E. 7 geldb̄
,p . 1111 . hid̄ . 7 11' . partibʒ uni hidæ . T̄ra . ē . 1111 . car̄ . De ea ſt in dn̄io
.11 . hidæ . 7 una v̄ træ . 7 11 . partes uni v̄ . 7 ibi . 11 . car̄ . 7 11 . ſerui . 7 v . uilli .
7 xv . bord̄ cū . 11 . car̄ . Ibi molin redd̄ . x . ſot . 7 xvi . ac̄ p̄ti . Paſtura
.v . q̄ʒ̄ lḡ . 7 111 . q̄ʒ̄ lat̄ . Silua . vi . q̄ʒ̄ lḡ . 7 11 . q̄ʒ̄ lat̄ . Valuit 7 ual . c . folid̄ .
Rex ten̄ *WINBVRNE* Ode tenuit T.R.E. Ibi . ē dim hida 7 nunq
geldau . T̄ra . ē . 11 . car̄ . In dn̄io . ē . 1 . v̄ . 7 1 . car̄ . 7 11 . ſerui . 7 1111 . uilli 7 vii .
bord̄ cū . 11 . car̄ . Ibi . x1111 . ac̄ p̄ti . Silua . 1 . q̄ʒ̄ lḡ . 7 tntd̄ lat̄ . -
Valuit 7 ual . 1111 . lib . h̄ tra n̄ p̄tin ad firmā de *WINBVRNE* .
Has|infra sc̄|ptas tras tenuit Hvgo de Regina.
Waia tenuit Aluuin T.R.E. 7 geldb̄ ,p hida 7 dim . T̄ra . ē . 1 . car̄ .
Ibi ſt . 11 . bord̄ . 7 v . q̄rent paſturæ . Valet . xxx ſot .
Rex ten̄ *LANGETONE* . Aluuard tenuit T.R.E. 7 geldb̄ ,p . 1 . hida 7 dim .
T̄ra . ē . 11 . car̄ . Ibi ſt . 11 . ſerui . 7 vii . bord̄ 7 un redd̄ . xxx . den̄ . Ibi . viii . ac̄
p̄ti . 7 paſtura , v . q̄ʒ̄ lḡ . 7 111 . q̄ʒ̄ lat̄ . Valet . xxx . folid̄ .
Rex ten̄ *TARENTE* . Aluric tenuit T.R.E. 7 geldb̄ ,p . 111 . hid̄ 7 dim
T̄ra . ē . 1111 . car̄ . De ea ſt in dn̄io . 11 . hidæ . 7 ibi dim car̄ . 7 v . ſerui . 7 vi . uilli
7 111 . bord̄ cū . 11 . car̄ . Ibi paſtura . vii . q̄rent lḡ . 7 11 . q̄ʒ̄ lat̄ .

19   HAMPRESTON. Saul held it before 1066. It paid tax for 2 hides   E
and 1 virgate of land. Land for 2 ploughs, of which 1 hide is   E
in lordship; 1 plough there; 2 slaves;   30
     5 villagers and 4 smallholders with 1 plough and 3 virgates and 6 acres.   E a 1
     Meadow, 40 acres; pasture 1 league long and 5 furlongs wide;
     woodland, 2 acres. 1 cob; 15 cattle; 11 pigs; 40 sheep.
It pays 50s.

20   WITCHAMPTON. Two thanes held it before 1066. It paid tax for 4   E
hides and 2 parts of 1 hide. Land for 4 ploughs, of which 2 hides,
1 virgate of land and 2 parts of 1 virgate are in lordship; 2 ploughs   30
there; 2 slaves;   a 2
     5 villagers and 15 smallholders with 2 ploughs and 2 hides and 1 virgate.   E
     A mill which pays 10s; meadow, 16 acres; pasture 5 furlongs
     long and 3 furlongs wide; woodland 6 furlongs long and
     2 furlongs wide. 2 cows; 2 pigs; 40 sheep.
The value was and is 100s.   E

21   WIMBORNE (Minster). Odo the Treasurer held it before 1066.   E 30
½ hide there; it has never paid tax. Land for 2 ploughs.   b 1
In lordship 1 virgate; 1 plough; 2 slaves;   E
     4 villagers and 7 smallholders with 2 ploughs and the other virgate.
     Meadow, 14 acres; woodland 1 furlong long and as wide.   E
     2 cattle; 10 pigs; 127 sheep; 30 goats.
The value was and is £4.   E
This land does not belong to the revenue of Wimborne (Minster).   E

    HUGH SON OF GRIP HELD THE 8 LANDS WRITTEN BELOW FROM THE QUEEN   E

22   Alwin held 'WEY' before 1066. It paid tax for 1½ hides.   E
Land for 1 plough.
     2 smallholders.   31
     Pasture, 5 furlongs.   a 1
Value 30s.

  The King holds
23   LANGTON (Herring). Alward Colling held it before 1066.
It paid tax for 1½ hides. Land for 2 ploughs. 2 slaves.
     8 smallholders; 1 who pays 30d.   31
     Meadow, 8 acres; pasture 5 furlongs long and 3 furlongs wide.   a 2
Value 30s.

24   'TARRANT'. Aelfric held it before 1066. It paid tax for 3½ hides.
Land for 4 ploughs, of which 2 hides are in lordship; ½ plough
there; 5 slaves;
     6 villagers and 3 smallholders with 2 ploughs and 1½ hides.   31
     Pasture 7 furlongs long and 2 furlongs wide;   a 3

Silua . v . q̃rent lḡ ˖7 iiii˖q̃ɫ lat̄ . Valuit ˖ iiii . lib̄ ˖ M̃odo̅ . c̃ . ſolid̃˖

Huic ꝏ ptĩn una v̄ træ ˖ quã Aluric habuit in uadimonio pro

dimid Mark auri ˖7 necdũ ˖ ē redēpta.

Rᴇx teñ ᴛᴀʀᴇɴᴛᴇ . Aluuĩn tenuit T.R.E.˖7 geldb̄ ꝑ dĩm hida˖

T̃ra . ē . i . car̄ . Ibi ſt̄ . ii . bord̃ . Valet . x . ſolid̃.

Rᴇx teñ ᴛᴀʀᴇɴᴛᴇ . Duo taini tenuer̄ T.R.E.˖7 geldb̄ ꝑ.iii.hid̃

7 una v̄ træ . T̃ra . ē . iii . car̄ . De ea ſt̄ in dñio . ii . hidæ.˖7 iii.v̄ tre˖

7 ibi . i . car̄.˖7 iiii . ſerui.˖7 ii . uilłi 7 iiii . bord̃.   Ibi moliñ

redd̃ . iiii . ſoł.˖7 xiii . ãc ꝓti . Paſtura . iiii. q̃ɫ lḡ.˖7 tũtd̃ lat̄.

Valuit . iiii . lib̄ . Modo . iii . lib̄.

Rᴇx teñ ꜱᴄᴇᴛʀᴇ . Vluiet tenuit T.R.E.˖7 geldb̄ ꝑ . v . hid̃.

T̃ra.ē.iiii . car̄.De ea ſt̄ in dñio . iii ˖ hidæ 7 dim̃.˖7 ibi . i . car̄.

7 v . ſerui.˖7 vi . uilłi 7 iii . bord̃ cũ . i . car̄ . Ibi . iiii ˖ ãc ꝓti.Paſtura.

ii . q̃ɫ lḡ.˖7 ii . lat̄ . Silua . iii . q̃ɫ lḡ.˖7 iii . lat̄ . Valuit.vi.lib̄.m̃˖c.ſoł

Rᴇx teñ ɴᴏʀᴛꜰᴏʀᴅᴇ . Aluric tenuit T.R.E.˖7 geldb̄ ꝑ.ii . hid̃

7 dimid̃ . T̃ra . ē . ii . car̄ . Ibi ſt̄ . ii . ſerui.˖7 iii . coſcez .˖7 viii .ãc ꝓti˖

Paſtura . i . q̃ɫ lḡ .˖7 i . lat̄ . Valuit 7 ual . xxv . ſolid̃.

Rᴇx teñ ᴡᴀᴛʀᴇᴄᴏᴍᴇ . Aluric tenuit T.R.E.˖7 geldb̄ ꝑ . i . hida.

T̃ra . ē . i . car̄ . Ibi . ē uñ coſcet.˖7 dim̃ moliñ redd̃ . iiii . ſoł.paſtura

una leu lḡ.˖7 una q̃ɫ . Redd̃ . xv . ſolid̃.

Qui has t̃ras T.R.E. teneb̄: poteraʄ ire ad quē dñm uolebant.

Rᴇx teñ ᴍᴇʟᴄᴏᴍᴇ . Herald abſtulit injuſte S ᴍᴀʀɪᴁ Sceftesbiæ.

T.R.E.geldb̄ ꝑ.x.hid̃ . T̃ra.ē.x.car̄. De ea ſt̄ in dñio.vii.hidæ 7 dim̃.

7 una v̄ træ.˖7 ibi.ii.car̄.˖7 iiii.ſerui.˖7 ix . uilłi 7 xx . bord̃ cũ.vii.car̄.

woodland 5 furlongs long and 3 furlongs wide. 1 cob;   75 d
30 pigs; 300 sheep, less 10.
The value was £4; now 100s.   E
    To this manor belongs 1 virgate of land which Aelfric had in   E
pledge for ½ gold mark; it has not yet been redeemed.

25 'TARRANT'. Alwin held it before 1066. It paid tax for ½ hide.   31
    Land for 1 plough.   b 1
    2 smallholders.
    Value 10s.

26 'TARRANT'. Two thanes held it before 1066. It paid tax for
    3 hides and 1 virgate of land. Land for 3 ploughs, of which 2
    hides and 3 virgates of land are in lordship; 1 plough there;   32
    4 slaves;   a 1
        2 villagers and 4 smallholders (have) ½ hide.
    A mill which pays 4s; meadow, 13 acres; pasture 4 furlongs
        long and as wide. 15 pigs; 60 sheep.
    The value was £4; now £3.

27 *SCETRE*. Wulfgeat held it before 1066. It paid tax for 5 hides.
    Land for 4 ploughs, of which 3½ hides are in lordship;
    1 plough there; 5 slaves;   31
        6 villagers and 3 smallholders with 1 plough and 1½ hides.   b 2
    Meadow, 4 acres; pasture 2 furlongs long and 2 wide;
        woodland 3 furlongs long and 3 wide. 20 pigs; 120 sheep.
    The value was £6; now 100s.

28 NUTFORD. Aelfric held it before 1066. It paid tax for 2½ hides.   E
    Land for 2 ploughs. 2 slaves;   31
    3 Cottagers.   E b 3
    Meadow, 8 acres; pasture 1 furlong long and 1 wide.
        4 cattle; 80 sheep.
    The value was and is 25s.

29 WATERCOMBE. Aelfric held it before 1066. It paid tax for 1 hide.
    Land for 1 plough.
    1 Cottager.   31
    ½ mill which pays 4s; pasture 1 league long and 1 furlong [wide].   b 4
    It pays 15s.

The holders of these lands before 1066 could go to which lord they   E
would.

30 MELCOMBE (Horsey). Earl Harold wrongfully took it away from   E
    St. Mary's, Shaftesbury. Before 1066 it paid tax for 10 hides.
    Land for 10 ploughs, of which 7½ hides and 1 virgate of land   (·)
    are in lordship; 2 ploughs there; 4 slaves;
        9 villagers and 20 smallholders with 7 ploughs.

Ibi . v , ac p̄ti . 7 una leū ſiluæ . Paſtura . i . leū l̄g . 7 viii . q̄ꝗ laꝼ.

7 xii . ac p̄ti præſtitæ fueꝛ W̄lgaro . p̱tin eid ꝏ . Modo ten W̄iſſs belet.

Huic ꝏ adjunx̄ Goda . iii . v̄ træ 7 dimiꝺ . q̄s teneƀ tres liƀi taini

T.R.E . 7 ꝑ tanto geldƀ . Tra . ē . i . caꝛ . q̄ ibi . ē cū . iii . uiſſis . 7 xv . ac

p̄ti . 7 v . ac ſiluæ . Hæ . iii . v̄ 7 dim ſt in BOCHELANDE HVND.

Toꝼ ualuit 7 uaſ . xvi . liƀ . Goda comitiſſa tenuit.

76 a, b

▷Rᴇx ten HINETONE . Goda tenuit T.R.E . 7 geldƀ ꝓ . comitiſſa

xiiii . hiꝺ 7 una v̄ træ . Tra . ē . xii . caꝛ . De ea ſt in dn̄io

vi . hidæ 7 una v̄ træ . 7 ibi . ē una caꝛ . 7 viii . uiſſi 7 xiiii . borꝺ

hn̄t . iii . caꝛ . Ibi moliñ redd . x . ſoliꝺ . 7 xxxvii . ac p̄ti.

Paſtura . v . q̄ꝗ l̄g . 7 tn̄td laꝼ . Silua . i . leū l̄g . 7 dimiꝺ

leū laꝼ . Valet . xiii . liƀ . 7 v . ſoliꝺ.

╱De hac ead tra tenuit q̄dā pƀr . i . hidā jn tainlande

. 7 poterat cū ea ire q̄ uoleƀ . Modo . ē in dn̄io regis.

╱De ead tra tenuit alt pƀr . ii . hiꝺ 7 dimiꝺ . Harū unā hꝼ eꝓs

Lixouienſis in dn̄io . 7 ualet . xx . ſoliꝺ . Pƀr ū huj ꝏ hꝼ alterā

hidā 7 dimiꝺ . 7 ibi hꝼ . ii . caꝛ cū . iiii . uiſſis 7 ii . borꝺ . 7 moliñ

redd . v . ſoliꝺ . 7 xi . acs p̄ti . 7 unā q̄ꝗ ſiluæ in l̄g . 7 dim q̄ꝗ in laꝼ.

7 in Winburne . xi . domos . Toꝼ ualet . xxx . ſoliꝺ.

Hic pƀr cū ſua tra poterat ire q̄ uoleƀ T.R.E.

╱De ipſa ead tra ten alius pƀr| in TARENTE . unā hiꝺ 7 tciā partē manens

. i . hidæ . 7 ibi hꝼ . iii . uiſſos 7 iiii . borꝺ cū . i . caꝛ . 7 i . ac p̄ti.

7 v . q̄ꝗ paſturæ in l̄g . 7 una q̄ꝗ in laꝼ . Valet . xxx . ſoliꝺ.

╱De ipſa ead tra ten Vluric unā v̄ træ . 7 ualet . ii . ſoliꝺ.

╱De ead ipſa tra p̱tin ad æcclam de WINBVRNE . i . hida . 7

dimiꝺ . 7 dimiꝺ v̄ træ . Mauricius eꝓs tenet . 7 ibi hꝼ . vi . borꝺ

7 viii . burḡſes . 7 moliñ redd . v . ſoliꝺ . 7 xv . acs p̄ti . 7 dimiꝺ leū

paſturæ in l̄g . 7 iiii . q̄ꝗ in laꝼ . Valet . vi . liƀ . 7 vii . ſoſ . 7 vi . den.

Meadow, 5 acres; woodland, 1 league; pasture 1 league long
and 8 furlongs wide. 12 acres of meadow which belong to
this manor were leased to Wulfgar White; now William
Bellett holds them.
Goda attached to this manor 3½ virgates of land which three
free thanes held before 1066. They paid tax for as much.
Land for 1 plough, which is there, with
    3 villagers.
Meadow, 15 acres; woodland, 5 acres.
These 3½ virgates are in Buckland Hundred.
The value of the whole was and is £16.
    Countess Goda held it.

Ψ *Column 75d continues after 1,31*

Entered on an inserted piece of parchment, folio 76a,b; see note

Ψ31 HINTON (Martell). Countess Goda held it before 1066.   E 76 a,b
It paid tax for 14 hides and 1 virgate of land. Land for
12 ploughs, of which 6 hides and 1 virgate of land are in
lordship; 1 plough there.
    8 villagers and 14 smallholders have 3 ploughs.
    A mill which pays 10s; meadow, 37 acres; pasture 5 furlongs
        long and as wide; woodland 1 league long and ½ league wide.
Value £13 5s.   (·)
    Also of this land a priest held 1 hide in thaneland; he could
go where he would with it; now it is in the King's lordship.
    Another priest held 2½ hides of this land. The Bishop of
Lisieux has one of these in lordship; value 20s. A priest of
this manor has the other 1½ hides; he has 2 ploughs there, with
    4 villagers and 2 smallholders.
    A mill which pays 5s; meadow, 11 acres; woodland, 1 furlong
        in length and ½ furlong in width; 11 houses in Wimborne
        (Minster).
Value of the whole 30s.
    This priest could go where he would with his land before 1066.
    Also of this land another priest living in 'Tarrant' holds 1 hide
and the third part of 1 hide. He has
    3 villagers and 4 smallholders with 1 plough.
    Meadow, 1 acre; pasture, 5 furlongs in length and 1 furlong
        in width.
Value 30s.
    Also of this land Wulfric holds 1 virgate of land; value 2s.
    Also of this land 1½ hides and ½ virgate of land belong to
Wimborne Church. Bishop Maurice holds them; he has
    6 smallholders and 8 burgesses and
    a mill which pays 5s; meadow, 15 acres; pasture, ½ league
        in length and 4 furlongs in width.
Value £6 7s 6d.

.II.   TERRA EPI SARISBERIENSIS.

EPS SARISBER ten CERMINSTRE . T.R.E.geldb ꝑ.x.hiđ.
Tra.ē.viii.car̄. In dñio sꝶ.ii. car̄.7 iiii.serui.7 xiiii.uilli.
7 xii.borđ.cū.vi.car̄. Ibi moliñ redđ.vi.sot.7 xv.ac ꝑti.
paſtura.i.leū lḡ.7 iii.q̇ᵹ lat̄. Silua.ii.q̇ᵹ lḡ.7 una q̇ᵹ lat̄.
In Warhā.ii.burḡſes cū.xii.acris træ.7 In Doreceſtre.i.burḡs
cū.x.acris træ ꝑtiñ huic ꝏ.Valuit 7 ualet.xvi.lib.
De hac tra ten unus ꝓpoſit regis.i.hiđ.7 ibi hꝶ.i.car̄ cū.iii.borđ.
In ipſo ꝏ hꝶ eꝑs tanꝶ træ.quanꝶ poſſunt arare.ii.car̄.ħ nunꝗ gelđ.
Idē eꝑs ten ALTONE . T.R.E.geldb ꝑ.vi.hiđ.Tra.ē.vi.car̄.
ꝓter hanc hꝶ tra̅.ii.car̄ in dñio.quæ nunꝗ geldauit.7 ibi hꝶ
.ii.car̄.7 iiii.seruos.7 vi.uillos 7 x.borđ cū.i.car̄.Ibi moliñ redđ
.xv.soliđ.7 vii.ac ꝑti.Paſtura.vi.q̇ᵹ lḡ.7 ii.q̇ᵹ lat̄.Silua.ii.
q̇ᵹ lḡ.7 una q̇ᵹ lat̄.
De eađ tra hꝶ Eduuard.ii.hiđ.7 dim̅.Pagen.ii.hiđ 7 dimiđ.
Ibi sꝶ.iii.car̄.7 i.uillos 7 v.borđ cū.i.car̄.7 paſtura.iiii.q̇ᵹ lḡ.7 ii.lat̄.
Dñium eꝑi ualet.xii.lib.Homiñ û.́uat.iiii.lib.
Idē eꝑs ten OBCERNE . T.R.E.geldb ꝑ.ii.hiđ 7 dim̅.Tra.ē.iiii.
car̄.De ca.ē in dñio.i.hida 7 dim̅.7 ibi.iii.car̄.7 vi.serui.7 iiii.
uilli 7 viii.borđ cū.i.car̄.Ibi moliñ redđ.xv.sot.7 vii.ac ꝑti.
paſtura.i.leū lḡ.7 iii.q̇ᵹ lat̄.Valet.x.lib.Robꝶ ten de eꝑo.
Idē eꝑs ten ETIMINSTRE.T.R.E.geldb ꝑ.xv.hiđ.Tra.ē.xx.car̄.
ꝓter hanc hꝶ tra̅.vi.car̄.ꝗ nunꝗ geldauit T.R.E.Ibi sꝶ.iiii.
car̄ in dñio.7 vi.serui.7 xxv.uilli 7 xxv.borđ.cū.viii.car̄.
Ibi moliñ redđ.v.sot.7 xxx.ac ꝑti.paſtura.ii.q̇ᵹ lḡ.7 una q̇ᵹ
lat̄.Silua.i.leū lḡ.7 alia lat̄.Valuit 7 uat.xxii.lib.

Column 75d continued

2   **LAND OF THE BISHOP OF SALISBURY**   E

1 The Bishop of Salisbury holds CHARMINSTER. Before 1066 it paid
tax for 10 hides. Land for 8 ploughs. In lordship 2 ploughs;
4 slaves;
   14 villagers and 12 smallholders with 6 ploughs.
A mill which pays 6s; meadow, 15 acres; pasture 1 league
   long and 3 furlongs wide; woodland 2 furlongs long and
   1 furlong wide.
In Wareham 2 burgesses with 12 acres of land. In Dorchester
   1 burgess with 10 acres of land. They belong to this manor.
The value was and is £16.
A reeve of the King's holds 1 hide of this land; he has 1
plough there, with 3 smallholders.
   In this manor the Bishop has as much land as 2 ploughs can
plough; it has never paid tax.

  The Bishop also holds
2 ALTON (Pancras). Before 1066 it paid tax for 6 hides.
Land for 6 ploughs. Besides this he has land for 2 ploughs
in lordship which has never paid tax. He has 2 ploughs there
and 4 slaves and
   6 villagers and 10 smallholders with 1 plough.
A mill which pays 15s; meadow, 7 acres; pasture 6 furlongs
   long and 2 furlongs wide; woodland 2 furlongs long and
   1 furlong wide.
Also of this land Edward has 2½ hides, Payne 2½ hides. 3
ploughs there.
   1 villager and 5 smallholders with 1 plough.
   Pasture 4 furlongs long and 2 wide.
Value of the Bishop's lordship £13; value of the men's, £4.

3 UP CERNE. Before 1066 it paid tax for 2½ hides. Land for 4
ploughs, of which 1½ hides are in lordship; 3 ploughs there;
6 slaves;
   4 villagers and 8 smallholders with 1 plough.
A mill which pays 15s; meadow, 7 acres; pasture 1 league
   long and 3 furlongs wide.
Value £10.
Robert holds from the Bishop.

4 YETMINSTER. Before 1066 it paid tax for 15 hides. Land for
20 ploughs. Besides this he has land for 6 ploughs which
never paid tax before 1066. 4 ploughs in lordship; 6 slaves;
   25 villagers and 25 smallholders with 8 ploughs.
A mill which pays 5s; meadow, 30 acres; pasture 2 furlongs long
   and 1 furlong wide; woodland 1 league long and another wide.
The value was and is £22.

De hac ead tra ten Wilts de ep̄o.vi.hid.7 ibi hr̄.iiii.car.7 iiii.

ſeruos.7 vi.uiłłos.7 x.bord.cū.ii.car̄.7 moliñ.7 xii.acs p̄ti.

7 Silua.iii.q̊ʒ l̄g.7 una q̊ʒ lat̄.Valet.iiii.lib̄.

Qui teneb̄.T.R.E.ñ poterant ab æccła ſeparari.

Id̄e ep̄s teñ LYM.Tra.ē.i.car̄.Nunɋ geldauit.Piſcatores teneꞃ

7 redd.xv.ſolid monachis ad piſces.Ibi st̄.iiii.ac̄ p̄ti.

Ibi hr̄ ep̄s.i.domū redd.vi.denar̄.

77 a

Ip̄ſe ep̄s teñ SCIREBVRNE.Eddid regina tenuit.7 ante eā

Aluuold ep̄s.T.R.E.geldb̄ ꝑ.xl.iii.hid.Tra.ē.xlvi.car̄.

De hac tra ten ep̄s.xii.hid.7 ibi hr̄.xxv.uiłłos 7 xiiii.bord

cū.xii.car̄.Ibi.cxxx.ac̄ p̄ti.de ɋbʒ.iii.ac̄ st̄ in Sūmerſete

juxta Meleburne.Paſtura.i.leū l̄g.7 una lat̄.Silua.ii.

leū l̄g.7 tntd lat̄.

De ead tra huj ꝳ teñ de ep̄o Otbold.iiii.hid.Sinod.v.hid.

7 dim.Ingelbert.v.hid.Waleran.iii.hid.Radulf.iii.hid.

f. Grip

Vxor Hugonis.ii.hid.In his.xxii.hid 7 dim st̄.xxi.car̄.

7 xxxiii.uiłłi.7 xv.bord.7 x.coſcez.7 iiii.ſerui.

Ibi.iiii.molini redd.xviii.ſolid.7 dimid.

De ead etiā tra ten.vi.taini.viii.hid 7 dimid.7 ibi hñt.viii.

car̄.7 iiii.ſeruos.7 xvii.uiłłos.7 xix.bord.7 iii.moliñ redd

In hoc ꝳ SCIREBVRNE pt ſup̄dict̄a tram ⌐xxx.denar̄.

hr̄ ep̄s in dñio.xvi.carucat træ.H tra nunɋ ꝑ hid diuiſa

fuit neqʒ geldauit.Ibi st̄ in dñio.v.car̄.7 xxvi.uiłłi

7 xxvi.bord 7 viii.ſerui cū.xi.car̄.Ibi moliñ redd.x.ſoł.

De hac q̇eta tra ten Sinod de ep̄o.i.car̄ træ.7 Eduuard

aliā.Ibi st̄.ii.car̄.7 ii.ſerui.7 viii.bord.

III. In hac ead SCIREBVRNE ten monachi ejd̄e ep̄i.ix.caru

catas træ 7 dim.q̇ nec ꝑ hid diuiſæ fuer̄.nec unɋ geldauer̄.

William holds 6 hides also of this land from the Bishop.
He has 4 ploughs there and 4 slaves and
6 villagers and 10 smallholders with 2 ploughs.
A mill; meadow, 12 acres; woodland 3 furlongs long and
1 furlong wide.
Value £4.
The holders before 1066 could not be separated from the church.

5 LYME (Regis). Land for 1 plough. It has never paid tax.
Fishermen hold it; they pay 15s to the monks for fish.
Meadow, 4 acres.
The Bishop has 1 house there which pays 6d.

6 The Bishop holds SHERBORNE himself. Queen Edith held it, and   77 a
before her Bishop Alfwold. Before 1066 it paid tax for 43 hides.
Land for 46 ploughs. The Bishop holds 12 hides of this land;
he has
25 villagers and 14 smallholders with 12 ploughs.
Meadow, 130 acres of which 3 acres are in Somerset near
Milborne (Port); pasture 1 league long and 1 wide; woodland
2 leagues long and as wide.
Also of this manor's land Odbold holds 4 hides from the Bishop,
Sinoth 5½ hides, Engelbert 5 hides, Waleran 3 hides, Ralph 3
hides the wife of Hugh son of Grip 2 hides. On these 22½ hides
are 21 ploughs.
33 villagers, 15 smallholders, 10 Cottagers and 4 slaves.
4 mills which pay 18½s.
Six thanes hold 8½ hides also of this land. They have 8 ploughs
and 4 slaves and
17 villagers and 19 smallholders.
3 mills which pay 30d.
In this manor (of) Sherborne, besides the said land, the Bishop
has in lordship 16 carucates of land. This land was never divided
into hides and did not pay tax. In lordship 5 ploughs;
26 villagers, 26 smallholders and 8 slaves with 11 ploughs.
A mill which pays 10s.
Of this exempt land Sinoth holds 1 carucate of land from the
Bishop, and Edward another. 2 ploughs there; 2 slaves; 8 smallholders.

3   [LAND OF THE MONKS OF SHERBORNE]   E

1 In this same SHERBORNE the monks of this Bishop hold 9½ carucates
of land which were not divided into hides and never paid tax.

Ibi st̄ in dn̄io . III . car̄ 7 dim̄.7 IIII . ſerui .7 x . uil̄li 7 x.borð

cū . v . car̄ .7 III . molini redð xxII . ſol̄.7 xx . ac̄ p̄ti . Silua

una leū lḡ.7 IIII . q̄ƺ lat̄

De hac t̄ra monachoƺ ten̄ Lanbt de eis . I . car̄ træ.7 ibi

ht̄ . I . car̄.7 molin̄ redð . v . ſoliđ

Qð ht̄ ep̄s in dn̄io in hoc M̄ .'ualet . L . lib̄ . Qð monachi .'

vI . lib̄ 7 x . ſoliđ . Qð milites ep̄i .'xxvII . lib̄.Qð taini .'vI.lib̄.

Sup h̄ adhuc ten̄ Sinod de ep̄o . I . hiđ in eað uilla.7 ibi

ht̄ . I . car̄.7 II . ſeruos.7 II . borð . Valet xII . ſoliđ

H hiđā tenuit Aluuarð de rege . E . ſed tam̄ pus fuerat de ep̄atu.

Iđē ep̄s ten̄ WOCBVRNE . T . R . E . geldb̄ ᵽ . v . hiđ . T̄ra .ē . IIII .

car̄ . De ea st̄ in dn̄io . II . hidæ.7 ibi . I . car̄.7 II . ſerui.7 vI.uil̄li

7 v . borð cū . III . car̄ . Ibi . vIII . ac̄ p̄ti.7 IIII.ac̄ ſiluæ minutæ.

Valet . IIII . lib̄.

Iđē ep̄s ten̄ TORNEFORD . T . R . E . geldb̄ ᵽ . vII . hiđ . T̄ra .ē

vI . car̄ . De ea st̄ in dn̄io . III . hidæ.7 ibi.II . car̄ . cū . I . ſeruo.

7 vII . uil̄li 7 vII . borð cū . IIII . car̄ . Ibi molin̄ redð . xII . ſoliđ

7 vI . den̄.7 xvI . ac̄ p̄ti . Silua . x . q̄ƺ lḡ.7 una q̄ƺ lat̄

Valet . c . ſoliđ.

Iđē ep̄s ten̄ BRADEFORD . T . R . E.geldb̄ ᵽ.x.hiđ . T̄ra.ē.x.car̄.

De ea.ē in dn̄io.I.hida 7 dim̄.7 ibi.III.car̄.7 vII.ſerui.7 vIII.

uil̄li 7 vII .borð cū.vII . car̄ . Ibi molin̄ redð.xv.ſoliđ.7 xx.

ac̄ p̄ti.7 III.ac̄ ſiluæ minutæ . Valet . x . lib̄.

Iđē ep̄s CONTONE . T . R . E.geldb̄ ᵽ.vI.hiđ.7 III.v̄ træ.T̄ra.ē

vIII.car̄.De ea ē in dn̄io.I.hida 7 III.v̄ træ.7 ibi.II.car̄.

7 vI.ſerui.7 xIII.uil̄li 7 x.borð.cū.vI.car̄.Ibi molin̄ redð

x.ſoliđ.7 xvI.ac̄ p̄ti.Silua.II.q̄ƺ lḡ 7 lat̄.Valet.vI.lib̄.

Iđē ep̄s ten̄ STAPLEBRIGE . T . R . E.geld ᵽ.xx.hiđ.T̄ra.ē

xvI.car̄.De ea st̄ in dn̄io.vI.hidæ.7 ibi.II.car̄.cū.I.ſeruo.

In lordship 3½ ploughs; 4 slaves;
10 villagers and 10 smallholders with 5 ploughs.
3 mills which pay 22s; meadow, 20 acres; woodland 1 league
long and 4 furlongs wide.
Of this land of the monks Lambert holds 1 carucate of land
from them; he has 1 plough there; a mill which pays 5s.
Value of what the Bishop has in lordship in this manor, £50;
of what the monks (have), £6 10s; of what the Bishop's men-at-
arms (have), £27; of what the thanes (have), £6.
Further, in addition to this, Sinoth holds 1 hide from the
Bishop in the same village; he has 1 plough there, 2 slaves
and 2 smallholders. Value 12s. Alward held this hide from
King Edward, but previously, however, it had been (part) of
the Bishopric.

The Bishop also holds
2 OBORNE. Before 1066 it paid tax for 5 hides. Land for 4 ploughs,
of which 2 hides are in lordship; 1 plough there; 2 slaves;
6 villagers and 5 smallholders with 3 ploughs.
Meadow, 8 acres; underwood, 4 acres.
Value £4.

3 THORNFORD. Before 1066 it paid tax for 7 hides. Land for 6
ploughs, of which 3 hides are in lordship; 2 ploughs there,
with 1 slave;
7 villagers and 7 smallholders with 4 ploughs.
A mill which pays 12s 6d; meadow, 16 acres; woodland 10
furlongs long and 1 furlong wide.
Value 100s.

4 BRADFORD (Abbas). Before 1066 it paid tax for 10 hides. Land
for 10 ploughs, of which 1½ hides are in lordship; 3 ploughs
there; 7 slaves;
8 villagers and 7 smallholders with 7 ploughs.
A mill which pays 15s; meadow, 20 acres; underwood, 3 acres.
Value £10.

5 COMPTON. Before 1066 it paid tax for 6 hides and 3 virgates of
land. Land for 8 ploughs, of which 1 hide and 3 virgates of land
are in lordship; 2 ploughs there; 6 slaves;
13 villagers and 10 smallholders with 6 ploughs.
A mill which pays 10s; meadow, 16 acres; woodland 2 furlongs
long and wide.
Value £6.

6 STALBRIDGE. Before 1066 it paid tax for 20 hides. Land for 16
ploughs, of which 6 hides are in lordship; 2 ploughs there, with
1 slave;

7 XIX . uiłłi 7 II . borđ cū . XI . cař . Ibi moliñ redđ . xv . foliđ.

7 XXV . ãc p̃ti . paſtura . IIII . q̃ʒ l̄g.7 II . q̃ʒ lař . Silua . I . leū

l̄g.7 III . q̃ʒ lař.　　Valet . XII . lib.　　∫ Valet xx . fol.

De eađ tra teñ Lanbt . II . hiđ.7 ibi h̃ . I . cař . cū . VI . borđ.

De eađ etiā tra teñ Manaſſes . III . virg . q̃s . W . fili⁹ regis tulit

ab æccła fine confenfu ep̃i 7 monachoʒ . Ibi . ē . I . cař.

Ipfe ep̃s teñ WESTONE . T . R . E . geldb ₚ . VIII . hiđ . Tra.ē.VI.

cař . De ea s̃t in đñio . v . hidæ 7 ibi . II . cař . cū . I . feruo.7 VII.

uiłłi 7 VII . borđ cū . III . cař . Ibi . XII . ãc p̃ti . Silua modica

IIII . q̃ʒ l̄g .7 una q̃ʒ lař . Valet . VII . lib.

Iđe ep̃s teñ CORSCVBE . T . R . E . geldb ₚ . x . hiđ una v̄ min.⁹

Tra.ē.IX.cař.De ea s̃t in đñio . IIII . hidæ . 7 III·uirgatæ ibi . III . cař . cū . I . feruo.

7 VII . uiłłi 7 VII . cofcez cū . VII . cař . Ibi moliñ redđ . v . foliđ.

7 x . ãc p̃ti . Paſtura . IX . q̃ʒ l̄g.7 IIII . q̃ʒ lař . Silua . I . leū l̄g.

7 IIII . q̃ʒ lař . Valet . VII . lib.

Iđe ep̃s teñ STOCHE . T . R . E . geldb ₚ . VI . hiđ 7 dim . Tra.ē.VII.

cař . Præter hanc s̃t ibi . II . carucatæ træ q̃ nunq̃ diuifæ s̃t

p hiđ.7 ibi in đñio . ē . I . cař . cū . I . feruo.7 VI . cofcez.

77 b

Ibi . VIII . uiłłi h̃ñt . IIII . cař .7 II . taini teñ . II . hiđ.7 dim.7 ibi h̃ñt

. II . cař .7 XII . cofcez 7ᵢv . feruos.7 moliñ redđ . v . foliđ.

Paſtura . v . q̃ʒ l̄g .7 III . q̃ʒ lař . Silua modica . III . q̃ʒ l̄g .7 II . q̃ʒ lař.

Dñium ualet . VI . lib . Qđ taini teñ . XL . foliđ.

H̃ NOVĒ DESCRIPTA MANER SVÑ DE VICTV MONACHOʒ SCIREBVRÑ.

Ep̃s iđe teñ BEIMINSTRE . T . R . E . geldb ₚ . XVI . hiđ 7 una v̄ træ

Tra.ē.XX.cař.Præt hanc trā h̃t in đñio . II . carucat træ q̃ nunq̃

geldaueř .7 ibi h̃t . II . cař .7 moliñ redđ . xx . deñ.Sub ep̃o s̃t . XIX . uiłłi.

7 xx . borđ .7 v . ferui .7 XXXIII . ãc p̃ti . paſtura . I . leū l̄g .7 dim leū lař.

Silua . I . leū 7 dim l̄g .7 dim leū lař.

19 villagers and 2 smallholders with 11 ploughs.

A mill which pays 15s; meadow, 25 acres; pasture 4 furlongs long and 2 furlongs wide; woodland 1 league long and 3 furlongs wide.

Value £12.

Lambert holds 2 hides also of this land. He has 1 plough there, with 6 smallholders. Value 20s.

Also of this land Manasseh holds 3 virgates which W(illiam) son of the King took from the church without the agreement of the Bishop and monks. 1 plough there.

7 The Bishop holds (Stalbridge) WESTON himself. Before 1066 it paid tax for 8 hides. Land for 6 ploughs, of which 5 hides are in lordship; 2 ploughs there, with 1 slave;

7 villagers and 7 smallholders with 3 ploughs.

Meadow, 12 acres; a small wood 4 furlongs long and 1 furlong wide.

Value £7.

The Bishop also holds

8 CORSCOMBE. Before 1066 it paid tax for 10 hides, less 1 virgate. Land for 9 ploughs, of which 4 hides and 3 virgates are in lordship; 3 ploughs there, with 1 slave;

7 villagers and 7 Cottagers with 7 ploughs.

A mill which pays 5s; meadow, 10 acres; pasture 9 furlongs long and 4 furlongs wide; woodland 1 league long and 4 furlongs wide.

Value £7.

9 STOKE (Abbott). Before 1066 it paid tax for 6½ hides. Land for 7 ploughs. Besides this there are 2 carucates of land which have never been divided into hides. In lordship 1 plough, with 1 slave; 6 Cottagers.

8 villagers have 4 ploughs.

Two thanes hold 2½ hides; they have 2 ploughs and 12 Cottagers and 5 slaves.

A mill which pays 5s; ... pasture 5 furlongs long and 3 furlongs wide; a small wood 3 furlongs long and 2 furlongs wide.

Value of the lordship £6; of what the thanes hold, 40s.

77 b

THESE NINE MANORS DESCRIBED ARE FOR THE SUPPLIES OF THE MONKS OF SHERBORNE

10 BEAMINSTER. Before 1066 it paid tax for 16 hides and 1 virgate of land. Land for 20 ploughs. Besides this land he has in lordship 2 carucates of land which have never paid tax; he has 2 ploughs there; a mill which pays 20d. Under the Bishop are

19 villagers, 20 smallholders and 5 slaves.

Meadow, 33 acres; pasture 1 league long and ½ league wide; woodland 1½ leagues long and ½ league wide.

De ead tra ten de epo Algar.ii.hid.H.de cartrai.ii.hid una v min.

Sinod.v.hid.Brictuin.i.hid 7 dim.Ibi st.ix.car.7 xi.ferui.7 xix.

bord.7 ii.uitti 7 ii.cofcez.7 ii.molini redd.xxviii.den.7 xl.ac pti.

Paftura.iiii.q̄ lḡ.7 ii.q̄ lat.7 adhuc.xxx.ii.ac pafturæ.Silua.xiii.
q̄ lḡ.7 ix.q̄ lat.

Dnium epi.ualet.xvi.lib.Houm u.vii.lib.

Ide eps ten NIDERBERIE.T.R.E.geldb p.xx.hid.Tra.e.xx.car.

Pter hanc ht in dnio.ii.carucat træ q̄ nunq geldau.7 ibi st.ii.car.

Ibi.xviii.uitti 7 xxii.bord.7 vi.ferui.cu.viii.car.Ibi molin redd.x.fot.

7 xvi.ac pti.7 iii.q̄ pafturæ.Silua.ix.q̄ lḡ.7 una q̄ lat.

De ead tra ten de epo Tezelin.v.hid 7 iii.v træ.Wilts.ii.hid.Godefrid
ii.hid.Serlo.i.hid.Ibi st.x.car.7 xii.uitti 7 xxiiii.bord 7 v.ferui.

Ibi molin redd.v.fot.7 xxi.ac pti.7 iiii.q̄rent filuæ in lḡ 7 lat.

Dnium epi ualet.xvi.lib.Hominu.viii.lib 7 x.folid.

In BRIDEPORT ht eps dimid acr redd.vi.denar.

Ide eps ten CERDESTOCHE.7 ii.milites de eo Walt 7 Wilts.T.R.E.geldb
p.xii.hid.Tra.e.xx.car.De ea st in dnio.iiii.hidæ.7 ibi.iiii.car.7 vi.
ferui.7 xlv.uitti 7 xxi.bord.cu.xvii.car.Ibi.ii.molini redd.xx.fot.

7 x.ac pti.Paftura.iii.leu lḡ.7 una leu 7 dim lat.Silua.ii leu lḡ 7 lat.

7 in alia parte.iii.q̄ filuæ minutæ lḡ.7 ii.q̄ lat.Tot ualet.xvi.lib.

HAS TRAS QUÆ SVBTERSCRIBVNT.HABET EPS p EXCABIO DE SCIPELEIA.

In CERNEL ht eps.i.hid 7 dim 7 x.acs træ.Algar tenuit T.R.E.Tra.e.i.car.

Hanc ht ibi una femina 7 ten de epo.cu.iiii.bord.7 iii.acs pti.paftura
.ii.q̄ lḡ.7 una q̄ lat.Valet.xx.folid.

Also of this land Algar holds 2 hides from the Bishop,
H(umphrey) of Carteret 2 hides less 1 virgate, Sinoth 5 hides,
Brictwin 1½ hides. 9 ploughs there; 11 slaves.
19 smallholders, 2 villagers and 2 Cottagers.
2 mills which pay 28d; meadow, 40 acres; pasture 4 furlongs
long and 2 furlongs wide; a further 32 acres of pasture;
woodland 13 furlongs long and 9 furlongs wide.
Value of the Bishop's lordship £16; of the men's, £7.

11   NETHERBURY. Before 1066 it paid tax for 20 hides. Land for 20
ploughs. Besides this he has in lordship 2 carucates of land
which have never paid tax; 2 ploughs there.
18 villagers, 22 smallholders and 6 slaves with 8 ploughs.
A mill which pays 10s; meadow, 16 acres; pasture, 3 furlongs;
woodland 9 furlongs long and 1 furlong wide.
Also of this land Tesselin holds 5 hides and 3 virgates of
land from the Bishop, William 2 hides, Godfrey 2 hides,
Serlo 1½ hides. 10 ploughs there.
12 villagers, 24 smallholders and 5 slaves.
A mill which pays 5s; meadow, 21 acres; woodland, 4
furlongs in length and width.
Value of the Bishop's lordship £16; of the men's, £8 10s.

12   In BRIDPORT the Bishop has ½ acre which pays 6d.

13   The Bishop also holds CHARDSTOCK, and two men-at-arms, Walter
and William, from him. Before 1066 it paid tax for 12 hides.
Land for 20 ploughs, of which 4 hides are in lordship; 4 ploughs
there; 6 slaves;
45 villagers and 21 smallholders with 17 ploughs.
2 mills which pay 20s; meadow, 10 acres; pasture 3 leagues
long and 1½ leagues wide; woodland 2 leagues in both
length and width; elsewhere underwood, 3 furlongs long
and 2 furlongs wide.
Value of the whole £16.

THE BISHOP HAS THE UNDERMENTIONED LANDS IN EXCHANGE
FOR SHIPLEY

14   In 'CERNE' the Bishop has 1½ hides and 10 acres of land.
Aelmer held it before 1066. Land for 1 plough; a woman has it
there and holds from the Bishop, with
4 smallholders;
meadow, 3 acres; pasture 2 furlongs long and 1 furlong wide.
Value 20s.

Idē ēps ten PIDELE.7 uxor hug de eo . Agelric tenuit de rege.E.7 geldb
,p . iiii . hid . Tra . e . iii . car . In dnio . e una 7 iii . bord .7 xxxiiii . ac pti.
7 vi . q̈ꝗ pafturæ . Valuit . iiii . lib . modo . iii . lib.

Idē ēps ten PIDELE .7 Otbold de eo . Agelric tenuit T.R.E.7 geldb ,p.iiii.hid.
Tra.e.ii.car.q̄ ibi st cu.i.uitto 7 v.bord.7 v.feruis.Ibi molin redd
lx.vii . den.7 xx . ac pti.7 xx . ac pafturæ.7 v.q̈ꝗ filuæ . Valuit 7 uat

Idē ēps ten BOVEWODE .7 iii . milit de eo . Godefrid Ofwar 7 Elfric ⨍iii.lib. ★
Tres taini tenuer T.R.E.7 geldb ,p . vi . hid . Tra . e . vi . car.Ibi st.v.car.
7 iii . ferui .7 xiiii . uitti 7 xviii . bord . Ibi . iiii . ac pti 7 dim.7 x.ac pa
fturæ.7 xii . ac filuæ minutæ . Valet tot . lxx . folid.

Idē ēps ten BOCHENHA.7 Walter de eo . Tres taini teneb T.R.E.7 geldb
,p.iii.hid.Tra.e.iii.car.De ea st in dnio.ii.hidæ.7 i.v træ.7 ibi.i.car.
7 ii.ferui.7 iii.uitti 7 iiii.bord cu . ii . car . Ibi . iiii . ac pti.7 xxx.ac pa
fturæ . Silua.iiii.q̈ꝗ lg .7 ii . q̈ꝗ lat . Valet.xxx . folid . ⨍Ofmar tenet
Huic ꝏ adjacet.i.hida in WELLE.Tra.e.i.car.Ibi.e.i.bord.Valet.xl.den.

.IIII. ## TERRA EPI BAIOCENSIS.

Eps Baiocsis ten RAMESHA.7 Wadard de eo . Leuuin tenuit T.R.E.
7 geldb ,p.vi.hid.Tra . e . vi . car . De ea st in dnio . iii . hidæ.7 ibi.ii.car.
cu . i . feruo.7 x.uitti 7 vi.bord.cu . iii . car . Ibi.xii.ac pti . Paftura.i.leu
7 dimid.7 ii.q̈ꝗ lg.7 una leu 7 i.q̈ꝗ lat.Silua.i.leu 7 ii.q̈ꝗ lg.7 una leu 7 i.q̈ꝗ lat.
Valuit . x . lib . Modo.vi . lib .   ⨍fe vertere poterant.

Cu hoc ꝏ tenuit hacten Wadard.iii.v træ.q̈s teneb.v.taini T.R.E.7 q̈ uoleb

The Bishop also holds
15 'BARDOLFESTON'. Hugh's wife holds from him. Aethelric held it
from King Edward. It paid tax for 4 hides. Land for 3 ploughs.
In lordship 1;
3 smallholders.
Meadow, 34 acres; pasture, 6 furlongs.
The value was £4; now £3.

16 ATHELHAMPTON. Odbold holds from him. Aethelric held it before
1066. It paid tax for 4 hides. Land for 2 ploughs, which are
there, with
1 villager, 5 smallholders and 5 slaves.
A mill which pays 67d; meadow, 20 acres; pasture, 20 acres;
woodland, 5 furlongs.
The value was and is £3.

17 BOWOOD. Three men-at-arms, Godfrey, Osmer and Aelfric, hold
from him. Three thanes held it before 1066. It paid tax for 6
hides. Land for 6 ploughs. 5 ploughs there; 3 slaves.
14 villagers and 18 smallholders.
Meadow, 4½ acres; pasture, 10 acres; underwood, 12 acres.
Value of the whole 70s.

18 BUCKHAM. Walter holds from him. Three thanes held it before
1066. It paid tax for 3 hides. Land for 3 ploughs, of which 2 hides
and 1 virgate of land are in lordship; 1 plough there; 2 slaves;
3 villagers and 4 smallholders with 2 ploughs.
Meadow, 4 acres; pasture, 30 acres; woodland 4 furlongs long
and 2 furlongs wide.
Value 30s.
1 hide in WELLWOOD is attached to this manor. Land for 1
plough. 1 smallholder. Value 40d. Osmer holds it.

4   LAND OF THE BISHOP OF BAYEUX   E

1 The Bishop of Bayeux holds RAMPISHAM, and Wadard from him.
Leofwin held it before 1066. It paid tax for 6 hides. Land for
6 ploughs, of which 3 hides are in lordship; 2 ploughs there,
with 1 slave;
10 villagers and 6 smallholders with 3 ploughs.
Meadow, 12 acres; pasture 1½ leagues and 2 furlongs long
and 1 league and 1 furlong wide; woodland 1 league and 2
furlongs long and 1 league and 1 furlong wide.
The value was £10; now £6.
Hitherto Wadard held with this manor 3 virgates of land which
five thanes held before 1066; they could turn where they would.

TERRA EPI CONSTANTIENSIS.

EPS CONSTANTIENS ten WINTREBVRNE .7 Osbn de eo. Turmund tenuit T.R.E.7 geldb ₽.IIII. hid 7 dim . Tra . e .IIII. car . De ea st in dnio.III.hidæ 7 una v træ.7 ibi.II.car.7 II.ferui.7 v. uilli.7 III.bord cu.I.car. Ibi molin redd.XVI.denar.7 VIII.q̃ pasturæ. Silua.III.q̃ 7 dim lg.7 IIII.acs. 7 II.lat. Valuit.LX.solid.modo.c.solid.

Ide eps ten WINTREBVRNE. Duo frs tenuer T.R.E.7 geldb ₽.II.hid. Tra.e.II.car.In dnio.e.I.car.7 III.ferui.7 VI.cotar.Ibi molin redd.XV. denar.7 VIII.q̃ pasturæ lg.7 una q̃ lat.Valuit.XXX.sol.modo.L.sol. Osbn ten de epo.

TERRA EPI LISIACENSIS.

EPS LISIACENSIS ten TARENTE .Wluuard tenuit T.R.E.7 geldb ₽.V.hid.Tra.e.III.car.De ea st in dnio.III.hidæ 7 una v træ.7 ibi.II.car. 7 IIII.ferui.7 II.uilli 7 XIII.bord cu.I.car.Ibi molin redd.V.sol.7 IX. ac pti.Pastura.V.q̃ lg.7 una q̃ lat.Silua.II.q̃ lg.7 II.lat. Valuit.IIII.lib.Modo.c.solid.

Idem eps ten PRESTETVNE .Eduuard tenuit T.R.E.7 geldb ₽ una hida.Tra.e.I.car.Ibi.e dimid ac pti.7 pastura.IIII.q̃ lg.7 tntd lat.

Ide ejs ten TARENTE .Herling tenuit T.R.E.   ꟼValuit 7 ual.XX.sol. 7 geldb ₽.X.hid 7 tcia parte dim hidæ. Tra.e.VIII.car.De ea st in dnio.V.hidæ 7 dim.7 ibi.III.car.7 VI.ferui.7 XII.uilli.7 XIIII. bord cu.IIII.car.Ibi.II.molini redd XXX.sol 7 mille anguill. 7 LXXVI.ac pti.7 XXII.q̃ pasturæ in lg 7 lat.Silua.VIII.q̃ lg.7 totid lat.Valuit 7 ual.XIII.lib.

5   LAND OF THE BISHOP OF COUTANCES

1 The Bishop of Coutances holds 'WINTERBORNE', and Osbern from him. Thormund held it before 1066. It paid tax for 4½ hides. Land for 4 ploughs, of which 3 hides and 1 virgate of land are in lordship; 2 ploughs there; 2 slaves;
     5 villagers and 3 smallholders with 1 plough.
     A mill which pays 16d; pasture, 8 furlongs; woodland 3½ furlongs long and 4 acres and 2 wide.
The value was 60s; now 100s.

2 The Bishop also holds 'WINTERBORNE'. Two brothers held it before 1066. It paid tax for 2 hides. Land for 2 ploughs. In lordship 1 plough; 3 slaves;
     6 cottagers.
     A mill which pays 15d; pasture 8 furlongs long and 1 furlong wide.
The value was 30s; now 50s.
Osbern holds from the Bishop.

6   LAND OF THE BISHOP OF LISIEUX

1 The Bishop of Lisieux holds TARRANT (Crawford). Wulfward held it before 1066. It paid tax for 5 hides. Land for 3 ploughs, of which 3 hides and 1 virgate of land are in lordship; 2 ploughs there; 4 slaves;
     2 villagers and 13 smallholders with 1 plough.
     A mill which pays 5s; meadow, 9 acres; pasture 5 furlongs long and 1 furlong wide; woodland 2 furlongs long and 2 wide.
The value was £4; now 100s.

2 The Bishop also holds PRESTON. Edward the clerk held it before 1066. It paid tax for 1 hide. Land for 1 plough.
     Meadow, ½ acre; pasture 4 furlongs long and as wide.
The value was and is 20s.

3 The Bishop also holds TARRANT (Keyneston). Herling held it before 1066. It paid tax for 10 hides and the third part of ½ hide. Land for 8 ploughs, of which 5½ hides are in lordship; 3 ploughs there; 6 slaves;
     12 villagers and 14 smallholders with 4 ploughs.
     2 mills which pay 30s and 1,000 eels; meadow, 76 acres; pasture, 22 furlongs in length and width; woodland 8 furlongs long and as many wide.
The value was and is £13.

Idē eр̄s teñ C̄OME.Aluric tenuit T.R.E.7 geldb̄ p.x.hid.Tra.ē

vii.car̄.De ea st̄ in dñio.vi.hidæ 7 una v̄ træ.7 ibi.ii.car̄.7 iiii.

ferui.7 vi.uilti 7 ix.bord cū.v.car̄.Ibi.xx.ac p̄ti.7 viii.q̃ƶ

paſturæ in lḡ.7 totid lat̄.Silua.vi.q̃ƶ lḡ.7 tñtd lat̄.Valet.vii.lib̄.

.VII.   EP̄I LVNDONIENSIS.

Eр̄s Lvndon ten dimid hid in ODEHA.Aluric dod tenuit T.R.E.

Tra.ē dimid car̄.7 tam̄ ē ibi.i.car̄.7 viii.ac p̄ti.7 Silua.i.q̃ƶ

lḡ.7 dim q̃ƶ lat̄.Valuit 7 ual xii.ſol 7 vi.denar̄.

     TERRA S̄C̄Æ MARIE GLASTINGBERIENSIS.

.VIII Eccl̄a S̄ Marie Glastingber teñ NEWENTONE.T.R.E.geldb̄ pro

xxii.hid.Tra.ē.xxxv.car̄.P̄ter hanc ē tra.xiiii.car in dñio ibi.

q̃ nunq geldau.Ibi st̄.xxi.uilt 7 xviii.bord 7 x.cotar̄.7 xiii.colib̄ti

7 xv.ſerui.   Ibi.iii.molini redd.xl.ſol.7 lxvi.ac p̄ti.Silua

.ii.leū 7 dim lḡ.7 una leū lat̄.Valuit.xxx.lib̄.modo.xxv.lib̄.

De tra iſta huj M̄ teñ Waleran.vi.hid.Rogeri.i.hid.Chetel.i.hid

Hæ.viii.hidæ poſ arari.xi.car̄.Valeƞ́.vii.lib̄.

De ead tra ten Goſcelm de rege.iiii.hid.Ibi ht̄.ii.car̄.7 ii.ſeruos.7 v.

uillos 7 vi.bord cū.iiii.car̄.7 molin̄ redd.iii.ſol 7 ix.deñ.7 xvi.ac̄s p̄ti.

Silua dimid leū lḡ.7 una q̃ƶ lat̄.Valuit 7 ual.iiii.lib̄.

Ipſa æccla ten ADFORD.7 milites de ea.Quatuor taini tenuer̄ T.R.E.

7 geldb̄ p.viii.hid.Tra.ē.xvi.car̄.In dñio st̄.iiii.car̄.7 x.ſerui.7 xv.

uilti 7 xv.bord cū.vii.car̄.Ibi molin̄ redd.v.ſol.7 xxi.ac p̄ti.Paſtura   ★

vi.q̃ƶ lḡ.7 iii.q̃ƶ lat̄.Silua.ix.q̃ƶ lḡ.7 vi.q̃ƶ lat̄.Valuit 7 ual.xii.lib̄.

Vxor hugon ht̄.iiii.hid.Alured.ii.hid.Chetel.ii.hid.

4   The Bishop also holds COOMBE (Keynes). Aelfric held it before
1066. It paid tax for 10 hides. Land for 7 ploughs, of which 6
hides and 1 virgate of land are in lordship; 2 ploughs there;
4 slaves;
    6 villagers and 9 smallholders with 5 ploughs.
Meadow, 20 acres; pasture, 8 furlongs in length and as many
    wide; woodland 6 furlongs long and as wide.
Value £7.

7   [LAND] OF THE BISHOP OF LONDON   E

1   Bishop Maurice of London holds ½ hide in 'ODENHAM'. Aelfric
Doda held it before 1066. Land for ½ plough; 1 plough there,
however.
    Meadow, 8 acres; woodland 1 furlong long and ½ furlong wide.
The value was and is 12s 6d.

8   LAND OF ST. MARY'S, GLASTONBURY   E

1   St. Mary's Church, Glastonbury, holds (Sturminster) NEWTON.
Before 1066 it paid tax for 22 hides. Land for 35 ploughs. Besides
this there is land for 14 ploughs in lordship there which has never
paid tax.
    21 villagers, 18 smallholders, 10 cottagers, 13 freedmen
    and 15 slaves.
    3 mills which pay 40s; meadow, 66 acres; woodland 2½ leagues
    long and 1 league wide.
The value was £30; now £25.
    Of this manor's land Waleran holds 6 hides, Roger 1 hide,
Ketel 1 hide. These 8 hides can be ploughed by 11 ploughs.
Value £7.
    Gotshelm Cook holds 4 hides of this land from the King.
He has 2 ploughs there and 2 slaves and
    5 villagers and 6 smallholders with 4 ploughs.
    A mill which pays 3s 9d; meadow, 16 acres; woodland ½
    league long and 1 furlong wide.
The value was and is £4.

2   The Church holds OKEFORD (Fitzpaine) itself, and the men-at-arms
from it. Four thanes held it before 1066. It paid tax for 8 hides.
Land for 16 ploughs. In lordship 4 ploughs; 10 slaves;
    15 villagers and 15 smallholders with 7 ploughs.
    A mill which pays 5s; meadow, 21 acres; pasture 6 furlongs
    long and 3 furlongs wide; woodland 9 furlongs long and
    6 furlongs wide.
The value was and is £12.
    Hugh's wife has 4 hides, Alfred 2 hides, Ketel 2 hides.

Ipſa æccła teñ *Bochelande* .T.R.E.geldb ꝑ.xv.hid.Tra.e̅.xxiiii.car̅.

Pter hanc e̅ in dn̄io tra.viii.car̅.q̄ nunq̄ geldau.Ibi.in dn̄io.iiii.car̅.

⁊ iiii.ſerui ⁊ xxii.uilłi ⁊ xxii.bord.⁊ xxii.cotar̅.cu̅.viii.car̅.Ibi.xx.ac̅

p̊ti.Paſtura.ii.leu̅ łg.⁊ dim̅ leu̅ lat̅.⁊ tn̄td ſiluæ.

De ead̅ tra huj ꞏ ten de abbe uxor hug̅.vii.hid.⁊ una̅ v træ ⁊ dim̅.

⁊ Warmund.ii.hid.Ibi ſt̅ in dn̄io.iii.car̅.⁊ iiii.ſerui.⁊ iii.uilłi ⁊ vii.

bord cu̅.i.car̅.⁊ iii.ac̅ p̊ti.⁊ Silua.ii.q̂ꝫ łg.⁊ una q̂ꝫ lat̅.

Dn̄ium ækkłæ ualet.xx.lib.Hominu̅:vi.lib ⁊ x.ſolid.

Ipſa æccła teñ *Odiete*.⁊ uxor.H.de abbe.T.R.E.geldb ꝑ.iiii.hid.Tra.e̅

iiii.car̅.In dn̄io ſt̅.iii.hidæ ⁊ una v træ.⁊ ibi.i.car̅.⁊ iii.ſerui.⁊ ii.uilłi.

⁊ v.bord   Ibi paſtura.xvi.q̂ꝫ ⁊ dimid int łg ⁊ lat̅.Silua.vii.

q̄rent łg.⁊ v.q̂ꝫ ⁊ dim̅ lat̅.Valuit.iiii.lib.Modo.xl.ſoł.

Ipſa æccła tenuit *Pentric*.T.R.E.⁊ geldb ꝑ.vi.hid.Tra.e̅.vi.car̅.

Rex ten m̊ in dn̄io.⁊ ht̅.i.car̅ ibi.⁊ iiii.ſeruos.⁊ vi.uilłos.⁊ vi.bord

cu̅.iii.car̅.Ibi paſtura.viii.q̂ꝫ łg.⁊ iiii.q̂ꝫ lat̅.Silua.i.leu̅ łg.⁊ iii.q̂ꝫ

lat̅.Valet.vi.lib.Vluuard q̄ teneb.T.R.E:n̅ poterat ab æccła ſepari.

Ipſa æccła teñ *Lym*.T.R.E.geldb ꝑ.iii.hid.Tra.e̅.iiii.car̅.Vluiet

tenuit ⁊ teñ de abbe.⁊ ibi ht̅.ii.car̅.⁊ ix.uilłos ⁊ vi.bord.⁊ iiii.ac̅s

p̊ti.Paſtura.iiii.q̂ꝫ łg.⁊ ii.q̂ꝫ lat̅.⁊ x.ac̅ ſiluæ.Ibi.xiiii.ſalinarij.

redd.xiii.ſolid.Tot̅ ualet.lx.ſolid.

.IX.   TERRA ABBATIÆ S PETRI WINTONIENS.

Eccla̅ S Petri Winton teñ *Pidrie* .T.R.E.geldb ꝑ.xxx.hid.

Tra.e̅.xvii.car̅.De ea ſt̅ in dn̄io.xv.hidæ.⁊ ii.v træ ⁊ dim̅.

3 The Church holds BUCKLAND (Newton) itself. Before 1066 it paid tax for 15 hides. Land for 24 ploughs. Besides this there is in lordship land for 8 ploughs which has never paid tax. In lordship 4 ploughs; 4 slaves;
    22 villagers, 22 smallholders and 22 cottagers with 8 ploughs. Meadow, 20 acres; pasture 2 leagues long and ½ league wide; woodland, as much.
Of this manor's land Hugh's wife holds 7 hides and 1½ virgates of land from the Abbot, and Warmund 2 hides. In lordship 3 ploughs; 4 slaves;
    3 villagers and 7 smallholders with 1 plough. Meadow, 3 acres; woodland 2 furlongs long and 1 furlong wide.
Value of the Church's lordship £20; of the men's, £6 10s.

4 The Church holds WOODYATES itself, and H(ugh)'s wife (holds) from the Abbot. Before 1066 it paid tax for 4 hides. Land for 4 ploughs. In lordship 3 hides and 1 virgate of land; 1 plough there; 3 slaves;
    2 villagers and 5 smallholders ....
Pasture 16½ furlongs in both length and width; woodland 7 furlongs long and 5½ furlongs wide.
The value was £4; now 40s.

5 The Church held PENTRIDGE itself before 1066. It paid tax for 6 hides. Land for 6 ploughs. The King holds it now in lordship; he has 1 plough there and 4 slaves and
    6 villagers and 6 smallholders with 3 ploughs.
Pasture 8 furlongs long and 4 furlongs wide; woodland 1 league long and 3 furlongs wide.
Value £6.
    Wulfward who held it before 1066 could not be separated from the church.

6 The Church holds LYME (Regis) itself. Before 1066 it paid tax for 3 hides. Land for 4 ploughs. Wulfgeat held and holds it from the Abbot. He has 2 ploughs and
    9 villagers and 6 smallholders and
    meadow, 4 acres; pasture 4 furlongs long and 2 furlongs wide; woodland, 10 acres.
    13 salt-workers who pay 13s.
Value of the whole 60s.

9   LAND OF ST. PETER'S ABBEY, WINCHESTER   E 77 d

1 St. Peter's Church, Winchester, holds PIDDLETRENTHIDE.
Before 1066 it paid tax for 30 hides. Land for 17 ploughs, of which 15 hides and 2½ virgates of land are in lordship;

7 ibi.v.caɾ.7 xx.ſerui.7 xx.uiłłi 7 xxx.borđ.cū.viii.caɾ.

Ibi.iii.molini redđ.lx.ſolid.7 xvi.ãc p̃ti.Paſtura.ii.leū lḡ.7 dim̃ leu̓ lat̓.

De eađ t̓ra ten̓.i.miłes 7 q̃dã uidua.iii.hiđ.7 ibi hn̄t.ii.caɾ.

Dn̄iū æcclæ.ualet.xxviii.lib̄.Aliud.ual̓.xl.ſolid.

Hoc ᴍ̃ tenueɾ Almar 7 Aluerd T.R.E.p̃.ii.Maneɾ.de rege.E.

7 n̄ poteraꝗ̓ cū t̓ra iſta ire ad quēlibet đn̄m.

Poſtea tenuit Rogeri de rege. W.

_{arundel}

.X.   TERRA SC̃Æ MARIÆ CRENEBVRNENS̃.

Eccl̄a S̃ Mariæ Creneʙvrn̓ ten̓ *Ingelingehã*.T̓ra.ē

ii.caɾ.Ibi ſt̓.v.borđ 7 vii.ãc p̃ti.Valuit.lx.ſol̓.m̊.xx.ſol̓.

Hanc t̓ra accep̃ Hugo de firma regis.7 deđ æcclæ huic.

Ipſa æccl̄a ten̓ *Bovehric*.Brictric tenuit T.R.E.7 geldb̄ p̃.v.hiđ.T̓ra.ē.vii.caɾ.De ea ſt̓ in dn̄io.ii.hidæ 7 dim̃.

7 ibi.ii.caɾ.7 x.ſerui.7 v.uiłłi 7 ix.borđ cū.iii.caɾ.Ibi mo linū redđ.vi.ſol̓.paſtura.ix.q̃ꝗ 7 dim̃ in lḡ 7 lat̓.Bruaria. ii.leū lḡ 7 lat̓.Silua.i.leū lḡ.7 dim̃ leū lat̓.

Valuit 7 ual̓.c.ſolid.De hac t̓ra ten̓ Joħs.ii.virg̓ t̓ræ 7 dim̃.

Ipſa æccl̄a ten̓ *Winbvrne*.T.R.E.geldb̄ p̃.v.hiđ.T̓ra.ē vi.caɾ.De ea .ē in dn̄io.i.hida.7 ibi.ii.caɾ.7 vii.ſerui.

7 vii.uiłłi 7 vii.borđ.cū.iiii.caɾ.Ibi.x.ãc p̃ti.Paſtura. una leū lḡ.7 dim̃ leū lat̓.Silua.iiii.q̃ꝗ lḡ.7 ii.q̃ꝗ lat̓.

De eađ t̓ra ten̓ Radulf̓.i.hiđ.Tot̓ ualuit 7 ual̓.c.ſol̓.

Ipſa æccl̄a ten̓ *Levetesford*.7 Joħs de abbe.Ibi.ē dimiđ hida 7 ii.caɾ cū.iiii.uiłł 7 i.borđ.7 iiii.ãc p̃ti.Val̓.xv.ſol̓.

5 ploughs there; 20 slaves;
20 villagers and 30 smallholders with 8 ploughs.
3 mills which pay 60s; meadow, 16 acres; pasture 2 leagues
long and ½ league wide.
Of this land 1 man-at-arms and a widow hold 3 hides; they
have 2 ploughs there.
Value of the Church's lordship £28; value of the other (holding), 40s.
Aelmer and Aethelfrith held this manor before 1066 as two
manors from King Edward; they could not go with this land to
whichever lord they would. Later on, Roger Arundel held it from
King William.

| 10 | LAND OF ST. MARY'S, CRANBORNE | E |

1 St. Mary's Church, Cranborne, holds in GILLINGHAM. Land for 2
ploughs.
5 smallholders.
Meadow, 7 acres.
The value was 60s; now 20s.
Hugh received this land from the King's revenue and gave it
to this Church.

The Church itself holds
2 BOVERIDGE. Brictric held it before 1066. It paid tax for 5 hides.
Land for 7 ploughs, of which 2½ hides are in lordship; 2 ploughs
there; 10 slaves;
5 villagers and 9 smallholders with 3 ploughs.
A mill which pays 6s; pasture 9½ furlongs in length and width;
heathland 2 leagues long and wide; woodland 1 league long
and ½ league wide.
The value was and is 100s.
Of this land John holds 2½ virgates of land.

3 WIMBORNE (St. Giles). Before 1066 it paid tax for 5 hides. Land
for 6 ploughs, of which 1 hide is in lordship; 2 ploughs there;
7 slaves;
7 villagers and 7 smallholders with 4 ploughs.
Meadow, 10 acres; pasture 1 league long and ½ league wide;
woodland 4 furlongs long and 2 furlongs wide.
Ralph holds 1 hide of this land.
The value of the whole was and is 100s.

4 'LEFTISFORD'. John holds from the Abbot. ½ hide and 2 ploughs,
with
4 villagers and 1 smallholder.
Meadow, 4 acres.
Value 15s.

Ipſa æccła ten̅ dimid̅ hid̅ in *LANGEFORD*.T̅ra.e̅.ı.car̅.

Hanc hn̅t ibi.ıı.uiłłi.7 ıı.q̊ɫ paſturæ in lg̅.7 lat̅.Siluæ

una q̊ɫ in lg̅ 7 lat̅.Valet.v.ſolid̅.

Ipſa æccła ten̅ *TARENTE*.T.R̅.E.gełdb̅ ꝑ.x.hid̅.T̅ra.e̅

vııı.car̅.De ea ſt̅ in dn̅io.ıııı.hidæ 7 dim̅.7 ibi.ı.car̅.

7 ıııı.ſerui.7 xıı.uiłłi 7 xıı.bord̅ cu̅.ııı.car̅.Ibi molin̅

redd̅.v.ſolid̅.7 xxxv.ac̅ ꝑti.Paſturæ.ı.leu̅ 7 dim̅ in lg̅ 7 lat̅.

Siluæ.x.q̊ɫ in lg̅ 7 lat̅.Valuit.xıı.lib̅.Modo.x.lib̅.

.XI.   TERRA SC̅I PETRI DE CERNEL.

Eccl̅a S̅ petri CERNELIENS ten̅ *CERNELI*.T.R.E.gełdb̅

ꝑ.xxıı.hid̅.T̅ra.e̅.xx.car̅.De ea ſt̅ in dn̅io.ııı.hidæ

7 ibi.ııı.car̅.7 v.ſerui.7 xxvı.uiłłi 7 xxxıı.bord̅ cu̅.xıııı.

car̅.Ibi molin̅ redd̅.xx.ſolid̅.7 xx.ac̅ ꝑti.Paſtura.ıı.leu̅

lg̅.7 vııı.q̊ɫ lat̅.Silua.ı.leu̅ lg̅.7 vııı.q̊ɫ lat̅.

De ead̅ t̅ra ten̅ Brictuin̅.ıııı.hid̅ de abbe.7 ibi ht̅.ıııı.car̅.

Hic tenuit ſimilit̅ T.R.E.7 n̅ potuit reced̅e ab æccła nec poteſt.

Dn̅iu̅ æcclæ ualuit 7 ual̅.xxı.lib̅.Brictuini:c.ſolid̅.

Ipſa æccła ten̅ *LITELPIDRE*.Witłs de abbe.T.R.E.gełdb̅

ꝑ.ııı.hid̅ 7 dim̅.T̅ra.e̅.ıı.car̅.In dn̅io.e̅.ı.car̅.7 ıı.ſerui.

7 ı.uiłłs 7 ııı.bord̅ cu̅ dim̅ car̅.Ibi.ıııı.ac̅ ꝑti.Paſtura

.ıı.q̊ɫ lg̅.7 una q̊ɫ lat̅.Valuit 7 ual̅.L.ſolid̅.

Ipſa eccła ten̅ *RETPOLE*.T.R.E.gełdb̅ ꝑ.ııı.hid̅.T̅ra.e̅.ııı.

car̅.De ea.e̅ in dn̅io medietas.7 ibi.ı.car̅.cu̅.ı.ſeruo.7 ı.uiłło

7 v.bord̅ hn̅t.ıı.car̅.Ibi.x.ac̅ ꝑti.7 v.q̊ɫ paſturæ.Valet

Ipſa æccła ten̅ *BLOCHESHORDE*.T.R.E.gełdb̅ ⌐xL.ſolid̅.

ꝑ.v.hid̅. |⁷ dimid̅ T̅ra.e̅.vı.car̅.De ea ſt̅ in dn̅io.ıı.hidæ.7 ibi.ıı.car̅.

7 ııı.ſerui.7 xııı.uiłłi 7 ıx.bord̅ 7 vıı.cotar̅ cu̅.ıııı.car̅.7 dim̅.

5 in 'LANGFORD' ½ hide. Land for 1 plough.
2 villagers have it there.
Pasture, 2 furlongs in length and width; woodland, 1 furlong
in length and width.
Value 5s.

6 TARRANT (Monkton). Before 1066 it paid tax for 10 hides. Land
for 8 ploughs, of which 4½ hides are in lordship; 1 plough there;
4 slaves;
12 villagers and 12 smallholders with 3 ploughs.
A mill which pays 5s; meadow, 35 acres; pasture, 1½ leagues in
length and width; woodland, 10 furlongs in length and width.
The value was £12; now £10.

11   LAND OF ST. PETER'S OF CERNE (ABBAS)

1 St. Peter's Church, Cerne, holds CERNE (Abbas). Before 1066 it   E
paid tax for 22 hides. Land for 20 ploughs, of which 3 hides are   36
in lordship; 3 ploughs there; 5 slaves;   a 1
26 villagers and 32 smallholders with 14 ploughs and 15 hides.
A mill which pays 20s; meadow, 20 acres; pasture 2 leagues
long and 8 furlongs wide; woodland 1 league long and 8
furlongs wide. 3 cobs; 6 cattle; 14 pigs; 500 sheep.
Brictwin holds 4 hides of this land from the Abbot; he has 4   E
ploughs there. He held them likewise before 1066; he could
not withdraw from the Church, nor can he.
The value of the Church's lordship was and is £21; of Brictwin's,   E
100s.

The Church itself holds
2 LITTLE PUDDLE. William of Moutiers holds from the Abbot. Before   E
1066 it paid tax for 3½ hides. Land for 2 ploughs. In lordship 1   E
plough; 2 slaves; 3 hides.   36
1 villager and 3 smallholders with ½ plough and ½ hide.   a 2
Meadow, 4 acres; pasture 2 furlongs long and 1 furlong wide.
2 cows; 160 sheep.
The value was and is 50s.   E

3 RADIPOLE. Before 1066 it paid tax for 3 hides. Land for 3 ploughs,
of which half is in lordship; 1 plough there, with 1 slave and
1 villager; 5 smallholders have 2 ploughs and 1½ hides.   36
Meadow, 10 acres; pasture, 5 furlongs. 1 cob; 20 pigs; 100 sheep.   b 1
Value 40s.

4 BLOXWORTH. Before 1066 it paid tax for 5½ hides. Land for 6
ploughs, of which 2 hides are in lordship; 2 ploughs there; 3 slaves;
13 villagers, 9 smallholders and 7 cottagers with 4½ ploughs   E 36
and 3½ hides.   b 2

Ibi.viii.ac̄ p̄ti.7 viii.ac̄ ſiluæ.7 viii.q̄ʒ paſturæ in lḡ.7 tn̄tđ

Ipſa eccła ten̄ *AFFAPIDELE.*   ⌐lat̄.Valet.vii.lib̄.7 x.ſot.

T.R.E.geldb̄ ᵱ.ix.hiđ.T̄ra.e̅.vi.car̄.De ea ſt in dn̄io.iiii.

hidæ.7 ibi.ii.car̄.7 iii.ſerui.7 vi.uiłłi 7 iiii.borđ cū.iiii.car̄.

Ibi.ii.molini redđ.xv.ſoliđ.7 lv.ac̄ p̄ti.Paſtura.xii.q̄ʒ

lḡ.7 vi.q̄ʒ lat̄.Silua.vii.q̄ʒ lḡ.7 tn̄tđ

78 a

Ipſa æccła ten̄ *POCHESWELLE.*T.R.E.geldb̄ ᵱ.vi.hiđ.T̄ra.e̅

vii.car̄.De ea.e̅ in dn̄io.i.hida 7 dim̄.7 ibi.ii.car̄.cū.i.

ſeruo.7 iiii,uiłłi 7 viii.borđ cū.iii.car̄.Ibi.xv.ac̄ p̄ti.

Paſtura.viii.q̄ʒ 7 xxvi.virḡ lḡ.7 iii.q̄ʒ 7 xiiii.p̄tic lat̄.

De ead̄ t̄ra ten̄ uxor.Huḡ.iii.hiđ.7 ibi.e̅ una car̄.h̄ t̄ra

fuit de dn̄ica firma monachoʒ.7 ualet.xl.ſoliđ.

Dn̄ium æcclæ ualet.vii.lib̄.

Ipſa æccła ten̄ *WERDESFORD.*T.R.E.geldb̄ ᵱ.ii.hiđ 7 dimiđ.

T̄ra.e̅.ii.car̄.q̄ ibi ſt cū.iiii.uiłłis 7 iii.borđ.7 v.ſeruis.Valet

Ipſa æccła ten̄.iii.virḡ t̄ræ in *ÆLFATVNE.*   ⌐xxx.ſoliđ.

Valuer̄ 7 uat.v.ſoliđ.

Ipſa æccła ten̄.i.hiđ in *VERGROH.*7 ᵱ tanto geldb̄ T.R.E.

Ibi ſt.ii.ſerui.7 molin̄ dimiđ.7 viii.ac̄ p̄ti.Tot uat.xv.ſot.

Ipſa æccła ten̄ *LITELBRIDE.*T.R.E.geldb̄ ᵱ.xi.hiđ.T̄ra.e̅

vi.car̄.De ea ſt in dn̄io.v.hidæ.7 ibi.ii.car̄.7 v.ſerui.

7 vi.uiłłi 7 v.borđ.cū.vi.car̄.Ibi.xii.ac̄ p̄ti.Paſtura

una leū lḡ.7 altera lat̄.Silua.i.leū lḡ.7 ii.q̄ʒ lat̄.

Valuit 7 uat.xvi.lib̄

Ipſa æccła ten̄ *WINTREBVRNE.*T.R.E.geldb̄ ᵱ.x.hiđ.

T̄ra.e̅.x.car̄.De ea ſt in dn̄io.v.hidæ.7 ibi.iiii.car̄.

7 iii.ſerui.7 x.uiłłi 7 vii.coſcez cū.iii.car̄.Ibi.xx.ac̄ p̄ti.

Paſtura.xi.q̄ʒ lḡ.7 x.q̄ʒ lat̄.Silua.ii.q̄ʒ lḡ.7 una q̄ʒ lat̄.

Valuit 7 uat.xvi.lib̄.

Meadow, 8 acres; woodland, 8 acres; pasture, 8 furlongs in
length and as wide. 1 cob; 17 pigs; 26 [sheep?].   E
Value £7 10s.

5 AFFPUDDLE. Before 1066 it paid tax for 9 hides. Land for 6 ploughs,
of which 4 hides are in lordship; 2 ploughs there; 3 slaves;
6 villagers and 4 smallholders with 4 ploughs and 5 hides.   E
2 mills which pay 15s; meadow, 55 acres; pasture 12 furlongs   36
long and 6 furlongs wide; woodland 7 furlongs long and   b 3
as [wide]. 9 oxen; 12 sheep; 1 cob; 12 pigs.
This manor pays £7 10s a year.

When the Abbot acquired them, the said two manors were worth 100s more (than now),   E
because they have (since) been plundered for (the benefit of) Hugh son of Grip.

6 POXWELL. Before 1066 it paid tax for 6 hides. Land for 7 ploughs,   78 a
of which 1½ hides are in lordship; 2 ploughs there, with 1 slave;
4 villagers and 8 smallholders with 3 ploughs and 1½ hides.   E
Meadow, 15 acres; pasture 8 furlongs and 26 'rods' long and   37
3 furlongs and 14 perches wide. 1 cob; 6 pigs; 200 sheep.   a 1
Hugh's wife holds 3 hides also of this land; 1 plough there.   E
This land was (part) of the monks' lordship revenue; value 40s.   E
Value of the Church's lordship £7.

7 WOODSFORD. Before 1066 it paid tax for 2½ hides. Land for   E
2 ploughs, which are there, with   37
4 villagers, 3 smallholders and 5 slaves. 4 pigs.   a 2
Value 30s.

8 in HETHFELTON 3 virgates of land.   E 37
The value was and is 5s.   E a 3

9 in WORGRET 1 hide. It paid tax for as much before 1066. 2 slaves.   E
½ mill; meadow, 8 acres.   37
Value of the whole, 15s.   a 4

10 LITTLEBREDY. Before 1066 it paid tax for 11 hides. Land for 6
ploughs, of which 5 hides are in lordship; 2 ploughs there; 5 slaves;
6 villagers and 5 smallholders with 6 ploughs and 6 hides.
Meadow, 12 acres; pasture 1 league long and another wide;   37
woodland 1 league long and 2 furlongs wide. 12 pigs; 550 sheep.   a 5
The value was and is £16.   E

11 WINTERBORNE (Abbas). Before 1066 it paid tax for 10 hides. Land   E
for 10 ploughs, of which 5 hides are in lordship; 4 ploughs there;
3 slaves;   37
10 villagers and 7 Cottagers with 3 ploughs and 5 hides.   b 1
Meadow, 20 acres; pasture 11 furlongs long and 10 furlongs
wide; woodland 2 furlongs long and 1 furlong wide. 12 pigs;
116 sheep; 18 goats.
The value was and is £16.

Ipſa æccła teñ *LANGEBRIDE* .T.R.E.geldɓ ֹp.ıx.hiđ.Tra.e̅

ıx.caɼ.De ea ſt in dñio.ııı.hidæ.7 ibi.ııı.caɼ.7 ııı.ſerui.7 vıı.

uiłłi 7 ıx.coſcez cu̅.v.caɼ.7 un̊ tain̊ ht̅.ı.hida̅ 7 ibi.ı.caɼ.

Ibi moliñ redđ.vı.ſoł.7 xı.ac̅ p̊ti.Paſtura.ı.leu̅ łg̅.7 tn̊tđ

lat̅.Silua dim̊ leu̅ łg̅.7 ııı.q̊⁊ lat̅.Totu̅ ualet.xxı.liɓ.

Ipſa æccła teñ *NETELCOME*.T.R.E.geldɓ ֹp.v.hiđ.Tra.e̅

   De ea.e̅ in dñio hida 7 dim̊.7 dim̊ v̊ træ.7 ibi.ı.caɼ.

De eaɗ tra
ten un miles
.ıı.hiɗ.

7 ıı.ſerui.7 v.uiłłi 7 vıı.coſcez.cu̅.ıı.caɼ.Ibi.x.ac̅ p̊ti.

Paſtura.ı.leu̅ łg̅.7 ıııı.q̊⁊ lat̅.Silua.ı.leu̅ łg̅.7 vııı.q̊⁊ lat̅.

Valuit.xıı.liɓ.Modo aɓɓi.̓vııı.liɓ.Militi.̓lv.ſoliđ.

Ipſa æccła teñ *MIDELTONE*.T.R.E.geldɓ ֹp.ıııı.hiđ.Tra.e̅

ıııı.caɼ.De ea ſt in dñio.ıı.hidæ.7 ibi.ı.caɼ.7 ıı.ſerui.

7 v.uiłłi 7 xııı.borđ cu̅.v.caɼ.Ibi moliñ redđ.lxv.denaɼ.

7 xvı.ac̅ p̊ti.Paſtura.ı.leu̅ łg̅.7 ıııı.q̊⁊ lat̅.Silua.ııı.q̊⁊

łg̅.7 ıı.q̊⁊ lat̅.Valuit.x.liɓ.Modo.ıx.liɓ.

Ipſa æccła teñ *CAMERIC*.T.R.E.geldɓ ֹp.v.hiđ.Tra.e̅.ıııı.

caɼ.De ea ſt in dñio.ııı.hidæ.una v̊ 7 dim̅ min̊.7 ibi.ıı.caɼ.

cu̅.ı.ſeruo.7 ıı.uiłłi 7 vııı.borđ cu̅.ıı.caɼ.Ibi.xvııı.ac̅

p̊ti.paſtura.vı.q̊⁊ łg̅.7 ıı.q̊⁊ lat̅.Valuit 7 uał.vııı.liɓ.

Ipſa æccła teñ *ROMESCVBE*.T.R.E.geldɓ ֹp.v.hiđ 7 una v̊

træ.Tra.e̅.vı.caɼ.De ea ſt in dñio.ıı.hidæ 7 ııı.v̊ træ.

7 ibi.ıı.caɼ.7 ııı.ſerui.7 vıı.uiłłi 7 vıı.borđ

Ibi.xıı.ac̅ p̊ti.paſtura.ı.leu̅ łg̅.7 x.q̊⁊ lat̅.Silua infruc

tuoſa.v.q̊⁊ łg̅.7 una q̊⁊ lat̅.Valuit 7 uał.vııı.liɓ.

Ipſa æccła teñ *SIMONDESBERGE* .T.R.E.geldɓ ֹp.xıx.hiđ.

Tra.e̅.xx.caɼ.De ea ſt in dñio.v.hidæ.7 ibi.ıı.caɼ.cu̅.ı.

12 LONG BREDY. Before 1066 it paid tax for 9 hides. Land for 9   E
ploughs, of which 3 hides are in lordship; 3 ploughs there; 3 slaves;   37
7 villagers and 9 Cottagers with 5 ploughs and 5 hides.   E b 2
A thane has 1 hide; 1 plough there.   E
A mill which pays 6s; meadow, 11 acres; pasture 1 league long
and as wide; woodland ½ league long and 3 furlongs wide.
1 cob; 15 pigs; 353 sheep; 20 goats.
Value of the whole £21.   E

13 NETTLECOMBE. Before 1066 it paid tax for 5 hides. Land for ....   E
of which 1½ hides and ½ virgate of land are in lordship; 1 plough   38
there; 2 slaves;   a 1
5 villagers and 7 Cottagers with 2 ploughs and 1 hide and 1½ virgates.   E
Meadow, 10 acres; pasture 1 league long and 4 furlongs wide;
woodland 1 league long and 8 furlongs wide. 25 sheep; 5 goats.   E
A man-at-arms holds 2 hides also of this land.   E
The value was £12; (value) now to the Abbot £8; to the man-at-   E
arms 55s.

14 (West) MILTON. Before 1066 it paid tax for 4 hides. Land for 4
ploughs, of which 2 hides are in lordship; 1 plough there; 2 slaves;
5 villagers and 13 smallholders with 5 ploughs and 2 hides.   E
A mill which pays 65d; meadow, 16 acres; pasture 1 league long   38
and 4 furlongs wide; woodland 3 furlongs long and 2   a 2
furlongs wide. 16 sheep; 5 goats.
The value was £10; now £9.   E

15 KIMMERIDGE. Before 1066 it paid tax for 5 hides. Land for 4
ploughs, of which 3 hides, less 1½ virgates, are in lordship;
2 ploughs there, with 1 slave;   38
2 villagers and 8 smallholders with 2 ploughs and 2 hides and 1½ virgates.   b 1
Meadow, 18 acres; pasture 6 furlongs long and 2 furlongs wide.
1 cob; 2 cows; 16 pigs; 250 sheep.
The value was and is £8.

16 RENSCOMBE. Before 1066 it paid tax for 5 hides and 1 virgate of
land. Land for 6 ploughs, of which 2 hides and 3 virgates of land
are in lordship; 2 ploughs there; 3 slaves;
7 villagers and 7 smallholders (have) 3 hides and 1 virgate.   38
Meadow, 12 acres; pasture 1 league long and 10 furlongs wide;   b 2
unproductive woodland 5 furlongs long and 1 furlong wide.
1 cob; 2 cows; 12 pigs; 250 wethers; 8 goats.
The value was and is £8.   E

17 SYMONDSBURY. Before 1066 it paid tax for 19 hides. Land for 20
ploughs, of which 5 hides are in lordship; 2 ploughs there, with 1

feruo .7 xx . uiłłi 7 x . borð cū. xɪɪɪɪ . car̄ . Ibi . xɪɪɪɪ. ac p̄ti.
Paſtura . v . q̃⁊ l̄g .7 una q̃⁊ lat̄ . x . virg min . Silua
dimid leū l̄g.7 una q̃⁊ lat̄. Valuit 7 uał . xxɪ . lib̄.

.XII. Terra Abbatiæ Middeltvnensis.

Eccl̄a Middeltvnens ten Sidelince . T .R.E.geldb̄
p̄ .xxɪx. hid . Tra . e . xx . car̄ . De his ſt in dn̄io . vɪ . hidæ
7 ibi . ɪɪ . car̄ .7 vɪ . ſerui.7 xxv . uiłłi 7 x. borð cū. xɪɪɪ . car̄.
Ibi . ɪɪ. molini redd . vɪɪ . soł.7 vɪ. den̄.7 xɪɪ . ac p̄ti .Paſtura
.ɪɪ. leū 7 dimid l̄g .7 vɪ . q̃⁊ lat̄ . Silua . ɪ . leū l̄g .7 tntd lat̄.
Valet . xxv . lib̄.

78 b

Ipſa æccła ten Midelitvne 7 eſt caput abbatiæ .T.R.E.geldb̄ p̄.xxɪɪɪɪ.hid·
Tra.e.xvɪɪɪ.car̄.De ea ſt in dn̄io. x. hide una v min.7 ibi.ɪɪ.car̄.
7 vɪ. ſerui.7 xxvɪɪ. uiłłi 7 xx. borð cū. xɪɪɪ. car̄.Ibi molin̄ redd.xv.soł.
7 xl.ac p̄ti.Paſtura . ɪɪɪ. leū l̄g.7 una leū lat̄.Valet. xx.lib̄.
Ipſa æccła ten Contone .T.R.E.geldb̄ p̄.v.hid.Tra. e . ɪɪɪ.car̄.
De ea ſt in dn̄io.ɪɪɪ.hide.7 ibi.ɪ.car̄.7 ɪɪɪ.ſerui.7 vɪ.uiłłi 7 v.borð
Ibi. x . ac p̄ti.7 paſtura.ɪ.leū l̄g.7 ɪɪ.q̃⁊ lat̄.Valet.ɪɪɪɪ .lib̄.
Ipſa æccła ten Stoche .T.R.E.geldb̄ p̄.x.hid.Tra.e.vɪ.car̄.De ea
ſt in dn̄io.ɪɪɪ.hidæ.7 ibi.ɪ.car̄.7 vɪ.ſerui.7 xɪɪ.uiłłi 7 v.borð cū.v.
car̄.Ibi molin̄ redd.xv.denar̄.7 xvɪɪɪ.ac p̄ti.Paſtura . ɪ .leū l̄g.
7 ɪɪ.q̃⁊ lat̄.Silua.vɪ.q̃⁊ l̄g.7 ɪɪɪɪ.q̃⁊ lat̄.Valet.vɪ.lib̄.
Ipſa æccła ten Pidele .T.R.E.geldb̄ p̄.ɪɪɪ . hid . Tra.e.ɪɪ.car̄.De
ea ſt in dn̄io.ɪɪ.hidæ 7 dim̄.7 ibi.ɪɪ.car̄.7 ɪɪɪɪ.ſerui.7 v.borð

slave;
    20 villagers and 10 smallholders with 14 ploughs and 14 hides.   38
    Meadow, 14 acres; pasture 5 furlongs long and 1 furlong wide,   b 3
    less 10 'rods'; woodland ½ league long and 1 furlong wide.
    1 cob; 100 sheep; 12 goats.
The value was and is £21.

12   LAND OF MILTON ABBEY   E

1 The Church of Milton (Abbas) holds SYDLING. Before 1066 it paid E
tax for 29 hides. Land for 20 ploughs; of these 6 hides are in
lordship; 2 ploughs there; 6 slaves;   43
    25 villagers and 10 smallholders with 13 ploughs and 23 hides. a 1
    2 mills which pay 7s 6d; meadow, 12 acres; pasture 2½ leagues
    long and 6 furlongs wide; woodland 1 league long and as wide.
    3 cobs; 10 cattle; 250 sheep.
Value £25.

  The Church itself holds   78 b
2 MILTON (Abbas); it is the head of the Abbey. Before 1066 it paid
tax for 24 hides. Land for 18 ploughs, of which 10 hides, less 1
virgate, are in lordship; 2 ploughs there; 6 slaves;   43
    27 villagers and 20 smallholders with 13 ploughs and 14 hides b 5
    and 1 virgate.
    A mill which pays 15s; meadow, 40 acres; pasture 3 leagues
    long and 1 league wide. 2 cobs; 20 pigs; 450 sheep; 50 goats.
Value £20.

3 (West) COMPTON. Before 1066 it paid tax for 5 hides. Land for
3 ploughs, of which 3 hides are in lordship; 1 plough there;
3 slaves;   43
    6 villagers and 5 smallholders (have) 2 hides and 2 ploughs. a 2
    Meadow, 10 acres; pasture 1 league long and 2 furlongs wide. E
    1 cob; 150 sheep.
Value £4.

4 CATTISTOCK. Before 1066 it paid tax for 10 hides. Land for
6 ploughs, of which 3 hides are in lordship; 1 plough there;
6 slaves;
    12 villagers and 5 smallholders with 5 ploughs and 7 hides. 43
    A mill which pays 15d; meadow, 18 acres; pasture 1 league long a 3
    and 2 furlongs wide; woodland 6 furlongs long and 4 furlongs
    wide. 2 cobs; 14 pigs; 150 sheep.
Value £6.

5 BURLESTON. Before 1066 it paid tax for 3 hides. Land for 2 ploughs, 43
of which 2½ hides are in lordship; 2 ploughs there; 4 slaves; b 1
    5 smallholders (have) ½ hide.   E

Ibi molin redd.xl.denar.7 xvi.ac p̄ti.Valet.xl.folid.

Ipſa æccła ten CLIVE.T.R.E.geldb ꝑ.ii.hid.Tra.ē.ii.car.Ibi ſt
v.uiłłi.Valet.xx.folid.

Ipſa æccła ten OSMENTONE.T.R.E.geldb ꝑ.x.hid.Tra.ē.x.car.
De ea ſt in dn̄io.iiii.hidæ.7 ibi.ii.car.7 iii.ſerui.7 xvi.uiłłi
7 vii.bord cū.vi.car.Ibi molin redd.v.folid.7 v.ac p̄ti.
7 una leū paſturæ.Valet.viii.lib.

Ipſa æccła ten WIDECOME.T.R.E.geldb ꝑ.vi.hid.Tra.ē.vi.
car.De ea ſt in dn̄io.iiii.hidæ.7 ibi.i.car.7 ii.ſerui.7 vii.uiłłi
7 v.bord cū.iii.car.Ibi.v.ac p̄ti.7 Paſtura.xiii.q̄ʒ lḡ.7 ii.q̄ʒ
lat.Valet.iiii.lib 7 x.ſol.

Ipſa æccła ten LISCOME.T.R.E.geldb ꝑ.iii.hid.Tra.ē.ii.car.
De ea ſt in dn̄io.ii.hidæ.7 ibi.i.car.7 ii.ſerui.7 iii.uiłłi 7 v.bord
cū.i.car.Ibi paſtura.vi.q̄ʒ lḡ.7 iii.q̄ʒ lat.Valet.xl.folid.

Ipſa æccła ten WINLANDE.T.R.E.geldb ꝑ.v.hid.Tra.ē.iiii.
car.De ea ſt in dn̄io.ii.hidæ.7 ibi.i.car.7 iii.ſerui.7 v.uiłłi
7 v.bord cū.ii.car.Ibi.viii.ac p̄ti.Silua.vii.q̄ʒ lḡ.7 iiii.q̄ʒ lat.

Ipſa æccła ten WINTREBVRNE.T.R.E.geld   ⌐Valet.lx.folid.
ꝑ.ii.hid 7 una v træ.Tra.ē.i.car 7 dimid.De ea.ē in dn̄io
una hida.7 ibi.i.car.cū.i.feruo.7 ii.bord.Ibi.vi.ac p̄ti.
7 x.ac paſturæ.Valet.xxv.folid.

Ipſa æccła ten HOLVERDE.T.R.E.geldb ꝑ.v.hid.Tra.ē.v.
car.De ea ſt in dn̄io.iii.hidæ.7 ibi.ii.car.7 iiii.ſerui.7 iiii.
uiłłi 7 v.coſcez cū.ii.car.Ibi.iii.ac p̄ti.7 paſtura.v.q̄ʒ
lḡ.7 totid lat.Valet.iii.lib.7 ſextariū mellis.

Ipſa æccła ten ORA.T.R.E.geldb ꝑ.iii.hid.Ibi nulla car habet.ſed.xiii.
ſalinarij redd.xx.folid.

A mill which pays 40d; meadow, 16 acres. 1 cob; 3 cattle; 115 sheep.
Value 40s.

6 CLYFFE. Before 1066 it paid tax for 2 hides. Land for 2 ploughs.   43
5 villagers hold them.   b 2
Value 20s.

7 OSMINGTON. Before 1066 it paid tax for 10 hides. Land for 10 ploughs, of which 4 hides are in lordship; 2 ploughs there; 3 slaves;
16 villagers and 7 smallholders with 6 ploughs and 6 hides.   43
A mill which pays 5s; meadow, 5 acres; pasture, 1 league.   b 3
2 cobs; 3 pigs; 127 sheep.   E
Value £8.

8 WHITCOMBE. Before 1066 it paid tax for 6 hides. Land for 6 ploughs, of which 4 hides are in lordship; 1 plough there;
2 slaves;
7 villagers and 5 smallholders with 3 ploughs and 2 hides.   43
Meadow, 5 acres; pasture 13 furlongs long and 2 furlongs wide.   b 4
1 cob; 86 sheep.
Value £4 10s.

9 LYSCOMBE. Before 1066 it paid tax for 3 hides. Land for 2 ploughs, of which 2 hides are in lordship; 1 plough there; 2 slaves;   44
3 villagers and 5 smallholders with 1 plough and 1 hide.   a 1
Pasture 6 furlongs long and 3 furlongs wide.
1 cow; 3 pigs; 50 sheep.
Value 40s.

10 WOOLLAND. Before 1066 it paid tax for 5 hides. Land for 4 ploughs, of which 2 hides are in lordship; 1 plough there; 3 slaves;
5 villagers and 5 smallholders with 2 ploughs and 3 hides.   44
Meadow, 8 acres; woodland 7 furlongs long and 4 furlongs wide.   a 2
1 cob; 8 pigs; 60 sheep; 16 goats.
Value 60s.

11 WINTERBORNE (Whitechurch). Before 1066 it paid tax for 2 hides and 1 virgate of land. Land for 1½ ploughs, of which 1 hide is in lordship; 1 plough there, with 1 slave;
2 smallholders (have) 1 hide and 1 virgate.   44
Meadow, 6 acres; pasture, 10 acres.   a 3
Value 25s.

12 HOLWORTH. Before 1066 it paid tax for 5 hides. Land for 5 ploughs, of which 3 hides are in lordship; 2 ploughs there; 4 slaves;
4 villagers and 5 Cottagers with 2 ploughs and 2 hides.   44
Meadow, 3 acres; pasture 5 furlongs long and as many wide.   b 1
1 cob; 4 cows; 224 sheep.
Value £3 and a sester of honey.

13 OWER. Before 1066 it paid tax for 3 hides. No plough is recorded   E 44
there, but 13 salt-workers who pay 20s.   b 2

Ipſa æccła ten *ERTACOMESTOCHE*.7 Herueus de abbe.T.R.E.geldb ‚p.x. hid.Tra.ē.xvi.cař.De ea ſt in dnio.iiii.hidæ.7 ibi.ii.cař.7 iiii.ſerui. 7 xl.uiłłi hnt.xx.cař.Ibi.iii.molini redd xxxvii.den.7 xx.iii.ac pti. Silua.xiii.q̊ʒ lg.7 xii.lat.Valet.ix.lib

Hoc m̄ fuit ſep de dnio monachoʒ ad uictu 7 ueſtitu eoʒ.

Ipſa æccła ten *PIDRE*.T.R.E.geldb ‚p.ii.hid.Tra.ē.i.cař.q̊ ibi eſt. 7 xii.ac pti.7 ii.ac ſiluæ.Paſtura.i.leu lg.7 iii.q̊ʒ lat.Valet.x.ſolid. Ipſa æccła ten *CERNE*.7 Aiulf de abbe.T.R.E.geldb ‚p.i.hida 7 dim. Tra.ē.ii.cař.De ea.ē in dnio hida 7 una v̄ ✝ 7 ibi.i.cař ✝ v.acs min. Ibi ſt.v.bord.7 molin redd.xx.denar.7 xiii.ac pti.7 xix.ac paſturæ. Valuit.x.ſoł.Modo.xxv.ſolid.Qui teneb T.R.E. n̄ poterat ab æccła

f ſeparari.

.XIII.   TERRA ABBATIE ABEDESBERIENS.

Eccla Abodesberiens ten *ABEDESBERIE*.T.R.E.geldb ‚p.xxi. hida.Tra.ē.xvi.cař.De ea ſt in dnio.viii.hidæ.7 ibi.v.cař.7 xiiii. ſerui.7 xxxii.uiłłi.7 xvi.bord.cu.xvi.cař.Ibi.ii.molini redd xvi.ſoł 7 iii.den.7 xxxvi.ac pti.Paſtura.xxvii.q̊ʒ lg.7 una leu 7 iii.q̊ʒ lat.Siluæ.viii.qrent.Valet.xxvi.lib.

Huic m̄ ptin una hida.T.R.E.ad uictu monachoʒ erat.Hanc Hugo accep injuſte 7 retinuit.7 adhuc uxor ej ui detinet.

78 c

Ipſa æccła ten *PIDELE*.T.R.E.geldb ‚p.xviii.hid.Tra.ē.xii.cař.De ea ſt in dnio.viii.hidæ.7 ibi.iii.car.7 iiii.ſerui.7 xvi.uiłłi 7 xiiii.coſcez cu.v.cař.Ibi.ii.molini redd.xx.ſolid.7 vi.q̊ʒ pti.7 xviii.q̊ʒ paſturæ Valet.xii.lib.

14 STOCKLAND. Hervey son of Ansger holds from the Abbot. Before
1066 it paid tax for 10 hides. Land for 16 ploughs, of which
4 hides are in lordship; 2 ploughs there; 4 slaves.
    40 villagers have 20 ploughs and 6 hides.
    3 mills which pay 37d; meadow, 23 acres; woodland 13 furlongs
    long and 12 wide. 4 cattle; 7 pigs; 20 goats.
Value £9.
    This manor was always (part) of the monks' lordship for their
supplies and clothing.

44
b 3

E

15 (Little) PUDDLE. Before 1066 it paid tax for 2 hides. Land for 1
plough, which is there.
    Meadow, 12 acres; woodland, 2 acres; pasture 1 league long
    and 3 furlongs wide. 5 cattle.
Value 10s.
This (manor) is (part) of the lordship revenue of the Abbot.

E
44
b 4

16 'CERNE'. Aiulf holds from the Abbot. Before 1066 it paid tax for
1½ hides. Land for 2 ploughs, of which (1) hide and 1 virgate,
less 5 acres, are in lordship; 1 plough there.
    5 smallholders (have) 1 virgate and 5 acres.
    A mill which pays 20d; meadow, 13 acres; pasture, 19 acres.
    12 cattle; 2 pigs; 65 sheep.
The value was 10s; now 25s.
    The holder before 1066 could not be separated from the Church.

45
a 1

E
E

E
E

13   LAND OF ABBOTSBURY ABBEY

E

1 Abbotsbury Church holds ABBOTSBURY. Before 1066 it paid tax
for 21 hides. Land for 16 ploughs, of which 8 hides are in
lordship; 5 ploughs there; 14 slaves;
    32 villagers and 16 smallholders with 16 ploughs and 13 hides.
    2 mills which pay 16s 3d; meadow, 36 acres; pasture 27 furlongs
    long and 1 league and 3 furlongs wide; woodland, 8 furlongs.
    4 cobs; 23 cattle; 30 pigs; 600 sheep.
Value £26.
    To this manor belongs 1 hide; before 1066 it was for the monks'
supplies. Hugh son of Grip received it wrongfully and kept it; his
wife still retains it by force.

ς
39
a 3

E

The Church itself holds
2 TOLPUDDLE. Before 1066 it paid tax for 18 hides. Land for 12
ploughs, of which 8 hides are in lordship; 3 ploughs there; 4 slaves;
    16 villagers and 14 Cottagers with 5 ploughs and 10 hides.
    2 mills which pay 20s; meadow, 6 furlongs; pasture, 18 furlongs.
    2 cobs; 10 cattle; 20 pigs; 300 sheep.
Value £12.

78 c
39
a 1

Ipſa æccɫa teñ ELTONE .T.R.E. geldƀ ₚ xviii . hiđ . Tra. ē . x . car.

De ea ſt in dñio. ix . hidæ 7 una v̄ træ.7 ibi.iii.car̄.7 viii.ſerui.7 xvii.

uiɫɫi 7 xii . borđ cū . vii.car̄ . Ibi moliñ redđ . xx . denar̄.7 x .ac̄ p̃ti.

Paſtura.i.leū l̄g .7 dim̄ leū lāt . Siluæ . iii . q̃rent . Valet . xv . liƀ.

Ipſa eccɫa teñ PORTESIIA. T .R.E.geldƀ ₚ. xii . hiđ . Tra. ē . ix . car̄.

De ea ſt in dñio. v . hidæ 7 ibi. iiii . car̄.7 xii. ſerui.7 xii.uiɫɫi 7 x . borđ

cū. v . car̄ . Ibi moliñ redđ . x . ſoɫ.7 xxiiii .ac̄ p̃ti . Paſtura.i.leū l̄g.

7 ii .q̃ᵶ lāt . Valet . xii . liƀ.

Huic ɑ) ₚtiñ una v̄ træ quā Hugo injuſte accep̄.7 uxor ej adhuc tenet.

ħ erat in uiĉtu monachoᵶ T.R.E.

Ipſa æccɫa teñ SEVEMETONE . T .R.E.geldƀ ₚ.v.uirg̃ træ. Tra.ē.i.car̄.

q̨ ibi.ē cū.i.ſeruo 7 i.borđ.Ibi.vi.ac̄ p̃ti.7 iii.q̃ᵶ paſturæ.Valet.xv.ſoɫ.

Ipſa æccɫa teñ WIDETONE.T.R.E.geldƀ ₚ.ii.hiđ 7 dimiđ. £ 7 vi.deñ.

Tra.ē.iiii.car̄.De ea.ē in dñio . i . hida.7 ibi . ii . car̄.7 iiii . ſerui.

7 iiii.uiɫɫi cū.ii.car̄ . Ibi.v.ac̄ p̃ti.7 iii.q̃ᵶ paſturæ.7 iii.q̃ᵶ ſiluæ.

Ipſa æccɫa teñ dimiđ hiđ in BOVRTONE. £ Valet.xl.ſoliđ.

Tra.ē.i.car̄.Hanc hñt ibi.ii.uiɫɫi.7 iii.q̃ᵶ ſiluæ .Valet. x . ſoliđ.

Ipſa eccɫa teñ ATREM.7 Bollo de abƀe.T.R.E.geldƀ ₚ.ii.hiđ.Tra.ē

.ii.car̄.q̨ ibi ſt.7 ii.ſerui.7 i.uiɫɫs 7 iii.borđ.Ibi.v.ac̄ p̃ti.7 iii.q̃ᵶ ſiluæ.

£ Valet. xx . ſoɫ.

3   HILTON. Before 1066 it paid tax for 18 hides. Land for 10 ploughs, of which 9 hides and 1 virgate of land are in lordship; 3 ploughs there; 8 slaves;   39

    17 villagers and 12 smallholders with 7 ploughs and 9 hides, less   a 2
    1 virgate.

    A mill which pays 20d; meadow, 10 acres; pasture 1 league long and ½ league wide; woodland, 3 furlongs. 3 cobs; 8 cattle; 20 pigs; 406 sheep; 25 goats.

    Value £15.

4   PORTESHAM. Before 1066 it paid tax for 12 hides. Land for 9 ploughs, of which 5 hides are in lordship; 4 ploughs there; 12 slaves;

    12 villagers and 10 smallholders with 5 ploughs and 7 hides.

    A mill which pays 10s; meadow, 24 acres; pasture 1 league long   39
    and 2 furlongs wide. 3 cobs; 13 cattle; 20 pigs; 250 sheep.   b 1

    Value £12.

    To this manor belongs 1 virgate of land which Hugh son of Grip received wrongfully, and his wife still holds it by force. Before 1066 it was for the monks' supplies.

5   SHILVINGHAMPTON. Before 1066 it paid tax for 5 virgates of land. Land for 1 plough, which is there, in lordship, with 1 slave;

    1 smallholder.   39

    Meadow, 6 acres; pasture, 3 furlongs. 100 sheep.   b 2

    Value 15s 6d.

    Bolle the priest holds it now from the Abbot; he cannot withdraw from the Church with this land.

6   (Abbotts) WOOTTON. Before 1066 it paid tax for 2½ hides. Land for 4 ploughs, of which 1 hide is in lordship; 2 ploughs there; 4 slaves;

    4 villagers with 2 ploughs and 1½ hides.   40

    Meadow, 5 acres; pasture, 3 furlongs; woodland, 3 furlongs.   a 1
    1 cob; 4 cattle; 100 sheep; 20 goats.

    Value 40s.

7   in POORTON ½ hide. Land for 1 plough.   40

    2 villagers have it there.   E   a 2

    Woodland, 3 furlongs.

    Value 10s.

8   ATRIM. Bolle the priest and a widow hold from the Abbot. Before   E
    1066 it paid tax for 2 hides. Land for 2 ploughs, which are there.   E
    2 slaves.   40

    1 villager and 3 smallholders.   E   a 3

    Meadow, 5 acres; woodland, 3 furlongs. 1 cob; 2 cattle; 20 sheep.

    Value 20s.

    These (holders) cannot be separated from the Church with this land.

.XIIII.   TERRA ABBATIÆ HORTVNENSIS.

ECCLA HORTVNENS ten *HORTVNE* .T.R.E.geldb ꝓ.vii.hid.Tra.ē
vii.caṝ.De ea s̄ in dñio.ii.hidæ.7 ibi.ii.caṝ.7 iii.ferui.7 iiii.uiłłi
7 x.bord cū.i.caṝ.Ibi.ii.molini redd.xv.folid.7 vi.aͨc pti.Paſtura.
ii.leū lḡ 7 laͭ.Silua.i.leū lḡ.7 dim leū laͭ.Valet.iiii.lib.
Duas meliores hidas de his.vii.ten rex in forefta de Winburne.
Ad hanc æcclam ptin ecclefiola.una in *WINBVRNE* .7 tra duabʒ
domibʒ.7 in *WARHA* una æccla 7 v.dom.redd.lxv.denar
7 In Doreceftre.una dom.

.XV.   TERRA·ABBATIE ADELINGIENSIS.

ECCLA ADELINIENS ten *CANDEL* .T.R.E.geldb ꝓ.iiii.hid 7 una v̄
træ 7 dim.Tra.ē.iiii.caṝ.De ea s̄ in dñio.iiii.hidæ.7 ibi.i.caṝ.
7 ii.uiłłi 7 xiiii.bord cū.ii.caṝ.Ibi.xiiii.aͨc pti.Silua.iii.q̃ʒ lḡ.
7 ii.q̃ʒ laͭ.De hac tra ten Alured.unā v̄ træ 7 dimid.
Totū ualet.lxvii.folid 7 vi.denar.

.XVI.   TERRA ABBATIÆ TAVESTOCH.

ECCLA TAVESTOCH ten *OSCHERWILLE* .T.R.E.geldb ꝓ.iii.hid.
Tra.ē.vi.caṝ.De ea.ē in dñio.i.hida.7 ibi.ii.caṝ.7 iiii.ferui.7 vii.
uiłłi 7 xvii.bord cū.iiii.caṝ.Ibi.ii.molini redd.vii.fol.7 ix.aͨc pti.
Paſtura.xv.q̃ʒ lḡ.7 ii.q̃ʒ laͭ.7 ii.cenfores redd.xv.folid.Valet.vi.lib.
Ipfa æccla ten *POWRTONE* .T.R.E.geldb ꝓ.ii.hid.Tra.ē.ii.caṝ.De ea
.ē in dñio.i.hida.7 ibi.i.caṝ.7 v.uiłłi 7 iii.bord.7 ii.aͨc pti.7 xvi.aͨc filuæ.
Paſtura.viii.q̃ʒ lḡ.7 ii.q̃ʒ laͭ.Valuit.xxv.folid.Modo.xl.folid.

14   LAND OF HORTON ABBEY   E

1 Horton Church holds HORTON. Before 1066 it paid tax for 7 hides.
Land for 7 ploughs, of which 2 hides are in lordship; 2 ploughs
there; 3 slaves;
   4 villagers and 10 smallholders with 1 plough.
   2 mills which pay 15s; meadow, 6 acres; pasture 2 leagues long
     and wide; woodland 1 league long and ½ league wide.
Value £4.
   The King holds two better hides of these seven in the Forest
of Wimborne.
   To this Church belongs a small church in Wimborne (Minster)
and land for 2 houses; in Wareham a church and 5 houses which
pay 65d; in Dorchester a house.

15   LAND OF ATHELNEY ABBEY   E

1 Athelney Church holds (Purse) CAUNDLE. Before 1066 it paid tax
for 4 hides and 1½ virgates of land. Land for 4 ploughs, of which
4 hides are in lordship; 1 plough there;
   2 villagers and 14 smallholders with 2 ploughs and 1½ virgates.
   Meadow, 14 acres; woodland 3 furlongs long and 2 furlongs wide.
   Of this land Alfred the Butler holds 1½ virgates of land.
Value of the whole 67s 6d.
Seven thanes held it before 1066; they could go to whichever lord they would.

41
a 1
E
E

16   LAND OF TAVISTOCK ABBEY   E

1 Tavistock Church holds ASKERSWELL. Before 1066 it paid tax
for 3 hides. Land for 6 ploughs, of which 1 hide is in lordship;
2 ploughs there; 4 slaves;
   7 villagers and 17 smallholders with 4 ploughs and 2 hides.
   2 mills which pay 7s; meadow, 9 acres; pasture 15 furlongs
     long and 2 furlongs wide. 9 cattle; 13 pigs; 260 sheep.
   2 tributaries who pay 15s.
Value £6; when he acquired it, 100s.

E
42
a 1
E

2 The Church holds POORTON itself. Before 1066 it paid tax for 2
hides. Land for 2 ploughs, of which 1 hide is in lordship;
1 plough there;
   5 villagers and 3 smallholders (have) 1 hide and 1 plough.
   Meadow, 2 acres; woodland, 16 acres; pasture 8 furlongs long
     and 2 furlongs wide. 7 pigs.
The value was 25s; now 40s.

42
a 2
E
E

TERRA SCI STEFANI DE CADOM.

Eccla S Stefani Cadom ten Frantone.Gida tenuit T.R.E.⁊ geldb
⅌.xxv.hid ⁊ dim.Tra.e tot.d car.De ea st in dnio.ix hidæ ⁊ dimid.
⁊ ibi.vii.car.⁊ xxvii.ferui.⁊ xxiiii.bord.⁊ vi.cotar.cu.xiiii.car.
Ibi.ii.molini redd.xx.folid.⁊ lxvii.ac pti.Paftura.i.leu ⁊ dim lg.
⁊ dimid leu lat.Silua.viii.q̃ lg.⁊ iii.q̃ lat.
Huic.CO adjuncte st.ii.hidæ quas Mathildis regine ded S Stefano.
Totu ualuit ⁊ reddit.xl.lib.
Ipfa æccla ten Beincome.Herald comes tenuit T.R.E.⁊ geldb ⅌.viii.hid.
Tra.e.vi.car.De ea st in dnio.v.hidæ.⁊ ibi.ii.car.⁊ iii.ferui.⁊ ii.uiłłi
⁊ x.bord cu.i.car.Ibi.xx.ac pti.⁊ ii.leu pafturæ.Valuit ⁊ redd.xii.lib.

★ Eccla S Wandregisili ten æcclam de Bridetone.⁊ de Brideport.
⁊ de Witcerce.His ptin ; iiii.hidæ.Redd.vii.lib.
Ipfa æccla ten una æcclam de rege in Warham.ad qua ptin.i.
hida.⁊ ibi.e.i.car cu.ii.bord.Valet.lxx.folid cu append fuis.

78 d
TERRA ABBATIÆ SCEPTESBERIENS.

Eccla S Mariæ Sceptesber ten Hanlege.T.R.E.
geldb ⅌.xx.hid.Tra.e.xx.car.De ea st in dnio.iiii.hidæ
una v min.⁊ ibi.iiii.car ⁊ dim.⁊ iiii.ferui.⁊ xxx.uiłłi ⁊ xv.
bord cu.xii.car.Ibi.vii.ac pti.⁊ Silua.i.leu lg.⁊ dimid leu
lat.Valuit ⁊ ual.xii.lib.De hac tra ten.ii.angli libi.iiii.hid.
Ipfa æccla ten Haintone.T.R.E.geldb ⫯ ⁊ hnt ibi.iii.car.
⅌.viii.hid.Tra.e.ix.car.De ea st in dnio.iii.hidæ ⁊ ibi.
iii.car.⁊ iii.ferui.⁊ xvi.uiłłi ⁊ ix.bord cu.vi.car.Ibi molin
redd.x.folid.⁊ xxx.ac pti.Siluæ.i.q̃ lg.⁊ tntd lat.
⁊ Pafturæ fimilit.Valuit.viii.lib.Modo.x.lib.

17   LAND OF ST. STEPHEN'S OF CAEN   E

1   St. Stephen's Church, Caen, holds FRAMPTON. Gytha held it before 1066. It paid tax for 25½ hides. Land for as many ploughs, of which 9½ hides are in lordship; 7 ploughs there; 27 slaves; 24 smallholders and 6 cottagers with 14 ploughs.
2 mills which pay 20s; meadow, 67 acres; pasture 1½ leagues long and ½ league wide; woodland 8 furlongs long and 3 furlongs wide.
To this manor are attached 2 hides which Queen Matilda gave to St. Stephen's.
The whole was valued at and pays £40.

2   The Church holds BINCOMBE itself. Earl Harold held it before 1066. It paid tax for 8 hides. Land for 6 ploughs, of which 5 hides are in lordship; 2 ploughs there; 3 slaves; 2 villagers and 10 smallholders with 1 plough.
Meadow, 20 acres; pasture, 2 leagues.
It was valued at and pays £12.

18   [LAND OF ST. WANDRILLE'S ABBEY]   E

1   St. Wandrille's Church holds the church of BURTON (Bradstock), of BRIDPORT and of WHITCHURCH (Canonicorum). 4 hides belong to them. They pay £7.   E   28   a 4

2   The Church itself holds from the King a church in WAREHAM, to which 1 hide belongs; 1 plough there, with 2 smallholders.
Value 70s, with its dependencies.   E   28   b 1

19   LAND OF SHAFTESBURY ABBEY   E   78 d

1   St. Mary's Church, Shaftesbury, holds (Sixpenny) HANDLEY. Before 1066 it paid tax for 20 hides. Land for 20 ploughs, of which 4 hides, less 1 virgate, are in lordship; 4½ ploughs there; 4 slaves; 30 villagers and 15 smallholders with 12 ploughs.
Meadow, 7 acres; woodland 1 league long and ½ league wide.
The value was and is £12.
Of this land 2 free Englishmen hold 4 hides; they have 3 ploughs there.

The Church itself holds
2   HINTON (St. Mary). Before 1066 it paid tax for 8 hides. Land for 9 ploughs, of which 3 hides are in lordship; 3 ploughs there; 3 slaves; 16 villagers and 9 smallholders with 6 ploughs.
A mill which pays 10s; meadow, 30 acres; woodland 1 furlong long and as wide; pasture, the same.
The value was £8; now £10.

Ipſa æccła teñ *STVRE* . T.R.E.geldb̵ ҏ . xvii . hiđ . T̓ra.ē . x.

cař . De ea ſt in dñio . x . hidæ . una v̓ �7 dim̃ min̊ .7 ibi . ii . cař.

7 xxv . uiłłi 7 xviii . borđ cū . v . cař . Ibi . iii . molini redđ

xxx . foł .7 x . ac̃ p̊ti . Paſtura . viii . q̃ɀ l̄g .7 vi . q̃ɀ lař.

Valuit . viii . lib̵ . modo . x . lib̵.

Ipſa æccła teñ *FONTEMALE* . T.R.E.geldb̵ ҏ . xv . hiđ . T̓ra . ē

xvi . cař . De ea ſt in dñio . iii . hidæ 7 una v̓ træ .7 ibi . ii . cař.

7 iii . ferui .7 xlv . uiłłi 7 xx . borđ cū . xiiii . cař . Ibi . iii . molini

redđ . xi . foliđ .7 vii . deñ .7 viii . ac̃ p̊ti .7 iiii . q̃rent paſturæ.

7 viii . q̃ɀ 7 ii . ac̃ filuæ . Valuit . x . lib̵ . Modo . xv . lib̵.

Ipſa æccła teñ *CVNTONE* . T.R.E.geldb̵ ҏ . x . hiđ . T̓ra.ē . x.

cař . De ea ſt in dñio . iiii . hidæ .7 una v̓ træ .7 ibi . ii . cař.

Ibi . xviii . uiłłi 7 xiiii . borđ cū . viii . cař . Ibi moliñ redđ . l . deñ.

7 iii . ac̃ p̊ti . Paſtura dimiđ leū l̄g .7 ii . q̃ɀ lař . Valet x . lib̵.

Ipſa æccła teñ *MELEBERIE* . T.R.E. geldb̵ ҏ . x . hiđ . T̓ra . ē

xii . cař . De ea ſt in dñio . iii . hidæ .7 ibi . vi . cař .7 xxvii . uiłłi

7 xx . cofcez cū . vi . cař . Ibi . iiii . molini redđ . xv . foł 7 iii . deñ.

paſtura dim̃ leū l̄g .7 ii . q̃ɀ lař . Silua . viii . q̃ɀ l̄g .7 ii . q̃ɀ lař.

Valuit . ix . lib̵ . Modo . xiii . lib̵.

Ipſa æccła teñ *EVNEMINSTRE* . T.R.E.geldb̵ ҏ . xviii . hiđ . T̓ra.ē

xvi . cař . De ea ſt in dñio . v . hidæ 7 dim̃ .7 ibi . ii . cař .7 xxix.

uiłłi 7 xxi . borđ cū . xiiii . cař . Ibi . iii . molini redđ . xvii . foliđ.

7 xviii . ac̃ p̊ti⊙ Paſtura . x . q̃ɀ l̄g .7 ii . q̃ɀ lař . Valuit x . lib̵.

Ipſa æccła teñ *TARENTE* . T.R.E.geldb̵ ҏ . x . hiđ ⎰modo xiiii . lib̵.

T̓ra . ē . viii . cař . De ea ſt in dñio . ii . hidæ 7 dimiđ .7 ibi . ii . cař.

7 iii . ferui .7 xviii . uiłłi 7 xiiii . borđ cū . vi . cař . Ibi . xviii . ac̃

p̊ti . Paſtura . i . leū l̄g .7 dim̃ leū lař . Silua . l . ptic̃ l̄g .7 xl . lař

Valuit . vi . lib̵ . Modo . x . lib̵ . ⎰ In *EVNEM* Silua . i . leū l̄g .7 dim̃ lař.

3 STOUR. Before 1066 it paid tax for 17 hides. Land for 10 ploughs, of which 10 hides, less 1½ virgates, are in lordship; 2 ploughs there;
   25 villagers and 18 smallholders with 5 ploughs.
   3 mills which pay 30s; meadow, 10 acres; pasture 8 furlongs long and 6 furlongs wide.
The value was £8; now £10.

4 FONTMELL (Magna). Before 1066 it paid tax for 15 hides. Land for 16 ploughs, of which 3 hides and 1 virgate of land are in lordship; 2 ploughs there; 3 slaves;
   45 villagers and 20 smallholders with 14 ploughs.
   3 mills which pay 11s 7d; meadow, 8 acres; pasture, 4 furlongs; woodland, 8 furlongs and 2 acres.
The value was £10; now £15.

5 COMPTON (Abbas). Before 1066 it paid tax for 10 hides. Land for 10 ploughs, of which 4 hides and 1 virgate of land are in lordship; 2 ploughs there.
   18 villagers and 14 smallholders with 8 ploughs.
   A mill which pays 50d; meadow, 3 acres; pasture ½ league long and 2 furlongs wide.
Value £10.

6 MELBURY (Abbas). Before 1066 it paid tax for 10 hides. Land for 12 ploughs, of which 3 hides are in lordship; 6 ploughs there;
   27 villagers and 20 Cottagers with 6 ploughs.
   4 mills which pay 15s 3d; pasture ½ league long and 2 furlongs wide; woodland 8 furlongs long and 2 furlongs wide.
The value was £9; now £13.

7 IWERNE MINSTER. Before 1066 it paid tax for 18 hides. Land for 16 ploughs, of which 5½ hides are in lordship; 2 ploughs there;
   29 villagers and 21 smallholders with 14 ploughs.
   3 mills which pay 17s; meadow, 18 acres; ⊙pasture 10 furlongs long and 2 furlongs wide.
The value was £10; now £14.

8 TARRANT (Hinton). Before 1066 it paid tax for 10 hides. Land for 8 ploughs, of which 2½ hides are in lordship; 2 ploughs there; 3 slaves;
   18 villagers and 14 smallholders with 6 ploughs.
   Meadow, 18 acres; pasture 1 league long and ½ league wide; woodland 50 perches long and 40 wide.
The value was £6; now £10.
   ⊙In IWERNE MINSTER woodland 1 league long and ½ wide.

Ipſa æccła teñ *FIFHIDE* .T.R.E.geldb ꝑ.v.hid.Tra.ē.IIII.caꝛ.

De ea ſt in dñio.III.hidæ 7 dimid.7 ibi.II.caꝛ.7 II.ſerui.7 IIII.uiłłi

7 III.bord cū.II.caꝛ.Ibi moliñ redd.v.ſolid.7 vI.ǎc ꝑti.Silua

IIII.q̊ꝫ l͞g.7 III.q̊ꝫ laꝋ.Valet.III.lib.Chetel teñ de abbatiſſa.

Ipſa æccła teñ *CHINGESTONE* .T.R.E.geldb ꝑ.xvI.hid.Tra.ē

xx.caꝛ.De ea ſt in dñio.III.hidæ.7 III.v̇ træ.7 ibi.II.caꝛ.7 II.

ſerui.7 xxII.uiłłi 7 xvI.bord cū.xvIII.caꝛ.Ibi.xII.ǎc ꝑti.

☞ Paſtura.I.leu l͞g.7 tñtd laꝋ.Valuit.xvI.lib.Modo.xxIII.lib.

Ipſa æccła teñ *STOCHE*.T.R.E.geldb ꝑ.v.hid.Tra.ē.IIII.caꝛ.

De ea ſt in dñio.III.hidæ 7 una v̇ træ.7 ibi.II.caꝛ.7 IIII.ſerui.

7 vII.uiłłi 7 IIII.bord cū.II.caꝛ.Ibi moliñ redd.xII.denaꝛ.

7 xv.ǎc ꝑti.paſtura.vI.q̊ꝫ l͞g.7 una q̊ꝫ laꝋ.Silua.xII.q̊ꝫ

l͞g.7 IIII.q̊ꝫ laꝋ.Valuit 7 uał.IIII.lib.

Ipſa æccła teñ *MAPLEDRETONE* T.R.E.geldb ꝑ.xI.hid.Tra.ē

IIII.caꝛ.De ea ſt in dñio.vII.hide 7 una v̇ træ.7 ibi.II.caꝛ.

cū.I.ſeruo.7 vI.uiłłi 7 IIII.bord cū.II.caꝛ.Ibi.vII.ǎc ꝑti.Int

paſturā 7 ſiluā.xI.q̊ꝫ l͞g.7 tñtd laꝋ.Valuit.xxx.ſoł.m̄.c.ſolid.

Ipſa æccła teñ *CESEBVRNE*.T.R.E.geldb ꝑ.xvI.hid.Tra.ē

De ea ſt in dñio.II.hidæ 7 III.virg.7 ibi.III.caꝛ.7 v.ſerui.7 xxI.uiłłs

7 x.bord cū.vIII.caꝛ.Ibi moliñ redd.xv.ſoł.7 x.ǎc ꝑti.Paſtura

una leu 7 dimid l͞g.7 una leu laꝋ.Valuit 7 uał.xvI.lib.

Iſtū Maneꝛ 7 *STVRE*.abſtulerat Herald S *MARIÆ*.T.R.E.ſed.W.rex

eā fecit reſaiſiri.q̊a in ipſa æccła inuent.ē breuis cū ſigillo.R.E.

ꝑcipieꝜ ut æcclæ reſtituerent cū *MELECOME*.quē rex adhuc teñ.

Ipſe etiā Herald abſtulit ab æccła *PIDELE*.Comes moriton tenet.

9 FIFEHEAD (St. Quintin). Before 1066 it paid tax for 5 hides.
Land for 4 ploughs, of which 3½ hides are in lordship; 2
ploughs there; 2 slaves;
    4 villagers and 3 smallholders with 2 ploughs.
    A mill which pays 5s; meadow, 6 acres; woodland 4 furlongs
       long and 3 furlongs wide.
Value £3.
Ketel holds from the Abbess.

10 KINGSTON. Before 1066 it paid tax for 16 hides. Land for 20
ploughs, of which 3 hides and 3 virgates of land are in lordship;
2 ploughs there; 2 slaves;
    22 villagers and 16 smallholders with 18 ploughs.
    Meadow, 12 acres; pasture 1 league long and as wide.
The value was £16; now £23.

ψ *The rest of 19,10 and all of 19,11 are written at the bottom of col. 78d after 19,14, directed
by transposition signs to their correct position in the text*

12 STOKE (Wake). Before 1066 it paid tax for 5 hides. Land for
4 ploughs, of which 3 hides and 1 virgate of land are in lordship;
2 ploughs there; 4 slaves;
    7 villagers and 4 smallholders with 2 ploughs.
    A mill which pays 12d; meadow, 15 acres; pasture 6 furlongs
       long and 1 furlong wide; woodland 12 furlongs long and 4
       furlongs wide.
The value was and is £4.

13 MAPPERTON. Before 1066 it paid tax for 11 hides. Land for 4
ploughs, of which 7 hides and 1 virgate of land are in lordship;
2 ploughs there, with 1 slave;
    6 villagers and 4 smallholders with 2 ploughs.
    Meadow, 7 acres; pasture and woodland, between them, 11
       furlongs long and as wide.
The value was 30s; now 100s.

14 CHESELBOURNE. Before 1066 it paid tax for 16 hides. Land for ....
of which 2 hides and 3 virgates are in lordship; 3 ploughs there;
5 slaves;
    21 villagers and 10 smallholders with 8 ploughs.
    A mill which pays 15s; meadow, 10 acres; pasture 1½ leagues
       long and 1 league wide.
The value was and is £16.
    Earl Harold took this manor and STOUR away from St. Mary's
before 1066, but King William restored them to its possession
because in the Church itself was found a writ with the seal of
King Edward ordering that they should be restored to the Church
with MELCOMBE (Horsey) which the King still holds. Earl Harold
himself also took away 'PIDDLE' from the Church; the Count of
Mortain holds it.

☞ De ꝏ Chingestone hͭ rex.ɪ.hiđ.in qua feͨ caſtellū Warha.7 ꝑ ea deđ
S̅ Marie æcclam de Gelingeha.cū Appendic̀ ſuis.q̄ uaɫ.xl.ſolid.
De eođ ꝏ hͭ Wiɫɫs de Braioſe unā v̄ træ.q teneƀ æccɫa T.R.E.
Ipſa æccɫa teñ in Ferneha.ɪ.hiđ.quā teñ de ea Aiulf9 7 uxor Hug.f.grip.

79 a
.XX.   TERRA ABBATIE WILTVNIENSIS.
Ecclā S̅ Mariæ Wiltvniens teñ Dedilintone.T.R.E.geldƀ
ꝑ.vɪ.hiđ.Tra.ē.v.car̄.De ea ſͭ in dñio.ɪɪ.hidæ 7 ɪɪɪ.virḡ træ.
7 ibi.ɪɪ.car̄.7 ɪɪɪɪ.ſerui.7 vɪɪ.uiɫɫi 7 xɪɪ.borđ cū.ɪɪ.car̄.
Ibi moliñ redđ.xɪɪ.ſoliđ 7 vɪ.deñ.7 xxxvɪ.ac̄ p̃ti.Paſtura
dimiđ leū lḡ.7 tntđ laͭ.Silua.ɪ.leū lḡ.7 dimiđ leū laͭ.
Valet.vɪɪ.liƀ.
Ipſa æccɫa teñ Winbyrne.T.R.E.geldƀ ꝑ.ɪɪɪ.hiđ 7 dimiđ.
Tra.ē.ɪɪ.car̄.In dñio.ē tota p̃t unā v̄.7 ibi.ɪ.car̄.7 ɪɪ.ſerui.
cū.ɪ.uiɫɫo 7 vɪ.borđ.Ibi moliñ redđ.vɪɪ.ſoɫ 7 vɪ.denaͭ.
7 vɪɪ.ac̄ p̃ti.Paſturæ.ɪɪɪɪ.q̄ɇ int lḡ 7 laͭ.Siluą.ɪɪɪ.q̄ɇ lḡ.
7 una q̄ɇ laͭ.Valuit.xl.ſoliđ.Modo.xxx.ſoliđ.
.XXI.   TERRA SC̃Æ K̃INITATIS DE CADOM.
Ecclā S̅ k̃init Cadom teñ Tarente.Briͨtric tenuit T.R.E.
7 geldƀ ꝑ.x.hiđ.Tra.ē.vɪɪɪ.car̄.De ea ſͭ in dñio.ɪɪɪɪ.hidæ.ɪɪɪɪ.ac̄s
min.7 ibi.ɪɪ.car̄.7 xɪɪɪɪ.ſerui.7 ɪx.uiɫɫi 7 ɪ.borđ cū.ɪɪɪɪ.car̄.
Ibi.xxxvɪɪɪ.ac̄ p̃ti.Paſtura xxxɪɪɪ.q̄ɇ int lḡ 7 laͭ.Silua.xv.
q̄ɇ int lḡ 7 laͭ.Valuit.xɪ.liƀ.Modo.xɪɪɪɪ.liƀ.
.XXII.   TERRA CANONICOȥ CONSTANͭ ÆCCLÆ.
Canonici Conſtantienſes teñ Wintrebyrne.T.R.E.geldƀ ꝑ.vɪɪɪ.
hiđ.Tra.ē.ɪx.car̄.De ea ſͭ in dñio.ɪɪɪ.hidæ 7 ɪɪɪ.v̄ træ.7 ibi.ɪɪɪɪ.car̄.

Entered at the foot of col. 78d and directed by transposition signs to their correct position in the text

19,10 continued

Of the manor of KINGSTON the King has 1 hide, on which he built WAREHAM Castle; for it he gave to St. Mary's the church of Gillingham, with its dependencies, whose value is 40s.

Also of this manor William of Braose has 1 virgate of land, which the Church held before 1066.

11 The Church itself holds in FARNHAM 1 hide, which Aiulf and Hugh son of Grip's wife hold from it.

20 LAND OF WILTON ABBEY E 79 a

1 St. Mary's Church, Wilton, holds DIDLINGTON. Before 1066 it paid tax for 6 hides. Land for 5 ploughs, of which 2 hides and 3 virgates of land are in lordship; 2 ploughs there; 4 slaves;
  7 villagers and 12 smallholders with 2 ploughs.
  A mill which pays 12s 6d; meadow, 36 acres; pasture ½ league long and as wide; woodland 1 league long and ½ league wide.
Value £7.

2 The Church itself holds WIMBORNE (St. Giles). Before 1066 it paid tax for 3½ hides. Land for 2 ploughs. The whole of it is in lordship except 1 virgate; 1 plough there; 2 slaves, with
  1 villager and 6 smallholders.
  A mill which pays 7s 6d; meadow, 7 acres; pasture, 4 furlongs in both length and width; woodland 3 furlongs long and 1 furlong wide.
The value was 40s; now 30s.

21 LAND OF HOLY TRINITY OF CAEN E

1 Holy Trinity Church, Caen, holds TARRANT (Launceston). Brictric held it before 1066. It paid tax for 10 hides. Land for 8 ploughs, of which 4 hides, less 4 acres, are in lordship; 2 ploughs there; 14 slaves;
  9 villagers and 1 smallholder with 4 ploughs.
  Meadow, 38 acres; pasture 33 furlongs in both length and width; woodland 15 furlongs in both length and width.
The value was £11; now £14.

22 LAND OF THE CANONS OF COUTANCES CHURCH E

1 The Canons of Coutances hold WINTERBORNE (Stickland). Before 1066 it paid tax for 8 hides. Land for 9 ploughs, of which 3 hides and 3 virgates of land are in lordship; 4 ploughs there;

7 v.ſerui.7 xii.uiłłi 7 xx.borđ cū.iiii.cař.Ibi moliñ redđ.xii.ſoł.
7 vi.den.Paſtura.xxvi.q̃ɫ l̄g.7 iiii.q̃ɫ laŧ.Silua.v.q̃ɫ l̄g.7 iiii.
q̃ɫ laŧ.Valuit.x.liƀ.Modo.xv.liƀ.

.XXIII.   TERRA SC̄Æ MARIÆ VILLARIS MONASTERIJ.
Eccl̄a S̃ MARIÆ VILLAR ten WADONE.Tres taini tenuer̄ T.R.E.
7 geldƀ p.vi.hiđ.Tra.ē.v.cař.De ea ſŧ in dñio.v.hidæ 7 dimiđ.
7 ibi.iii.cař.7 iiii.ſerui.7 ii.uiłłi 7 vii.borđ.cū.ii.cař.Ibi.xx.ac̃
pti.7 xv.q̃ɫ paſturæ.Valuit 7 uał.x.liƀ
Hanc trā deđ Hūgo eiđ æccłæ .f. grip .De ea habeƀ æccła ABODESBER T.R.E
vi ac̃s meſſis 7 iii.circſcez de c̄ſuetuđ.ſed Hugo nunɋ dedit.

.XXIIII.   TERRA ELEMOSINARIOɀ REGIS.
BRISTVARD pƀr ten̄ æccłā de Doreceſtre 7 BERE.7 decimas.
Ibi ptin̄.i.hida 7 xx.ac̃ træ.Valeɴ̄.iiii.liƀ.   ⨍ Valet.x.ſolid.
Bollo pƀr hŧ æcclam de WINFRODE.cū una v̄ træ.Ibȳ.ē dimiđ cař.
Bollo pƀr æcclam hŧ de PITRETONE.7 de Caluedone.7 de Flote.
His adjacet.i.hida 7 dimiđ.Redđ.lvii.ſoliđ.7 vi.denar̄.
RAINBALDVS pƀr ten̄ de rege POLEHAM.Ipſe tenuit T.R.E.7 geldƀ
p.x.hiđ.Tra.ē.x.cař.De ea ſŧ in dñio.iiii.hidæ.   7 ii.ſerui.
7 ix.uiłłi.7 v.borđ cū.iiii.cař.Ibi.viii.q̃ɫ pti.int̄ l̄g 7 laŧ.7 ii.leū
ſiluæ int̄ l̄g 7 laŧ.Valet.c.x.ſoliđ
WALTER diacon ten̄ de rege CERNEL.7 Bernarđ de eo.Goduin tenuit
T.R.E.7 geldƀ p.iii.hiđ.Tra.ē.v.cař.In dñio ſŧ.ii.cař.7 iii.ſerui.7 viii.
uiłłi 7 vi.borđ cū.ii.cař.Ibi moliñ redđ.x.ſoliđ.7 iii.ac̃ pti.7 vii.q̃ɫ
paſturæ in l̄g.7 vi.q̃ɫ laŧ.Valuit.c.ſoł.Modo.vi.liƀ.

5 slaves;
  12 villagers and 20 smallholders with 4 ploughs.
  A mill which pays 12s 6d; pasture 26 furlongs long and 4
    furlongs wide; woodland 5 furlongs long and 4 furlongs wide.
The value was £10; now £15.

23   LAND OF ST. MARY'S, MONTIVILLIERS   E

1 St. Mary's Church, (Monti)villiers, holds WADDON. Three thanes
  held it before 1066. It paid tax for 6 hides. Land for 5 ploughs,
  of which 5½ hides are in lordship; 3 ploughs there; 4 slaves;
    2 villagers and 7 smallholders with 2 ploughs.
    Meadow, 20 acres; pasture, 15 furlongs.
  The value was and is £10.
    Hugh son of Grip gave this land to this Church. Before 1066
  Abbotsbury Church had from it 6 acres of harvest and 3 church
  taxes in customary dues, but Hugh never gave them.

24   LAND OF THE KING'S ALMSMEN   E

1 Brictward the priest holds the church of DORCHESTER and BERE
  (Regis) and the tithes. 1 hide belongs there and 20 acres of land.
  Value £4.
  27 b 2

2 Bolle the priest has the church of WINFRITH (Newburgh), with 1
  virgate of land. ½ plough there.
  Value 10s.
  E 28 a 2

3 Bolle the priest has the church of PUDDLETOWN, of CHALDON and
  of FLEET. 1½ hides are attached to these.
  They pay 57s 6d.
  28 a 5

4 Reinbald the priest holds PULHAM from the King. He held it
  himself before 1066. It paid tax for 10 hides. Land for 10
  ploughs, of which 4 hides are in lordship; ...; 2 slaves;
    9 villagers and 5 smallholders with 4 ploughs.
    Meadow, 8 furlongs in both length and width; woodland, 2
      leagues in both length and width.
  Value 110s.
  (·)

5 Walter the deacon holds 'CERNE' from the King, and Bernard from
  him. Godwin, a free man, held it before 1066. It paid tax for 3
  hides. Land for 5 ploughs. In lordship 2 ploughs; 3 slaves;
    8 villagers and 6 smallholders with 2 ploughs.
    A mill which pays 10s; meadow, 3 acres; pasture, 7 furlongs
      in length and 6 furlongs wide.
  The value was 100s; now £6.
  (·)

C. .XXV. TERRA ALANI COMITIS.

COMES ALANVS ten̄ de rege *DEVENIS* . Bri⟨c⟩tric tenuit T.R.E.
7 geldb̄ ℘.xv.hiđ.Tra.ē.xv.car̄.De ea sī in dn̄io.v.hidæ./ ibi.iiī.car̄.
7 xiii.ſerui.7 xix.uiłłi 7 vi.borđ cū.vi.car̄.Ibi.xv.ac̄ p̄ti.Paſ
tura.xxiii.q̂ẕ int̄ lḡ 7 lat̄.Silua.vi.q̂ẕ in lḡ 7 lat̄.Valuit
7 ualet.xx.iii.lib̄.

79 b
.XXVI. TERRA COMITIS MORITONIENSIS.

COMES MORITON ten̄ *WESTONE*.7 Haimo de eo.Godric 7 Bruno ⁱⁿ ᵖᵃʳᵃᵍᵇ
tenuer̄ T.R.E.℘.ii.Maner̄.7 geldb̄ ℘.vii.hiđ.Tra.ē.vi.car̄.In dn̄io
sī.ii.car̄.7 v.ſerui.7 xiiii.uiłłi 7 vii.borđ.cū.i.car̄ 7 dim̄.Ibi.xl.
ac̄ p̄ti.7 Silua dimiđ leū lḡ.7 tn̄tđ lat̄.Valuit.iiii.lib̄.m̄.vii.lib̄.

Iđē com̄ ten̄.ii.hiđ in *ILAND*.7 Drogo de eo.Tra.ē.i.car̄.Vaſta.ē.

Ipſe.Co.ten̄ *HANFORD*.Aluuard tenuit T.R.E.7 geldb̄ ℘.iiii.ᵒʳ
hiđ.Tra.ē.iii.car̄.In dn̄io sī.ii.car̄.7 iiii.ſerui.7 ii.uiłłi 7 ii.borđ
cū.i.car̄.Ibi.ii.molini redđ.xvi.ſol.7 xxxv.ac̄ p̄ti.7 xv.ac̄ ſiluæ.
Paſtura.i.leū lḡ.7 una q̂ẕ lat̄.Valuit 7 ual̄.c.ſoliđ.

Ipſe.co.ten̄ *ACFORD*.Aluuin tenuit T.R.E.7 geldb̄ ℘.v.hiđ.
Tra.ē.vi.car̄.In dn̄io sī.ii.car̄.cū.i.ſeruo.7 vi.uiłłi 7 xvii.borđ
cū.v.car̄.Ibi medietas.ii.molinoẕ redđ.x.ſol.7 xl.ac̄ p̄ti.
7 tn̄tđ paſturæ Silua.ii.q̂ẕ 7 dim̄ lḡ.7 una q̂ẕ 7 dim̄ lat̄.
Valuit 7 ual̄.vii.lib̄.

Iđē.Co.ten̄ in *CERNEL*.i.hiđ 7 dim̄.7 ꝗda femina de eo.Brungar
tenuit T.R.E.Tra.ē.i car̄.q̄ ibi.ē 7 iii.ac̄ p̄ti.paſtura.ii.q̂ẕ lḡ.
7 una q̂ẕ lat̄.Valet.x.ſoliđ.

25   LAND OF COUNT ALAN   E

1 Count Alan holds DEWLISH from the King. Brictric held it before 1066. It paid tax for 15 hides. Land for 15 ploughs, of which 5 hides are in lordship; 3 ploughs there; 13 slaves;
     19 villagers and 6 smallholders with 6 ploughs.
Meadow, 15 acres; pasture 23 furlongs in both length and width; woodland 6 furlongs in length and width.
The value was and is £23.

26   LAND OF THE COUNT OF MORTAIN   E   79 b

1 The Count of Mortain holds (Buckhorn) WESTON, and Hamo from him. Godric and Brown held it jointly before 1066 as two manors. It paid tax for 7 hides. Land for 6 ploughs. In lordship 2 ploughs; 5 slaves;
     14 villagers and 7 smallholders with 1½ ploughs.
Meadow, 40 acres; woodland ½ league long and as wide.
The value was £4; now £7.

2 The Count also holds 2 hides in NYLAND, and Drogo from him. Land for 1 plough.
It is waste.

3 The Count holds HANFORD himself. Alward held it before 1066. It paid tax for 4 hides. Land for 3 ploughs. In lordship 2 ploughs; 4 slaves;
     2 villagers and 2 smallholders with 1 plough.
2 mills which pay 16s; meadow, 35 acres; woodland, 15 acres; pasture 1 league long and 1 furlong wide.
The value was and is 100s.

4 The Count holds (Child) OKEFORD himself. Alwin held it before 1066. It paid tax for 5 hides. Land for 6 ploughs. In lordship 2 ploughs, with 1 slave;
     6 villagers and 17 smallholders with 5 ploughs.
Half of 2 mills which pays 10s; meadow, 40 acres; pasture, as much; woodland 2½ furlongs long and 1½ furlongs wide.
The value was and is £7.

5 The Count also holds 1½ hides in 'CERNE', and a woman from him. Brungar held it before 1066. Land for 1 plough, which is there.
Meadow, 3 acres; pasture 2 furlongs long and 1 furlong wide.
Value 10s.

Idē.Co.ten̈ _FROME_.7 Wilłs de eo.Aluuard tenuit T.R.E.7 geldƀ
ᵽ.iiii.hid.T̄ra.ē.iii.car̄.In dn̄io sꝼ.ii.7 xv.ac̄ ᵽti.Paſtura.iiii.
q̃ꝛ lḡ.7 ii.q̃ꝛ lar̄.Valuit.xl.ſoł.Modo.lx.ſolid.
Roƀtus ten̈ de.Co._STANFORD_.Britnod tenuit T.R.E.7 geldƀ
ᵽ.iii.hid.T̄ra.ē.ii.car̄.Ibi.ē un̈ uiłłs 7 iii.bord.cū dim̃ car̄.
Ibi molin̄.iiii.ſolid.7 xxx.ac̄ ᵽti.Paſtura.i.leū lḡ.7 iii.q̃ꝛ lar̄.
Anſger ten de.Co._CERNE_.Duo taini tenuer̄ ſ̃ Valet.xx.ſolid.
T.R.E.7 geldƀ ᵽ.iii.hid.T̄ra.ē.ii.car̄.q̃ ibi sꝼ in dn̄io.7 ii.uiłłi
7 vi.bord.Ibi molin̄.v.ſolid.7 iiii.ac̄ ᵽti.Paſtura.v.q̃ꝛ lḡ.
7 iii.q̃ꝛ lar̄.Valuit 7 uał.iii.liƀ.
Radulf ten de.Co._CERNE_.Decē taini tenuer̄ T.R.E.7 geldƀ
ᵽ.iii.hid.T̄ra.ē.ii.car̄.In dn̄io.ē una.7 ii.uiłłi.7 ii.bord.7 ii.ſerui
entes francig̃ cū.i.car̄.Ibi.iii.ac̄ ᵽti.Paſtura.v.q̃ꝛ lḡ.7 iii.lar̄.
Ipſe.Co.ten in _CERNE_.ii.hid 7 dim̃.Sex taini ſ̃ Valet.xl.ſoł.
tenuer̄ T.R.E.T̄ra.ē.ii.car̄.Ibi.ii.bord cū.i.car̄.7 molin̄ redd
xl.denar̄.7 iii.ac̄ ᵽti.Paſtura.iii.q̃ꝛ lḡ.7 ii.q̃ꝛ lar̄.Valet.l.ſoł.
Anſger ten de.Co._CERNE_.Brictuin̈ tenuit T.R.E.7 geldƀ
ᵽ.ii.hid.T̄ra.ē.i.car̄.Valet.xv.ſolid.
Bretel ten de.Co.in _FROME_.i.hid.T̄ra.ē.i.car̄.Ibi sꝼ.v.ac̄
ᵽti.7 xxx.ac̄ paſturæ.Valet.xii.ſolid.
Roƀt ten de.Co I _WINTREBVRNE_.i.hid.Alured tenuit T.R.E.
T̄ra.ē.i.car̄.q̃ ibi.ē cū.iii.uiłłis.Valuit 7 uał.x.ſolid.

6 The Count also holds BHOMPSTON, and William from him. Alward held it before 1066. It paid tax for 4 hides. Land for 3 ploughs. In lordship 2.

Meadow, 15 acres; pasture 4 furlongs long and 2 furlongs wide. The value was 40s; now 60s.

7 Robert holds STAFFORD from the Count. Brictnoth held it before 1066. It paid tax for 3 hides. Land for 2 ploughs.

1 villager and 3 smallholders with ½ plough.

A mill, 4s; meadow, 30 acres; pasture 1 league long and 3 furlongs wide.

Value 20s.

8 Ansger holds 'CERNE' from the Count. Two thanes held it freely before 1066. It paid tax for 3 hides. Land for 2 ploughs, which are there, in lordship;

2 villagers and 6 smallholders.

A mill, 5s; meadow, 4 acres; pasture 5 furlongs long and 3 furlongs wide.

The value was and is £3.

9 Ralph holds 'CERNE' from the Count. Ten thanes held it jointly before 1066. It paid tax for 3 hides. Land for 2 ploughs. In lordship 1;

2 villagers, 2 smallholders and 2 Frenchmen who serve with 1 plough.

Meadow, 3 acres; pasture 5 furlongs long and 3 wide.

Value 40s.

10 The Count holds 2½ hides in 'CERNE' himself. Six thanes held them jointly before 1066. Land for 2 ploughs.

2 smallholders with 1 plough.

A mill which pays 40d; meadow, 3 acres; pasture 3 furlongs long and 2 furlongs wide.

Value 50s.

11 Ansger holds 'CERNE' from the Count. Brictwin held it before 1066. It paid tax for 2 hides. Land for 1 plough.

Value 15s.

12 Bretel holds 1 hide in BHOMPSTON from the Count. Land for 1 plough.

Meadow, 5 acres; pasture, 30 acres.

Value 12s.

13 Robert holds 1 hide in 'WINTERBORNE' from the Count. Alfred held it before 1066. Land for 1 plough, which is there, with 3 villagers.

The value was and is 10s.

Dodeman ten de. Co. *WAI*. Scireuuold 7 Vluuard tenueř in parag' T.R.E.

7 geldb ꝑ.II.hiđ.Tra.ē.I.car 7 dim.In dnio.ē.I.car cū.I.ſeruo.

7 II.borđ.Ibi.II.molini redđ.xx.ſol.7 xII.ac ꝑti.Paſtura.v.q̊ꝗ

lg̅.7 II.lat.Valuit 7 ual.xL.ſoliđ.

Amun ten de Co. *WAI*. Nouē taini tenueř libe T.R.E.7 geldb ꝑ.IIII.

hiđ.Tra.ē.IIII.car.In dnio.ē.I.car.7 III.coſcez cū.I.uillo hn̅t.I.car.

Ibi.II.molini redđ.xxxII.ſol.7 xII.ſalinæ.7 Ix.ac ꝑti.7 Ix.q̊ꝗ Paſturæ.

Robt ten de.Co.*WAI*.Octo taini tenueř libe.T.R.E. Valet.IIII.lib.

7 geldb ꝑ.IIII.hiđ una v min.Tra.ē.III.car.Ibi ſt.II.borđ 7 vII.ac

ꝑti.Paſtura.vII.q̊ꝗ lg̅.7 IIII.q̊ꝗ lat.Valet.xL.ſol.

Bretel ten de. Co. *HALEGEWELLE*.Aluuin tenuit T.R.E.7 geldb ꝑ.II.

hiđ.Tra.ē.I.car 7 dim.Ibi ſt.xII.ac ꝑti.7 Paſtura.vII.q̊ꝗ lg̅.

7 una q̊ꝗ lat.Valet.x.ſoliđ.

Robt ten de.Co.*WINTREBVRNE*.Alured tenuit T.R.E.7 geldb

ꝑ.III.hiđ.Tra.ē.II.car.In dnio.ē.I.car.7 II.ſerui.7 I.uills 7 III.borđ

Ibi.x.ac ꝑti.7 paſtura.v.q̊ꝗ lg̅.7 III.q̊ꝗ lat.Valuit.xL.ſol.m̅.xxx.ſol.

Robt ten de.Co.*WINTREBVRNE*.Duo taini tenueř in parag'.T.R.E.7 geldb

ꝑ.II.hiđ 7 dim.Tra.ē.I.car 7 dimiđ.q̊ ibi ſt cū.II.uiltis.7 II.ſeruis.

Ibi.II.ac ꝑti.Paſtura.v.q̊ꝗ lg̅.7 una q̊ꝗ lat.Valuit 7 ual.xL.ſol.

Abbatia majoris Monaſt ten de.Co.*PIDELE*.Duo taini tenueř

T.R.E.ꝑ.II.Maneř.7 geldb ꝑ.x.hiđ.Tra.ē.vII.car.De ea ſt

in dnio.v.hidæ.7 ibi.II.car.7 III.ſerui.7 xIII.uilti.7 vIII.borđ

cū.III.car.Ibi.xxxIII.ac ꝑti.7 xv.q̊ꝗ paſturæ.Valet.x.lib.

14 Dodman holds 'WEY' from the Count. Sheerwold and Wulfward held it jointly before 1066. It paid tax for 2 hides. Land for 1½ ploughs. In lordship 1 plough, with 1 slave; 2 smallholders.
2 mills which pay 20s; meadow, 12 acres; pasture 5 furlongs long and 2 wide.
The value was and is 40s.

15 Amund holds 'WEY' from the Count. Nine thanes held it freely before 1066. It paid tax for 4 hides. Land for 4 ploughs. In lordship 1 plough.
3 Cottagers with 1 villager have 1 plough.
2 mills which pay 32s; 12 salt-houses; meadow, 9 acres; pasture, 9 furlongs.
Value £4.

16 Robert holds 'WEY' from the Count. Eight thanes held it freely before 1066. It paid tax for 4 hides, less 1 virgate. Land for 3 ploughs.
2 smallholders.
Meadow, 7 acres; pasture 7 furlongs long and 4 furlongs wide.
Value 40s.

17 Bretel holds HOLWELL from the Count. Alwin held it before 1066. It paid tax for 2 hides. Land for 1½ ploughs.
Meadow, 12 acres; pasture 7 furlongs long and 1 furlong wide.
Value 10s.

18 Robert holds 'WINTERBORNE' from the Count. Alfred held it before 1066. It paid tax for 3 hides. Land for 2 ploughs. In lordship 1 plough; 2 slaves;
1 villager and 3 smallholders.
Meadow, 10 acres; pasture 5 furlongs long and 3 furlongs wide.
The value was 40s; now 30s.

19 Robert holds 'WINTERBORNE' from the Count. Two thanes held it jointly before 1066. It paid tax for 2½ hides. Land for 1½ ploughs, which are there, with
2 villagers and 2 slaves.
Meadow, 2 acres; pasture 5 furlongs long and 1 furlong wide.
The value was and is 40s.

20 The Abbey of Marmoutier holds PIDDLEHINTON from the Count. Two thanes held it before 1066 as two manors. It paid tax for 10 hides. Land for 7 ploughs, of which 5 hides are in lordship; 2 ploughs there; 3 slaves;
13 villagers and 8 smallholders with 3 ploughs.
Meadow, 33 acres; pasture, 15 furlongs.
Value £10.

Hunfrid ten de.Co.*PIDELE*.Vn tain tenuit T.R.E.7 geldb ‚p. ɪ.

hida 7 dim.Tra.ē.ɪ.caŕ.Ibi sŧ.ɪɪɪɪ.bord cū dimid caŕ Ibi moliñ

★ edd.xʟ.deñ.7 ɪɪɪɪ.ac p̄ti.7 v.q̃ʒ̃ paſturæ.Valuit.xxx.ſot.Modo.xʟ.ſot.

Hunfrid ten de.co.*PIDELE*.Duo taini tenueŕ T.R.E.7 geldb ‚p.ɪɪ.

hid 7 dimid.Tra.ē.ɪɪ.caŕ.Ibi.ē una caŕ cū.ɪ.ſeruo.7 vɪɪ.bord.

Ibi moliñ redd.xʟ.denaŕ.7 ac 7 dimid p̄ti.Paſtura.ɪɪɪ.q̃ʒ̃ lḡ.

7 una q̃ʒ̃ 7 dimid lat.Valet.ʟ.ſolid.

Ipſe Com̄ ten *MAPLEDRE*.Brictric tenuit T.R.E.7 geldb ‚p.ɪɪɪ.virg

7 dimid.7 vɪɪ.acris træ.Tra.ē.ɪ.caŕ.Ibi.ē uñ ſeruus.7 xɪɪ.ac p̄ti.

Silua.ɪɪ.q̃ʒ̃ lḡ.7 una q̃ʒ̃ lat.Valuit.xx.ſot.Modo.xɪɪ.ſolid.

Robt ten de.Co.*MORDONE*.Duo taini tenueŕ T.R.E.7 geldb

‚p una hida.Tra.ē.ɪ.caŕ.Ibi sŧ.ɪɪ.uitti 7 moliñ redd.vɪ.ſot 7 ɪɪɪ.

denaŕ.7 v.ac p̄ti.7 dimid leū paſturæ.Valuit.xx.ſot.Modo.xv.ſot.

Ipſe.Co.ten *SPESTEBERIE*.Tres taini tenueŕ T.R.E.7 geldb ‚p.ɪ.hida

7 dimid.Tra.ē dimid caŕ.Ibi.ē uñ bord 7 uñ uitts.7 xvɪ.ac p̄ti.

7 xxxɪɪɪɪ.ac paſturæ.De hac tra hŧ com̄ una v træ 7 ɪɪɪ.acs.7 Robt

ɪɪɪ.virg 7 vɪ.acs.Tot ualet.xvɪɪɪ.ſolid.

Anſgeri ten de.Co.*SIDELINCE*.Edmar tenuit T.R.E.7 geldb ‚p.v.

hid.Tra.ē.ɪɪɪɪ.caŕ.In dñio sŧ.ɪɪ.caŕ.7 v.ſerui.7 ɪɪɪɪ.uitti 7 ɪɪɪɪ.bord

cū.ɪ.caŕ.Ibi moliñ redd.v.ſot.7 xɪɪ.ac p̄ti.Paſtura.ɪ.leū lḡ.

7 ɪɪɪɪ.q̃ʒ̃ lat.Valuit 7 uat.ɪɪɪɪ.lib.

Amund ten de.Co.*SIDELINCE*.Suain tenuit T.R.E.7 geldb ‚p.ɪ.

hida.Tra.ē.ɪ.caŕ.Ibi sŧ.ɪɪɪɪ.q̃ʒ̃ paſturæ|lḡ.7 ɪɪ.q̃ʒ̃ lat.Valet.x.ſot.

21 Humphrey holds 'PIDDLE' from the Count. A thane held it freely before 1066. It paid tax for 1½ hides. Land for 1 plough.
4 smallholders with ½ plough.
A mill which pays 40d; meadow, 4 acres; pasture, 5 furlongs.
The value was 30s; now 40s.

22 Humphrey holds 'PIDDLE' from the Count. Two thanes held it freely before 1066. It paid tax for 2½ hides. Land for 2 ploughs. 1 plough there, with 1 slave;
7 smallholders.
A mill which pays 40d; meadow, (1)½ acres; pasture 3 furlongs long and 1½ furlongs wide.
Value 50s.

23 The Count holds MAPPOWDER himself. Brictric held it before 1066. It paid tax for 3½ virgates and 7 acres of land. Land for 1 plough. 1 slave.
Meadow, 12 acres; woodland 2 furlongs long and 1 furlong wide.
The value was 20s; now 12s.

24 Robert holds MORDEN from the Count. Two thanes held it before 1066. It paid tax for 1 hide. Land for 1 plough.
2 villagers.
A mill which pays 6s 3d; meadow, 5 acres; pasture, ½ league.
The value was 20s; now 15s.

25 The Count holds SPETISBURY himself. Three thanes held it before 1066. It paid tax for 1½ hides. Land for ½ plough.
1 smallholder and 1 villager.
Meadow, 16 acres; pasture, 34 acres.
Of this land the Count has 1 virgate of land and 3 acres,
Robert 3 virgates and 6 acres.
Value of the whole, 18s.

26 Ansger holds SYDLING from the Count. Edmer held it before 1066. It paid tax for 5 hides. Land for 4 ploughs. In lordship 2 ploughs; 5 slaves;
4 villagers and 4 smallholders with 1 plough.
A mill which pays 5s; meadow, 12 acres; pasture 1 league long and 4 furlongs wide.
The value was and is £4.

27 Amund holds SYDLING from the Count. Swein held it before 1066. It paid tax for 1 hide. Land for 1 plough.
Pasture, 4 furlongs in length and 2 furlongs wide.
Value 10s.

Bretel ten de.Co.*LITELTONE*.Vluiet tenuit T.R.E.7 geldħ
￫.v.hiđ.Tra.ē.III.cař.In dñio.ē una cař.7 VI.borđ.7 II.ſerui.
Ibi moliñ redđ.VII.ſoł.7 VI.deñ.7 xx.ac p̃ti.7 xxx.ac paſturæ.
Valuit.IIII.liħ.Modo.XL.ſolid.
Bretel ten de.Co.*BLENEFORD*.Aluuarđ tenuit T.R.E.7 geldħ ￫.I.
hida 7 dimiđ.Tra.ē.I.cař.Redđ.XII.ſoł.Valuit.xx.ſolid.
Roħt ten de.Co.*WINTREBVRNE*.Goduin tenuit T.R.E.7 geldħ
￫.II.hiđ.Tra.ē.I.cař.ꝗ ibi.ē cū.III.borđ.7 III.q̃ᵹ paſturæ.Valet
Roħt ten de.Co.*WINTREBVRNE*.Aluuarđ   ꞁxx.ſolid
tenuit T.R.E.7 geldħ ￫.III.hiđ.Tra.ē.II.cař.Ibi ſt.VII.coſcez
cū dimiđ cař.7 II.q̃ᵹ ſiluæ.7 Paſtura.III.q̃ᵹ lḡ.7 una q̃ᵹ laī.Valet
Ipſe.Ro.ten *WINBVRNE*.de Co.Aſchil tenuit T.R.E. ꞁxxx.ſolid.
7 geldħ ￫.III.hiđ.Tra.ē.II.cař.In dñio.ē una cař cū.I.ſeruo.7 v.
borđ.Ibi moliñ redđ.II.ſoł.7 II.ac p̃ti 7 dim.Paſtura.I.leū
lḡ.7 IIII.q̃ᵹ laī.Silua.VI.q̃ᵹ lḡ.7 II.q̃ᵹ laī.Valuit 7 ual.III.liħ.
Huħt ten de.Co.*WINTREBVRNE*.Duo taini tenueř. T.R.E.
7 geldħ ￫.v.hiđ.Tra.ē.III.cař.In dñio ſt.II.cař.7 II.uiłłi
7 IIII.borđ cū dim cař.Ibi.xx.ac p̃ti.Paſtura.II.q̃ᵹ lḡ.7 una
laī.Silua.III.q̃ᵹ lḡ.7 II.q̃ᵹ laī.Valuit.IIII.liħ.Modo.XL.ſoł.
Malger ten I *WINTREBVRNE*.de Co.Tres taini tenueř.T.R.E.
Tra.ē.I.cař.ꝗ ibi.ē cū.I.uiłło.Ibi.III.q̃ᵹ paſturæ.Valet.xx.ſoł.

28 Bretel holds LITTLETON from the Count. Wulfgeat held it before 1066. It paid tax for 5 hides. Land for 3 ploughs. In lordship 1 plough;
6 smallholders and 2 slaves.
A mill which pays 7s 6d; meadow, 20 acres; pasture, 30 acres.
The value was £4; now 40s.

29 Bretel holds BLANDFORD (St. Mary) from the Count. Alward held it before 1066. It paid tax for 1½ hides. Land for 1 plough.
It pays 12s; the value was 20s.

30 Robert holds 'WINTERBORNE' from the Count. Godwin held it before 1066. It paid tax for 2 hides. Land for 1 plough, which is there, with
3 smallholders.
Pasture, 3 furlongs.
Value 20s.

31 Robert holds 'WINTERBORNE' from the Count. Alward held it before 1066. It paid tax for 3 hides. Land for 2 ploughs.
7 Cottagers with ½ plough.
Woodland, 2 furlongs; pasture 3 furlongs long and 1 furlong wide.
Value 30s.

32 R(obert) holds 'WIMBORNE' himself from the Count. Askell held it before 1066. It paid tax for 3 hides. Land for 2 ploughs.
In lordship 1 plough, with 1 slave;
5 smallholders.
A mill which pays 2s; meadow, 2½ acres; pasture 1 league long and 4 furlongs wide; woodland 6 furlongs long and 2 furlongs wide.
The value was and is £3.

33 Hubert holds 'WINTERBORNE' from the Count. Two thanes held it jointly before 1066. It paid tax for 5 hides. Land for 3 ploughs.
In lordship 2 ploughs;
2 villagers and 4 smallholders with ½ plough.
Meadow, 20 acres; pasture 2 furlongs long and 1 wide; woodland 3 furlongs long and 2 furlongs wide.
The value was £4; now 40s.

34 Mauger holds 2 hides in 'WINTERBORNE' from the Count. Three thanes held them before 1066. Land for 1 plough, which is there, with
1 villager.
Pasture, 3 furlongs.
Value 20s.

Dodeman teñ *MELESBERIE* de.Co.Tres taini tenueŕ T.R.E.

7 geldb ꝑ.ıı.hiđ 7 dim.Tra.e.ıı.caŕ.Ibi.e uñ faber.7 ıı.borđ

7 ıı.ſerui.7 ıx.ac p̄ti.Silua.vııı.q̄ʒ lḡ.7 ıı.q̄ʒ lat.Valet.xx.ſol.

Dodeman teñ de.Co.*WINTREBVRNE*.Alric tenuit T.R.E.

7 geldb ꝑ.ı.hida 7 dim.Tra.e.ı.caŕ.Ibi.e uñ borđ cū.ı.ſeruo.

7 vı.ac p̄ti.7 ıı.q̄ʒ 7 dimiđ paſturæ.Valet.xv.ſoliđ.

In eađ uilla hŕ comes.v.uirg træ 7 dim.Tra.e.ı.caŕ.Ibi

ſt.xııı.ac p̄ti.7 una q̄ʒ 7 dim paſturæ.Valuit 7 ual.xıııı.ſol.

Dodeman teñ *BLANEFORD*.Sared 7 fŕ ej tenueŕ T.R.E.

7 geldb ꝑ.ı.hida 7 dim.Tra.e dimiđ caŕ.Ibi ſt.ııı.borđ 7 ıı.

ſerui 7 ıx.ac p̄ti.7 v.q̄ʒ paſturæ.Valet.xv.ſoliđ.

Ipſe.Co.hŕ.ıı.hiđ in *MANITONE*.Tra.e.ı.caŕ.Aluric tenuit.

Ibi ſt.ııı.uilti 7 ıı.borđ.cū.ı.caŕ.Paſtura.ı.leū lḡ.7 dim

leū lat.Siluæ dimiđ leū in lḡ 7 lat.Valet.xx.ſoliđ.

Hubt teñ de.Co.*HEMEDESWORDE*.Vñ tain tenuit.T.R.E.

7 geldb ꝑ.ı.hida.Tra.e.ı.caŕ 7 dim.q̄ ibi ſt cū.ı.ſeruo

7 ııı.borđ.Ibi paſturæ.ııı.q̄ʒ in lḡ 7 lat.7 tntđ ſiluæ.Valet

Hubt teñ de.Co.*WICHEMETVNE*.   ſ xxv.ſoliđ.

Vñ tain tenuit T.R.E.7 geldb ꝑ.ıı.hiđ.Tra.e.ı.caŕ

7 dimiđ.Ibi.e uñ uilts 7 ııı.borđ cū.ı.caŕ.7 moliñ redđ

.v.ſoliđ.7 vııı.ac p̄ti.paſtura.ıı.q̄ʒ lḡ.7 una q̄ʒ lat.

Silua.una q̄ʒ lḡ.7 vııı.acs lat.Valuit 7 ual.xxv.ſol.

Ibi hŕ Hubt unā v træ 7 tciā parte uni v.de q̄ nunq̄ deđ gelđ.

35 Dodman holds MELBURY from the Count. Three thanes held it jointly before 1066. It paid tax for 2½ hides. Land for 2 ploughs.
A smith, 2 smallholders and 2 slaves.
Meadow, 9 acres; woodland 8 furlongs long and 2 furlongs wide.
Value 20s.

36 Dodman holds 'WINTERBORNE' from the Count. Alric held it before 1066. It paid tax for 1½ hides. Land for 1 plough.
1 smallholder with 1 slave.
Meadow, 6 acres; pasture, 2½ furlongs.
Value 15s.
Also in this village the Count has 5½ virgates of land. Land for 1 plough.
Meadow, 13 acres; pasture, 1½ furlongs.
The value was and is 14s.

37 Dodman holds (Langton Long) BLANDFORD from the Count. Saered and his brother held it jointly before 1066. It paid tax for 1½ hides. Land for ½ plough.
3 smallholders and 2 slaves.
Meadow, 9 acres; pasture, 5 furlongs.
Value 15s.

38 The Count has 2 hides in MANNINGTON himself. Land for 1 plough. Aelfric held it.
3 villagers and 2 smallholders with 1 plough.
Pasture 1 league long and ½ league wide; woodland, ½ league in length and width.
Value 20s.

39 Hubert holds HEMSWORTH from the Count. A thane held it before 1066. It paid tax for 1 hide. Land for 1½ ploughs, which are there, with 1 slave;
3 smallholders.
Pasture, 3 furlongs in length and width; woodland, as much.
Value 25s.

40 Hubert holds WITCHAMPTON from the Count. A thane held it before 1066. It paid tax for 2 hides. Land for 1½ ploughs.
1 villager and 3 smallholders with 1 plough.
A mill which pays 5s; meadow, 8 acres; pasture 2 furlongs long and 1 furlong wide; woodland 1 furlong long and 8 acres wide.
The value was and is 25s.
Hubert has there 1 virgate of land and the third part of 1 virgate on which he has never paid tax.

Girard ten de.Co.ɪ.hiđ ad *Lodre*.Vluiet tenuit T.R.E.Trã
ẽ.ɪ.car̃.ḡ ibi.ẽ cũ.v.borđ.Ibi moliñ.ɪɪɪ.foliđ 7 ɪɪɪɪ.ãc p̃ti.
7 xxvɪ.ãc pafturæ.Valet.xxv.foliđ.

Ipfe.Co.teñ.ɪ.hiđ ad *Lodre*.Aluric tenuit T.R.E.Tra.ẽ.ɪ.
car̃.Ibi fĩ.vɪ.borđ cũ.ɪ.feruo.7 ɪɪ.ãc p̃ti.7 xxx.ãc pafturæ
Valet.xxv.foliđ.Alured teñ de.Co.medietaṫ huj hidæ.

Anfger teñ de.Co.in *Chenoltvne*.ɪɪ.hiđ.Ailmer tenuit
T.R.E.|Tra.ẽ.ɪ.car̃.ḡ ibi.ẽ cũ.ɪ.feruo 7 ɪ.borđ.Ibi moliñ
redđ.xɪɪ.foliđ 7 vɪ.deñ.Valuit 7 ual.xxv.foliđ.

Ipfe.Co.teñ *Gessic*.Edmer tenuit T.R.E.7 geldƀ p.xv.hiđ.
Tra.ẽ.xɪɪ.car̃.In dñio fĩ.ɪɪɪ.car̃.7 ɪx.ferui.7 vɪɪɪ.uiłti 7 xvɪɪt.
borđ cũ.v.car̃.Ibi moliñ redđ.xxv.foliđ.7 ɪx.ãc p̃ti.Paftura
ɪɪ.leũ lḡ.7 una leũ laĩ.7 tñtđ filuæ.Valuit 7 ual.xv.liƀ.

Witts teñ de.Co.*Dervinestone*.Quinꝗ taini tenueř
T.R.E.7 geldƀ p.ɪɪ.hiđ 7 dim.Tra.ẽ.ɪɪ.car̃.ḡ ibi fĩ in dñio.
7 ɪɪ.ferui.7 ɪɪ.uiłti 7 v.borđ cũ.ɪ.car̃.Ibi.vɪɪɪ.ãc p̃ti.7 vɪɪ.q̃ꝗ
pafturæ.7 una q̃ꝗ filuæ minutæ in lḡ 7 laĩ.Val.ʟ.foliđ.

Ipfe.Co.teñ *Blaneford*.Edmer tenuit T.R.E.7 geldƀ p x.hiđ.Tra.ẽ
.vɪ.car̃.In dñio fĩ.ɪɪɪ.car̃.7 vɪɪɪ.ferui.7 vɪɪ.uiłti 7 ɪx.borđ cũ.ɪɪ.car̃.
Ibi moliñ redđ.xx.foł.7 xx.ãc p̃ti.paftura.ɪx.q̃ꝗ lḡ.7 ɪɪɪ.q̃ꝗ laĩ.
Siluæ.v.q̃rent 7 dimiđ.Valuit.x.liƀ.modo.xɪ.liƀ.

Ipfe.Co.teñ *Brochemtvne*.Godric tenuit 7 geldƀ p.ɪ.hida 7 dim.Tra.ẽ
.ɪ.car̃.ḡ ibi.ẽ.7 x.ãc p̃ti.7 paftura.ɪɪ.q̃ꝗ lḡ.7 una q̃ꝗ laĩ.Valet.xx.foł.

26

41 Gerard holds 1 hide at LODERS from the Count. Wulfgeat held
it before 1066. Land for 1 plough, which is there, with
   5 smallholders.
A mill, 3s; meadow, 4 acres; pasture, 26 acres.
Value 25s.

42 The Count holds 1 hide at LODERS himself. Aelfric held it before
1066. Land for 1 plough.
   6 smallholders with 1 slave.
Meadow, 2 acres; pasture, 30 acres.
Value 25s.
Alfred holds half of this hide from the Count.

43 Ansger holds 2 hides in KNOWLTON from the Count. Aelmer held
them before 1066. It paid tax. Land for 1 plough, which is there,
with 1 slave;
   1 smallholder.
A mill which pays 12s 6d.
The value was and is 25s.

44 The Count holds GUSSAGE himself. Edmer held it before 1066.
It paid tax for 15 hides. Land for 12 ploughs. In lordship 3
ploughs; 9 slaves;
   8 villagers and 18 smallholders with 5 ploughs.
A mill which pays 25s; meadow, 60 acres; pasture 2 leagues
      long and 1 league wide; woodland, as much.
The value was and is £15.

45 William holds KNIGHTON from the Count. Five thanes held it
before 1066. It paid tax for 2½ hides. Land for 2 ploughs,
which are there, in lordship; 2 slaves;
   2 villagers and 5 smallholders with 1 plough.
Meadow, 8 acres; pasture, 7 furlongs; underwood, 1 furlong
      in length and width.
Value 50s.

   The Count himself holds
46 BRYANSTON. Edmer held it before 1066. It paid tax for 10 hides.
Land for 6 ploughs. In lordship 3 ploughs; 8 slaves;
   7 villagers and 9 smallholders with 2 ploughs.
A mill which pays 20s; meadow, 20 acres; pasture 9 furlongs
      long and 3 furlongs wide; woodland, 5½ furlongs.
The value was £10; now £11.

47 BROCKINGTON. Godric held it. It paid tax for 1½ hides. Land for
1 plough, which is there.
   Meadow, 10 acres; pasture 2 furlongs long and 1 furlong wide.
Value 20s.

Ipſe.Co.teñ *WINTREBVRNE*.Alured 7 ɪɪ.alij tenueͬ T.R.E.7 geldℏ ꝑ.ɪ.hida 7 una v̾ trǣ.Tͬa.e̅.ɪ.caͬ.Ibi ſt.ɪɪɪ.borđ.7 Paſtura.ɪɪɪɪ.q̊ƺ l̄g. 7 ɪɪ.q̊ƺ laͭ.Silua.ɪɪ.q̊ƺ l̄g.7 ɪɪ.laͭ.Valet.xx.ſoͭ.Dodeman teñ.ɪɪ.v̾ trǣ huj.

Ipſe.Co.teñ *BEASTEWELLE*.Edmar tenuit T.R.E.7 geldℏ ꝑ.ɪɪɪ.hiđ. Tͬa.e̅.ɪ.caͬ 7 dim̅.In dñio.e̅.ɪ.caͬ.7 ɪɪɪɪ.ſerui.7 ɪɪɪɪ.coͭ.7 uñ uiƚƚ cū dim̅ caͭ.Ibi.xx.ac̅ p̊ti.7 xx.ac̅ paſturæ.Silua.ɪɪ.q̊ƺ l̄g.7 una q̊ƺ laͭ. Valuit.xxx.ſoliđ.Modo.ʟx.ſoliđ.

Ipſe.Co.teñ *LOLOWORDE*.Alſi tenuit T.R.E.7 geldℏ ꝑ.ɪɪɪ.hiđ 7 dim̅. Tͬa.e̅.ɪɪ.caͬ.In dñio.e̅ una caͬ.cū.ɪ.ſeruo.7 ɪɪɪɪ.borđ Ibi.ɪɪ.ac̅ p̊ti.Paſtura.ɪɪɪ.q̊ƺ l̄g.7 una q̊ƺ laͭ.Valuit.ʟx.ſoͭ.m̅.xxx.ſoͭ.

Ipſe.Co.teñ *LOLOWORDE*.Trauuiñ tenuit T.R.E.7 geldℏ ꝑ.ɪɪ.hiđ. Tͬa.e̅.ɪ.caͬ 7 dim̅.In dñio.e̅.ɪ.caͬ.7 ɪɪ.borđ.7 ɪɪ.ac̅ p̊ti.Paſtura.ɪɪ. q̊ƺ l̄g.7 ɪɪ.laͭ.Valuit.xʟ.ſoͭ.Modo.xx.ſoliđ.

Ipſe Comes tenet *STOCHES*.Edmer tenuit T.R.E.7 geldℏ ꝑ.ɪɪ.hiđ. Tͬa.e̅.ɪɪ.caͬ.q̄ ibi ſt in dñio.7 ɪɪ.ſerui.7 ɪɪ.uiƚƚi 7 ɪɪɪ.borđ.cū.ɪ.caͬ. Ibi moliñ redđ.xv.ſoͭ.7 xx.ac̅ p̊ti.Paſtura.v.q̊ƺ l̄g.7 tñtđ laͭ. Valuit 7 uaͭ.ʟ.ſoliđ.   ⌐xʟ.ſoliđ

Ipſe.Co.hͭ in *STANBERGE*.ɪ.moliñ cū dimiđ hida.7 ɪɪɪ.borđ.Toͭ ualet Bretel teñ de Co.*CRIST*.Sireuuald tenuit T.R.E.7 geldℏ ꝑ.ɪɪ.hiđ. Tͬa.e̅.ɪ.caͬ.q̄ ibi.e̅ cū.ɪ.uiƚƚo 7 ɪ.borđ.7 ɪɪɪɪ.ac̅ p̊ti.Paſtura.vɪ.q̊ƺ l̄g.7 tñtđ laͭ.7 una dom̅ in Warhā.Valuit.xx.ſoͭ.Modo.xʟ.ſoͭ.

Bretel teñ de.Co.*TIGEHA*.Sex taini tenueͬ.T.R.E.7 geldℏ ꝑ.ɪɪɪ.hiđ. 7 dimiđ.Tͬa.e̅.ɪɪɪ.caͬ.Ibi ſt.ɪɪɪ.uiƚƚi 7 ɪɪɪɪ.borđ 7 ɪɪ.ac̅ p̊ti.Paſtura v.q̊ƺ l̄g.7 ɪɪ.q̊ƺ laͭ.Valuit 7 uaͭ.xʟ.vɪɪ.ſoliđ.

48 'WINTERBORNE'. Alfred and two others held it before 1066. It paid tax for 1 hide and 1 virgate of land. Land for 1 plough.
3 smallholders.
Pasture 4 furlongs long and 2 furlongs wide; woodland 2 furlongs long and 2 wide.
Value 20s.
Dodman holds 2 virgates of this land.

49 BESTWALL. Edmer held it before 1066. It paid tax for 3 hides. Land for 1½ ploughs. In lordship 1 plough; 4 slaves;
4 cottagers and 1 villager with ½ plough.
Meadow, 20 acres; pasture, 20 acres; woodland 2 furlongs long and 1 furlong wide.
The value was 30s; now 60s.

50 LULWORTH. Alsi held it before 1066. It paid tax for 3½ hides. Land for 2 ploughs. In lordship 1 plough, with 1 slave;
4 smallholders. ...
Meadow, 2 acres; pasture 3 furlongs long and 1 furlong wide.
The value was 60s; now 30s.

51 LULWORTH. Traswin held it before 1066. It paid tax for 2 hides. Land for 1½ ploughs. In lordship 1 plough;
2 smallholders.
Meadow, 2 acres; pasture 2 furlongs long and 2 wide.
The value was 40s; now 20s.

52 (East) STOKE. Edmer held it before 1066. It paid tax for 2 hides. Land for 2 ploughs, which are there, in lordship; 2 slaves;
2 villagers and 3 smallholders with 1 plough.
A mill which pays 15s; meadow, 20 acres; pasture 5 furlongs long and as wide.
The value was and is 50s.

53 The Count himself has in STOBOROUGH 1 mill with ½ hide;
3 smallholders.
Value of the whole, 40s.

54 Bretel holds CREECH from the Count. Sheerwold held it before 1066. It paid tax for 2 hides. Land for 1 plough, which is there, with
1 villager and 1 smallholder.
Meadow, 4 acres; pasture 6 furlongs long and as wide; a house in Wareham.
The value was 20s; now 40s.

55 Bretel holds TYNEHAM from the Count. Six thanes held it before 1066. It paid tax for 3½ hides. Land for 3 ploughs.
3 villagers and 4 smallholders.
Meadow, 2 acres; pasture 5 furlongs long and 2 furlongs wide.
The value was and is 47s.

R̅obt̅ ten̅ de.Co.*MORTVNE*.Sex taini tenuer̅ T.R.E.⁊ geldɓ ⹁p.iii.hiđ.
T̅ra.e̅.iii.car̅.Has hn̅t ibi.vi.uilti cu̅.iii.cofcez.Ibi molin̅ redđ.iii.fot.
⁊ xxx.ac̅ p̅ti.paftura.i.leu̅ lg̅.⁊ tn̅tđ lat̅.Valuit ⁊ uat.iiii.liɓ.
R̅obt̅ ten̅ de.co.*WARMWELLE*.Leuuin̅ tenuit T.R.E.⁊ geldɓ ⹁p.i.hida.
T̅ra.e̅.i.car̅.Ibi ft̅.iii.borđ.⁊ ix.q̅ƶ pafturæ in lg̅.⁊ una in lat̅.Valet
I̅pfe.Co.ten̅ *LODRE*.Brictric tenuit T.R.E.⁊ geldɓ ⹁p una ⌐xvi.fot.
hida ⁊ dim̅.T̅ra.e̅.ii.car̅.g̅ ibi ft̅ cu̅.i.cofcet ⁊ iii.feruis.⁊ xv.ac̅ p̅ti.
⁊ vi.q̅ƶ pafturæ in lg̅.⁊ una q̅ƶ lat̅.Valuit ⁊ uat.xlvii.fot ⁊ vi.den̅.
W̅itts ten̅ de.Co.*LAHOC*.Aluric tenuit T.R.E.⁊ geldɓ ⹁p.ii.hiđ.T̅ra.e̅
.iii.car̅.In dn̅io ft̅.ii.car̅.cu̅.i.feruo.⁊ iiii.uilti ⁊ iii.borđ cu̅.ñcar̅.
Ibi molin̅ redđ.vi.foliđ.⁊ vi.ac̅ p̅ti.⁊ v.q̅ƶ pafturæ.⁊ iiii.q̅ƶ filuæ.
Valuit ⁊ uat.xl.foliđ.
B̅retel ⁊ Malger ten̅ de.Co.*WELLE*.Tres taini tenuer̅ T.R.E.⁊ geldɓ ^p.ii.Maner.
⹁p.i.hida ⁊ iii.v̅ træ.T̅ra.e̅.i.car̅ ⁊ dim̅.Ibi ft̅.ii.uilti ⁊ vi.cofcez.
Ibi.iiii.ac̅ p̅ti.Paftura.v.q̅ƶ lg̅.⁊ ii.q̅ƶ lat̅.Valuit ⁊ uat.xxiii.foliđ.
H̅aimo ten̅ de.Ço.*STOLLANT*.Almar tenuit T.R.E.⁊ geldɓ ⹁p.iii.hiđ
⁊ dimiđ.T̅ra.e̅.iiii.car̅.In dn̅io ft̅.ii.car̅.⁊ vi.ferui.⁊ v.uilti ⁊ xiii.borđ
80 a
P̅aftura.i.leu̅ lg̅.⁊ tn̅tđ lat̅.Silua.ii.q̅ƶ lg̅.⁊ una q̅ƶ lat̅.
Ibi ft̅.xxxii.falinæ.redđ.xl.foliđ.Tot̅ ualet.viii.liɓ.
A̅lured ten̅ de.Co.in *STANTONE* dimiđ hiđ.Eduui tenuit T.R.E.
T̅ra.e̅.vi.car̅.In dn̅io ft̅.ii.car̅ ⁊ dimiđ.⁊ v.ferui.⁊ iii.uilti
⁊ viii.borđ cu̅.iii.car̅ ⁊ dimiđ.Ibi.xxiiii.ac̅ p̅ti.⁊ ii.leu̅ ⁊ dim̅
pafturæ.⁊ ii.q̅rent filuæ.Valuit ⁊ uat.lx.foliđ.

56 Robert holds MORETON from the Count. Six thanes held it before
1066. It paid tax for 3 hides. Land for 3 ploughs.
   6 villagers with 3 Cottagers have them there.
   A mill which pays 3s; meadow, 30 acres; pasture 1 league long
     and as wide.
The value was and is £4.

57 Robert holds WARMWELL from the Count. Leofwin held it before
1066. It paid tax for 1 hide. Land for 1 plough.
   3 smallholders.
   Pasture, 9 furlongs in length and 1 in width.
Value 16s.

58 The Count holds LODERS himself. Brictric held it before 1066.
It paid tax for 1½ hides. Land for 2 ploughs, which are there, with
   1 Cottager and 3 slaves.
   Meadow, 15 acres; pasture, 6 furlongs in length and 1 furlong
     wide.
The value was and is 47s 6d.

59 William holds HOOKE from the Count. Aelfric held it before 1066.
It paid tax for 2 hides. Land for 3 ploughs. In lordship 2 ploughs,
   with 1 slave;
   4 villagers and 3 smallholders with 1 plough.
   A mill which pays 6s; meadow, 6 acres; pasture, 5 furlongs;
     woodland, 4 furlongs.
The value was and is 40s.

60 Bretel and Mauger hold WOOL from the Count. Three thanes held
it before 1066 as two manors. It paid tax for 1 hide and 3 virgates
of land. Land for 1½ ploughs.
   2 villagers and 6 Cottagers.
   Meadow, 4 acres; pasture 5 furlongs long and 2 furlongs wide.
The value was and is 23s.

61 Hamo holds STUDLAND from the Count. Aelmer held it before
1066. It paid tax for 3½ hides. Land for 4 ploughs. In lordship 2
ploughs; 6 slaves;
   5 villagers and 13 smallholders.
   Pasture 1 league long and as wide; woodland 2 furlongs   80 a
     long and 1 furlong wide; 32 salt-houses which pay 40s.
Value of the whole £8.

62 Alfred holds ½ hide in 'STANTON (St. Gabriel)' from the Count.
Edwy held it before 1066. Land for 6 ploughs. In lordship 2½
ploughs; 5 slaves;
   3 villagers and 8 smallholders with 3½ ploughs.
   Meadow, 24 acres; pasture, 2½ leagues; woodland, 2 furlongs.
The value was and is 60s.

Bretel ten de. Co.*WODETONE* . Edmer tenuit T.R.E.7 geldb

p . ii . hid . Tra . e . vii . car . In dnio st . ii . car . 7 ii . ferui . 7 xii . uilli

7 ix . bord cu . v . car . Ibi molin redd . xv . den . 7 vi . ac pti . 7 vii.

qrent 7 iiii . acs pafturæ . 7 una leu 7 v . q҃z filuæ . Valet . c . fot.

Wills ten de Co.*CERNELI* . Aldebert tenuit T.R.E. 7 geldb

p . iii . hid . Tra . e . iiii . car . In dnio st . ii . car . 7 v . ferui . 7 vi . uilti

7 ii . bord . cu . ii . car . Ibi molin redd . iii . denar . 7 viii . ac

pti . Paftura . x . q҃z lg . 7 una q҃z lat . Silua . ii . q҃z lg . 7 ii . lat.

Valuit 7 ual . lx . folid.

In ead uilla ten . W . dim hida . q fuit de dnica firma Cerne T.R.E.

Ide . W . ten de . Co. *CORIESCVBE* . Leuuin tenuit T.R.E.

7 geldb p . i . hida . Tra . e . i . car . 7 dim . q ibi st cu . i . uillo 7 vii.

bord 7 ii . feruis . Ibi paftura . i . q҃z lg . 7 dimid q҃z lat . 7 tntd filuæ.

Valuit 7 ual . xv . folid.

Drogo ten de . Co. *TOLRE* . Almar tenuit T.R.E. 7 geldb

p . iii . hid . Tra . e . iii . car . In dnio . e . i . car . cu . vi . bord . Ibi dim

ac pti . Paftura . v . q҃z lg . 7 ii . q҃z lat . Valuit . xx . fot . Modo . xl . fot.

Robt ten de . Co. *CERNEMVDE* . Algar tenuit T.R.E. 7 geldb

p . iii . hid . Tra . e . iii . car . In dnio st . ii . car . 7 iii . ferui . 7 iii . uilti

cu . ii . car . Ibi . xvi . falinarij . 7 xvi . ac pti . Paftura . iii . q҃z

lg . 7 una q҃z lat . Silua . vii . q҃z lg . 7 una q҃z lat . Valet . lx.

Ipfe . Co . ten *SCILFEMETVNE* . Tres taini|tenuer T.R.E. ∫ folid.

7 geldb p . i . hida 7 una v . Tra . e . i . car . q ibi . e cu . i . cofcet.

Ibi paftura . ii . q҃z lg . 7 ii . lat . Valuit 7 ual . xv . folid.

63 Bretel holds WOOTTON (Fitzpaine) from the Count. Edmer held it
before 1066. It paid tax for 2 hides. Land for 7 ploughs.
In lordship 2 ploughs; 2 slaves;
12 villagers and 9 smallholders with 5 ploughs.
A mill which pays 15d; meadow, 6 acres; pasture, 7 furlongs
and 4 acres; woodland, 1 league and 5 furlongs.
Value 100s.

64 William holds CATHERSTON (Leweston) from the Count. Aldbert
held it before 1066. It paid tax for 3 hides. Land for 4 ploughs.
In lordship 2 ploughs; 5 slaves;
6 villagers and 2 smallholders with 2 ploughs.
A mill which pays 3d; meadow, 8 acres; pasture 10 furlongs
long and 1 furlong wide; woodland 2 furlongs long and 2 wide.
The value was and is 60s.
Also in this village William holds ½ hide which was (part) of
the lordship revenue of 'Cerne' before 1066.

65 William also holds CORSCOMBE from the Count. Leofwin held it
before 1066. It paid tax for 1 hide. Land for 1½ ploughs, which
are there, with
1 villager, 7 smallholders and 2 slaves.
Pasture 1 furlong long and ½ furlong wide; woodland, as much.
The value was and is 15s.

66 Drogo holds TOLLER (Whelme) from the Count. Aelmer held it
before 1066. It paid tax for 3 hides. Land for 3 ploughs.
In lordship 1 plough, with
6 smallholders.
Meadow, ½ acre; pasture 5 furlongs long and 2 furlongs wide.
The value was 20s; now 40s.

67 Robert holds CHARMOUTH from the Count. Algar held it before
1066. It paid tax for 3 hides. Land for 3 ploughs. In lordship 2
ploughs; 3 slaves;
3 villagers with 2 ploughs. 16 salt-workers.
Meadow, 16 acres; pasture 3 furlongs long and 1 furlong wide;
woodland 7 furlongs long and 1 furlong wide.
Value 60s.

68 The Count holds SHILVINGHAMPTON himself. Three thanes held it
jointly before 1066. It paid tax for 1 hide and 1 virgate. Land
for 1 plough, which is there, with
1 Cottager.
Pasture 2 furlongs long and 2 wide.
The value was and is 15s.

Bretel ten̄ de.Co. *WODETONE* . Vlfret tenuit T.R.E.⁊ geld℔
⫯ dim̄ hida. Ṫra . ē . ɪ . car̄ . Ibi s̄ . ɪɪ . uiℓℓi cū dim̄ car̄.⁊ v. ac̄
p̄ti .⁊ ɪɪɪɪ . ac̄ filuæ . Valet . v . folið.

Ipſe. Co. ten̄ *CANDEL* . Alſtan̄ tenuit T.R.E.⁊ geld℔ ⫯.ɪ.hida.
Ṫra .ē.ɪ.car̄.Ibi sī. ɪɪɪ.borð ⁊ ɪɪ.ferui.⁊ vɪ.ac̄ p̄ti.⁊ vɪɪɪ.ac̄ filuæ
minutæ. Valuit. xx . folið . Modo. x . folið.

Aluuin̄ ten̄ de . Co. *CANDEL* . Alueua tenuit T.R.E.⁊ geld℔
⫯ . ɪɪɪ.hið.Ṫra.ē. ɪɪɪ.car̄ . q̄ ibi sī cū . ɪ . feruo.⁊ ɪɪ.uiℓℓis.⁊ v .borð.
Ibi.ɪɪɪ.ac̄ p̄ti.⁊ Silua.ɪɪɪɪ.q̄℥ lḡ.⁊ tn̄tð lat̄ . Valuit ⁊ ual.xL.fot.
Om̄s q́ has tras habe℔ T.R.E. liℬe tenebaℵ.

.XXVII. TERRA COMITIS HVGONIS.

Comes Hvgo ten̄ *FIFHIDE* .⁊ Giℓleℏt de eo . Alnoð tenuit
T.R.E.⁊ geld℔ ⫯ . v . hið . Ṫra.ē.v.car̄.In dn̄io sī.ɪɪɪ . car̄.⁊ ɪɪɪɪ. ⁊ vɪ.ferui.
uiℓℓi ⁊ ɪɪɪɪ.borð cū . ɪɪ . car̄ . Ibi . ɪɪ.molini redð.xxɪɪ.folið.⁊ vɪ.
den̄ .⁊ xxx.ac̄ p̄ti.Silua.ɪɪɪɪ.q̄℥ lḡ.⁊ ɪɪ.q̄℥ lat̄.Valuit ⁊ ual

Wiℓℓs ten̄ de.Co.*ELSANGTONE* . Elnod tenuit ⨍ vɪɪ.liℬ.
T.R.E.⫯ Heraldū q́ eā abſtulit cuidā clerico.Tc̄ geld℔ ⫯.ɪɪ.hið.
Ṫra.ē.ɪ.car̄ ⁊ dimið.q̄ ibi.ē.⁊ molin̄.⁊ vɪɪɪ.ac̄ p̄ti.⁊ paſturæ
v . q́rent.⁊ ɪɪɪ.q́rent̄ filuæ.Valuit ⁊ ual.xx.folið.

Wiℓℓs ten̄ de.Co.*TINCLADENE* . Ednod tenuit T.R.E.⁊ geld℔
⫯.ɪɪ.hið.Ṫra.ē.ɪɪ.car̄.In dn̄io.ē.ɪ.car̄.cū.ɪ.feruo.⁊ ɪ.uiℓℓo.
⁊ ɪɪɪɪ.borð.Ibi.v.ac̄ p̄ti.⁊ v.q̄℥ paſturæ.⁊ ɪɪ.q̄℥ filuæ. Valet

Wiℓℓs ten̄ de.Co. *MAINE*.Ednod tenuit T.R.E. ⨍ xx.folið.
⁊ geld℔ ⫯.ɪɪɪ. hið .Ṫra.ē.ɪɪ.car̄.In dn̄io.ē.ɪ.car̄.⁊ ɪɪɪ.ferui.⁊ vɪ.
uiℓℓi ⁊ ɪɪ.borð cū.ɪ.car̄.Ibi.ɪɪɪ.ac̄ p̄ti.⁊|xL.ac̄ paſturæ.
In Warham una dom̄ redð.v.den̄.Valuit ⁊ ual.xL.folið.

69 Bretel holds WOOTTON (Fitzpaine) from the Count. Wulfred held
it before 1066. It paid tax for ½ hide. Land for 1 plough.
2 villagers with ½ plough.
Meadow, 5 acres; woodland, 4 acres.
Value 5s.

70 The Count holds (Stourton) CAUNDLE himself. Alstan held it
before 1066. It paid tax for 1 hide. Land for 1 plough.
3 smallholders and 2 slaves.
Meadow, 6 acres; underwood, 8 acres.
The value was 20s; now 10s.

71 Alwin holds (Stourton) CAUNDLE from the Count. Aelfeva held it
before 1066. It paid tax for 3 hides. Land for 3 ploughs, which
are there, with 1 slave and
2 villagers and 5 smallholders.
Meadow, 3 acres; woodland 4 furlongs long and as wide.
The value was and is 40s.

All the holders of these lands before 1066 held them freely.

27   LAND OF EARL HUGH   E

1 Earl Hugh holds FIFEHEAD (Magdalen), and Gilbert from him.
Alnoth held it before 1066. It paid tax for 5 hides. Land for
5 ploughs. In lordship 3 ploughs; 6 slaves;
4 villagers and 4 smallholders with 2 ploughs.
2 mills which pay 22s 6d; meadow, 30 acres; woodland 4
furlongs long and 2 furlongs wide.
The value was and is £7.

William holds from the Earl
2 ILSINGTON. Alnoth held it before 1066 through Earl Harold who
took it from a clerk. Then it paid tax for 2 hides. Land for 1½
ploughs, which are there.
A mill; meadow, 8 acres; pasture, 5 furlongs; woodland, 3
furlongs.
The value was and is 20s.

3 TINCLETON. Ednoth held it before 1066. It paid tax for 2 hides.
Land for 2 ploughs. In lordship 1 plough, with 1 slave and
1 villager and 4 smallholders.
Meadow, 5 acres; pasture, 5 furlongs; woodland, 2 furlongs.
Value 20s.

4 MAYNE. Ednoth held it before 1066. It paid tax for 3 hides.
Land for 2 ploughs. In lordship 1 plough; 3 slaves;
6 villagers and 2 smallholders with 1 plough.
Meadow, 3 acres; pasture, 140 acres; in Wareham a house
which pays 5d.
The value was and is 40s.

W̅itts ten̅ de.Co.*MAINE*.Edric᷉ tenuit T.R.E.⁊ geldb̅ ⫽p.ıı.hid.
T̅ra.ē.ı.car̅ ⁊ dim̄.In dn̄io.ē.ı.car̅ cū.ı.feruo.⁊ ıııı.bord̅.
Ibi.ııı.ac̅ p̄ti.Paſtura.vııı.q̊⁊ l̅g.⁊ una q̊⁊ lat̅.Valet.xL.fot.
W̅itts ten̅ de.Co.*CLISTONE*.Ednod tenuit T.R.E.⁊ geldb̅ ⫽p.vı.
hid̅.T̅ra.ē.ıııı.car̅.In dn̄io ſt.ııı.car̅.⁊ ııı.uitti ⁊ xıııı.bord̅
cū.ıı.car̅.Ibi molin̄ redd̅.x.folid̅.⁊ xıı.ac̅ p̄ti.Silua.vııı.
q̊rent̅ l̅g.⁊ ıııı.q̊⁊ lat̅.Valuit ⁊ uat.vı.lib̅.

80 b

Huic c͡ᴗ Cliſtone ſt adjunc̄t̊æ.ııı.hidæ in *K̄ELLE*.q̊s tͤneb̅ in parag᷉
tres taini T.R.E.⁊ ⫽p.ııı.hid geldb̅.T̅ra.ē.ıı.car̅.Ibi ſt.ııı.
uitti ⁊ ıııı.bord̅ cū.ı.car̅.⁊ molin̄ redd̅.L.den̅.⁊ vııı.ac̅
p̄ti.Silua.vı.q̊⁊ l̅g.⁊ ıı.q̊⁊ lat̅.Valuit ⁊ uat.ııı.lib̅.
W̅itts ten̅ de.Co.*WARMEMOILLE*.Duo taini tenuer̅.T.R.E.
⁊ geldb̅ ⫽p.ıı.hid ⁊ una v̅ træ.Pt̅ ħ eſt ibi una v̅ træ quæ
nūnq̅ geldau̅.T̅ra.ē.ıı.car̅.In dn̄io.ē.ı.car̅.cū.ı.feruo.
⁊ ıı.uitti ⁊ vıı.bord̅ cū dim̄ car̅.Ibi molin̄ redd̅.v.folid̅.
Paſtura.ıx.q̊⁊ l̅g.⁊ ıı.q̊⁊ lat̅.Valet.L.folid̅.
I̅dē.W.ten̅ de.Co.in *TINGEHA*.ı.hid ⁊ una v̅ træ.Alnod
tenuit T.R.E.T̅ra.ē.ı.car̅.Ibi ſt.ııı.uitti ⁊ una ac̅ p̄ti.
⁊ vı.ac̅ filuæ.⁊ ıııı.q̊⁊ paſturæ.Valuit ⁊ uat.xx.fot.
I̅dē.W.ten̅ de.Co.*PEDRET*.Alnod tenuit T.R.E.⁊ geldb̅
⫽p.v.hid.T̅ra.ē.v.car̅.In dn̄io ſt.ıı.car̅.⁊ ııı.ferui.
⁊ vı.uitti ⁊.xıııı.bord̅ cū.ııı.car̅.Ibi molin̄ redd̅.ıı.fot.
⁊ xıı.ac̅ p̄ti.Paſtura.xıııı.q̊⁊ l̅g.⁊ ııı.q̊⁊ lat̅.Silua.
vıı.q̊⁊ l̅g.⁊ v.q̊⁊ lat̅.Valuit.c.fot.Modo.vı.lib̅.
Hoc c͡ᴗ emit Alnod ab ep̄o Aluuoldo.tant̅ in uita fua.
tali c̅uentione ut poſt ej morte᷉ reſtitueret̅ æcclæ.

27

5 MAYNE. Edric held it before 1066. It paid tax for 2 hides.
Land for 1½ ploughs. In lordship 1 plough, with 1 slave;
4 smallholders.
Meadow, 3 acres; pasture 8 furlongs long and 1 furlong wide.
Value 40s.

6 CLIFTON (Maybank). Ednoth held it before 1066. It paid tax
for 6 hides. Land for 4 ploughs. In lordship 3 ploughs;
3 villagers and 14 smallholders with 2 ploughs.
A mill which pays 10s; meadow, 12 acres; woodland 8
furlongs long and 4 furlongs wide.
The value was and is £6.
To this manor of Clifton (Maybank) are attached 3 hides in   80 b
TRILL which three thanes held jointly before 1066. They paid
tax for 3 hides. Land for 2 ploughs.
3 villagers and 4 smallholders with 1 plough.
A mill which pays 50d; meadow, 8 acres; woodland 6 furlongs
long and 2 furlongs wide.
The value was and is £3.

7 WARMWELL.Two thanes held it before 1066. It paid tax for 2
hides and 1 virgate of land. Besides this there is 1 virgate of land
there which has never paid tax. Land for 2 ploughs. In lordship
1 plough, with 1 slave;
2 villagers and 7 smallholders with ½ plough.
A mill which pays 5s; pasture 9 furlongs long and 2 furlongs wide.
Value 50s.

8 William also holds 1 hide and 1 virgate of land in TYNEHAM from
the Earl. Alnoth held it before 1066. Land for 1 plough.
3 villagers.
Meadow, 1 acre; woodland, 6 acres; pasture, 4 furlongs.
The value was and is 20s.

9 William also holds (South) PERROTT from the Earl. Alnoth held it
before 1066. It paid tax for 5 hides. Land for 5 ploughs.
In lordship 2 ploughs; 3 slaves;
6 villagers and 14 smallholders with 3 ploughs.
A mill which pays 2s; meadow, 12 acres; pasture 14 furlongs
long and 3 furlongs wide; woodland 7 furlongs long and
5 furlongs wide.
The value was 100s; now £6.
Alnoth bought this manor from Bishop Alfwold for his lifetime
only on such agreement that after his death it should be restored
to the church.

Idē teñ de . Co. *CATESCLIVE* . Alnod tenuit T.R.E. 7 geldb̄ _{Ibi . ē una v træ}
,p. i. hida . Tra .ē. i. cař 7 dimid̄. Ibi . ē . i . uiłłs . 7 iii . bord̄   ^{de q̄ celař . ē ɡeld . T.R:W}
cū . i . feruo . 7 xii . ac̄ p̄ti . Paſtura . iiii . q̄ɀ lḡ . 7 tñtd̄ lat̄.
Silua . i . q̄ɀ lḡ . 7 una q̄ɀ lat̄ . Valuit . v . fol . Modo . x . fol.
7 Hanc trā fimilit emit Alnod ab ep̄o Aluuoldo . ea c̄uenti
one ut poſt ej morte ad æcclam rediret .
Idē . W . teñ *BVREVVINESTOCH* . Vñ tain tenūit T . R . E.
7 Alnod tulit ab eo . T. R . W. 7 geld ,p . iii . hid̄ . Tra . ē . iii . cař.
In dñio .ē . i . cař 7 dimid̄ . 7 iii . ferui . 7 iiii . uiłłi 7 v . bord̄ cū . i.
cař 7 dim̄ . Ibi . viii . ac̄ p̄ti . 7 paſtura . ii . q̄ɀ lḡ . 7 ii . q̄ɀ lat̄.
Valuit . xx . fol . Modo . xl . folid̄.

.XXVIII.   TERRA ROGERIJ DE BELMONT.

Rogerivs De Belmont teñ de rege *STVR* . Alured
tenuit T.R.E. 7 geldb̄ ,p . vii . hid̄ . Tra .ē. ix . cař . De ea ſt in dñio
iiii . hidæ 7 dimid̄ . 7 ibi . ii . cař . 7 vi . ferui . 7 xii . uiłłi . 7 xii . bord̄
cū . iii . cař . Ibi moliñ redd̄ . c . denař . 7 xx . ac̄ p̄ti . Silua . i . leū
7 dim̄ lḡ . 7 dimid̄ leū lat̄ . Valuit . ix . lib̄ . Modo . viii . lib̄.
Idē Rog teñ *STVRMINSTRE* . ^{arcñ} Stigand tenuit T.R.E. 7 geldb̄
,p . xxx . hid̄ . Tra .ē. xxv . cař . De ea ſt in dñio . xii . hide 7 dim̄
7 ibi . iii . cař . 7 viii . ferui . 7 lxiiii . uiłłi 7 xxvi . bord̄ cū . xv.
cař . Ibi . ii . molini redd̄ . xxviii . fol . 7 cxxiiii . ac̄ p̄ti . Paſtura
. iii . leū lḡ . 7 una leū 7 dim̄ lat̄ . Silua . i . leū lḡ . 7 dim̄ leū lat̄.
Valeb̄ . lxvi . lib̄ qdo recep̄ . Modo . lv . lib̄.
Idē Rog teñ *CRIZ* . Colebrand tenuit T.R.E. 7 geldb̄ ,p . ii . hid̄.
Tra .ē. ii . cař . q̄ ibi ſt cū . ii . uiłłis 7 iiii . feruis . Ibi . iiii . ac̄ p̄ti.
paſtura . vi . q̄rent lḡ . 7 tñtd̄ lat̄ . Silua . vi . q̄ɀ lḡ . 7 iii . q̄ɀ lat̄.
Valuit 7 ual . xl . folid̄.

80 b

10 He also holds CATSLEY from the Earl. Alnoth held it before 1066. It paid tax for 1 hide. 1 virgate of land, the tax on which was concealed after 1066. Land for 1½ ploughs.
1 villager and 3 smallholders with 1 slave.
Meadow, 12 acres; pasture 4 furlongs long and as wide; woodland 1 furlong long and 1 furlong wide.
The value was 5s; now 10s.
Alnoth bought this land likewise from Bishop Alfwold on the agreement that after his death it should return to the church.

11 William also holds BURSTOCK. A thane held it before 1066. Alnoth took it from him after 1066. It paid tax for 3 hides. Land for 3 ploughs. In lordship 1½ ploughs; 3 slaves;
4 villagers and 5 smallholders with 1½ ploughs.
Meadow, 8 acres; pasture 2 furlongs long and 2 furlongs wide.
The value was 20s; now 40s.

28   LAND OF ROGER OF BEAUMONT   E

1 Roger of Beaumont holds STOUR from the King. Alfred held it before 1066. It paid tax for 7 hides. Land for 9 ploughs, of which 4½ hides are in lordship; 2 ploughs there; 6 slaves;
12 villagers and 12 smallholders with 3 ploughs.
A mill which pays 100d; meadow, 20 acres; woodland 1½ leagues long and ½ league wide.
The value was £9; now £8.

Roger also holds
2 STURMINSTER (Marshall). Archbishop Stigand held it before 1066. It paid tax for 30 hides. Land for 25 ploughs, of which 12½ hides are in lordship; 3 ploughs there; 8 slaves;
64 villagers and 26 smallholders with 15 ploughs.
2 mills which pay 28s; meadow, 124 acres; pasture 3 leagues long and 1½ leagues wide; woodland 1 league long and ½ league wide.
Value when he acquired it, £66; now £55.

3 CREECH. Colbran held it before 1066. It paid tax for 2 hides. Land for 2 ploughs, which are there, with
2 villagers and 4 slaves.
Meadow, 4 acres; pasture 6 furlongs long and as wide; woodland 6 furlongs long and 3 furlongs wide.
The value was and is 40s.

Idē.R.ten STIPLE.Leuuin tenuit T.R.E.7 geldℏ ⫏p.ii.hid 7 dim.
Tra.ē.iii.car.In dnio.ē.i.car.7 ii.ferui.7 un uitts 7 iii·bord
cū.i.car.Ibi.iiii.ac p̃ti.7 iii.ac filuæ.paftura.iii.q̃ʒ lg.7 una
q̃ʒ lat.Valuit 7 ual.l.folid.

Idē.R.ten GLOLE.Tres taini|tenuer̄ T.R.E.7 geldℏ ⫏p.iii.hid
7 dim.Tra.ē.iii.car.Ibi.ē pℏr 7 un uitt 7 i.bord cū.i.car.
Ibi.iii.ac p̃ti.7 paftura.iii.q̃ʒ lg.7 una q̃ʒ lat.Valuit 7 ual.xl.fot.

Idē.R.ten ALVRONETONE.Alueron tenuit T.R.E.7 geldℏ ⫏p.ii.
hid.Tra.ē.ii.car.ᵹ ibi st cū.ii.uittis ii.bord.Ibi.ii.ac p̃ti 7 dim. ★
7 ii.ac filuæ.Paftura.iiii.q̃ʒ lg.7 una q̃ʒ lat.Valuit 7 ual.l.fot.

Idē.Ro.ten ALVRETONE.Leodmar tenuit T.R.E.7 geldℏ ⫏p dimid
hida.7 iiii.acris træ.Tra.ē.i.car.Ibi st.ii.uitti·Valet.vii.fot 7 vi.den.

.XXIX.   TERRA ROGERIJ DE CVRCELLE.
Rogerivs de Cvrcelle ten de rege CORFETONE·Duo taini in parag
tenuer̄ T.R.E.7 geldℏ ⫏p.v.hid.Tra.ē.iiii.car.In dnio st.ii.car.
7 xii.bord.7 xv.ac p̃ti.Paftura.i.leū lg.7 dimid leū lat.
Valuit.ix.liℏ.modo.vii.liℏ.Vitalis ten de Rog.

.XXX.   TERRA ROBERTI FILIJ GEROLDI.
Robertvs fili Geroldi ten de rege CORF.Wada 7 Egelric
tenuer̄ T.R.E.7 geldℏ ⫏p.x.hid.Tra.ē.x.car.De ea st in
dnio.vii.hidæ 7 dimid.7 ibi.i.car.7 iiii.ferui.7 xii.uitti 7 xii.
bord cū.v.car.Ibi molin redd.xx.folid.7 cii.ac p̃ti.Paftura
ii.leū| lg 7 lat.Silua.ii.leū lg.7 una leū lat.Valuit 7 ual.xv.
ʄlib.

4 STEEPLE. Leofwin held it before 1066. It paid tax for 2½ hides. Land for 3 ploughs. In lordship 1 plough; 2 slaves; 1 villager and 3 smallholders with 1 plough. Meadow, 4 acres; woodland, 3 acres; pasture 3 furlongs long and 1 furlong wide. The value was and is 50s.

5 (Church) KNOWLE. Three thanes held it jointly before 1066. It paid tax for 3½ hides. Land for 3 ploughs. A priest, 1 villager and 1 smallholder with 1 plough. Meadow, 3 acres; pasture 3 furlongs long and 1 furlong wide. The value was and is 40s.

6 AFFLINGTON. Alfrun held it before 1066. It paid tax for 2 hides. Land for 2 ploughs, which are there, with 2 villagers and 2 smallholders. Meadow, 2½ acres; woodland, 2 acres; pasture 4 furlongs long and 1 furlong wide. The value was and is 50s.

7 AFFLINGTON. Ledmer held it before 1066. It paid tax for ½ hide and 4 acres of land. Land for 1 plough. 2 villagers. Value 7s 6d.

29   LAND OF ROGER OF COURSEULLES   E

1 Roger of Courseulles holds CORTON from the King. Two thanes held it jointly before 1066. It paid tax for 5 hides. Land for 4 ploughs. In lordship 2 ploughs; 12 smallholders. Meadow, 15 acres; pasture 1 league long and ½ league wide. The value was £9; now £7. Vitalis holds it from Roger.

30   LAND OF ROBERT SON OF GERALD   E   80 c

1 Robert son of Gerald holds CORFE (Mullen) from the King. Wada and Aethelric held it before 1066. It paid tax for 10 hides. Land for 10 ploughs, of which 7½ hides are in lordship; 1 plough there; 4 slaves; 12 villagers and 12 smallholders with 5 ploughs. A mill which pays 20s; meadow, 102 acres; pasture 2 leagues in length and width; woodland 2 leagues long and 1 league wide. The value was and is £15.

Idē.Ro.teñ *LEGE*.Duo taini tenueɼ T.R.E.7 geldb̄

ᵱ.ɪ.hida.Tra.ē.ɪ.caɼ.Hanc hn̄t ibi.ɪɪɪ.uiɫɫi.Ibi.ɪɪ.ac p̄ti.

Silua.ɪ.q̊ɀ lḡ.7 v.uirg̊ laɼ.Valuit.xɪɪɪ.foɫ.Modo.xx.foliđ.

Robt teñ de Robto teñ *IWERNE*.Duo fɼs|tenueɼ T.R.E.7 geld

ᵱ.ɪɪɪ.hiđ.Tra.ē.ɪɪ.caɼ 7 dim̄.In dn̄io.ē.ɪ.caɼ.7 vɪ.uiɫɫi 7 ɪɪɪ.borđ

cū.ɪ.caɼ.Ibi molin̄ redđ.ɪɪɪ.foɫ.7 x.ac p̄ti.Paſtura.ɪɪɪ.q̊ɀ

lḡ.7 una q̊ɀ laɼ.Silua.v.q̊ɀ lḡ.7 ɪɪɪ.q̊ɀ laɼ.Valuit 7 uaɫ.ɪɪɪ.lib̄.

Ipſe.Ro.teñ *POVINTONE*.Almar tenuit T.R.E.7 geldb̄ ᵱ.vɪɪɪ.

hiđ 7 dim̄.Tra.ē.vɪ.caɼ.In dn̄io ſt̄.ɪɪɪ.caɼ.7 vɪɪɪ.ſerui.7 ɪɪɪɪ.

uiɫɫi 7 v.borđ cū.ɪɪɪ.caɼ.Ibi molin̄ redđ.xxv.foɫ.7 vɪɪɪ.ac p̄ti.

7 vɪ.ac filuæ.Paſtura.vɪ.q̊ɀ lḡ.7 tñtđ laɼ.Valuit 7 uaɫ.xɪ.lib̄.

Huj ꝏ molin̄ calūniaɼ.ē ad op̊ regis.

.XXXI.   TERRA EDWARDI SARISBEɼ.

Edward Sarisbeɼ teñ de rege *CHENEFORD*.Vluuen tenuit

T.R.E.7 geldb̄ ᵱ.xxv.hiđ.Tra.ē.xvɪɪɪ.caɼ.De ea ſt̄ in dn̄io

xɪ.hidæ 7 dim̄.7 ibi.ɪɪɪ.caɼ.7 ɪx.ſerui.7 xxxv.uiɫɫi 7 xɫ.borđ

cū.xv.caɼ.Ibi molini.ɪɪ.redđ.xv.foliđ.7 cxvɪɪɪ.ac p̄ti.Paſtura.

.ɪɪ.leū int̄ lḡ 7 laɼ.Silua:una leū lḡ.7 dim̄ leū laɼ.   ꝼbrocæ

Ad Winburne.ɪɪɪ.borđ 7 una dom̄ ᵱtin̄ huic ꝏ.7 ibi una leū

Idē Edw teñ *CHINESTANESTONE*.Wluuen tenuit T.R.E.

7 geldb̄ ᵱ.xɪɪɪ.hiđ.Tra.ē.ɪx.caɼ.De ea ſt̄ in dn̄io.v.hidæ

7 una v træ.7 ibi.ɪɪ.caɼ.7 vɪɪ.ſerui.7 xvɪɪɪ.uiɫɫi 7 xɪɪɪɪ.cofcez.

7 ɪɪɪɪ.cotar cū.vɪɪ.caɼ.Ibi molin̄ redđ.v.foliđ.7 una ac filuæ.

7 c.ac p̄ti.v.min̄.Paſtura.ɪɪɪ.leū lḡ.7 ɪɪ.leū laɼ.ɪɪɪ.q̊ɀ min̄.

H̄.ɪɪ.Maner qdo receᵽ ualeb̄.ɫ.lib̄.Modo.ʟxx.lib̄.

2   Robert also holds LEIGH. Two thanes held it before 1066. It paid
tax for 1 hide. Land for 1 plough.
 3 villagers have it there.
 Meadow, 2 acres; woodland 1 furlong long and 5 'rods' wide.
The value was 13s; now 20s.

3   Robert holds RANSTON from Robert. Two brothers held it jointly
before 1066. It paid tax for 3 hides. Land for 2½ ploughs. In
lordship 1 plough;
 6 villagers and 3 smallholders with 1 plough.
 A mill which pays 3s; meadow, 10 acres; pasture 3 furlongs
  long and 1 furlong wide; woodland 5 furlongs long and 3
  furlongs wide.
The value was and is £3.

4   Robert holds POVINGTON himself. Aelmer held it before 1066.
It paid tax for 8½ hides. Land for 6 ploughs. In lordship 3
ploughs; 8 slaves;
 4 villagers and 5 smallholders with 3 ploughs.
 A mill which pays 25s; meadow, 8 acres; woodland, 6 acres;
  pasture 6 furlongs long and as wide.
 In Wareham a burgess who pays 2s.
The value was and is £11.
This manor's mill is claimed for the King's use.

31   LAND OF EDWARD OF SALISBURY   E

1   Edward of Salisbury holds CANFORD (Magna) from the King.
Wulfwen held it before 1066. It paid tax for 25 hides. Land
for 18 ploughs, of which 11½ hides are in lordship; 3 ploughs
there; 9 slaves;
 35 villagers and 40 smallholders with 15 ploughs.
 2 mills which pay 15s; meadow, 118 acres; pasture 2 leagues
  in both length and width; woodland 1 league long and ½
  league wide.
 At Wimborne (Minster) 3 smallholders and a house belong
to this manor; water-meadow, 1 league there.

2   Edward also holds KINSON. Wulfwen held it before 1066. It paid
tax for 13 hides. Land for 9 ploughs, of which 5 hides and 1
virgate of land are in lordship; 2 ploughs there; 7 slaves;
 18 villagers, 14 Cottagers and 4 cottagers with 7 ploughs.
 A mill which pays 5s; woodland, 1 acre; meadow, 100 acres,
  less 5; pasture 3 leagues long and 2 leagues wide, less
  3 furlongs.
Value of these two manors when he acquired them £50; now £70.

TERRA ERNVLFI DE HESDING.

ERNVLFVS ten de rege *CHINTONE* . Edric tenuit T.R.E.7 geldb
⊙7 una v tre ꝓ.VI.hid ⊙Tra.e.v.car.De ea ſt in dnio.IIII . hidæ 7 III.v træ.
7 ibi.II.car.7 VI.ſerui.7 VI.uiłłi 7 I.bord cu.II.car.Ibi.xx.ac p̊ti.
7 una q̅ꝫ ſiluæ.Valuit 7 uał.IIII.lib.Vrſo ten de Ernulfo.

VR ſo ten de Ern *MELESBERIE*.Tres taini∥tenuer. T.R.E.7 geldb
ꝓ.IIII.hid 7 dim.Tra.e.IIII.car.In dnio ſt.III.car.cu.I.uiłło
7 VII.bord cu dim car.Ibi.XII.ac p̊ti.Silua.VIII.q̅ꝫ lg̅.7 IIII.q̅ꝫ
lat.Valuit.XL.ſolid.modo.IIII.lib.

IPſe.Er.ten *CHIMEDECOME*.Quinq̅ taini tenuer T.R.E.7 geldb
ꝓ.III.v træ 7 IIII.parte uni v.Tra.e.I.car.Hanc hnt ibi.v.uiłłi
7 ibi.III.ac p̊ti.7 Paſtura.VIII.q̅ꝫ lg̅.7 II.q̅ꝫ lat.Valet.x.ſoł.

☞IPſe.Er.ten *MAPERETONE*.Septe taini tenuer.T.R.E.7 geldb
ꝓ.III.hid 7 III.v træ.Tra.e.III.car 7 dim.In dnio ſt.II.car.
7 III.uiłłi 7 x.bord cu.I.car 7 dim.Ibi.VIII.ac p̊ti.Paſtura
una leu lg̅.7 IIII.q̅ꝫ lat.Silua.v.q̅ꝫ lg̅.7 IIII.q̅ꝫ lat.
Valuit.XL.ſoł.Modo.LX.ſolid.

TERRA TVRSTINI FILIJ ROLF.

TVRSTINVS filius Rolf ten de rege *GELINGHAM* 7 Ber
nard de eo.Aluuold tenuit T.R.E.7 geldb ꝓ.III.hid 7 dim.
Tra.e.IIII.car.In dnio ſt.II.car.7 VIII.ſerui.7 I.uiłłs cu.II.
car.Ibi.XII.ac p̊ti.Valuit 7 uał.LX.ſolid.

Rannulf ten de.T.*INLANDE*.Edric 7 Dachelin 7 Aluuard
In paragio
tenuer T.R.E.7 geldb ꝓ.II.hid.Tra.e.II.car.In dnio.e.I.car.

32   LAND OF ARNULF OF HESDIN   E

1 Arnulf holds KINGTON from the King. Edric held it before 1066.
It paid tax for 6 hides and 1 virgate of land. Land for 5 ploughs,
of which 4 hides and 3 virgates of land are in lordship; 2 ploughs
there; 6 slaves;
   6 villagers and 1 smallholder with 2 ploughs.
Meadow, 20 acres; woodland, 1 furlong.
The value was and is £4.
Urso holds from Arnulf.

2 Urso holds MELBURY from Arnulf. Three thanes held it jointly
before 1066. It paid tax for 4½ hides. Land for 4 ploughs.
In lordship 3 ploughs, with
   1 villager and 7 smallholders with ½ plough.
Meadow, 12 acres; woodland 8 furlongs long and 4 furlongs wide.
The value was 40s; now £4.

3 Arnulf holds KINGCOMBE himself. Five thanes held it before 1066.
It paid tax for 3 virgates of land and the fourth part of 1 virgate.
Land for 1 plough.
   5 villagers have it there.
Meadow, 3 acres; pasture 8 furlongs long and 2 furlongs wide.
Value 10s.

ψ *32,4 is entered at the foot of col. 80c in the middle of 33,4, directed by transposition signs
to its correct place in the text.*

5 Arnulf holds MAPPERTON himself. Seven thanes held it before
1066. It paid tax for 3 hides and 3 virgates of land. Land for
3½ ploughs. In lordship 2 ploughs;
   3 villagers and 10 smallholders with 1½ ploughs.
Meadow, 8 acres; pasture 1 league long and 4 furlongs wide;
   woodland 5 furlongs long and 4 furlongs wide.
The value was 40s; now 60s.

33   LAND OF THURSTAN SON OF ROLF   E

1 Thurstan son of Rolf holds GILLINGHAM from the King, and
Bernard from him. Alwold held it before 1066. It paid tax
for 3½ hides. Land for 4 ploughs. In lordship 2 ploughs; 8 slaves;
   1 villager with 2 ploughs.
Meadow, 12 acres.
The value was and is 60s.

2 Ranulf holds NYLAND from Thurstan. Edric, Dachelin and
Alward held it jointly before 1066. It paid tax for 2 hides.
Land for 2 ploughs. In lordship 1 plough,

cū.ı.feruo.7 ıı.uiłłi 7 ıı.borđ cū dimiđ cař.Ibi.vııı.ac̄ p̄ti.

Bernard·ten̄ de.T.in· eađ uilla.ı.hidā. ⌐Valuit 7 uał.xx.foł.

Dode tenuit T.R.E.Ibi.ē.ı.cař.7 uał.x.foł.Valuit.v.foliđ.

Ipfe.T.ten̄ ADELINGTONE.Brictui tenuit T;R.E.7 geldb̄
p.ıııׂhiđ.Tra.ē.ıı.cař.In dn̄io ſt.ıı.cař.7 xıı.borđ cū dim̄
cař.7 ıx.cenfores redđ.xı.foł.Ibi molin̄ redđ.xv.foliđ.

☞ Idē.Er.ten̄ POVERTONE.Septē taini tenuer̄ T.R.E.7 geldb̄ p dim̄ hida.
Tra.ē.ı.cař.Hanc hn̄t ibi.vıı.uiłłi 7 ıı.q̄ɫ̄ paſturæ in łḡ 7 lat̄.Valet
⌐xx.foł 7 vı.den̄.   ★

80 d

7 x.ac̄ p̄ti.7 vı.ac̄ filuæ.Paſtura.vıı.q̄ɫ̄ 7 dim̄ łḡ.7 una
q̄rent lat̄.Valuit.ııı.lib̄.Modo.ıııı.lib̄.

Rannulf⁹ ten̄ de.T.STOCHES.Vluiet tenuit T.R.E.7 geldb̄
hid
p.ı.cař.Tra.ē.ı.cař.q̄ ibi.ē cū.ı.feruo.7 v.borđ.Ibi.x.ac̄·
p̄ti.7 xvı.ac̄ filuæ.Valet.xx.foliđ.

Rannulf⁹ ten̄ de.T.STOCHES.Brictuin tenuit T.R.E.7 geldb̄
p.ııı.v træ.Tra.ē.ı.cař.q̄ ibi.ē.7 ıııı.ac̄ p̄ti.7 xvı.ac̄ filuæ.
Valet.x.foliđ.

.XXXIIII.   TERRA WILLELMI DE OW.

Willelm⁹ DE OW.ten̄ de rege TORENTONE.7 Wiłłs de eo.
Aleſtan tenuit T.R.E.7 geldb̄ p.ıı.hiđ.Tra.ē.ııı.cař.In dn̄io st
.ıı.cař.7 ıııı.ferui.7 ııı.uiłłi 7 vı.borđ cū.ı.cař.Ibi.x.ac̄ p̄ti.Silua
.ııı.q̄ɫ̄ łḡ.7 ıı.q̄ɫ̄ lat̄.Valuit 7 uał.xɫ.foliđ.

80 c, d

with 1 slave;
    2 villagers and 2 smallholders with ½ plough.
    Meadow, 8 acres.
The value was and is 20s.

3   Bernard holds 1 hide from Thurstan in this village. Doda held it before 1066. 1 plough there.
Value 10s; the value was 5s.

4   Thurstan holds ALLINGTON himself. Brictwy held it before 1066. It paid tax for 3 hides. Land for 3 ploughs. In lordship 2 ploughs;
    12 smallholders with ½ plough; 9 tributaries who pay 11s.
    A mill which pays 15s;

Ψ   *32,4 entered at the foot of col. 80c, directed to its correct place by transposition signs*

32,4   Arnulf also holds POORTON. Seven thanes held it before 1066. It paid tax for ½ hide. Land for 1 plough.
    7 villagers have it there.
    Pasture, 2 furlongs in length and width.
Value 12s 6d.

33,4 continued

    meadow, 10 acres; woodland, 6 acres; pasture 7½ furlongs   **80 d**
      long and 1 furlong wide.
The value was £3; now £4.

5   Ranulf holds 'STOKE (Wallis)' from Thurstan. Wulfgeat held it before 1066. It paid tax for 1 hide. Land for 1 plough, which is there, with 1 slave;
    5 smallholders.
    Meadow, 10 acres; woodland, 16 acres.
Value 20s.

6   Ranulf holds 'STOKE (Wallis)' from Thurstan. Brictwin held it before 1066. It paid tax for 3 virgates of land. Land for 1 plough, which is there.
    Meadow, 4 acres; woodland, 16 acres.
Value 10s.

34   LAND OF WILLIAM OF EU   E

1   William of Eu holds THORNTON from the King, and William from him. Alstan held it before 1066. It paid tax for 2 hides. Land for 3 ploughs. In lordship 2 ploughs; 4 slaves;
    3 villagers and 6 smallholders with 1 plough.
    Meadow, 10 acres; woodland 3 furlongs long and 2 furlongs wide.
The value was and is 40s.

Idē Wills ten de . W . *Bradeford* . Tol tenuit T.R.E.⁊ geldb ꝑ.xvii.
hid . Tra . ē . viii . car̄ . In dn̄io st̄ . ii . car̄ .⁊ iiii . ſerui .⁊ x . uilli ⁊ xiii.
bord . cū . v . car̄ . Ibi . ii . molini redd . xx . ſol.⁊ xxx . ac̄ pti . Paſtura
.x . q̇ꝛ lḡ.⁊ iiii . q̇ꝛ lat̄ . Valuit ⁊ ual . xii . lib.

Wills ten de . W . in *Hiwes* . i . hidā . Tra . ē dim̄ car̄ . Valet . xx . ſol.

Hugo ten de . W . *Mapledre* . Vluuard ⁊ Almar tenuer̄ T.R.E.
⁊ geldb ꝑ . iii . virg træ . Tra . ē . i . car̄ . Ibi . iiii . ac̄ pti .⁊ v . ac̄ ſiluæ.
Valuit . xv . ſol . Modo . vii . ſolid.

Idē . H . ten de . W . *Lichet* . Tholi tenuit T.R.E.⁊ geldb ꝑ.xii . hid.
Tra . ē . viii . car̄ . In dn̄io st̄ . ii . car̄ .⁊ iii . ſerui .⁊ xvi . uilli ⁊ xi . coſcez.
cū . v . car̄ . Ibi . xl . ac̄ pti . Paſturæ xi . q̇ꝛ . ſilua dimid leu|lḡ ⁊ lat̄.
Brocæ . i . leu in lḡ ⁊ lat̄ . In Warhā . ii . ortos ⁊ i . bord
Valuit . ix . lib . Modo . x . lib.

Wills ten de . W . *Bleneford* . Tou tenuit T.R.E.⁊ geldb ꝑ.iii.hid
⁊ dim̄ . Tra . ē . ii . car̄ . In dn̄io . ē . i . car̄ .⁊ iii . ſerui .⁊ iii . bord.
Ibi . xii . ac̄ pti .⁊ lvi . ac̄ paſture , Valuit ⁊ ual . xl . ſol.
In ipſa uilla ten Wills dim̄ hid . quā Tou habuit p uadimon̄ .⁊ fuit
adꝗetata . quā cep̄ Rad de Limeſi cū iſta alia tra . Poſtea n̄ habuit rex
geld de ea . Valet . iii . ſolid.

Hugo ten de . W . *Wellecome* . Briſmar tenuit T.R.E.⁊ geldb
ꝑ.v . hid . Tra . ē . iiii . car̄ . In dn̄io . ē . i . car̄ .⁊ ii . ſerui .⁊ ii . uilli .⁊ viii . bord
cū . i . car̄ .⁊ iii . cotar̄ . |viii . ac̄ pti . Paſtura . viii . q̇ꝛ lḡ .⁊ ii . q̇ꝛ lat̄.
Silua . ii . q̇ꝛ lḡ .⁊ una q̇ꝛ lat̄ . Valuit ⁊ ual . l . ſolid.

2   William also holds BRADFORD (Peverell) from William. Toli held it before 1066. It paid tax for 17 hides. Land for 8 ploughs. In lordship 2 ploughs; 4 slaves;
    10 villagers and 13 smallholders with 5 ploughs.
    2 mills which pay 20s; meadow, 30 acres; pasture 10 furlongs long and 4 furlongs wide.
The value was and is £12.

3   William holds 1 hide in HIWES from William. Land for ½ plough. Value 20s.

4   Hugh holds MAPPOWDER from William. Wulfward and Aelmer held it before 1066. It paid tax for 3 virgates of land. Land for 1 plough.
    Meadow, 4 acres; woodland, 5 acres.
The value was 15s; now 7s.

5   Hugh also holds LYTCHETT (Matravers) from William. Toli held it before 1066. It paid tax for 12 hides. Land for 8 ploughs. In lordship 2 ploughs; 3 slaves;
    16 villagers and 11 Cottagers with 5 ploughs.
    Meadow, 40 acres; pasture, 11 furlongs; woodland ½ league in both length and width; water-meadow(?), 1 league in length and width; in Wareham 2 gardens and 1 smallholder.
The value was £9; now £10.

6   William holds BLANDFORD (St. Mary) from William. Toli held it before 1066. It paid tax for 3½ hides. Land for 2 ploughs. In lordship 1 plough; 3 slaves;
    3 smallholders.
    Meadow, 12 acres; pasture, 56 acres.
The value was and is 40s.
    In this village William holds ½ hide which Toli had by way of a pledge. It was discharged. Ralph of Limesy took it with that other land. Later on the King did not have tax from it. Value 3s.

7   Hugh holds WOOLCOMBE from William. Brictmer held it before 1066. It paid tax for 5 hides. Land for 4 ploughs. In lordship 1 plough; 2 slaves;
    2 villagers and 8 smallholders with 1 plough; 3 cottagers.
    Meadow, 8 acres; pasture 8 furlongs long and 2 furlongs wide; woodland 2 furlongs long and 1 furlong wide.
The value was and is 50s.

Wills ten de.W.*SVERE*.Tol tenuit T.R.E.7 geldb ⁊p.ıx.hıd.
Tra.e.vıı.car.In dnio st.ııı.car.7 v.ſerui.7 v.uilli 7 xı.borđ
cu.ııı.car.Ibi molin redđ.xvı.ſol.7 xxx.ac pti.Paſtura.vıı.q̃⁊
lg.7 una q̃⁊ lat.Valuit 7 ual.ıx.lıb.

In iſta uilla ten.W.quandā parte træ q̃ nunq̃ geldaū T.R.E.
ſed erat in dnio 7 in firma regis.Hanc preſtiterat Toxos q̃đa ppoſit ★
regis.deinde reſupſit ea in manu regis.Toxus u̅ p rege.E.iteru fuit
ſaiſit ſic dicit.7 ita tenuit ea in uita 7 in morte regis.E.7 tpr Heraldi.
Prius erat paſcualis.m̃ ſeminabilis.

Ipſe.W.ten in dnio *WENFROT*.Aleſtan tenuit T.R.E.7 geldb ⁊p.xıı.
hıd.Tra.e.xı.car.In dnio st.vı.hidæ de ea tra.7 ibi.ııı.car.7 ıı.
ſerui.7 xııı.uilli 7 xvııı.borđ cu.vııı.car.Ibi molin redđ.x.ſolid.
7 vııı.ac pti.Paſtura.ıı.leu lg.7 una leu 7 ıııı.q̃⁊ lat.Silua.v.q̃⁊
lg.7 ııı.q̃⁊ lat.Valuit.xıı.lıb.Modo.xıx.lıb.

Ansfrid ten de.W.*FROME*.Aleſtan tenuit.T.R.E.7 geldb ⁊p.vı.hıd.
Tra.e.ııı.car.In dnio.e.ı.car.7 ıı.ſerui.7 ıııı.uilli.7 vııı.borđ cu.ıı.
car.Ibi molin redđ.x.ſol.7 x.ac pti.Paſtura.vı.q̃⁊ lg.7 ıı.q̃⁊ lat.
Silua.ıı.q̃⁊ lg.7 una q̃⁊ lat.Valeb.ııı.lıb.Modo.ıııı.lıb.

Ipſe.W.ten *CIRCEL*.Aleſtan tenuit T.R.E.7 geldb ⁊p.xıı.hıd.
Tra.e.ıx.car.De ea st in dnio.vıı.hidæ 7 dimiđ.7 ibi.ıı.car.
7 vııı.ſerui.7 ııı.ancillæ.7 xııı.uilli 7 vıı.borđ cu.ıııı.car.Ibi.ıı.
ac pti.Paſtura.xx.q̃⁊ lg.7 ııı.q̃⁊ lat.Silua.ııı.q̃⁊ lg.7 ıı.q̃⁊ lat.
Valuit.x.lıb.Modo.xv.lıb.

8   William holds SWYRE from William. Toli held it before 1066.
It paid tax for 9 hides. Land for 7 ploughs. In lordship 3
ploughs; 5 slaves;
>   5 villagers and 11 smallholders with 3 ploughs.
>   A mill which pays 16s; meadow, 30 acres; pasture 7 furlongs
>   long and 1 furlong wide.

The value was and is £9.
In that village William holds a part of the land which never
paid tax before 1066 but was in lordship and in the King's
revenue. A King's reeve had leased it to Toxus (the priest?), then
retook it into the King's hands. Toxus was put in possession of
it again by King Edward, so he states, and so he held it during
King Edward's life and at the (time of his) death and in the
time of Harold. Previously it was pasture, now arable.

9   William holds WYNFORD (Eagle) himself in lordship. Alstan held
it before 1066. It paid tax for 14 hides. Land for 11 ploughs.
In lordship 6 hides of this land; 3 ploughs there; 2 slaves;
>   13 villagers and 18 smallholders with 8 ploughs.
>   A mill which pays 10s; meadow, 8 acres; pasture 2 leagues
>   long and 1 league and 4 furlongs wide; woodland 5 furlongs
>   long and 3 furlongs wide.

The value was £12; now £19.

10   Ansfrid holds FROME (Vauchurch) from William. Alstan held it
before 1066. It paid tax for 6 hides. Land for 3 ploughs. In
lordship 1 plough; 2 slaves;
>   4 villagers and 8 smallholders with 2 ploughs.
>   A mill which pays 10s; meadow, 10 acres; pasture 6 furlongs
>   long and 2 furlongs wide; woodland 2 furlongs long and
>   1 furlong wide.

The value was £3; now £4.

11   William holds (Long) CRICHEL himself. Alstan held it before 1066.
It paid tax for 12 hides. Land for 9 ploughs, of which 7½ hides
are in lordship; 2 ploughs there; 8 male and 3 female slaves;
>   13 villagers and 7 smallholders with 4 ploughs.
>   Meadow, 2 acres; pasture 20 furlongs long and 3 furlongs
>   wide; woodland 3 furlongs long and 2 furlongs wide.

The value was £10; now £15.

Wills teñ de.W.*TERENTE*.Toul tenuit T.R.E.7 geldb ᵽ.iii.

hid 7 dimid.Tra.e.iii.car̃.In dñio.e.i.car̃.7 ii.ſerui.7 iiii.uilli

7 ii.bord cũ.i.car̃ 7 dim.Ibi paſtura.v.q̃ɤ lg.7 iii.q̃ɤ lat̃.Silua

viii.q̃ɤ lg.7 iiii.q̃ɤ lat̃.Valuit.xx.ſol.Modo.iiii.lib.

Ansfrid teñ de.W.*ALEVRDE*.Aleſtan tenuit T.R.E.7 geldb

ᵽ.ii.hid.Tra.e.ii.car̃.In dñio.e.i.car̃.cũ.i.ſeruo.7 iii.uilli

82 a

7 iiii.bord cũ.i.car̃.Ibi.viii.ac pti.7 paſtura.iii.q̃ɤ lg.

7 ii.q̃ɤ lat̃.Valuit 7 ual.lx.ſolid.

Hugo teñ *STOCHES*.Toul tenuit T.R.E.7 geldb ᵽ.i.hida.

Tra.e.iii.car̃.Has hñt ibi.viii.uilli 7 iii.bord.Ibi.viii.ac

pti.Silua.x.q̃ɤ lg.7 iiii.q̃ɤ lat̃.Valuit 7 ual.l.ſolid.

Hanc trã teneb Toul in uadimonio T.R.E.de tra Scireburne.

Ide.H.teñ de.W.*CANDEL*.Toul tenuit T.R.E.7 geldb ᵽ.iiii.

hid 7 dim.Tra.e.iii.car̃.In dñio.e.i.car̃.7 ii.ſerui.7 iiii.

uilli 7 ii.bord cũ.i.car̃.Ibi.vii.ac pti.7 paſtura.iiii.q̃ɤ

lg.7 una q̃ɤ lat̃.Valuit 7 ual.lx.ſolid.

XXXV. TERRA WILLI DE FALEISE.

Wills de FALEISE teñ de rege *SELTONE*.Vluuard

tenuit T.R.E.7 geldb ᵽ.viii.hid.Tra.e.viii.car̃.

In dñio ſt.ii.car̃.7 vi.ſerui.7 viii.uilli 7 x.bord cũ.iiii.car̃.

Ibi.iii.molini redd.v.ſolid.7 xx.ac pti.Silua.i.leu lg.

7 dim leu lat̃.Valuit.xi.lib.Modo.vi.lib.

Cũ hac tra teñ id Wills.i.hid 7 dimid v træ.Tra.e.i.car̃.

hanc hñt ibi.iii.uilli.7 ualet.x.ſolid.Hanc trã teneb

Vluuard in uadimonio T.R.E.de q̃dã ᵽpoſito ejus.

12 William holds ʼTARRANTʼ from William. Toli held it before 1066. It paid tax for 3½ hides. Land for 3 ploughs. In lordship 1 plough; 2 slaves;
    4 villagers and 2 smallholders with 1½ ploughs.
    Pasture 5 furlongs long and 3 furlongs wide; woodland 8 furlongs long and 4 furlongs wide.
The value was 20s; now £4.

13 Ansfrid holds ELWORTH from William. Alstan held it before 1066. It paid tax for 2 hides. Land for 2 ploughs. In lordship 1 plough, with 1 slave;
    3 villagers and 4 smallholders with 1 plough.
    Meadow, 8 acres; pasture 3 furlongs long and 2 furlongs wide.
The value was and is 60s.

82 a

14 Hugh holds STOCK (Gaylard) from William. Toli held it before 1066. It paid tax for 1 hide. Land for 3 ploughs.
    8 villagers and 3 smallholders have them there.
    Meadow, 8 acres; woodland 10 furlongs long and 4 furlongs wide.
The value was and is 50s.
    Toli held this land in pledge before 1066 from the land of Sherborne.

15 Hugh also holds (Stourton) CAUNDLE from William. Toli held it before 1066. It paid tax for 3½ hides. Land for 3 ploughs. In lordship 1 plough; 2 slaves;
    4 villagers and 2 smallholders with 1 plough.
    Meadow, 7 acres; pasture 4 furlongs long and 1 furlong wide.
The value was and is 60s.

35   LAND OF WILLIAM OF FALAISE   E

1 William of Falaise holds SILTON from the King. Wulfward White held it before 1066. It paid tax for 8 hides. Land for 8 ploughs. In lordship 2 ploughs; 6 slaves;
    8 villagers and 10 smallholders with 4 ploughs.
    3 mills which pay 5s; meadow, 20 acres; woodland 1 league long and ½ league wide.
The value was £11; now £6.
    William also holds with this land 1 hide and ½ virgate of land. Land for 1 plough.
    3 villagers have it there.
Value 10s.
    Wulfward held this land in pledge before 1066 from a reeve of his.

Cū ipſa t̕ra adhuc ten̕ id Wilts . i . hidā . T̕ra . ē . i . car̕.
q̄ ibi . ē in dn̄io . 7 ualet . xx . ſolid . Hanc hidā emit
Vluuard ab ep̄o execeſtr̕ . T . R . E . ſed n̄ ptineb ad ipſū m̄.
Cū ead p̄dicta t̕ra ten̕ id Wilts . iii . hid in MILTETONE.
7 Roger de eo . Wicnod tenuit T . R . E . T̕ra . ē . i . car̕ 7 dim̄.
Ibi ſt . v . bord cū . i . car̕ . 7 moliñ redd . xv . denar̕.
7 viii . ac̄ p̄ti . 7 Silua . viii . q̄z̧ lḡ . 7 ii . q̄z̧ lat̄ . Valuit 7 ual̄

⌐ xx . ſolid.

TERRA WILLELMI DE MOION.

Wills de MOIONE ten̕ de rege TODEBERIE . 7 Goiſ
frid de eo . Godric tenuit T . R . E . 7 geldb p . ii . hid . T̕ra . ē
ii . car̄ . q̄ ibi ſt in dn̄io . 7 moliñ redd . x . ſolid . 7 xii . ac̄
p̄ti . Silua . dimid leū lḡ . 7 una q̄z̧ lat̄ . Valuit . iii . lib . M . ii . lb.
Ipſe . W . ten̕ SPEHTESBERIE . Ageluuard 7 Godric
tenuer̄ p . ii . m̄ T . R . E . 7 geldb p . vii . hid 7 una v̄ t̕ræ 7 vi.
acris . T̕ra . ē . vi . car̄ . In dn̄io ſt . iiii . car̄ . 7 vi . ſerui . 7 x . uilti
7 xii . bord cū . iii . car̄ . Ibi moliñ redd . xii . ſolid 7 vi . den.
7 l . ac̄ p̄ti . 7 paſtura . v . q̄z̧ 7 dimid lḡ . 7 ii . q̄z̧ lat̄ . 7 alio
loco ſup aquā paſtura . ii . q̄z̧ lḡ . 7 dimid . 7 i . q̄z̧ 7 dim̄ lat̄.
Valuit . c . ſolid . Modo . vii . lib 7 x . ſolid.
Ogiſus ten̕ de . W . WINTREBVRNE . Aluuard tenuit
T . R . E . 7 geldb p . ii . hid 7 dimid . T̕ra . ē . ii . car̄ . Ibi ſt . iiii.
bord cū . i . ſeruo . 7 ii . ac̄ p̄ti . 7 vi . q̄z̧ paſturæ . 7 xiii . ac̄ ſiluæ
minutæ . Valuit . l . ſolid . Modo . xl . ſolid.

Further, with this land William also holds 1 hide. Land for 1 plough, which is there, in lordship. Value 20s.
Wulfward bought this hide from the Bishop of Exeter before 1066, but it did not belong to this manor.
With this said land William also holds 3 hides in MILTON (on Stour), and Roger from him. Wihtnoth held it before 1066. Land for 1½ ploughs.
5 smallholders with 1 plough.
A mill which pays 15d; meadow, 8 acres; woodland 8
   furlongs long and 2 furlongs wide.
The value was and is 20s.

36   LAND OF WILLIAM OF MOHUN

1 William of Mohun holds TODBER from the King, and Geoffrey   E
Mallory from him. Godric held it before 1066. It paid tax for 2   47
hides. Land for 2 ploughs, which are there, in lordship.   E   a 2
   A mill which pays 10s; meadow, 12 acres; woodland ½ league
   long and 1 furlong wide. 1 cob; 8 cattle; 12 pigs; 100 sheep.
The value was £3; now £4.   E

2 William holds SPETISBURY himself. Aethelward and Godric held it   E
as two manors before 1066. It paid tax for 7 hides and 1 virgate   47
of land and 6 acres. Land for 6 ploughs. In lordship 4 ploughs;   b 1
6 slaves; 3 hides and 1 virgate and 10 acres.
   10 villagers and 12 smallholders with 3 ploughs and 4 hides,
   less 4 acres.
   A mill which pays 12s 6d; meadow, 50 acres; pasture 5½
   furlongs long and 2 furlongs wide; in another place,
   overlooking the water, pasture 2½ furlongs long and 1½   E
   furlongs wide. 2 cobs; 5 cattle; 30 pigs; 166 sheep.
The value was 100s; now £7 10s.   E

3 Ogis holds WINTERBORNE (Houghton) from William. Alward held   E
it before 1066. It paid tax for 2½ hides. Land for 2 ploughs.   E
In lordship 2 hides and ½ virgate.   47
   A villager has ½ virgate. 4 smallholders, with 1 slave.   b 2
   Meadow, 2 acres; pasture, 6 furlongs; underwood, 13 acres.   E
   4 cattle; 4 pigs; 10 sheep.
The value was 50s; now 40s.
   Of these 2½ hides Hugh of Boscherbert holds 1 virgate wrongfully from the wife of   E
   Hugh son of Grip. Now Ogis holds it from William.

Column 82a continues after 36,11

☞ Idem Wilts de Moion ten *Poleha*.Viginti 7 un tein tenuer T.R.E.7
geldb ᵽ.x.hid.Tra.e.viii.car.In dnio st.iii.car.7 vi.ferui.
7 xiiii.uilti 7 xxv.bord cu.vii.car.Ibi molin redd.xl.denar.7 xxxii.
ac pti.Silua.ii.leu lg.7 viii.q̃ʒ lat.Valuit x.lib.m̃.viii.lib.
Ide Wilts ten *Hame*.Godric tenuit T.R.E.7 geldb ᵽ.v.hid.Tra
.e.iiii.car.In dnio st.ii.car.7 iiii.ferui.7 vi.uilti 7 v.bord.
cu.ii.car.Ibi molin redd.vii.folid.7 vi.den.7 l.ac pti.7 iii.q̃ʒ
pafturæ in lg.7 una q̃ʒ in lat.Valuit.lx.fot.modo.c.folid.
Ide.W.ten *Frome*.Tres taini tenuer.T.R.E.7 geldb ᵽ.x.hid.Tra.e
.vi.car.In dnio st.iiii.car.7 iiii.ferui.7 iiii.uilti 7 vii.bord.
Ibi molin de.iii.fot.7 xx.ac pti.7 ix.ac filuæ.Paftura.xvii.
q̃ʒ lg.7 tntd lat.Valuit 7 uat.vi.lib.Duo hoes ten de Witto.
Robt ten de.W.*Frome*.Aluuard tenuit T.R.E.7 geldb ᵽ.iiii.
hid.Tra.e.ii.car.q̃ ibi st in dnio.cu.i.feruo.7 ix.bord.
Ibi molin redd.x.folid 7 vii.ac pti.7 vii.q̃ʒ pafturæ in lg.7 v.
q̃ʒ in lat.Valuit.iiii.lib.Modo.iii.lib.
Rannulf ten de.W.*Celberge*.Godric tenuit T.R.E.7 geldb ᵽ.iii.hid.
Tra.e.iii.car.In dnio.e.i.car.7 un uilts 7 v.bord cu.i.car.

36,4–11 are written on an inserted piece of parchment, folio 81c,d, and directed here by transposition signs

4 William of Mohun also holds PULHAM. Twenty-one thanes held it before 1066. It paid tax for 10 hides. Land for 8 ploughs. In lordship 3 ploughs; 6 slaves; 4 hides and 1 virgate and 6 acres. 14 villagers and 25 smallholders with 7 ploughs and 5½ hides and 4 acres. A mill which pays 40d; meadow, 32 acres; woodland 2 leagues long and 8 furlongs wide. A garden in Wareham which pays 3d. 2 cobs; 6 cattle; 25 pigs; 170 sheep; 15 goats. The value was £10; now £8.

E 81 c,d
48
a 1
E

5 William also holds HAMMOON. Godric held it before 1066. It paid tax for 5 hides. Land for 4 ploughs. In lordship 2 ploughs; 4 slaves; 3 hides and 8 acres. 6 villagers and 5 smallholders with 2 ploughs and 2 hides, less 12 acres. A mill which pays 7s 6d; meadow, 50 acres; pasture, 3 furlongs in length and 1 furlong in width. 2 cobs; 14 cattle; 24 pigs; 67 sheep. The value was 60s; now 100s. Thurstan holds it now from William.

E
48
a 2

6 William also holds CHILFROME. Three thanes held it jointly before 1066. It paid tax for 10 hides. Land for 6 ploughs. In lordship 4 ploughs; 4 slaves; 4 villagers and 7 smallholders. A mill at 3s; meadow, 20 acres; woodland, 9 acres. pasture 17 furlongs long and as wide. The value was and is £6. Two men hold it from William. William claims these three manors as two.

D
48
b 1
E
E
E
E

7 Robert holds CRUXTON from William. Alward held it before 1066. It paid tax for 4 hides. Land for 2 ploughs, which are there, in lordship, and 3 hides and 8 acres, with 1 slave; 9 smallholders (who have) 1 hide, less 8 acres, and 1 plough. A mill which pays 10s; meadow, 7 acres; pasture, 7 furlongs in length and 5 furlongs in width. 1 cob; 6 pigs; 80 sheep. The value was £4; now £3.

48
b 2

8 Ranulf holds CHELBOROUGH from William. Godric held it before 1066. It paid tax for 3 hides. Land for 3 ploughs. In lordship 1 plough; 2½ hides. 1 villager and 5 smallholders with 1 plough and ½ hide.

49
a 1

Ibi.x.ac̄ p̄ti.7 vii.q̄ɫ paſturæ in l̄g.7 iii.q̄ɫ in laɫ.Valuit 7 ual
.iii.lib̄.Has.iii.hid̄ calūniaɫ filius Odon̄ camerarij.

Goisfrid̄ ten̄ de.W.*WERNE*.Goduin̄ tenuit T.R.E.7 geldb̄ ꝑ.iii.
hid̄.Tra.e̅.iii.car̄.In dn̄io ſt.ii.car̄.7 ii.ſerui.7 vi.uilli
7 vi.bord̄ cū.i.car̄.Ibi.viii.q̄ɫ ſiluæ.7 x.q̄ɫ paſturæ in l̄g.7
iii.q̄ɫ in laɫ.Valuit 7 ual.iiii.lib̄.

Idem.W.ten̄ *WINDRESORIE*.Aluuard̄ tenuit T.R.E.7 geldb̄ ꝑ.iiii.
hid̄.Tra.e̅.iii.car̄.In dn̄io ſt.ii.car̄.7 ii.ſerui.7 ix.uilli
7 ii.bord̄ cū.i.car̄.Ibi.xxx.ac̄ p̄ti.7 viii.q̄ɫ paſture in l̄g.7 vi.q̄ɫ
in laɫ.7 vi.q̄ɫ ſiluæ in l̄g.7 iii.q̄ɫ in laɫ.Valet.lx.ſolid̄.

Idem.W.ten̄ *MALPERETONE*.Elmer tenuit T.R.E.7 geldb̄ ꝑ.v.
hid̄ 7 una v̄ træ.Tra.e̅.iiii.car̄.In dn̄io ſt.iii.car̄.
7 vi.ſerui.7 vi.uilli 7 vii.bord̄.cū.i.car̄.Ibi molin̄ redd̄.v.ſoɫ.7
viii.ac̄ p̄ti.7 xii.ac̄ paſturæ.Silua.vi.q̄ɫ in l̄g.7 iiii.q̄ɫ laɫ.
Valet.lxx.ſolid̄.

82 a *continued*

XXXVII.   TERRA WILLI DE BRAIOSE.

Wills de Braiose ten̄ de rege *WIDETONE*.7 Radulf
de eo.Abb̄ de Middeltun tenuit T.R.E.7 geldb̄ ꝑ.iii.hid̄.
Tra.e̅.iii.car̄.In dn̄io.e̅.i.car̄.cū.i.ſeruo.7 iii.uilli 7 iiii.
bord̄ cū.i.car̄.Ibi.xvi.ac̄ p̄ti.7 iiii.ac̄ paſturæ.Silua
.v.q̄ɫ l̄g.7 iiii.q̄ɫ laɫ.Valuit 7 ual.iii.lib̄.

Meadow, 10 acres; pasture, 7 furlongs in length and 3 furlongs
in width; woodland, 1 league long and ½ wide. 6 pigs.   E
The value was and is £3.
The son of Odo the Chamberlain claims these 3 hides. The King   E
has ordered that he should have the right to them.
Of these 3 hides, there is 1 which did not pay tax.

9 Geoffrey holds IWERNE (Stepleton) from William. Godwin held it
before 1066. It paid tax for 3 hides. Land for 3 ploughs.
In lordship 2 ploughs; 2 slaves; 1½ hides.   49
    6 villagers and 6 smallholders with 1 plough and 1½ hides. a 2
Woodland, 8 furlongs; pasture, 10 furlongs in length and 3
    furlongs in width. 1 cob; 6 cattle; 282 sheep.
The value was and is £4.

10 William also holds LITTLEWINDSOR. Alward held it before 1066.   E
It paid tax for 4 hides. Land for 3 ploughs. In lordship 2 ploughs;
2 slaves; 3 hides and 1 virgate.   49
    9 villagers and 2 smallholders with 1 plough and ½ hide and 1 virgate. b 1
Meadow, 30 acres; pasture, 8 furlongs in length and 6 furlongs
    in width; woodland, 6 furlongs in length and 3 furlongs in
    width. 1 cob; 10 cattle; 3 pigs; 10 sheep.
Value 60s; when he acquired it, 40s.

11 William also holds MAPPERTON. Aelmer held it before 1066.   E
It paid tax for 5 hides and 1 virgate of land. Land for 4 ploughs.
In lordship 3 ploughs; 6 slaves; 3 hides.   49
    6 villagers and 7 smallholders with 1 plough and 2 hides and 1 virgate. b 2
A mill which pays 5s; meadow, 8 acres; pasture, 12 acres;
    woodland 6 furlongs in length and 4 furlongs wide.
    2 cobs; 14 cattle; 16 pigs; 47 wethers; 30 goats.
Value 70s; when he acquired it, 60s.

Column 82a continued

37   **LAND OF WILLIAM OF BRAOSE**   E

1 William of Braose holds (Glanvilles) WOOTTON from the King, and
Ralph from him. The Abbot of Milton held it before 1066. It
paid tax for 3 hides. Land for 3 ploughs. In lordship 1 plough,
with 1 slave;
    3 villagers and 4 smallholders with 1 plough.
Meadow, 16 acres; pasture, 4 acres; woodland 5 furlongs long
    and 4 furlongs wide.
The value was and is £3.

Radulf ten de.W.in ead uilla.II.hid.Tra.ē.I.car.Ibi
st.II.ferui.7 I.bord.7 VI.ac pti.7 II.ac pasturæ.Silua.v.q̃z̃
lḡ.7 II.q̃z̃ lat.Valuit.xxx.fot.Modo.xL.folid.
Ipfe.W.ten dimid hid in HOLTONE.Tra.ē dim car.Valet
Dauid ten de.W.AISSE.Duo taini tenuer ⌐x.folid.
T.R.E.7 geldb ,p.II.hid.|Tra.ē.II.car.Ibi.ē.I.car.7 IIII.ferui. ✶
7 III.cofcez.7 x.ac pti.7 pastura.x.q̃z̃ lḡ.7 II.q̃z̃ lat.
Valuit 7 uat.xL.folid.
Ricard ten de.W.CVNELIZ.Brictuold tenuit T.R.E.
7 geldb ,p.I.hida 7 dim.Tra.ē.I.car 7 dim.In dñio.ē.I.car.
7 IIII.ac pti.7 Pastura.II.q̃z̃ lḡ.7 una q̃z̃ lat.Valuit 7 uat
Idē.W.ten in CRIC.dim hid 7 Walt de eo. ⌐xxx.folid.
Ednod tenuit T.R.E.Ibi st.II.bord 7 III.ac pti.7 III.ac filuæ
7 Pastura.VII.q̃z̃ lḡ.7 IIII.q̃z̃ lat.Valuit 7 uat.x.folid.
Idē Walt ten de.W.in ALVRETONE.III.virg tre 7 dim.
Tra.ē.I.car.q̃ ibi.ē cū.II.bord.7 una ac pti.7 I.q̃z̃ pasturæ.
82 b   ⌐Valuit 7 uat.xvi.fot.
Idē Walt ten de.W.in CHENOLLE.I.hid.Tra.ē.I.car.Ibi una ac pti.
Pastura.IIII.q̃z̃ lḡ.7 II.q̃z̃ lat.Valet.xx.folid.Sauuin tenuit T.R.E.
Idē.W.ten in RISTONE.I.hid 7 dimid.Tra.ē.I.car.q̃ ibi.ē 7 molin.   Burde tenuit
7 xx.ac pti.7 una leū pasturæ.Redd.xxx.fot.7 IIII.fextar mellis.
Idē.Walt ten de.W.in WEREGROTE.I.hid 7 III.v træ.Brictuin
tenuit T.R.E.Tra.ē.I.car 7 dimid.Ibi.ē uñ uilts 7 I.bord 7 dimid
molin redd.x.folid.Redd tot.xxvIII.folid.

2   Ralph holds 2 hides from William also in this village. Land for 1
plough. 2 slaves.
    1 smallholder.
    Meadow, 6 acres; pasture, 2 acres; woodland 5 furlongs long
      and 2 furlongs wide.
The value was 30s; now 40s.

3   William holds ½ hide in HOLTON himself. Land for ½ plough.
Value 10s.

4   David holds ASH from William. Two thanes held it before 1066.
It paid tax for 2½ hides. Land for 2 ploughs. 1 plough there;
3 slaves.
    3 Cottagers.
    Meadow, 10 acres; pasture 10 furlongs long and 2 furlongs wide.
The value was and is 40s.

5   Richard holds KIMMERIDGE from William. Brictwold held it before
1066. It paid tax for 1½ hides. Land for 1½ ploughs. In lordship
1 plough.
    Meadow, 4 acres; pasture 2 furlongs long and 1 furlong wide.
The value was and is 30s.

6   William also holds ½ hide in CREECH, and Walter from him.
Ednoth held it before 1066.
    2 smallholders.
    Meadow, 3 acres; woodland, 3 acres; pasture 7 furlongs long
      and 4 furlongs wide.
The value was and is 10s.

7   Walter also holds 3½ virgates of land from William in AFFLINGTON.
Land for 1 plough, which is there, with
    2 smallholders.
    Meadow, 1 acre; pasture, 1 furlong.
The value was and is 16s.

8   Walter also holds 1 hide from William in (Church) KNOWLE.   82 b
Land for 1 plough.
    Meadow, 1 acre; pasture 4 furlongs long and 2 furlongs wide.
Value 20s.
    Saewin held it before 1066.

9   W(illiam) also holds 1½ hides in RUSHTON. Land for 1 plough,
which is there. Burde held it.
    A mill; meadow, 20 acres; pasture, 1 league.
It pays 30s and 4 sesters of honey.

10   Walter also holds 1 hide and 3 virgates of land from William in
WORGRET. Brictwin held it before 1066. Land for 1½ ploughs.
    1 villager and 1 smallholder.
    ½ mill which pays 10s.
The whole pays 28s.

Robt́ teñ de.W. in *HAFELTONE*.II.hid́ træ.Ædelflete tenuit
T.R.E.Tra.e.I.car̃.Ibi st́.II.uilti cū.I.feruo.7 x.ac̃ p̃ti.Paſtura
una leū lḡ.7 dimid́ leū lat́.Valuit 7 ual.x.folid́.

Ricard́ teñ de.W. in *METMORE*.dimid́ hid́.Tra.e dimid́ car̃.
Ibi.e uñ uilts 7 uñ feruus.7 III.ac̃ p̃ti.Valet.x.folid́.

Ricard́ teñ de.W.in *HVNDRET PORBICHE*.VII.hid́ dimid́ v̄ miñ.
Duodecī taini tenueŕ T.R.E.7 poteraŕ ire q́ uoleb́.Tra.e.VII.car̃.
In dño st́.II.car̃.7 IIII.uilti 7 II.bord́.Valet.LXX.folid́.

De hac t́ra parte teñ uxor Hugoń.7 ibi ht́.II.car̃.7 IIII.uiltos.
7 v.bord́.7 Paſturā.I.leū lḡ.7 VI.q́ lat́.Valet.IIII.lib́.

Hunfrid́ teñ de.W.*ORGARESTONE*.Quinq̨ taini tenueŕ T.R.E.
7 geldb́ p.II.hid́.IIII.acris miñ.Tra.e.II.car̃.Ibi st́.VI.uilti.
7 VIII.ac̃ p̃ti.paſtura dimid́ leū lḡ.7 una q́ lat́.Valet.XL.fol.

XXXVIII.   TERRA WILLELMI DE SCOHIES.

Wilts de Scohies teñ de rege *CHENISTETONE*.Duo taini tenueŕ in paraǵ.
T.R.E.7 geldb́ p.VI.hid́.Tra.e.IIII.car̃.In dño st́.II.car̃.7 VI.ferui.7 v.uilti
7 v.bord́ cū.I.car̃.Ibi.II.molini redd́.XII.folid́.7 xx.ac̃ p̃ti.7 xx.ac̃ filuæ.
7 CCL.ac̃ paſturæ.Valuit.VII.lib́.Modo.VI.lib́.

Id́e.W.ten trā.v.taino̧ p uno Maner.in *CANDELLE*.Ibi st́.v.hidæ.
De ea st́ in dño.III.hidæ 7 dimid́.7 ibi.II.car̃.7 III.ferui.7 VII.uilti 7 III.
bord́ cū.III.car̃.Ibi moliñ redd́.IX.folid́.7 x.ac̃ p̃ti.7 XII.ac̃ filuæ.
Paſtura.VI.q́ lḡ.7.III.q́ lat́.Valuit 7 ual.VII.lib́.

11 Robert holds 2 hides of land from William in HETHFELTON. Aethelfled held them before 1066. Land for 1 plough.
2 villagers with 1 slave.
Meadow, 10 acres; pasture 1 league long and ½ league wide.
The value was and is 10s.

12 Richard holds ½ hide from William in SMEDMORE. Land for ½ plough.
1 villager and 1 slave.
Meadow, 3 acres.
Value 10s.

13 Richard holds 7 hides, less ½ virgate, from William in PURBECK Hundred. Twelve thanes held them before 1066; they could go where they would. Land for 7 ploughs. In lordship 2 ploughs;
4 villagers and 2 smallholders.
Value 70s.
The wife of Hugh son of Grip holds part of this land. She has 2 ploughs there and
4 villagers and 5 smallholders and
pasture 1 league long and 6 furlongs wide.
Value £4.

14 Humphrey holds WOOLGARSTON from William. Five thanes held it before 1066. It paid tax for 2 hides, less 4 acres. Land for 2 ploughs.
6 villagers.
Meadow, 8 acres; pasture ½ league long and 1 furlong wide.
Value 40s.

38   LAND OF WILLIAM OF ÉCOUIS   E

1 William of Écouis holds (West) KNIGHTON from the King. Two thanes held it jointly before 1066. It paid tax for 6 hides. Land for 4 ploughs. In lordship 2 ploughs; 6 slaves;
5 villagers and 5 smallholders with 1 plough.
2 mills which pay 12s; meadow, 20 acres; woodland, 20 acres; pasture, 250 acres.
The value was £7; now £6.

2 William also holds the land of 5 thanes as one manor in (Stourton) CAUNDLE. 5 hides, of which 3½ hides are in lordship; 2 ploughs there; 3 slaves;
7 villagers and 3 smallholders with 3 ploughs.
A mill which pays 9s; meadow, 10 acres; woodland, 12 acres; pasture 6 furlongs long and 3 furlongs wide.
The value was and is £7.

XXXIX. TERRA WALSCINI DE DWAI.

Walscin⁹ de Dvai ten⁷ de rege _WINTREBVRNE_.7 Walcher⁹
de eo.Aluuard⁷ᴬˡᵘᵘⁱⁿ tenuer̄ T.R.E.p.ɪɪ.Man̄.7 geldb p.vɪ.hid.Tra⁷.ē
ɪɪɪɪ.car̄.In dn̄io sē.ɪɪ.car̄.7 ɪɪɪ.ſerui.7 v.uiłłi 7 ɪɪɪ.borđ cū dim⁷ car̄.
Ibi.xɪɪ.āc p̄ti.7 vɪɪɪ.āc ſiluæ.Paſtura.ɪɪɪɪ.q̂ʑ lḡ.7 ɪɪɪ.q̂ʑ lat̄.
Valuit.vɪ.lib.Modo.ɪɪɪɪ.lib.

Wimer⁹ ten̄⁷ de.W.CANDELLE.Alſi tenuit T.R.E.7 geldb p.ɪɪɪ.hid.
Tra⁷.ē.ɪɪɪ.car̄.In dn̄io sē.ɪɪ.car̄.7 ɪɪ.ſerui.7 ɪɪ.uiłłi.7 ɪɪ.borđ cū.ɪ.
car̄.Ibi molin̄ redđ.ɪɪɪ.ſolid.7 x.āc p̄ti.7 ɪɪɪ.āc ſiluæ minutæ.
Valuit 7 ual.xʟ.ſolid.

.XL. TERRA WALERANNI.

Waleran̄ ten̄⁷ de rege _MANESTONE_.7 Warenger de eo.Traſmund⁹
tenuit T.R.E.7 geldb p.v.hid.Tra⁷.ē.vɪɪɪ.car̄.In dn̄io sē.ɪɪ.car̄.
7 ɪɪɪ.ſerui.7 x.uiłłi.7 vɪ.borđ cū.ɪɪ.car̄.Ibi.ɪɪ.molini redđ.xɪɪ.ſol.
7 xxv.āc p̄ti.Silua.ɪɪɪɪ.q̂ʑ lḡ.7 una q̂ʑ lat̄.Valuit.vɪ.lib.M̊.c.ſol.
Rannulf⁹ ten̄⁷ de.W.CHINTONE.Leuiet tenuit T.R.E.7 geldb p.ɪɪɪ.
hid.Tra⁷.ē.ɪɪ.car̄.In dn̄io.ē.ɪ.car̄ 7 dim⁷.7 ɪɪ.ſerui.7 vɪɪ.borđ cū dim⁷
car̄.Ibi.vɪɪɪ.āc p̄ti.7 ɪɪɪɪ.āc paſturæ.Valuit.xxx.ſol.Modo.ʟ.ſol.
Ipſe.W.ten̄ SVDTONE.Godmund⁹ tenuit T.R.E.7 geldb p.vɪɪɪ.hid.
Tra⁷.ē.vɪ.car̄.In dn̄io.ē.ɪ.car̄.cū.ɪ.ſeruo.7 xɪ.uiłłi 7 xɪɪ.borđ cū.ɪɪɪ.
car̄.Ibi molin̄ redđ.vɪɪ.ſot 7 vɪ.den̄.7 vɪ.āc p̄ti.7 xʟ.āc ſiluæ.
Valuit 7 ual.vɪɪɪ.lib.

39   LAND OF WALSCIN OF DOUAI   E

1   Walscin of Douai holds 'WINTERBORNE' from the King, and Walkhere from him. Alward and Alwin held it before 1066 as two manors. It paid tax for 6 hides. Land for 4 ploughs. In lordship 2 ploughs; 3 slaves;
    5 villagers and 3 smallholders with ½ plough.
    Meadow, 12 acres; woodland, 8 acres; pasture 4 furlongs long and 3 furlongs wide.
The value was £6; now £4.

2   Wimer holds (Stourton) CAUNDLE from William. Alsi held it before 1066. It paid tax for 3 hides. Land for 3 ploughs. In lordship 2 ploughs; 2 slaves;
    2 villagers and 2 smallholders with 1 plough.
    A mill which pays 3s; meadow, 10 acres; underwood, 3 acres.
The value was and is 40s.

40   LAND OF WALERAN   E

1   Waleran holds MANSTON from the King, and Warengar from him. Thrasemund held it before 1066. It paid tax for 5 hides. Land for 8 ploughs. In lordship 2 ploughs; 3 slaves;
    10 villagers and 6 smallholders with 2 ploughs.
    2 mills which pay 12s; meadow, 25 acres; woodland 4 furlongs long and 1 furlong wide.
The value was £6; now 100s.

2   Ranulf holds KINGTON from Waleran. Leofgeat held it before 1066. It paid tax for 3 hides. Land for 2 ploughs. In lordship 1½ ploughs; 2 slaves;
    7 smallholders with ½ plough.
    Meadow, 8 acres; pasture, 4 acres.
The value was 30s; now 50s.

3   Waleran holds SUTTON (Waldron) himself. Godmund held it before 1066. It paid tax for 8 hides. Land for 6 ploughs. In lordship 1 plough, with 1 slave;
    11 villagers and 12 smallholders with 3 ploughs.
    A mill which pays 7s 6d; meadow, 6 acres; woodland, 40 acres.
The value was and is £8.

Vrſo ten de . W .*WINTREBVRNE* . Alured tenuit T.R.E.7 geldb
ք.iiii.hid.Tra.ē.ii.caſ.q̄ ibi ſt.7 iii . ſerui.7 vi.uiłłi.7 q̄t xx.ac ք̄aſturæ
7 xxx.v.ac ք̄ti.Silua.ix.q̄ꝗ lḡ.7 ꝑna q̄ꝗ lat . Valuit 7 ual . xl . ſolid.

Azelin ten *DODESBERIE* . de Wat . Goduin tenuit T.R.E.7 ք.i.hida
geldb.Tra.ē.i.caſ.q̄ ibi.ē cū.iiii.bord.7 vii.ac ք̄ti.7 vi . ac ſiluæ.
paſtura.dimid leū lḡ.7 v.q̄ꝗ lat . Valuit 7 ual.xx . ſolid.

Ingelramn ten de.W.*FIFHIDE*.Vn tain tenuit T.R.E.7 geldb ք.v.
hid.Tra.ē.iii.caſ.q̄ ibi ſt cū.iiii.bord 7 iiii . ſeruis.Ibi moliñ redd
xl.den.7·xv.ac ք̄ti . Silua.viii . q̄ꝗ lḡ.7 iiii.q̄ꝗ lat.Valet.iiii.lib.

Beulf ten de Wat.*CNOLLE*.Vn tain tenuit T.R.E.7 lib erat cū hac tra.
7 geldb ք.i.hida.Tra.ē.i.caſ.q̄ ibi.ē cū.iii.ſeruis.Ibi paſtura.ii.q̄ꝗ lḡ.
7 tntd lat . Silua . i . q̄ꝗ lḡ.7 tntd lat . Valet . xxv . ſolid.
Hanc tenuit Waler de Wiłło comite . Modo ut dicit ten de rege.

82 c

Ipſe Waler ten *NEWETONE* . Aluuard tenuit T.R.E.7 geldb ք.vi.hid.
Tra.ē.vii.caſ.De ea.ē dim hida in dñio.7 ibi.ii.caſ.7 v.ſerui.7 vii .uiłłi
7 xiiii.bord cū.v.caſ.Ibi.ii.molini redd.xx.ſolid.7 xviii.ac ք̄ti.Paſ
tura.xiiii.q̄ꝗ lḡ.7 vii.q̄ꝗ lat . Silua . v.q̄ꝗ lḡ.7 iii.q̄ꝗ lat . Valet.x .lib.

Ogeri ten de.W.*TOLRE*.Aluuard tenuit T.R.E.7 geldb ք.v.hid.
Tra.ē.iiii.caſ.In dñio ſt.ii.caſ.7 iii.ſerui.7 iiii.uiłłi 7 v.bord.cū.i.caſ.
Ibi moliñ redd.xxx.den.7 xv.ac ք̄ti.Paſtura.xii.q̄ꝗ lḡ.7 x.q̄ꝗ lat.
Silua.v.q̄ꝗ lḡ.7 iii.q̄ꝗ lat.Valuit.iii.lib.Modo.iiii.lib.

4 Urso holds 'WINTERBORNE' from Waleran. Alfred held it before
   1066. It paid tax for 4 hides. Land for 2 ploughs, which are there;
   3 slaves.
   6 villagers.
   Pasture, 80 acres; meadow, 35 acres; woodland 9 furlongs long
       and 1 furlong wide.
   The value was and is 40s.

5 Azelin holds DUDSBURY from Waleran. Godwin held it before
   1066. It paid tax for 1 hide. Land for 1 plough, which is there,
   with
   4 smallholders.
   Meadow, 7 acres; woodland, 6 acres; pasture ½ league long and
       5 furlongs wide.
   The value was and is 20s.

6 Ingelrann holds FIFEHEAD (Neville) from Waleran. A thane held it
   before 1066. It paid tax for 5 hides. Land for 3 ploughs, which
   are there, with
   4 smallholders and 4 slaves.
   A mill which pays 40d; meadow, 15 acres; woodland 8 furlongs
       long and 4 furlongs wide.
   Value £4.

7 Beowulf holds (Church) KNOWLE from Waleran. A thane held it
   before 1066; he was free with this land. It paid tax for 1 hide.
   Land for 1 plough, which is there, with 3 slaves.
   Pasture 2 furlongs long and as wide; woodland 1 furlong long
       and as wide.
   Value 25s.
   Waleran held it from Earl William. Now, as he states, he holds
   it from the King.

8 Waleran holds (Maiden) NEWTON himself. Alward held it before   82 c
   1066. It paid tax for 6 hides. Land for 7 ploughs, of which ½
   hide is in lordship; 2 ploughs there; 5 slaves;
   7 villagers and 14 smallholders with 5 ploughs.
   2 mills which pay 20s; meadow, 18 acres; pasture 14 furlongs
       long and 7 furlongs wide; woodland 5 furlongs long and 3
       furlongs wide.
   Value £10.

9 Oger holds TOLLER from Waleran. Alward held it before 1066.
   It paid tax for 5 hides. Land for 4 ploughs. In lordship 2 ploughs;
   3 slaves;
   4 villagers and 5 smallholders with 1 plough.
   A mill which pays 30d; meadow, 15 acres; pasture 12 furlongs
       long and 10 furlongs wide; woodland 5 furlongs long and 3
       furlongs wide.
   The value was £3; now £4.

TERRA WALTERIJ DE CLAVILE.

Walterivs de Glanvile ^{t Clavile} teñ de rege *ALVERONETVNE*. Briꝗric te
nuit T.R.E.7 geldb ꝑ.ii.hid 7 una v̅ træ 7 dim̅.Tra.e̅.ii.car̅ 7 dimid.
In dn̅io st̅.ii.car̅.cu̅.i.feruo 7 i.bord.Ibi.iii.ac̅ p̅ti.7 iiii.ac̅ filuæ minutæ.
Pafturæ.iiii.q̇ꝛ in lg̅ 7 lat̅.Valuit 7 ual.l.folid.

Ide̅ teñ *CNOLLE*.Bern tenuit T.R.E.7 geldb ꝑ.ii.hid.Tra.e̅.ii.car̅.
In dn̅io.e̅.i.car̅ cu̅.i.feruo.7 ii.uiꞁꞁi 7 iii.ac̅ p̅ti.7 iii.q̇ꝛ pafturæ lg̅.7 tntd
in lat̅.Valuit 7 ual xl.folid.

Ide̅ ter̅ *HOLNE*.Eldred tenuit T.R.E.7 geldb ꝑ.ii.hid.7 una v̅ træ.Tra.e̅
ii.car̅.In dn̅io.e̅.i.car̅.7 iiii.uiꞁꞁi.7 x.ac̅ p̅ti.7 iii.ac̅ filuæ.Paftura.vi.
q̇rent lg̅.7 tntd lat̅.Valuit 7 ual.xx.folid.

Ide̅ teñ *CVME*.Duo taini tenuer̅ T.R.E.7 geldb ꝑ.iii.hid.Tra.e̅.iii.car̅.
In dn̅io.e̅.i.car̅.7 ii.ferui.7 ii.uiꞁꞁi 7 i.bord cu̅.i.car̅ 7 dim̅.Ibi.ii.ac̅
p̅ti.7 ii.q̇ꝛ pafturæ int lg̅ 7 lat̅.Valuit 7 ual.lx.fot.

Ide̅ teñ *MORDVNE*.Quatuor taini tenuer̅ T.R.E.7 geldb ꝑ.iii.hid
7 ii.v̅ træ 7 dim̅.Tra.e̅.iii.car̅.In dn̅io.e̅.i.car̅.7 viii.uiꞁꞁi 7 x.bord
cu̅.ii.car̅.Ibi moliñ redd.xlv.denar̅.7 xiiii.ac̅ p̅ti.7 iii.leu̅ paf
✿ture int lg̅ 7 lat̅.Silua.ii.q̇ꝛ lg̅.7 una q̇ꝛ lat̅.Valuit 7 ual.lx.folid.

41   LAND OF WALTER OF CLAVILLE   E

1 Walter of Glanville or Claville holds AFFLINGTON from the King.
Brictric held it before 1066. It paid tax for 2 hides and 1½
virgates of land. Land for 2½ ploughs. In lordship 2 ploughs, with
1 slave;
   1 smallholder.
   Meadow, 3 acres; underwood, 4 acres; pasture, 4 furlongs in
     length and width. 2 cobs; 10 cattle; 8 pigs; 50 sheep.
The value was and is 50s.

E
E
62
a 1
E
E

  He also holds

2 (Church) KNOWLE. Beorn held it before 1066. It paid tax for 2
hides. Land for 2 ploughs. In lordship 1 plough and 1 hide and 1 virgate,
with 1 slave;
   2 villagers (who have) 3 virgates.
   Meadow, 3 acres; pasture, 3 furlongs long and as much in width.
    1 cob; 11 cattle; 57 sheep.
The value was and is 40s.

E
62
a 2

3 (East) HOLME. Aldred held it before 1066. It paid tax for 2 hides
and 1 virgate of land. Land for 2 ploughs. In lordship 1 plough;
½ hide.
   4 villagers (have) 1½ hides and 1 virgate.
   Meadow, 10 acres; woodland, 3 acres; pasture 6 furlongs long
    and as wide. 1 cob; 5 cattle.
The value was and is 20s.

E
62
a 3

4 COOMBE (Keynes). Two thanes held it before 1066. It paid tax for
3 hides. Land for 3 ploughs. In lordship 1 plough; 2 slaves; 2 hides.
   2 villagers and 1 smallholder with 1½ ploughs and 1 hide.
   Meadow, 2 acres; pasture, 2 furlongs in both length and width.
    2 cobs; 5 cattle; 5 pigs.
The value was and is 60s.

E
62
b 1

5 MORDEN. Four thanes held it before 1066. It paid tax for 3 hides
and 2½ virgates of land. Land for 3 ploughs. In lordship 1 plough;
1½ virgates.
   8 villagers and 10 smallholders with 2 ploughs and 3 hides and 1 virgate.
   A mill which pays 45d; meadow, 14 acres; pasture, 3 leagues
    in both length and width; woodland 2 furlongs long and 1
    furlong wide. 14 pigs; 85 sheep; 5 goats.
✠ The value was and is 60s.

E
62
b 2

Column 82c continues after Ch. 42

TERRA BALDVINI.

.XLII. B^{viceco̅m}ALDVINVS ten de rege *WERNE* . Seuuard tenuit T.R.E.7 geldb̄ ꝑ.VIII . hid . Tra . e̅ . VIII . car̄ . In dn̄io s̅t . III . car.

7 IIII . ferui . 7 IIII . uilłi 7 IX . bord cu̅ . IIII . car̄ . Ibi . II . molini redd . XII . foł . 7 XXX . ãc p̄ti . Paſtura . IX . q̃ʒ lg̅ . 7 VI . q̃ʒ lat̅.

Valuit . XV . lib̄ . Modo . X . lib̄.

.XLIII. TERRA BERENGER GIFARD.

B^{Gifard}ERENGER ten de rege *BRIDIE* . Harding tenuit T.R.E.7 geldb̄ ꝑ.IIII.

hid . Tra . e̅ . III . car̄ . In dn̄io . e̅ . I . car̄ . 7 II . ferui . 7 V . uilłi 7 VII . bord cu̅ . II.

car̄ . Ibi molin̄ redd . X . foł . 7 XV . ãc p̄ti . 7 paſtura . III . q̃ʒ lg̅ . 7 una lat̅.

Valet . III . lib̄ . modo . IIII . lib̄.

.XLII. TERRA OSBERNI GIFARD.

O^{Gifard}SBERNVS ten de rege *HILLE* . Trafmund tenuit T.R.E.7 geldb̄ ꝑ . II . hid . Tra . e̅ . I . car̄ . q̃ ibi . e̅ in dn̄io . 7 XX . ãc p̄ti . 7 XX . ãc paſturæ.

Valuit 7 uał . XX . folid.

.XLV. TERRA ALVREDI HISPANENSIS

A⁹LVRED Hiſpaniens ten de rege *TORNEWORDE* . Aluui tenuit T.R.E.7 geldb̄ ꝑ . V . hid . Tra . e̅ . VI . car̄ . In dn̄io s̅t . IIII . car̄ . 7 IIII . ferui.

7 VII . uilłi . 7 VIII . bord . cu̅ . I . car̄ . Ibi . X . ãc p̄ti . 7 X . q̃ʒ paſturæ in lg̅.

7 IIII . In lat̅ . Silua . X . q̃ʒ in lg̅ . 7 V . q̃ʒ in lat̅ . Valuit . VI . lib̄ . modo . X . lib̄.

Ch. 42 is written on an inserted piece of parchment, folio 81 a,b, and directed here by transposition signs

LAND OF BALDWIN   E   81 a,b

42

1 Baldwin the Sheriff holds IWERNE (Courtney) from the King.
Siward held it before 1066. It paid tax for 8 hides. Land for 8
ploughs. In lordship 3 ploughs; 4 slaves;
   4 villagers and 9 smallholders with 4 ploughs.
   2 mills which pay 12s; meadow, 30 acres; pasture 9 furlongs
     long and 6 furlongs wide.
The value was £15; now £10.

Column 82c continued

LAND OF BERENGAR GIFFARD   E

43

1 Berengar Giffard holds BREDY from the King. Harding held it
before 1066. It paid tax for 4 hides. Land for 3 ploughs. In
lordship 1 plough; 2 slaves;
   5 villagers and 7 smallholders with 2 ploughs.
   A mill which pays 10s; meadow, 15 acres; pasture 3 furlongs
     long and 1 wide.
Value £3; now £4.

LAND OF OSBERN GIFFARD   E

44

1 Osbern Giffard holds (Gold) HILL from the King. Thrasemund
held it before 1066. It paid tax for 2 hides. Land for 1 plough,
which is there, in lordship.
   Meadow, 20 acres; pasture, 20 acres.
The value was and is 20s.

LAND OF ALFRED OF 'SPAIN'   E

45

1 Alfred of 'Spain' holds TURNWORTH from the King. Alwy held it
before 1066. It paid tax for 5 hides. Land for 6 ploughs. In
lordship 4 ploughs; 4 slaves;
   7 villagers and 8 smallholders with 1 plough.
   Meadow, 10 acres; pasture, 10 furlongs in length and 4 in
     width; woodland 10 furlongs in length and 5 furlongs
     in width.
The value was £6; now £10.

.XLVI. TERRA MATHIV DE MORETANIA.

Mathew de Moretanie teñ de rege *MELEBVRNE* . Johs tenuit
T.R.E.7 geldb ᵱ.v.hid.Tra.e̅.iiii.car̅.In dn̅io st̅.ii.car̅.cu̅.i.uillo
7 ix.bord.Ibi moliñ redd.xxxii.denar̅.7 v.ac̅ p̃ti.7 vi.q̃ʑ filuæ minutæ.
Ide̅ teñ *OGRE* . Johs tenuit T.R.E.7 geldb ⸋⸍Valuit 7 ual.c.fol.
ᵱ.x.hid una v̊ miñ.Tra.e̅.viii.car̅.In dn̅io st̅.ii.car̅.7 vi.ferui.
7 vii.uilti 7 vi.cofcez cu̅.v.car̅.Ibi moliñ redd.vi.fol.7 xx.ac̅ p̃ti.
7 una leu̅ pafturæ in lḡ.7 dim̅ leu̅ lat̅.Valuit 7 ual.x.lib

.XLVII. TERRA ROGERIJ ARVNDEL.

Rogerivs Arundel teñ de rege *WINDELHA̅* . Alnod̊ tenuit T.R.E.
7 geldb ᵱ.ii.hid.Tra.e̅.i.car̅ 7 dim̅.In dn̅io.e̅.i.car̅.cu̅.i.feruo.Ibi.iii.ac̅
p̃ti.7 iiii.q̃ʑ filuæ.Valuit.xxx.fol.Modo.xx.fol.Rog teñ de Rogerio.
Ipfe Rog teñ *MELEBERIE* . Bricnod tenuit T.R.E.7 geldb ᵱ.vi.hid.
Tra.e̅.iiii.car̅.Ibi st̅.iiii.uilti 7 vii.bord 7 iiii.ferui.cu̅.ii.car̅.Ibi moliñ
redd.v.folid.7 xii.ac̅ p̃ti.7 iii.q̃ʑ pafturæ.Silua.x.q̃ʑ lḡ.7 iiii.q̃ʑ lat̅.
Valuit 7 ual.iiii.lib.
Ipfe teñ *CELBERGE* . Aluert tenuit T.R.E.7 geldb ᵱ.v.hid.Tra.e̅.ii.
car̅.In dn̅io.e̅.i.car̅.cu̅.i.feruo.7 iiii.uilti 7 vii.bord cu̅.i.car̅.Ibi.ii.ac̅
p̃ti.7 una q̃ʑ pafturæ in lḡ.7 una lat̅.Silua.iiii.q̃ʑ lḡ.7 ii.q̃ʑ lat̅.Valuit
Robt̅.teñ de Rog *BLENEFORD* . Aieluert tenuit T.R.E ⸋⸍7 ual.l.folid.
7.geldb ᵱ.v.hid.Tra.e̅.iiii.car̅.In dn̅io st̅.iii.car̅.7 iiii.ferui.7 i.uilts

46   LAND OF MATTHEW OF MORTAGNE   E

1 Matthew of Mortagne holds MILBORNE (St. Andrew) from the King. John held it before 1066. It paid tax for 5 hides. Land for 4 ploughs. In lordship 2 ploughs, with
  1 villager and 9 smallholders.
  A mill which pays 32d; meadow, 5 acres; underwood, 6 furlongs.
The value was and is 100s.

2 He also holds OWERMOIGNE. John held it before 1066. It paid tax for 10 hides, less 1 virgate. Land for 8 ploughs. In lordship 2 ploughs; 6 slaves;
  7 villagers and 6 Cottagers with 5 ploughs.
  A mill which pays 6s; meadow, 20 acres; pasture, 1 league in
    length and ½ league wide.
The value was and is £10.

47   LAND OF ROGER ARUNDEL   E

1 Roger Arundel holds WYNDLAM from the King. Alnoth held it before 1066. It paid tax for 2 hides. Land for 1½ ploughs. In lordship 1 plough, with 1 slave.
  Meadow, 3 acres; woodland, 4 furlongs. 4 cattle; 8 pigs.
The value was 30s; now 20s.
Roger *de Margella* holds from Roger.   E 50 / a 1 / E

2 Roger holds MELBURY himself. Brictnoth held it before 1066. It paid tax for 6 hides. Land for 4 ploughs. Roger has 3 hides and 1 virgate.
  4 villagers, 7 smallholders and 4 slaves with 2 ploughs
  and 2 hides and 3 virgates.
  A mill which pays 5s; meadow, 12 acres; pasture, 3 furlongs;
  woodland 10 furlongs long and 4 furlongs wide. 3 cattle; 15 pigs.
The value was and is £4.   E 50 / a 2

3 He holds CHELBOROUGH himself. Aethelfrith held it before 1066. It paid tax for 5 hides. Land for 2 ploughs. In lordship 1 plough and 3 hides, with 1 slave;
  4 villagers and 7 smallholders with 1 plough and 2 hides.
  Meadow, 2 acres; pasture, 1 furlong in length and 1 wide;
  woodland 4 furlongs long and 2 furlongs wide. 12 unbroken mares; 5 cattle; 5 pigs.
The value was and is 50s.   50 / a 3 / E / E

4 Robert Tilly holds (Langton Long) BLANDFORD from Roger. Aethelfrith held it before 1066. It paid tax for 5 hides. Land for 4 ploughs. In lordship 3 ploughs; 4 slaves; 4 hides.   50 / b 1

7 ıı.borđ Ibi.ıııɪ.ač p̃ti.7 vı.q̃ɀ paſturæ in l̄g.7 ıııı.q̃ɀ in lat̃,
Valuit 7 ual.ıııı.lib.

Ipſe Rog̃ ten̄ *Bessintone*. Ailmar tenuit T.R.E.;7 gelđɓ
p.ıx.hiđ 7 dım̃.Tra.ē.vıı.car̃.In dñio ſt̃.ıı.car̃.7 vııı.ſerui.
7 ıııı.uiłłi 7 vııı.borđ cū.ıııı.car̃.Ibi.ıııı.ač p̃ti.7 vııı.q̃ɀ
paſture in l̄g.7 una q̃ɀ ı̃ lat̃.Valuit.ıııı.lib.modo.vı.lib.
Hugo ten̄ de Rog̃ *Povrestoch*.Ailmar tenuit T.R.E.
7 gelđɓ p.vı.hiđ.Tra.ē.vı.car̃.In dñio ſt̃.ıı.car̃ 7 dım̃.
7 v.ſerui.7 v.uiłłi 7 ıx.borđ cū.ıı.car̃ 7 dım̃.Ibi.ıı.mơ
lini redđ.ıı.ſơł.7 xııı.ač p̃ti.7 xv.q̃ɀ paſturæ in l̄g.
7 ıı.q̃ɀ lat̃.Silua.xı.q̃ɀ l̄g.7 ıı.q̃ɀ 7 dım̃ lat̃.
Valuit.ıııı.lib.Modo.vı.lib.
Radulf̃ ten̄ de.Ro.*Brocheshale*.Ailmar tenuit T.R.E.
7 gelđɓ p.x.hiđ.Tra.ē.vııı.car̃.In dñio ſt̃.ıı.car̃.7 ıııı.
ſerui.7 ıııı.uiłłi 7 xıııı.borđ cū.ıı.car̃.Ibi molin̄ redđ.v.ſơł.
7 v.ač p̃ti.7 vııı.q̃ɀ paſturæ in l̄g.7 ıı.q̃ɀ 7 dım̃ lat̃.Silua.
vııı.q̃ɀ l̄g.7 ıı.q̃ɀ lat̃.Valet.c.ſoliđ   ſ̃ ıı.lib.
In ead̃ uilla ten̄ Wiłłs de Rog̃.ııı.hiđ.Ibi ſt̃.ıııı.uiłłi.Valej̃
7 un̄ miles ten̄ de Rog̃.ı.hidã.7 ualet.xx.ſoliđ.
Int̃ tot̃ ualet c̃ɀ.ıx.lib.Q̃do recep̃.ıııı.lib.
Wido ten̄ de Rog̃ *Povertone*.Aluuin̄ 7 Vlf tenuer̃
p.ıı.hiđ.Tra.ē.ıı.car̃.In dñio.ē.ı.car̃.7 ibi ſt̃.ıx.coſcez.
7 vı.ač p̃ti.7 xv.q̃ɀ paſturæ in l̄g 7 lat̃.Valet.xxx.ſoliđ.

1 villager and 2 smallholders.
Meadow, 4 acres; pasture, 6 furlongs in length and 4 furlongs
in width. 15 pigs; 140 sheep.   E
The value was and is £4.

5   Roger holds BEXINGTON himself. Aelmer held it before 1066.   82 d
It paid tax for 9½ hides. Land for 7 ploughs. In lordship 2
ploughs; 8 slaves; 4 hides and ½ virgate.
    4 villagers and 8 smallholders with 4 ploughs and 5 hides, less   50
1 virgate.   b 2
Meadow, 4 acres; pasture, 8 furlongs in length and 1 furlong
in width. 2 cows; 5 pigs; 136 sheep.
The value was £4; now £6.

6   Hugh holds POWERSTOCK from Roger. Aelmer held it before 1066.
It paid tax for 6 hides. Land for 6 ploughs. In lordship 2½
ploughs; 5 slaves; 3 hides.   50
    5 villagers and 9 smallholders with 2½ ploughs and 3 hides.   b 3
2 mills which pay 3s; meadow, 13 acres; pasture, 15 furlongs
in length and 2 furlongs wide; woodland 11 furlongs long
and 2½ furlongs wide. 2 cobs; 4 cattle; 13 pigs; 158 sheep; 16 goats.
The value was £4; now £6.

7   Ralph holds WRAXALL from Roger. Aelmer held it before 1066.   E
It paid tax for 10 hides. Land for 8 ploughs. In lordship 2   51
ploughs; 4 slaves; 3½ hides.   a 1
    4 villagers and 14 smallholders with 2 ploughs and 2½ hides.
A mill which pays 5s; meadow, 5 acres; pasture 8 furlongs in
length and 2½ furlongs wide; woodland 8 furlongs long and
3 furlongs wide. 2 cows; 17 pigs; 60 sheep.
Value 100s.
    Also in this village William holds 3 hides from Roger.   E
4 villagers.   E
Value £3.
    A man-at-arms holds 1 hide from Roger; value 20s.   E
In total, value of the manor £9; when he acquired it £4.

8   Guy holds POORTON from Roger. Alwin and Ulf held it as (...)   E
2 hides. Land for 2 ploughs. In lordship 1 plough; 1 hide and 1 virgate.   E
9 Cottagers (have) 3 virgates.   51
Meadow, 6 acres; pasture, 15 furlongs in length and width.   E   a 2
Woodland, 15 acres. 1 mare; 13 cattle; 32 pigs; 108 sheep; 32 goats.
Value 30s; when Roger received it, 20s.

Ipfe Rog̵ ten̄ O*RDE* . Ailuert tenuit T.R.E. 7 geld̵b ꝑ. xvi. de rege.
hid̵ 7 dimid̵. 7 dimid̵ v̄. Tra. ē. xii . car̄. In dn̄io s̄t . iiii . car̄.
7 viii . ſerui. 7 ix . uilti 7 viii . bord̵ cū . ix . car̄, Ibi molin̄
redd̵. vii . fot 7 dimid̵. 7 xv. ac̄ p̄ti. 7 xv. q̄q̄ | in l̄g 7 in lat̄. paſturæ
7 vii . q̄q̄ ſiluæ int̄ l̄g 7 lat̄ . Valuit 7 ual̄. xvi. lib̵ 7 vii . fot
Rob̄t ten̄ de Rog̵ R*AGINTONE* . Noū̄e taini �eꝑ 7 vi . den̄
libe tenuer̄ T.R.E. 7 geld̵b ꝑ. ii . hid̵. 7 dimid̵. 7 iiij . parte uni. v̄ min̄. ta
Tra. ē. ii . car̄ . Ibi. iiii . ac̄ p̄ti. 7 xiiii . q̄q̄ paſturæ in l̄g
7 lat̄ . Valet . xl. ſolid̵.
Ipfe. R. ten̄ *WRDE* . Aluuard̵ tenuit T.R.E. 7 geld̵b ꝑ dim̄
hida. Tra. ē dim̄ car̄. q̄ ibi. ē cū . iii . bord̵ . Valet . x . fot.
Ipfe Rog̵ ten̄ H*ERESTONE* . Her tenuit T.R.E. 7 geld̵b
ꝑ. ii . partib̵ uni hidæ. Tra. ē dim̄ car̄. Ibi. ii . ac̄ p̄ti 7 dim̄. ab̵
Valet . x . ſolid̵.

.XLVIII.   TERRA SERLONIS DE BVRCI.
Serlo de Bvrci ten̄ de rege P*IDERE* . Herald̵ tenuit com̄
T.R.E. 7 geld̵b ꝑ. x . hid̵ . Tra. ē. vi . car̄. In dn̄io s̄t. iii . car̄
7 ii . ſerui. 7 xii . uilti 7 xii . bord̵ cū . iii . car̄. Ibi molin̄ redd̵
. iii . fot. 7 xl . ac̄ p̄ti. 7 xx. ac̄ ſiluæ . Paſtura. xvi. q̄q̄ l̄g.
7 iiii . q̄q̄ lat̄ . Valet . x . lib̵.
Id̄e ten̄ *WITECLIVE*. Aluuard̵ tenuit T.R.E. 7 geld̵b ꝑ. iii .
hid̵. Tra. ē. iii . car̄. In dn̄io s̄t . ii . car̄. 7 ii . ſerui. 7 i . uilts
7 iiii . bord̵. Ibi. vi. q̄q̄ paſturæ in l̄g. 7 una q̄q̄ lat̄.
Valuit 7 ual̄. lx . ſolid̵.

9 Roger holds WORTH (Matravers) himself. Aethelfrith held it from
the King before 1066. It paid tax for 16½ hides and ½ virgate.
Land for 12 ploughs. In lordship 4 ploughs; 8 slaves; 3½ hides
and ½ virgate.
    9 villagers and 8 smallholders with 9 ploughs and 13 hides.
A mill which pays 7½s; meadow, 15 acres; pasture, 15 furlongs
in length and in width; woodland, 7 furlongs in both length
and width. 13 pigs; 250 sheep.
The value was and is £16 7s 6d.

      E
      51
      b 1
      E

10 Robert Tilly holds ROLLINGTON from Roger. Nine thanes held it
freely before 1066. It paid tax for 2½ hides, less the fourth part
of 1 virgate. Land for 2 ploughs.
    Meadow, 4 acres; pasture, 14 furlongs in length and width.
Value 40s.

      E
      51
      b 2

11 Roger holds WORTH (Matravers) himself. Alward held it before
1066. It paid tax for ½ hide. Land for ½ plough, which is there,
with
    3 smallholders.
Value 10s.

      E
      E
      52
      a 1

12 Roger holds HERSTON himself. Her held it before 1066. It paid tax
for 2 parts of 1 hide. Land for ½ plough.
    Meadow, 2½ acres.
Value 10s.

      E
      52
      a 2

48   LAND OF SERLO OF BURCY   E

1 Serlo of Burcy holds WATERSTON from the King. Earl Harold held
it before 1066. It paid tax for 10 hides. Land for 6 ploughs. In
lordship 3 ploughs; 2 slaves; 6 hides and 1 virgate.
    12 villagers and 12 smallholders with 3 ploughs and 3 hides
and 3 virgates.
    A mill which pays 3s; meadow, 40 acres; woodland, 20 acres;
pasture 16 furlongs long and 4 furlongs wide.
1 cob; 10 cattle; 400 sheep, less 7.
Value £10.

      53
      E a 1
      E

2 He also holds WHITECLIFF. Alward held it before 1066. It paid tax
for 3 hides. Land for 3 ploughs. In lordship 2 ploughs; 2 slaves;
2½ hides.
    1 villager and 4 smallholders (have) ½ hide.
    Pasture, 6 furlongs in length and 1 furlong wide. 50 sheep.
The value was and is 60s.

      E
      53
      a 2
      E

Aivlfvs ten de rege *BLANEFORDE* . Leueua tenuit T.R.E.
7 geldb ꝑ una hida 7 dim . Tra.ē.ɪ.car.q̄ ibi.ē.7 v.ac p̄ti.
7 ɪɪ.q̄ꝗ̄ pasturæ . Valuit . xx . sol , Modo . xxx . solid.

Ipfe Aiulf ten *MORDVNE* . Ailueua tenuit T.R.E.7 geldb
ꝑ.ɪɪɪ.v̄ træ . Tra.ē dimid car. Valet . xxv . solid.

Ipfe Aiulf ten *HAME* . Quinꝗ̄ taini tenuer T.R.E.7 geldb
ꝑ.vɪ.hid . Tra.ē. v. car . In dn̄io st̄. ɪɪ. car . 7 ɪɪɪɪ.ferui.7 vɪ.
bord cū . ɪɪ. car. Ibi.xx.ac p̄ti.7 vɪɪɪ.q̄ꝗ̄ pasturæ in lḡ.7 totid
in lat̄.7 ɪɪɪɪ.q̄ꝗ̄ siluæ in lḡ.7 totid lat̄ . Valet . ɪɪɪɪ.lib 7 x. sol.

Ipfe.A.ten *SELAVESTVNE* . Duo taini tenuer T.R.E.
7 geldb ꝑ.ɪɪɪɪ . hid.7 una v̄ tre 7 dim . Tra.ē.ɪɪɪ. car.In dn̄io
st̄.ɪɪ.car̄.7 ɪɪ.ferui.7 v.uilli 7 ɪ.bord cū.ɪ.car̄.Ibi.xxx.
ac p̄ti.7 ɪɪɪɪ.q̄ꝗ̄ pasturæ in lḡ.7 ɪɪ.q̄ꝗ̄ lat̄. Valet . lx . solid.

Ide.A.ten *TERENTE*. Vn̄ lib hō tenuit T.R.E.7 geldb ꝑ.ɪɪ.
hid. Tra.ē.ɪ.car̄.q̄ ibi.ē in dn̄io.7 ɪɪɪ.uilli 7 ɪɪ.bord
7 ɪɪ.ferui.Ibi.xv.ac pasturæ.7 tantd siluæ. Valet . xl . sol.

Ide.A.ten *STIBEMETVNE*. Vn̄ tain tenuit T.R.E.7 geldb
ꝑ una hida . Tra.ē.ɪ.car̄.q̄ ibi.ē in dn̄io.7 ɪɪɪɪ.ferui.
Ibi. ɪɪɪ.ac pasturæ.7 xxv.ac siluæ. Valet . xx . solid.

83 a

Ide Aiulf ten *CEOTEL*.7 Airard de eo.Vn̄ tain tenuit T.R.E.
7 geldb ꝑ.ɪ.hida.Tra.ē.ɪ.car̄.Ibi st̄ xɪɪ.ac pasturæ. Valet
Ipfe.A.ten *FERNHA*.un̄ tain tenuit T.R.E.ʄ xx.solid.

49 LAND OF AIULF THE CHAMBERLAIN E

1 Aiulf holds BLANDFORD (St. Mary) from the King. Leofeva held it before 1066. It paid tax for 1½ hides. Land for 1 plough, which is there.

Meadow, 5 acres; pasture, 2 furlongs.

The value was 20s; now 30s.

2 Aiulf holds MORDEN himself. Aelfeva held it before 1066. It paid tax for 3 virgates of land. Land for ½ plough.

Value 25s.

3 Aiulf holds HAMPRESTON himself. Five thanes held it before 1066. It paid tax for 6 hides. Land for 5 ploughs. In lordship 2 ploughs; 4 slaves;

6 smallholders with 2 ploughs.

Meadow, 20 acres; pasture, 8 furlongs in length and as many in width; woodland, 4 furlongs in length and as many wide.

Value £4 10s.

4 Aiulf holds *SELAVESTUNE* himself. Two thanes held it before 1066. It paid tax for 4 hides and 1½ virgates of land. Land for 3 ploughs. In lordship 2 ploughs; 2 slaves;

5 villagers and 1 smallholder with 1 plough.

Meadow, 30 acres; pasture, 4 furlongs in length and 2 furlongs wide.

Value 60s.

5 Aiulf also holds 'TARRANT'. A free man held it before 1066. It paid tax for 2 hides. Land for 1 plough, which is there, in lordship;

3 villagers, 2 smallholders and 2 slaves.

Pasture, 15 acres; woodland, as much.

Value 40s.

6 Aiulf also holds STUBHAMPTON. A thane held it before 1066. It paid tax for 1 hide. Land for 1 plough, which is there, in lordship; 4 slaves.

Pasture, 3 acres; woodland, 25 acres.

Value 20s.

7 Aiulf also holds CHETTLE, and Aethelhard from him. A thane held it before 1066. It paid tax for 1 hide. Land for 1 plough. 83 a

Pasture, 12 acres.

Value 20s.

8 Aiulf holds FARNHAM himself. A thane held it before 1066.

7 geldb ꝑ.ıı.hıđ q̄ ibi sꞇ cū.ı.ſeruo.7 ıııı.borđ.Ibi.x.

ãc paſturæ.7 ııı.q̂⁊ ſıluæ in l͞g.7 ıı.q̂⁊ in laꞇ.Valet.xxx.

Iđē.A.teñ BRADELEGE.Vñ taiñ tenuit T.R.E.∠ſolıđ.

7 geldb ꝑ.ıııı.hıđ.Ťra.ē.ıı.caꞃ.In dn̄io.ē.ı.caꞃ.7 ıı.ſerui.

7 uñ uıꞛꞇs 7 ıı.borđ cū dım̄ caꞃ.Ibı.ı.aꞓ p̂ti.7 ıı.q̂⁊ paſturæ.

7 una q̂⁊ ſılue in l͞g.7 dım̄ in laꞇ.Valuit.xL.ſol.m̊.Lx.ſol.

Ipſe.A.teñ TATETVN.Vñ taiñ tenuit T.R.E.de eccꞗa

cernelienſi 7 n̄ poterat ab ea ſeparari.7 geldb ꝑ.ııı.hıđ.

Ťra.ē.ıı.caꞃ.In dn̄io.ē.ı.caꞃ.7 ıı.ſerui.7 uñ uıꞛꞇs 7 ıııı.borđ.

Ibi.ıııı.ãc p̂ti.7 ıı.q̂⁊ paſturæ in l͞g 7 laꞇ.Valet.Lxxv.ſol.

Ipſe.A.teñ DERWINESTONE.Tres taini tenueꞃ.T.R.E.

7 geldb ꝑ.ıııı.hıđ 7 dım̄.Ťra.ē.ııı.caꞃ.In dn̄io sꞇ.ıı.caꞃ.

7 ıııı.ſerui.7 vııı.borđ cū.ı.caꞃ.Ibı.ıı.ãc uıneæ.7 xv.ãc

p̂ti.7 ııı.q̂⁊ paſturæ ın l͞g.7 una q̂⁊ laꞇ.Silua.ııı.q̂⁊ l͞g.

7 ıı.q̂⁊ laꞇ.Valuit.Lx.ſolıđ.Modo.ıııı.lıb 7 x.ſolıđ.

Ipſe.A.teñ ODETVN.Bricſi tenuit miles regis.E.7 geldb

ꝑ.xıı.hıđ.Ťra.ē.xvı.caꞃ.De ea sꞇ in dn̄io.ıııı.carucatæ.

7 ibi.ııı.caꞃ.7 vı.ſerui.7 xıı.uıꞛꞇi 7 xı.borđ cū.ıx.caꞃ.

Ibi.ıı.molini redđ.xv.ſol.7 ıı.arpenz uıneæ.7 L.ãc p̂ti.

7 xL.ãc ſıluæ.7 una leū paſturæ in l͞g.7 tntđ laꞇ.

Valuit.x.lıb.Modo.xx.lıb.

Iđē.A.teñ unā v̄ træ ad BRIGE.Sauuarđ tenuit T.R.E.

Ťra.ē.ıı.boū.Ibi sꞇ.ıı.piſcatores.7 redđ.v.ſolıđ.

Iđē.A.teñ unā hıđ 7 dım̄ in HAFELTONE.Azor tenuit T.R.E.

Ťra.ē.ı.caꞃ.q̄ ibi.ē in dn̄io.7 v.ãc p̂ti.7 vı.q̂⁊ paſturæ.

Valuit.v.ſolıđ.Modo.xL.ſolıđ.

It paid tax for 2 hides, which are there, with 1 slave;
4 smallholders.
Pasture, 10 acres; woodland, 3 furlongs in length and 2 furlongs
in width.
Value 30s.

9 Aiulf also holds BRADLE. A thane held it before 1066. It paid tax
for 4 hides. Land for 2 ploughs. In lordship 1 plough; 2 slaves;
1 villager and 2 smallholders with ½ plough.
Meadow, 1 acre; pasture, 2 furlongs; woodland, 1 furlong
in length and ½ in width.
The value was 40s; now 60s.

10 Aiulf holds TATTON himself. A thane held it before 1066 from
Cerne Church; he could not be separated from it. It paid tax for
3 hides. Land for 2 ploughs. In lordship 1 plough; 2 slaves;
1 villager and 4 smallholders.
Meadow, 4 acres; pasture, 2 furlongs in length and width.
Value 75s.

11 Aiulf holds DURWESTON himself. Three thanes held it before 1066.
It paid tax for 4½ hides. Land for 3 ploughs. In lordship 2
ploughs; 4 slaves;
8 smallholders with 1 plough.
A vineyard, 2 acres; meadow, 15 acres; pasture, 3 furlongs in
length and 1 furlong wide; woodland 3 furlongs long and
2 furlongs wide.
The value was 60s; now £4 10s.

12 Aiulf holds WOOTTON (Fitzpaine) himself. Brictsi, a man-at-arms
of King Edward's, held it. It paid tax for 12 hides. Land for 16
ploughs, of which 4 carucates are in lordship; 3 ploughs there;
6 slaves;
12 villagers and 11 smallholders with 9 ploughs.
2 mills which pay 15s; vineyard, 2 *arpents*; meadow, 50 acres;
woodland, 40 acres; pasture, 1 league in length and as wide.
The value was £10; now £20.

13 Aiulf also holds 1 virgate of land at BRIDGE. Saeward held it
before 1066. Land for 2 oxen.
2 fishermen; they pay 5s.

14 Aiulf also holds 1½ hides in HETHFELTON. Azor held them before
1066. Land for 1 plough, which is there, in lordship.
Meadow, 5 acres; pasture, 6 furlongs.
The value was 5s; now 40s.

Ipſe.A.ten̄ *LVLVORDE*.Alured tenuit T.R.E.7 geldb̄
p̄.viii.hid̄ 7 iii.v trǣ.Tra.ē.v.car̄.In dn̄io sꝉ.iii.car̄.7 iii.
ſerui.7 iii.uiꝉli 7 viii.bord̄ cū.i.car̄.Ibi.xii.ac̄ p̄ti.7 vi.q̄ƶ
paſturæ in lḡ.7 tn̄td̄ in lat̄.Valuit.vi.lib̄.Modo.vii.lib̄.
Ipſe.A.ten̄ *CHIRCE*.Aluric tenuit T.R.E.7 geldb̄ p̄.iiii.
hid̄.Tra.ē.iii.car̄.In dn̄io sꝉ.ii.car̄.7 ii.ſerui.7 iiii.uiꝉli
7 vii.bord̄ cū dim̄ car̄.Ibi molin̄ redd̄.xx.ſoꝉ.7 xviii.ac̄
p̄ti.7 iiii.q̄ƶ paſturæ in lḡ.7 una q̄ƶ lat̄.7 vi.q̄ƶ ſiluæ lḡ.
7 una q̄ƶ lat̄.Valuit.xl.ſoꝉ.Modo.lxv.ſoꝉ.7 viii.den̄.
Hanc ten̄ Aiulf de rege.quādiu erit uicecomes.
Id̄ē.A.ten̄ *FERNHA*.quā tenuit un̄ tain̄ T.R.E.de æccꝉa
Sceptesbie.7 n̄ poterat ab ea ſeparari.7 geldb̄ p̄ dimid̄ hida.
Tra.ē dimid̄ car̄.Ibi.i.q̄ƶ paſturæ in lḡ.7 dimid̄ in lat̄.
7 ii.q̄ƶ ſiluæ in lḡ.7 una q̄ƶ lat̄.Valet.xxx.ſolid̄.

.L.   TERRA HVNFRIDI CAMERARIJ.
Hvnfrid̄ ten̄ de rege *AMEDESHA*.Dodo tenuit
T.R.E.7 geldb̄ p̄.i.hida 7 dim̄.Tra.ē.i.car̄ 7 dim̄.q̄ ibi sꝉ
cū.i.uiꝉlo.7 ii.bord̄ 7 i.ſeruo.Ibi molin̄ redd̄.xxx.denar̄.
7 una ac̄ p̄ti 7 dim̄.7 viii.q̄ƶ paſturæ in lḡ.7 iii.q̄ƶ i lat̄.
7 v.q̄ƶ ſiluæ in lḡ.7 una q̄ƶ 7 dim̄ in lat̄.Valet.lx.ſolid̄.
Id̄ē ten̄ *MEDESHA*.T.R.E.geldb̄ p̄.i.hida| Tra.ē.i.car̄
q̄ ibi.ē.Valet.xxx.ſoꝉ.Eddeua ten̄ de Hunf̄.
Id̄ē ten̄ *HEMEDESWRDE*.Vn̄ lib̄ tain̄ tenuit T.R.E.7 geldb̄
p̄.i.hida.Tra.ē.i.car̄.q̄ ibi.ē cū.i.ſeruo.7 iii.bord̄.Ibi.ii.ac̄
p̄ti.7 ii.q̄ƶ paſturæ in lḡ.7 una q̄ƶ in lat̄.Valuit 7 uaꝉ.lx.ſoꝉ.

15 Aiulf holds LULWORTH himself. Alfred the Sheriff held it before 1066. It paid tax for 8 hides and 3 virgates of land. Land for 5 ploughs. In lordship 3 ploughs; 3 slaves;
   3 villagers and 8 smallholders with 1 plough.
   Meadow, 12 acres; pasture, 6 furlongs in length and as much in width.
The value was £6; now £7.

16 Aiulf holds (Long) CRICHEL himself. Aelfric held it before 1066. It paid tax for 4 hides. Land for 3 ploughs. In lordship 2 ploughs; 2 slaves;
   4 villagers and 7 smallholders with ½ plough.
   A mill which pays 20s; meadow, 18 acres; pasture, 4 furlongs in length and 1 furlong wide; woodland, 6 furlongs long and 1 furlong wide.
The value was 40s; now 65s 8d.
   Aiulf holds it from the King for as long as he shall be Sheriff.

17 Aiulf also holds FARNHAM, which a thane held before 1066 from Shaftesbury Church; he could not be separated from it. It paid tax for ½ hide. Land for ½ plough.
   Pasture, 1 furlong in length and ½ in width; woodland, 2 furlongs in length and 1 furlong wide.
Value 30s.

50   LAND OF HUMPHREY THE CHAMBERLAIN   E

1 Humphrey holds EDMONDSHAM from the King. Doda held it before 1066. It paid tax for 1½ hides. Land for 1½ ploughs, which are there, with
   1 villager, 2 smallholders and 1 slave.
   A mill which pays 30d; meadow, 1½ acres; pasture, 8 furlongs in length and 3 furlongs in width; woodland, 5 furlongs in length and 1½ furlongs in width.
Value 60s.

2 He also holds EDMONDSHAM. Before 1066 it paid tax for 1½ hides. Land for 1 plough, which is there.
Value 30s.
   Edeva holds it from Humphrey.

3 He also holds HEMSWORTH. A free thane held it before 1066. It paid tax for 1 hide. Land for 1 plough, which is there, with 1 slave;
   3 smallholders.
   Meadow, 2 acres; pasture, 2 furlongs in length and 1 furlong in width.
The value was and is 60s.

Idē ten̄ *STVRE* Aluuard tenuit T.R.E.7 geldƀ ⸝p.vı.hiđ.

7 una v̄ træ 7 diṁ.Tra.ē.ııı.cař.In dn̄io sͣ.ıı.cař.cū uno

feruo.7 vı.uiłłi 7 vıı.borđ cū.ı.cař 7 diṁ.Ibi moliṅ redđ

.ııı.fol.7 xʟ.ac̄ p̄ti.7 vııı.q̄ʒ pafturæ in łḡ.7 v.q̄ʒ in lať.

☞ Valuit.ıııı.liƀ 7 x.folid.Modo.vı.liƀ.

.LII.   TERRA HVGONIS DE S͛ QVINTINO.

Hvɢo de S͛ qͣntino ten̄ de rege *STITEFORD*.Sex taini in paraḡ

tenueř T.R.E.7 geldƀ ⸝p.ıı.hiđ.7 ıı.v̄ træ 7 diṁ.Tra.ē.ıı.cař.

q̄ ibͦ sͣ in dn̄io.7 ııı.uiłłi 7 ıı.borđ cū.ı.cař.Ibi.xxııı.ac̄ p̄ti.

7 ıı.q̄ʒ pafturæ in łḡ.7 una q̄ʒ lať.Valuit 7 ual.xv.folid.

Idē ten̄ *RINGESTEDE*.Q̄ttuo taini |tenueř T.R.E.7 geldƀ
⸝p.ıı.hiđ.Tra.ē.ıı.cař.q̄ ibi sͣ in dn̄io.cū.vı.borđ.Ibi

dimiđ moliṅ.redđ.ıııı.fol.7 vııı.ac̄ p̄ti.7 xıı.q̄ʒ pafturæ in łḡ.

7 una q̄ʒ in lať.Valuit.xxx.fol.Modo.xʟ.folid.

.LIII Hvɢo de Bofchherƀti ten̄ de rege *CERNEL*.Goduiṅ tenuit T.R.E.

7 geldƀ ⸝p.ı.hida 7 diṁ.Tra.ē.ı.cař.q̄ ibi.ē in dn̄io cū.ı.feruo.

7 ıı.uiłłis 7 ı.borđ.Ibi.ı.ac̄ p̄ti 7 diṁ.7 ııı.q̄ʒ pafturæ in łḡ.7 una

in lať.Valuit.xxv.fol.Modo.xx.folid.

Idē ten̄ uṅ Maneriū q̄ duo frs tenueř T.R.E.7 geldƀ ⸝p.x.hiđ.

Tra.ē.vııı.cař.In dn̄io sͣ.ıı.cař.7 vı.ferui.7 ıx.uiłłi 7 v.borđ

cū.ıııı.cař.Ibi moliṅ redđ.xxx.denař.7 xıı.ac̄ p̄ti.Paftura.ı.leū

7 ıııı.q̄ʒ łḡ.7 una leū lať.Valuit.vı.liƀ.Modo.ıx.liƀ.

4 He also holds STOURPAINE. Alward held it before 1066. It paid
tax for 6 hides and 1½ virgates of land. Land for 4 ploughs. In
lordship 2 ploughs, with 1 slave;
  6 villagers and 7 smallholders with 1½ ploughs.
  A mill which pays 3s; meadow, 40 acres; pasture, 8 furlongs
  in length and 5 furlongs in width.
The value was £4 10s; now £6.

*Ch. 51 is entered at the foot of col. 83b after Ch. 54 and is directed by transposition signs
to its correct position in the text.*

52   LAND OF HUGH OF ST. QUENTIN   E

1 Hugh of St. Quentin holds STINSFORD from the King. Six thanes
held it jointly before 1066. It paid tax for 2 hides and 2½ virgates
of land. Land for 2 ploughs, which are there, in lordship;
  3 villagers and 2 smallholders with 1 plough.
  Meadow, 23 acres; pasture, 2 furlongs in length and 1 furlong wide.
The value was and is 15s.

2 He also holds RINGSTEAD. Four thanes held it jointly before 1066.
It paid tax for 2 hides. Land for 2 ploughs, which are there, in
lordship, with
  6 smallholders.
  ½ mill which pays 4s; meadow, 8 acres; pasture, 12 furlongs   83 b
  in length and 1 furlong in width.
The value was 30s; now 40s.

53   [LAND OF HUGH OF BOSCHERBERT]   E

1 Hugh of Boscherbert holds 'CERNE' from the King. Godwin held
it before 1066. It paid tax for 1½ hides. Land for 1 plough, which
is there, in lordship, with 1 slave and
  2 villagers and 1 smallholder.
  Meadow, 1½ acres; pasture, 3 furlongs in length and 1 in width.
The value was 25s; now 20s.

2 He also holds one manor which two brothers held before 1066.
It paid tax for 10 hides. Land for 8 ploughs. In lordship 2
ploughs; 6 slaves;
  9 villagers and 5 smallholders with 4 ploughs.
  A mill which pays 30d; meadow, 12 acres; pasture 1 league
  and 4 furlongs long and 1 league wide.
The value was £6; now £9.

.LIII Hⱽᴳᴼ de Lᴠʀɪ.ten de rege trā in tribȝ Locis.quā tenueř.xɪ.taini

7 geldƀ ᵽ.ᴠ.hid.Tra.e.ɪɪɪɪ.cař.Radulf ten de Hug.In dñio.e dim

cař.7 xɪɪ.uiłti cū.ɪɪɪ.cař 7 dimid.Ibi.x.ac ᵽti.7 ᴠ.q̃ȝ paſturæ in lḡ.

7 ɪɪ.q̃ȝ in lat.Valuit 7 ual.ɪɪɪɪ.liƀ.

Hⱽᴳᴼ Silueſtris ten in Cᴀɴᴅᴇʟ dimid hid træ.Leuerone tenuit

T.R.E.Tra.e dim cař.Ibi st.ɪɪ.bord 7 ɪɪ.ac ᵽti.Nil āplius.

Fⱽʟᴄʀᴇᴅ ten Wᴀɪᴀ.ᵈᵉ ʳᵉᵍᵉWateman tenuit T.R.E.7 geldƀ ᵽ.ɪɪ.hid

7 dim.Tra.ɪɪ.cař.In dñio.e.ɪ.cař.7 ɪɪɪ.ſerui.7 ɪ.uiłts.7 ɪɪ.bord.

Ibi.ɪɪɪɪ.ac ᵽti.7 ᴠɪɪ.q̃ȝ paſturæ.Valet.xxx.ſolid.

Fⱽʟᴄʀᴇᴅ ten Mᴏʀᴅᴀᴀᴛ.Alric tenuit T.R.E.7 geldƀ ᵽ.ɪɪ,hid.

Tra.e.ɪɪ.cař.g̃ ibi st in dñio.7 ɪɪɪ.uiłti 7 ɪɪɪɪ.bord.Ibi.xɪ.ac ᵽti.

7 ʟ.ac paſture.7 xxx.ac ſiluæ.Valet.xxx.ſol.

Rɪᴄᴀʀᴅ de Reduers ten Mᴏʀᴛᴇsᴛᴏʀɴᴇ.Ælmer tenuit T.R.E.

7 geldƀ ᵽ.ᴠɪ.hid.Tra.e.ᴠ.cař.In dñio st.ɪɪ.cař.7 ᴠ.ſerui.7 ᴠɪɪɪ.uiłti

7 ᴠ.bord.cū.ɪɪɪ.cař.Ibi molin redd.ᴠɪɪ.ſol 7 ᴠɪ.den.7 xxx.ac ᵽti.

Silua.ɪ.leū lḡ.7 dimid leū lat.Valuit 7 ual.xɪɪ.liƀ.

Sᴄʜᴇʟɪɴ ten Aʟꜰᴏʀᴅ.Herald tenuit T.R.E.7 geldƀ ᵽ.xᴠɪ.hid.

Tra.e.xᴠɪ.cař.In dñio st.ɪɪɪ.cař.7 ᴠ.ſerui.7 xᴠ.uiłti 7 xxᴠɪ.

bord cū.ᴠɪɪɪ.cař.Ibi molin redd xxɪɪɪ.ſol 7 ᴠɪ.den.7 cc.ac ᵽti.

xᴠɪɪ.min.Paſtura.xʟɪɪ.q̃ȝ lḡ.7 ᴠɪɪɪ.q̃ȝ lat.Silua.xxɪɪɪ.q̃ȝ

lḡ.7 ɪx.q̃ȝ lat.Valuit.xᴠɪ.liƀ.Modo.xɪx.liƀ.

Dᴀᴠɪᴅ intpres ten Pᴏᴠʀᴛᴏɴᴇ.Octo taini tenueř T.R.E.7 geldƀ

ᵽ.ɪ.hida 7 ɪɪ.ᴠ træ 7 dim.Tra.e.ɪɪ.cař.g̃ ibi st cū.ᴠɪɪɪ.uiłtis.

[LAND OF HUGH OF IVRY AND OTHER FRENCHMEN]   E

1   Hugh of Ivry holds land in three places from the King, which
    eleven thanes held. It paid tax for 5 hides. Land for 4 ploughs.
    Ralph holds it from Hugh. In lordship ½ plough;
       12 villagers with 3½ ploughs.
       Meadow, 10 acres; pasture, 5 furlongs in length and 2
          furlongs in width.
    The value was and is £4.

2   Hugh Silvester holds ½ hide of land in (Stourton) CAUNDLE.
    Leofrun held it before 1066. Land for ½ plough.
       2 smallholders.
       Meadow, 2 acres; nothing more.
    [Value ....]

3   Fulcred holds 'WEY' from the King. Hwaetmann held it before
    1066. It paid tax for 2½ hides. Land for 2 ploughs. In lordship
    1 plough; 3 slaves;
       1 villager and 2 smallholders.
       Meadow, 4 acres; pasture, 7 furlongs.
    Value 30s.

4   Fulcred holds MOORBATH. Alric held it before 1066. It paid tax
    for 2 hides. Land for 2 ploughs, which are there, in lordship;
       3 villagers and 4 smallholders.
       Meadow, 11 acres; pasture, 50 acres; woodland, 30 acres.
    Value 30s.

5   Richard of Reviers holds MOSTERTON. Aelmer held it before 1066.
    It paid tax for 6 hides. Land for 5 ploughs. In lordship 2 ploughs;
    5 slaves;
       8 villagers and 5 smallholders with 3 ploughs.
       A mill which pays 7s 6d; meadow, 30 acres; woodland 1
          league long and ½ league wide.
    The value was and is £12.

6   Azelin holds SHILLINGSTONE. Earl Harold held it before 1066.
    It paid tax for 16 hides. Land for 16 ploughs. In lordship 3
    ploughs; 5 slaves;
       15 villagers and 26 smallholders with 8 ploughs.
       A mill which pays 23s 6d; meadow, 200 acres, less 17;
          pasture 42 furlongs long and 8 furlongs wide; woodland
          23 furlongs long and 9 furlongs wide.
    The value was £16; now £19.

7   David the Interpreter holds POORTON. Eight thanes held it before
    1066. It paid tax for 1 hide and 2½ virgates of land. Land for 2
    ploughs, which are there, with
       8 villagers.

Ibi moliñ 7 ɪɪɪɪ . ac ſiluæ .7 ɪɪ . q̊ʒ paſturæ in l͞g .7 dimid q̊ʒ in lat̄.

Valuit 7 ual . xxx . ſolid . Godeſcal ten de Dauid.

A f. ameline
Nschitil ten TINGEHA . Brictric tenuit T.R.E .7 geldb ꝑ . ɪɪɪ.

hid . T̄ra . e͞ . ɪɪɪ . car̄ . In d͞nio ſt̄ . ɪɪ . car̄ .7 ɪx . ſerui .7 ɪɪɪɪ . uilti cu͞ . ɪ.

car̄ . Ibi . ɪɪɪɪ . ac p͡ti .7 vɪɪɪ . q̊ʒ paſturæ in l͞g .7 ɪɪɪɪ . q̊ʒ in lat̄.

Valuit . ɪɪɪ . lib . modo . ɪɪɪɪ . lib . Hanc t̄ra tenuit Anſchit de regina

ut dicit . ſed poſt morte ej rege non reqſiuit.

Radvlfvs ten TARENTE . Brictric tenuit T.R.E .7 geldb ꝑ . ɪɪ . hid

Tra . e͞ . ɪ . car̄ 7 dimid . In d͞nio . e͞ . ɪ . car̄ .7 ɪɪ . ſerui .7 ɪɪ . uilti 7 ɪɪ . coſcez.

cu͞ dimid car̄ . Ibi . ɪɪɪ . ac p͡ti .7 vɪɪ . q̊ʒ paſturæ in l͞g .7 una q̊ʒ 7 dim

in lat̄ . Silua . ɪ . q̊ʒ l͞g .7 ɪɪɪɪ . ac lat̄ . Valuit 7 ual . xL . ſolid.

Radvlfvs de Creneburne ten PERLAI . Briſnod tenuit T.R.E.

7 geldb ꝑ . ɪɪ . hid . T̄ra . e͞ . ɪɪ . car̄ . q̄ ibi ſt̄ .7 v . uilti 7 ɪɪɪɪ . bord .7 ɪɪ.

ſerui .7 xv . ac p͡ti . Paſtura . ɪ . leu͞ l͞g .7 vɪɪ . q̊ʒ lat̄ . Silua . ɪɪɪɪ . q̊ʒ

l͞g .7 una q̊ʒ lat̄ . Valuit 7 ual . xxx . ſolid.

Odo fili Eurebold ten FERNHA . Vluiet tenuit T.R.E .7 geldb

ꝑ . ɪɪ . hid . Tra . e͞ . ɪɪ . car̄ . q̄ ibi ſt̄ in d͞nio .7 ɪɪɪɪ . ſerui .7 ɪɪɪ . bord.

Paſturæ . x . ac int l͞g 7 lat̄ . Silua . ɪɪɪ . q̊ʒ l͞g .7 ɪɪ . q̊ʒ lat̄ . Valet . xL.

Idem ten MELEBVRNE . Dodo tenuit T.R.E .7 geldb ſolid.

ꝑ . ɪɪ . hid . T̄ra . e͞ . ɪ . car̄ . q̄ ibi . e͞ in d͞nio .7 ɪɪɪɪ . ac p͡ti .7 ɪɪ . q̊ʒ

paſturæ . Valuit . xLɪɪɪ . ſot . Modo . xxx . ſolid.

Filius Eurebold ten . ɪɪɪ . v træ in RISTONE . Tra . e͞ . ɪ . car̄.

quæ ibi . e͞ cu͞ . ɪɪɪɪ . uiltis .7 una ac p͡ti .7 ɪɪɪɪ . ac ſiluæ .7 una leu͞

paſturæ in l͞g 7 lat̄ . Valet . x . ſolid.

A mill; woodland, 4 acres; pasture, 2 furlongs in length and
½ furlong in width.
The value was and is 30s.
Godescal holds it from David.

8 Ansketel son of Amelina holds TYNEHAM. Brictric held it before
1066. It paid tax for 3 hides. Land for 3 ploughs. In lordship 2
ploughs; 9 slaves;
4 villagers with 1 plough.
Meadow, 4 acres; pasture, 8 furlongs in length and 4 furlongs
in width.
The value was £3; now £4.
Ansketel held this land from the Queen, as he states, but after
her death he did not petition the King (for it).

9 Ralph holds 'TARRANT'. Brictric held it before 1066. It paid tax
for 2 hides. Land for 1½ ploughs. In lordship 1 plough; 2 slaves;
2 villagers and 2 Cottagers with ½ plough.
Meadow, 3 acres; pasture, 7 furlongs in length and 1½ furlongs
in width; woodland 1 furlong long and 4 acres wide.
The value was and is 40s.

10 Ralph of Cranborne holds (West) PARLEY. Brictnoth held it before
1066. It paid tax for 2 hides. Land for 2 ploughs, which are there.
5 villagers, 4 smallholders and 2 slaves.
Meadow, 15 acres; pasture 1 league long and 7 furlongs wide;
woodland 4 furlongs long and 1 furlong wide.
The value was and is 30s.

11 Odo son of Everbold holds FARNHAM. Wulfgeat held it before
1066. It paid tax for 2 hides. Land for 2 ploughs, which are there,
in lordship; 4 slaves;
3 smallholders.
Pasture, 10 acres in both length and width; woodland 3
furlongs long and 2 furlongs wide.
Value 40s.

12 He also holds MILBORNE (Stileham). Doda held it before 1066.
It paid tax for 2 hides. Land for 1 plough, which is there, in
lordship.
Meadow, 4 acres; pasture, 2 furlongs.
The value was 44s; now 30s.

13 The son of Everbold holds 3 virgates of land in RUSHTON. Land
for 1 plough, which is there, with
4 villagers.
Meadow, 1 acre; woodland, 4 acres; pasture, 1 league in
length and width.
Value 10s.

Idẽ ten̄ *PETRISHESHÃ*. Sauuard tenuit T.R.E.7 geldb̄ ꝓ. III. virḡ træ. Tra. ẽ. I. car̄. Ꝗ ibi. ẽ. 7 VI. ac̄ p̄ti.

☞ TERRA HVḠ DE PORTH.

.LI. HVGO de Porth ten̄ de rege *CONTONE*. Bundi tenuit T.R.E.7 geldb̄ ꝓ. x. hid̄. Tra. ẽ. VIII.
★ car̄. In dñio st̄. II. car̄. 7 III. ferui. 7 x. uitti 7 XII. bord̄ cũ. III. car̄. Ibi. XXXII. ac̄ p̄ti. Paftura. XVIII. q̃z lḡ. 7 una leũ lat̄. Valuit 7 uat. xx. lib̄.

83 c

.LV. TERRA VXORIS HVGONIS FILIJ GRIP.

VXOR HVGONIS .F. Grip ten̄ de rege *WINTREBVRNE*. Noue̅ taini in paragio. tenuer̄. T.R.E. 7 geldb̄ ꝓ. VI. hid̄. Tra. ẽ. VI. car̄. In dñio de ea tra st̄. III. hide. 7 ibi. II. car̄. 7 v. ferui. 7 XVII. bord̄ cũ. II. car̄. Ibi molin̄ redd̄ XVI. denar̄. 7 XIII. ac̄ p̄ti. Paftura. IX. q̃z lḡ. 7 VIII. q̃z lat̄. Valuit. x. lib̄. Modo. VI. lib̄.

Witts ten̄ de ea *FROME*. Godric tenuit T.R.E. 7 geldb̄ ꝓ. IIII. hid̄. Tra. ẽ. III. car̄. In dñio st̄. II. car̄. cũ. I. feruo. 7 VIII. bord̄ 7 IIII. cotar̄. Ibi molin̄ redd̄. v. fol̄. 7 XXX. ac̄ p̄ti. Paftura. IIII. q̃z lḡ. 7 II. q̃z lat̄. Valuit. XL. folid̄. Modo. IIII. lib̄.

Roger̄ ten̄ de ead̄ *CEOSELBVRNE*. Elgar 7 Alftan̄ tenuer̄ T.R.E. 7 geldb̄ ꝓ. II. hid̄. Tra. ẽ. II. car̄. In dñio. ẽ. I. car̄. cũ. VI. bord̄. Ibi molin̄ redd̄. XXX. denar̄. 7 v. ac̄ p̄ti. 7 una q̃z pafturæ. Valuit. L. fol̄. m̃. XXV. fol̄. Hanc tr̃a tenuit Hugo de abb̄e Abedefber̄. ut hoẽs ej̄ dicu̅t. f; abb̄ negat.

14 He also holds PETERSHAM. Saeward held it before 1066. It paid
tax for 3 virgates of land. Land for 1 plough, which is there.
Meadow, 6 acres.
[Value ....]

*Ch. 51 entered at the foot of col. 83b and directed by transposition signs to its correct
position in the text.*

51   LAND OF HUGH OF PORT   E

1 Hugh of Port holds COMPTON (Valence) from the King. Bondi
held it before 1066. It paid tax for 10 hides. Land for 8 ploughs.
In lordship 3 ploughs; 3 slaves;
10 villagers and 12 smallholders with 3 ploughs.
Meadow, 32 acres; pasture 18 furlongs long and 1 league wide.
The value was and is £20.

55   LAND OF THE WIFE OF HUGH SON OF GRIP   83 c

1 The wife of Hugh son of Grip holds MARTINSTOWN from the King.
Nine thanes held it jointly before 1066. It paid tax for 6 hides.   E
Land for 6 ploughs. In lordship 3 hides of this land; 2 ploughs
there; 5 slaves;
17 smallholders with 2 ploughs and 3 hides.   54
A mill which pays 16d; meadow, 13 acres; pasture 9 furlongs   a 1
  long and 8 furlongs wide. 1 cob; 8 pigs; 380 sheep.
The value was £10; now £6.   E

2 William holds FROME (Whitfield) from her. Godric held it before
1066. It paid tax for 4 hides. Land for 3 ploughs. In lordship 2   E
ploughs and these 4 hides, with 1 slave;
8 smallholders and 4 cottagers.   54
A mill which pays 5s; meadow, 30 acres; pasture 4 furlongs   a 2
  long and 2 furlongs wide. 1 cob; 15 cattle; 30 pigs; 250 sheep; 1 ass.
The value was 40s; now £4.

3 Roger Bushell holds '(Little) CHESELBOURNE' also from her. Algar
and Alstan held it before 1066. It paid tax for 2 hides. Land for
2 ploughs. In lordship 1 plough, with
6 smallholders.
A mill which pays 30d; meadow, 5 acres; pasture, 1 furlong.   54
50 sheep.   a 3
The value was 50s; now 25s.
Hugh son of Grip held this land from the Abbot of Abbotsbury,
as his men state, but the Abbot denies it.

Ipſa femina ten̄ *BOCHELAND*.Quattuor taini tenuer̄ ^{in paragio}.T.R.E.7 geldb̄
‚p.IIII.hid.Tra.ē.III.car̄.In dn̄io ſt.II.car̄.cū.I.ſeruo.7 II.uilli 7 v.
bord cū.I.car̄.Ibi molin̄ redd.xx.ſol.7 x.ac̄ p̄ti.Paſtura.xv.q̃q̃
lḡ.7 una q̃q̃ lat̄.Valuit 7 ual.c.ſolid.

Ipſa ten̄.*WAIA*.Noue͞ taini tenuer̄ ^{in paragio}.T.R.E.7 geldb̄ ‚p.IIII.hid 7 una
v trӕ.Tra.ē.IIII.car̄.In dn̄io ſt.II.car̄.7 III.ferui.7 vI.bord
Ibi.III.molini redd.xxxv.ſolid.7 p̄tū.Ix.q̃q̃ lḡ.7 una q̃q̃ lat̄.Paſ
tura.III.q̃q̃ lḡ.7 una q̃q̃ lat̄.Valuit.vI.lib̄.Modo.c.ſolid.

Ipſa ten̄ *WAIA*.Quinq̃ taini tenuer̄ ^{libe} T.R.E.7 geldb̄ ‚p.vI.hid.Tra.ē
v.car̄.In dn̄io ſt.II.car̄.cū.I.ſeruo.7 I.uilt 7 x.bord cū.I.car̄.
Ibi.III.molini redd.xxxvII.ſol.7 vI.denar̄.7 xxv.ac̄ p̄ti.Paſtura
xx.q̃q̃ lḡ.7 III.q̃q̃ lat̄.Valuit.vII.lib̄.Modo.x.lib̄.

Azo ten̄ de ea *WINTREBVRNE*.Almar tenuit T.R.E.7 geldb̄ ‚p.I.
hida.Tra.ē dimid car̄.Ibi ſt.II.bord.7 una ac̄ p̄ti.7 II.q̃q̃ paſturӕ
in lḡ.7 una q̃q̃ lat̄.Valet.x.ſolid.

Hugo 7 Wilts ten̄ de ea *STAFORD*.Tres taini tenuer̄ ^{in paragio.} T.R.E.‚p.II.
Maner̄.7 geldb̄ ‚p.vI.hid.Tra.ē.III.car̄.In dn̄io ſt.II.car̄ cū.I.ſeruo.
7 vIII.bord.Ibi.xxIIII.ac̄ p̄ti.   7 xvI.q̃q̃ paſturӕ.7 vIII.ac̄.
Valeb̄.IIII.lib̄.Modo.Lxx.ſolid.

Ipſa femina ten̄ *WINTREBVRNE*.Alric tenuit T.R.E.7 geldb̄ ‚p.vIII.
hid.Tra.ē.IIII.car̄.In dn̄io ſt.II.car̄.7 III.ferui.7 III.uilli 7 v.bord
cū dimid car̄.Ibi.Ix.ac̄ p̄ti.7 cc.ac̄ paſturӕ.Valuit 7 ual.vI.lib̄.

4 The woman holds BUCKLAND (Ripers) herself. Four thanes held it
  jointly before 1066. It paid tax for 4 hides. Land for 3 ploughs.   E
  In lordship 2 ploughs and 3 hides and 1 virgate, with 1 slave;
    2 villagers and 5 smallholders with 1 plough and 3 virgates.   54
  A mill which pays 20s; meadow, 10 acres; pasture 15 furlongs   b 1
    long and 1 furlong wide. 1 cob; 4 pigs; 200 sheep.
  The value was and is 100s.

5 She holds 'WEY' herself. Nine thanes held it jointly before 1066.
  It paid tax for 4 hides and 1 virgate of land. Land for 4 ploughs.
  In lordship 2 ploughs; 3 slaves; 3 hides and 3 virgates.
    6 smallholders (have) ½ hide.   54
    3 mills which pay 35s; meadow 9 furlongs long and 1 furlong   E b 2
    wide; pasture 3 furlongs long and 1 furlong wide.   E
    1 cob; 2 cows; 9 pigs; 130 sheep.
  The value was £6; now 100s.

6 She holds 'WEY' herself. Five thanes held it freely before 1066.   E
  It paid tax for 6 hides. Land for 5 ploughs. In lordship 2 ploughs   55
  and 4 hides and 1 virgate, with 1 slave;   a 1
    1 villager and 10 smallholders with 1 plough and 2 hides, less 1 virgate.
  3 mills which pay 37s 6d; meadow, 25 acres; pasture 20
    furlongs long and 3 furlongs wide. 1 cob; 330 sheep.
  The value was £7; now £10.

7 Azo holds 'WINTERBORNE' from her. Aelmer held it before 1066.
  It paid tax for 1 hide. Land for ½ plough.   E
    2 smallholders.   55
  Meadow, 1 acre; pasture, 2 furlongs in length and 1 furlong   a 2
    wide. 3 cattle; 100 sheep.
  Value 10s.

8 Hugh and William hold STAFFORD from her. Three thanes held it   D
  jointly before 1066 as two manors. It paid tax for 6 hides. Land   E
  for 3 ploughs. In lordship 2 ploughs, with 1 slave;
    8 smallholders.   55
  Meadow, 24 acres; pasture, 16 furlongs and 8 acres.   b 1
  The value was £4; now 70s.   E

9 The woman holds 'WINTERBORNE' herself. Alric held it before 1066.
  It paid tax for 8 hides. Land for 4 ploughs. In lordship 2 ploughs;
  3 slaves; 6 hides, less 1 virgate.   55
    3 villagers and 5 smallholders with ½ plough and 2 hides and 1 virgate. b 2
  Meadow, 9 acres; pasture, 200 acres. 1 cob; 6 cows; 10 pigs; 304 sheep.
  The value was and is £6.

Wills ten de ea MORDONE . Alnod tenuit T.R.E.7 geldɓ ꝑ.v. uirg
træ . Tra.ē.1.caᷓ.   Valuit.xxv.ſol.m̄.xx.ſol.

Ipſa ten WINTREBVRNÉ . Tres taini tenueᷓ T.R.E.7 geldɓ ꝑ.v.
hiđ.Tra.ē.iii.caᷓ.In dn̄io.ē una caᷓ.7 ii.ſerui.7 v.uilli 7 iiii.borđ.
Ibi.iiii.ac̄ p̄ti.7 v.q̇ꝗ̇ paſturæ in lḡ.7 tn̄tđ laᷓ.Valuit.c.ſol.m̄.xl.ſol.
Radulf⁹ ten de ea unā v̆ træ 7 dim in WINTREBVRNE.Tra.ē.iii.boū.
Goduin⁹ tenuit T.R.E. 7 ualuit 7 ual.iii. ſol.

Wills ten de ea WINBVRNE . Alduin⁹ tenuit T.R.E.7 geldɓ ꝑ.i.hida.
Tra.ē.i.caᷓ.Ibi ſᷓ.ii.borđ.7 tcia pars molini redđ xv . denaᷓ.
Ibi paſturæ.iiii.q̇ꝗ̇ in lḡ 7 laᷓ.Silua.i.q̇ꝗ̇ lḡ.7 dimiđ q̇ꝗ̇ laᷓ.
Valuit . xx . ſoliđ . Modo . v . ſoliđ.

Idē.W.ten de ea. HAME . Ageluuarđ⁹ tenuit T.R.E.7 geldɓ ꝑ.i. hida.
Tra.ē.i . caᷓ.Ibi.ē un⁹ uills 7 ii.borđ.7 ii.ac̄ p̄ti.7 una q̇ꝗ̇ ſiluæ
in lḡ.7 altera in laᷓ . Valuit 7 ual.xii. ſoliđ.

Wills ten de ea BERE . Leomer tenuit T.R.E.7 geldɓ ꝑ dim hida.
Tra.ē dimid caᷓ q̄ ibi.ē.7 molin̄ redđ.xx.ſol.7 i.borđ.7 vi.ac̄ p̄ti.
7 vi.ac̄ paſturæ.Valet.xxx. ſoliđ.
Wills ten de ea.unā v̆ træ 7 dimiđ . Redđ . xx . ſoliđ.

Walteri⁹ ten de ea PIDELE .Gerling tenuit T.R.E.7 geldɓ ꝑ.vi.
hiđ.Tra.ē.iii.caᷓ.In dn̄io ſᷓ.ii.caᷓ.7 iiii.ſerui.7 ii.uilli 7 iiii.borđ
cū dim caᷓ.Ibi.x.ac̄ p̄ti.7 xx.ac̄ ſiluæ.Paſtura.xii.q̇ꝗ̇ lḡ.7 vi.laᷓ.
Valuit ; iii . liɓ .Modo.iiii . liɓ.

10 William Chernet holds MORDEN from her. Alnoth held it before
1066. It paid tax for 5 virgates of land. Land for 1 plough.
In lordship 3½ virgates.
    The villagers have 1½ virgates.
The value was 25s; now 20s.

56
a 1
E
E

11 She holds 'WINTERBORNE' herself. Three thanes held it before
1066. It paid tax for 5 hides. Land for 3 ploughs. In lordship
1 plough; 2 slaves; 3 hides.
    5 villagers and 4 smallholders (have) 1½ hides.
Meadow, 4 acres; pasture, 5 furlongs in length and as wide.
    5 pigs; 100 sheep.
The value was 100s; now 40s.

56
a 2

E

12 Ralph holds 1½ virgates of land from her in 'WINTERBORNE'.
Land for 3 oxen. Godwin held it before 1066.
The value was and is 3s.

56
a 3

13 William Chernet holds WIMBORNE (St. Giles) from her. Aldwin held
it before 1066. It paid tax for 1 hide. Land for 1 plough.
    2 smallholders.
    The third part of a mill which pays 15d; pasture, 4 furlongs
        in length and width; woodland 1 furlong long and ½
        furlong wide.
The value was 20s; now 5s.

56
E   a 4

14 William Chernet also holds HAMPRESTON from her. Aethelward held
it before 1066. It paid tax for 1 hide. Land for 1 plough.
    1 villager and 2 smallholders.
    Meadow, 2 acres; woodland, 1 furlong in length and another
        in width.
The value was and is 12s.

E   56
     b 1

15 William of Moutiers holds BERE (Regis) from her. Leofmer held it
before 1066. It paid tax for ½ hide. Land for ½ plough, which
is there.
    A mill which pays 20s.
    1 smallholder.
    Meadow, 6 acres; pasture, 6 acres. 10 cattle; 45 sheep; 28 pigs; 1 cob.
Value 30s.

E   56
     b 2

E

15a William holds 1½ virgates of land from her; they pay 20s.

56
b 3

16 Walter Thunder holds (Turners) PUDDLE from her. Gerling held it
before 1066. It paid tax for 6 hides. Land for 3 ploughs. In
lordship 2 ploughs; 4 slaves; 4½ hides.
    2 villagers and 4 smallholders with ½ plough and ½ hide.
    Meadow, 10 acres; woodland, 20 acres; pasture 12 furlongs
        long and 6 wide. A mill at 10s a year. 20 cattle; 12 mares with their
        foals; 2 cobs; 80 sheep; 20 pigs; 40 goats.
The value was £3; now £4.

E
E

56
b 4

E

Hugo ten̓ de ea.*WINTREBVRNE*.Vlgar tenuit T.R.E.7 geldb̵
p̸.ii.hid̓ 7 una v̓ tr̓æ.Tra.ē.i.car̄ 7 dim̄.In d̄nio.ē.i.car̄ cū.i.feruɔ.
7 ii.uil̵li 7 ii.bord̓.cū dim̄ car̄.Ibi.xiiii.ac̄ filuæ minutæ.7 vi.q̓᷒
pafturæ in l̄g.7 vi.in lat̄.Valuit.xx.folid̓.Modo.xxx.folid̓.
Cū hòc ꝏ ten̓ id̓ Hugo.unā v̓ tr̓æ injufte.q̄ ptin̓ ad Wil̵lm de Moione.

83 d

Hugo ten̓·de ead̓ fem̄.unā v̓ tr̓æ ad *BRIGA̅*.Tra.ē.ii.boū.
7 ibi.ē un̓ uil̵ls.Valuit 7 val̄.x.folid̓.
Wil̵ls ten̓ de ead̓ *STERTE*.Aluric tenuit T.R.E.7 geldb̵
p̸.v.hid̓.Tra.ē.iiii.car̄.In d̄nio sꝽ.ii.car̄.7 iiii.ferui.7 ii.
uil̵li 7 iiii.bord̓ cū.i.car̄ 7 dim̄.Ibi molin̄ redd̓.vi.fol 7 iii.den̓.
7 xxvii.ac̄ p̓ti.Paftura.iiii.q̓᷒ l̄g.7 una q̓᷒ lat̄.
Valuit.iiii.lib̵.Modo.c.folid̓.
Wil̵ls ten̓ de ead̓ *GRAVSTAN*.Aluuard tenuit T.R.E.7 geldb̵
p̸.ii.hid̓ 7 dimid̓.Tra.ē.ii.car̄.In d̄nio.ē.i.car̄.7 ii.ferui.7 i̓.uil̵ls
7 viii.bord̓ cū dim̄ car̄.Ibi molin̄ redd̓.vii.fol 7 vi.den̓.7 xvi.
ac̄ p̓ti.Valuit.xl.fol.Modo.lx.folid̓.
Il̵btus ten̓ de ead̓ dim̄ hid̓ in *FERNHA̅*.Tra.ē dimid̓ car̄.7 tam̄
ē ibi.i.car̄.7 i.q̓᷒ 7 dim̄ pafturæ in l̄g.7 i.q̓᷒ lat̄.Valet.x.fol.
Aluuin̓ tenuit hanc tr̄a de æccta Sceftesb̵ie.7 n̄ poterat ab ea fepari.
Wil̵ls ten̓ de ead̓ *POMACANOLE*.Aluuard tenuit T.R.E.7 geldb̵
p̸.v.hid̓.Tra.ē.iiii.car̄.In d̄nio sꝽ.ii.car̄.7 iiii.ferui.7 iiii.uil̵li
7 v.bord̓.cū.ii.car̄.Ibi molin̄ redd̓.xii.folid̓ 7 vi.den̓.7 xxxv.
ac̄ p̓ti.7 xxx.ac̄ filuæ.7 iii.q̓᷒ pafturæ.Valuit.lx.fol.m̄.c.fol.

17 Hugh holds WINTERBORNE (Houghton) from her. Wulfgar held it before 1066. It paid tax for 2 hides and 1 virgate of land. Land for 1½ ploughs. In lordship 1 plough and 2 hides, less ½ virgate, with 1 slave;
    2 villagers and 2 smallholders with ½ plough and 1½ virgates. Underwood, 14 acres; pasture, 6 furlongs in length and 6 in width. 300 sheep.
The value was 20s; now 30s.
    With this manor Hugh also holds wrongfully 1 virgate of land which belongs to William of Mohun.

57
a 1

E

18 Hugh holds 1 virgate of land at BRIDGE also from this woman. Land for 2 oxen. Aelmer held it in 1066.
    1 villager.
The value was and is 10s.

83 d

57
a 2

19 William of Daumeray holds STURTHILL also from her. Aelfric held it before 1066. It paid tax for 5 hides. Land for 4 ploughs. In lordship 2 ploughs; 4 slaves; 3 hides.
    2 villagers and 4 smallholders with 1½ ploughs and 2 hides.
A mill which pays 6s 3d; meadow, 27 acres; pasture 4 furlongs long and 1 furlong wide. 17 cattle; 7 pigs; 8 sheep.
The value was £4; now 100s.

57
b 1

20 William holds GRASTON also from her. Alward held it before 1066. It paid tax for 2½ hides. Land for 2 ploughs. In lordship 1 plough; 2 slaves; 1½ hides.
    1 villager and 8 smallholders with ½ plough and 1 hide.
A mill which pays 7s 6d; meadow, 16 acres. 15(?) cattle; 7 pigs; 25 sheep.
The value was 40s; now 60s.

E
57
b 2

E

21 Ilbert holds ½ hide also from her in FARNHAM. Land for ½ plough; however, 1 plough there.
    Pasture, 1½ furlongs in length and 1 furlong wide. 1 cow; 6 pigs; 40 sheep; 20 goats.
Value 10s; when H(ugh) acquired it, as much.
    Alwin held this land from Shaftesbury Church; he could not be separated from it.

E
57
b 3

22 William of Moutiers holds PUNCKNOWLE from her. Alward held it before 1066. It paid tax for 5 hides. Land for 4 ploughs. In lordship 2 ploughs; 4 slaves; 3 hides.
    4 villagers and 5 smallholders with 2 ploughs and 2 hides.
A mill which pays 12s 6d; meadow, 35 acres; woodland, 30 acres; pasture, 3 furlongs. 1 cob; 12 cattle; 13 pigs; 153 sheep.
The value was 60s; now 100s.

58
a 1

Ipſa femina teñ.ii.hid in TATENTONE.q̄ eraſ de dñio abbatiæ de Cernel. T.R.E.duo teini teneb preſtito.has hugo ſup abbem accepit.Val.xx.ſolid.

Walter teñ de ead.i.hid ad LODRA.Duo taini tenuer T.R.E. Tra.ē.i.car.q̄ ibi.ē in dñio cū.i.ſeruo.7 i.uillo.7 iiii.bord. Ibi.ii.ac p̃ti.7 xxx.ac p̃ſte. Valuit.xx.ſol.Modo.xxx.ſolid.

Ipſa teñ dimid hid in TARENTE.Tra.ē.i.car.Ibi.ē.i.uills 7 i.bord.7 ii.ac p̃ti.7 iii.q̄z paſturæ in lḡ.7 i.q̄z lat.Valet

Robt teñ de ead DERVINESTONE.Aluric   x.ſolid. tenuit T.R.E.7 geldb p.ii.hid.Tra.ē.ii.car.In dñio.ē una car.cū.iii.bord.Ibi.viii.ac p̃ti.7 iiii.q̄z paſturæ in lḡ.7 ii. q̄z in lḡ.Valuit 7 ual.xl.ſolid.

Rotbt teñ de ead WINTREBVRNE.Goduin tenuit T.R.E. 7 geldb p.i.hida 7 dim.Tra.ē.i.car 7 dimid.In dñio.ē.i.car. cū.i.ſeruo.7 iiii.bord.Ibi molin redd.v.ſol.Siluæ.i.q̄z 7 dimid.7 iii.q̄z paſturæ in lḡ.7 una q̄z in lat.Valet.xxx.ſol.

In Wintreburne teñ Robt.i.hid 7 una v træ. In dñio.ē dim car.cū.i.bord.Valuit.xxv.ſol.Modo.xx.ſol.

Radulf teñ de ead TARENTE.Vn tain tenuit T.R.E. 7 geldb p.v.hid.Tra.ē.iii.car.In dñio.ē.i.car.7 iiii.ſerui.

23 The woman holds 2 hides in TATTON herself, which were (part) of the lordship of the Abbey of Cerne. Before 1066 two thanes held them by lease. Hugh received them despite the Abbot. Value 20s.

E
58
E a 2

24 Walter holds 1 hide at LODERS also from her. Two thanes held it before 1066. Land for 1 plough, which is there, in lordship, and ½ hide, with 1 slave and
1 villager and 4 smallholders (who have) ½ hide.
Meadow, 2 acres; pasture, 30 acres. 24 sheep.
The value was 20s; now 30s.

58
E a 3

25 She holds ½ hide in 'TARRANT' herself. Land for 1 plough.
Aelmer held it in 1066; he could go with his land to whichever lord he would.
In lordship 1 virgate.
1 villager and 1 smallholder.
Meadow, 2 acres; pasture, 3 furlongs in length and 1 furlong wide.
Value 10s; when Hugh acquired it, as many (shillings).

58
E a 4

26 Robert holds DURWESTON also from her. Aelfric held it before 1066. It paid tax for 2 hides. Land for 2 ploughs. In lordship 1 plough and 1½ hides, with
3 smallholders (who have) ½ hide and ½ plough.
Meadow, 8 acres; pasture, 4 furlongs in length and 2 furlongs in [width]. 14 pigs.
The value was and is 40s.

58
b 1

27 Robert holds 'WINTERBORNE' also from her. Godwin held it before 1066. It paid tax for 1½ hides. Land for 1½ ploughs. In lordship 1 plough and 1 hide and 1 virgate, with 1 slave;
4 smallholders (who have) 1 virgate.
A mill which pays 5s; woodland, 1½ furlongs; pasture, 3 furlongs in length and 1 furlong in width. 1 cow; 172 sheep.
Value 30s; when H(ugh) acquired it, as much.

58
b 2

28 In 'WINTERBORNE' Robert holds 1 hide and 1 virgate of land, which Aelfric held in 1066. In lordship ½ plough, with
1 smallholder.
2 cattle; 100 sheep, less 12.
The value was 25s; now 20s.
King William has never had his tax from 1 virgate.

E
58
b 3
E

29 Ralph holds 'TARRANT' also from her. A thane held it before 1066. It paid tax for 5 hides. Land for 3 ploughs. In lordship 1 plough; 4 slaves; 4½ hides.

59
a 1

7 ɪɪ.uilłi 7 ɪɪɪɪ.borđ.cū.ɪ.caɼ.Ibi moliñ redđ.xxx.denaɼ.

7 xvɪ.ac p̃ti.Paſtura.ɪɪɪ.q̃ɀ lḡ.7 ɪɪ.q̃ɀ laɼ.7 in alio loco

vɪɪɪ.q̃ɀ paſturæ.Valuit.c.ſoliđ.Modo.ɪɪɪɪ.liɓ.

Berolđ teñ dè eađ TARENTE.Vñ tain tenuit T.R.E

7 gelđɓ ꝑ.ɪ.hida 7 ɪɪɪ.v́ træ.T́ra.e̅.ɪ.caɼ 7 dim̃.Ibi sɼ.ɪɪɪ.

borđ.cū.ɪ.ſeruo.7 vɪɪ.ac p̃ti.7 ɪɪ.q̃ɀ paſturæ in lḡ.7 ɪɪ.laɼ.

Valuit.xL.ſoliđ.Modo.xv.ſoliđ.

Ipſa teñ LANGETONE.Vñ tain tenuit T.R.E.7 gelđɓ

ꝑ.ɪ.hida 7 dim̃.T́ra.e̅.ɪɪɪ.caɼ.In dñio sɼ.ɪɪ.caɼ.cū.ɪ.ſeruo.

7 ɪ.uilł 7 vɪɪ.borđ.cū.ɪ.caɼ.Ibi.ɪɪɪɪ.ac p̃ti.7 xL.ac paſturæ

Valuit.xxx.ſoł.Modo.xL.ſoliđ.

Duo milites teñ de eađ dimiđ hiđ in RISTONE.Tres taini

libere tenueɼ.T.R.E.7 ꝑ tanto gelđɓ.T́ra.e̅ dimiđ caɼ.Ibi.xx.ac

p̃ti.7 cc.ac paſturæ.Valet.x.ſoliđ.

Hugo teñ de eađ CELVEDVNE.Nouē taini tenueɼ T.R.E. in paragio.

7 gelđɓ ꝑ.v.hiđ.T́ra.e̅.ɪɪɪɪ.caɼ.In dñio sɼ.ɪɪ.caɼ.7 ɪɪ.ſerui.

7 v.uilłi.7 vɪɪɪ.borđ.cū.ɪɪ.caɼ.Ibi.ɪɪɪ.ac p̃ti.7 vɪɪ.q̃ɀ paſ

turæ in lḡ.7 v.q̃ɀ in laɼ.Valuit.x.liɓ.Modo.vɪɪɪ.liɓ.

Hugo teñ de eađ RINGESTEDE.Vlnod tenuit T.R.E. libe

7 gelđɓ ꝑ.ɪ.hida.T́ra.e̅.ɪ.caɼ.Ibi sɼ.ɪɪ.uilłi 7 ɪɪ.borđ

7 vɪɪɪ.ac p̃ti.7 ɪɪ.q̃ɀ paſturæ in lḡ.7 una q̃ɀ in laɼ.

Valuit.xxx.ſoł.Modo.xxv.ſoliđ.

Turolđ teñ de eađ WARMEWELLE.Almæɼ tenuit T.R.E.

7 gelđɓ ꝑ.ɪ.hida 7 dim̃.T́ra.e̅.ɪɪ.caɼ.q̄ ibi sɼ in dñio.7 v.

borđ.Ibi moliñ redđ.v.ſoliđ.Paſtura dimiđ leū 7 ɪɪɪ.q̃ɀ

lḡ.7 ɪɪɪ.q̃ɀ laɼ.Valuit.xxx.ſoliđ.Modo.xL.ſoliđ.

2 villagers and 4 smallholders with 1 plough and ½ hide.
A mill which pays 30d; meadow, 16 acres; pasture 3 furlongs   E
long and 2 furlongs wide; in another place pasture,   E
8 furlongs; woodland, 6 furlongs in length and 2 furlongs in width. 2 cattle;   E
20 pigs; 120 sheep.
The value was 100s; now £4.   E

30 Berold holds 'TARRANT' also from her. A thane held it before
1066. It paid tax for 1 hide and 3 virgates of land. Land for
1½ ploughs. In lordship 1½ hides.   59
3 smallholders with 1 slave (have) 1 virgate.   a 2
Meadow, 7 acres; pasture, 2 furlongs in length and 2 wide.
The value was 40s; now 15s.   E

31 She holds LANGTON (Herring) herself. A thane held it before 1066.
It paid tax for 1½ hides. Land for 3 ploughs. In lordship 2 ploughs
and 3 virgates, with 1 slave;   59
1 villager and 7 smallholders with 1 plough and 3 virgates.   a 3
Meadow, 4 acres; pasture, 40 acres. 6 pigs; 170 sheep; 1 cob.
The value was 30s; now 40s.

32 Two men-at-arms hold ½ hide in RUSHTON also from her. Three   E
thanes held it freely before 1066. It paid tax for as much. Land   59
for ½ plough.   b 1
Meadow, 20 acres; pasture, 200 acres.
Value 10s.

33 Hugh holds CHALDON also from her. Nine thanes held it jointly   E
before 1066. It paid tax for 5 hides. Land for 4 ploughs. In
lordship 2 ploughs; 2 slaves; 2½ hides.   59
5 villagers and 8 smallholders with 2 ploughs and 2½ hides.   b 2
Meadow, 3 acres; pasture, 7 furlongs in length and 5 furlongs
in width. 3 cattle; 302 sheep.
The value was £10; now £8; in Hugh's lifetime it paid £11.

34 Hugh holds RINGSTEAD also from her. Wulfnoth held it freely   E
before 1066. It paid tax for 1 hide. Land for 1 plough. In lordship   60
3 virgates, less 5 acres.   a 1
2 villagers and 2 smallholders (have) 1 virgate and 5 acres and ½ plough.
Meadow, 8 acres; pasture, 2 furlongs in length and 1 furlong
in width. 100 sheep, less 7.
The value was 30s; now 25s.

35 Thorold holds WARMWELL also from her. Aelmer held it before   E
1066. It paid tax for 1½ hides. Land for 2 ploughs, which are   E
there, in lordship, and 1 hide and 1 virgate.   60
5 smallholders (have) ½ hide.   a 2
A mill which pays 5s; pasture ½ league and 3 furlongs long
and 3 furlongs wide. 10 pigs; 200 sheep.
The value was 30s; now 40s.

Radulf[9] ten̄ de ead̄ *RINGESTEDE* . Onouuin̄[9] tenuit T.R.E.

7 geldb̄ ⸱p. i. hida 7 dim̄. Ťra. ē. ii. car̄. In dn̄io. ē. i. car̄.

7 i. uills 7 iii. bord̄ cū dim̄ car̄.7 iiii. q̄ӡ pasturæ . Valet . xl . sol.

84 a

Rob̄t[9] ten̄ de ead̄ fem̄.*CRIZ*. Boln tenuit T.R.E.7 geldb̄

⸱p dim̄ hida . Ťra. ē dim̄ car̄. q̄ ibi. ē cū. iiii. bord̄.7 iii. ac̄

p̄ti.7 vii. q̄ӡ pasturæ in lḡ.7 iii. q̄ӡ in lat̄. Valet. x .sol.

Rob̄t[9] ten̄ de ead̄ *HERPERE* . Aluuard̄[9] tenuit T.R.E.

7 geldb̄ ⸱p. iii. hid̄. Ťra. ē. iii . car̄ . In dn̄io. ē. i. car̄ 7 dimid̄.

7 iii. serui.7 ii. coscez. Ibi molin̄ redd̄. xx. denar̄.7 ix. ac̄

p̄ti.7 iiii. q̄ӡ pasturæ .7 i. q̄ӡ siluæ.7 uñ burḡs redd̄. viii.

denar̄. Valuit. c .solid̄. Modo. iiii. lib̄.

In ead̄ uilla ten̄ Rob̄t de ipsa fem̄ dimid̄ hid̄. Sauuin̄[9] tenuit

⸱p Maner̄ T.R.E. Ťra. ē dim̄ car̄. Valet. xii . sol.7 vi. denar̄.

Ipsa ten̄ *WILCESWDE* . Aluuard̄ tenuit T.R.E.7 geldb̄ ⸱p. iii.

hid̄ 7 dim̄.7 ii. partibӡ uni v̄. Ťra. ē. iii . car̄ 7 dim̄. In dn̄io. ē. i. car̄.

7 ii. serui.7 ii. uilli 7 iiii. bord̄. cū. i. car̄.7 ii. ac̄ p̄ti.7 iiii. q̄ӡ siluæ

Valuit 7 ual. iiii . lib̄.

Ipsa ten̄ *TACATONE* . Aluuard̄ tenuit T.R.E.7 geldb̄ ⸱p. ii. hid̄

7 dim̄. Ťra. ē. ii. car̄. In dn̄io. ē. i. car̄.7 iii. serui.7 ii. uilli.7 i. bord̄

cū. i. car̄. Ibi molin̄ redd̄. xii . sol.7 vi. den̄. Silua. ii. q̄ӡ lḡ.

7 una q̄ӡ 7 dim̄ lat̄. Valuit. lx. sol. Modo. xl. solid̄.

Walter[9] ten̄ de ead̄ *SVVANWIC* . Aluuard tenuit[in parag'.] T.R.E.

7 geldb̄ ⸱p. i. hida 7 dim̄. Ťra. ē. i. car̄. q̄ ibi. ē cū. i. seruo.7 i. bord̄.

Ibi. vii. ac̄ p̄ti. Valuit. xx . sol. Modo. xxv. solid̄.

36 Ralph the Steward holds RINGSTEAD also from her. Hunwine held it
before 1066. It paid tax for 1½ hides. Land for 2 ploughs. In
lordship 1 plough; 1 hide and ½ virgate.
  1 villager and 3 smallholders with ½ plough and ½ virgate.
  Pasture, 4 furlongs. 1 cob; 4 cattle; 10 pigs; 53 sheep.
Value 40s; when Hugh acquired it, as much.

60
a 3
E

37 Robert the Corn-dealer holds CREECH also from this woman. Bolle
held it before 1066. It paid tax for ½ hide. Land for ½ plough,
which is there, with
  4 smallholders.
  Meadow, 3 acres; pasture, 7 furlongs in length and 3 furlongs
    in width. 1 cob.
Value 10s.

84 a
E

60
b 1

38 Robert Boy holds HURPSTON also from her. Alward held it before
1066. It paid tax for 3 hides. Land for 3 ploughs. In lordship 1½
ploughs; 3 slaves; 3 hides.
  2 Cottagers.
  A mill which pays 20d; meadow, 9 acres; pasture, 4 furlongs;
    woodland, 1 furlong. 1 cob; 6 cattle; 20 pigs; 103 sheep.
  A burgess who pays 8d.
The value was 100s; now £4.

60
b 2

E

39 Also in this village Robert Boy holds ½ hide from the woman
herself. Saewin held it as a manor before 1066. Land for ½
plough.
Value 12s 6d.

E
60
b 3

E

40 She holds WILKSWOOD herself. Alward held it before 1066. It paid
tax for 3½ hides and 2 parts of 1 virgate. Land for 3½ ploughs.
In lordship 1 plough; 2 slaves; 2½ hides.
  2 villagers and 4 smallholders with 1 plough and 2 oxen and 1 hide.
  Meadow, 2 acres; woodland, 4 furlongs. 1 cob; 16 sheep.
The value was and is £4.

60
b 4

E

41 She holds ACTON herself. Alward held it before 1066. It paid tax
for 2½ hides. Land for 2 ploughs. In lordship 1 plough; 3 slaves;
2 hides.
  2 villagers and 1 smallholder with 1 plough and ½ hide.
  A mill which pays 12s 6d; woodland 2 furlongs long and 1½
    furlongs wide. 4 cattle.
The value was 60s; now 40s.

61
a 1

42 Walter Thunder holds SWANAGE also from her. Alward held it jointly
before 1066. It paid tax for 1½ hides. Land for 1 plough, which
is there, with 1 slave.
  1 smallholder.
  Meadow, 7 acres. 20 sheep; 5 pigs.
The value was 20s; now 25s.

E

61
a 2

Radulf⁹ ten de ead͛ . III . v͛ træ in *WIRDE* . Duo taini tenueŕ ^{in parag'.}

T.R.E.7 ᵱ tanto geldб . Tra . e̅ dim̅ caŕ . q̅ ibi . e̅ cu̅ . II . bord͛ . Valet

Walter ten de ead͛ *TORNE* . Aluric tenuit T.R.E. ^{in parag'.} ₤ xv . folid͛.

7 geldб ᵱ . I . hida . Tra . e̅ . I . caŕ.   Valet . xviii . fot.

Roбt ten de ead͛ *TORNE* . Sauuin tenuit T.R.E.7 geldб ᵱ . I . hida.

Tra . e̅ . I . caŕ . q̅ ibi . e̅ in dn̅io . Valuit . x . fot. Modo . xx . folid͛.

Hugo ten de ead͛ *BRVNESCVME* . Algar tenuit T.R.E.7 geldб ^{in paragio.}

ᵱ una v͛ træ . Tra . e̅ . I . caŕ . Ibi st̅ . III . bord͛.7 paftura dim̅ leu̅

lg̅ .7 IIII . q̅ꝛ lat̅ . Silua . IIII . q̅ꝛ lg̅ .7 una q̅ꝛ lat̅ . Valet . x . folid͛.

Ipfa ten *HORCERD* . Quattuor taini tenueŕ T.R.E.7 geldб

ᵱ una hida 7 dim̅ . Tra . e̅ . I . caŕ 7 dim̅ . Ibi st̅ . II . bord͛.7 uirgultu̅.

Hanc hida̅ ded͛ Hugo ᵱ anima fua æcc̅læ de   ₤ Valet . xx . fot.

Creneburne .7 Valet . xx . folid͛. Dimid͛ u̅ hid͛ ten̅ Vxor hug̅.

Durand⁹ ten̅ de ead͛ dim̅ hid͛ in *WILCHESODE* . Tra . e̅ dim̅ caŕ.

Valet . x . folid͛. Duo taini tenueŕ . T.R.E.

Om̅s taini q̅ T.R.E. has tras teneб:́ poteraɲ́ ire ad que̅ dn̅m uoleб

Iseldis ten̅ de rege *PITRICHESHA͂* . Wade tenuit T.R.E.

7 geldб ᵱ . I . hida . Tra . e̅ . I . caŕ . Ibi st̅ . xi . bord͛.7 molin̅ redd͛

v . folid͛ 7 x . den̅ .7 vii . ac̅ pti . Paftura . I . q̅ꝛ lg̅ .7 dim̅ q̅ꝛ lat̅.

Silua . I . q̅ꝛ lg̅ .7 alia lat̅ . Valet . xv . folid͛.

43 Ralph holds 3 virgates of land in WORTH (Matravers) also from her.   E
   Two thanes held them jointly before 1066. They paid tax for as   61
   much. Land for ½ plough, which is there, with   E   a 3
   2 smallholders.
   Value 15s.

44 Walter Thunder holds 'THORNE' also from her. Aelfric held it jointly
   before 1066. It paid tax for 1 hide. Land for 1 plough.   61
   Walter holds the whole (of the land) in lordship.   a 4
   Value 18s.

45 Robert, Hugh's nephew, holds 'THORNE' also from her. Saewin held it
   jointly before 1066. It paid tax for 1 hide. Land for 1 plough,   E
   which is there, in lordship.   61
   The value was 10s; now 20s.   b 1

46 Hugh of Boscherbert holds BRENSCOMBE also from her. Algar held it
   jointly before 1066. It paid tax for 1 virgate of land. Land for 1
   plough.
     3 smallholders.   61
     Pasture ½ league long and 4 furlongs wide; woodland 4   b 2
       furlongs long and 1 furlong wide.
   Value 10s.

47 She holds ORCHARD herself. Four thanes held it before 1066.   E
   It paid tax for 1½ hides. Land for 1½ ploughs.   61
     2 smallholders.   b 3
     An orchard.   E
   Hugh gave this hide to the Church of Cranborne for his   E
   soul('s sake); value 20s.
   But Hugh's wife holds the ½ hide; value 20s.   E

48 Durand Carpenter holds ½ hide in WILKSWOOD also from her. Land
   for ½ plough.   61
   Value 10s.   b 4
   Two thanes held it before 1066.

All the thanes who held these lands before 1066 could go to which   E
lord they would.

[55a]   [LAND OF ISOLDE]   E

1 Isolde holds PETERSHAM from the King. Wada held it before 1066.
  It paid tax for 1 hide. Land for 1 plough.
    11 smallholders.
    A mill which pays 5s 10d; meadow, 7 acres; pasture 1 furlong
      long and ½ furlong wide; woodland 1 furlong long and
      another wide.
  Value 15s.

TERRE TAINOƷ REGIS.

GVDMVND ten *MIDELTONE*.Ide tenuit T.R.E.⁊ geldb ͵p.IIII.hid ⁊ dim.Tra.e̅.III.car.In dn̅io.e̅.I.car.⁊ II.ferui.⁊ II.uiłł ⁊ VIII.bord cu̅.I.car.Ibi molin.XII.denar.⁊ x.ac pti.Silua.VIII.q̅ƺ lg̅. ⁊ dim q̅ƺ lat.Valuit.LX.fot.Modo.xxx.folid.

CHETEL ten *CHINTONE*.Dodo tenuit T.R.E.⁊ geldb ͵p.III.hid ⁊ III.v træ.Tra.e̅.III.car.In dn̅io st.II.car.cu̅.I.feruo.⁊ I.uiłł ⁊ III.bord.Ibi.xv.ac pti.⁊ v.ac filuæ.Valuit ⁊ uat.XL.folid

EDVIN ten una̅ v træ in *GELINGEHA̅*.Tra.e̅ dim car.Valet

GODRIC ten una̅ v træ in *GELINGEHA̅*.Tra.e̅ dimid car.ʄv.fot.

Ibi st.IIII.bord.⁊ III.ac pti.Valet.v.folid.   ʄvi.folid.

VLVVIN ten una̅ v træ ⁊ dim in *GELINGEHA̅*.Tra.e̅ dim car.Valet

ALVRIC ten.I.hid in *WINTREBVRNE*.Tra.e̅.I.car.Valet.x.folid.

BOLLO ten *MAPLEDRE*.Ipfe tenuit cu̅ alijs.VII.tainis T.R.E. ⁊ geldb ͵p.v.hid ⁊ III.v træ.Tra.e̅.v.car.In dn̅io st.II.car.⁊ II. ferui.⁊ VIII.uiłłi ⁊ IIII.bord.cu̅.III.car.Ibi aliqtu̅ pti.⁊ Silua IIII.q̅ƺ lg̅.⁊ III.q̅ƺ lat.Valet.IIII.lib.

BOLLO ten *CICHERELLE*.Saulf tenuit.T.R.E.⁊ geldb ͵p.III.hid ⁊ dimid v træ.Tra.e̅.III.car.q̅ ibi st in dn̅io.⁊ IĻII.ferui.⁊ un uiłłs ⁊ vi.bord.Ibi.vi.ac pti.⁊ vii.q̅ƺ pafturæ.Valet.LX.fot.

BRICTVIN ten *WAIA*.Ipfe tenuit T.R.E.⁊ geldb ͵p.II.hid. Tra.e̅.II.car.q̅ ibi st in dn̅io.⁊ III.ferui.⁊ II.uiłłi ⁊ IIII.bord. Ibi molin redd.xv.folid.⁊ III.ac pti.⁊ II.ac pafturæ.Valet.XL.

                                        ʄ folid.

1   Godmund holds MILTON (on Stour). He also held it before 1066.
It paid tax for 4½ hides. Land for 3 ploughs. In lordship 1 plough;
2 slaves;
    2 villagers and 8 smallholders with 1 plough.
    A mill, 12d; meadow, 10 acres; woodland 8 furlongs long
       and ½ furlong wide.
The value was 60s; now 30s.

2   Ketel holds KINGTON. Doda held it before 1066. It paid tax for 3
hides and 3 virgates of land. Land for 3 ploughs. In lordship 2
ploughs, with 1 slave;
    1 villager and 3 smallholders.
    Meadow, 15 acres; woodland, 5 acres.
The value was and is 40s.

3   Edwin holds 1 virgate of land in GILLINGHAM. Land for ½ plough.
Value 5s.

4   Godric holds 1 virgate of land in GILLINGHAM. Land for ½ plough.
    4 smallholders.
    Meadow, 3 acres.
Value 5s.

5   Wulfwin holds 1½ virgates of land in GILLINGHAM. Land for ½
plough.
Value 6s.

6   Aelfric holds 1 hide in 'WINTERBORNE'. Land for 1 plough.
Value 10s.

7   Bolle the priest holds MAPPOWDER. He held it himself with another
7 free thanes before 1066. It paid tax for 5 hides and 3 virgates
of land. Land for 5 ploughs. In lordship 2 ploughs; 2 slaves;
    8 villagers and 4 smallholders with 3 ploughs.
    Meadow, 16 [acres?]; woodland 4 furlongs long and 3 furlongs
       wide.
Value £4.

8   Bolle holds CHICKERELL. Saewulf held it before 1066. It paid tax
for 3 hides and ½ virgate of land. Land for 3 ploughs, which are
there, in lordship; 4 slaves;
    1 villager and 6 smallholders.
    Meadow, 6 acres; pasture, 7 furlongs.
Value 60s.

9   Brictwin holds 'WEY'. He held it himself before 1066. It paid tax
for 2 hides. Land for 2 ploughs, which are there, in lordship;
3 slaves;
    2 villagers and 4 smallholders.
    A mill which pays 15s; meadow, 3 acres; pasture, 2 acres.
Value 40s.

BRICTVIN ten.I.hiđ 7 dimiđ in *WINTREBVRNE*.Ipſe tenuit T.R.E.
Tra.ē.I.caŕ.q̄ ibi.ē. Valet.xv.ſoliđ.

BRICTVIN ten unā v̄ træ in *LEWELLE*.Ipſe tenuit T.R.E.Valet.x.den̄.

ALVRIC ten̄ *GRAVEFORD*.7 Eduuard de eo.T.R.E.geldb̄ ꝑ.II.hiđ.
Tra.ē.I.caŕ 7 dim.Tam̄ ſt ibi.II.caŕ.cū.I.coſcet.7 III.ſerui.7 IIIi.pars
molini redđ.xxx.den̄.7 xII.ac̄ p̊ti.7 vI.q̄ʒ ſiluæ in lḡ.7 II.q̄ʒ laŕ.
Valuit.xxx.den̄.Valet.xL.ſoliđ.

VLVRIC ten̄ *MORDONE*.Pat eʒ tenuit T.R.E.7 geldb̄ ꝑ.II.hiđ 7 dim̄.
Tra.ē.II.caŕ.q̄ ibi ſt cū.II.uiłłis 7 vI.borđ.7 de parte molini.xI.den̄.
7 v.ac̄ p̊ti.7 una leū paſturæ in lḡ 7 laŕ.Valet.xxx.ſoliđ.   ſ̄ſoliđ.
Vxor fris Vlurici hī ibi.I.hiđ 7 dimiđ v̄ træ.Tra.ē.I.caŕ. Valet.xx.

EDVIN ten̄ *BLENEFORDE*. Aluuin tenuit T.R.E.7 geldb̄ ꝑ.v.hiđ
7 virg 7 dimiđ.Tra.ē.III.caŕ.In dn̄io.ē.I.caŕ.7 III.ſerui.7 II.uiłłi
7 I.borđ.7 III.cotaŕ cū.I.caŕ.Ibi.xvIII.ac̄ p̊ti.Paſtura.vIII.q̄ʒ lḡ.
7 II.q̄ʒ laŕ.Valuit.IIII.lib̄.Valet xL.ſoliđ.

ALWARD ten̄ *TORNECOME*. Ipſe tenuit T.R.E.7 geldb̄ ꝑ.II.hiđ.
Tra.ē.I.caŕ.q̄ ibi.ē cū.I.ſeruo.7 IIII.borđ.Valet.xx.ſoliđ.

VLVIET ten̄ *WINBVRNE*.Ipſe teneb̄ T.R.E.7 geldb̄ ꝑ.I.hida.
Ibi.ē.I.caŕ.cū.I.ſeruo.Paſtura.IIII.q̄ʒ lḡ.7 una laŕ.Silua.I.q̄ʒ
lḡ.7 dimiđ q̄ʒ laŕ.Valuit.xx.ſoliđ.Modo.x.ſoliđ.

BRICTVIN ten̄ *MELEBERIE*.T.R.E.geldb̄ ꝑ.v.hiđ.Tra.ē.IIII.caŕ.
In dn̄io ſt.II.caŕ.7 v.ſerui.7 IIII.uiłłi.7 Ix.borđ.cū.II.caŕ.
Ibi.III.ac̄ p̊ti.7 III.q̄ʒ ſiluæ in lḡ.7 III.in laŕ.Valet.Lx.ſoliđ.

10 Brictwin holds 1½ hides in 'WINTERBORNE'. He held them himself
before 1066. Land for 1 plough, which is there.
Value 15s.

11 Brictwin holds 1 virgate of land in LEWELL. He held it himself
before 1066.
Value 10d.

12 Aelfric holds '(Great) CRAWFORD', and Edward from him. Before
1066 it paid tax for 2 hides. Land for 1½ ploughs. However, 2
ploughs there, with
1 Cottager; 3 slaves.
The fourth part of a mill which pays 30d; meadow, 12 acres;
woodland, 6 furlongs in length and 2 furlongs wide.
The value was 30d; value 40s.

13 Wulfric holds MORDEN. His father held it before 1066. It paid tax
for 2½ hides. Land for 2 ploughs, which are there, with
2 villagers and 6 smallholders.
From part of a mill 11d; meadow, 5 acres; pasture, 1 league
in length and width.
Value 30s.
The wife of Wulfric's brother has 1 hide and ½ virgate of land
there. Land for 1 plough. Value 20s.

14 Edwin holds BLANDFORD (St. Mary). Alwin held it before 1066.
It paid tax for 5 hides and (1)½ virgates. Land for 3 ploughs.
In lordship 1 plough; 3 slaves;
2 villagers, 1 smallholder and 3 cottagers with 1 plough.
Meadow, 18 acres; pasture 8 furlongs long and 2 furlongs wide.
The value was £4; value 40s.

15 Alward holds THORNICOMBE. He held it himself before 1066. It paid
tax for 2 hides. Land for 1 plough, which is there, with 1 slave;
4 smallholders.
Value 20s.

16 Wulfgeat holds WIMBORNE (St. Giles). He held it himself before
1066. It paid tax for 1 hide. 1 plough there, with 1 slave.
Pasture 4 furlongs long and 1 wide; woodland 1 furlong long
and ½ furlong wide.
The value was 20s; now 10s.

17 Brictwin holds MELBURY. Before 1066 it paid tax for 5 hides.
Land for 4 ploughs. In lordship 2 ploughs; 5 slaves;
4 villagers and 9 smallholders with 2 ploughs.
Meadow, 3 acres; woodland, 3 furlongs in length and 3 in width.
Value 60s.

VLVRICVS teñ $TORNEHELLE$. Pāt ej tenuit T.R.E.7 geldb ꝓ dim hida.Tra.ē.ı.car̄.ḡ ibi.ē cū.v.borđ 7 v.cotar̄.7 v.ac̄ p̄ti.Valet.x

TORCHIL teñ $HAME$.T.R.E.geldb ꝓ.ııı.v træ 7 tcia parte ⨍ſoliđ. uni v.Tra.ē.ı.car̄.Ibi.ē dim car̄ cū.ı.borđ.7 vı.ac̄ p̄ti.7 ıı.q̄ꝗ ſiluæ.7 ıı.q̄ꝗ paſturæ l̄g.7 una q̄ꝗ lat̄.Valet.vııı.ſoliđ.

★ Hanc tr̄a deđ regina Schelm.modo h̄t rex in dn̄io.

Dodo teñ dimiđ hiđ.7 ꝓ tanto geldauit.T.R.E.Tra.ē dim car̄.Tam̄ ibi.ē.ı.car̄.7 moliñ redđ.x.ſoliđ.7 xıııı.ac̄ p̄ti.7 dimiđ ac̄ ſiluæ. paſtura dimiđ leū l̄g.7 ııı.q̄ꝗ lat̄.Valet.xvıı.ſoliđ.7 vı.deñ. Hanc tr̄a deđ regina dodoni in elemoſina.

Idē teñ in $WEDECHESWORDE$.ı.hiđ 7 ꝓ tanto geldb T.R.E.Tra.ē .ı.car̄.ḡ ibi.ē cū.ıı.ſeruis.7 ıı.uiłłis 7 ıı.borđ h̄ntes dimiđ car̄. Ibi.xıııı.ac̄ p̄ti.7 ıı.q̄ꝗ ſiluæ in l̄g.7 una q̄ꝗ lat̄.Valet.x.ſoliđ.

ALWARD teñ tcia partē uni virḡ træ.7 redđ xxx.denar̄.

AILRVN teñ $WEDECHESWORDE$.Ibi.ē.ı.hida.Tra.ē.ı.car̄. ḡ ibi.ē cū.ıı.borđ 7 ıı.ſeruis.7 paſtura.ıııı.q̄ꝗ l̄g.7 una q̄ꝗ lat̄. 7 tntđ ſiluæ.Valet.x.ſoliđ.

GODVIN teñ $WALTEFORD$.Almar tenuit T.R.E.7 geldb ꝓ.ı. hida.Tra.ē.ı.car̄.ḡ ibi.ē cū.ııı.borđ.7 vıı.ac̄ p̄ti.7 Paſtura .v.q̄ꝗ l̄g.7 ıı.q̄ꝗ lat̄.7 una q̄ꝗ ſiluæ.Valet.xv.ſoliđ.

AILWARD teñ in $RISTONE$ unā v træ.Tra.ē.ıı.boū.Valet.xxx.deñ.

18 Wulfric holds THORN HILL. His father held it before 1066. It paid
tax for ½ hide. Land for 1 plough, which is there, with
    5 smallholders and 5 cottagers.
    Meadow, 5 acres.
Value 10s.

19 Thorkell holds HAMPRESTON. Before 1066 it paid tax for 3 virgates
of land and the third part of 1 virgate. Land for 1 plough. ½
plough there, with
    1 smallholder.
    Meadow, 6 acres; woodland, 2 furlongs; pasture, 2 furlongs
        long and 1 furlong wide.
Value 8s.
    The Queen gave this land to Azelin; now the King has it in
lordship.

20 Doda holds ½ hide. It paid tax for as much before 1066. Land
for ½ plough. However, 1 plough there.
    A mill which pays 10s; meadow, 14 acres; woodland, ½ acre;
        pasture ½ league long and 3 furlongs wide.
Value 17s 6d.
    The Queen gave this land to Doda in alms.

21 He also holds 1 hide in WILKSWORTH. It paid tax for as much
before 1066. Land for 1 plough, which is there, with 2 slaves and
    2 villagers; 2 smallholders who have ½ plough.
    Meadow, 14 acres; woodland, 2 furlongs in length and 1
        furlong wide.
Value 10s.

22 Alward holds the third part of 1 virgate of land.
It pays 30d.

23 Aethelrun holds WILKSWORTH. 1 hide there. Land for 1 plough,
which is there, with
    2 smallholders and 2 slaves.
    Pasture 4 furlongs long and 1 furlong wide; woodland, as much.
Value 10s.

24 Godwin Hunter holds WALFORD. Aelmer held it before 1066. It
paid tax for 1 hide. Land for 1 plough, which is there, with
    3 smallholders.
    Meadow, 7 acres; pasture 5 furlongs long and 2 furlongs wide;
        woodland, 1 furlong.
Value 15s.

25 Alward holds 1 virgate of land in RUSHTON. Land for 2 oxen.
Value 30d.

G ͡ppofit· ꝯ ꞁ
ODVIN ten in *WINTREBVRNE*.ı.hiđ.Ipſe tenuit T.R.E.Tᷓra
ē.ı.caͬ.Ibi.ē uꝴ borđ.Valet.xıı.ſoliđ 7 vı.denaͬ.

G uenator ꝯ ꞁ ꞁ ꞁ
ODVIN teñ unā v træ 7 ıııı.aćs.7 ibi hͭ dimiđ caͬ cū.v.borđ.
7 ıx.aćs p̄ti.Valet.x.ſoliđ.Godricus tenuit T.R.E.

S ꞁ ꝯ
VAIN ten *WINTREBVRNE*.Paͭ ej tenuit T.R.E.7 geldᵬ
ꝑ.x.hiđ.Tᷓra.ē.vı.caͬ.In dn̄io sͭ.ıı.caͬ:7 v.ſerui.7 vıı.uiꞇꞇi
7 xvıı.borđ cū.ııı.caͬ.Ibi.x.ac̄ p̄ti.Paſtura.ı.leū 7 dimiđ
lͬg.7 dimiđ laͭ.Silua.ı.leū 7 dimiđ lͬg.7 ıııı.q̄ꝗ laͭ.
Valuit.c.ſoliđ.Modo.vııı.liᵬ.Roᵬt teñ de Suain

I ꝯ ꝯ
đē Suain teñ *PLVBERE*.7 Radulf de eo.Paͭ ej tenuit T.R.E.
7 geldᵬ ꝑ.v.hiđ.Tᷓra.ē.ııı.caͬ.In dn̄io.ē una caͬ.7 ıııı.ſerui.
7 ııı.uiꞇꞇi 7 vı.borđ cū.ı.caͬ.Ibi.xv.ac̄ p̄ti.Silua.v.q̄ꝗ lͬg.
7 ııı.q̄ꝗ laͭ.Valuit.xxx.ſoliđ.Modo.ʟx.ſoliđ.

V uenator ꞁ ꝯ
ʟurıc teñ.ı.hiđ de rege.Paͭ ej tenuit T.R.E.7 ꝑ tanto geldᵬ.
Tᷓra.ē.ı.caͬ.Ibi sͭ.ııı.borđ.7 ııı.ac̄ p̄ti.Valet.x.ſoliđ.

E ꝯ ꞁ
dvıñ teñ *BLENEFORD*.Aluui tenuit T.R.E.7 geldᵬ ꝑ.v.hiđ.
Tᷓra.ē.ıııı.caͬ.In dn̄io.ē.ı.caͬ 7 dimiđ.7 ııı.ſerui.7 ııı.uiꞇꞇi cū
pᵬro 7 vı.borđ 7 ııı.cotaͬ cū.ı.caͬ.Ibi moiñ redđ.xvııı.ſoꞁ 7 ıııı. ★
denaͬ.7 xvııı.ac̄ p̄ti.Paſtura.v.q̄ꝗ lͬg.7 ıı.q̄ꝗ laͭ.Valet.ıııı.liᵬ.

E ꝯ ꞁ
dvıñ teñ *WERNE*.Aluuard tenuit T.R.E.7 geldᵬ ꝑ.ııı.hiđ.
Tᷓra.ē.ıı.caͬ.q̄ ibi sͭ cū.ı.uiꞇꞇo 7 ııı.coſcez.7 ııı.ſeruis.Ibi mo
liñ redđ.ıı.ſoliđ 7 ıııı.q̄ꝗ paſturæ 7 dim in lͬg.7 ıı.q̄ꝗ laͭ.Silua

84 c
vı.q̄ꝗ lͬg.7 ıı.q̄ꝗ laͭ.Valuit.ʟx.ſoliđ.Modo.xxx.ſoliđ.

26   Godwin the reeve holds 1 hide in 'WINTERBORNE'. He held it himself before 1066. Land for 1 plough.
    1 smallholder.
Value 12s 6d.

27   Godwin Hunter holds 1 virgate of land and 4 acres. He has ½ plough, with
    5 smallholders;
    meadow, 9 acres.
Value 10s.
    Godric held it before 1066.

28   Swein holds WINTERBORNE (Houghton). His father held it before 1066. It paid tax for 10 hides. Land for 6 ploughs. In lordship 2 ploughs; 5 slaves;
    7 villagers and 17 smallholders with 3 ploughs.
    Meadow, 10 acres; pasture 1½ leagues long and ½ wide; woodland 1½ leagues long and 4 furlongs wide.
The value was 100s; now £8.
    Robert holds it from Swein.

29   Swein also holds PLUMBER, and Ralph from him. His father held it before 1066. It paid tax for 5 hides. Land for 3 ploughs. In lordship 1 plough; 4 slaves;
    3 villagers and 6 smallholders with 1 plough.
    Meadow, 15 acres; woodland 5 furlongs long and 3 furlongs wide.
The value was 30s; now 60s.

30   Wulfric Hunter holds 1 hide from the King. His father held it before 1066. It paid tax for as much. Land for 1 plough.
    3 smallholders.
    Meadow, 3 acres.
Value 10s.

31   Edwin holds (Langton Long) BLANDFORD. Alwy held it before 1066. It paid tax for 5 hides. Land for 4 ploughs. In lordship 1½ ploughs; 3 slaves;
    3 villagers with a priest, 6 smallholders and 3 cottagers with 1 plough.
    A mill which pays 18s 4d; meadow, 18 acres; pasture 5 furlongs long and 2 furlongs wide.
Value £4.

32   Edwin holds LAZERTON. Alward held it before 1066. It paid tax for 3 hides. Land for 2 ploughs, which are there, with
    1 villager, 3 Cottagers and 3 slaves.
    A mill which pays 2s; pasture, 4½ furlongs in length and 2 furlongs wide; woodland 6 furlongs long and 2 furlongs wide.
                           84 c
The value was 60s; now 30s.

Idē Eduiñ tēñ *SILFEMETONE*. Aluui tenuit T.R.E.7 geldb
,p. ii. hid 7 dim . Tra.ē.ii.car.Ibi.ē uñ uilts 7 v. ferui cū dim
car.7 xv. ac p̄ti.7 iii.q̄ꝥ pafturæ in lḡ 7 lat.Valet.xl.folid.
Vlviet teñ *BLENEFORD*.Ipfe tenuit T.R.E.7 geldb ,p.i.hida.
Tra.ē.i.car.Ibi st.iiii.cofcez.7 iii.ac p̄ti.7 v.ac pafturæ.
Valuit 7 ual.x.folid.
Brictvin teñ *CILTECOME*.Ipfe tenuit T.R.E.7 geldb ,p.iii.hid.
Tra.ē.iii.car.In dñio st.ii.car.7 v.ferui.7 uñ uilts 7 viii.bord
cū dimid car.Ibi moliñ redd.v.folid.7 xxv.ac p̄ti.7 xx.ac pa
fturæ.Valet.lx.folid.
Idē teñ *WADONE*.Aluuard tenuit T.R.E.7 geldb ,p.ii.hid.
Tra.ē.ii.car.q̄ ibi st in dñio.7 iiii.ferui.7 i.uilts 7 iii.bord.
Ibi.xvi.ac p̄ti.7 xiiii.ac pafturæ.Valet.xl.folid.
Hanc trā cābiuit Hugo Briċtuino.Qꝺ modo teñ Comes morit.
7 ipfū Scābiū ualet duplū.
Idē Briċtuiñ teñ in *MORTVNE*.i.hidā 7 viii.acs træ.Ipfe
tenuit T.R.E.Tra.ē.i.car.Hanc hñt ibi.iii.uilti 7 iiii.bord.
Ibi.xi.ac p̄ti.7 vi.q̄ꝥ pafturæ in lḡ.7 iiii.q̄ꝥ in lat.
Valet.xxi.folid 7 iii.denar.
Idē.B.teñ *GAVELTONE*,Ipfe tenuit T.R.E.7 geldb ,p.ii.hid
7 una v træ 7 dimid.Tra.ē.ii.car.In dñio.ē.i.car.7 iii.ferui.
7 ii.uilti 7 vi.cotar.Ibi moliñ redd.xii.fot.7 vi.den.7 ii.ac
p̄ti.7 viii.q̄ꝥ pafture in lḡ.7 iii.q̄ꝥ in lat.Valet.xl.folid.
Idē.B.teñ.i.hid in *RINGESTEDE*.Ipfe tenuit T.R.E.Tra.ē
.i.car.Sex hōes teñ eā ad firmā.Valet.xxv.folid.

33 Edwin also holds SHILVINGHAMPTON. Alwy held it before 1066.
It paid tax for 2½ hides. Land for 2 ploughs.
1 villager and 5 slaves with ½ plough.
Meadow, 15 acres; pasture, 3 furlongs in length and width.
Value 40s.

34 Wulfgeat holds BRYANSTON. He held it himself before 1066.
It paid tax for 1 hide. Land for 1 plough.
4 Cottagers.
Meadow, 3 acres; pasture, 5 acres.
The value was and is 10s.

35 Brictwin holds CHILCOMBE. He held it himself before 1066. It paid
tax for 3 hides. Land for 3 ploughs. In lordship 2 ploughs;
5 slaves;
1 villager and 8 smallholders with ½ plough.
A mill which pays 5s; meadow, 25 acres; pasture, 20 acres.
Value 60s.

36 He also holds WADDON. Alward held it before 1066. It paid tax
for 2 hides. Land for 2 ploughs, which are there, in lordship;
4 slaves;
1 villager and 3 smallholders.
Meadow, 16 acres; pasture, 14 acres.
Value 40s.
Hugh son of Grip exchanged this land with Brictwin. The
Count of Mortain now holds it. The exchange(d land) itself
is worth twice as much.

Brictwin also holds
37 in MORETON 1 hide and 8 acres of land. He held it himself before
1066. Land for 1 plough.
3 villagers and 4 smallholders have it there.
Meadow, 11 acres; pasture, 6 furlongs in length and 4 furlongs
in width.
Value 21s 3d.

38 GALTON. He held it himself before 1066. It paid tax for 2 hides
and 1½ virgates of land. Land for 2 ploughs. In lordship 1 plough;
3 slaves;
2 villagers and 6 cottagers.
A mill which pays 12s 6d; meadow, 2 acres; pasture, 8 furlongs
in length and 3 furlongs in width.
Value 40s.

39 in RINGSTEAD 1 hide. He held it himself before 1066. Land for 1
plough. Six men hold it at a revenue.
Value 25s.

Idē.B.ten.ii.virg tre 7 dimid in *STINGTEFORD*.7 Aiulf de eo.
Tra.ē dimid car.Ibi st.iii.bord.Valet.vii.folid.
Idē ten unā v træ in *BRIGE*.Tra.ē.ii.boū.Ibi st.ii.pifcatores.
Valet.v.folid.Has tras id Brictuin teneb.T.R.E.

Edric ten.i.hid in *RISTONE*.q̄rta parte uni v min.Sauuin
tenuit T.R.E.Tra.ē.i.car.Ibi st.v.ac p̄ti 7 dimid.Val.ix.fot 7 ii.den.
Id ten.i.hid ad *HOLNE*.Tra.ē.i.car.Valet.xx.folid.
Id ten.i.hid ad *STOCHE*.Tra.ē.ii.car.In dñio.ē.i.car.7 ii.ferui.
7 un uitts 7 viii.bord cū dimid car.Ibi molin redd.xl.den.
7 xiiii.ac p̄ti.7 xvi.ac filuæ.7 xii.ac pafturæ.Valet.xxx.fot.
Id ten.ii.hid ad *SLITLEGE*.Tra.ē.ii.car.In dñio.ē.i.car.7 ii.
ferui.7 ii.uitti 7 iii.bord cū.i.car 7 dimid.Ibi.v.ac p̄ti.7 iii.ac
filuæ.7 una q̄⅜ pafturæ in lḡ.7 altera in lat.Valet.xxv.folid.
Id ten *PILESDONE*.T.R.E.geldb ꝑ.iii.hid.Tra.ē.iiii.car.
Ibi st.vii.uitti 7 viii.bord cū.iii.car.7 xii.ac p̄ti.7 c.ac pafturæ.
Valuit.xx.fot.Modo.xl.folid.
Id ten unā v tre ad *STODLEGE*.Tra.ē dimid car.Valet.v.fot.
Has tras Edrici tenuit Sauuin T.R.E.

Godric ten *PIDELE*.Azor tenuit T.R.E.7 geldb ꝑ.v.hid.
Tra.ē.iii.car.In dñio.ē.i.car.7 vii.ferui.7 ii.uitti 7 iiii.bord
cū.ii.car.Ibi molin redd.vii.folid 7 vi.denar.7 xxxviii.ac p̄ti.
7 xii.ac filuæ.7 xi.q̄⅜ pafturæ in lḡ.7 iiii.lat.Valet.iiii.lib.

40 in STINSFORD 2½ virgates of land. Aiulf holds from him. Land
for ½ plough.
3 smallholders.
Value 7s.

41 He also holds 1 virgate of land in BRIDGE. Land for 2 oxen.
2 fishermen.
Value 5s.
Brictwin also held these lands before 1066.

42 Edric holds in RUSHTON 1 hide, less the fourth part of 1 virgate.
Saewin held it before 1066. Land for 1 plough.
Meadow, 5½ acres.
Value 9s 2d.

He also holds
43 at (East) HOLME 1 hide. Land for 1 plough.
Value 20s.

44 at 'STOKE (Wallis)' 1 hide. Land for 2 ploughs. In lordship 1
plough; 2 slaves;
1 villager and 8 smallholders with ½ plough.
A mill which pays 40d; meadow, 14 acres; woodland, 16 acres;
pasture, 12 acres.
Value 30s.

45 at 'STUDLEY' 2 hides. Land for 2 ploughs. In lordship 1 plough;
2 slaves;
2 villagers and 3 smallholders with 1½ ploughs.
Meadow, 5 acres; woodland, 3 acres; pasture, 1 furlong in
length and another in width.
Value 25s.

46 PILSDON. Before 1066 it paid tax for 3 hides. Land for 4 ploughs.
7 villagers and 8 smallholders with 3 ploughs.
Meadow, 12 acres; pasture, 100 acres.
Value 20s; now 40s.

47 at 'STUDLEY' 1 virgate of land. Land for ½ plough.
Value 5s.

Saewin held these lands of Edric's before 1066.

48 Godric holds BRIANTSPUDDLE. Azor held it before 1066. It paid
tax for 5 hides. Land for 3 ploughs. In lordship 1 plough;
7 slaves;
2 villagers and 4 smallholders with 2 ploughs.
A mill which pays 7s 6d; meadow, 38 acres; woodland, 12
acres; pasture, 11 furlongs in length and 4 wide.
Value £4.

Edric ten unā v̄ træ in *TIGEHA*. Tra . ē . II . boū . Valet . LXV . den.

Dodo ten unā v̄ træ in *WELLACOME* . Tra . ē . II . boū . Ibi st̄ . II.
ac pti . 7 III . q̇ꝫ pasturæ in lḡ 7 lat̄ . Valuit 7 ual̄ . XX . denar.

Alvric 7 Brictric ten dimid hid in *LODRE* . Tra . ē . I . car̄.
Ibi . v . ac pti . 7 XX . ac pasturæ . Valuit 7 ual̄ . X . solid.

Alvric ten *BLACHEMANESTONE* . Ipse tenuit T . R . E . 7 geldb
p una hida . Tra . ē . I . car̄.

Svain ten *MELEBORNE* . 7 Osmund de eo . Pat Suain tenuit
T . R . E . Tra . ē . II . car̄ . Ibi st̄ . VII . bord cū . I . seruo . 7 molin redd
XXV . denar . 7 X . ac pti . 7 XXX . ac pasturæ . Valuit 7 ual̄ . XX . sol.

Godric ten . I . hid in *CANDELE* . Leueron tenuit T . R . E . Tra
ē . I . car̄ . Ibi st̄ . II . serui . cū . I . bord . 7 VI . ac pti . 7 X . ac pasturæ.
7 II . q̇ꝫ siluæ minutæ . Valet . X . solid.

Saward ten in *CANDELE* . II . v̄ træ 7 dimid . Ipse tenuit T . R . E.
Tra . ē dimid car̄ . Ibi . ē una ac pasturæ . Valet . v . solid.

84 d

Duo bord ten q̇rtā parte uni v̄ træ . Valet . XV . denar.

Ipsi libe tenuer T . R . E.

Alvric ten *COME* . Ipse tenuit T . R . E . 7 geldb p . v . hid
7 una v̄ træ Tra . ē . III . car̄ . In dnio st̄ . II . car̄ . 7 IIII . serui.
7 un uilts 7 IIII . bord .   Ibi . VI . ac pti . 7 IIII . q̇ꝫ silue
in lḡ . 7 II . q̇ꝫ lat̄ . Valet . VI . lib.

Svain ten *ALEOVDE* . Azor tenuit T . R . E . 7 geldb p . v . hid
una v̄ min . Tra . ē . VI . car̄ . In dnio st̄ . III . car̄ . cū . I . seruo.
7 uno uilto 7 uno coscet . Ibi . X . ac pti . 7 VIII . q̇ꝫ pasturæ
in lḡ . 7 una q̇ꝫ lat̄ . Silua . I . leū lḡ . 7 tntd lat̄.
Valuit 7 ual̄ . XL . solid . Vxor hugonis ten de Suain.

49 Edric holds 1 virgate of land in TYNEHAM. Land for 2 oxen.
Value 65d.

50 Doda holds 1 virgate of land in WOOLCOMBE. Land for 2 oxen.
Meadow, 2 acres; pasture, 3 furlongs in length and width.
The value was and is 20d.

51 Aelfric and Brictric hold ½ hide in LODERS. Land for 1 plough.
Meadow, 5 acres; pasture, 20 acres.
The value was and is 10s.

52 Aelfric holds BLACKMANSTON. He held it himself before 1066.
It paid tax for 1 hide. Land for 1 plough. ...

53 Swein holds MILBORNE (Stileham), and Osmund from him.
Swein's father held it before 1066. Land for 2 ploughs.
7 smallholders with 1 slave.
A mill which pays 25d; meadow, 10 acres; pasture, 30 acres.
The value was and is 20s.

54 Godric holds 1 hide in (Stourton) CAUNDLE. Leofrun held it
before 1066. Land for 1 plough. 2 slaves, with
1 smallholder.
Meadow, 6 acres; pasture, 10 acres; underwood, 2 furlongs.
Value 10s.

55 Saeward holds 2½ virgates of land in (Purse) CAUNDLE. He held
them himself before 1066. Land for ½ plough.
Pasture, 1 acre.
Value 5s.

56 Two smallholders hold the fourth part of 1 virgate of land.   **84 d**
Value 15d.
They held it freely themselves before 1066.

57 Aelfric holds COOMBE. He held it himself before 1066. It paid tax
for 5 hides and 1 virgate of land. Land for 3 ploughs. In lordship
2 ploughs; 4 slaves;
1 villager and 4 smallholders....
Meadow, 6 acres; woodland, 4 furlongs in length and 2
furlongs wide.
Value £6.

58 Swein holds AILWOOD. Azor held it before 1066. It paid tax for 5
hides, less 1 virgate. Land for 6 ploughs. In lordship 3 ploughs,
with 1 slave and
1 villager and 1 Cottager.
Meadow, 10 acres; pasture, 8 furlongs in length and 1 furlong
wide; woodland 1 league long and as wide.
The value was and is 40s.
Hugh's wife holds it from Swein.

ALVRIC ten BOVINTONE . Ipſe tenuit T.R.E.7 geldꝸ pro
.IIII. hiđ . Tra . ē . III . caꝛ . In dīnio . ē . I . caꝛ . cū . I . ſeruo.
7 III . uiłłi cū . II .caꝛ . Ibi . XL . ac̄ p̄ti . Paſtura . I . leū l̄g.
7 dimiđ leū laꝛ . Valet . XL . ſoliđ.
ALVRIC ten WINTREBVRNE . Ipſe tenuit T.R.E.7 geldꝸ
ꝓ una hida . Tra . ē . I . caꝛ . Ibi s̄ī . V . borđ cū . I . ſeruo.
7 V . ac̄ p̄ti . 7 VIII . q̂ꝗ paſturæ in l̄g . 7 IIII . q̂ꝗ in laꝛ . Valet
Decē taini ten CHIMEDECOME . Ipſi tenueꝛ̄   ⌐xx . ſoliđ.
T.R.E. ꝓ uno ꝳ . 7 geldꝸ ꝓ una hida . 7 IIĪ . partibꝥ uni̇ v̇
Tra . ē . I . caꝛ . q̄ ibi eſt.
ALWARD ten WILLE . Ipſe tenuit T.R.E.7 geldꝸ ꝓ . I . hida
7 dimiđ . Tra . ē . I . caꝛ . q̄ ibi . ē in dīnio . cū . I . uiłło 7 II . borđ.
Ibi . VII . ac̄ p̄ti 7 dim̄ . 7 II . ac̄ paſturæ . Valet . XV . ſoliđ.
ALMARVS ten WILLE . Aluuard tenuit T.R.E.7 geldꝸ
ꝓ una v̇ tre . Tra . ē . II . boū . Valet . II . ſoliđ.
GODVIN ten CORISCVBE . Alduin tenuit T.R.E.7 geldꝸ
ꝓ una hida Tra . ē . I . caꝛ 7 dimiđ . Ibi . ē un̄ uiłłs cū . I.
caꝛ 7 IIII . borđ . 7 I . ſeruo . 7 dimiđ q̂ꝗ paſturæ . 7 II . q̂ꝗ ſiluæ.
Valuit . XXX . ſoliđ . Modo . XX . ſoliđ.
ALVRIC ten . I . hiđ in BLACHEMANESTONE . Ipſe tenuit
T.R.E. Tra . ē . I . caꝛ . Valet . XX . ſoliđ.
EDWARD uenator ten dimiđ v̇ træ in GELINGEHA̅ . Anſchil te
nuit T.R.E. Tra . ē . III . boū . Valet xxx . denaꝛ.
Om̄s q̣ has tras T.R.E. teneꝸ ꞏ poteraꞃ ire ad quē dn̄m uoleꝸ.

59 Aelfric holds BOVINGTON. He held it himself before 1066. It paid tax for 4 hides. Land for 3 ploughs. In lordship 1 plough, with 1 slave;
  3 villagers with 2 ploughs.
  Meadow, 40 acres; pasture 1 league long and ½ league wide.
  Value 40s.

60 Aelfric holds 'WINTERBORNE'. He held it himself before 1066. It paid tax for 1 hide. Land for 1 plough.
  5 smallholders with 1 slave.
  Meadow, 5 acres; pasture, 8 furlongs in length and 4 furlongs in width.
  Value 20s.

61 Ten thanes hold KINGCOMBE. They held it themselves before 1066 as one manor. It paid tax for 1 hide and 3 parts of 1 virgate. Land for 1 plough, which is there. ...

62 Alward holds WOOL. He held it himself before 1066. It paid tax for 1½ hides. Land for 1 plough, which is there, in lordship, with 1 villager and 2 smallholders.
  Meadow, 7½ acres; pasture, 2 acres.
  Value 15s.

63 Aelmer holds WOOL. Alward held it before 1066. It paid tax for 1 virgate of land. Land for 2 oxen.
  Value 2s.

64 Godwin holds CORSCOMBE. Aldwin held it before 1066. It paid tax for 1 hide. Land for 1½ ploughs.
  1 villager with 1 plough, 4 smallholders and 1 slave.
  Pasture, ½ furlong; woodland, 2 furlongs.
  The value was 30s; now 20s.

65 Aelfric holds 1 hide in BLACKMANSTON. He held it himself before 1066. Land for 1 plough.
  Value 20s.

66 Edward Hunter holds ½ virgate of land in GILLINGHAM. Askell held it before 1066. Land for 3 oxen.
  Value 30d.

All the holders of these lands before 1066 could go to which lord they would.

TERRE SERVIENᵗ REGIS

Wͥₗₗₛ Belot ten� de rege *FROME*. Vluuard⁹ tenuit T.R.E. ★

7 geldɓ ꝑ.III.hid. Tͬra.ē.II.caƦ.Taɱ sͭ ibi.III.caƦ.

7 VI.ſerui.7 II.uilli cū.I.borđ.Ibi moliñ redđ.v.folid.

7 XXIII.aͦc ꝑti.Paſtura.III.q̃ɀ lḡ.7 II.q̃ɀ laͭ.Valet.VI.liɓ.

HᵥGO ten.III.v̊ træ in *LIWELLE*.Aluuarđ tenuit T.R.E.

Tͬra.ē.II.boū.Ibi sͭ.II.borđ.redđ.xx.denaƦ.

Wͥₗₗₛ ten *WINTREBVRNE*.Duo taini| tenueƦ T.R.E.

7 geldɓ ꝑ.II.hiđ 7 diɱ.Tͬra.ē.I.caƦ 7 diɱ.Taɱ sͭ ibi.II.

caƦ.7 v.ſerui.7 XVIII.aͦc ꝑti.Paſtura.VI.q̃ɀ lḡ.7 III.q̃ɀ

laͭ.Valuit.XL.folid.Modo.IIII.liɓ 7 xv.folid.

Wͥₗₗₛ de DALMARI ten̊ tras triū tainoɀ.q̃ geldɓ

T.R.E.ꝑ.III.hiđ 7 II.v̊ træ 7 dimiđ.Tͬra.ē.II.caƦ.q̃ ibi sͭ.

7 v.ſerui.7 v.borđ.Ibi.III.partes molini redđ.IX.folid.

7 IIII.aͦc ꝑti.Silua.VI.q̃ɀ lḡ.7 III.q̃ɀ laͭ.Valet.LX.folid.

HᵥGO[Gosbert] ten unā v̊ træ.Saulf tenuit T.R.E.Valet.xxx.den̊.

Idē Hugo ten *WINTREBVRNE*.Duo taini tenueƦ T.R.E.

7 geldɓ ꝑ diɱ hida.Tͬra.ē dimiđ caƦ.Ibi sͭ.II.uilli.Valet

Iđ.H.ten̊ unā v̊ træ in *WIREGROTE*.Almar ⫦ xL.den̊.

tenuit T.R.E.Tͬra.ē.II.boū.Valuit 7 ual.XII.denaƦ.

Iđ.H.ten̊.III.v̊ træ in *WILECOME*.Dode monach⁹ tenuit

T.R.E.7 ꝑ tanto geldɓ.Tͬra.ē.I.caƦ.q̃ ibi.ē cū.II.borđ.

7 IIII.aͦc ꝑti.7 VI.q̃ɀ paſturæ.7 VIII.aͦc filuæ minutæ.

Valuit.v.folid.Modo.xv.folid.

1 William Bellett holds 'FROME (Billet)' from the King. Wulfward and Brictferth held it as two manors before 1066. It paid tax for 3 hides. Land for 2 ploughs. However, 3 ploughs there; 6 slaves; 2 villagers with 1 smallholder.
A mill which pays 5s; meadow, 23 acres; pasture 3 furlongs long and 2 furlongs wide.
Value £6.

2 Hugh holds 3 virgates of land in LEWELL. Alward held them before 1066. Land for 2 oxen.
2 smallholders who pay 20d.

3 William holds 'WINTERBORNE (Belet)'. Two thanes held it jointly before 1066. It paid tax for 2½ hides. Land for 1½ ploughs. However, 2 ploughs there; 5 slaves.
Meadow, 18 acres; pasture 6 furlongs long and 3 furlongs wide.
The value was 40s; now £4 15s.

4 William of Daumeray holds the land of three thanes which paid tax before 1066 for 3 hides and 2½ virgates of land. Land for 2 ploughs, which are there; 5 slaves; 5 smallholders.
3 parts of a mill which pay 9s; meadow, 4 acres; woodland 6 furlongs long and 3 furlongs wide.
Value 60s.

5 Hugh Gosbert holds 1 virgate of land. Saewulf held it before 1066.
Value 30d.

6 Hugh also holds 'WINTERBORNE'. Two thanes held it before 1066. It paid tax for ½ hide. Land for ½ plough.
2 villagers.
Value 40d.

7 Hugh also holds 1 virgate of land in WORGRET. Aelmer held it before 1066. Land for 2 oxen.
The value was and is 12d.

8 Hugh also holds 3 virgates of land in WOOLCOMBE. Doda the monk held them before 1066. They paid tax for as much. Land for 1 plough, which is there, with 2 smallholders.
Meadow, 4 acres; pasture, 6 furlongs; underwood, 8 acres.
The value was 5s; now 15s.

H^{cubiculariꝰ}ERVEVS ten _WINBVRNE_ . Brictric tenuit T.R.E.7 geldb
ꝑ . II . hid 7 dim . Tra . e . III . car . In dnio . e . I . car . 7 v . uilli 7 v . bord
cu . II . car . In molino uillæ . xxII 7 dim.   Ibi . II . ac pti.
7 paſtura . I . leu lg . 7 III . q᷄ʒ lat . Silua . vI . q᷄ʒ lg . 7 II . q᷄ʒ lat.
Valuit . xxx . ſolid . Modo . L . ſolid.

J oħs ten _WINTREBVRNE_ . Aluuold tenuit T.R.E . 7 geldb
ꝑ . II . hid 7 una v 7 dim . Tra . e . II . car . In dnio . e . I . car 7 dim.
7 III . ſerui . 7 II . uilli . 7 III . bord cu dimid car . Ibi paſtura
v . q᷄ʒ lg . 7 tntd lat . Valuit 7 ual . xL . ſolid.

WILLS de DALMARI ten _WALDIC_ . Aluui tenuit T.R.E.
7 geldb ꝑ . II . hid . Tra . e . I . car . q̄ ibi . e in dnio cu . I . ſeruo.
7 I . uills 7 vIII . bord cu dimid car . Ibi molin redd . xL . v.
denar . 7 IIII . ac pti . Silua . IIII . q᷄ʒ lg . 7 una q᷄ʒ lat.
Valuit 7 ual . xL . ſolid.

W^{belet}ills ten _NODFORD_ . Alnod tenuit T.R.E . 7 geldb ꝑ una
hida 7 II . v træ 7 dim . Tra . e . I . car . Tam ſt ibi . II . car . 7 III.
ſerui . 7 vIII . ac pti . Paſtura . III . q᷄ʒ lg . 7 una q᷄ʒ lat
Valuit . xv . ſolid . Modo . xxx . ſolid.

I de . W . ten _WARDESFORD_ . Leuegar tenuit T.R.E . 7 geldb
ꝑ . II . hid 7 dim . Tra . e . II . car . q̄ ibi ſt in dnio . 7 IIII . ſerui.
7 II . uilli . 7 II . bord . Ibi molin redd . vI . ſolid . 7 xxvIII . ac pti.
7 xII . q᷄ʒ paſturæ in lg 7 lat Valuit . c . ſolid . Modo . Lx . ſolid.

I de . W . ten _LIME_ . Alueue tenuit T.R.E . 7 geldb ꝑ . I . hida.
Tra . e . I . car . Ibi . e un uills cu dim car . 7 xIIII . ſalinarij.
Ibi molin redd . xxxIx . denar . 7 III . ac pti . Paſtura . IIII . q᷄ʒ
lg . 7 una q᷄ʒ lat . 7 una q᷄ʒ ſiluæ in lg 7 lat . Valet . Lx . ſolid.

9 Hervey the Chamberlain holds WIMBORNE (St. Giles). Brictric held it before 1066. It paid tax for 2½ hides. Land for 3 ploughs. In lordship 1 plough; 5 villagers and 5 smallholders with 2 ploughs. In the village mill 22½ .... Meadow, 2 acres; pasture 1 league long and 3 furlongs wide; woodland 6 furlongs long and 2 furlongs wide. The value was 30s; now 50s.

85 a

10 John holds 'WINTERBORNE'. Alwold held it before 1066. It paid tax for 2 hides and 1½ virgates. Land for 2 ploughs. In lordship 1½ ploughs; 3 slaves; 2 villagers and 3 smallholders with ½ plough. Pasture 5 furlongs long and as wide. The value was and is 40s.

11 William of Daumeray holds WALDITCH. Alwy held it before 1066. It paid tax for 2 hides. Land for 1 plough, which is there, in lordship, with 1 slave; 1 villager and 8 smallholders with ½ plough. A mill which pays 45d; meadow, 4 acres; woodland 4 furlongs long and 1 furlong wide. The value was and is 40s.

12 William Bellett holds NUTFORD. Alnoth held it before 1066. It paid tax for 1 hide and 2½ virgates of land. Land for 1 plough. However, 2 ploughs there; 3 slaves. Meadow, 8 acres; pasture 3 furlongs long and 1 furlong wide. The value was 15s; now 30s.

13 William also holds WOODSFORD. Leofgar held it before 1066. It paid tax for 2½ hides. Land for 2 ploughs, which are there, in lordship; 4 slaves; 2 villagers and 2 smallholders. A mill which pays 6s; meadow, 28 acres; pasture, 12 furlongs in length and width. The value was 100s; now 60s.

14 William also holds LYME (Regis). Aelfeva held it before 1066. It paid tax for 1 hide. Land for 1 plough. 1 villager with ½ plough; 14 salt-workers. A mill which pays 39d; meadow, 3 acres; pasture 4 furlongs long and 1 furlong wide; woodland, 1 furlong in length and width. Value 60s.

H^{f. Odini}ᵛⁿᵍᵉʳᵛˢ teñ *WINDESORE* . Bondi tenuit T.R.E. 7 geldƀ
ꝓ. xx. hiđ. Tra. ē. xx. cař. In dñio sť. ii . cař .7 vii . ferui.7 xxxviii.
uitti 7 xii . borđ cū. xvi . cař. Ibi .xii .ac ṕti .7 xxx .q̃ʒ filuæ
in lg.7 viii.q̃ʒ lať.7 viii . q̃ʒ paſturæ. Valuit 7 uat. xx .liƀ.
In eađ uilla hť Hunger . i . hiđ træ quã tenuit uñ liƀ hō T.R.E.
O^{piſtor}ˢᵐᵛⁿᴅ teñ in *GALTONE* . i . hiđ 7 dim v̊ træ . Quattuor
liƀi hões tenueř T.R.E.Tra.ē. i . cař. Ibi sť .iiii .hões redđ
xii .fot .7 iiii . denař.   Valuit. xv . foliđ.
Iđ. O. teñ in *WINDESTORTE* . iii . v̊ træ. Tres liƀi hões teneƀ
T.R.E.Tra.ē.vi . boū. Ibi sť . ii .borđ. Valuit 7 uat . vii .fot 7 vi.
Qui has tras teneƀ T.R.E. poterant ire quo uolebaɴ.   ſdenař.
W^{belet}itts teñ unā hiđ 7 ii .virg træ 7 dim in *STVRE* de rege. Alnod
☞ tenuit de Eduuardo lipe.7 ñ poterat feparari a dño fuo.

TERRA COMITISSE BOLONIENŚ.

LVIII Cᴏᴍɪᴛɪꜱꜱᴀ ʙᴏʟᴏɴɪᴇⁿˢ teñ *BOCHEHATONE* T.R.E.^{ſde rege.W.}
geldƀ ꝓ. iiii . hiđ. Tra.ē. iii . cař. In dñio. ē . i . cař cū . i . feruo.
7 iiii . uitti cū . i . borđ hñt . ii .cař. Ibi moliñ redđ .v . foliđ.
7 xx .ac ṕti .7 iiii . q̃ʒ filuæ in lg .7 una q̃ʒ lať. Valet. iii .liƀ.

15 Hundger son of Odin holds BROADWINDSOR. Bondi held it before 1066. It paid tax for 20 hides. Land for 20 ploughs. In lordship 2 ploughs; 7 slaves;
    38 villagers and 12 smallholders with 16 ploughs.
    Meadow, 12 acres; woodland, 30 furlongs in length and 8 furlongs wide; pasture, 8 furlongs.
The value was and is £20.

16 Also in this village Hundger has 1 hide of land which a free man held before 1066.
[Value ...]

17 Osmund the Baker holds 1 hide and ½ virgate of land in GALTON. Four free men held it before 1066. Land for 1 plough.
    4 men who pay 12s 4d.
The value was 15s.

18 Osmund also holds 3 virgates of land in WOODSTREET. Three free men held them before 1066. Land for 6 oxen.
    2 smallholders.
The value was and is 7s 6d.

The holders of these lands before 1066 could go where they would.

19 William Bellett holds 1 hide and 2½ virgates of land in STOURPAINE from the King. Alnoth held them from Edward Lip; he could not be separated from his lord.

╞ *57,20–22 are written at the bottom of col. 85a, after Ch. 58, directed by transposition signs to their correct position in the text.*

58   LAND OF THE COUNTESS OF BOULOGNE

1 The Countess of Boulogne holds BOCKHAMPTON from King William. Before 1066 it paid tax for 4 hides. Land for 3 ploughs. In lordship 1 plough and 2 hides, with 1 slave.
    4 villagers with 1 smallholder have 2 ploughs and 2 hides.
    A mill which pays 5s; meadow, 20 acres; woodland, 4 furlongs in length and 1 furlong wide.
Value £3; when the Countess acquired it, as much.

    E

    33
    a 1

Ead ten *WINTREBVRNE* . T . R . E . geldb ᵱ . vi . hid . Tra.ē.v.

caᷓ . In dīnio sᷓ . ii . caᷓ . 7 iiii . ſerui . 7 iiii . uilti 7 ii . bord cū . ii . caᷓ.

Ibi . ix . aᷓc p̃ti . 7 ix . q̃ʒ paſturæ in lḡ . 7 iii . q̃ʒ laᷓt . Valet . vi . lib.

Ead ten *SONWIC* . T.R.E.geldb ᵱ . i . hida . 7 tcia parte uni v.

Tra . ē . i . caᷓ . Hanc hᷓt ibi . i . uilts . 7 ibi . iiii . aᷓc p̃ti . Valet . xv . ſol.

Hæc tria ᴹ tenuit Vlueua T . R . E . 7 poterat ire cū tra quo uoleb.

☞ Dᵛᴿᴬᴺᴰ carpent". ten *ALFRVNETONE* . Leuuin tenuit T . R . E . 7 geldb

ᵱ una v træ . Tra . ē dimid caᷓ . Valet . vi . ſolid.

Id ten *MOLEHAM* . Tres taini tenueᷓr T.R.E. 7 geldb ᵱ una

hida . Tra . ē . i . caᷓ . ḡ ibi . ē cū . i . cotaᷓ . Ibi molin redd . vi.

denaᷓr . 7 una aᷓc p̃ti . Valuit . v . ſol . Modo . xxx . ſolid.

Godefrid Scutulari ten unā v træ in *HERSTUNE* . Pat ej

tenuit T . R . E . 7 geldb ᵱ una v træ 7 iiii . acris . Has

2 She also holds WINTERBORNE (Monkton). Before 1066 it paid tax
for 6 hides. Land for 5 ploughs. In lordship 2 ploughs; 4 slaves;
4½ hides.
    4 villagers and 2 smallholders with 2 ploughs and 1½ hides.
    Meadow, 9 acres; pasture, 9 furlongs in length and 3 furlongs
      wide. 5 cows; 16 pigs; 105 sheep.
Value £6; when the Countess acquired it, as much.

33
a 2

3 She also holds SWANAGE. Before 1066 it paid tax for 1 hide and
the third part of 1 virgate. Land for 1 plough.
    1 villager has it there.
    Meadow, 4 acres.
Value 15s.
    King William has never had the tax from this manor.

33
a 3

Wulfeva held these three manors before 1066. She could go with the
land where she would.

E

⊢⊂ *Ch. 57 continued, directed by transposition signs to the correct position in the text*

57,20 Durand Carpenter holds AFFLINGTON. Leofwin held it before
1066. It paid tax for 1 virgate of land. Land for ½ plough.
Value 6s.

21 He also holds 'MOULHAM'. Three thanes held it before 1066.
It paid tax for 1 hide. Land for 1 plough, which is there, with
1 cottager.
A mill which pays 6d; meadow, 1 acre.
The value was 5s; now 30s.

22 Godfrey Scullion holds 1 virgate of land in HERSTON. His father
held it before 1066. It paid tax for 1 virgate of land and 4 acres.
These ....

HOLDINGS IN DORSET IN 1086,
ENTERED ELSEWHERE IN THE SURVEY

The Latin text for these entries will be found in the county volumes concerned
(Exon. references are in the right margin and additions in small type within the translation)

In the SOMERSET folios

19   LAND OF THE COUNT OF MORTAIN   91 d

E 1 86 The Count holds 'BISHOPSTONE' himself*, in lordship. His   93 a
castle, called Montacute, is there. This manor paid tax for
9 hides before 1066; it was (part) of Athelney Abbey and
for it the Count gave that church the manor called (Purse)
Caundle. In this manor (of) 'Bishopstone', land for 7
ploughs, of which 2½ hides are in lordship; 2 ploughs there;
4 slaves;   280
4 villagers and 3 smallholders with 2 ploughs and 1 hide.   a 3
A mill which pays 50d; meadow, 15 acres. 1 cob; 100 sheep.
Of these 9 hides† Alfred the Butler holds 1½ hides from the
Count, Drogo 1 hide, Bretel 1 hide, Duncan 1 hide.
5 ploughs there, with 1 slave;
19 smallholders.
Value of this manor to the Count £6; to the men-at-arms
£3 3s.

* Exon. adds ". . . which the Abbot of Athelney (*Aliennia*) held in 1066".

† Exon. provides details of these sub-tenancies, which are as follows:

Alfred the Butler has 1½ ploughs (in lordship) and 6 smallholders, 1 slave, 80
sheep; the value of his 1½ hides in 1086 is 28s.

Drogo has 1½ ploughs (in lordship) and 5 smallholders; the value of his 1 hide
in 1086 is 10s.

Bretel has 1 plough (in lordship) and 2 smallholders; the value of his 1 hide in
1086 is 10s.

Duncan has 1 plough in lordship and 6 smallholders; the value of his 1 hide in
1086 is 15s.

In the WILTSHIRE folios

23   LAND WHICH WAS EARL AUBREY'S   69 a

E 2 10 GUSSAGE paid tax for 10 hides before 1066. Land for 12
ploughs. Of this land 4½ hides in lordship; 2 ploughs there;
8 slaves.
5 villagers and 8 smallholders with 4 ploughs.
Meadow, 40 acres; pasture 1 league long and ½ league
wide; woodland, as much.
The value was £40, when Aubrey acquired it; now £10.

Azor held these three manors before 1066. All this land was
Earl Aubrey's; now it is in the King's hands.

E 3   5   Fulcred holds 3 virgates of land in GILLINGHAM. Algar held   73 c
them before 1066. Land for 2 ploughs, which are there, with
1 smallholder.
The value was and is 15s.

HOLDINGS OUTSIDE DORSET IN 1086,
LATER TRANSFERRED TO THE COUNTY

Noted here to complete the description of the modern county.
See the county volumes concerned for the full text.
(The Exon. references for each entry are in brackets)

In the DEVONSHIRE folios

16   LAND OF BALDWIN THE SHERIFF   105 d
ED 1   165   THORNCOMBE   108 b   (313
a 3)

In the SOMERSET folios

[3]   LAND OF THE BISHOP OF SALISBURY   87 d
ES 1   1   SEABOROUGH ... Another SEABOROUGH   (154
a 1-2)

[5]   LAND OF THE BISHOP OF COUTANCES   87 d
ES 2   69   WEATHERGROVE   89 a   (152
a 1)

19   LAND OF THE COUNT OF MORTAIN   91 d
ES 3   70   GOATHILL   92 c,d   (278
b 1)

ES 4   74   ADBER   93 a   (279
a 2)

ES 5   75   TRENT   (279
a 3)

ES 6   76   POYNTINGTON   (279
a 4)

24   LAND OF WALTER OF DOUAI   95 a
ES 7   37   ADBER   95 c   (355
b 1)

45   LAND OF HUMPHREY [THE CHAMBERLAIN]   98 c
ES 8   5   SANDFORD (Orcas)   99 b   (466
b 4)

47   LANDS OF THE KING'S THANES   98 d
ES 9   11   ADBER   99 a   (493
b 2)

Notes on the Text and Translation
including:

Bibliography and Abbreviations

Introductory Notes:
1. Places: 2. The Dorset Rivers; 3. The County Boundary

General Notes

Exon. Notes

Details Table

Appendix: The Dorset Hundreds
including:

The Tax Return Hundreds, Detachments,
Later Hundreds, Tithings, Liberties,
The Hundred Names

Persons Index

Places Indices

Maps and Map Keys

Systems of Reference

Technical Terms

NOTES ON THE TEXT AND TRANSLATION

BIBLIOGRAPHY and ABBREVIATIONS used in the Notes
AN ... Anglo-Norman.
Anderson ... O. S. Anderson *The English Hundred Names: The South-Western Counties*, Lund 1939 (Lunds Universitets Årsskrift N.F. Avd. 1 Bd. 37 Nr. 1).
ASC ... *The Anglo-Saxon Chronicle* (translated G. N. Garmonsway), London 1960.
Bach ... Adolf Bach *Deutsche Namenkunde* 1, Part 1, *Personennamen* (2nd edn., Heidelberg 1952).
BCS ... W. de Gray Birch (ed.) *Cartularium Saxonicum*, 4 vols. with index, London 1885-1899 (reprinted 1964).
BJRL ... Bulletin of the John Rylands Library.
Boswell ... E. Boswell *The Civil Division of the County of Dorset*, Sherborne 1795.
Cal. Inq. Misc. ... *Calendar of Inquisitions Miscellaneous* (HMSO State Papers), London 1916 on.
Cal. Inq. PM ... *Calendar of Inquisitions Post Mortem* (HMSO State Papers), London 1904 on.
Dauzat and Rostaing ... A. Dauzat and Ch. Rostaing *Dictionnaire Étymologique des Noms de Lieux en France*, 2nd edition Paris 1978.
Davis MCGB ... G. R. C. Davis *Medieval Cartularies of Great Britain*, London 1958.
DB ... Domesday Book.
DB1-4 ... Domesday Book, associated texts, introduction and indices published by the Record Commission, London 1783-1816.
DB3 ... *Libri Censualis Vocati Domesday Book, Additamenta ex Codic. Antiquiss.*, comprising Exon. Domesday, Inquisitio Eliensis, Liber Winton', Boldon Book; vol. 3 of the Record Commission's edition of DB, London 1816 (vol. 4 in some bindings).
DEPN ... E. Ekwall *The Concise Oxford Dictionary of English Placenames*, 4th edn., Oxford 1960.
Details Table ... Details of Holdings omitted in DB and given in Exon.; see after the Exon. Notes below.
DG ... H. C. Darby and G. R. Versey *Domesday Gazetteer*, Cambridge 1975.
DGSW ... H. C. Darby and R. Welldon Finn *The Domesday Geography of South-West England*, Cambridge 1967.
Drew ... C. D. Drew *The Manors of the Iwerne Valley, Dorset*, in PDNHAS vol. 69 (1947) pp. 45-50.
Drew ... C. D. Drew *Earnley: A Lost Place-name Recovered*, in PDNHAS vol. 71 (1949) pp. 84-87.
Du ... Dutch.
Ducange ... G. A. L. Henschel (ed.) *Glossarium Mediae et Infimae Latinitatis*, Niort and London 1884-7.
ECW ... H. P. R. Finberg *The Early Charters of Wessex*, Leicester 1964.
EHR ... English Historical Review.
Ekwall (ERN) ... E. Ekwall *English River-Names*, Oxford 1928.
El(s) ... Element(s).
Ellis ... H. Ellis (ed.) *Exon. Domesday* in DB3 (see above).
Ellis (DTG) ... C. S. Ellis *On the Landholders of Gloucestershire Named in Domesday Book*, in TBGAS iv (1879-1880) pp. 86-198.
Ellis (Introduction) ... H. Ellis *A General Introduction to Domesday Book*, 2 vols., 1833 (reprint 1971); folio edition DB4 1816, pp. i-cvii. References in these Notes are to the 2-volume edition.
English Place-Name Elements ... A. H. Smith *English Place-Name Elements*, parts i-ii (EPNS vols. 25-26), Cambridge 1956.
EPNS ... English Place-Name Society. References are to the Dorset volumes edited by A. D. Mills unless otherwise stated. Only volumes i (1977) and ii (1980) were available to the editors.
Exon. (Book) ... in DB3 (see above).
Exon. Notes ... Exon. Extra Information and Discrepancies with DB; see below after the General Notes.
Eyton (*Dorset*) ... R. W. Eyton *A Key to Domesday ... Analysis and Digest of the Dorset Survey*, London 1878.
Eyton (*Somerset*) ... R. W. Eyton *Domesday Studies: An Analysis and Digest of the Somerset Survey*, 2 vols., London and Bristol 1880.
FA ... *Inquisitions and Assessments relating to Feudal Aids with other analogous Documents preserved in the Public Records Office AD 1284-1431*, HMSO 1899-1920, 6 vols.
Fägersten ... A. Fägersten *The Place Names of Dorset*, Uppsala 1933 (reprinted East Ardsley 1978).
Farley ... Abraham Farley, editor of DB1 (see above).
Fees ... *Book of Fees (Testa de Nevill)*, 3 vols., HMSO 1920-31.
Fellows-Jensen ... G. Fellows-Jensen *Scandinavian Personal Names in Lincolnshire and Yorkshire*, Copenhagen 1968.

FF ... E. A. Fry and G. S. Fry (eds.) *Full Abstracts of the Feet of Fines relating to the County of Dorset, remaining in the Public Record Office, London, from their Commencement in the Reign of Richard I [1195-1485]*, Dorset Records vols. 5 and 10 (1896 and 1910).
Finn (*Introduction*) ... R. Welldon Finn *An Introduction to Domesday Book*, London 1963.
Finn (LE) ... R. Welldon Finn *Domesday Studies: The Liber Exoniensis*, London 1964.
Finn (MDD) ... R. Welldon Finn *The Making of the Dorset Domesday*, in PDNHAS vol. 81 (1959) pp. 150-157.
Forssner ... T. Forssner *Continental-Germanic Personal Names in England in Old and Middle English Times*, Uppsala 1916.
Fr ... French.
Freeman ... E. A. Freeman *The History of the Norman Conquest of England*, 6 vols., Oxford 1867-79.
Galbraith ... V. H. Galbraith *The Making of Domesday Book*, Oxford 1961.
Gallia Christiana ... D. Sammarthani and others (eds.) *Gallia Christiana*, 16 vols. in 15, Paris 1715-1865 (2nd edition 1744-1877).
GC ... Dom Aelred Watkin *The Great Chartulary of Glastonbury*, vols. i-iii SRS 59,63-64 (1944, 1948,1949-50).
GF ... F. W. Weaver *A Feodary of Glastonbury Abbey*, SRS 26 (1910).
GR ... Grid Reference.
Harmer ... F. E. Harmer *Anglo-Saxon Writs*, Manchester 1952.
Hassall ... W. O. Hassall *The Dorset Properties of the Nunnery of St. Mary, Clerkenwell*, in PDNHAS vol. 68 (1946) pp. 43-51.
HD ... Sir H. C. Maxwell-Lyte *Documents and Extracts Illustrating the History of the Honour of Dunster*, SRS 33 (1917-18).
Hutchins ... J. Hutchins and others *The History and Antiquities of the County of Dorset*, (3rd edition) 4 vols. 1861-1870 (reprinted East Ardsley 1973).
JMcND ... John McN. Dodgson, see Acknowledgements below.
KCD ... J. M. Kemble *Codex Diplomaticus Aevi Saxonici*, 6 vols., London 1839-48.
Ker ... N. R. Ker *Medieval Manuscripts in British Libraries*, vol. ii, Oxford 1977.
Leland ... John Leland (ed. L. Toulmin Smith) *Itinerary*, 5 vols., London 1906-1910.
Lennard ... R. Lennard *Rural England: 1086-1135, A study of Social and Agrarian Conditions*, Oxford 1959.
LG ... Low German.
Little Domesday ... Essex, Norfolk and Suffolk in DB2 (see above).
Longnan ... A. Longnan *Les Noms de Lieux de la France*, Paris 1923.
LSR ... R. E. Glasscock (ed.) *The Lay Subsidy of 1334*, British Academy Records of Social and Economic History, New Series II, London 1975.
Maitland (DBB) ... F. W. Maitland *Domesday Book and Beyond*, Cambridge 1897.
MC ... *Cartulary of the Cluniac Priory of Montacute* in H. C. Maxwell-Lyte and T. S. Holmes *Bruton and Montacute Cartularies*, SRS 8 (1894).
MDu ... Middle Dutch.
ME ... Middle English.
ML ... Medieval Latin.
Mod.E ... Modern English.
Mod.Fr ... Modern French.
Mod.G ... Modern German.
Mon. Ang. ... W. Dugdale *Monasticon Anglicanum*, 6 vols. in 8, London 1817-30.
Morgan ... M. Morgan (later Chibnall) *The English Lands of the Abbey of Bec*, London 1946.
MS ... Manuscript.
OE ... Old English.
OEB ... G. Tengvik *Old English Bynames*, Uppsala 1938 (Nomina Germanica 4).
OED ... *Oxford English Dictionary* (formerly the *New English Dictionary*, 10 vols., Oxford 1884-1921), 12 vols., Oxford 1933; micrographic reprint in 2 vols., 1977.
OFr ... Old French.
OHG ... Old High German.
ON ... Old Norse.
Orderic Vitalis ... A. Le Prévost (ed.) *Historia Ecclesiastica*, 5 vols., Paris 1838-1855. A new edition edited by M. Chibnall has recently been completed (Oxford 1969-1981). References are to the old edition.

OS ... Ordnance Survey. First Edition One-inch Maps (early 19th century) were reprinted Newton Abbot 1969 on.
OScand ... Old Scandinavian.
PDNHAS ... Proceedings of the Dorset Natural History and Archaeological Society.
PNDB ... O. von Feilitzen *Pre-Conquest Personal Names of Domesday Book*, Uppsala 1937 (Nomina Germanica 3).
Pipe Roll ... J. Hunter (ed.) *Magnum Rotulum Scaccarii vel Magnum Rotulum Pipae de Anno tricesimo-primo regni Henrici Primi*, Record Commission 1833 (reprint 1929, ed. H. C. Johnson).
RBE ... H. Hall (ed.) *The Red Book of the Exchequer*, Rolls Series no. 99, 3 vols., London 1896.
RCHM ... Royal Commission on Historical Monuments, England. *Dorset* vol. i (West) 1952; vol ii (South East) 1970; vol. iii (Central) 1970; vol. iv (North) 1974; vol. v (East) 1975.
Reaney ... P. H. Reaney *Dictionary of British Surnames*, 2nd edition, London 1976.
Rectitudines ... *Rectitudines Singularum Personarum* in F. Liebermann *Die Gesetze der Angelsachsen* 1, Halle 1903, translated in part in D. C. Douglas (ed.) *English Historical Documents* vol. 2 no. 172 (London 1968).
Regesta ... H. W. C. Davis, C. Johnson and H. A. Cronne (eds.) *Regesta Regum Anglo-Normannorum* vol. i, Oxford 1913; vol. ii, Oxford 1956.
RH ... *Rotuli Hundredorum*, Record Commission 1812-18, 2 vols.
RMLWL ... R. E. Latham *Revised Medieval Latin Word-List*, London 1965.
Robertson ... A. J. Robertson *Anglo-Saxon Charters*, Cambridge 1939; 2nd edition 1956.
Round (CDF) ...J. H. Round *Calendar of Documents preserved in France*, vol. i 918-1206, London 1899 (HMSO State Papers).
Round (FE) ... J. H. Round *Feudal England*, London 1909.
Round (KS) ... J. H. Round, *The King's Serjeants and Officers of State*, London 1911.
Sanders ... I. J. Sanders *English Baronies: A Study of their Origin and Descent 1066-1327*, Oxford 1960.
Sawyer (1) ... P. H. Sawyer *Anglo-Saxon Charters: An Annotated List and Bibliography*, London 1968.
Sawyer (2) ... P. H. Sawyer *The 'Original Returns' and Domesday Book*, in EHR lxx (1955) pp. 177-197.
Searle ... W. G. Searle *Onomasticon Anglo-Saxonicum*, Cambridge 1897.
SRS ... Somerset Record Society.
Stenton (ASE) ... F. M. Stenton *Anglo-Saxon England*, Oxford 1943.
Tax Return ... Tax Returns for the Dorset Hundreds, Exon. folios 17a–24a; see Appendix and the beginning of Introductory Note 1.
Taylor ... C. C. Taylor *Lost Dorset Placenames*, in PDNHAS vol. 88 (1966) pp. 207-215.
TBGAS ... Transactions of the Bristol and Gloucestershire Archaeological Society.
TE ... *Taxatio Ecclesiastica of Pope Nicholas IV*, Record Commission, London 1802.
Traskey ... J. P. Traskey *Milton Abbey, A Dorset Monastery in the Middle Ages*, Tisbury 1978.
TRHS ... Transactions of the Royal Historical Society.
VCH ... *The Victoria History of the Counties of England*: Dorset vol. ii (1908); vol. iii (1968).
Vol. iii contains an Introduction to the Domesday Survey with a translation of the Exchequer and Exon. versions and a translation and analysis of the Tax Returns by Ann Williams.
Vinogradoff ... P. Vinogradoff *English Society in the Eleventh Century*, Oxford 1908.
Zachrisson ... R. E. Zachrisson *A Contribution to the Study of Anglo-Norman Influence on English Place-names*, Lund 1909.
Zupko ... R. E. Zupko *A Dictionary of English Weights and Measures from Anglo-Saxon Times to the Nineteenth Century*, University of Wisconsin Press 1968.

Acknowledgements
The Editors are deeply grateful to John McN. Dodgson of University College, London, who, besides seeing the present series through the press, has given advice about place and personal names with unfailing care and kindness, even when most pressed by his many other obligations; to Miss Daphne Gifford of the Public Record Office, Chancery Lane, for consulting the Exchequer Domesday Manuscript on various points arising from Caroline Thorn's earlier examination of it and for answering several other queries; to Mrs. Audrey Erskine of Exeter Cathedral Library for the loan of microfilm and for allowing frequent consultation of the manuscript of the Exeter Domesday, always providing a welcome and facilities for study in Exeter; to the staff of the Dorset Record Office; and finally to Mr. J. D. Foy for reading through the translation and Notes and checking the Indices and for making numerous helpful suggestions.

Note 1

INTRODUCTORY NOTES

1. PLACES

In the text of the south-western counties, neither the Exchequer Domesday nor the Exon. Book includes the Hundred rubrication that is an important aid to the identification of places. This lack is felt especially in the case of Dorset where many places, are named only from the rivers on which they lie, such as *Frome, Cerne, Tarente, Wintreburne* (see Introductory Note 2), and where a single DB form can represent more than one modern place at opposite ends of the County. Thus *Bocheland* can represent Buckland Newton or Buckland Ripers, *Bradeford* can be Bradford Peverel or Bradford Abbas, *Hame* can be Hammoon or Hampreston, while *Stoche* or *Stoches* can be Cattistock, Stoke Abbott, Stoke Wake, 'Stoke Wallis', East Stoke or Stock Gaylard.

The absence of Hundred information can in part be made good from the evidence of the Exon. Book Tax Returns for Dorset (folios 17a-24a), printed by Ellis in DB3, translated and annotated in VCH iii pp. 115-148 and briefly discussed below in the Appendix. The Tax Return for each Hundred gives the total hidage for the Hundred, then the amount of the (exempt) lordship land (in total and in detail), followed by details of holdings for which tax is owed or has been waived, and finally the tax the King actually receives. No place-names are included, but when the personal names and the extents of land given in the Returns are compared with DB, most entries can be satisfactorily identified and located. A clear resumé of the problems encountered in dating the Tax Returns is given in VCH iii pp. 117-118.

The present editors hope to publish their analysis of the Tax Returns separately. In this county volume, the evidence of a Tax Return for individual holdings is cited only where it is reasonably certain. Since the Tax Returns also give the total hidage for each Hundred, it is sometimes possible to deduce all the constituent villages of a Hundred simply by adding together the hidage of places considered likely to be in the Hundred, then adjusting the list until the correct total is obtained. But this sole reliance on totals, when there are many discrepancies between the Tax Returns and DB and when many villages have the same hidage figures, must be regarded as unreliable evidence. This method is adopted by Eyton (*Dorset*) who claims to have identified every village in each Hundred, although he rarely cites any evidence, and a number of his identifications can certainly be shown to be wrong. The VCH volume wisely refrains from such wholesale reconstructions and distinguishes carefully between lands that are certainly in a given Hundred and those that are only possibly there. This is a sensible precaution in view of the large numbers of 'Winterborne' and 'Tarrant' villages that still await precise identification. A similar caution is followed in this volume. References to the Tax Return Hundreds are given in Roman numerals; the relation of the Tax Return Hundreds to the 'modern' (that is mid-19th century) Hundreds is given at the beginning of the Appendix and of 'modern' Hundreds to those of the Tax Returns at the head of the Map Keys.

A secondary source of place-name identification from within the Exchequer and Exon. Domesday volumes themselves is the order in which places are entered within each fief. In some counties where Hundred rubrication is full, lands are found to be entered in a consistent order of Hundreds within each chapter, probably as the scribe re-arranged into fiefs information that was first returned by Hundreds; see Sawyer (2). Among the south-west counties, Cornwall, Devon and Somerset show a consistent sequence of Hundreds within each chapter in the order of the Exon. Domesday. Moreover, in Somerset this sequence is that of a list of Hundreds included among the folios of the Exon. Book (folios 64a,b, see DB Somerset Appendix I). In Cornwall, and to a lesser extent in Somerset and Devon, the order of Exchequer DB differs from that of Exon.; while in Dorset the two orders are very similar where Exon. has survived, except for the King's land (see Ch. 1 note) and Chs. 12 and 13 where the chief manor, Milton and Abbotsbury respectively, has been brought closer to the head of the fief (see VCH iii p. 3). Even so, in Dorset it is difficult to find a consistent order of Hundreds within individual chapters. This may partly be because no list of the Hundred returns that formed the basis of DB survives. It is clear from Somerset DB that the Tax Return Hundreds and the Hundreds whose information was used to compile DB differed in a number of respects, the Tax Return often grouping together into a single 'Hundred' smaller 'Hundreds' or composite manors each of which produced a Return for the DB commissioners. The same may well have been the case in Dorset.

From the study of separate chapters, however, certain patterns do emerge, suggesting that places were entered in some chapters in a sequence of groups of Hundreds. These patterns have been systematised by Finn in MDD, but a re-examination of the evidence suggests that the groupings are not as clear as Finn states and are found mainly in the chapters of lay landholders (Chs. 25–53;55), being absent from the Land of the King (Ch. 1), from those of the Churches as well as from Ch. 54 (which is grouped by sub-tenants not by Hundreds) and from Ch. 57.

In view of this, it is unwise to identify places only from the supposed sequence of Hundreds; thus in the notes below, the only evidence of this kind normally used is where a place of uncertain identity falls within a group of places that appear from the Tax Returns to have lain within the same Hundred.

Total and secure identification of places depends on a study of early name-forms and later manorial history, both outside the scope of this edition. Fägersten's pioneering study of place-names is invaluable but is now being superseded by the EPNS volumes of A.D. Mills. In due course the appearance of further VCH volumes can be expected to trace the descent of individual DB holdings with greater precision and bring some new or more exact identifications. In the meantime, while the notes below do not claim to be exhaustive, they attempt to offer enough later information, where this has been found, to support identifications which might otherwise be reasonably disputed.

A number of adjacent modern villages in Dorset, now distinguished by affixes such as 'East' and 'West', 'St. Quintin', 'St. Michael' or 'All Saints', share the same DB place-name form. The existence of separate villages is rarely evidenced in Dorset, the few examples relating to rivers (see Introductory Note 2). Such places are not normally distinguished in the translation and the Indices of this volume, the grid reference referring to the larger village. Where these modern separate villages can be traced from individual DB holdings, this fact is recorded in the notes below. It is possible, however, for modern editions to be over precise. DB manors often comprise a large number of hides and will have contained, but do not mention, several separate villages. It would thus be unwise to identify *Sture* 19,3, a manor of 17 hides, as one particular 'Stour' village.

On the other hand, to avoid confusion, affixes are included where two places of the same basic name are in different parts of the County, or in different Hundreds. Thus (Maiden) Newton appears in order to distinguish it from the distant (Sturminster) Newton, but the adjacent villages of East and West Chelborough appear simply as Chelborough.

A number of identifications in this edition differ from those of VCH or DG. For convenience, the major discrepancies are set out below in a table. The VCH identifications are those of the DB translation, not of the notes nor in the Tax Returns. Differentiation of adjacent places of the same basic name is ignored, as are variant spellings and alternative forms (e.g. Compton Abbas for West Compton). Moreover, only identifications that actually conflict are noticed; where one identification is more precise than another but still in the same parish (e.g. 'Colway' for Lyme Regis) or on the same river (e.g. South Winterborne for 'Winterborne Belet'), it is usually ignored. It should be noted that the South Winterborne river is called Winterborne western in DG. Places within inverted commas are identifiable but now lost or not located; a dash indicates that the place has not been identified.

DB column	Chapter and Section	DB Form	VCH	DG	This edition
75b	1,3	*Chirce*	Crichel	Long and Moor Crichel	Moor Crichel
75b	1,4	*Frome*	–	Chilfrome and Frome Vauchurch	'Frome'
75b	1,6	*Wintreburne*	–	Winterborne (Eastern)	'Winterborne'
75b	1,8	*Mapertune*	?Mapperton in Almer	Mapperton near Beaminster	Mappowder

Note 1

DB column	Chapter and Section	DB Form	VCH	DG	This edition
75d	1,25	Tarente	?Tarrant Gunville	'Tarrant'	as DG
75d	1,26	Tarente	?Tarrant Rushton	'Tarrant'	as DG
75d	1,27	Scetre	Shitterton in Bere Regis	—	as DG
77b	3,18	Welle	Wool	Wellwood	as DG
77b	5,1-2	Wintreburne	—	Winterborne (Eastern)	'Winterborne' (unidentified)
77c	7,1	Odeham	—	—	'Odenham'
77d	10,5	Langeford	Langford in Stratton	—	'Langford' in West Parley
78b	12,11	Wintreburne	—	Winterborne (Eastern)	Winterborne Whitechurch
78b	12,15	Pidre	Little Puddle	Briants or Turners Puddle	as VCH
78b	12,16	Cerne	—	Godmanstone	'Cerne'
78c	13,7	Bourtone	Burcombe in North Poorton	as VCH	Poorton
78d	19,14	Pidele	—	Tolpuddle, Athelhampton, Piddlehinton or Bardolfeston	'Piddle'
79a	24,5	Cernel	—	Godmanstone	'Cerne'
79b	26,6;12	Frome	Bhompston	Frome Billet and Frome Whitfield	as VCH
79b	26,13	Wintreburne	—	Winterborne St. Martin	'Winterborne' (South)
79b-c	26,21-22	Pidele	—	Tolpuddle, Athelhampton, Piddlehinton or Bardolfeston	'Piddle'
79c	26,32	Winburne	—	Wimborne Minster	'Wimborne'
79c	26,29	Bleneford	—	Blandford St. Mary	as DG
79c	26,31	Wintreburne	—	Winterborne Kingston	'Winterborne' (Eastern)
79c	26,37	Blaneford	Blandford St. Mary	as VCH	Langton Long Blandford
79d	26,46	Blaneford	?Blandford Forum	Bryanston	as DG
79d	26,47	Brochemtune	Brockhampton in Buckland Newton	Brockington	as DG
79d	26,52	Stoches	Stock Gaylard	East Stoke	as DG
80b	28,5	Glole	Church Knowle	Lutton Gwyle	as VCH
81c,d	36,4	Poleham	?Hazelbury Bryan	Pulham	as DG
82c	44,1	Hille	Hill farm in Iwerne Minster	as VCH	Gold Hill in Child Okeford

DB column	Chapter and Section	DB Form	VCH	DG	This edition
82d	48,1	*Pidere*	Waterston	Tolpuddle, Piddlehinton, Athelhampton or Bardolfeston	as VCH
82d	49,5	*Terente*	?Tarrant Gunville	'Tarrant'	as DG
83d	55,27-28	*Wintreburne*	Winterborne Stickland	Winterborne (Eastern)	as DG
84a	55,44-45	*Torne*	–	Thornham	'Thorne'
84b	56,12	*Craveford*	Tarrant Crawford	'Great Crawford'	as DG
84b	56,28	*Wintreburne*	–	Winterborne (South)	Winterborne Houghton
84c	56,34	*Bleneford*	Langton Long Blandford	as VCH	Bryanston
84c	56,55	*Candele*	Stourton Caundle	Caundle Marsh	Purse Caundle
85a	57,10	*Wintreburne*	–	Winterborne (South)	Winterborne (Eastern)
85a	58,2	*Wintreburne*	Winterborne Monkton	Winterborne (Eastern)	as VCH

2. THE DORSET RIVERS

In Dorset DB a particular problem is posed by the large number of places that are named from the rivers on whose banks they stand. This problem is found in Devon and in Wiltshire, with other less complex examples elsewhere. In Dorset, major groups of places are so named from the rivers Cerne, Frome, Piddle, Tarrant and Wey and from the two rivers Winterborne. Smaller groups are associated with the Caundle, the Bride, the Iwerne and the Stour, the Allen (formerly the Wimborne) and the Char (originally a second 'Cerne' river). In modern times, such places are differentiated by suffixes, prefixes or secondary names and this process had begun by 1086. Thus *Obcerne*, *Piretone*, *Litelfrome*, *Litelpidele*, *Affapidele*, *Cernemude*, *Cerminstre* and *Opewinburne* had already become distinguished from their parent names.

On the other hand, many places are indicated only by the plain river name. In such cases, evidence has to be sought elsewhere, in the Tax Returns, in the order of entries within a fief or in the later history of manors. But even where the lands of a particular DB holding can be traced in later documents, it is often difficult to make an exact identification when a 1086 tenant-in-chief holds several lands of the same name. Thus in Ch. 26 the Count of Mortain holds 6 places called 'Cerne', 3 called 'Wey', 9 'Winterbornes', 3 'Piddles' and 2 'Fromes'.

In some cases, a place can be assigned confidently to a particular Hundred, even though its precise identity remains in doubt, while some places remain completely unidentified, for example several 'Winterbornes' (1,6. 5,1-2. 39,1).

In view of these uncertainties, it is difficult to be sure that a modern place named from a river was in fact a DB site. Where a place is given in the Places Index under a river name, but without a chapter and section reference, it has been included as a likely DB place, following Fägersten and the EPNS volumes, even though both have been influenced by Eyton's conjectures. Such places are usually parish names and have been chosen to show the likely geographical spread of a name. Other possibilities within parishes, including lost names, are given both in the General Notes and in the river notes below. Even where a river-derived place-name is given a chapter and section reference, it may be that other unassigned references belong to it.

In the lists below, the places that can be certainly identified in Tax Return Hundreds are given first, then the distribution of all places named from the river among their 'modern' Hundreds.

Note 2

River Cerne
The DB name applied to two rivers; one, now the river Char, joins the sea at Charmouth (*Cernemude*) separately distinguished by DB, and flows through Catherston Leweston ('Cerne', see 26,64 note). The other river joins the Frome just to the north of Dorchester; lying on it DB distinguishes Up Cerne (*Obcerne*) and Charminster (*Cerminstre*). This latter river will have passed through the Tax Return Hundreds of 'Stone' (ix), Modbury (xxxiii) and Dorchester (xxxii), the 'modern' Hundreds of Sherborne (1) where Up Cerne lies; of Cerne, Totcombe and Modbury (14) which includes Cerne Abbas and possibly Godmanstone (11,1 and 24,5 notes), and of St. George (20). In addition to Charminster in this last Hundred, Forston, Herrison and Pulston are probably places named 'Cerne' in 1086; see 26,5 note and RCHM iii pp. 71-72.

River Frome
The river names a number of places of which DB only distinguishes *Litelfrome*, now Frome St. Quintin. The river will have passed through the Tax Return Hundreds of Tollerford (xiv) where Chilfrome, Cruxton and Frome Vauchurch can probably be identified; Modbury (xxxiii) which certainly contained Frome St. Quintin; Frampton (xxxviii) and Dorchester (xxxii) in which latter lay 'Frome Billett'. These and other places named from the river now lie in the following 'modern' Hundreds: in Tollerford (13) lie Chilfrome, Cruxton, Frome St. Quintin and Frome Vauchurch; in St. George (20) lie Bhompston and Frome Whitfield, also possibly 'Frome Cranchen' (EPNS i p. 368); in Cullifordtree (26) lies 'Frome Billett' (but see the 'Tithings' note in the Appendix).

River Piddle
Places named from the river can be identified in the Tax Return Hundreds of 'Stone' (ix) where Piddletrenthide is found; of Puddletown (viii) which included Tolpuddle and where DB distinguishes Puddletown (*Piretone*) and Little Puddle (*Litelpidel*); and of Bere (xv) which contained Briantspuddle, Turners Puddle and Affpuddle (*Affapidele* in DB). These places and others, probably named from the river in 1086, are distributed among 'modern' Hundreds as follows: in Cerne, Totcombe and Modbury (14) lies Piddletrenthide; in Puddletown Hundred (21) lie Athelhampton, 'Bardolfeston', Burleston, Piddlehinton, Little Puddle, Puddletown, Tolpuddle and Waterston. Lovard, Muston and 'Combe Deverel' should probably be added to these 'Piddles' (26,21 note). Lying in Bere and Barrow Hundred (22) are Affpuddle, Briantspuddle and Turners Puddle; EPNS (i p. 290) would add Throop.

River Tarrant
DB makes no distinction between the numerous 'Tarrant' villages which probably lay in the Tax Return Hundreds of Badbury (vi) which certainly included Tarrant Crawford, and of *Langeberga* (xxii) which contained Tarrants Hinton, Keyneston, Monkton, and Launceston and possibly Tarrants Gunville, Rawston and Rushton (see 1,24 and 54,9 notes). The relationship between the Tax Return Hundreds and the 'modern' Hundreds in this corner of Dorset is extremely complex (see the Appendix) and the various Tarrants now lie as follows: in Cranborne Hundred (6) lie Tarrant Gunville and Tarrant Rushton; in Badbury Hundred (17) is Tarrant Crawford; in Pimperne Hundred (9) are Tarrant Hinton, Tarrant Keyneston, Tarrant Launceston and Tarrant Rawston. Tarrant Monkton lies now in Monkton Up Wimborne Hundred, but is here mapped in Pimperne (9); see the Appendix.

River Wey
All the villages named in DB from this river lay and lie in Cullifordtree Hundred (26); three modern parishes — Broadwey, Upwey and Weymouth — represent the name and the first two of these contained other 'Wey' manors that may have DB ancestors. In Broadwey lay Causeway, 'Crecketway', 'Rowaldsway', 'Southway' and 'Wayhoughton' (EPNS i pp. 200-201), while Upwey contained 'Stottingway' (EPNS i p. 247) and Westbrook; see notes to 1,22. 26,14-16. 55,5-6 and 56.9.

Rivers Winterborne
Winterburne is the most frequent river-derived place-name in Dorset; none of the occurrences of the name is distinguished by affixes. The name applies to two rivers. Of these, the eastern river is a tributary of the Stour, the South Winterborne of the Frome.

Places on the **eastern Winterborne** lay in at least three Tax Return Hundreds, those of *Hunesberga* (xxv) which contained Winterborne Stickland and Quarleston (55,1 note); of Combsditch (xvi) containing Anderson and Winterbornes Whitechurch, Clenston, and Tomson and perhaps also Winterborne Muston and Winterborne Houghton and a part of Winterborne Kingston; of Bere (xv) which contained Winterborne Kingston. The 'modern' Hundreds distribute these and other eastern Winterbornes differently. In Pimperne Hundred (9) lie Quarleston, Winterborne Houghton and Winterborne Stickland; in Bere and Barrow Hundred (22) lies Winterborne Kingston which has absorbed Winterborne Muston from Combsditch (see 'Tithings' note in the Appendix). Combsditch Hundred itself (16) includes Anderson, Winterborne Clenston (within which 'Phelpston' and 'Nicholston' may be DB places, 26,13 note), Winterborne Whitechurch (including Whatcombe (26,13 and 55,1 notes) and Winterborne Tomson. Winterborne Zelston, here included in Combsditch Hundred for convenience, is in the late Hundred of Rushmore (see the Appendix).

The villages on the **South Winterborne** river likewise lay in at least three Tax Return Hundreds: those of Eggardon (iv) which included Winterborne Abbas; of Dorchester (xxxii) including Martinstown; and of Cullifordtree (xxxvii) which contained Ashton (55,1 note), 'Winterborne Belet' and Winterborne Monkton. The villages situated beside this river now fall into four 'modern' Hundreds: in Eggardon (19) lies Winterborne Abbas; in St. George (20) lie Ashton and Martinstown; in Cullifordtree (26) are found Winterborne Came (which includes 'Winterborne Hundyngton' EPNS i p. 263; see 17,1 note below) and Winterbornes Farringdon, Herringston, 'Belet' and Monkton. A further Winterborne, Winterborne Steepleton, lies in Uggescombe Hundred (25).

Less major problems are caused by smaller groups of places named from other rivers. Thus, various places named Caundle (26,70-71 note) can be identified in the Tax Returns for Brownshall (xxviii) and Sherborne (xxxiv) Hundreds. On the river Stour DB distinguishes Sturminster, and from later evidence it is possible to separate East and West Stour, Stour Provost and Stourpaine from each other. On the river Allen (formerly Wimborne) holdings are grouped around Wimborne Minster or Wimborne St. Giles. The river Bride names various villages now called Bredy as well as Burton Bradstock (1,2 note); while on the river Iwerne, DB distinguishes Iwerne Minster (*Euneminstre*) from the other holdings which also lie in different Hundreds, see 30,3 note. Loders may also be an original river name, see 1,13 note.

Further information will be found in Ekwall (ERN), and in DGSW pp. 72-76 and under individual village names in Fägersten and the EPNS volumes, the last of which will contain a study of the river names.

3. THE COUNTY BOUNDARY

19th and 20th century boundary changes have made some adjustments to the border of the DB County. In 1086 Thorncombe was in Devon, being transferred to Dorset in 1844; while Chardstock, Stockland (Chs. 2-3 note) and Dalwood (1,4 and 12,14 notes) were originally in Dorset, the first being given to Devon in 1896, the others in 1832. On the same side of the County, Hawkchurch, including 'Philleyholme', neither separately mentioned in DB (see 11,1 and 17,1 notes), was transferred to Devon in 1896.

Larger adjustments have been made on the boundary with Somerset. In 1086, Holwell (not mentioned separately in DB) was a detached part of Milborne Port parish (Somerset) lying completely within Dorset, to which county it was transferred in 1844. Also transferred from Somerset, all in 1896, were Adber, Goathill, Poyntington, Sandford Orcas, Seaborough, Trent and Weathergrove and in the same year Wambrook (not mentioned in DB, see 3,13 note) was transferred from Dorset to Somerset.

Before April 1974, the only change on the border with Hampshire was the transfer of Kinson from Dorset in 1930. The 1974 boundary changes, otherwise ignored in this edition, push the Dorset boundary eastwards to the river Avon south of Fordingbridge, bringing into Dorset a number of places, including Bournemouth and Christchurch, and thus returning Kinson to the County.

B

GENERAL NOTES

The Manuscript is written on either side of leaves, or folios, of parchment (sheepskin) measuring about 15 by 11 ins. (38 by 28 cms.). On each side, or page, are two columns, making four to each folio. The folios were numbered in the 17th century and the four columns of each are here lettered a, b, c, d. The Manuscript emphasises words and usually distinguishes chapters and sections by the use of red ink. Underlining in the MS indicates deletion.

From a study of the MS it would appear that Dorset, though not as untidy a county as Hereford-shire, or Gloucestershire, was hurriedly compiled, with several spaces left by the scribe for information to be added when available, a number of marginal additions and the unusual entering on separate slips of parchment of 1,31. 36,4–11 and Ch. 42. Farley also seems to have had difficulties in transcription, and attention is drawn in the Notes below to more than a dozen mistakes of his, ranging from capitals for lower-case letters and vice versa to figure and name errors.

Details from the Tax Returns for Dorset (Exon. 17 a 1 to 24 a 3; see Introductory Note 1 and the Appendix) have only been given in the General Notes and Exon. Notes in the following instances: where they support a place-name identification; where they supply or suggest a byname for a holder given only a simple name in DB; where they record tax unpaid in cases where the identifi-cation of the holding is fairly certain. Not included are conjectural identifications, nor exact identifications where the Return adds no information to DB, nor where there are large discrepancies in the lordship land.

When Latin is quoted in these Notes, words are extended only where there is no reasonable doubt. The Anglo-Saxon *þ* and *ð* are reproduced as *th*.

These Notes follow the correct order of the text, ignoring displacements in the MS; thus the notes for Ch. 51 (which was added later) follow those for Ch. 50, rather than those for Ch. 54.

References to other DB counties are to the Chapters and Sections of the editions in the present series.

Bracketed references in arabic numerals after the Hundred names are to the 'modern' Hundreds (as mapped in this edition), those in Roman numerals are to the Tax Return Hundreds; see the Appendix.

DORSET. *Dorsete* is written across the top of cols. 75a,b-75c,d; 77a,b-80c,d; 82a,b-85a inclusive in red capitals and also at the head of the list of landholders on 75a and in 1,8. The inserted pieces of parchment, 76a,b and 81a,b,c,d, have no county heading.

B   THE DETAILS of only 4 boroughs are listed here, but there appears to have been a fifth borough in Dorset in 1086, Wimborne Minster. Although never actually called a borough, it had burgesses and houses (1,31. 31,1 etc.). The information on it appears in several places in DB Dorset (see Places Index). Details of boroughs in the adjacent Somerset are similarly scattered across the text of that county.

B 1   172 HOUSES ... 88 HOUSES THERE ... 100 ... DESTROYED. If one of these figures is not in error, the difference probably suggests new building since Hugh's time. ANSWERED FOR. *Se defendeba(n)t pro* is a common phrase in other DB counties (e.g. Sussex, Bucks., Beds., Herts.) where it means the same as *geldaba(n)t pro* 'paid tax for'. Here the meaning is slightly different.
HIDES. The hide is a unit of land measurement, either of productivity, of extent or of tax liability, and contained 4 virgates. Administrators attempted to standardize the hide at 120 acres, but incomplete revision and special local reductions left hides of widely differing extents in different areas. See 36,4 note and Dr. J. Morris in DB Sussex Appendix.
1 SILVER MARK. That is, 13s 4d.
FOR THE USE OF THE GUARDS. *ad opus Huscarlium*. The meaning of the fairly common DB phrase *ad opus* varies with the context: here the silver mark is for the guards' upkeep. In Herefords. 1,2 *opus* is 'use' where a contrast is implied between money going to the King and what the Sheriff receives for administering the land; see also 30,4 last note below. Exon. sometimes has, for example, "value to the Bishop" where DB has "value for the Bishop's use" (see Somerset General Notes 6,1) and see 11,1 Exon. Notes below for a correspondence between 'lordship' and 'use' in the value statement. The predominant Latin meaning of *opus*, however, is 'work' and there are occasions in DB where this is the appropriate rendering. It can also mean 'benefit'; see Devon Exon. Notes 15,67 and Worcs. H 2 in DB Worcs. App. V.

NIGHT'S REVENUE. See 1,2 note. Dorchester on its own did not pay one night's revenue, but combined with others in 1,4 to provide it. Similarly for Bridport and Wareham. See Round FE pp. 113-114.

MONEYERS ... COINAGE WAS CHANGED. See DB Herefords. C 9 (col. 179a) where on the renewal of the coinage each of the 7 moneyers gave 18s for acquiring the dies and then had a month in which to pay the King 20s. In DB Shrops. C 11 (col. 252a) the 20s had to be paid on the 15th day after the moneyers bought their dies.

PAYING ... 20s. DB uses the old English currency system which lasted for a thousand years until 1971. The pound contained 20 shillings, each of 12 pence, abbreviated respectively as £(ibrae), s(olidi) and d(enarii). DB often expresses sums above a shilling in pence (as 35d in 1,2) and above a pound in shillings (e.g. 110s in 1,3).

100 HAVE BEEN COMPLETELY DESTROYED. Opinion seems to be divided on the cause of the destruction of so many houses here and in Wareham and Shaftesbury. According to C. S. Taylor 'The Norman Settlement of Gloucestershire' p. 61 in TBGAS xl (1917) they were probably destroyed when in 1068 King William and his men marched towards Exeter (which had refused to surrender to him). Eyton *Dorset* p. 72 believes that the destruction was perhaps due to internal conflicts between the English and Norman burgesses. Other views, which the phraseology of Exchequer and Exon. DB appear to support, are that Hugh the Sheriff (see next note) was responsible for the devastation, perhaps when clearing ground for work on the castles (cf. DB Glos. G 4 col. 162a); see W. A. Morris 'The Office of Sheriff in the Early Norman Period' in EHR xxxiii (1918) p. 162 note 148; VCH iii p. 27.

HUGH THE SHERIFF. Hugh son of Grip (also called Hugh of Wareham; see 23,1 note) was Sheriff of Dorset before Aiulf the Chamberlain (see Ch. 49 note). He was dead by the date of the Tax Returns (1084-86), if not earlier (see Ch. 49 note), and his wife held many of his lands (see Ch. 55). He took lands from the churches of Shaftesbury, Abbotsbury (see 13,1 note) and Cerne, as well as from lay tenants. Exon. 36 b 3 (= DB 11,5) is outspoken about the losses caused by his depredations (see DB Worcs. Ch. 26 note for the similar behaviour of Urso of Abetot, Sheriff of Worcs.). For a discussion of the injustices caused by Sheriffs, as well as their judicial, military and financial duties, see W. A. Morris in EHR xxxiii (1918) p. 158 ff.

B 3 ST. WANDRILLE'S. See Ch. 18 note.

B 4 KING'S GUARDS. In the MS and Farley there is a full stop after *regis*; the facsimile does not reproduce it.

ABBESS. Of St. Mary's, Shaftesbury (Ch. 19).

L NOTES ON MAJOR LANDHOLDERS appear at the heads of their respective chapters. Notes referring to other individuals are under their first occurrence in the text.

IT WOULD SEEM that in Dorset the scribe had already begun at least the *Terra Regis* when he came to write the Landholders' List (and possibly also the Boroughs, though these may have been written first of all) and that he had left himself insufficient room for the List. Normally the Landholders are indexed in 2 columns of more or less equal length; in Dorset, however, no account is taken of the rulings and in the first column 24 entries (I-XXIV) are squeezed in and in the second 27 entries (XXV-LI) occupy almost the same length of parchment (not as Farley prints). LII to LVII are then written on the last ruled line of the folio, across cols. 75a and b; LVIII is added below LVII. The transposition signs are as in the translation, not the 'hands' that Farley prints. Alfred of 'Spain' was omitted from the list and a number given to the land of Isolde; see Ch. 45 note. In this edition the Latin has been cut to fit the page, the entries at the bottom of col. 75b (L 54-58 inclusive, though L 55-58 in the text) forming a further three lines, indented.

L 8 GLASTONBURY. In the MS *GlastingbeRy,* not *Glastingbez,* as Farley prints, the abbreviation sign being the one he normally uses in *q̃* (= *quãrentina* 'furlong').

L 22 FOR THE DISCREPANCY between the numbering of the Landholders' List and that of
-23 the text, see Chs. 22-23 note.

L 45 FOR THE DISCREPANCY between the numbering of the Landholders' List and that of
-55 the text, see Ch. 45 note.

Ch. 1 THE LAND OF THE KING is entered by Exchequer DB in four distinct groups: 1,1-6 groups of royal manors forming the *vetus dominicum coronae* (land held TRE by King Edward), each group providing a half or one night's revenue; 1,7-14 lands formerly held by 'Earl' Harold; 1,15-29 lands held by and from Queen Matilda (William's queen, died 1083); 1,30-31 lands held by Countess Goda, King Edward's sister. Exon. Domesday enters the manors somewhat differently (see Exon. Notes to 1,1;15;22;30-31) and in

the King's lands includes DB Ch. 18 and 24,1-3 and an entry for 'Winterborne' not in DB (see 1,6 note and Exon. Notes to Ch. 49). The sections of Exchequer DB fall in the following order in Exon.: 1,7-8;14;9-10;1;11-13;2-4. 24,1. 1,5-6. 24,2. 18,1. 24,3. 18,2. (*Dominicatus Regis*); 1,15-21 (lordship land of Queen Matilda) and 1,22-25;27-29;26 (land held from Queen Matilda). 1,30-31 are not in the extant portion of the Exon. Book. There is a discussion of the arrangement and a table of the supposed members of the royal manors in Eyton *Dorset* pp. 78-101.
The rubricator has omitted the *I* beside the chapter heading; in a great many counties in DB the initial chapter numbers are omitted, probably in error.

1,1-6 THESE MANORS ARE GROUPED partly on a geographical basis, but made up so that each group can contribute one night's revenue; see VCH iii p. 28. Similar groupings are found in the other Wessex shires of Somerset, Hampshire and Wiltshire.

1,1 THE KING HOLDS. Repeated at the beginning of 1,1-21 and 1,23-31.
PORTLAND. The land probably included *Wik'* and *Helewill'* [Wyke Regis, GR SY 6577, and Holwell in Radipole, GR SY 6583 (rather than Elwell in Upwey, Fägersten p. 158), see Fees p. 90, Hutchins ii p. 850 and EPNS i p. 267] as well as Melcombe Regis (SY 6880) and Weymouth (SY 6779) (see next note).
KING EDWARD HELD IT DURING HIS LIFE. Exon. has "which King Edward held on the day he was alive", omitting *et mortuus* "and dead", its usual formula for pre-1066 tenure. This lends some support to the idea that King Edward did bequeath Portland to Old Minster, Winchester, but the writ announcing this bequest is of doubtful authenticity; see Harmer no. 112 and pp. 385-7. The bequest was presumably to take effect after King Edward's death, but was ignored by King William and no claim by the monks of Winchester appears in DB. However, in a writ of Henry I, dated 1100-7, the monks of St. Swithun's of Winchester are to hold Portland given them by King Edward (and also *Wike, portum Waimuth* and *Melecumbe* with their dependencies); V. H. Galbraith 'Royal Charters to Winchester' in EHR xxxv (1920) p. 390 no. xviii; see *Regesta* ii p. 52 no. 745.
DURING HIS LIFE ... The rest of the line has been left blank after this, perhaps for the plough estimate. Exon. does not give any additional information. Other examples of gaps left in DB being paralleled by lack of information in Exon. include 1,26. 11,13;16. 55,28 and perhaps 55,10.
100 SMALLHOLDERS. *Bordarii*, apparently from a Frankish word *borda* 'a wooden hut'. In DB they are usually listed after the villagers, but before the cottagers, who, though very similar in many respects (see notes to 1,2;8), seem to have been poorer. *Bordarii* form almost half the recorded population in DB Dorset. They frequently hold land (e.g. in 12,16. 55,5 and 56,56), as well as ploughs, and in 1,23 1 smallholder paid 30d and in 57,2 2 smallholders paid 20d (see note). It would seem probable that smallholders also owed their lords some form of labour service (see DB Herefords. 19,1). See DB Middlesex Appendix on a summary of the land holdings of smallholders, among other classes, in that county, and R. Lennard 'The Economic Position of the Bordars and Cottars of Domesday Book' pp. 342-371 of The Economic Journal vol. lxi (June 1951).
100 LESS 10. This edition keeps to the exact translation here and elsewhere with *minus* rather than translating as 90, because sometimes the reason for the subtraction is noted (e.g. in DB Wilts. 2,1 "100 hides, less 3" where the removal of the 3 hides is explained). Exon. has the same phrase.
ACRES. *Acra* (Exon. *agra, ager*) is used in DB both as a linear measure (as in 5,1. 26,40. 54,9;11) and as a square measure, as here. See 5,1 note on the linking of furlongs and acres in measurements and 36,4 note on the number of acres in a hide.
FURLONGS. DB *quarentina*, Exon. *quadragenaria*, a sub-division of the league (see 1,2 note), reckoned at 220 yards, an eighth of a mile. The largest number of furlongs recorded in one entry in Dorset is pasture 42 furlongs long in 54,6. In a great number of cases in DB the furlong is used linearly, both measurements of the land being given, as here. In many other instances, however, only one measurement is given, as in 1,7 "pasture, 2 furlongs"; it is possible that here the furlong is being used as a square measure, the pasture measuring 2 furlongs by 1 furlong (so Eyton *Dorset* p. 31 ff.). However, there is a good deal of evidence to suggest that to the Exchequer scribe the phrase "pasture, 2 furlongs" meant "pasture, 2 furlongs in length and 2 furlongs in width" (= 4 square furlongs of pasture): see Exon. Notes to 55,29;36;38;40 where, in the first instance, for DB's plain "pasture, 8 furlongs" Exon. has "pasture, 8 furlongs in both length and width". The facts that on several occasions Exon. also gives just the one measurement (as for 1,11 "pasture, 6 furlongs") and that DB often has the phrase (as in 41,1) "pasture, 4 furlongs in length and width" suggest that the phrases were interchangeable when the length and width of the land were the same.

COBS. *Roncini*, probably pack-horses. However, see DB Somerset Exon. Notes 8,5 where *roncinos* is glossed above *caballos* which is ordinarily to be translated 'riding horses', 'war horses', but in that case ML *caballus* may be reflecting OE *capel*, ON *kapall* 'a nag'.

CATTLE. *Animalia*, commonly called *animalia otiosa* 'idle animals' elsewhere, i.e. beef or dairy cattle in contrast to ploughing oxen, though occasionally in DB they seem to be oxen (see Somerset Exon. Notes 25,41; Cornwall Exon. Notes 4,23; Devon Exon. Notes 17,28;39 and Northants. 48,13). Cattle and other animals were generally omitted from Exchequer DB, though sometimes they were mistakenly not eliminated when the original returns were abstracted (see Glos. 3,7 and note); sometimes they may have been included to make a particular point, as probably in Herts. 31,8 where a catalogue of livestock etc. is given for land wrongfully appropriated by Bishop Odo.

PIGS. Without doubt there were a great many more pigs in Dorset than Exon. records, as only those pigs which formed part of the lordship are given, whereas according to Lennard p. 255 ff. the pigs were largely the responsibility of the special pig-farmers (*porcarii*) or the 'villagers' themselves. See DB Devon 1,18 General Notes.

SHEEP. *Oues* 'ewes', providing milk, cheese, wool and mutton. Sheep were extremely important in the economy of Dorset, several hundred frequently being recorded on individual manors in the surviving portion of Exon.

BLANCHED. *albas*, also *candidas* and *blancas* in DB. A sample of coin was melted as a test for the presence of alloy or baser metal. Money could also be said to be blanched when, without a test by fire, a standard deduction was made to compensate for alloying or clipping; see *Dialogus de Scaccario* (ed. C. Johnson, 1950) p. 125.

1,2 **A GROUP OF ROYAL MANORS** lying predominantly in the south-west of the County to which have been added Bere Regis and Colber. Outlying portions of some of the manors of this group may have been Kingston Russell (GR SY 5891), held as *Kingeston'* by John *Russel* in Fees p. 92 (see Fees p. 1268), and possibly Litton Cheney (GR SY 5590) a major holding not so far identified with any DB land, but which may have been the holding of Hugh of Boscherbert (53,2 note); see Cal. Inq. PM vol. vi (Ed. II) no. 724 and Hutchins ii p. 749.

BURTON (BRADSTOCK). DB *Bridetone*, named like the Bredys from the river Bride, see Fägersten p. 256. Burton lay in Godderthorn Hundred (18), see FA ii pp. 34, 54.

BERE (REGIS). Held later by the Earl of Hereford, see FA ii p. 11; sometimes called *Kyngesber'*, FA ii pp. 28, 44, 48. See 1,27 note.

COLBER. Now represented by Colber Crib House in Sturminster Newton, Fägersten p. 48.

SHIPTON (GORGE). In Godderthorn Hundred (18), held by Thomas *de Gorges* from the Countess of Albemarle (*de Albemarlie*) in FA ii p. 10; see Fees p. 425 and FA ii pp. 34, 54.

BRADPOLE. Fees p. 1268 records 1½ virgates outlying at *Kenilecumb'* [Lower Kingcombe GR SY 5599] ; see Fees p. 92 and 47,7 second note; Kingsland in Netherbury (GR SY 4597) was probably an outlying part (Hutchins ii p. 109).

CHIDEOCK. See 26,63 note.

THEY DID NOT PAY TAX. Or perhaps 'it', referring to the group of places as a whole (see DB's use of 'this manor' in the value statement). See Exon. Notes for this entry. Similarly for 1,3-6.

LAND FOR 55 PLOUGHS. This estimate of the ploughlands, very common in the south-west counties and elsewhere in DB, but rare in Glos., Worcs. and Herefords., is a convenient way of giving the true arable extent without the complexities associated with the hide (see B 1 note). It does not always agree with the details of the ploughs recorded in lordship and on the villagers' land. On a little less than half the occasions where both details are given do they tally with the assessment, and on about the same number of occasions (as here) they fall short (sometimes, as in 24,4. 26,50 and 56,57 a space has been left for one or other of the details). In some twenty-nine instances more ploughs are recorded than are estimated, sometimes as many as six more (as in 12,14); in some seven entries (e.g. 7,1) attention is expressly drawn to this fact. On the frequent artificiality of the numbers in the plough assessment, see R. Welldon Finn p. 97 ff. of 'The Teamland of the Domesday Inquest' in EHR lxxxiii (1968). See also J. S. Moore 'The Domesday Teamland: a reconsideration' in TRHS 5th ser. xiv (1964) pp. 109-130.

41 VILLAGERS. *xli uill(anu)s.* The singular occurs regularly in DB with 21,31 etc. Cf. *pro xxi hida* in 13,1. But see 36,4 *viginti 7 unus teinus tenuerunt.*

7 FREEDMEN. *Coliberti*; former slaves. A continental term, not otherwise found in England; used in DB to render a native term, stated on three occasions to be *(ge)bur* (Worcs. 8,10a and Hants. 1,10;23). The *coliberti* are found mainly in the counties in

Wessex and western Mercia, particularly in Wiltshire and Somerset. There were 33 freedmen in Dorset, 20 on the King's land and 13 on Glastonbury land, some of them being listed with the villagers and holding ploughs (as here), others (as in 1,4-5) appearing with the slaves and so perhaps working the lordship ploughs. In other counties in DB some held land (Som. 2,1 etc.) and paid dues (Herefords. 1,6; Worcs. 8,7 etc.). See Vinogradoff pp. 468-9; Maitland DBB pp. 36-7, 328-30; DB Oxon. 1,6 note on boors.

74 COTTAGERS. *Cotarii*, inhabitants of a *cote*, sometimes with land of their own (as in DB Middx. 2,1. 3,1 etc.; see the Appendix to that county), but in Dorset they are only stated as having a share in the ploughs and land. See 1,8 note on the allied group *coscez* 'Cottagers'. The terms *cotarius* and *bordarius* ('smallholder'; see 1,1 note) were sometimes confused: in the summary of the Glastonbury lordship holding in Exon. 527 b 4 the 72 *bordarii* correspond to the 40 *bordarii* and 32 *cotarii* of DB 8,1;3. See also Lennard pp. 346, 353 ff. and in The Economic Journal lxi (1951) p. 352 ff. Likewise two of the Exon. scribes dealing with Devon material never use the terms *cotarii* and *coceti* but only *bordarii*, and it is more likely that the former categories were included with the latter, than that there were no 'cottagers' on so many manors; Finn LE p. 50.

LEAGUES. DB *leuga, leuua, leuuede*. A measure of length, usually of woodland and pasture, traditionally reckoned at a mile and a half. If so, some will have been of enormous length (see Round in VCH Northants. vol. i p. 280 and DB Worcs. 1,1c note). The league is used regularly as a linear measure, both measurements being given for the land, as here. In the numerous entries where only one measurement is given, it is possible that the league, like the furlong apparently (see 1,1 note), is not being used as a square measure (as Eyton *Dorset* p. 31 ff.), but that the same figure represents both the length and width. Thus in 17,2 ('pasture, 2 leagues') the pasture actually measured 2 leagues in length and 2 leagues in breadth.

WOODLAND ... WIDE. The scribe may have intended to leave blank the rest of the line after this for more information to be added when available. Or the gap may be the usual one left before the 'value' statement, as appears regularly in other counties (e.g. Worcs. and Glos.). A similar gap occurs in 1,4. 3,6. 10,2. 55,10;44 etc.

ONE NIGHT'S REVENUE. Many royal manors, especially in the south-west, had to pay this revenue which took the place of the normal tax payment, the manors not usually being assessed in hides. Originally this meant the amount of food needed to support the King and his household for one night, though by the 11th century these food rents were generally commuted. From examples in Somerset and Hampshire £80 appears to be a probable figure before 1066, and £100 after, for one night's revenue; see R. L. Poole *The Exchequer in the Twelfth Century* (Oxford 1912) p. 29. It would seem that in Dorset, as in Gloucestershire (DB Glos. 1,9;11;13) and sometimes in Wiltshire (e.g. 1,2-4), these rents were not commuted. In DB Somerset, as here, there are several instances of manors combining to provide this rent (see Somerset General Notes 1,2;10). Latin *firma* here represents OE *feorm* 'a food rent'; see OED *farm* sb. i. See Exon. Notes 1,9 for another sense of *firma* and also DB Herefords. 1,1 notes on revenue.

SCRUBLAND AT 'HAWCOMBE'. In the MS *Boscus de havocūbe*; Farley misprints *Boscus ten havocūbe*, as if *Boscus* were a personal name, the holder of 'Hawcombe'. 'Hawcombe' is a lost name in the area of Shipton Hill (GR SY 5092); see Hutchins ii p. 284. It is placed by Eyton (*Dorset* p. 85) in Burton Bradstock parish and by Fägersten (p. 260) in Shipton Gorge parish.

(AND BELONGED) IN SUCH A WAY. The Exchequer scribe seems to have had trouble with the *ita ut* phrase in Exon. (see Exon. Notes), hence the need for the bracketed words in the translation.

EARL EDWIN. In Exon. 'Earl Godwin', which is probably correct, as his wife, Gytha, held Frampton (17,1) before 1066, to which the third oak of 'Hawcombe' belonged by 1086. Earl Godwin was earl of the West Saxons and father of Earl (King) Harold and Edith (wife of King Edward); he died in 1053.

1,3 THESE MANORS lie in the eastern part of the County. For Knowlton, which would form a natural geographical grouping with them, see 1,6.

WIMBORNE (MINSTER) ... WIMBORNE (ST. GILES). DB *Winborne, Opewinburne*. Between them the two 'Wimbornes' must have covered a considerable area although the hidage was not known in 1086. Wimborne Minster included the manors of *Kyngeston'* and *Bernardesleye* [Kingston Lacy in Pamphill, GR SZ 9701, EPNS ii p. 167, and Barnsley farms also in Pamphill, GR SZ 9903], FA ii p. 14, see pp. 32, 51; Fees p. 91; RH i p. 97a.

'Up Wimborne', conveniently distinguished by DB, will have included at least

Winterborn' Malemains, Fees p. 750, otherwise *Up Wymburn Malemeyns*, FA ii p. 28, held from the Honour of Gloucester, that is the parish of Wimborne St. Giles (EPNS ii p. 263), as well as All Hallows farm (EPNS ii p. 264; GR SU 0212) and Monkton Up Wimborne (EPNS ii p. 265; GR SU 0113). For 'Philipston' see 20,2 note. For the river name, see Introductory Note 2.

SHAPWICK. See FA ii p. 14, Fees p. 91 and RH i p. 97a.

(MOOR) CRICHEL. DB *Chirce*. There are now two parishes, Moor Crichel in Badbury Hundred (17) and Long Crichel in Knowlton Hundred (10). The latter is found in the same Hundred in 1086 (34,11 and 49,16 notes), but the former does not occur in a Tax Return. Since DB does not give its extent, it is not clear whether the land involved both Crichels or only one. There was certainly royal land at Moor Crichel in Badbury Hundred in FA ii p. 14, held as *Kerchil Sifrast* from the Honour of Chewton in Fees p. 753 (see 56,14 note), also at *Parva Kerchelle* in FA ii p. 14 ['Little Crichel' lost in Moor Crichel, EPNS ii p. 141] and at *Kerchel Freinel* in Badbury Hundred which was granted with Shapwick and 'Up Wimborne' to the Count of Meulan by Henry I (Fees p. 91). This is also identified with 'Little Crichel' by EPNS ii p. 141.

GOATS. *Caprae*, she-goats, important for their milk.

A GROUP OF ROYAL MANORS mainly close to Dorchester, but including Gillingham in the north of the County.

DORCHESTER. Royal land, either part of Dorchester or of the unidentified 'Frome' below lay at *Kyngeston Crubbe* [Kingston Maurward in Stinsford parish, GR SY 7191] in FA ii pp. 17, 31, and probably at *Cherleton* [Charlton GR SY 6895 in Charminster parish] held by Thomas *de Hyneton* from the Earl of Lincoln in FA ii pp. 31, 51, as well as at *Wolfeton* [Wolfeton GR SY 6792 in Charminster parish] held by Thomas *Maubaunk* from William *de Byngeham* in FA ii pp. 31, 51. All these places are in St. George Hundred (20); see notes to 26,5;8-11 and 27,4-5 and 53,1.

FORDINGTON. This former Liberty occupied a crescent-shaped area to the east, south and west of Dorchester, Fordington being marked at GR SY 6990 on the first edition one-inch OS map (sheet 17 of 1811, reprint sheet 92 of 1969); Fordington fields are south of the Borough and Fordington Down is at GR SY 6691 on current maps; see EPNS i p. 348. In Fees pp. 88-89 it included *Witewill'* [Frome Whitwell GR SY 6791, now in Bradford Peverell parish, possibly the unidentified 'Frome' below, see Fees p. 379], *Burton'* [Burton GR SY 6891, now in Charminster parish], *Herleg* (or *Ertleg'* in Fees p. 379, *Hertleye* in Cal. Inq. PM vol. v (Ed. II) no. 404] [Hartley farm in Minterne Magna, GR ST 6406] and *Dalewde* [Dalwood GR ST 2400, formerly a detached part of Dorset, transferred to Devon in 1832; see RH i p. 100]. The Liberty of Fordington also included 'Loops' (in Dorchester) and Hermitage parish (GR ST 6407); see EPNS i pp. 334, 363 and Hutchins ii pp. 414, 791.

SUTTON (POYNTZ). In Cullifordtree Hundred (26). It later formed part of the Honour of Gloucester and was held from it in Fees p. 95 by Nicholas *Puinz*. In FA ii p. 18 it is said to include *Prestone* [Preston GR SY 7083], *Podintone* [Putton in Chickerell, SY 6580], *Estchykerel* [East Chickerell; for West Chickerell see 56,8 note] and *Sutwaye* ['Southwey' lost in Broadwey, EPNS i p. 201]; see FA ii pp. 38, 57 and Cal. Inq. PM vol. iv (Ed. II) no. 346.

GILLINGHAM. A *villa regalis* in FA ii p. 21.

'FROME'. This holding which cannot at present be identified is named from the river Frome; see Introductory Note 2 above. DG identifies Chilfrome and Frome Vauchurch, but without supporting evidence; see notes on Dorchester and Fordington above.

HIDES ARE THERE. *hidae sint ibi*, subjunctive, here and in 1,5-6; s̄t in 1,2-3 which could abbreviate *sint* or *sunt*. Exon. has s̄t throughout. *Sint* occurs in the same phrase in the first chapter of Wilts., Somerset and Devon. The subjunctive and indicative are interchangeable in indirect questions in Medieval Latin. But see Round FE p. 109.

THESE MANORS lie within four miles of one another in the eastern central part of the County.

PIMPERNE. Probably included Blandford Forum, not separately mentioned in DB; see 26,29 note and RH i p. 97a. It was later associated with Kingston Lacy (see 1,3 note, Hutchins i p. 217).

CHARLTON (MARSHALL). Presumably an outlier of Pimperne in 1086; it was later a detached part of Cogdean Hundred (24), though locally in Combsditch (16). Charlton Marshall, like Sturminster Marshall, belonged after 1086 to the Count of Meulan who in 1099 gave the tithes and church of *Cerlentone* and *Posteberies* [Spetisbury] for the souls

of King William and Queen Matilda; Round CDF p. 111 no. 326 and p. 118 no. 352. Charlton Marshall will have included a part of Spetisbury and of 'Great Crawford'. The Abbot of Préaux (Ch. 28 note) holds *Sp'ttebury* and *Cherleton* in TE p. 184b and in FA ii p. 44 he holds *Crauford* in Loosebarrow Hundred (23); see Cal. Inq. PM vol. iv (Ed. I) no. 34 and Hutchins iv p. lxxvii.
THIS MANOR. In the MS *Hooc M̄*, a scribal error for *Hoc M̄*. On this occasion Farley does not correct the scribe's mistake, as he does at 9,1 and 37,4.
HALF OF ONE NIGHT'S REVENUE. The other half of the one night's revenue may have been provided by the group of manors in 1,6. See 1,2 note.

1,6   THESE MANORS appear (with the exception of Knowlton, see first note under 1,3) to lie in the south-east of the County.
WINFRITH (NEWBURGH). Held by John *de Novo Burgo* (Newburgh) in FA ii p. 9; see Fees p. 425. The holding seems to have included *Knysteton* and *Buriton* [East Knighton GR SY 8185 and Burton GR SY 8386, both in Winfrith parish], FA ii p. 10; see Fees p. 89.
LULWORTH. Certainly included East Lulworth, held as *Est Loleworth* in FA ii p. 29 by John *de Novo Burgo*; see 26,50-51 note.
'WINTERBORNE'. The grouping of manors suggests a place on the eastern river Winterborne. Winterborne Zelston, whose 1086 hundred is unknown, but which later formed (with West Morden tithing) the Hundred of Rushmore, is possible, especially since, like many royal manors, it is later held by the Honour of Gloucester (*Winterborn' Maureward'*, Fees p. 750; see FA ii p. 25, EPNS ii p. 68, Hutchins i p. 336 and Eyton *Dorset* pp. 97, 100). Convincing evidence is lacking and the descent of Winterborne Kingston also requires further study.
    The next Exon. entry contains the details of a part of Winfrith held by Bolle the priest (see 24,2 and Exon. Notes to Ch. 24), followed by another part of 'Winterborne' (presumably the same place), held as reeveland by Aiulf the Sheriff. This latter entry does not appear in Exchequer Domesday (see Exon. Notes to Ch. 49); although it rightly belongs in DB Ch. 1, this brief entry was probably missed by the Exchequer scribe when excerpting, because it was amongst alms' lands.
KNOWLTON. Only a few houses now remain, but the medieval village has left impressive mounds, see RCHM vol. v p. 113. It is held in Fees p. 750 from the Honour of Gloucester; see Fees p. 91.
AS WIDE. In the MS *tấntd' lat̄*; Farley omits the *a* in *tấntd'* in error. The abbreviation sign over the *a* is not needed, as no letter is omitted; the scribe probably added it by mistake at the same time as the one over the *tntd'* later in the line.
AS MUCH WOODLAND IN LENGTH AND WIDTH. The Latin is ambiguous and could mean either that the woodland measured the same in length and width (cf. the phrase 'woodland, 7 furlongs in both length and width', 47,9) or that it measured the same as the pasture (although here one would expect *totidem* 'as many (leagues)' to be used in place of *tantundem* and cf. *pasturae similiter* in 19,2). However, Exon. shows that in fact both meanings are correct in this case, the woodland, like the pasture, measuring 3 leagues by 3 leagues.

1,7   EARL HAROLD. Son of Earl Godwin and brother of Queen Edith; King of England 6th Jan.-14th Oct. 1066. William the Conqueror did not recognise his title to the crown, hence the persistent use in DB of 'Earl' instead of 'King'. Harold was Earl of East Anglia (1045), received half of Swein's earldom (1046), was Earl of the West Saxons on his father's death in 1053, and Earl of Hereford (1058).
(CHILD) OKEFORD. The place can be identified in the Tax Return for Farrington Hundred (xxxv) whereas Okeford Fitzpaine is in that for *Hunesberga* (xxv); 8,2 note. A third 'Okeford' is now Shillingstone, 54,6 note. *Child Acford* in Gillingham and Redlane Hundred (4), into which Farrington Hundred was absorbed, is held by the Countess *de Albamara* in FA ii p. 22; see Fees pp. 91, 753.
OF WHICH. *De ea* 'of it', referring to *terra* 'land' (see 55,1), not *car(ucas)* 'ploughs'.
2 MILLS WHICH PAY 20s. There were 2 mills in Child Okeford, the King having 10s from them (see Exon. Notes here) and the Count of Mortain having 10s (see 26,4 and note).
PASTURE, 2 FURLONGS. The same phrase occurs in Exon.; see 1,1 note above.
VALUE. *Valet* (*valebat, valuit*, past tenses) normally means the sums due to lords from their lands (e.g. 'Value to him of this castle ...' in DB Herefords. 24,13; 'Value to Gerald ...' in Devon 45,3; where 'him' and 'Gerald' are the 1086 holders). Cf. 'Value of the Bishop's lordship' in 2,2. Exon. frequently has 'value when he (1086 holder) acquired it' for DB's plain past tense (but see 28,2 and 47,7); see 1,9 Exon. Notes.
    For evidence that DB's simple *valet* sometimes concealed the fact that a manor was being held at a revenue (was being 'farmed') either by an individual not resident on the

estate or by the villagers themselves, see R. S. Hoyt 'Farm of the Manor and Community of the Vill in Domesday Book' in Speculum xxx (1955) and Lennard Ch. V. See also 47,7 note below and DB Devon General Notes to 25,28 and 26,1.

reddit, reddidit 'pays, paid' would seem to have a similar meaning (see 1,19, and also 17,1-2 and 26,29 where both occur together). The two verbs appear to be interchangeable, especially in Exon., which often has *reddit* for DB's *valet* or vice versa, both in the main 'Value' statement and in the payment of mills etc. However, there is a belief that when *reddit* is used it means that the manor is being 'farmed' (see Hoyt and Lennard op. cit.); and that Exon.'s frequent interlineations of *reddit* above *valet* and vice versa, possibly in correction (see Exon. Notes 1,7), are intended to draw the distinction between the two terms (but see Lennard's reservation on p. 123).

1,8 PUDDLETOWN. In Puddletown Hundred (Tax Return viii). Two-thirds of *Pideleton'* are held in Fees p. 91 by the *Comes de Insula* (de Lisle), a frequent later holder of Ch. 1 land; see FA ii p. 15 and 26,21-22 note.

TAX FOR ½ HIDE. This would appear to be an example of beneficial hidation, considering the number of plough-teams, the population and the value of the manor.

29 COTTAGERS. DB *coscet* singular, *coscez, cozets* plural, indeclinable (Exon. *cocetus* singular, *cotseti, coceti* plural, 2nd declension), represent Anglo-Norman versions of OE *cot-seta* singular, *cot-setan* plural, 'a cottage-dweller; cottage holder' (OE *cot, saeta*, see *English Place-name Elements* s.v. *cot-saeta*; OED s.v. *cotset*): the Anglo-Norman letter *z* represents the sound *ts* and the spelling *sc* a miscopied *st* representing metathesis of *ts*, so *coscet* = *cotset, coscez* and *cozets* = *cotsets*. The plural in *-s* represented by *cozets* (= *cotsets*) is the result of either a French adaptation or an OE change of inflexion, and is the form used in DB Wilts. Ch. 1,1-15.

'Cottagers' are almost entirely confined to the south-west counties in DB, Wiltshire providing about 80% of the total entries. In Dorset there are 209 Cottagers on some 30 manors, ranging in number from 29 here and 20 at Melbury Abbas (19,6) to single Cottagers at Watercombe (1,29), Loders (26,58) etc. Unlike in DB Somerset where, with one exception, they occur on the eastern side of the county, in Dorset they are recorded for manors throughout. They are normally listed after the villagers (but see 3,9. 26,15) and in 31,2 they appear before cottagers (*cotarii*) who were apparently a different class, though the distinction is obscure. In DB Wilts. *coscez* and *cotarii* regularly occur in the same entry, suggesting that they were not identical. The *bordarii* 'smallholders' (see 1,1 note) also had aspects in common with the *coscez*. It is interesting that in the Domesday satellite Bath A (see DB Somerset App. II) *coceti* are replaced in the corresponding Exon. and DB entries by *bordarii*. See Lennard pp. 346, 353ff. and in the Economic Journal vol. lxi (1951) p. 352ff.

Not much is known about the status and economic position of *coscez*, though as can be seen from this entry and many others they shared ploughs with other 'villagers' and 7 Cottagers in 26,31 had ½ plough on their own, but in 3,9 the 6 Cottagers are excluded from a share in the 4 ploughs. They also had some land, as can be seen from the corresponding entries in the surviving portion of Exon., such as for 1,28 and 47,8, and shared land with other 'villagers' in 11,11-13. 12,12 and 13,2. A class of person called in OE *cotsetla* 'cottage-dweller', which seems equivalent to that of the *coscet*, has its obligations detailed in the 10th-11th century *Rectitudines Singularum Personarum* pp. 445-6. His rights varied according to local custom: in some places he had to work for his lord every Monday throughout the year or (so Anglo-Saxon version; 'and' in the Latin) 3 days a week at harvest; in some places every day at harvest, reaping 1 acre of oats or ½ acre of other corn; he was to be allowed his sheaf by the steward; he was not to pay land-tax; he was to have 5 acres of his own, more where customary, but less would be too little because his duty-labour was frequently called for; he was to pay his hearth-penny at Holy Thursday like every free man, to relieve his lord's demesne, if required, of its obligations to sea-defences, royal deer parks and such things, according to his condition, and pay his church-dues at Martinmas.

IN 'PURBECK'. Purbeck is the name of the hill which crosses the Isle of Purbeck from west to east, Purbeck Hills on OS six-inch map, Purbeck Hill on OS one-inch 1st Edition of 1811 (sheet 16, reprint sheet 93 of 1969), in Steeple and Tyneham parishes. The reference here could be to a lost settlement name derived from the hill; but it is more likely that 'Hundred' has been omitted, Purbeck Hundred being an alternative name for the Tax Return Hundred of Ailwood (xix) now Rowbarrow Hundred (29); see 37,13 and EPNS i p. 2. 1½ hides held by Harold's villagers, from which the King had no tax, occur in the Tax Return for Ailwood Hundred (xix) and are probably this land, which was possibly at *Lesseton'* [Leeson in Langton Matravers parish, GR SZ 0078] held from the Honour of Gloucester in Fees p. 750; but see Hutchins i p. 633.

MAPPOWDER. DB *Mapertone* identified by VCH tentatively with Mapperton in Almer and by DG with Mapperton near Beaminster. The DB form may be a confusion between Mapperton and Mappowder both of which have the same origin: OE *mapuldor* 'mapletree'. Elsewhere in DB Mappowder is *Mapledre*. In this instance OE *tūn* seems to have been attached. More decisive evidence is the Tax Return for Buckland Hundred (xxxvi) where the King is said to have ½ hide of Harold's land in lordship. Mappowder is in Buckland Hundred (8).

LAND FOR 1½ PLOUGHS. The rest of the line in the MS has been left blank after this, either for more details to be added or because the scribe wanted a gap before the separate information about the third penny. Cf. the space after the woodland details in 3,1 and after the mill in 3,9.

THIRD PENNY OF ... DORSET. This is the third penny of the pleas of the county, as in DB Warwicks. 1,6 and note, to which Earl Harold was entitled as holder of the manor. This and the third penny of a Hundred (see DB Shrops. 4,1,1 and Herefords. 19,2 and note) are not to be confused with the third penny of a Borough's total revenues (see DB Glos. B 1 note).

AIULF. Probably Aiulf the Sheriff who would have had the 'farming' of this manor as well as Frome St. Quintin 1,15 (see Exon. Notes). The name represents OE *Aethelwulf.*

1,9   CHARBOROUGH. In the MS the *R* and *E* of *CEREBERIE* have been written over an erasure and the *R* has a long tail to link it to the *E*. The land was in Charborough (Loosebarrow) Hundred (Tax Return xviii); see Fees p. 88 and FA ii p. 44.
VILLAGERS ... 1½ HIDES. According to the Tax Return for Charborough Hundred (xviii) the King did not have tax from 1½ hides held by the villagers from Harold's land.

1,10   IBBERTON. In Whiteway Hundred (15), Hilton Hundred Tax Return (xi), held by the *Comes de Insula* as *Hedbredinton'* in Fees p. 90; *Ethbrichinton* in FA ii p. 13.

1,11   FLEET. The Tax Return for Uggescombe Hundred (iii) states that Fulcred (see Exon. Notes under 1,10) paid tax in another Hundred on 1½ hides of Harold's land. In Fees p. 93 Hawisia *de Ripariis* (Rivers) holds *Flete* in Uggescombe Hundred (25) from the Earl of Devon; see Fees p. 426 and FA ii p. 6.

1,12   CHALDON. Chaldon Herring or East Chaldon, distinct from the holding at 55,33; see Hutchins i p. 339. *Chavedon' Hareng* is a fee of the Earl of Warwick in Fees p. 425. It lay in Winfrith Hundred (Tax Return xxx).

1,13   LODERS. Possibly an old river name, referring in DB to a number of settlements on its banks, such as Loders itself, Up Loders and Loders Lutton, now Matravers, all within the modern parish of Loders; see Fägersten p. 257. Of these Loders and Matravers can be confidently identified with individual DB holdings and Eyton *Dorset* (pp. 127-8) would go further. The King's land here has its own Tax Return (xxxix). Other holdings seem to have fallen into two Tax Return Hundreds, Eggardon (iv) and Godderthorn (x); see notes to 26,41-42;58. 55,24 and 56,51. In Fees p. 92 the Abbey of *Monteburc* [Montebourg] holds *Lodres* by gift of Richard *de Revers*. The same land in FA ii p. 11 in Godderthorn Hundred (18) includes *Bothenamtone* [Bothenhampton, GR SY 4791] and *Pymor* [Pymore, GR SY 4694, in Allington and Bradpole parishes].
VILLAGERS ... 10 HIDES. According to the Tax Return for Loders Hundred (xxxix) the King did not have tax from 10 hides the villagers hold from land once belonging to Earl Harold.
2 HIDES (OF) THANELAND WHICH DO NOT BELONG THERE. These 2 hides are also entered in the Tax Return for Loders Hundred (xxxix): they were added to the manor and the King did not have tax from them. Cf. DB Herefords. 1,75. Generally thaneland was part of the lordship land (see DB Som. 8,16) of either a lay or an ecclesiastical landholder, set aside to maintain a thane, armed and mounted. In return for the land the thane would provide certain services, often military. This land, especially if it was part of the church's land, was usually inalienable: the holder was not free to transfer his allegiance to another lord nor to sell the land (see 49,10;17 and Exon. Notes to 11,2 and 11,13; but cf. 1,31). Thaneland was not automatically hereditable, though it could sometimes be granted for a period of 'three lives' (a common length of lease). The holder of thaneland was not necessarily a thane, however; see 1,31 where he is a priest and 11,13 Exon. Notes where he is a French man-at-arms. From several entries, this one included, it would seem that thaneland was often simply land once held by a thane.

1,14 LITTLE PUDDLE. In Puddletown Hundred (Tax Return viii); see Fees p. 425, FA ii
pp. 15, 34, 54, and Cal. Inq. PM vol. ii (Ed. I) no. 689 where *Litele Pydele* is held from
Stephen *de Baiocis* (see 1,22 note).
EARL HAROLD'S MOTHER. Countess Gytha, wife of Earl Godwin.
IT PAID TAX. Or perhaps 'she paid tax' here and elsewhere with *geldb'*. However, see
1,7-13 etc., where the subject of *geldb'* must be the manor; also 57,4 where *q̄ geldb'*
must refer to the lands of the thanes. See 26,43 note.
1,15 QUEEN MATILDA. Wife of King William; she died in 1083.
FROME (ST. QUINTIN). DB *Litelfrome*. This holding can be deduced from the Tax
Return for Modbury Hundred (xxxiii). It is later in Tollerford Hundred (13), held from
the Earl of Gloucester; see Fees pp. 426, 750, FA ii pp. 35, 55, Cal. Inq. PM vol. i
(Henry III) no. 530 and vol. iii (Ed. I) no. 371.
VALUE WAS £12. The scribe originally wrote *xiiii*, then erased the first two minims
(although they are still visible in the facsimile) to make *xii*.
NOW £18. The scribe originally wrote *xii*, then corrected it to *xviii* by joining the *ii*
together, adding a *i* after them and interlining *ii* above. All these corrections to the value
are done in a darker ink.
1,16 CRANBORNE. In *Albretesberga* Hundred (v), according to the evidence of the Tax
Return; later in Cranborne Hundred (6), held by the Earl of Gloucester, FA ii pp. 26, 39.
PASTURE 2 LEAGUES LONG AND 1 FURLONG AND 1 LEAGUE WIDE. Or perhaps,
as one would expect the league to precede its subdivision the furlong (as in 4,1. 13,1 etc.),
the scribe omitted the *una q̄₄* before the *lḡ* and the meaning should be 'pasture 2 leagues
and 1 furlong long and 1 league wide'. See 5,1 note for another case where the scribe
may have added part of a length measurement. Exon., however, also gives the width as
'1 furlong and 1 league', but gives the length as 2½ leagues.
THEY PAY £3 APART FROM SERVICE. In both Exchequer DB and Exon. *excepto
seruitio* which is ambiguous. The meaning could be either that the thanes owed service as
well as £3, or that the £3 was instead of doing service. However, the Exon. addition to
11,1 (see Exon. Notes) suggests that the £3 was paid to exempt the thanes from doing
service, in other words the service was commuted to a render. VCH iii p. 67 translates
'render £3 excepting service'.
1,17 ASHMORE ... 4 HIDES. According to the Tax Return for *Langeberga* Hundred (xxii) the
King had no tax from 4 hides of the Queen's land. Ashmore is later in Cranborne Hundred
(6) and held from the Earl of Gloucester; Fees p. 750 and FA ii pp. 26, 39, 46.
BRICTRIC. Almost certainly Brictric son of Algar, a great English thane who had held
much land in the west. Many of his lands passed to Queen Matilda before going to the
King on her death in 1083. A romantic tale told by the Continuator of Wace and others
(Freeman iv App. Note O) alleges that Matilda had seized his lands because in youth he
had spurned her hand. See also 10,2 note.
1,18 EDMONDSHAM. DB *Medesham*: for the spelling see EPNS ii p. 217. The land was in
Albretesberga Hundred in 1086 (Tax Return v), later in Cranborne (6); see FA ii pp. 27,
39, 46.
DODA. Probably the same Doda who was the TRE holder of another part of
Edmondsham (50,1).
1,19 HAMPRESTON. DB *Hame*, see EPNS ii p. 224. The land can be identified in the Tax
Return for *Canendona* Hundred (vii) where the King had no tax from 2 hides 1 virgate
held by a thane at a revenue from him (this thane might be William Bellett; see Exon.
Notes). Hampreston is later in Cranborne Hundred (6).
TAX FOR 2 HIDES AND 1 VIRGATE. The details given for the lordship and villagers'
land total 1 hide, 3 virgates and 6 acres. Other examples in Dorset of the total hidage
details not agreeing with the tax include 11,16. 15,1. 36,5. 47,4(?)-5. 55,11;16;40. The
details can only be checked against the tax total in the Dorset entries for which Exon.
survives, as the villagers' land holding is not given in Exchequer DB for this county, and
only where Exon. gives both lordship and villagers' land (see 1,18 Exon. Notes). There are
a large number of manors in Exon. for Dorset for which no detail of villagers' and lordship
land and ploughs is given.
1,20 WITCHAMPTON. This holding and that at 26,40 can be identified in the Tax Return for
Badbury Hundred (vi). Witchampton is later in Cranborne Hundred (6), where the land
formed part of the Honour of Gloucester; Fees p. 750 and FA ii pp. 26, 39, 45.
2 PARTS OF 1 HIDE. Latin *pars, partis* is ambiguous, the fraction of the whole varying:
see 1,31 'the third part of 1 hide'; 47,10 'the fourth part of 1 virgate'; DB Northants.

1

18,54 'the fifth part of 1 hide'. In this case, however, the parts of the hide, and of the virgate in lordship, must be thirds or the details of the lordship and villagers' land would not add up to the taxed hidage, which they generally do (see 1,19 note, however).

1,21   WIMBORNE (MINSTER). DB *Winburne*; it can be identified from the Tax Return for Badbury Hundred (vi); see 1,3 note.
ODO THE TREASURER. Exon. *thesaurarius*. He seems to have given his name to 'Odenham' a lost part of Wimborne Minster, see 7,1 note.

1,22   'WEY'. This holding is to be found in the Tax Return for Cullifordtree Hundred (xxxvii). The various DB lands named from the river Wey cannot all be identified with certainty, see Introductory Note 2. This land appears to have been at *Waye Bause* (derived from Stephen *de Baiocis*, a representative of a family which came from Bayeux in Normandy), held in FA ii pp. 18–19 by Peter *de Rabeyne*, the same man who holds 1,14. The same land later appears (in FA ii p. 57) as *Upweye* [Upwey] ; see Cal. Inq. PM vol. ii (Ed. I) no. 689, EPNS i p. 199 and pp. 245–6; also notes to 26,14-16 and 55,5–6. Melcombe Regis in Weymouth was royal land (see 1,1 note), although part seems to have belonged to Cerne Abbey in 1086, being surveyed as part of Radipole (11,3); see Hutchins ii p. 448 and 1,1 second note above.

1,23   THE KING HOLDS. See 1,1 first note.
LANGTON (HERRING). The royal land can be identified in the Tax Return for Uggescombe Hundred (iii). *Langetun* in Uggescombe Hundred (25) is held from the Earl of Gloucester by Hugh *Poynz* and from him by Philip *Harang* in FA ii p. 6. Another part of the village is held by the wife of Hugh, see 55,31 note.
ALWARD COLLING. Exon. *Alwardus colinus*; a man of the same name is a 1086 holder of land in DB Wilts. 67,14. On the form Alward, see 3,1 note.
8 SMALLHOLDERS; 1 WHO PAYS 30d. It is not clear from the Latin whether or not the 1 smallholder is separate from the 8. Exon. has '7 smallholders' with 'and 1 smallholder who pays 30d a year' interlined with no omission sign (by the same scribe as the rest of the entry and in the same colour ink, so obviously not a later addition). The fact that the Exchequer scribe corrected *vii bord'* to *viii* by interlining *i*, perhaps as a result of a closer look at the Exon., suggests that there were 8 smallholders altogether, 1 of whom paid 30d.

1,24   'TARRANT'. See Introductory Note 2. Both 1,24 and 1,26 are required by the Tax
-26   Return for *Langeberga* Hundred (xxii) and the order of entries suggests that 1,25 was there as well. The 'Tarrants' concerned may have been Tarrant Gunville (*Tarente Gundevil'* or *Gundevyleston*) and Tarrant Rushton (*Tarente Petri de Russell', Tarente Vilers, Tarrante Russeaston*), held from the Earl of Gloucester in FA ii pp. 26, 39 and Fees p. 750 in Cranborne Hundred (6); see Cal. Inq. PM vol. i (Henry III) no. 530 and vol. iii (Ed. I) no. 371.

1,24   3 SMALLHOLDERS. In the MS and Farley *iii bord'*, but the facsimile does not reproduce the *iii* clearly.
PASTURE 7 FURLONGS LONG AND 2 FURLONGS WIDE. In the MS there is a smear of pale orange/brown paint or ink (or perhaps a water blot), probably contemporary, over *7 ii* and under the preceding words, but there is no difficulty in reading them. See 55,15 note for a similar blot.
½ GOLD MARK. That is, £3.

1,26   2 VILLAGERS AND 4 SMALLHOLDERS. A gap of about 7 letters' width has been left after this in the MS, presumably for the villagers' ploughs, which Exon. also omits. A similar gap for the villagers' ploughs appears in 8,4. 11,16. 26,50 and 56,57. Cf. the fourth note under 1,1 above and 24,4 note on the space left for lordship ploughs.

1,27   *SCETRE*. Possibly to be identified with Shitterton (or Sitterton) GR SY 8495, in Bere Regis Hundred, see EPNS i p. 276. The order of the entries at this point, however, suggests a place in *Langeberga* Tax Hundred (xxii) or in Pimperne (xxvi) where this land seems to be required to make up the holding of the Queen. There is a Shitley in Winterborne Houghton (EPNS ii p. 130) which may be derived from *Scetre*, but Pimperne Hundred is unlikely to have stretched this far west in 1086. Sitterton, which included *Westmauston* ['Westmyngton' lost in Turners Puddle, EPNS i p. 295], *Suthbroke* [Southbrook GR SY 8494] and *Fulcume* [now a field name, see EPNS i p. 281] may have been counted as part of Bere Regis (1,2) in 1086; see FA ii p. 42.

1,28   NUTFORD. In Pimperne Hundred (Tax Return xxvi). The name is now represented by two places, less than a mile from each other, Nutford in Pimperne parish and France farm, earlier Nutford Lockey in Stourpaine. Eyton *Dorset* pp. 137-8 identifies the second DB holding (57,12) with France farm, so called from the holding there of the Norman Abbey

---

of Fontevrault. But from Round CDF p. 385 no. 1085, it is clear that the gift by Robert, Earl of Leicester, of *Nutford, Pimpre* [Pimperne 1,5] and *Beneford* [Blandford 1,5 note] must have been out of royal land. Thus 1,28 is France farm.

1,29 WATERCOMBE ... ½ MILL. The ½ mill at 4s complements that at Ringstead (52,2) which lay to the south. The land can be identified in the Tax Return for 'Chilbury' Hundred (xxxi), part of the later Hundred of Winfrith (27).
PASTURE ... 1 FURLONG [WIDE]. The scribe omitted *lat̄* 'wide' in error; it has been supplied from Exon.
THE HOLDERS ... COULD GO TO WHICH LORD THEY WOULD. They were free to choose any lord as their patron and protector of their lands. Many other lands were 'tied' to a particular manor or lord, as is seen in 2,4. 11,1 etc. Cf. Exon. Notes to 47,9 'Aethelfrith ... could not be separated from the King's service'.

1,30 THIS ENTRY is written in a smaller script and compressed. It would seem that the scribe stopped after 1,29, leaving a space for the remaining land of the King, but this did not prove large enough for both this entry and 1,31. The fact that neither 1,30 nor 1,31 is with the rest of the King's lands in the surviving portion of Exon. helps to confirm the idea that the information on these lands came in late, probably because of their complexity, but see also Exon. Notes here.
MELCOMBE (HORSEY). Now incorporating Melcombe Bingham and Binghams Melcombe, the manorial names representing grants of royal land later than DB. The land is required by the Tax Return for Hilton Hundred (xi), later renamed Whiteway Hundred (15); see Fees p. 90, RBE ii p. 544 and FA ii pp. 13, 36, 40. Another Melcombe — Melcombe Regis — is probably surveyed as part of Portland or Weymouth (1,1;22 notes).
EARL HAROLD WRONGFULLY TOOK IT AWAY ... COUNTESS GODA HELD IT. Goda was the sister of King Edward (DB Glos. 24,1) and wife first of Count Drogo of Mantes and then the first wife of Count Eustace of Boulogne; she died *c.* 1056. She presumably bequeathed this manor to Shaftesbury Abbey and then Earl Harold seized it. He also took Cheselbourne and Stour from Shaftesbury, and though these were returned to the Abbey because of the discovery of a writ of King Edward ordering it, King William kept Melcombe Horsey in his possession; see 19,14.
TO WULFGAR WHITE. *Wlgaro uuit*; *Wlgaro* may be a scribal error for *Ulwardo*, see Eyton *Dorset* p. 112 note 6. For Wulfward White, see 35,1 note.
THREE FREE THANES. *Tres lib(er)i taini*; perhaps a mistake for '3 thanes held them freely', as the thane was basically a free man (see Maitland DBB p. 161ff.; Vinogradoff p. 81ff.). Unless they were thanes holding church land (e.g. 49,10;17 and Exon. Notes to 11,1) they were usually free to choose their lord (e.g. 4,1. 15,1 and see Exon. Notes to 55,34). However, the phrase 'free thanes' does occur elsewhere in Dorset (e.g. 50,3. 56,7).
3½ VIRGATES ... IN BUCKLAND NEWTON. These seem to be the ½ hide and ½ virgate which in the Tax Return for Buckland Hundred (xxxvi) are said not to have paid tax and to have been taken from a thane by Robert d'Oilly and placed in the King's revenue of *Melecome* [Melcombe]. In DB the action is attributed to Countess Goda.
IN BUCKLAND HUNDRED. In the MS these words are written in capitals the same size as *MELCOME*, similarly lined through in red, not as Farley prints them. Cf. 37,13.

1,31 THIS ENTRY is written right across (i.e. not in columns) a small separate piece of parchment, cut off from the side of a presumably spoiled sheet which had already been ruled out, so that the original horizontal rulings are seen as vertical scores. This piece was set into a larger sheet (probably in the 19th century) to make it the same size as the other folios. As the entry is rubricated the addition was an early one by the scribe. A transposition sign indicates its correct position in the chapter. In this edition each Latin line is set as two lines, an indentation marking the break thus introduced. The other side of the parchment (76c,d) is blank. Apart from folio 81 (see 36,4-11 and Ch. 42 below), there are only two other cases in DB of material being added on a separate piece of parchment: Surrey 8,23-27 (folio 33) and Hants. Ch. 4 and 6,13-17 (folio 42); see notes to these.
HINTON (MARTELL). The 6 hides 1 virgate in lordship appear in the Tax Return for Canendona Hundred (vii). *Hyneton Martel* and *Parva Hyneton* [Hinton Parva, GR SU 0004] are held respectively from the heirs of Roger *Martel* and the Countess *de Insula* in Badbury Hundred (17) in FA ii p. 15, representing the holdings of the Honour of Chewton and of the *Comes de Insula* in Fees pp. 425, 753. Hinton Parva in Fees p. 753 includes *Esseton'* [now Ashton farm, GR SU 0004]; see EPNS ii p. 149.

PRIEST HELD 1 HIDE IN THANELAND. According to Ellis *Introduction* i p. 299 he held it in hereditary succession. See 1,13 note on thaneland.
BISHOP OF LISIEUX ... 1 HIDE. Gilbert Maminot. This hide duly appears in his fief as Preston (6,2).
MEADOW, 11 ACRES. *Acras*, accusative after *habet*, as also the woodland measurements, and houses, and probably the mill. Cf. third note below.
WIMBORNE CHURCH. The 1½ hides and ½ virgate are unnamed, but appear as 1½ hides in the Tax Return for Badbury Hundred (vi) held by the Bishop of London.
BISHOP MAURICE. Bishop of London from April 1086 to 1107.
MEADOW, 15 ACRES. *Acras* is in the accusative after *habet* 'has'. The mill and the pasture may also be the objects of *habet*. Cf. 2,4 and note.

Chs.   BISHOP OF SALISBURY; MONKS OF SHERBORNE. The two chapters together
2-3   represent the lands of the former see of Sherborne. Sherborne and Ramsbury were united in 1058 and the episcopal seat was transferred to Salisbury between 1075 and 1078. The compiler of DB is uncertain how to treat the resulting division of lands; thus he enters a *III* in the left-hand margin of col. 77a to indicate land held by the monks of Sherborne, but omits a chapter head and includes the value of 2,6 in 3,1; moreover, subsequent entries in Ch. 3 are held by the Bishop of Salisbury, although 'for the monks' supplies' (see notes to 3,2 and 3,6 on the Tax Return treatment). In other counties, e.g. Worcestershire, Herefordshire, such divisions are made within a single chapter. The diocese of Sherborne had originally been larger and was split under Edward the Elder *c.* 909 into three based on Sherborne, Wells and Crediton (see Stenton ASE p. 433). From that time Sherborne seems to have possessed 300 hides, but some lands had already been alienated early in the 11th century according to a letter of Bishop Aethelric (*c.* 1001–*c.* 1012); see VCH iii p. 41. There is a confirmation charter addressed to the Church by Aethelred II (*c.* 978–1016) concerning Bradford Abbas, Compton, Oborne, Stalbridge, Stalbridge Weston, Thornford and Lyme Regis (KCD no. 701 = ECW no. 614 p. 174 = Sawyer (1) no. 895); a grant by the same King of Corscombe (KCD no. 1309 = ECW no. 617 = Sawyer (1) no. 933) and one by Cnut (1016–1035) of 16 *mansae* also in Corscombe (KCD no. 1322 = ECW no. 623 = Sawyer (1) no. 975). Lyme Regis had been a grant of Cynewulf (757–786), Bradford Abbas and Stalbridge of Athelstan (*c.* 924–939) and Oborne of Edgar (959–975) (BCS nos. 224, 695–6, 1308 = ECW nos. 562, 578–9, 611 = Sawyer (1) nos. 263, 422-3, 813). Aethelred's confirmation includes land in Stockland (see 12,14) and Halstock not separately mentioned in DB, also at *Wulfheardigstoke* and *Osanstoke*, both probably parts of Stoke Abbot (3,9).

Ch. 2   BISHOP OF SALISBURY. Osmund, bishop from 1078 to 1099; he was also Chancellor from *c.* 1073 to *c.* 1078–1082 before Bishop Maurice of London (*Regesta* i pp. xvi-xvii).
2,1   BISHOP OF SALISBURY HOLDS. The scribe has omitted the abbreviation sign over *ten*; Farley does not correct the error, as he does on several occasions (e.g. 9,1. 37,4).
CHARMINSTER. This large holding in St. George Hundred (20) also included land at Stratton (GR SY 6593) and Grimstone (SY 6494); Fees p. 94, RH i p. 100 and FA ii p. 17. See 3,14 note.
AS MUCH LAND AS 2 PLOUGHS CAN PLOUGH. That is, 2 carucates of land (see 2,6 and note), not hidated and so not paying tax. Similarly in 2,2;4-5. 8,1;3.
2,2   THE BISHOP ALSO HOLDS. Repeated at the beginning of 2,2-5.
ALTON (PANCRAS). The land may well have lain in 'Stone' Hundred (ix) in 1086; in FA ii pp. 4, 36, 41 it is in Sherborne Hundred (1).
6 VILLAGERS. Originally written *vi villo* in the MS and corrected to *villos*, the added *s* being squashed in very close to the *7*. Or it is possible that it was the *7* that was the addition.
VALUE ... £13. Originally *xii* with *i* interlined in correction; Farley does not show the small hair-line below and between the *xi* and *i* which was intended to indicate the position of the omitted *i*.
2,3   UP CERNE. Held by the Bishop of Salisbury in Sherborne Hundred (1) in FA ii p. 4; see FA ii pp. 36, 58. It may well have lain in 'Stone' Hundred (ix) in 1086.
2,4   YETMINSTER. In Yetminster Hundred (Tax Return i). It is *Iatmynstre* in FA ii p. 41 where it is coupled with *Legh* [Leigh GR ST 6108] and *Chateknoll* [Chetnole GR ST 6008]. *Rym* [Ryme Intrinseca GR ST 5810, so called to distinguish it from 'Ryme Extrinseca' in Long Bredy, Hutchins iv p. 491] held from the Bishop of Salisbury by Humphrey *de Bello Campo* in FA ii pp. 36, 41, was also probably part of Yetminster.
MEADOW, 12 ACRES. *Acras* is in the accusative after *habet*; the mill should also be. The woodland is probably not, however, although it is hard to tell because the tail of the *7* in

the line above covers where the abbreviation line over the *a* of *silua* would be to make it accusative. Cf. 1,31 and notes.

HOLDERS ... COULD NOT BE SEPARATED. See 1,29 note.

2,5   LYME (REGIS). In 1316 part of the Borough of Lyme (Regis) was held by the Abbot of Sherborne (FA ii p. 45) in Whitchurch Hundred (11).

PAY 15s TO THE MONKS FOR FISH. As no 'value' statement is given for this entry, it would appear that this clause replaces it, the fishermen's payment being for the right to fish (cf. 49,13). Or it could be a commuted money payment, the fishermen paying 15s instead of so many fish to the monks in rent (cf. the use of *ad pisces* in DB Herefords. 1,10a). See notes to 12,13. 47,7 and 57,2; cf. 54,2 note on omitted value statements.

2,6   SHERBORNE. The 43 hides will have included a number of villages. From FA ii pp. 4-5 it is clear that apart from Sherborne itself (*Schireburn Camel*), the Bishop held *Buryton* [Longburton GR ST 6412], *Wotton* or *Wotton Episcopi* [North Wootton ST 6514], *Caundel Episcopi* [Bishops Caundle ST 6913, see 26,70-71 note], *Holnest* [Holnest ST 6509], *Combe* [Coombe in Castleton, ST 6218], *Folke* and *Alveston* [Folk ST 6513, no doubt including Bishops Down ST 6712, and Allweston ST 6614], *Pyneford* [Pinford ST 6617], *Lydelinch* [Lydlinch ST 7413; see also FA ii p. 8], *Bere* [Beer Hackett ST 5911]; *Lyllington* [Lillington ST 6212], *Prinnesle* ['Prinsley' lost in Castleton, Fägersten p. 211], *Haydon* or *Haddon* [Haydon ST 6715] and *Leweston* [Leweston ST 6312]. A place *Dewelepole*, recorded in FA ii pp. 7-8 is perhaps to be associated with Poll Bridge farm in Caundle Marsh (ST 6812), Fägersten p. 212. Caundle Marsh (*Le Marsh* or *Le Merssh*) was also part of the Bishop's land, Hutchins iv p. 141.

QUEEN EDITH. Wife of King Edward the Confessor, daughter of Earl Godwin. She died in 1075.

BISHOP ALFWOLD. Alfwold (Aelfweald) II, Bishop of Sherborne from 1045 to 1058.

SINOTH. OE *Sigenoth*; PNDB p. 360.

WIFE OF HUGH ... 2 HIDES. They were at Pinford (see above) according to FA ii p. 4 where Alfred *de Nichol* is a mistake for Alfred *de Lincoln*, as also in GF p. 31. The land also appears in the Cal. Inq. PM cited in Ch. 55 note.

16 CARUCATES. *Carucatae* here and elsewhere in the south-west counties and DB Glos. and Herefords. are not the carucates of the former Danish areas (which are equivalent to the hide), but are the same as 'land for *y* ploughs' (see 2,1 note). The fact that on many occasions, Exon. uses the term *carucatae terrae* where DB has *terra est ... car* proves that the two terms were synonymous (e.g. Exon. 527 b 4, the summary of Glastonbury Abbey lordship lands in Dorset, = DB 8,1;3; cf. DB Somerset Exon. Notes 2,1). As can be seen from this entry and 3,1;9-11 land was measured in carucates when it had not been hidated; it did not pay tax. In DB Herefords. there is a distinction between the newly conquered lands measured still in carucates and the older acquisitions assessed in hides.

OF THIS EXEMPT LAND. *Quieta*, commonly in DB meaning 'immune from dues or service' (see Herefords. 1,44), 'free from tax' (as here, referring to the 16 carucates) or 'quit, settled, discharged' (as in Worcs. 2,74 and Herefords. C 14).

Ch. 3   [LAND OF THE MONKS OF SHERBORNE]. See Ch. 2 note.

3,1-5   ALL THESE PLACES can be identified in the Tax Return for Sherborne Hundred (xxxiv).

3,1   WOODLAND ... The rest of the line in the MS is blank after this; see sixth note under 1,8 on a similar space left.

VALUE OF WHAT THE BISHOP ... MEN-AT-ARMS ... THANES (HAVE). Referring to 2,6.

ALWARD. *Aluuardus* is a common reduction in DB for OE *Aethelweard* or *Aelfweard*; see PNDB §§ 109, 111 and pp. 155-157 s.n. *Al-weard* and pp. 188-189 s.n. *Aethelweard*. As it is usually impossible to discern which form is intended, the present editors on the advice of JMcND have decided to keep the base form *Alward*. See notes to 36,2 and 36,7.

OBORNE. DB *Wocburne*. For the grant, see BCS no. 1308 = ECW no. 611 p. 173 = Robertson 1 = Sawyer (1) no. 813. It is *Woburn* in FA ii pp. 5, 41.

3,3   THORNFORD. Originally a grant of 8 *cassati* to the Sherborne Cathedral clergy by Eadred, King of the West Saxons (946-955); ECW no. 594 p. 170 = BCS no. 894 = Sawyer (1) no. 516. See FA ii pp. 5, 41.

3,4   BRADFORD (ABBAS). Originally a grant of 10 *cassati* at *Bradan-forda* by King Athelstan (c.924-939) ECW no. 578 p. 166 = BCS no. 695 = Sawyer (1) no. 422. The land involved part of Castleton (GR ST 6417) lying to the east of Sherborne, now surviving only as a parish name; see 2,6 note. *Bradeford* is associated with *Wyke* [Wyke farm in Castleton, GR ST 6014, formerly in Bradford Abbas, see Fägersten p. 211] in FA ii pp. 5, 41.

3

3,5   COMPTON. The land included both Over and Nether Compton (Fägersten p. 213 and
FA ii pp. 36, 41) and *Stawell* [Stallen in Compton, GR ST 6016], FA ii pp. 4-5. It is
Cumpton Hauwey in FA ii pp. 36, 58.
3,6-7 STALBRIDGE ... (STALBRIDGE) WESTON. In the Tax Return for Brownshall Hundred
(xxviii) it is the monks of Sherborne, rather than the Bishop as in DB, who hold the 6
hides of lordship land in these two manors. The Abbot of Sherborne holds *Stapulbrigg* and
Weston in Brownshall Hundred (2) in FA ii p. 40; see FA ii p. 8.
3,6   MANASSEH. Manasseh Cook, from whom the King did not have tax on the 3 virgates he
held in the Tax Return for Brownshall Hundred (xxviii).
W(ILLIAM) SON OF THE KING. William Rufus, King of England 1087-1100. His
seizures of church land began early.
3,7   (STALBRIDGE) WESTON. Also Weston (Abbot), Fägersten p. 38.
A SMALL WOOD. *Silua modica*, as also in 3,9. Perhaps the same as *silua minuta*, here
translated 'underwood' (as in 3,4): DB Somerset 1,26 and 5,12;17 have *silua modica*
where the corresponding Exon. entries have *nemusculus*, the normal equivalent of DB's
silua minuta.
3,8   THE BISHOP ALSO HOLDS. Repeated at the beginning of 3,8-11.
CORSCOMBE. In Beaminster Hundred (Tax Return xii). It is *Coriscumbe* in FA ii pp. 7,
41. *Halghestok* [Halstock GR ST 5307], held by the Abbot of Sherborne in FA ii p. 4,
may have been part of it.
3,9   STOKE (ABBOTT). See Chs. 2-3 note. In the order of DB this *Stoche* appears between
two Beaminster Hundred places (xii); see FA ii p. 7 (*Stoke Abbatis*) and TE p. 179b.
A MILL WHICH PAYS 5s ... The rest of the line has been left blank after this in the MS,
perhaps for details of meadow; or possibly for some pence to be added to the mill's render,
although there is a dot after *solid'*. See sixth note under 1,8.
NINE MANORS ... FOR THE SUPPLIES OF THE MONKS. The revenues from 3,1-9 are
devoted to supplying the monks of Sherborne with provisions, and perhaps clothing as
in 12,14.
3,10   BEAMINSTER. According to FA ii pp. 7-8, 41, the land was at *Bemenistre* [Beaminster],
Langedon [Langdon in Beaminster, GR ST 5001], *Cedindon* or *Codyngton* [Cheddington
ST 4805], *Axnolre* [Axnoller farms ST 4803 and 4904], *Pikiete* [Picket farm in South
Perrot, ST 4705], *La Chapele* [Chapel Marsh in Beaminster, ST 4804] and *Seweberge*
[probably a part of Seaborough, Somerset (ST 4206) lying in Dorset; the Church held
Seaborough in Somerset DB 3,1. Seaborough is now entirely in Dorset, see ES 1].
Cotteleye [Cotleigh farm in Mapperton, GR SY 5199] may have been a part of Beaminster
or of Netherbury (3,11).
H(UMPHREY) OF CARTERET. The *H.* probably abbreviates *Hunfridus* who occurs in
the Tax Return for Witheridge Hundred (Devon; Exon. 66 b 3). Mauger of Carteret,
probably a relation, occurs in DB Somerset and Devon. Carteret is in the département of
Manche, France; OEB p. 81.
19 SMALLHOLDERS, 2 VILLAGERS. Unusually, the villagers do not head the list of
population, as also in 26,15;25;49.
3,11   NETHERBURY. FA ii pp. 7-8, 36, 41 list land at *Nitherbury* [Netherbury], *Mangertone*
[Mangerton GR SY 4895], *Melepes* or *Melepleychs* [Melplash SY 4898], *Worth* [now
Bingham's farm, GR SY 4796, in Netherbury, Fägersten p. 275] and *Esse* [Ash in
Netherbury, GR SY 4695; see FA ii p. 8 and Fägersten p. 275]. Mangerton and Melplash
may have been associated with Bowood (3,17).
2 PLOUGHS THERE. In the MS *ibi h̄t .ii. car̄* 'he has 2 ploughs there' with the *h̄t*
corrected to *s̄t* 'there are', although *h̄t* occurs in the similar phrase in 3,10, and as the 2
ploughs are obviously in lordship *h̄t* would not be out of place.
3,13   CHARDSTOCK. An outlying part of Beaminster Hundred (12) in the Middle Ages. The
12 hides probably included Wambrook (GR ST 2907) granted as *Awanbruth* by Egbert
King of the West Saxons (802-839) (ECW p. 121 no. 402 = Mon. Ang. i p. 337); see VCH
Somerset iv p. 222. In FA ii p. 36 Wambrook is held *cum membris* from the Bishop of
Salisbury and is coupled with Chardstock in FA ii p. 41. Modern boundary changes have
placed Chardstock in Devon, but Wambrook in Somerset; see Introductory Note 3 on the
County Boundary.
WOODLAND 2 LEAGUES. Originally written *iii leū*, but corrected to *ii* with *as* (for *duas*)
interlined to emphasise the correction.
3,14   'SHIPLEY'. In DB Wilts. 3,5 under the land of the Bishop of Salisbury, Charnage is said
to have been exchanged for 'Shipley'. There is no indication in Wilts. nor in Dorset DB of

the date of the exchange, nor is 'Shipley' surveyed elsewhere. It is possibly the place of that name in Aldbourne (Wilts.) GR SU 2278; see EPNS (Wilts.) p. 293; in that case the 'exchange' may have been connected with the adjustments that took place in the sees of Ramsbury, Sherborne and Salisbury in the 11th century or between the Bishop of Salisbury and the monks of Sherborne (see Chs. 2-3 note).

'CERNE'. An unidentified land named from the river (see Introductory Note 2) in St. George (20) or Cerne (14) Hundreds. In FA ii p. 8 the Bishop of Salisbury holds *Wolwowetone* [Wolfeton in Charminster, GR SY 6792, see notes to 1,4 and 26,5;8-11]. This might be a part of Charminster (2,1) or this present holding.

AELMER. Originally written *Algar* with an *m* interlined above the *g* in correction, but with no line or dot under the *g* to indicate its deletion. The name represents OE *Aethelmaer*.

A WOMAN HAS IT THERE. The *hanc* refers to the plough, not the land, although she also holds the land in this instance. This DB phrase is regularly made clear by Exon.'s fuller wording. Also, see 26,56 and 34,14 where *has* can only refer to the 3 ploughs in each entry (but cf. DB Devon 22,2 where in a similar phrase the *hanc* must refer to the land, perhaps in error; see the Exon. Note to it). See notes to 13,7 and 58,3 below.

4 SMALLHOLDERS. In the MS and Farley *iiii bord'*; the facsimile reproduces the *b* of *bord'* badly so that it looks like *hord'* which does not make sense.

MEADOW, 3 ACRES. *Acras* is in the accusative after *tenet*. From the Latin it does not appear that the woman held the pasture as well.

VALUE 20s. Originally written *x solid'* but a second *x* has been squashed in to correct the value to *xx solid'*.

3,15   THE BISHOP ALSO HOLDS. Repeated at the beginning of 3,15-18.

3,15   'BARDOLFESTON', ATHELHAMPTON. In Puddletown Hundred (21), formerly *Pidele*
-16   *Bardalston* and *Pidele Athelamston* held from the Bishop of Salisbury in FA ii pp. 16, 35, 54. Both seem required to make up the total for Puddletown Tax Return (viii). For the lost 'Bardolfeston' see Fägersten p. 176, EPNS i p. 315, RCHM iii p. 229. The holding at 3,15 must have been 'Bardolfeston' since it is held in 1086 by the wife of Hugh and is found among the lands held by Alfred of Lincoln from the Bishop of Salisbury in the Cal. Inq. PM cited in Ch. 55 note.

3,17   BOWOOD. See FA ii pp. 7-8, 41 and 3,11 note.
        OSMER AND AELFRIC. In the MS *Osmar* clearly; Farley misprints *Oswar*. *Elfric* was written over the erasure of a smaller word, so is compressed.

3,18   BUCKHAM. *Bukeham* in FA ii pp. 7-8, 36.
        WELLWOOD. *Welle* attached to Buckham is unlikely to be Wool (VCH text); this hide seems to be needed for a full reconstruction of the Tax Return for Beaminster Hundred (xii), and is more likely to have lain within the Hundred than to have been remote from it; see VCH ii p. 133.
        VALUE 40d. Written in darker ink, not quite aligned, with the *xl deñ* in the right margin; probably added later.

Ch. 4   BISHOP OF BAYEUX. Odo, half-brother of King William and elder brother of Count Robert of Mortain. Earl of Kent 1066/7 to 1082, then 1087 to 1088. He was 'regent' during some of King William's absences abroad, notably in 1067 with Earl William of Hereford. At the time when DB was written he was in prison in Rouen and many of his lands (e.g. those in Glos. and Worcs.) were treated as forfeited to the King. He was released by King William on his deathbed in 1087 and returned to England, but rebelled against William Rufus, was defeated in 1088 and all his lands in England confiscated. He fled to Normandy and died in 1097. Bayeux is in the département of Calvados, France.

4,1   RAMPISHAM. In Tollerford Hundred (Tax Return xiv).

Ch. 5   BISHOP OF COUTANCES. Geoffrey of Mowbray, one of King William's chief justices. He held a great deal of land in the south-west, especially in Somerset and Devon. He is also sometimes (as in DB Glos. 6,1 and the Somerset Tax Returns) called the Bishop of St. Lô, which is near Coutances in the département of Manche, France.

5,1-2   'WINTERBORNE'. It has not proved possible to identify this land in a particular Hundred or even on one of the two rivers. It is identified by Eyton *Dorset* p. 121 as Winterborne Houghton, a view followed by VCH iii p. 7, but without supporting evidence. Geoffrey's land might be expected to descend to the Honour of Gloucester and might be *Winterborn' Clench* or *Clencheston* [Winterborne Clenston] held from that Honour in Fees p. 750, FA ii p. 29 in Combsditch Hundred (16).

5,1   WOODLAND 3½ FURLONGS LONG AND 4 ACRES AND 2 WIDE. There are two possible interpretations of these dimensions as they stand: the scribe may have originally omitted the '4 acres' from the length (although it is unusual for acres and furlongs to be mixed in measurements, there are several instances in Dorset — 19,4. 26,40;63. 54,9. 55,8 — and in Devon 1,53); or the width may be 4 + 2 acres. The scribe may also have omitted q^i for *quarentinas* 'furlongs' after $\frac{as}{u}$, making the translation either 'woodland 3½ furlongs and 4 acres long and 2 furlongs wide' or 'woodland 3½ furlongs long and 4 acres and 2 furlongs wide'. On the accusative case of *acras* see 26,40 note. Cf. 1,16 note.

5,2   PASTURES. *pasturae*, nominative plural, or perhaps genitive singular 'of pasture 8 furlongs ...', although the genitive is not normally used in this particular phrase; it is possible that *in* was omitted before *lg* as in 6,3. Cf. the plural used in the Exon. Notes 48,1, and see Devon General Notes 1,57 for another example of *pasturae*.

Ch. 6   THE BISHOP OF LISIEUX. Gilbert Maminot, King William's doctor and chaplain, Bishop of Lisieux 1077–1101 (Orderic Vitalis ii pp. 311–312). Lisieux is in the département of Calvados, France. Hugh Maminot (his son; Sanders p. 97) holds from him in the Tax Return for Badbury Hundred (vi); the latter's daughter married Ralph *de Keynes* whence the names Tarrant Keyneston, Coombe Keynes below and Somerford Keynes (Wilts. DB, now in Gloucestershire).

6,1   TARRANT (CRAWFORD). Later *Parva Crawford* to distinguish it from 'Great Crawford' (DB *Craveford*) in Spetisbury, see 56,12 and EPNS ii p. 181. It is adjacent to Tarrant Keyneston (6,3) and required by the Tax Return for Badbury Hundred (vi).

6,2   PRESTON. Now in Tarrant Rushton and so a part of Cranborne Hundred (6), but it seems to be needed to reconstruct the Tax Return for Badbury Hundred (vi) and later seems to have been partly in Pimperne (9) and partly in Badbury (17) Hundreds, straddling the river Tarrant (FA ii p. 14; LSR (1334) p. 76). It is sometimes called Tarrant Preston; see EPNS ii p. 252. Before 1066 it had been part of the royal manor of Hinton Martell; 1,31 note.
EDWARD THE CLERK. Latin *clericus* can refer to a lay job or to an ecclesiastical office, and DB rarely indicates which is intended. The English 'clerk' preserves the ambiguity of the Latin. According to Lennard p. 404 there is no real distinction between the terms *clerici, canonici* and *presbiteri*: in DB Staffs. Ch. 7 the holders are called the *canonici* of Wolverhampton in the Landholders' List (col. 246a), but both the *clerici* and *canonici* in Ch. 7 itself, and the *presbiteri* of Wolverhampton in 12,1.
NO VILLAGE POPULATION is recorded for this holding, perhaps in error. There are some eighty entries in Dorset where no 'villagers' are mentioned; although many of these entries are by no means full (as 3,12. 19,11 etc.) about half record ploughs, mills, meadows etc., with no one, apparently, to work them, not even in most cases any slaves on the lordship land. Cf. 54,2 note on omitted value statements.

6,3   TARRANT (KEYNESTON). The land is identifiable in the Tax Return for *Langeberga* Hundred (xxii). In Fees p. 87 William *de Kaines* holds *Tarent'* in *Langeber'* Hundred. The same holding is *Tarente de Kaynes* in FA ii p. 1 and *Tarente Keyneston* in FA ii p. 27, both in Pimperne Hundred (9); see FA ii pp. 43, 46, EPNS ii p. 123 and Cal. Inq. PM vol. ii (Ed. I) no. 433 and vol. viii (Ed. III) no. 504.
1,000 EELS. From the mill-pond, a common render from mills in DB Herefords., but the only one in Dorset.

6,4   COOMBE (KEYNES). *Cumb'* is held by William *de Kaines* in Winfrith Hundred (27) in Fees p. 87 and by the heirs of Robert *de Kaynnes* in FA ii p. 9; see FA ii pp. 29, 49. It is required by the reconstruction of the Tax Return for Winfrith Hundred (xxx). A separate settlement, now lost, was 'Southcombe'; see Hutchins i p. 347, Taylor p. 215, EPNS i p. 116 and Cal. Inq. PM vol. ii (Ed. I) no. 637.

Ch. 7   [LAND] OF THE BISHOP OF LONDON. *Terra* omitted in error in the MS, as happens on several occasions.

7,1   BISHOP MAURICE. Bishop of London 1086–1107; also Chancellor after Bishop Osmund of Salisbury (*Regesta* i p. xvii; see Ch. 2 note).
'ODENHAM'. A lost place in the parish of Wimborne Minster, see EPNS ii p. 189 and 1,21 note. It is required by the Tax Return for Badbury Hundred (vi).
LAND FOR ½ PLOUGH; 1 PLOUGH THERE, HOWEVER. See also 55,21. 56,12;20 and 57,1;3;12 and cf. DB Herefords. 2,5 'the villagers have more ploughs than ploughable land'. See also DB Cambs. 26,18 and note for another example of actual ploughs on the land exceeding the estimate.

8,1   (STURMINSTER) NEWTON. Sometimes called *Sturminster Abbatis* from Glastonbury Abbey's holding, Fägersten p. 48. It is *Niweton'* in Newton Hundred in Fees p. 87. The Feodary of Glastonbury Abbey (GF), dating from 1342, pp. 30–50 gives a survey of all the Abbey's Dorset lands, with additional details. The 30 hides of Sturminster Newton consisted of 8 at Okeford Fitzpaine (listed separately in DB at 8,2), 5 hides of the Abbot's lordship at Newton itself and 7 hides 1 virgate of his lordship at *Kentlesworth qui modo dicitur Marnhulle* ['Kentleworth', lost in Marnhull, Fägersten p. 42; Marnhull is GR ST 7818]. Land held by sub-tenants consisted of 5 hides 3 virgates in *Kentlesworth*, 2½ hides in *Colbere* [Colber, GR ST 7714; see 1,2], 2½ hides in *Stoche* [?Hewstock GR ST 786154 on the 1st edition OS one-inch map (sheet 18 of 1811, reprinted 1969 as sheet 84), Yewstock on the six-inch map of 1886] and 2 hides in *Bagber* [Bagber in Sturminster Newton, GR ST 7615]. The 5 hides 3 virgates of *Kentlesworth* are further sub-divided by the Feodary into 2 hides 3 virgates there [also called *Kentlesworth'*, *Burton vel Marnhulle*, pointing to Burton Street in Marnhull GR ST 776187] held by Alfred of Lincoln (a descendant of the wife of Hugh son of Grip who held other Glastonbury land in 1086, see 8,2 and Ch. 55 notes); 1 hide in *Knyghtestrete* ['Knightstreet' lost in Marnhull, Fägersten p. 43; perhaps the same as Marnhull Street, 1st edition OS one-inch map GR ST 7719] held by William *de Sancto Martino* (see note on Waleran below); 1 hide in *Yerdegrove* [Yardgrove in Marnhull, GR ST 7717, Fägersten p. 44], and a further 1 hide in *Kentlesworth*. See also FA ii p. 42; Hutchins iv p. 314.

LAND FOR 14 PLOUGHS. That is, 14 carucates: together with the 'land for 8 ploughs' in 8,3, these formed the '22 carucates of land not paying tax' in the summary of the Glastonbury lordship lands in Dorset (Exon. 527 b 4). See notes to 2,1 and 2,6.

VILLAGERS ... Though DB does not mention their ploughs, it would seem from the summary of Glastonbury lordship lands in Dorset (Exon. 527 b 4) that they had 12 ploughs: 20 ploughs are given for the "villagers" for the lordship sections of the manors of Sturminster Newton and Buckland Newton (8,3), and 8 "villagers' " ploughs are recorded in DB for the latter. Similarly the lordship ploughs can be worked out at 5 here (9 in all and 4 are recorded at Buckland Newton).

WALERAN HOLDS 6 HIDES. The 6 hides are probably those found in GF as 2½ hides each at *Colbere* and *Stoche* and 1 hide at 'Knightstreet' (see above) held by William *de Sancto Martino*. Members of this family hold some of the lands of Waleran that descend from his fief, Ch. 40 note. In FA ii pp. 37, 56, *Esse* [not Ash in Stourpaine (FA index), but Nash Court in Marnhull, GR ST 7819, Fägersten p. 58] is held by Roger *de Sancto Quintino*.

ROGER 1 HIDE. In FA ii pp. 37, 56 Robert *filius Pagani* (Fitzpaine) holds *Baggeber'* [Bagber, GR ST 7615] from the Abbot of Glastonbury. Many of Roger Arundel's lands (Ch. 47) descend from this Robert and it is probable that the 1086 tenant here is thus Roger Arundel.

KETEL 1 HIDE. Perhaps represented by 'Kentleworth' in Marnhull, Taylor p. 208; see above.

THESE 8 HIDES CAN BE PLOUGHED BY 11 PLOUGHS. This formula is one of the common ones used by Exon. where DB has 'Land for so many ploughs', the estimate of the arable. It is an unusual phrase in DB (but see Wilts. 13,2 and cf. Herefords. 25,7). It may be that the scribe in this instance failed to alter the formula he was copying to fit in with the usual DB phraseology.

VALUE £7. Originally written *Valet*, but corrected to *Valent* to agree with the *viii hidae*. However, the singular is often used in the 'value' statement where the plural would be grammatically correct, as in the next statement of Gotshelm's 4 hides.

4 HIDES ... FROM THE KING. Glastonbury land also appears in the King's hands in DB Somerset, owing to the difficulty Thurstan had in controlling his Church (ASC 'E' version for 1083 pp. 214-215). This portion of Bagber became permanently alienated and passed to the Earl of Gloucester, becoming an outlying part of his Hundred of Cranborne (6); Fees p. 87, FA ii pp. 26, 39, 46 and Cal. Inq. PM vol. i (Henry III) no. 530. The other portion of Bagber (above) remained in Sturminster Newton Hundred (3).

MEADOW, 16 ACRES. *Acras*, accusative, after *habet* 'has'; the mill may also be an object, but apparently not the woodland.

8,2   OKEFORD (FITZPAINE). Identifiable in the Tax Return for *Hunesberga* Hundred (xxv), although later a part of Sturminster Newton Hundred (3). It is held there by Robert *filius Pagani* (Fitzpaine) from the Abbot of Glastonbury in FA ii p. 37. *Adford* appears to be an error for *Acford*; see 1,7 and 54,6 notes. The land included *Southgarston*, a lost place (Fägersten p. 47), held from the Abbot of Glastonbury by Robert *filius pagani* in Cal. Inq. PM vol. v (Ed. II) no. 607.

FROM IT. In the MS *de ea*, feminine to agree with *ecclesia*, has been corrected from the masculine *eo*.

MEADOW, 21 ACRES. In the MS *xxi a̅c̄ p̄ti,*; Farley omits the abbreviation sign over *ac* in error.

HUGH'S WIFE HAS 4 HIDES. The land was at *Lollebrok* [Lowbrook farm in Okeford Fitzpaine, GR ST 7809], held in FA ii pp. 37, 56 by William *de Gouiz*; see Ch. 55 note.
ALFRED 2 HIDES. The Tax Return for *Hunesberga* Hundred (xxv) states that the King had no tax from 2½ hides held by Alfred of 'Spain' from Glastonbury. As no other Alfred is mentioned in DB as holding from Glastonbury, it would appear that this Alfred is Alfred of 'Spain': perhaps he originally had more than 2 hides of the 8 in Okeford Fitzpaine.

8,3   BUCKLAND (NEWTON). Buckland Newton and *Plussh'* [Plush, a detached part of Buckland Newton parish, GR ST 7102] were granted by King Edmund (939–946) to *Elfleda* and later sold to Glastonbury Abbey, see ECW no. 584 p. 168 (= BCS no. 768 = Sawyer (1) no. 474). See also ECW no. 606 p. 173 (= BCS no. 1177 = Sawyer (1) no. 742). The land is held by Glastonbury in FA ii p. 30. The Feodary (GF pp. 30-50) divides Buckland into 7 hides 1½ virgates at *Dontyssh'* and *Hermyngeswell'* [Duntish GR ST 6907 and Armswell ST 7203], 2 hides in *Knolle* [Knoll in Buckland Newton, ST 7004], 2½ virgates in *Plussh'* [Plush, GR ST 7102, a detached part of Buckland Newton parish] and 1 hide in *Brochamton'* [Brockhampton GR ST 7106] divided into 3 holdings one of which, 1 virgate held by Robert *Belet*, was at *Othull* [unidentified]. The land at Duntish and Armswell is the 7 hides 1½ virgates held by the wife of Hugh in 1086, by Alfred of Lincoln in GF and by William *de Gouiz* (Ch. 55 note) in FA ii pp. 30, 42, 50. Godlingston (GR SZ 015802) in Swanage is said to have been an outlying part of Duntish manor; it is perhaps surveyed here or under the land of the wife of Hugh 55,42; see Cal. Inq. Misc. vol. iii no. 614 and Hutchins i p. 662.
LAND FOR 8 PLOUGHS. 8 carucates; see 8,1 second note.

8,4   WOODYATES. The Glastonbury land consisted only of East Woodyates in later times; Hutchins iii p. 441. West Woodyates had a different subsequent history, passing into the hands of Tarrant Abbey; Hutchins iii p. 607. West Woodyates was later fully in Wimborne St. Giles Hundred, East Woodyates remaining a tithing of Cranborne Hundred (6); see 'Tithings' note in the Appendix.
H(UGH)'S WIFE. *Uxor H.*, the wife of Hugh son of Grip, the Sheriff, a large landholder in Dorset. The land is held in GF p. 30 by Alfred of Lincoln, to whom Hugh's fief descended (Ch. 55 note).
2 VILLAGERS AND 5 SMALLHOLDERS ... There is a gap of about 9 letters' width in the MS after this, presumably left for the villagers' ploughs. See 1,26 note.

8,5   PENTRIDGE. Originally granted with *Domerham* [Damerham] and *Mertone* [Martin], both formerly in Wiltshire (DB Wilts. 7,1), now transferred to Hampshire, as 100 *mansae*, see ECW p. 169 no. 63 (= BCS no. 817 = Sawyer (1) no. 513), by King Edmund (939–946) to Aethelfled his Queen for life with reversion to St. Mary's of Glastonbury. The land was alienated from the Church in 1086 (hence *ipsa aecclesia tenuit* for the usual *ipsa aecclesia tenet*) and never subsequently returned, becoming part of the Honour of Gloucester, in Cranborne Hundred (6); see 8,1 penultimate note and FA ii p. 26; Cal. Inq. PM vol. i (Henry III) no. 530.
WULFWARD. Wulfward White, from whom the King did not have tax on the 1 hide 3 virgates he held (*tenuit*; Ellis misprints *tenent*) from Glastonbury in the Tax Return for *Albretesberga* Hundred (v).

8,6   LYME (REGIS). DB *Lym*. The holding was at 'Colway' now represented by the Colway Lane estate see Fägersten p. 287, Hutchins ii p. 40, VCH iii p. 56 and p. 74 note 83. It is *Colbegh iuxta Netherlym* or *coleheygh' inter Uplym in Devonia* at *Netherelym in Dorset'* in GF p. xxx and pp. 31, 49. The Abbey holds Up Lym just over the border in Devonshire (DB Devon 4,1).
WULFGEAT. His sub-tenancy seems to have passed to the wife of Hugh son of Grip or her descendants, *Coleweye* being held from Alfred of Lincoln in Fees p. 751; see Ch. 55 note.
13 SALT-WORKERS. At Lyme Regis itself; see 26,15 note.

Ch. 9   ST. PETER'S ABBEY, WINCHESTER. That is, the New Minster, renamed Hyde Abbey when it was moved in 1110 from its original situation near the Old Minster (Winchester Cathedral) to Hyde outside the city walls. Probably founded in 901 and dedicated to the Holy Trinity, the Virgin Mary and St. Peter, it was originally for secular canons, but they misbehaved and were replaced by Benedictine monks.

9,1   PIDDLETRENTHIDE. In 'Stone' Hundred in 1086 (Tax Return ix); DB *pidrie* to which the hidage in French (*trente hides*, '30 hides') has been attached. For the probable grant to the New Minster at Winchester see ECW no. 621 p. 176 (= Mon. Ang. ii p. 436), although Roger Arundel's tenure suggests a more complex history. It is held in Fees p. 92 by the Abbot of Hyde as *Pidele Trentehydes* to clothe his monks (*ad vestiendum suos monachos*); see Mon. Ang. ii p. 436; TE p. 179a).

VALUE OF THE CHURCH'S LORDSHIP. In the MS *Dniū* in error for *Dñiū* (as in 11,1 etc.). Farley corrects to *Dñiū*, though he does not always correct the scribe's mistakes (e.g. 1,5. 2,1).

Ch. 10 ST. MARY'S, CRANBORNE. It was founded *c*. 980, most of the community moving to Tewkesbury in 1102 whereupon Cranborne became a cell of the latter; see VCH ii pp. 70–71 and Mon. Ang. iv p. 465.

10,1 IN GILLINGHAM. In the MS *INGELINGEHA̅*, one word in error for two. Normally when the scribe states that a holding is 'in' a village or town, he gives the hidage (e.g. 10,5). HUGH ... GAVE IT ... Another gift of Hugh (son of Grip) to Cranborne Church is Orchard 55,47. Neither gift is cross-referenced in DB.

10,2 THE CHURCH ITSELF HOLDS. Repeated at the beginning of 10,2-6.
BOVERIDGE. In *Albretesberga* Hundred (Tax Return v).
BRICTRIC. Probably Brictric son of Algar; VCH iii p. 31. See 1,17 note on him.
2½ HIDES. In the MS there is an ink blot covering the ẹ and part of the 7 of the *hidẹ* 7.
HEATHLAND. *Bruaria*, from late Latin *brucus* (Mod.Fr *bruyère*). This is the only reference to it in DB, but see 34,5 note on water-meadow.

10,3 WIMBORNE (ST. GILES). The place lies in DB in a group of manors that were certainly in *Albretesberga* Hundred (v) or in *Langeberga* (xxii) in 1086; it is probably Monkton Up Wimborne in Wimborne St. Giles parish, held as *Wymburne Abbatis* in FA i p. 39 by the Abbot of Tewkesbury, with which Cranborne Abbey was associated; see EPNS ii p. 265 and Ch. 10 note. The Abbey of Cranborne received part of the revenues of the church of *Wymborn Karentlim* in TE p. 178b, now All Hallows (farm) in the same parish, (EPNS ii p. 264).

10,4 'LEFTISFORD'. A lost place in Verwood parish, described in an Inquisition of 1416 as *juxta le Fairewode*, see EPNS ii p. 256.

10,5 'LANGFORD'. The order of DB suggests a place in *Albretesberga* Hundred (v) or *Langeberga* (xxii), so the manor is unlikely to be Langford in the parish of Stratton suggested tentatively by Hutchins ii p. 571, VCH iii p. 74, and EPNS i p. 373. It is more probably 'Langford' in West Parley, EPNS ii p. 232.
2 VILLAGERS HAVE IT THERE. The plough; see fourth note under 3,14.

10,6 TARRANT (MONKTON). The land is in the Tax Return for *Langeberga* Hundred (xxii) and is later held by the Abbey of Tewkesbury, being transferred to Monkton Up Wimborne Hundred; see EPNS ii p. 292.

Ch. 11 CERNE ABBEY. The list of lands given in DB should be compared with the foundation charter (ECW no. 613 p. 174 = KCD no. 656 = Sawyer (1) no. 1217), a grant by the ealdorman Aethelmaer, son of Aethelweard. The lands include 6 *cassati* at Minterne (GR ST 6504) not mentioned separately in DB and the holdings at Winterborne Abbas, Renscombe, Poxwell, Affpuddle, Bloxworth and 'Cerne'. The 6 hides at *Bridian* and the 12 in *ulteriore Bridian* seem to correspond to DB's 11 hides at Little Bredy and 9 hides in Long Bredy, 11,10;12 below. Most of the lands reappear in a list of fees in Fees p. 92. See VCH iii p. 43.

11,1 CERNE (ABBAS). In 'Stone' Hundred in 1086 (Tax Return ix). The 22 hides probably included Nether Cerne [*Nithercerne*], GR SY 6698, and Minterne Magna [*Minterne*], GR ST 6504, whose churches are held by the Abbey in TE p. 184a; see Hutchins iv pp. 17, 469. Hawkchurch [*Havekechirche*, TE p. 183a], now in Devon and remote from Cerne, was a possession of the Abbey and a tithing in Cerne, Totcombe and Modbury Hundred (14) and may have been included in these hides; see the 'Red Book of Cerne' (Cambridge University Library MS Ll.1.10, see Davis MCGB p. 26 no. 218) in PDNHAS xxviii (1907) p. 68 and Hutchins iv p. 46. *Godmanston* [Godmanstone GR SY 6697] and *Sydelinch* or *Up Sidelinch* [Up Sydling GR ST 6201] may also have been part of this land, FA ii pp. 39, 58.
BRICTWIN HOLDS 4 HIDES. According to the Tax Return for 'Stone' Hundred (ix), the King did not have tax from 2½ hides that Brictwin held from the Abbot of Cerne.
HE HELD THEM LIKEWISE. The 4 hides.

11,2 THE CHURCH ITSELF HOLDS. Repeated at the beginning of 11,2-17.
WILLIAM OF MOUTIERS. In the MS there is an erased (though still visible) 7 before *Will's*. It was probably erased because William was a sub-tenant of the Abbot, rather than of the Church (but see 8,4. 10,4 etc.). In Exon. *de monasterio* here and for 55,22, but *de monasteriis* for 55,15. Moutiers-Hubert is in the département of Calvados, France; OEB p. 102. Winterborne Muston is named after his descendants, as is Muston (GR SY 7295) which was probably part of this holding, Hutchins ii p. 802; see 26,21-22 note.

11,3 RADIPOLE. See 1,22 note. It lay in Cullifordtree Hundred (26) in 1086 (Tax Return xxxvii) and is *Reppole* or *Rapely* in Cullifordtree Hundred in FA ii pp. 19, 38, 57.

OF WHICH HALF IS IN LORDSHIP. Half the land, 1½ hides, see third note under 1,7.
WITH ... 1 VILLAGER; 5 SMALLHOLDERS HAVE 2 PLOUGHS & 1½ HIDES.
Ibi ... cū ... i uitto 7 v bord' hūt ii car ... . Either *hūt* (= *habent*) is a scribal error for
hūntibus (= *habentibus*: 'with ... 1 villager and 5 smallholders who have 2 ploughs ...') or
uitto is an error for the nominative *uitts* (= '1 villager and 5 smallholders have 2 ploughs ...').
Exon. supports this latter, stating that the villagers (used generically) have 1½ hides and 2
ploughs and that (the Abbot) has there 1 villager and 5 smallholders etc. Cf. 56,21 note.

11,4   BLOXWORTH. Held by the Abbot of Cerne as *Blockysworth* in Combsditch Hundred
(16) in FA ii pp. 29, 43, 48. It is required by a reconstruction of the Tax Return for
Combsditch (xvi).
LAND FOR ... In the MS *Tra*; Farley omits the abbreviation sign in error, probably
because it occurs in the middle of the interlined 7 *dimid'* (of '5½ hides').

11,5   AFFPUDDLE. In Bere Hundred (Tax Return xv) it is Aeffa's or Aelfrith's
'Puddle', given by Aelfrith to Cerne Abbey in 987; see Ch. 11 note, TE p. 179a and EPNS
i p. 289. The land was later in Barrow Hundred and included *Palyngton* [Pallington GR SY
7891], FA ii pp. 21, 36, 42.
[WIDE]. Supplied from Exon. The DB scribe appears to have omitted the end of the
entry, perhaps because he was not sure of the meaning of the last sentence in Exon., or
because it might have been written later; see Exon. Notes here. There is no full-stop after
ūtd', but an illegible erasure of a few letters, with the rest of the line blank. The scribe
may have intended to finish it later, began a new folio for the next entry and promptly
forgot it.
SAID TWO MANORS. Bloxworth and Affpuddle.

11,6   POXWELL. The Abbot of Cerne holds *Pokeswell* in FA ii pp. 9, 30, 49 and part of
Upryngstede ['Up Ringstead'] in FA ii p. 29, now Upton (GR SY 7483) adjacent to
Poxwell. See notes to 52,2 and 55,34. The land lay in 'Chilbury' Hundred in 1086 (Tax
Return xxxi).
HUGH'S WIFE. That is, Hugh son of Grip; Roger Bushell (see Exon. Notes here) is also
a tenant of hers on alienated church land at 55,3 (see note there).
26 'RODS'. *Virg'* here (and also in 11,17 and 30,2) may abbreviate *uirgas* or *uirgates*.
Exon. regularly uses *uirga* where Exchequer DB has *uirgata* 'virgate' in the hidage statement (see B 1 note above). The measure intended here, however, appears to be linear not
areal (which the virgate is) and is of uncertain length. *Virga* is the Latin for a rod or pole
or measuring stick and like many DB measurements its size seems to have been subject to
local variations or is not attested by contemporary evidence. From 11,17 it would appear
that more than 10 *uirgae* constituted a furlong. See RMLWL s.v. *uirga*.
PERCHES. DB *pertica* or *perca*, a measure of length, usually reckoned at 5½ yards,
though a 20-foot perch was in use for measuring woodland until last century; see Zupko
s.v. *perch*. In Dorset it is used as a measure of both pasture (as here) and woodland (as
in 19,8).

11,7   WOODSFORD. East Woodford, held as *Estwerdesford* by the Abbot of Cerne in FA ii
pp. 9, 30 in Winfrith Hundred (27). For West Woodsford, see 57,13.

11,8   HETHFELTON. Part or all of the village may have been in Bere Tax Return Hundred
(xv) in 1086, though later in Winfrith (27), see 49,14 note. In FA ii pp. 39, 58 the Abbot
of Cerne holds *Welesbrigg* in Barrow Hundred (probably the same as *Celebrigg* in FA ii
p. 37), that is Wool Bridge in East Stoke (GR SY 8487), probably a part of this holding;
see the 'Red Book of Cerne' (11,1 note) p. 69.

11,9   WORGRET. Part or all was in Bere Hundred in 1086 (Tax Return xv), see 49,14 and
57,7 notes. It was later locally in Hasler Hundred (28), though a tithing of Barrow
Hundred, a later subdivision of Bere (22). It is included in Barrow Hundred in FA ii p. 42.
½ MILL. The other half of the mill in Worgret is recorded in 37,10.

11,10;   LITTLEBREDY; LONG BREDY. Held by the Abbot of Cerne in Fees p. 92 as *Langebrid'*
12   and *Litlebrid'*. Littlebredy can be deduced from the Tax Return for Uggescombe
Hundred (iii), Long Bredy from that for Eggardon (iv). *Lytelebridye* and *Langebridie* are
both held from the Abbot in Uggescombe Hundred (25) in FA ii pp. 6, 33-34, 53.

11,11   WINTERBORNE (ABBAS). See Tax Return for Eggardon Hundred (iv); and FA ii pp. 3,
33. In the latter it is *Wynterborn Waterlyse* (Fägersten p. 242).

11,13   NETTLECOMBE; (WEST) MILTON. In Eggardon Hundred (Tax Return iv). The holdings
-14   seem to have included Mappercombe in Powerstock (GR SY 5195), FA ii pp. 3, 33.

11,13   LAND FOR ... A gap of about 7 letters' width has been left after this in the MS for the
number of ploughs to be added when known. Cf. 19,14 and see fourth note under 1,1 on
similar omissions by both DB and Exon.

11,14 (WEST) MILTON. So called to distinguish it from Milton Abbas, Fägersten p. 242. It is required by the reconstruction of the Tax Return for Eggardon Hundred (iv).

11,15 KIMMERIDGE. In Hasler Hundred in 1086 (Tax Return xxix). *Cumerygge* in Hasler Hundred (28) is held by the Abbot in FA ii p. 23 and associated with an unidentified *Hamelton* (see EPNS i p. 71) in FA ii p. 37.

11,16 RENSCOMBE. It seems to be required by the Tax Return for Hasler Hundred (xxix) although it has since been transferred to Rowbarrow (29); see FA ii p. 44.
5 HIDES AND 1 VIRGATE. The details of the lordship and villagers' holdings amount to 6 hides. See 1,19 note.
7 VILLAGERS AND 7 SMALLHOLDERS. In the MS there is a gap of about 16 letters' width after this, presumably for the villagers' ploughs; Exon. similarly omits them (see fourth note under 1,1 and 1,26 note).
UNPRODUCTIVE WOODLAND. *Silua infructuosa*; it did not provide beechmast and acorns for pigs (see Exon. Notes 11,13). The pigs that Exon. records must have fed elsewhere. Woodland was also used to provide fuel and timber for building and repairing houses and for salt-houses, as well as for hunting; see DB Worcs. 2,15;31 and Wilts. 13,10.
WETHERS. *Berbices*: male sheep kept for mutton. The milk for this manor was presumably provided by the cows and goats.

11,17 SYMONDSBURY. *Symondesbergh* in Whitchurch Hundred (11), FA ii p. 45; see Tax Return ii.
10 'RODS'. See 11,6 note.

Ch. 12 THE LIST OF HOLDINGS in DB should be compared with Athelstan's Charter of which a Latin and a Middle English version exist, BCS nos. 738-9 (= KCD nos. 1119 and 375 = ECW no. 580 p. 167 = Sawyer (1) no. 391). Land is granted at *Muleborn* 26 hides [probably Milton Abbas, 24 hides in DB 12,2]; at *Wonlonde* 5 hides [Wolland 12,10]; at *Fromemuthe* ['Fromemouth'] 3 hides of which 2 are on *Ye* [Green Island] and 1 at *Ore* [Ower, where DB places all 3 hides, 12,13; see EPNS i p. 13]; *Clyve* 3 hides [Clyffe 2 hides 12,6]; *Liscombe* 3½ hides [Lyscombe 12,9]; *Bordelestone* 1 hide [Burleston 3 hides 12,5]; *Litele Pidele* 1 hide [Little Puddle 2 hides 12,15]; *Sidelyng* 30 hides [Sydling 29 hides 12,1]; *Stoke* (or *Cattestoke* in ME version) 5 hides [Cattistock 10 hides 12,4]; *Cumptune* 6 hides [West Compton 5 hides 12,3]; *Osmingtone* 5 hides [Osmington 10 hides 12,7]; *Wydecombe* 2 hides [Whitcombe 6 hides 12,8]; *Holewourthe* 6 hides [Holworth 5 hides 12,12]; and *Stokelonde* or Yarcombe [GR ST 2408; *Ercecombe* in ME version] 10 hides [Stockland 12,14]. The charter also grants 2 hides in Chalmington (in Cattistock, GR ST 5900) and 6 hides at *Hyllefeyld* [Hilfield GR ST 6305] which are not separately mentioned in DB. The charter is summarised in Fees p. 90; see VCH iii p. 44. The possessions of the Abbey are usefully studied in Traskey.

12,1 SYDLING. This holding can be identified with Sydling St. Nicholas (Tax Return xxxiii for Modbury Hundred). The missing 1 hide of the original 30 hides may be held by the Count of Mortain, 26,27). In an Inquisition *ad quod damnum* cited in Hutchins (iv pp. lxxvii-lxxx) Sydling consists of 38 hides and contains *Brodesidlinge* [Sydling St. Nicholas] with *Hulfeld* [Hilfield, see above], *La Halfehid* ['Halfhide', see Fägersten p. 202], *Upsidlinge* [Upsydling], *Eliston* [Ellston GR ST 6302], *Chalminton* [Chalmington, see above], and *Blakmore* [either Blackmore in Glanvilles Wootton, GR ST 6709, or Blackmore Vale or Forest; Fägersten p. 208].
OF THESE. *de his*, probably a scribal error for the more usual *de ea* 'of this (land)' (see 1,7 third note), unless it refers back to the 29 hides.

12,2 THE CHURCH ITSELF HOLDS. Repeated at the beginning of 12,2-16.
MILTON (ABBAS). The holding can be identified in the Tax Return for Hilton (Whiteway) Hundred (xi); see FA ii pp. 13, 40.
IT IS THE HEAD OF THE ABBEY. *caput*; the chief manor and head of the Abbey's fief.

12,3 (WEST) COMPTON. Formerly Compton Abbas West, see 19,5 note. It is locally in Tollerford Hundred (13) although in fact a detachment of Cerne, Totcombe and Modbury Hundred (14). It was in the same situation in 1086, being identifiable in the Tax Return for Modbury Hundred (xxxiii).
6 VILLAGERS AND 5 SMALLHOLDERS. There is no dot after *bord'* in the MS, but, as there is no marginal ruling here (so that gaps left at ends of lines are hard to determine), it is unclear whether the DB scribe intended to add the villagers' ploughs at a later stage; there is no apparent reason, however, why he did not include the 2 ploughs mentioned in Exon. (similarly the villagers' ploughs in 16,2. 36,7 and 55,26;34).

12,4 CATTISTOCK. DB *Stoche*, but see Ch. 12 note. It can be found in the Tax Return for Modbury Hundred (xxxiii). In the Inquisition cited in 12,1 note, Cattistock is said to consist of *Doudeleshegh* ['Dudley Moor', Fägersten p. 195], *Witham* [Witcham GR ST 568021], *Bestedene* ['Bestedon', Fägersten p. 195] and *Chantmerle* [Chantmarle GR ST 5802], all places in Cattistock parish.

12,5;   BURLESTON; (LITTLE) PUDDLE. The foundation charter (Ch. 12 note) grants
15   Burleston and Little Puddle to Milton Abbey. The two DB holdings at *Pidele* and *Pidre* are likely to represent these, but it is not clear which is which.

12,6   CLYFFE. The Abbot of Milton's 1 hide of lordship in the Bere Hundred Tax Return (xv) may represent this holding, which is later in Puddletown Hundred (21).
      5 VILLAGERS HOLD THEM. The two ploughs; see fourth note under 3,14.

12,7   OSMINGTON; WHITCOMBE. Held by the Abbot in Cullifordtree Hundred (26) in FA ii
-8   pp. 19-20; see Tax Return xxxvii.

12,9   LYSCOMBE; WOOLLAND. Required by the Tax Return for Hilton (Whiteway)
-10   Hundred (xi).

12,10   WOOLLAND. Held by the Abbot in Whiteway Hundred (15) in FA ii p. 13.

12,11   WINTERBORNE (WHITECHURCH). The manor can be identified in the Tax Return for Combsditch Hundred (xvi); it included land at *La Leye* [La Lee GR ST 8301] in TE p. 184b; see EPNS ii p. 83. The Prior of Milton Abbey receives a portion of the revenues of the church of *Albi Monasterii*, that is (Winterborne) Whitechurch, in TE p. 178b.

12,12   HOLWORTH. The Abbot of Milton holds *Holeworth* in Winfrith Hundred (27) in FA ii p. 9; it is required by the Tax Return for 'Chilbury' Hundred (xxxi).
      SESTER OF HONEY. The sester is a measure, sometimes of liquid, as here, sometimes dry; of uncertain and probably variable size (see DB Glos. G 1 and 19,2 notes). It was reckoned at 32 oz. for honey; see Zupko p. 155. Sesters of honey also occur in the value statement of 37,9. See Lennard p. 126 on the significance of this render.

12,13ff. THE REST OF THE ENTRIES in this column are written smaller, though in the same colour ink; it may be that the scribe had a break after 12,12 and began again the next morning when the light was better. The writing shows a gradual increase in size from the top of col. 78b, suggesting perhaps that it was getting dark. Cf. 26,46-61 where the writing also suddenly becomes much smaller.

12,13   OWER. Required by the Tax Return for Ailwood (Rowbarrow) Hundred (xix). 1 hide was at Ower, 2 hides on the island of *Ye* (or *Sancte Elene* in the Inquisition cited in 12,1 note), that is Green Island; see Ch. 12 note.
      13 SALT-WORKERS WHO PAY 20s. Their payment may be a money-rent as there is no value statement for this entry (as is probably the case in 57,2; see note), but salt-workers also pay money in 8,6 and the value is given for that entry. See 54,2 note on omitted value statements.

12,14   STOCKLAND. Now in Devon, but long a detached part of Whitchurch Hundred (11). It is held there by the Abbot in FA ii p. 45. Dalwood (see 1,4 note) was a part of this land according to the Inquisition cited in 12,1 note.
      VALUE £9. As there is no full stop after *lib'*, it may be that the scribe intended to add the 1066 value of Buckland when available; it is not recorded in Exon. either.

12,15   (LITTLE) PUDDLE. See 12,5 note.

12,16   'CERNE'. The land was possibly the holding of the Abbot later called Little Minterne, or Minterne Parva, in Buckland Newton (GR ST 6603); see Hutchins iv p. 17.
      (1) HIDE. Plain *hida*; *i* or *una* is often omitted by the DB scribe; see also notes to 26,22 and 56,14.
      LESS 5 ACRES. Briefly omitted by the scribe and added at the end of the line with transposition signs (which are more interlined than Farley prints them). It is interesting that in Exon. *v agros min'* is interlined, and so could have been momentarily missed by the Exchequer scribe if, as seems likely, he was copying. See Exon. Notes here.

Ch. 13   ABBOTSBURY ABBEY. St. Peter's, Abbotsbury, was founded by Urk, a *huscarl* of Cnut and Edward the Confessor, and his wife Tole whose name distinguishes Tolpuddle (13,2); see *Regesta* no. 108 (= ECW no. 628 p. 177 = KCD no. 841 = Sawyer (1) no. 1064). In Fees p. 92 the Abbey holds *Abbedesbir', Portesham, Helton, Tolepidele* and *Wdeton* given *per Oro* (i.e. *Orc*) *et Tolam uxorem suam*. All these lands are held by the Abbey in DB; see VCH iii p. 44.

13,1   ABBOTSBURY. In Uggescombe Hundred (Tax Return iii). The land seems to have included *Raddun* [Rodden GR SY 6184] and an unidentified *Finelegh* [*Fynle* in LSR p. 77]; see FA ii pp. 5, 33, 53.
      1 HIDE. Hugh son of Grip appears to have despoiled this church of several lands; his wife holds part of Abbotsbury here and part of Portesham in 13,4. A further 'acquisition' is mentioned in 55,3, but none is cross-referenced in Domesday. See B 1 note on Hugh.

13,2   THE CHURCH ITSELF HOLDS. Repeated at the beginning of 13,2-8.
TOLPUDDLE. See Ch. 13 note. Abbotsbury Abbey holds *Tolle Pudele* in FA ii p. 15 in
Puddletown Hundred (21); see FA ii pp. 35, 54; TE p. 184a.
14 COTTAGERS. In the MS above the last *i* of *xiiii* is a small and irregular *l.*, more
probably a slip of the pen than a correction to the figure; Farley omits it.

13,3   HILTON. Held in Whiteway Hundred (15) by the Abbot in FA ii pp. 13, 36, 40, 55.

13,4   PORTESHAM. See FA ii pp. 5, 33, 53. The Church had also held the dues of the adjacent
village of Waddon (23,1) before 1066. Portesham was and is in Uggescombe Hundred
(Tax Return iii).
1 VIRGATE OF LAND. See 13,1 note. This land may have been at *Corfton* [Corton in
Portesham, GR SY 6385], given by a descendant of the wife of Hugh to East Holme
priory; Ch. 55 note.
HOLDS IT BY FORCE. *ui* 'by force' interlined. VCH ii p. 49 misreads it as *vi* 'six'.

13,5   SHILVINGHAMPTON. In Uggescombe Hundred (Tax Return iii).

13,6;   (ABBOTTS) WOOTTON; ATRIM. The taxable size of these two holdings (leaving aside
8   the 1 hide of lordship at *Widetone*) is 3½ hides. This amount is entered in the Tax Return
for Whitchurch Hundred (ii) where both places lay in 1086, as paid in another Hundred.
The 'other Hundred' is Uggescombe (iii) where Abbotsbury itself lay. The Abbot of
Abbotsbury holds *Wodeton Abbatis* in FA ii p. 45 in Whitchurch Hundred (11).

13,7   POORTON. Now North Poorton, a parish in Beaminster Hundred (12), and South
Poorton, a part of Powerstock parish in Eggardon Hundred (19). With the exception of
54,7, all the other four occurrences of Poorton can be accounted for in the Tax Return
for 'Redhone' (xiii) and are therefore probably North Poorton. The Tax Return records
the present entry in 'Redhone' Hundred, but mentions that ½ hide pays tax in another
Hundred, probably Uggescombe, for in the Tax Return for Uggescombe Hundred (iii)
payment is received on 4 hides that belong to other Hundreds: these are probably the
3½ hides of Abbotts Wootton and Atrim (13,6;8, see previous note) together with the
½ hide of the present holding.
     The DB form *Bourtone* is probably another form of *Povertone* rather than Burcombe
in North Poorton, Eyton *Dorset* pp. 137-8; see Fägersten p. 281.
2 VILLAGERS HAVE IT THERE. *Hanc*, referring to the plough; see fourth note under
3,14. However, according to Exon. the villagers also hold the ½ hide, though not the
woodland.

13,8   ATRIM. See 13,6 note.

Ch. 14   HORTON ABBEY. For the history of the Priory, see VCH ii p. 71 ff.

14,1   HORTON. Granted by King Cnut in 1033 as 7 *mansae* to his thane Bovi; see KCD no.
1318 = ECW p. 176 no. 622 = Sawyer (1) no. 969. It lay in *Canendona* Hundred in 1086
(Tax Return vii).
TWO BETTER HIDES. *meliores*, translated 'best' by VCH iii p. 80 and DGSW p. 103,
for which the corresponding Latin is rightly *optimas*. The implication here seems to be
that of the 7 hides some land (extent unspecified) is better than other land. Of this better
land, 2 hides are held by the King; not only has he taken land into his Forest, but some
of the more productive land.
FOREST OF WIMBORNE. Now Holt Forest, EPNS ii pp. 150-151.
IN THE LEFT MARGIN of the MS, level with lines 5 and 6 of this entry, is a large
comma-type mark, not shown by Farley but probably contemporary with DB; it resembles
similar marks checking royal land.

Ch. 15   ATHELNEY ABBEY. St. Peter's.

15,1   (PURSE) CAUNDLE. See 26,70-71 note. This land is to be identified with the unnamed
gift of 4 hides of land by King Alfred (871-899) in Sherborne Hundred (1) in Fees p. 90.
Purscaundel or *Pruscaundel* is held by Athelney Abbey in TE p. 178a, FA ii p. 41 and
RH i p. 103. From these last two entries, it is clear that the Abbot held half the village less
½ hide (see 56,55 note), the other half being held by the Abbess of Shaftesbury (see Cal.
Inq. PM vol. iii (Ed. I) no. 111 and Hutchins iv p. 143). Athelney Abbey's holding was
given by Count Robert of Mortain in exchange for 'Bishopstone' in Somerset, where he
raised his castle of Montacute; see E 1 below.
TAX FOR 4 HIDES AND 1½ VIRGATES. The details of lordship and villagers' land
together with Alfred's holding would appear to total 4 hides 3 virgates. However, Exon.
states that Alfred held '1½ virgates of these 4 hides': unless the 4 hides is a scribal error
for the total 4 hides 1½ virgates (and perhaps the villagers' 1½ virgates are also a mistake),
the scribe seems to be stating that Alfred's 1½ virgates were part of the lordship 4 hides.

This would be most unusual, but would make the details tally with the tax total. However, see 1,19 note for other examples of discrepancies between details and total.
ALFRED THE BUTLER. Exon. *Alueredus pincerna*. He was the Count of Mortain's butler and held a considerable amount of land from him in many other counties, including 1½ hides in 'Bishopstone' (DB Somerset 19,86 = E 1 below) which was exchanged with Purse Caundle.

16,1 ASKERSWELL. The Tax Return for 'Redhone' Hundred (xiii) records 2½ hides as paying tax in another Hundred. Askerswell is later in Eggardon Hundred (19); see FA ii pp. 3, 33, 53. Its status seems to have been uncertain in 1086; see VCH iii p. 133. Part of this land was apparently in Sturthill, Godderthorn Hundred (18), for in FA ii p. 11 the Abbot of Tavistock holds a half of *Stertel* (the other half being 55,19).
2 TRIBUTARIES. *Censores* here and in 33,4; in Exon. here *gablatores* from *gablum* [OE *gafol*] 'tribute, rent'. They paid 15s in rent (cf. the 5 *censarii* who paid 5s in DB Derbys. 6,38). See DB Notts. 10,3 note and Lennard p. 372 and his article in The Economic Journal, June 1951, p. 361 note 1.
VALUE ... WHEN HE ACQUIRED IT. Abbot Geoffrey; see Exon. Notes.

16,2 POORTON. Required by the Tax Return for 'Redhone' Hundred (xiii); see 13,7 note and Fees p. 425.

Ch. 17 LAND OF ST. STEPHEN'S AT CAEN. In the MS *STEFANI* is written over an erasure. Holy Trinity Church at Caen also held land in DB; see Ch. 21 below and Devon Ch. 13. St. Stephen's was founded in 1064 by Duke William and consecrated in 1066. Lanfranc, afterwards Archbishop of Canterbury, was the first Abbot. Caen is in the département of Calvados, France.

17,1 FRAMPTON ... 2 HIDES. The bulk of the manor forms the major part of Frampton Hundred Tax Return (xxxviii); the added 2 hides appear to have been in Cullifordtree (xxxvii). The wood at 'Hawcombe' is shared with the royal manor of Burton Bradstock, see 1,2 note. Frampton and Bincombe (17,2) are granted by William I to St. Stephen's in *Regesta* i no. 105 and confirmed in charters of Henry II and Richard, Archbishop of Canterbury (Round CDF nos. 453, 459 pp. 156, 162; see Mon. Ang. vi pp. 1070-1 and Fees p. 94). The confirmation charters given in Mon. Ang. and *Regesta* ii p. 224 no. 1575 list the members of the manor of *Frantona* and *Biencome* [Bincombe 17,2] as *Alphilicome* [?Philleyholme in Hawkchurch, GR ST 3500, now in Devon, see EPNS (Devon) ii p. 655], *Bethescome* [Bettiscombe parish, GR SY 3999, see Fägersten p. 283], *Omouskerigge* [unidentified], *Erneleys* ['Ernly', now Benville in Corscombe parish, GR ST 5303; see Drew's 1949 article and Boswell p. 77], *Sedelinch* [Sydling St. Nicholas GR SY 6399], *Wintreborna* [Winterborne Came GR SY 7088], *Ceirnell* [a holding on the river Cerne] and *Pubich* [land in Purbeck, i.e. Rowbarrow Hundred (29), see 1,8 note]. Winterborne Came, locally in Cullifordtree Hundred (26), was a member of Frampton Liberty, the name being derived from Caen; see EPNS i p. 261, TE p. 183b. Winterborne *Huntindon* [Winterborne Huntingdon] in Winterborne Came was probably a part of this land, being named from the Earls of Huntingdon who had a grant of part of Frampton (EPNS i p. 263, Fägersten p. 163; see FA ii pp. 38, 57). The land in Purbeck can be identified in the Tax Return for Ailwood (Rowbarrow) Hundred (xix), where tax on 1 hide is said to be paid in another Hundred. It lay in Swanage; see TE p. 183b and Hutchins i p. 661. In later times Frampton Liberty consisted of the tithings of Benville, Bettiscombe, Bincombe, Burton Bradstock, Winterborne Came and Compton Valence. Burton Bradstock was a gift of Henry I; see *Regesta* ii p. 175 no. 1341 and p. 24 no. 601.
QUEEN MATILDA. *Mathildis regina* with *regin* interlined, but the last letter was not completed, probably because the scribe realised there was no need for the interlineation. Farley prints *regine* (genitive) which would be the wrong case.
THE WHOLE WAS VALUED AT AND PAYS ... It is unusual for both *valuit* and *reddit* to appear in the same statement; see 1,7 note. Also occurs in 17,2 and 26,29.

17,2 BINCOMBE. Included in the Tax Return for Cullifordtree Hundred (xxxvii). See 17,1 note.
PAYS. Although *redd'* can abbreviate both the present *reddit* and the past *reddebat/reddidit*, the present is more likely here in view of *reddit* in the similar phrase in 17,1.

Ch. 18 [LAND OF ST. WANDRILLE'S ABBEY]. Farley omits the chapter number *XVIII* which is very clear in the MS. There is no chapter heading in the MS, however, due to lack of space. The first three words of 18,1 are written in the same size script as are the initial words in Chs. 14-17; not in large capitals as for a chapter heading as Farley prints them. St. Wandrille's, originally the Benedictine Abbey of Fontanelle, was founded in 654 by St. Wandregisilius (Mon. Ang. vi p. 1107) and lies on the Seine between Lillebonne and Rouen in the département of Seine-Maritime, France. King William also granted it lands in Surrey (DB Ch. 9) and Cambridgeshire (DB Ch. 10); see also B 3 above and DB Wilts. 1,23g and Northants. 56,61.

18,1 BURTON (BRADSTOCK), BRIDPORT, WHITCHURCH (CANONICORUM). There is a charter of William I confirming on St. Wandrille's *Mincherte* [Whitchurch] and *Bridetune* [Burton Bradstock see 1,2 note] ; *Regesta* i no. 110 (= Mon. Ang. vi p. 1108). A charter of Jocelyn, Bishop of Salisbury 1142-1184, confirms on St. Wandrille's the churches of *Witchercha, Bridiport* and *Britidon*, Round CDF p. 60 no. 174. These churches, like those of Ch. 24, were granted out of royal lands or boroughs and are entered in Exon. Domesday in the *Dominicatus Regis* (see Ch. 1 note). Burton Bradstock is called *Briditone Sancti Wandrigesili* in FA ii p. 11.

18,2 WAREHAM ... 1 HIDE. The hide is not named, but lay in Hasler Hundred (Tax Return xxix).

Ch. 19 SHAFTESBURY ABBEY. A charter of King Alfred grants 100 hides to the Church of Shaftesbury, of which there lay in Dorset 20 hides at *Hanlee* [Sixpenny Handley 19,1] and *Gissic* [Gussage 19,1 note], 10 hides at *Terente* [Tarrant Hinton 19,8]; 15 hides at *Ywern* [Iwerne Minster 19,7] and 15 at *Funtemel* [Fontmell Magna 19,4]. Iwerne Minster is 18 hides in DB (see 19,7 note), otherwise the hidages are the same. The Charter is in BCS nos. 531-532 = Robertson no. XIII = ECW no. 212 p. 165 = Sawyer (1) no. 357; see VCH iii p. 42. Two later surveys of Shaftesbury Abbey lands in British Library Harleian MS 61 ff. 37-89 can usefully be compared with DB. The Abbey also held land in Purse Caundle, not mentioned in DB; see 15,1 note.

19,1 (SIXPENNY) HANDLEY. See Fees p. 87 and FA ii pp. 31, 39. DB *Hanlege* to which the name of the Hundred has been added. Sixpenny (now represented by Sixpenny farm (GR ST 8416) near Pen Hill in the parish of Fontmell Magna and by the adjacent Sixpenny Covert), was originally the western half of the two-part Hundred which was surveyed as two separate Tax Return Hundreds. Handley has its own Tax Return (xx) and probably included Gussage St. Andrew, see 26,44 note.

19,3 THE CHURCH ITSELF HOLDS. Repeated at the beginning of 19,2-14.
HINTON (ST. MARY). The land lay in Newton (Sturminster Newton) Hundred (Tax Return xxi) in 1086 and later. 6½ of its 8 hides, however, paid tax in Handley Hundred (xx) which consisted entirely of Shaftesbury lands. Fees p. 87 and FA ii pp. 37, 42, 56 record this holding in Newton Hundred (3).

19,3 STOUR. The Shaftesbury lands no doubt encompassed both East and West Stour. *Sture Cosin* (see Fägersten p. 16) is held from the Abbess of Shaftesbury in FA ii p. 22 in Gillingham and Redlane Hundred (4); see FA ii p. 40. Part of the land may have been at *Liland'* now Nyland, Fees p. 87.

19,4 THESE VILLAGES are all accounted for in the Tax Return for Sixpenny Hundred (xxiv);
-7 see 19,7 note. *Ywerne, Fontemel* and *Melebury* are holdings of the Abbess of Shaftesbury in Sixpenny and Handley Hundreds (5) in FA ii pp. 30, 39, 50.

19,4 FONTMELL (MAGNA). Fontmell Parva has a different history, being a part of Child Okeford parish in Gillingham and Redlane Hundred (4).

19,5 COMPTON (ABBAS). Formerly Compton Abbas East to distinguish it from Compton Abbas West, now West Compton (12,3).

19,6 MELBURY (ABBAS). Also, sometimes, Melbury *Abbatissae*, 'Abbess' Melbury; Fägersten p. 27.

19,7 IWERNE MINSTER. Named from the river Iwerne (see Introductory Note 2 on Rivers and 30,3 note) but distinguished as *Euneminstre* by DB. In Alfred's grant the hidage is 15 and that number is implied by the Tax Return for Sixpenny Hundred (xxiv). The excess 3 hides may have lain south of the village in Pimperne Hundred (9) where in the Tax Return (xxvi) the Abbess of Shaftesbury has 1 hide ½ virgate in lordship, not otherwise accounted for.

19,8 TARRANT (HINTON). For Alfred's grant see Ch. 19 note. There is a separate grant of 12 hides at *Terenta* by King Athelstan (924-939) to the nuns of Shaftesbury, see ECW p. 168 no. 581 = BCS no. 708 = Sawyer (1) no. 429. The secondary name is OE *hīgna-tūn* 'farm of the monastic community'. The lordship land is accounted for in the Tax Return for *Langeberga* Hundred (xxii). Later, Tarrant Hinton is in Pimperne Hundred (9); see FA ii pp. 1, 27, 46. In 1086 and later, an outlying part of the manor, 1 hide, lay adjacent to Pimperne itself; Fees p. 87, Hutchins i p. 315 and VCH iii p. 140. It is now represented by Hyde farm (GR ST 906093) in a part of Pimperne parish transferred from Tarrant Hinton parish in 1933; EPNS ii p. 120.
IN IWERNE MINSTER WOODLAND ... Added in the space at the end of 19,8, directed by transposition signs to its correct position in 19,7.

19,9 FIFEHEAD (ST. QUINTIN). 'Fifehead' means 'five hides', other examples being 27,1 and
40,6. This Fifehead can be identified in the Tax Return for Newton Hundred (xxi), but
the land seems to have been alienated from the Church some time after 1086 and become
a part of the Honour of Gloucester and so of Cranborne Hundred (6); see 8,1 penultimate
note. Various members of the *de Sancto Quintino* family hold *Fifhyde* and its constituents
Belle and *Chaldewelle* from that Honour in Fees p. 750 and FA ii pp. 27, 39, 46. *Belle* and
Chaldewelle now form the parish of Belchalwell (GR ST 7909) which long contained
Fifehead St. Quintin. Since 1920 however, the latter has been part of Fifehead Neville
parish (see 40,6) and so of Pimperne Hundred (9); the former has been in Okeford
Fitzpaine, Sturminster Newton Hundred (3); see Fägersten pp. 53, 146, EPNS ii p. 95,
Eyton *Dorset* p. 135 and Tithings note in the Appendix.

19,10 KINGSTON. In Corfe parish, also called Kingston *Abbatissae*; see Fees p. 87, FA ii p. 44
and EPNS i p. 15. The land lay in two Tax Return Hundreds: 3 hides, less ¼ virgate, of
lordship in Ailwood (Rowbarrow) Hundred (xix) and 1 hide, less 6 acres, in Hasler (xxix).
See VCH iii p. 142. The holding seems to have included *Blachenewell* [Blashenwell in
Corfe, GR SY 9580] and *Enecumbe* [Encombe in Corfe parish, GR SY 9478], also a
detached portion at *Harn* [Arne, now a separate parish, formerly in Holy Trinity parish
Wareham, GR SY 9788], FA ii p. 23.

19,10 THE REST OF 19,10 and all of 19,11 are added below the bottom marginal ruling (with
-11 the exception of the first line), and some 3 letters into the central margin. There is no sign
that the scribe intended to add details of population, resources and value to 19,11,
probably because these are to be found in the fiefs of Aiulf and Hugh's wife.

19,10 WAREHAM CASTLE. *Castellum Warham*, now Corfe Castle, GR SY 9582. Fees p. 91
records that Shaftesbury Abbey holds the advowson of Gillingham church 'in exchange
for the land where Corfe Castle is situated' (*in escambium pro terra ubi castellum de corf'
positum est*); see EPNS i p. 11. The reason for the original omission of this detail may be
that the scribe thought it had been included in the return for the King's lands, or perhaps
information on this exchange came in late.
WILLIAM OF BRAOSE HAS 1 VIRGATE. This detail may have been omitted from the
main part of the Kingston entry because the scribe was unsure whether to include it under
William of Braose's fief in Ch. 37.

19,11 FARNHAM ... AIULF AND HUGH SON OF GRIP'S WIFE. The hide is divided between
Aiulf the Chamberlain (49,17) and the wife of Hugh (55,21), though there Aiulf and
Hugh's wife are tenants-in-chief, not sub-tenants. This entry may have been added later as
part of an attempt by Shaftesbury to recover the land in Farnham by informing the DB
Commissioners that the hide was only leased to Aiulf and Hugh's wife. The Abbey
succeeded in recovering Aiulf's ½ hide; see 49,17 note.

19,12 STOKE (WAKE). The land can be identified in the Tax Return for Hilton (Whiteway)
Hundred (xi). It is held by Shaftesbury Abbey in FA ii p. 13 and by John Wake from
Shaftesbury in Cal. Inq. PM vol. ix (Ed. III) no. 117.

19,13 MAPPERTON. Originally granted by King Edmund (939-946) as 11 *mansae* at
Mapeldertune (ECW p. 169 no. 586 = BCS no. 781 = Sawyer (1) no. 490). It is required by
the Tax Return for Charborough Hundred (xviii). It will have contained West Almer, Fees
p. 87 and Hutchins iii p. 495.
PASTURE AND WOODLAND, BETWEEN THEM ... *inter pasturam et siluam*... the
pasture was mixed in with the woodland, the whole measuring 11 furlongs by 11 furlongs.
Cf. "woodland, pasture in places, 16 furlongs long and 7 furlongs wide" in DB Rutland
R 5. See also DB Worcs. 8,6 note.

19,14 CHESELBOURNE. Sometimes called Long Cheselbourne to distinguish it from 'Little
Cheselbourne' (55,3). It can be identified in the Tax Return for Hilton (Whiteway)
Hundred (xi); and is held by the Abbess of Shaftesbury in Fees p. 87 and FA ii p. 13. The
land was granted as 16 *cassati* given by King Cnut (1016-1035) to his thane Agemund
(KCD no. 730 = ECW no. 619 p. 176 = Sawyer (1) no. 955).
LAND FOR ... There is a gap of only 2 letters' width after this. The scribe obviously
intended to write into the margin when the information became available. Cf. 11,13 note.
WRIT. *breuis*, an alternative and rarer form of *breue*, both originally derived from the
adjective meaning 'short, brief'. Here it has its more common meaning of the King's writ,
but in DB it can also mean 'return', referring to the returns made by landholders and the
King of their fiefs (e.g. Worcs. X 2-3). See Galbraith in EHR lvii (1942) pp. 171-5.
'PIDDLE'. The land was probably the 10 *cassati* granted by Wynflaed grandmother of
King Edgar to the Church of All Saints, Shaftesbury, in *Uppidelen* (ECW no. 607 p. 173
= BCS no. 1186 = Sawyer (1) no. 744), which Finberg identifies as part of Piddletrenthide.

The land is said in DB to be held by the Count of Mortain. The only 'Piddle' held by him and of sufficient size is 26,20 Piddlehinton (see note) granted by him to the monks of Marmoutier.
MELCOMBE (HORSEY) WHICH THE KING STILL HOLDS. See 1,30.

20,1   DIDLINGTON. The land can be identified in the Tax Return for *Canendona* Hundred (vii). The 6 hides probably originated in the grant of Edwy (*Eadwig*), King of Albion (955-959) to his nobleman Alfred (ECW no. 599 p. 171 = BCS no. 958 = Sawyer (1) no. 609) and will have consisted of 5 hides at Didlington and 1 at Uddens (GR SO 0402) in Holt parish. In FA ii p. 14, the Abbess of Wilton holds *Dudelyngton* in Badbury Hundred (17) with which *Canendona* was merged.

20,2   WIMBORNE (ST. GILES). The land was at 'Philipston' (*Felipston*') held by the Abbess of Wilton in Fees p. 426; it is *Phelipeston* in Knowlton Hundred (10) in FA ii p. 28. It survives as a field name 'Upper' and 'Lower Philipston' on the 1839 Tithe map of Wimborne St. Giles parish (GR SU 027108); see Taylor pp. 210-211, VCH iii p. 83 note 32 and EPNS ii p. 266. The land lay in Knowlton Hundred in 1086 (Tax Return xxiii).

Ch. 21   HOLY TRINITY OF CAEN. This nunnery was founded *c.* 1066 by Queen Matilda.

21,1   HOLDS. In the MS and Farley *ten* ; the facsimile fails to reproduce the abbreviation sign clearly. Cf. 23,1 first note.
TARRANT (LAUNCESTON). This *Tarente* can be identified in the Tax Return for *Langeberga* Hundred (xxii). For the grant of this manor and others in 1082 to the Abbey of Holy Trinity, Caen, see *Regesta* i no. 149 and Round CDF p. 141 no. 422 and p. 143 no. 427. The Abbey's holding here appears as *Tarente de Lowyneston* in FA ii p. 1 in Pimperne Hundred (9) and as *Tarent'* in *Langeburgh* Hundred in Fees p. 87. Part of the adjacent Tarrant Monkton may have been involved in it; see TE p. 184b.
BRICTRIC. Probably Brictric son of Algar; see 1,17 note.
VILLAGERS. According to the Tax Return for *Langeberga* Hundred (xxii) the King did not have tax from the 6 hides 4 acres that the villagers had there.

Chs. 22   IN THE LIST OF LANDHOLDERS these chapters are reversed, No. 22 being the Abbess
-23   of Montivilliers and No. 23 being the Canons of Coutances.

Ch. 22   CANONS OF COUTANCES. This is their only holding in England recorded in DB.

22,1   WINTERBORNE (STICKLAND). This 'Winterborne' can be identified in the Tax Return for *Hunesberga* Hundred (xxv); see FA ii p. 43 and TE p. 178b. In the confirmation charter of Herbert, Bishop of Salisbury 1194-1217, to the Canons of Coutances it is *Winterburn Stikellane*, Round CDF p. 344 no. 966, see TE p. 178b and Cal. Inq. Misc. vol. ii no. 1602. In the adjacent village of Quarleston lies a Normandy farm, which might recall the Coutances holding; EPNS ii p. 132, Fägersten p. 63.

Ch. 23   ST. MARY, MONTIVILLIERS. DB *Monasterium Villare* ('monastery on a country estate, or at a place there called Villare'), O Fr *Mouti(er)villier(s)*, is Montivilliers near Le Havre in the département of Seine-Maritime, France. See Longnan vol. 3 p. 353 and Dauzat and Rostaing p. 463 s.n. *Monastère*.

23,1   (MONTI)VILLIERS. In the MS and Farley *VILLAR* ; the facsimile does not reproduce the abbreviation sign. Cf. 21,1 first note.
WADDON. Broad Waddon, held as *Brodewaddon'* in Uggescombe Hundred of the fee of *Mustervilers*, Fees p. 93; see FA ii p. 7. It is also called Friar Waddon or Waddon Monks from the holding of Netley Abbey which acquired the land from the Abbey of Montivilliers.
HUGH SON OF GRIP GAVE THIS LAND TO THIS CHURCH. A copy of a charter granting Waddon to the church of St. Mary, Montivilliers, appears in *Gallia Christiana* (2nd edition) vol. xi Appendix col. 329 E. The grant is said to have been made by *Hawise* (*Haduidis*) daughter of Nicholas *de Baschelvilla* and wife of Hugh of Wareham (*de Varham*) son of Grip on the advice and with the consent of her husband for the sake of her soul and those of her husband and friends, with King William's assent, in the presence of various barons, including Bishop Odo, Earl Roger (of Montgomery), Walter Giffard, Geoffrey Martel (Hugh's brother) etc.
CHURCH TAXES. *Circscez*, plural (*circset* singular), also *circieti* plural; OE *ciric-sceat*. An obscure tax; see Maitland DBB p. 321 ff. It was due in kind and payable at Martinmas; see DB Worcs. 9,7 and the quotation from the *Rectitudines* on the duties and rights of the *cotsetla* in 1,8 note above.

Ch. 24   KING'S ALMSMEN. In the List of Landholders they are written 'Reinbald the Priest and other Clergy'.

24,1   THESE SIX CHURCHES have all been awarded from royal land: 1,4;2;6;8;12;11
-3   respectively, as is the case of some of the churches in DB Somerset Ch. 16 (Land of the

King's Clergy). In Exon. these entries are found in the *Dominicatus Regis*; see Ch. 1 note and Exon. Notes to Ch. 24.

24,1   BRICTWARD THE PRIEST. Probably the same man as Brictward the priest who in 1086 held the church of Bedwyn in DB Wilts. 1,23j.

24,4   REINBALD THE PRIEST. Reinbald, or Regenbald, was also called Reinbald of Cirencester (DB Berks. Ch. 61; and in 1130 Alfred of Lincoln paid 60 silver marks to have the manor of Pulham 'from the Honour of Cirencester', Pipe Roll 1130 p. 16), of which church he was dean or provost (Leland *Itinerary* i p. 128). Reinbald was probably also the first chancellor of England (see DB Herefords. 1,46 for this title) and held land in Somerset, Wilts., Glos., Herefords., Berks. and Bucks. See Round FE p. 421 ff; *Regesta* i pp. xiii, xv; W. H. Stevenson in EHR xi (1896) p. 731 note.
PULHAM. This land can be identified in the Tax Return for Buckland Hundred (xxxvi) and is probably a separate village from 36,4 (see note) which is in *Hunesberga* Hundred (xxv). It is possibly West Pulham, Hutchins iii p. 735. In FA ii p. 42 the land is held by the Abbot of Cirencester.
LORDSHIP; ... ; the gap of about 11 letters' width in the MS was presumably left for details of the ploughs in lordship. Cf. 1,26 note.

24,5   THE DEACON. In the MS *diacon'* is only partially visible, due to the parchment's being scraped rather messily here, perhaps as a result of ink being spilt.
'CERNE'. It appears that this 3-hide holding is needed to complete the Tax Return total for 'Stone' Hundred (ix). If so, it will have lain on the upper reaches of the river and may have been at Godmanstone (GR SY 6697); so Eyton *Dorset* pp. 133-134 although he included it in Modbury Hundred (11,1). The 3 hides with the 22 hides of Cerne Abbas (11,1) will have made a 25-hide unit.
THERE IS A GAP of about 13 lines after this entry, presumably left for further details of land held in alms to be added when and if available.

Ch. 25   COUNT ALAN. Count of Brittany and Earl of Richmond; married to Constance, King William's daughter. He held much land in the north, also in Cambs., Herts., Hants., Northants., Notts., etc.

25,1   DEWLISH. It can be identified in the Tax Return for Puddletown Hundred (viii), but was later sometimes included in Whiteway (15) as explained in FA ii p. 16.
BRICTRIC. Probably Brictric son of Algar because Dewlish was later part of the Honour of Gloucester (Fees p. 93) and Brictric's lands formed the nucleus of that Honour; VCH iii p. 31. Also Count Alan had been a protégé of Queen Matilda who had possession of most of Brictric's lands (see 1,17 note).

Ch. 26   COUNT OF MORTAIN. Robert, half-brother of King William and younger brother of Bishop Odo of Bayeux. He held more land in England than any other follower of King William (see Freeman iv p. 762), especially in Cornwall and other south-west counties. According to the summary of his fief in Dorset, Devon, Cornwall and Wiltshire in Exon. 531 a 2 he held 623 manors. He was the greatest lay landholder in Dorset after the King. He was responsible for the 'removal' of numerous parts of manors, illegally in many cases, and for the cessation of payment of various customary dues owed to royal manors in Somerset and Devon. In the 'exchanges' he made of manors he invariably got the better bargain (e.g. 56,36 and E 1). After rebelling against William Rufus in 1088, he was reconciled and died in 1091. When his fief escheated to the King, many of his tenants became tenants-in-chief, their lands forming separate baronies. Later fees or holdings are described as of Morton, Montague or Montacute; among principal later holders are the Beauchamps. Mortain is in the département of Manche, France.

26,1   (BUCKHORN) WESTON. This *Westone* is held as a Mortain fee in Gillingham Hundred (4) in Fees p. 91 and as *Bokeres Westone* in FA ii pp. 21, 32.
JOINTLY. *in parag(io)* here and elsewhere in DB Dorset, *pariter* in Exon., a form of land tenure whereby a man's estate was not physically divided among his heirs, often his children (as probably in 26,37 and 30,3), but enjoyed equally by them, with one heir being responsible to the lord and King for the services due from the land and the other heirs being answerable only to the first, thus preserving the unity of the manor. See VCH iii pp. 34-35 on the advantages of this type of tenure. Sometimes, as in Devon 16,7, it was not a man's sons or daughters who shared the manor. Moreover, there are numerous cases of just one person, often a thane, holding land 'jointly' (e.g. 55,42;44-46), for which see DB Somerset Exon. Notes Introduction p. 310 and DB Devon General Notes 1,15. In Dorset there are no occurrences of the phrase in the accounts of the King's land or of church land (though it appears there regularly in Devon), but some 27 occurrences thereafter, mostly in Chs. 26 and 55. The words *in parag'* are interlined in all but 4 cases

(where they are written at the end of a line, perhaps later; see 27,6 note). There is some evidence to suggest that they were added when the Exchequer scribe checked over the Exon. MS where the phrase appears more frequently than in DB; see Devon General Notes 15,47-52. The importance of knowing the way in which a manor was held in 1066 cannot be stressed too much when so many lands were acquired unlawfully: perhaps the reason why the phrase occurs so often in the fiefs of the two greatest land-thieves in Dorset — the Count of Mortain (Ch. 26) and Hugh son of Grip (Ch. 55). The phrases *pariter / libere / poterat ire ad quemlibet dominum / pro uno manerio / pro duobus maneriis* appear to be interchangeable in DB and Exon. (see Devon General Notes 1,15 for examples) and in Dorset all but two occurrences of *libere* and some of *pro duobus maneriis* are interlineations or marginal insertions, again suggesting the result of a check. Because so many of those who held 'jointly' are described as 'thanes' who were by their position free to choose whichever lord they would, it would seem that joint tenure implied free tenure and the land thus held possibly then having the status of a *manerium*, rather than a mere piece of land.

26,2   NYLAND. The land can be identified in the Tax Return for Gillingham Hundred (xxvii). DROGO. Drogo of Montacute: he gave 2 hides in Nyland to Shaftesbury Abbey when his daughter became a nun there; see the confirmation charter of 1121-2 in *Regesta* ii pp. 346-7 no. CLV (Calendar No. 1347).

26,3   HANFORD. It lay in Farrington Hundred in 1086 (Tax Return xxxv). Hanford in Gillingham Hundred (4) is a Mortain fee in Fees p. 91; see FA ii p. 22. In Fees p. 425 there is a Mortain fee at *Lathirton'* [Lazerton, see 30,3 and 56,32 notes] which may have been part of this land.

26,4   (CHILD) OKEFORD. *Chyldakford* is a Mortain fee in Gillingham Hundred (4) in FA ii pp. 22, 33. This land can be identified in the Tax Return for Farrington Hundred (xxxv). The 2 mills shared with the King (1,7; see next note) support the identification. HALF OF 2 MILLS WHICH PAYS 10s. *Redd'* here must have as its subject *medietas*, as, according to Exon., the King has the other half of the value of the 2 mills at 20s recorded in 1,7.

26,5;   'CERNE'. The order of DB suggests a group of holdings named from the river Cerne and
8-11   lying in St. George Hundred (20). Most of 26,8-11 can certainly be identified in the Tax Return for Dorchester (St. George) Hundred (xxxii). Mortain fees are later found at *Fosardeston'* [Forston] in Fees p. 425, held of the Honour of Odcombe, and in FA ii p. 18; at *Haringston'* [Herrison], held by Philip *Hareng* in Fees p. 425, see FA ii p. 18; and at *Pulleinston'* [Pulston], held by John *Pulein* in Fees p. 424, see FA ii pp. 17, 31. In RBE ii p. 218 Bernard *Pullus* holds *Cerna Pulli* from the Honour of Montacute in St. George Hundred. The Honour of Odcombe is formed later around the DB holdings of Ansger; thus either 26,8 or 26,11 will have been at Forston. In MC, among the grants by Count William of Mortain, son of Count Robert, frequent mention is made of 'the three *Cernels*', perhaps implying these three villages; see *Regesta* i pp. 180-181, nos. 1367-8 and 26,44 note. But there was also a Mortain interest in *Wolfeton* [Wolfeton in Charminster parish (1,4 note), now represented by Wolfeton Clump GR SY 6995, Wolfeton House SY 6792 and Wolfeton Eweleaze SY 6893] held from Cecilia *de Bello Campo* in FA ii p. 31 (see 26,6;12 note); also at *Cherleton* [Charlton in Charminster parish (1,4 note), GR SY 6895], where two Mortain fees are held in Fees p. 752; in FA ii p. 18 *Cherleton's* tax is paid with Herrison and it is held in FA ii p. 31 from Robert *Martin* who also holds Pulston.

26,6;   BHOMPSTON. DB *Frome*. The two holdings together form a 5-hide unit and may well
12   have involved several villages along the Frome river. In later times there was Mortain land at Bhompston in Stinsford parish in St. George Hundred (20), earlier *Frome Bonevileston* (FA ii p. 17), a half fee held by John *de Wytefeld* from John *Quintin* and he from John *de Bello Campo* in FA ii p. 17; in FA ii p. 31 it is held under Glastonbury Abbey. It is held as *Frome* by Philip *Quintyn* from Robert *de Bello Campo* in Fees p. 1468; see Cal. Inq. PM vol. ii (Ed. I) no. 609 and vol. viii (Ed. III) no. 470. The larger of these 'Frome' holdings (26,6) seems later to have been known as *Styntesford* [Stinsford] held in FA ii p. 31 as 1 fee by Walter *de Haddon* from Cecilia *de Bello Campo* (and by him from Glastonbury); see Cal. Inq. PM vol. vii (Ed. III) no. 431 and vol. viii (Ed. III) no. 470. In DB Stinsford is a name applied to two other holdings (52,1. 56,40). Neither 26,6 nor 26,12 can be identified in any Tax Return, but they fall in a group of Cullifordtree (26) and St. George (20) Hundred places in the order of the text.

26,7   STAFFORD. DB *Stanford*. In a group of Dorchester (St. George) Hundred places (20). The DB holdings are probably represented by the modern West Stafford parish (now in

Cullifordtree Hundred 26). 'East Stafford' is a lost place in West Knighton parish, EPNS i p. 209. See notes to 27,4-5 and 55,8.

ROBERT. Perhaps Robert son of Ivo, a sub-tenant of the Count of Mortain in several of his Somerset manors and his constable (possibly of Montacute Castle, see VCH Som. i p. 427 and Eyton *Somerset* i p. 97). The Tax Return for Cullifordtree Hundred (xxxvii) states that the King did not have tax from ½ hide he held from the Count. However, the holding could be 'Wey' (26,16).

26,8-11 'CERNE'. See 26,5 note.

26,8 FREELY. See 26,1 note on the correspondence between *libere* and *in paragio* etc.

26,9 RALPH. Probably Ralph the Clerk, from whom the King did not have tax from the 2 hides 1 virgate he held from the Count in the Tax Return for Dorchester Hundred (xxxii). 2 FRENCHMEN WHO SERVE. *Seruientes francig*; similarly in DB Worcs. 8,11. *Seruientes* is probably being used in the sense of *faciebant seruitium* 'did service' (see Worcs. 8,9b;14), rather than implying land held by serjeanty, on which see DB Leics. 13,63 note. But see Worcs. 10,16 note.
MEADOW, 3 ACRES. Originally written *.ii. ac̄*, but corrected to *iii* by the addition of a *i* at the beginning, covering the original dot.

26,12 BRETEL. Bretel here and elsewhere in this chapter may be Bretel of St. Clair (see OEB p. 112): in the Tax Return for the Somerset Hundred of Bulstone (Exon. 526 b 1) the King did not have tax on ½ hide held by *Britellus de sancto claro*, which holding can be identified with Somerset 19,15, Swell held by Bretel from the Count of Mortain. A Bretel was also the Count's sub-tenant on many of his manors in Somerset and Devon. See 26,28 note below.
BHOMPSTON. See 26,6 note.

26,13 'WINTERBORNE'. The nine Mortain 'Winterbornes' (26,13;18-19;30-31;33-34;36;48) are difficult to identify. Only one (26,36) can be found with certainty in a Tax Return, that for Combsditch (xvi). In the case of the others, the order of entries gives some indication. Thus 26,13;18-19 seem to fall in a group of St. George (20) or Cullifordtree Hundred (26) places, and therefore lie on the South Winterborne river; 26,30-31;33-34 are probably in a group of Combsditch Hundred (16) places and thus on the eastern Winterborne, while 26,48 falls before Bestwall which is identifiable in the Tax Return for Bere Hundred (xv) and probably also lay in that Hundred (22).
In the early feudal documents, Mortain or Beauchamp lands are found in St. George Hundred (20) at *Wynterborn Seint Martyn* [Martinstown, see 55,1 note] a holding which also included *La Rewe* [Rew GR SY 6389], Cal. Inq. PM vol. ii (Ed. I) no. 481, vol. viii (Ed. III) no. 470, vol. ix (Ed. III) no. 190. In the last two cases, the holder is John *de Bello Campo* and it is to the Beauchamps of Hatch Beauchamp (in Somerset) that the lands of Robert (if he is Robert the Constable) descend. This probably represents Robert's 1 hide of 26,13.
In Cullifordtree Hundred (26) Mortain lands lay at Winterborne *Germain* [Winterborne Farringdon in Winterborne Came] and at Winterborne *Harang* [Winterborne Herringston also called Winterborne *Beauchamp*] both held by the Beauchamp family in Fees p. 751, FA ii pp. 19-20, Cal. Inq. PM (Ed.I) vol. ii no. 609, vol. viii (Ed. III) no. 470; see EPNS i pp. 262, 265 and Hutchins ii p. 521. In Fees p. 1468, a list of the lands of Robert *de Bello Campo*, Robert *Blaunch'* holds one-third fee in *South' Wynterburne* in Dorset, and Philip *Germain* holds 1 fee in the same vill, that is probably in Winterborne *Germain* or Farringdon. These lands are likely to account for 26,18-19, held by Robert.
In Combsditch Hundred (16) are found Winterborne Clenston (*Clencheston*) held from John *de Bello Campo*, and Anderson (Winterborne *Fyhasse*), FA ii p. 29, the latter held by William *de Stokes* (see 26,52 note) from the heirs of John *de Burgo*, a frequent Mortain or Beauchamp tenant; see Cal. Inq. PM vol. iii (Ed. I) nos. 142-3 and Hutchins i p. 160. Some or all of the land in Winterborne Clenston may have been in 'Winterborne Phelpston' [a lost place in this parish, EPNS ii p. 80], possibly named from Philip, son of William *de Wynterburne*, who holds in Fees p. 1469 from Robert *de Beauchamp*. Some may also have been at *Winterborn Nichole* ['Winterborne Nicholston', EPNS ii p. 79], held by John *de Bello Campo* in Cal. Inq. PM vol. ii (Ed. I) no. 609 and vol. viii (Ed. III) no. 470. Also in Combsditch Hundred there was Mortain land at *Winterborn Wytchurche* [Winterborne Whitechurch] and at *Wynterborn Watecombe* [Whatcombe in Winterborne Whitechurch, GR ST 8301, EPNS ii p. 84], FA p. 44 and Cal. Inq. PM vol. viii (Ed. III) no. 470. These will account for the lands of 26,30-31;33-34, those of 26,30-31 held by Robert in 1086 being no doubt the lands later held by the Beauchamps.
Finally, in Fees p. 751 Winterborne *Musters* [Muston] in Bere Hundred (22) is held

from Robert *de Bello Campo* and may account for 26,48 (see 40,4 note). In Fees p. 1468 it is held from Robert *de Beauchamp* by William *de Wytefeld* and from him by William *de Monasterio* (*Moutiers* or *Musters*) as *Est Wynterburne juxta Warham*. Further, in FA ii p. 43, the Abbess of Tarrant holds *Turbervileston* [Winterborne Muston]; she likewise holds Gussage (26,44), Hanford (26,3) and Studland (26,61) from Mortain. Winterborne Muston with the holdings of 55,12 and 57,10 forms a five-hide unit.

26,14 'WEY'. See 1,22 and Introductory Note 2 on Rivers. The Mortain lands certainly included
-16 *Waye Hamondevill* [Upwey, EPNS i p. 246] in Cal. Inq. PM vol. viii (Ed. III) no. 470 and *Waywestbrok* [now Westbrook in Upwey, GR SY 6684; FA ii p. 38] and *Waye Rewald* ['Rowaldsway' lost in Broadwey, FA ii p. 19; see EPNS i p. 200]. The latter holding is identified by Hutchins ii p. 479 and Taylor (p. 215) with Causeway farm (GR SY 6581). The fact that one of the sub-tenants of 'Rowaldsway' in FA ii p. 19 is Geoffrey *de Wermewell* may suggest that both 'Wey' and Warmwell (26,57) had the same 1086 holders: a Robert holds both Warmwell and 'Wey' 26,16. William *Cruket*, who is a later Mortain tenant at Holwell (26,17), may have named 'Creketway' in Broadwey, see FA ii p. 38 and EPNS i p. 200. The salt-houses of 26,15 may suggest a coastal or tidal site such as Weymouth, but see Hutchins ii p. 420.

26,15 HOLDS. In the MS *teñ* instead of the usual *teñ'* which Farley prints, presumably in correction.
SALT—HOUSES. *Salinae* comprehend all kinds of salt workings from coastal pans, as here, to the boilers of Worcestershire and Cheshire, with their associated sheds and buildings. 'Salt-house' is the most comprehensive term. See DB Worcs. 1,3a note on salt extraction. In Dorset there were three areas of salt production: the Isle of Purbeck, the mouth of the Wey and Lyme Regis; see VCH iii pp. 22–23. The only other mention of salt-houses in Dorset is 26,61 where the Count has 32 at Studland. Salt-workers are mentioned at 8,6. 12,13. 26,67. 57,14.

26,16 ROBERT. See 26,7 note.
'WEY'. See 26,7 second note.

26,17 HOLWELL. *Halwell* or *Hallewolle* is a Mortain land held by William *Cruket* in Cullifordtree Hundred (26); FA ii pp. 19, 38, 57.

26,18 'WINTERBORNE'. On the South Winterborne river probably in Cullifordtree Hundred
-19 (26); see 26,13 note.

26,19 1½ PLOUGHS, WHICH ARE THERE. ... *quae ibi sunt*; normally the singular is used with '1½' in DB, as in 3,4 and 26,40 (see note to latter) and 27,2. The plural, however, also occurs in 26,39;65 and 50,1.

26,20 ABBEY OF MARMOUTIER. In Tours in the département of Indre-et-Loire, France. It was founded in the 4th century by St. Martin. Its importance gained it the name of 'the greater monastery' (*majoris monasterii*, genitive). Cf. the place-name Moutiers; 11,2 note.
PIDDLEHINTON 5 HIDES ... LORDSHIP. It had belonged to Matilda, Count Robert's wife, and was granted on her death and for her soul's sake by him and by King William c. 1082-84 to the Church of St. Mary, Mortain, which belonged to the monks of Marmoutier; Round CDF no. 1206 p. 435 (= *Regesta* i no. 204). See TE p. 184a and *Regesta* ii p. 32 no. 645. The grant is of 10 hides at *Pidele Hinctune*, of which only 4 hides are to pay tax, the remaining 6 hides being in lordship. This holding can also be identified in the Tax Return for Puddletown Hundred (viii), which states that the Abbot of Marmoutier has 5 hides 3 virgates in lordship from the land of the Countess of Mortain (Piddlehinton is his only holding in this Hundred). In FA ii p. 15 Piddlehinton, held by the Prior of Mortain, is *Hine Pudele* and is probably the same land as the 10 *cassati* at *Uppidelen* restored to Shaftesbury Abbey in 966 by King Edgar; VCH iii p. 43; see 19,14 note.

26,21 'PIDDLE'. These two holdings at *Pidele* appear to be needed to complete the Tax Return
-22 for Puddletown Hundred (viii), see VCH iii p. 130. There was later Mortain land at *Pideltun* (Puddletown, *Piretone* and *Pitretone* in DB) according to Fees pp. 93, 261, FA ii p. 15, but this appears to have been an exchange since in Fees p. 93 William *de Monte Acuto* is stated to hold a third of *Pideleton'* (the rest being 1,8) in exchange for the claim his predecessors had in *Huneton'* (Piddlehinton). The land belonging to the Count's fief in 1086 seems to have lain within the parishes of Piddlehinton and Puddletown. Thus in Fees p. 426 William *de Monte Acuto* holds in *Luveford*; and in FA ii p. 16 John *de Witefeld* and John *de Deverel* hold in *Pudele Loveford* from Simon of Montacute. This is 'Lovard', a lost place lying in both parishes, see EPNS i p. 318 and Taylor pp. 211–212. 'South Lovard' is probably to be identified with Higher Waterston (GR SY 7295). One of the holders of 'Lovard' in FA ii p. 35 is Richard *de Portes*. *Lytle Pydle* [Little Puddle] is also

held from him by Matilda *de Deverel* and *Musterston* [Muston farm GR SY 7295, in Piddlehinton, cf. Winterborne Muston 26,13 note] from him by Richard *de Musters* in FA ii p. 35. The Deverel family will also have held and named 'Combe Deverel', an alternative name for Little Puddle; see Fägersten p. 175; EPNS i p. 311. It is possible that Little Puddle and Muston were thus also Mortain lands, together with Druce farm in Puddletown (GR SY 7495) named perhaps from the later Drogo of Montacute (EPNS i p. 316).

26,21   1½ HIDES. In the MS and Farley *.i. hida 7 dim*ᵗ ; the facsimile fails to reproduce the 7 which is father faint.

WHICH PAYS. In the MS *redd*'; Farley has *edd*', undoubtedly a printing error as there is a space for a letter at the beginning of the line before *edd*'.

26,22   MEADOW. (1)½ ACRES. *ac*ᵗ *7 dimid*'; see 12,16 note.

26,23   COUNT HOLDS. There is a black ink blot over the *t* of *ten*ᵗ in the MS, identical to the one on the opposite folio (27,7 'held').

3½ VIRGATES. In the MS the *iii* has been corrected from *ii*.

26,24   ROBERT. Perhaps Robert son of Ivo (on whom see 26,7 note), from whom the King never had tax on 1 virgate he held from the Count in Charborough (Loosebarrow) Hundred (xviii).

MORDEN. Identifiable in the Tax Return for Charborough (Loosebarrow) Hundred (xviii). There was Mortain land at *West Mourden*, Cal. Inq. PM vol. viii (Ed. III) no. 470; Morden is a fee of Robert *de Bello Campo*, Fees p. 751 (see p. 1469). West Morden (see 41,5 note) was later a tithing in the post-Domesday Hundred of Rushmore, though in Morden parish; see Hutchins iii p. 511 and EPNS ii pp. 54, 58–59. East Morden seems to have been a part of Lytchett Matravers in 1086 (see 34,5 note), as well as a holding of Wulfric (56,13 note).

A MILL WHICH PAYS 6s 3d. Other mills at Morden are 41,5 (paying 45d) and 56,13 (part of a mill paying 11d).

26,25   SPETISBURY. The land can be identified in the Tax Return for Charborough Hundred (xviii).

COUNT HAS 1 VIRGATE. In the MS *una v*' in error for the accusative *unam* after *habet*; Farley does not correct this error (see 1,5 note).

26,26 -27   SYDLING. The 5-hide holding of 26,26 is probably 'Sydling Fifehead' (that is 'Five Hides'), a tithing in Sydling St. Nicholas parish, see Fägersten p. 202. The land will have included *Upseteling* [Upsydling GR ST 6201], a Mortain fee in Fees p. 425, held from the Honour of Odcombe to which Ansger's manors descended; see 12,1 note.

26,26   EDMER. Here and elsewhere in Dorset he is probably Edmer Ator who was one of the Count of Mortain's predecessors in Somerset and Devon and, as plain Edmer, in Cornwall. On the byname see DB Devon 15,12 General Note.

26,28   LITTLETON. Can be identified in the Tax Return for Combsditch Hundred (xvi). It was long in the parish of Langton Long Blandford in Pimperne Hundred, but since 1933 has been in Blandford St. Mary (Combsditch Hundred). It is, however, included in Combsditch Hundred (16) in FA ii p. 29 where Henry *de Lytleton* holds from John *de Sancto Claro*, probably a descendant of the 1086 holder, Bretel, who may thus be Bretel of St. Clair (see 26,12 note).

26,29   BLANDFORD (ST. MARY). DB *Blaneford, Bleneford*, probably represents variously Blandford St. Mary, Langton Long Blandford and Bryanston (EPNS ii p. 90). Blandford Forum, a further *Blaneford*, does not seem to be mentioned in DB, and was probably surveyed as part of Pimperne 1,5. Of the three other 'Blandfords', Blandford St. Mary lay in 1086 in Combsditch Hundred (16) (the holdings at 34,6. 49,1 and 56,14 being found in Tax Return xvi), and Langton Long Blandford lay in *Langeberga* (xxii), later Pimperne Hundred (9) (the holdings at 47,4 and 56,31). Bryanston (26,46 and 56,34 notes) lay in a third Tax Return Hundred, *Hunesberga* (xxv). Where the Tax Returns provide no clue, the Blandfords have to be identified from the order of the text or later evidence. In the case of the present entry this 'Blandford' seems to lie within a group of Combsditch Hundred places, begun by Littleton (26,28); it was later given to Clerkenwell priory, see Hassall and Hutchins i p. 163 and the Cartulary of St. Mary Clerkenwell (Camden 3rd Series vol. lxxi nos. 6, 9, 35, 37). There was also Mortain land at *Blaneford' Belet* (Langton Long Blandford) in Fees p. 752; held in FA ii pp. 27, 43 as *Langeton' Botyler* by Elizabeth *de Guldene* who holds Littleton (26,28) in FA ii p. 49; this is probably the entry at 26,37 which will have lain in *Langeberga* Hundred (xxii).

IT PAYS ... VALUE WAS. See 17,1 note.

26,30 -31; 33-34   'WINTERBORNE'. On the eastern Winterborne river, possibly in Combsditch Hundred (16); see 26,13 note.

26,32   RO(BERT) ... HIMSELF. In the MS *Ipse Ro.* has been written over an erasure and the *Ro.* is not absolutely clear, although 'Robert' is probably intended as the sub-tenant.

26,33   'WINTERBORNE'. See 26,30-31 note.
-34

26,33   HUBERT. Probably Hubert of St. Clair; see VCH iii p. 50.

26,34   IN 'WINTERBORNE'. In the MS *IN* is interlined with the *I* extended down to the line below, the normal method of indicating the position of an interlineation; Farley prints the *N* only as interlined, in error.

26,35   MELBURY. DB *Meleberie, Melesberie*, are now represented by Melbury Abbas in Sixpenny Handley Hundred (19,6 note) and by a separate group of three adjacent parishes — Melbury Osmond and Bubb in Yetminster Hundred (7) and Melbury Sampford in Tollerford Hundred (13). It has not been possible to identify all four DB entires (26,35. 32,2. 47,2. 56,17) with these three adjacent modern villages. All four DB holdings were in Yetminster Hundred in 1086 (Tax Return i), and if Melbury Sampford was among them it must later have been transferred to Tollerford Hundred. The holding at 47,2 can be confidently identified with Melbury Bubb and the Count of Mortain's land here with Melbury Osmond, given by his son William to Montacute Priory, see MC passim, TE p. 185a and VCH iii p. 86 note 49; Fägersten p. 226. Melbury Sampford is held in FA ii p. 35 by *Alda de Sanford* as *Mellbyry Turberevyle* from Hugh *Despensar*. The latter is a Mohun tenant at Winterborne Houghton (36,3; FA ii p. 27) and it is possible that Melbury Sampford was part of the Mohun holding of West Chelborough 36,8 and not separately accounted for in DB. Only Melbury Bubb and Melbury Osmond have been mapped and indexed.
2½ HIDES. The Tax Return for Yetminster Hundred (i) states that the King did not have tax from ½ hide held by Dodman from the Count of Mortain 'this year'. See VCH iii pp.117-8 on the dating of the Tax Returns.

26,36   'WINTERBORNE'. This 'Winterborne' can be identified in the Tax Return for Combsditch Hundred (xvi); see 26,13 note.

26,37   (LANGTON LONG) BLANDFORD. See 26,29 note.

26,38   MANNINGTON. The place can be identified in the Tax Return for *Canendona* Hundred (vii). It is later in Badbury Hundred (17).

26,39   HEMSWORTH. A Mortain fee in Fees p. 426; held from John *de Meriet* by John *de Cormayles* in Cranborne Hundred (6) in FA ii pp. 27, 46.

26,40   WITCHAMPTON. See 1,20 note and FA ii p. 29. It lay in Badbury Hundred (Tax Return vi) in 1086.
WOODLAND 1 FURLONG LONG AND 8 ACRES WIDE. *acras*, accusative of extent, as on several occasions (e.g. 5,1); however, the nominative appears in *una quarentina* and in numerous other instances. The number of different phrases used to describe the measurements of pasture, woodland etc. probably confused the scribe; for example, both the genitive *siluae* and the nominative *silua* are used in the phrase "woodland, *y* furlongs in both length and width". The accusative *acras* may, however, be the result of the DB scribe's copying of Exon.: in a great many Exon. entries all the details of population, livestock, pasture, woodland etc. are put in the accusative as the objects of *habet* (the subject being the holder of the manor).
ON WHICH HE HAS NEVER PAID TAX. On the 1 virgate and the third part of 1 virgate, rather than just on the one-third virgate (the singular *de qua* is normally used after 1 virgate and one-third virgate; but see 26,19 note): the Tax Return for Badbury Hundred (vi) states that the King never had tax from the third part of 1 hide which Picot holds from the Count of Mortain (Picot apparently holding before Hubert or being a sub-tenant, or a scribal error).

26,41   LODERS. The first of these holdings can be identified in the Tax Return for Godderthorn
-42   Hundred (x). In FA ii pp. 11, 34 two parts of *Lodres Luttone* in Godderthorn Hundred (18) [now Matravers in Loders parish, Fägersten p. 258] are Mortain fees, another part being derived from the land of the wife of Hugh, 55,24. See 1,13 note.

26,42   ALFRED. Probably Alfred the (Count's) Butler (*pincerna*) who is a sub-tenant of the Count of Mortain in Somerset (and perhaps Cornwall) and who in Dorset 15,1 holds part of Purse Caundle from Athelney Abbey, which the Count had given that Abbey in exchange for 'Bishopstone' (see E 1 below), where Alfred also held land. The Alfred in 26,62 is probably also Alfred the Butler.

26,43   KNOWLTON. Probably included Woodlands which has the same later descent; Hutchins iii p. 151. Woodlands is now the parish name.
IT PAID TAX. Or perhaps, in this case, 'he (Aelmer) paid tax (on the 2 hides)', as one would expect the plural *geldabant* referring to the *ii hid*, unless the scribe meant the singular *geldabat* to refer to the holding as a whole. See 1,14 note.

26,44 GUSSAGE. Three modern villages bear the name. Gussage St. Michael was an outlying part of Badbury Hundred (17), held in 1086 by Earl Aubrey and wrongly entered in the Wiltshire folios, see E 2 note below. Gussage St. Andrew was held by the Abbess of Shaftesbury (FA ii pp. 30, 39, 50) and was probably included by DB in the details of Handley (19,1). The present Mortain holding was Gussage All Saints, held as a Mortain fee in Fees p. 91 (see pp. 378, 752); see also MC no. 8 p. 124 and Hutchins iii p. 489. It is required by the Tax Return for Knowlton Hundred (xxiii). Portions of this holding were at *Boressen* [Bowerswain farm in Gussage All Saints, GR SU 0009; Fägersten p. 92, EPNS ii p. 279] held in FA ii p. 42 in Knowlton Hundred (10) by the Prior of Montacute; also *Hunecroft* and *Loverlay* ['Hunecroft' surviving only as a field name (EPNS ii p. 283) and Loverley GR SU 0008, both in this parish] confirmed on Montacute Priory by Henry I, *Regesta* ii pp. 180-181 nos. 1367-8.

26,45 WILLIAM HOLDS KNIGHTON ... 2½ HIDES. DB *Dervinestone*. William is probably William of Lestre (who as William *de Estra* in the Tax Return for Whitchurch Hundred (ii) holds from the Count land identifiable as Catherston Leweston; see 26,54 note): in 1212 (Fees p. 87) 2½ hides are held by Richard *de Estre* in *Knicteton'* in *Hundesburg'* Hundred, and in Fees p. 92 by Richard *de Atrio* in *Durewneston'*; (see Eyton *Dorset* p. 131; Fägersten p. 52; EPNS ii p. 93).

26,46 THESE ENTRIES are written in a smaller script and paler ink than the preceding ones;
-61 see 12,13 ff. note.

26,46 THE COUNT HIMSELF HOLDS. Repeated at the beginning of 26,46-52. BRYANSTON. DB *Blaneford*, see 26,29 note. This land is found in the Tax Return for *Hunesberga* Hundred (xxv) and is thus distinct from the two Blandfords; see EPNS ii p. 90 and Fägersten p. 51.

26,47 BROCKINGTON. DB *Brochemtune*. In Gussage All Saints parish; see EPNS ii p. 280. The holding can be identified in the Tax Return for *Albretesberga* Hundred (v) and is thus unlikely to be Brockhampton Green (VCH) in Buckland Newton.

26,48 'WINTERBORNE'. On the eastern Winterborne river, possibly in Bere Hundred (22), see 26,13 note.

26,49 BESTWALL. DB *Beastewelle* meaning '(place) to the east of the (town) wall' (EPNS i p. 158), the town being near Wareham. The holding can be located in the Tax Return for Bere Hundred (xv), though it is later in Winfrith Hundred (27); see 49,14 note. In FA ii p. 42 *Byestewall* is held by William *de Estok* in Barrow Hundred. The same man holds (East) Stoke 26,52.

26,50 LULWORTH. In Winfrith Hundred (Tax Return xxx). This land is included among fees
-51 of Robert *de Bello Campo* in Fees p. 751 and contained *Gatemerston* ['Gatemerston' GR SY 8481 in East Lulworth parish, see EPNS i p. 124] held from John *de Bello Campo* in FA ii p. 29; also *Sanctum Andream* and *Behylde Hywysche* [Saint Andrew's farm in West Lulworth, GR SY 8380, and Belhuish also in West Lulworth, GR SY 8282] held by Robert *filius Pagani* (Fitzpaine) in FA ii p. 29. In these last two the sub-tenant is William *de Stok* who holds Bestwall and East Stoke (26,49;52 notes); see Hutchins i p. 377. *Gatemershton* appears as a Mortain fee in Cal. Inq. PM vol. ii (Ed. I) no. 609 and vol. viii (Ed. III) no. 470; *Stokes St. Andrew* and *Bustewall* appear in Cal. Inq. PM vol. iii (Ed. I) nos. 142-3 concerning William *de Stokes*.

26,50 ALSI. DB *Alsi* represents OE *Aelfsige* or *Aethelsige*; see PNDB pp. 151-2. As with *Aluuardus* (3,1 note) safety indicates keeping to the base form. 4 SMALLHOLDERS ... The gap of about 11 letters' width left after this in the MS was presumably for their ploughs. See 1,26 note.

26,51 TRASWIN. *Trauuin'*, which occurs only here in DB, is either OG *Traswin* with AN loss of *s*, or a scribal error for *Frauuin'* 'Frawin'; PNDB pp. 388, 252. A 'Frawin' occurs four times as a TRE holder in DB Devon.

26,52 (EAST) STOKE. DB *Stoches*. In the order of the text, this place falls in a group of Winfrith and Hasler Hundred holdings (27-28) and is identified with East Stoke by Hutchins i p. 410, Eyton *Dorset* p. 142 and DG. VCH iii pp. 87, 142 identifies Stock Gaylard in Lydlinch but a Sherborne Hundred entry would not be expected at this point in the schedule. The location of West Stoke is uncertain, see EPNS i p. 145. In FA ii p. 9 East Stoke in Winfrith Hundred (27) is held by Robert *filius Pagani* who holds Wootton (26,63) from Mortain. The sub-tenant in FA, William *de Stok*, also holds Mortain land; see 26,49-50 notes; Hutchins i p. 410.

26,53 STOBOROUGH. In Hasler Hundred (Tax Return xxix).

26,54 CREECH. Now represented by the parish of East Creech and by Creech Grange and West Creech in Steeple parish. The form *Erlescrich* (1301), cited in Fägersten p. 133 and EPNS i

p. 90, may refer to the Count of Mortain. This holding falls in a group of Winfrith and Hasler Hundred places (27-28).

26,56 MORETON. In Winfrith Hundred (27). A Mortain fee, held with Hemsworth (26,39) and 'Winterborne' in Fees p. 426; see FA ii pp. 10, 30, 49.
6 VILLAGERS. In the MS the dot after the *vi* is written higher than usual, level with the top (rather than with the bottom) of the *i*; it is not an attempted correction to *vii*.

26,58 LODERS. This holding is found in the Tax Return for Eggardon Hundred (iv); see notes to 26,41-42 and 1,13.

26,59 HOOKE. In Eggardon Hundred (19); a Mortain fee in Fees p. 424 and FA ii pp. 2, 33, 53. The holder in Fees is William *de Lestre*, suggesting that the 1086 holder is the same William of Lestre who probably holds Knighton (26,45) and Catherston Leweston (26,64).

26,60 WOOL. DB *Welle*, which can be deduced from the Tax Return for Winfrith Hundred (xxx).

26,61 STUDLAND. In Rowbarrow Hundred (29). It is a Mortain fee in Fees p. 752; see RH i p. 101 and FA ii p. 44.
5 VILLAGERS AND 13 SMALLHOLDERS. The scribe may have omitted recording any ploughs they had, when he began a new folio for the rest of the entry; cf. 11,5 second note.
SALT-HOUSES. See 26,15 note.

26,62 ALFRED. See 26,42 note.
'STANTON (ST. GABRIEL)'. The name survives only as a parish and in St. Gabriel's House near the remains of the church.

26,63 WOOTTON (FITZPAINE). A Mortain fee held by Robert *filius Pagani* in Whitchurch Hundred (11), FA ii p. 38; see FA ii p.45. It is possible that one of the two Mortain holdings (26,63;69) was at *Merscwode* [Marshwood GR SY 3899] held by John *de Maundevile* in FA ii p. 38. Marshwood was *caput* of the Mandeville Barony (see VCH Devon i p. 563 ff. and Hutchins ii p. 260). The same John holds Buckhorn Weston (26,1) from Mortain in FA ii p. 32. Marshwood may equally have been an outlier of Chideock (1,2), with which it is associated in Cal. PM vol. ii (Ed. I) no. 154.

26,64 CATHERSTON (LEWESTON). DB *Cerneli*. The name 'Cerne' applies to the modern rivers Cerne and Char (see Introductory Note 2 on 'Rivers'). The Tax Return for Whitchurch Hundred (ii) records that the King never had tax 'from 1 hide which William *de Estra* [of Lestre, département of Eure, France; OEB pp. 94-5], holds from the Count of Mortain — half this hide belongs to the King's revenue'. This clearly refers to this entry and locates it on the river Char. It is identified by Eyton *Dorset* pp. 141-2 with Catherston Leweston, an identification not mentioned by Fägersten p. 284. Cerne Abbey holds it in FA ii p. 38 and it must be the same as 'Cerne' held in Fees p. 92 by Richard *de Altrio*, a descendant of William of Lestre; see VCH iii p. 60. The same man holds *Durewneston'* [Knighton 26,45] also held by William in 1086. In FA ii p. 45 *Cardeston Leuston* is held by John *de Pavely*, who is a Mortain tenant at Hooke (26,59) in FA ii p. 2; see Fees p. 426. Hooke was also held by William of Lestre in 1086.
(PART) OF THE LORDSHIP REVENUE OF 'CERNE'. In the Tax Return for Whitchurch Hundred (ii) this ½ hide is stated to be *de firma regis*. In Domesday, however, the King holds no manor of 'Cerne' and if the Tax Return is correct, the King may have been holding land belonging to Cerne Abbey, temporarily alienated, as was some of the land of Glastonbury Abbey (8,1 note). This may explain why Cerne Abbey holds the land in FA ii p. 38, it having been restored (see previous note).

26,66 DROGO. Probably Drogo of Montacute; see 26,2 note.
TOLLER (WHELME). The holding can be identified in the Tax Return for Beaminster Hundred (xii) and thus represents Toller Whelme, up river and in a different Hundred from Toller Fratrum and Toller Porcorum (40,9 note). The name is that of the river, Whelme being OE *ǣwielm* 'river-spring'. In Fees p. 426 William *de Monte Acuto* renders for 1 fee in *Tore* and *Luveford*, that is Toller and 'Lovard' (26,21-22 note).

26,67 CHARMOUTH. DB *Cernemude*, 'mouth of the (river) Cerne', now the Char, see 26,64 note and Introductory Note 2 on 'Rivers'. The land lay in Whitchurch Hundred (11) and was held from Robert *de Bello Campo* in Fees p. 751; see Fees pp. 94, 1468.

26,68 SHILVINGHAMPTON. A Mortain fee in Fees p. 426; it can be identified in the Tax Return for Uggescombe Hundred (iii).

26,69 WOOTTON (FITZPAINE). See 26,63 note.

26,70 (STOURTON) CAUNDLE. There are now four parishes representing DB *Candel*: Stourton Caundle (earlier Caundle Haddon) in Brownshall Hundred (2) and Purse Caundle, Caundle Marsh and Bishops Caundle all in Sherborne Hundred (1). The exact relation of these parishes to the nine DB entries is not entirely clear. Bishops Caundle and Caundle Marsh were probably accounted for in the 43 hides of Sherborne (2,6), since the Bishop of

Salisbury holds them in FA ii p. 4. Purse Caundle is the land held by Athelney Abbey (15,1) and probably also the 2½ virgates of 56,55 which were in Sherborne Hundred in 1086, although some of Purse Caundle may have been in Brownshall Hundred (Tax Return xxviii). The remaining Caundles have been provisionally assigned to Stourton Caundle, of which Caundle Wake was a hamlet (FA ii p. 40 Caundle *Bevin*; Fägersten pp. 211-212) before being absorbed by Bishops Caundle. In FA ii p. 40 Caundle Haddon is divided between 5 holders and thus in 1316 still seemed to preserve the mixed ownership of DB. Of these Caundle holdings those of 26,70. 38,2. 54,2 and 56,54 are identifiable in the Tax Return for Brownshall Hundred.

26,71   AELFEVA. OE *Aelfgifu*, feminine.

Ch. 27   EARL HUGH. Hugh of Avranches (département of Manche, France), nephew of King William; Earl of Chester 1071/77 to 1101. His daughter Matilda married Count Robert of Mortain and his sister Count William of Eu. His lands later form the Honour of Chester; on which see W. Farrer *Honours and Knights' Fees*, vol. ii, London 1924, pp. 284-287.

27,1   FIFEHEAD (MAGDALEN). Granted to the Canons of St. Augustine's, Bristol, by Robert fitz Harding, probably grandson of Ednoth the Staller, a gift confirmed by Earl Ranulf of Chester, Mon. Ang. vi p. 366; see FA ii pp. 22, 40. There is a confirmation by John (then Count of Mortain, later King) in R. B. Patterson *Earldom of Gloucester Charters*, Oxford 1973 p. 49, no. 31.

27,1-2   ALNOTH. Alnoth here and in 27,8-11 and Ednoth in 27,3-4;6 are probably one man — Alnoth (or Ednoth) the Constable who was Earl Hugh's predecessor in other counties as well. He was killed in battle against Earl Harold's sons in 1067. See DB Somerset General Notes 18,1 and 39,1.

27,2   WILLIAM HOLDS FROM THE EARL. Repeated at the beginning of 27,2-7. Here and elsewhere in this chapter William is probably William Malbank, a sub-tenant of Earl Hugh in other counties. Clifton Maybank (27,6) is named after him. See also 27,10 note.
ALNOTH HELD ... THROUGH EARL HAROLD. *Elnod tenuit* ... *per Heraldum*; the *per* implies that this was not a normal sub-tenancy: it would appear that Earl Harold obtained the manor illegally and gave it to Alnoth.
LAND FOR 1½ PLOUGHS, WHICH ARE THERE. ... *quae ibi est*, singular; see 26,19 note.

27,4-5   MAYNE. There are now three places, Broadmayne (GR SY 7286), Fryer Mayne (GR SY 7386) and Little Mayne (GR SY 7287), the first a detached parish of St. George Hundred (20) within Cullifordtree Hundred (26), the last two a part of West Knighton parish, Cullifordtree Hundred. The exact relation of the DB holdings to these is unclear, though it is likely that some of the land lay in 'Chilbury' Hundred in 1086 (Tax Return xxxi, part of the later Winfrith Hundred (27)). One of the DB lands was undoubtedly Little Mayne, earlier Mayne *Syrard* named from Sirard to whom it descended from the Earls of Chester and who gave it to St. Werburgh's Abbey, Chester (see FA ii pp. 19-20, Farrer cited in Ch. 27 note, Fägersten pp. 154-155 and EPNS i p. 208). The other may well have been Fryer Mayne, earlier *Mayne Ospitalis* (FA ii pp. 18, 20), held by the Knights Hospitalers. This seems to have had dependencies at *Stafford Ospitalis* ['East Stafford' in West Knighton parish coupled with Mayne in LSR p. 73, see EPNS i p. 209 and 26,7 note] and at *Waye* or *Westebroke Ospitalis* [Westbrook in Upwey, earlier *Weywestbrok*, GR SY 6684, see EPNS i p. 248 and 26,14-16 note]; see VCH ii pp. 90-91. Broadmayne is held at *Mayne Martel* in St. George Hundred (20) in FA ii pp. 31, 51 by Peter son of Reginald and Reginald son of Peter from John son of Peter or John *de Vyvonia*. Both the names of the holders and the fact that Broadmayne is a detachment of St. George Hundred suggest a different origin for this holding, which may have been part of the royal manor of Dorchester (1,4) in 1086; in Cal. Inq. PM vol. vi (Ed. II) no. 724, it is associated with *Hyneton* (1,31), *Mapoudre* (1,8), *Mapelerton* (Mapperton) and *Wolverton* (1,4 note).

27,6   CLIFTON (MAYBANK). In Yetminster Hundred; see 27,2 note.
TRILL. Lying to the east of the Wriggle river, tributary of the Yeo which divided Sherborne Hundred from Yetminster Hundred. It had belonged to Sherborne Abbey (Hutchins iv p. 431) and clearly had been unlawfully joined to Clifton. *Clifton* and *Tryll* are held in FA ii p. 41 in Yetminster Hundred by Philip *Maubank*.
JOINTLY. In the MS *in parag[h]* written into the right margin in darker ink, perhaps later, the first,[4] being faint and perhaps intended to be erased, as it is superfluous. Farley prints *in parag[h]* in correction (see 1,5 note).

27,7   HELD. An ink blot in the MS covers the *u* and part of the second *e* of *tenuēr*; see 26,23 note.

27,9   (SOUTH) PERROTT. North Perrott is in Somerset, held in 1086 by the Count of Mortain (DB Somerset 19,45).

ALNOTH BOUGHT THIS MANOR FOR HIS LIFETIME ONLY. In other words he purchased the lease of South Perrott for his own life only. Also in 27,10.
BISHOP ALFWOLD. Of Sherborne; see 2,6 note.
RESTORED TO THE CHURCH. Neither this manor nor Catsley (27,10) appears to have been restored to Sherborne.

27,10   1 VIRGATE ... AFTER 1066. Entered in the right margin with no transposition signs to indicate its correct position in the text. The Tax Return for Beaminster Hundred (xii) states that the King never had tax from 1 virgate which William Malbank (*Malbeenc*) holds from Earl Hugh. Cf. 55,16 (Exon. additions) and also DB Devon 19,6 where ½ virgate has been concealed with the result that the King has no tax from it.

Ch. 28   ROGER OF BEAUMONT. Roger, who also held land in Glos. (Ch. 40), appears to have been an old man by the time of Domesday Book. About 1094-1095 he entered the monastery of St. Pierre, at Préaux, which his father Humphrey of Vieilles had founded *c*. 1034. He died some years later; Orderic Vitalis ii p. 14 and iii pp. 426-7. Roger's son Robert inherited the title of the Count of Meulan through his mother Adeline and was a tenant-in-chief in Northants., Warwicks. and Leics. Another son, Henry, became Earl of Warwick *c*. 1089. Roger of Beaumont's lands passed to his son Count Robert of Meulan, then to Waleran (also Count of Meulan), and thence to his grand-daughter Mabel, wife of William of Redvers, Earl of Devon. Beaumont is most probably Beaumont-le-Roger in the département of Eure, France; OEB p. 71.

28,1   STOUR. DB *Stur*. The land was at Stour Provost in Gillingham Hundred (4), a corruption of Stour *Pratellorum* or *Préaux* from the Abbey of St. Léger of Préaux in Normandy (founded, like its twin monastery of St. Pierre, by Roger's father; see Ch. 28 note). Although there is no mention of the grant in DB, the Tax Return for Gillingham Hundred (xxvii) records 3½ hides of lordship land for the Abbess of Préaux and a further 3½ hides on which no tax has been paid, thus accounting for the 7 hides of the DB holding. See VCH iii pp. 37, 141 and Fägersten p. 17. In FA ii p. 22 the Abbess of Préaux holds *Sture Pratell(is)* from the Earl of Leicester; see TE p. 177a.

28,2   ROGER ALSO HOLDS. Repeated at the beginning of 28,2-7.
STURMINSTER (MARSHALL). Held by the Earl Marshall from the Count of Meulan in Fees p. 90; see VCH iii p. 55. The tithes were given in a charter of *c*. 1080 to the Abbey of Préaux by Robert, Count of Meulan, and Henry, Earl of Warwick, the sons of Roger of Beaumont; *Regesta* i no. 130; see Round CDF p. 85 nos. 251-2. The land is found in the Tax Return for Cogdean Hundred (xvii); see FA ii pp. 60-61 and 1,5 note above.
ARCHBISHOP STIGAND. Stigand was Bishop of Elmham (East Anglia) in 1043, then 1044-47, before becoming Bishop of Winchester in 1047, which see he held with the Archbishopric of Canterbury from 1052 until he was deposed in 1070. He died in 1072. See R. R. Darlington in EHR li (1936) p. 420 on Stigand's status as Archbishop of Canterbury.
VALUE WHEN HE ACQUIRED IT. Exon. regularly gives the former value of a manor as 'when acquired' by the 1086 holder, but this was usually changed to 'Value was' or 'Formerly' in Exchequer DB. Here and in 31,2 and 47,7 the Exchequer scribe may have copied Exon. too closely; however, this was also the case in a number of entries in DB Somerset and Devon. See 47,7 last note.

28,3-5   CREECH; STEEPLE; (CHURCH) KNOWLE. These places can be accounted for in the Tax Return for Hasler Hundred (xxix). In Fees p. 89 in Hasler Hundred (28), Geoffrey de Nevile holds *Knolle, Stupel* and *Crihz* as Gloucester fees, formerly held by Robert de Tebovill'. *Cnolle* and *Stypele* are also held of the Earl of Gloucester in FA ii p. 23; see Cal. Inq. PM vol. i (Henry III) no. 530 and Hutchins i p. 597.

28,5   (CHURCH) KNOWLE. Identified by DG with Lutton Gwyle; but see EPNS i p. 87.

28,6-7   AFFLINGTON. Now in Rowbarrow Hundred (29). In 1086 it was divided between Rowbarrow (the holding at 28,6-7 in Tax Return xix for Ailwood Hundred) and Hasler (28) (41,1 and 57,20 in the Tax Return for Hasler Hundred xxix). The entry at 37,7 cannot be identified in a Tax Return, but is sandwiched between two Hasler Hundred places. Afflington is named after *Alfrun*, the TRE holder of 28,6; Fägersten p. 117 and EPNS i p. 7.

28,6   2 VILLAGERS AND 2 SMALLHOLDERS. In the MS *ii uittis 7 ii bord'*; Farley omits the 7 in error.

Ch. 29   ROGER OF COURSEULLES. Also known as Roger Whiting; OEB p. 11. Courseulles-sur-Mer is in the département of Calvados, France.

29,1   CORTON. In Uggescombe Hundred (25); see FA ii pp. 6, 34, 53.

Ch. 30 ROBERT SON OF GERALD. For the descent of his lands see F. A. Cazel Jnr. *Norman and Wessex Charters of the Roumare Family* in P. M. Barnes and C. F. Slade *A Medieval Miscellany for Doris Mary Stenton*, Pipe Roll Society lxxvi (new series xxxvi for 1960), London 1962, pp. 77–88.

30,1 CORFE (MULLEN). Required by the Tax Return for Cogdean Hundred (xvii). The added name is from OFr *molin*, Latin *molendinum* (Mod.Fr *moulin*) 'mill' and perhaps refers to the valuable mill here in 1086. See EPNS ii p. 15. Later there were two manors here, *Corf Molyn* and *Corf Huberd*, held respectively by Henry *de Herdynton* and Hubert *La Veylle* as small Mortain fees in FA ii p. 28; see Fees p. 90.

WADA. Perhaps Wada son of Aethelgyth (*Wada aegelgethe sunu*); see PNDB p. 407 no. 2.

30,2 LEIGH. In Colehill parish. The identification is not secure, although the order of DB makes it not improbable; see Fägersten p. 79 and EPNS ii p. 137.

3 VILLAGERS HAVE IT THERE. The plough, see fourth note under 3,14.

5 'RODS'. See 11,6 note.

30,3 RANSTON. DB *Iwerne*. Iwerne is a river name, applied in DB to five settlements on its banks. Of these, Iwerne Minster (*Euneminstre* 19,7) is separately identified by DB and the identifications of Iwerne Courtney (42,1) and Iwerne Stepleton (36,9) rest on firm evidence. Of the remaining 'Iwernes', the land at 56,32 is identifiable in the Tax Return for Pimperne Hundred (xxvi) and it is probable that the present holding was there as well since it is entered at the wrong point in the chapter for a Gillingham (4) or Handley (5) Hundred place. The lands of 30,3 and 56,32 are represented by Ranston and Lazerton; EPNS ii p. 117, Eyton *Dorset* pp. 63, 137–8 and Fägersten pp. 11 and 59. Ranston is now in Iwerne Courtney (Gillingham and Redlane Hundred (4)) and Lazerton in Stourpaine, although they were both formerly in Pimperne Hundred (9). Ranston is possibly derived from Ranulf *le Meschin* who may have inherited Robert son of Gerald's estate (Fägersten p. 12). It is held as *Randolfeston* in Pimperne Hundred (9) from the Honour of *Cammel* [Queen Camel in Somerset] to which Robert's estates descended; see FA ii pp. 1, 43, 46 and Hutchins iii p. 95. Iwerne Stepleton or Stepleton Iwerne survives as a parish name; the name is also represented by Stepleton House (GR ST 8611).

IN THE CENTRAL MARGIN beside this entry is written a large backward sloping *f*, not printed by Farley. It is similar to the *f*'s, *n*'s and other marginal figures found in DB Glos. and which are discussed at the beginning of the Glos. Notes, and resembles the *f*'s in the margins of DB Norfolk, also not printed by Farley. This is the only occurrence of such a marginal figure in Dorset and, unlike the Glos. ones, is not written next to the first entry of the chapter.

30,4 POVINGTON. In Hasler Hundred (Tax Return xxix); granted by Robert son of Gerald to the Abbot of Bec-Hellouin in Normandy, see Fees p. 89, FA ii p. 24, VCH ii p. 118 note 91 and Morgan p. 141.

IN WAREHAM A BURGESS ... 2s. Written in the left margin of the MS by the same scribe as the rest and probably at an early stage because the two vertical ink lines surrounding it have been rubricated. No transposition signs indicate its correct position in the entry.

MILL ... FOR THE KING'S USE. The revenue from the mill went to the King. It is possible that the King was claiming the mill as part of the adjacent land at Lulworth, 1,6. On *opus* see B 1 note.

Ch. 31 EDWARD OF SALISBURY. Sheriff of Wiltshire in 1086.

31,1-2 WULFWEN. She was one of Edward of Salisbury's predecessors in Wiltshire and Somerset.

31,1 CANFORD (MAGNA). The 25 hides probably included the modern parishes of Hamworthy, Parkstone, Longfleet and Poole. Little Canford is in Hampreston, EPNS ii p. 2. Canford Magna is identifiable in the Tax Return for Cogdean Hundred (xvii). The Earl of Salisbury (a descendant of Edward) holds *Caneford* in Fees p. 90 and the Earl of Lincoln *Caneford* and *Kynstenston* [Kinson 31,2] in Cogdean Hundred (24) in FA ii pp. 28, 47.

WATER-MEADOW. *Broc̨*, genitive singular, a first declension Latinization of OE *broc*. See DB Herefords. 24,2 note for other forms. *Broc* came to mean 'a brook', but originally the word (like its cognates MDu, Du *brock*, LG *brok*, OHG and Mod.G *bruch*) meant 'marsh, bog' etc., a sense retained by *brook* 'water-meadow' in the Mod.E dialects of Kent, Sussex and Surrey and in medieval field names in Cambridgeshire and Essex and in some place-names; see DEPN s.v. *broc*. Canford Magna lies on the river Stour at a point where it winds slowly through a flat and formerly marshy valley. See 34,5 note.

31,2 KINSON. Identifiable in the Tax Return for Cogdean Hundred (xvii). It was transferred to Hampshire in 1930; see EPNS ii p. 22 and 31,1 note.

WHEN HE ACQUIRED THEM. See 28,2 note and last note under 47,7.

Ch. 32   ARNULF OF HESDIN. A large landholder in Wiltshire. Hesdin is in the département of Pas-de-Calais, France.

32,1   KINGTON. Identifiable in the Tax Return for Gillingham Hundred (xxvii). The name is now represented by the parish of Kington Magna and by Little Kington farm in West Stour parish (see 40,2 and 56,2 notes). Arnulf's holding was Kington Magna, which passed to the Earls of Salisbury and Lincoln, while the rest of his fief (see VCH iii p. 58). *Magna Kington'* is a fee of the Earl of Salisbury in Fees p. 753; see FA ii pp. 22, 33.

AND 1 VIRGATE OF LAND. Added in the left margin with transposition signs to show its correct position in the text. It is not well written and could have been by a different scribe.

32,2   MELBURY. Identifiable in the Tax Return for Yetminster Hundred (i); see 26,35 note.

4½ HIDES. The Tax Return for Yetminster Hundred (i) states that the King has never had tax from ½ hide which Urso holds from Arnulf of Hesdin.

32,3   KINGCOMBE. Possibly Higher Kingcombe, now in Toller Porcorum parish, Tollerford Hundred (13). It could well have lain in Eggardon Hundred (19) in 1086; see 47,7 second note.

32,4   THIS ENTRY is added below the last ruling on col. 80c, extending some 4 letters into the left margin, with a gap of a line (not shown by Farley) between it and 33,4.

POORTON. See 13,7 note.

VALUE 12s 6d. In the MS *xii sol' 7 vi den̂'*; Farley misprints *xx sol'* ... .

32,5   MAPPERTON. The position in the schedule suggests the Mapperton near Beaminster, probably North Mapperton, see Hutchins ii p. 158 and 36,11 note.

Ch. 33   THURSTAN SON OF ROLF. Perhaps the standard bearer at Hastings (see Ellis DTG pp. 186-7) who was rewarded with land in Glos., Somerset, Herefords., Dorset etc. His lands passed to Wynebald de Ballon; his grandson was Henry *de Neufmarché* (*de Novo Mercato*), and the lands are later divided between Ralph *Russel* and Nicholas *de Moels*, husbands of Henry's descendants.

33,1;3   BERNARD. Probably Bernard Pancevolt ('Paunch-face'; OEB pp. 324-5) who was a sub-tenant of Thurstan son of Rolf in Somerset and probably in Glos. too.

33,1   ALWOLD. DB *Aluuold* for OE *Aelfweald* or *Aethelweald*; see PNDB pp. 154-5. As with *Aluuardus* (see 3,1 note) safety indicates keeping to the base form.

33,2-3   NYLAND. Held in FA ii p. 33 by Nicholas *de Mortesthorn* from William *Rossel de Horsington* in Gillingham Hundred (4).

33,4   ALLINGTON. Avicia *de Mortesthorne* holds in Godderthorn Hundred (18) from William *Russel* in FA ii p. 10; see Fees p. 425.

TRIBUTARIES. *Censores*; see 16,1 note.

33,5-6   'STOKE (WALLIS)'. DB *Stoches*. This land can be identified in the Tax Return for Whitchurch Hundred (ii), although all 7 virgates pay tax in Godderthorn Hundred (x). 'Stoke Wallis' is a lost site in Whitchurch Canonicorum parish (Fägersten p. 297), recorded as Stoke on the 1st edition one-inch OS map (no. 18 of 1811, reprint no. 84 of 1969). Thurstanshay, another lost name in the same parish, may preserve Thurstan's name. In Cal. Inq. PM vol. x (Ed. III) no. 312 *Stok Waleys Whitchurch* is held from Eleanor *Russel* by knight service.

33,5   1 HIDE. The scribe originally wrote *car̄* ('plough') and then underlined it for deletion and interlined *hid'* in correction, positioning it mostly over the *car̄*, rather than to the left as Farley prints it.

Ch. 34   WILLIAM OF EU. William, Count of Eu (but see *Anglo-Saxon Chronicle* ed. D. Whitelock etc. p. 173 note 7 and Eyton *Dorset* p. 120 note 7), the second son of Count Robert of Eu. More than half his fief lay in Wiltshire and Dorset. His second wife was the sister of Earl Hugh of Chester. He rebelled against William Rufus in 1088 and in 1094 and was charged with treason in 1096, was blinded and castrated and probably died soon after; Orderic Vitalis iii p. 411. He was executed in 1096 according to Eyton *Dorset* p. 76. See DB Glos. W 16 note. Some of his lands were later held by the Earls Marshall, Earls of Pembroke. Some of the earlier entries in the Book of Fees record these lands as held by Adam *de Port*. On his exile, the fief was re-allotted. Eu is in the département of Seine-Maritime, France.

34,1   WILLIAM. In the MS and Farley *WILLELM'*; the facsimile fails to reproduce most of the abbreviation sign. Cf. 40,1 note.

THORNTON. This holding seems to be required for a full reconstruction of the Gillingham Hundred Tax Return (xxvii) to make up the total. It is now in Marnhull in Sturminster Newton Hundred (3), although a tithing of Redlane (4); see Fägersten p. 44. Adam *de Port* holds *Thornton'* in Gillingham Hundred (4) in Fees p. 91; see FA ii pp. 22, 52.

WILLIAM FROM HIM. Probably William Bellett; see 34,2 note.

ALSTAN. Most probably the great Anglo-Saxon thane Alstan of Boscombe, both here and elsewhere in this chapter; his lands in some nine counties had apparently passed to William of Eu, though first to Ralph of Limesy (see DB Glos. 31,4 and cf. 34,6 note below).

34,2   BRADFORD (PEVERELL). This *Bradeford* is required by the Tax Return for Dorchester Hundred (xxxii), where the King has no tax from 1 hide held by William Bellett from William of Eu. Bradford had belonged to Adam *de Port* (Fees p. 379) before being granted by King Richard to Robert Peverel; see Fees pp. 88, 260, 425 and FA ii p. 17. There is a separate place-name Peverell at GR SY 6492.

34,2;6;   TOLI. DB *Tou, Tol, Toul* from Old Danish *Tóli*, Latinized *Tolus, - i*, which must have
8;12;   developed from an anglicized derivative *Tól*. As Toli (called Toli the Dane in DB Hants.)
14-15   32,1) is the predecessor of many of William of Eu's lands (e.g. in Wilts., Devon, Hants.), and here as *Tholi* in 34,5), it would seem probable that *Tou, Tol* and *Toul* here represent *Tóli* rather than *Tholf* (as PNDB p. 389: in all other instances except Dorset and Hants. and one in Staffs., the forms mentioned there have the final *f*).

34,3   HIWES. Tentatively identified by Eyton *Dorset* (pp. 123-4) with Muckleford in Bradford Peverell parish. There is a Hewish in Portesham and in Milton Abbas, and a Huish in Sydling St. Nicholas and in Winterborne Zelston.

34,5   LYTCHETT (MATRAVERS). Probably named from the family of William's tenant Hugh, who appears as Hugh *Maltravers* in DB Somerset 26,5. He named the adjacent *Morden Matravers* [East Morden] which was probably part of this land in 1086; see Cal. Inq. PM vol. viii (Ed. III) no. 464, EPNS ii p. 58 and 26,24 note. John *Mautravers* holds from the Earl of Gloucester in FA ii pp. 28, 47 in Cogdean Hundred (24). There is a Strigoil fee in *Litsed* in Fees p. 426 (see 34,6 last note) and a Marshall fee in *Lischet* in Fees p. 753. The history of the other Lytchett, Lytchett Minster, which lies just to the south (GR SY 9693) is unclear; it may have been a part of this land (see next note) or of Sturminster Marshall (28,2, see EPNS ii p. 33), yet it appears to have connections with Great Canford (31,1, see Hutchins iii pp. 289, 360).

WATER-MEADOW(?). *Broce*, genitive singular; see 31,1 note. However, Lytchett Matravers lies on rising ground, the only likely places for water-meadow being on the Stour to the north, near Sturminster Marshall, if the holding stretched that far, or to the south of Lytchett Minster (if the latter was part of this holding in 1086, see previous note). So broca here might be a first declension Latin variant form of, or a simple error for, Latin *brucus* (whence **brucaria, bruaria*, Fr. *bruyère* 'brushwood, heathland'; see Fägersten p. 112 and cf. 10,2 note above). The reference would then be to Lytchett Heath (GR SY 9695).

34,6   BLANDFORD (ST. MARY). The two Blandfords are not easy to distinguish; see 26,29 note. In the present case, the Tax Return for Combsditch Hundred (xvi) records that the King never had tax from the 3 virgates which William of Moutiers holds from William of Audrieu. William of Audrieu is a tenant of William of Eu in other counties (e.g. Wilts.) and the 3 virgates may well represent the ½ hide from which the King did not have tax in 34,6.

HELD. In the MS ten' was originally written and immediately corrected to *tenuit* (although there are numerous cases in DB of ten' abbreviating the past tenses, especially when *TRE* is in the sentence), without the ' sign being erased. Farley does not remove the sign; see 1,5 note.

3 SMALLHOLDERS. In the MS *iii bord'* is clearly written; in the facsimile the dot after the *iii* is smudged upwards making the figure look like *iiii*.

RALPH OF LIMESY. William of Eu received many of his lands, as well as the Holding of Chepstow (see DB Glos. W 16 note). See last note under 34,1. Chepstow later becomes the *caput* of the Honour of Strigoil from which some of this chapter's lands are held in the feodaries. Limésy is in the département of Seine-Maritime, France.

34,7   WOOLCOMBE. In Melbury Bubb parish. John *Mautravers* holds *Wellecombe* in Yetminster Hundred (7) from the Earl of Gloucester in FA ii p. 41; see FA ii p. 36. It was sometimes called Woolcombe *Mautravers*, see Fägersten p. 225.

34,8   SWYRE. Later in Uggescombe Hundred (25), but it seems probable that it was in Godderthorn Hundred (18) in 1086, being needed to make up the Tax Return total (x); see VCH iii p. 131, Fees pp. 88, 260, RH i p. 102 and FA ii pp. 6, 34, 54. Part of this land may have been at *Berewyk* [Berwick in Swyre, GR SY 5289], see FA ii p. 6 and Cal. Inq. PM vol. ii (Ed. I) no. 2.

TO TOXUS (THE PRIEST?). In the MS *Toxo* with another letter (at least) interlined after it, extending down to *Toxo*. The letter appears to be a *p* rather than *ſ* (s), having a slight backwards hook at the top left-hand corner. Farley obviously took this letter as an *s*, however (though he does not show that the *s* is interlined), presumably intending *Toxos* to be nominative — despite the nominative form *Toxus* below — and the name of the King's reeve. (The translation would thus be 'Toxus, a King's reeve, had leased it, then returned it ...'.) There may be another letter after the *p* (if it is one), possibly an *r* (*pr* is the regular abbreviation for *presbiter* 'priest') or an *i*, but it is impossible to be sure because the *i* interlined over the *q* of *q̄dā* gets in the way. Also, the interlined letter(s) and the *xo* of *Toxo* are written over erasures. See Eyton *Dorset* p. 128 note 7.

BY KING EDWARD. In the MS *p* is interlined, the tail of the *p* extending down between *ů* and *regē*; Farley does not print it as an interlineation.

SO HE STATES. Perhaps at one of the Hundred or Shire courts where rival claims to land were discussed. Other examples of oral testimony in Dorset occur at 40,7. 54,8 and 55,3.

AT THE (TIME OF HIS) DEATH. King Edward died on 5th January 1066.

PREVIOUSLY IT WAS PASTURE, NOW ARABLE. One of the few explicit references in DB to colonization; DGSW p. 110. Cf. DB Sussex 13,52 where land for 1 plough was pasture, but is now settled (*hospitata*), and DB Herefords. 10,43 and note.

34,9   WYNFORD (EAGLE). Identifiable in the Tax Return for Tollerford Hundred (xiv); see FA ii p. 35.
        14 HIDES. In the MS *xii* with *ii* interlined to correct the figure to *xiiii*.

34,10   FROME (VAUCHURCH). This *Frome* falls in the text after Wynford Eagle which can be definitely located in Tollerford Hundred (13). It seems to be needed to make up the Tax Return total for the Hundred (xiv); see VCH iii p. 133. In Fees p. 425 *Frome* is a fee of the Honour of Strigoil (see 34,6 last note), like Lytchett (34,5) and Elworth (34,13). In FA ii p. 35 in Tollerford Hundred (13) John *de la Tour* (who also holds Elworth) holds *Frome Foechurch*; see Cal. Inq. PM vol. iv (Ed. I) no. 235.

34,11   (LONG) CRICHEL. This holding is required by the Tax Return for Knowlton Hundred (xxiii) where William's mother holds 7½ hides in lordship; see 1,3 note. In FA ii p. 28 *Lang Kyrchil* is held from the Earl Marshall (though a small Mortain fee), the other half of the village being held by John *de Gouys*; see 49,16 note.
        3 FEMALE SLAVES. The only occurrence in DB Dorset of *ancillae*, whereas in Gloucestershire, for example, they occur very frequently. Their almost complete absence from Dorset does not mean that they did not exist, merely that, like much of the female population, they were not counted.
        NOW £15. In the MS *xv* corrected from *xii*.

34,12   'TARRANT'. An unidentified *Tarente Grice* is a Marshall fee in Fees p. 753.

34,13   ELWORTH. 2 hides are held from the Honour of Strigoil (Chepstow) in Fees p. 93 in Uggescombe Hundred (25). John *de Turry* or *de la Tour* holds in FA ii pp. 6, 34, 53; see 34,10 note.
        3 VILLAGERS. After these last words on col. 80d, the text of this entry continues on col. 82a, as the inserted piece of parchment, folio 81 a, b, c, d, contains Ch. 42 and 36,4-11 (see note to latter).

34,14   STOCK (GAYLARD). Probably the 'Stoke' near Stourton Caundle (34,15) which has the same holders in FA ii p. 40. It was in Brownshall Hundred (2) in 1316 (FA ii p. 40), then in Lydlinch, Sherborne Hundred (1); see Fägersten p. 219. Like Lytchett Matravers (34,5) it is held by Hugh's descendants, see Hutchins iii p. 683, who states that there was a 'Matravers farm' in this parish.
        THE LAND OF SHERBORNE. Perhaps meaning that it was held by Sherborne, see Chs. 2 and 3, or that it was taken from the many hides of Sherborne (2,6. 3,1).

34,15   (STOURTON) CAUNDLE. See 26,70-71 note. The holding was probably adjacent to Stock Gaylard (34,14), the two being separated by the Caundle Brook; see Hutchins iii p. 664.

Ch. 35 WILLIAM OF FALAISE. He was married to the daughter of Serlo of Burcy (DB Som. 27,3). William's daughter Emma married William *de Curcy* and the lands pass to the Courcy family. Falaise is in the département of Calvados, France.

35,1   SILTON. In Gillingham Hundred (Tax Return xxvii). The land included *Poerstone* [Pierston farm, GR ST 7928], FA ii pp. 22, 32, 40, 52. Silton and Milton are held in Fees p. 607 by Margery of Redvers, daughter of Alice *de Curcy*, widow of Baldwin of Redvers, Earl of Devon.
        WULFWARD WHITE. *Uuit* here; also *Wit, Wite, albus* elsewhere in DB. He is called a thane of King Edward in DB Middx. 8,5. See 1,30 note.
        REEVE OF HIS. That is, a reeve of King Edward.
        BISHOP OF EXETER. Leofric, who was bishop from 1046 to 1072.
        MILTON (ON STOUR). Required by the Tax Return for Gillingham Hundred (xxvii).

Ch. 36   WILLIAM OF MOHUN. In DB *Moion, Moiun*; Exon. *Moione, Mouin*. Though he came from Moyon in the département of Manche, France, he is rendered as William of Mohun here in deference to the more popular 13th century spelling of the English form of his surname. He was Sheriff of Somerset from *c.* 1068 and 'farmed' various royal manors there (see DB Som. General Note 1,14). Dunster in Somerset was the seat of his Barony and his lands later formed the Honour of Dunster.

36,1   TODBER. Held from John *de Moun* in Gillingham Hundred (4) in FA ii pp. 22, 33, 40, 52. GEOFFREY MALLORY. In Exon. *Maloret*; OEB p. 351.
VALUE ... NOW £4. In the MS *ii* with *ii* interlined to correct the figure to *iiii*.

36,2   SPETISBURY. In Charborough (later Loosebarrow) Hundred in 1086, Tax Return xviii. AETHELWARD. DB *Ageluuard*; Exon. *Alwardus. Agel-* here and in 55,14 for *Aethel-*, see PNDB § 111 and pp. 188-9. Cf. 3,1 note.
PASTURE ... OVERLOOKING THE WATER. The river Stour winds slowly on the shallow valley floor at this point, nowadays being split into two channels in front of the village. *Aqua* was probably a stretch of marshland in 1086.

36,3   WINTERBORNE (HOUGHTON). Also *Winterbom' Moyun*, Fees p. 753, and simply *Howeton* (Pimperne Hundred 9) in FA ii p. 27; see Cal. Inq. PM vol. ii (Ed. I) nos. 306, 593 and EPNS ii p. 129. Maxwell-Lyte, historian of the Honour of Dunster, doubts this identification, considering that Winterborne Houghton was quite distinct from the original Mohun 'Winterborne', HD p. ii note 1.
HOLDS 1 VIRGATE WRONGFULLY. See 55,17.

36,4   THESE ENTRIES are added on a separate scrap of parchment, later numbered 81c,d, and
-11   are rubricated. Like Ch. 42 on the reverse and 1,31 (fol. 76) they are written acrosswise; see 1,31 note. In this edition each Latin line is set on two lines, an indentation marking the break thus introduced. The initial omission of these eight manors by the Exchequer scribe is odd, if, as seems probable, he was copying from Exon. (see Introduction to Exon. Notes): he cannot have lost a folio or two from Exon., as in Exon. the details of Winterborne Houghton (36,3) continue onto folio 48a and are immediately succeeded by those for Pulham, Hammoon (36,4-5) etc. (but see Finn's view in his article in BJRL xl (1957) p. 70). It is possible that the DB scribe broke off after 36,3 for some reason and when he (or another) resumed he mistakenly thought he had completed William's lands in Dorset and so began the next fief, but realised his error later.

36,4   PULHAM. This land can be identified in the Tax Return for *Hunesberga* Hundred (xxv). It lay some way to the west of the main body of the Hundred, and was possibly a detachment in 1086, later coming into Buckland Newton Hundred, where another part of Pulham lay in 1086 (Tax Return xxxvi). It is not found later in the Mohun fief and must soon have passed into other hands; see EPNS ii p. 100 and HD pp. ii, 3.
10 HIDES. The details of lordship and villagers' holdings suggest that there were 10 acres to a virgate (40 to a hide, instead of the more usually reckoned 120 acres; see B 1 note). A 40-acre geld-hide is also implied in the Wiltshire Tax Return for Calne Hundred, where one of the versions (Exon. 13 a 5) has two parts of a virgate and one part of a virgate while the other two (Exon. 1 a 4 and 7 b 1) have 7 acres and 3 acres (the virgate was always a quarter of a hide). Another 'small hide' of 48 acres for tax purposes has also been suggested; Eyton *Dorset* p. 14 ff. See DB Sussex Appendix; J. Tait "Large Hides and Small Hides" in EHR xvii (1902); DGSW pp. 80-81; Finn LE pp. 122-3. On a larger acre in Cornwall, see DB Cornwall 1,1 note. However, there are several examples in Dorset where the details of the lordship and villagers' land do not add up to the tax total given; see 1,19 note and cf. 36,5 note. Moreover, the Tax Return for *Hunesberga* Hundred (xxv) states that William of Mohun's lordship land there is 4½ hides less 4 acres, which then does add up to the 10 hides; this evidence, however, is not conclusive, because there are many discrepancies in the amount of lordship land in the Tax Return and in DB (even where a holding can be positively identified) and changes could have taken place between the dates of the two surveys.

36,5   HAMMOON. Earlier *Hamme Mohun*; see Fees p. 424, FA ii pp. 27, 43, 47, Fägersten p. 54 and EPNS ii p. 99. It was a detachment of Pimperne Hundred (9) in 1303 (FA ii p. 27) and was probably in *Hunesberga* Hundred (xxv) in 1086. It is here mapped in Sturminster New ton Hundred (3) which is geographically appropriate.
TAX FOR 5 HIDES. The details of lordship and villagers' land amount to 5 hides, less 4 acres. Although there are several instances in Dorset of the details not tallying with the tax total (see 1,19 note), it is probable that in this case the Exon. scribe wrote *viii* for *xii* in the acreage, or vice versa.

36,6-7 CHILFROME; CRUXTON. *Childefrome* and *Crokeston'* are Mohun holdings in Fees p. 424 and FA ii p. 35; see HD *passim* and Fägersten pp. 229, 233. Since Chilfrome is later held as two fees and Cruxton as one, it is probable that Cruxton is the smaller DB holding. Both appear to be required to make up the total for Tollerford Hundred Tax Return (xiv); see VCH iii p. 133.

36,6 WILLIAM CLAIMS THESE THREE MANORS AS TWO. He has combined the three manors of the three 1066 holders in Chilfrome into two manors, held by Dodman and Nigel (see Details Table).

36,7 ALWARD. DB *Aluuardus*, Exon. *Ailuuardus*, for Aethelward; see PNDB pp. 188–189. Exon. also has the form *Ailuuardus* for DB's *Aluuard(us)* in 55,40-42 and *Aelwardus* for DB's *Aluuard* in 36,10. DB has the form *Ailward* for 56,25. Cf. notes to 3,1 and 36,2.

36,8 CHELBOROUGH. The Mohun holding was West Chelborough; FA ii p. 35 and HD *passim*. It is required in the Tax Return for Tollerford Hundred (xiv). It is possible that this land included *Mellbyry Turberevyle* [Melbury Sampford], the next entry in FA ii p. 35; see notes to 26,35 and 47,3.
3 HIDES ... 1 WHICH DID NOT PAY TAX. The same information is given in the Tax Return for Tollerford Hundred (xiv).

36,9 IWERNE (STEPLETON). *Stepelton'* is a Mohun fee in Fees p. 426 and held from John *de Mohun* in FA ii p. 27. See 30,3 note; Hutchins i p. 298 and iv p. 85.

36,10 LITTLEWINDSOR. *Parva Windelessor'* is a Mohun fee in Fees p. 426.
ALWARD. In the MS there is an *7* after the place-name which is partially covered by the *A* of *Aluuard*, presumably in an attempt to hide it. Farley does not show it. Cf. notes to 56,39. 57,7;15.

36,11 MAPPERTON. Near Beaminster, held as *Mapelarton Bret* by William *le Bret* from the Honour of Dunster, HD p. 75, probably South Mapperton; see Fägersten p. 272, Hutchins ii p. 158.

Ch. 37 WILLIAM OF BRAOSE. Briouze in the département of Orne, France. Most of his land lay in Sussex.

37,1-2 (GLANVILLES) WOOTTON. This land is required by the reconstruction of the Tax Return for Buckland Hundred (xxxvi). It is held as *Wolfrenewotton* by Henry *de Glaunvyle* from William *de Brewes* (Braose) in FA ii p. 30; see FA ii pp. 42, 50 and VCH iii p. 59.

37,1 ABBOT OF MILTON. Or perhaps 'Abbey', as *Abb'* can abbreviate both *abbas* 'Abbot', *abbatia* 'Abbey', as well as occasionally *abbatissa* 'Abbess'. The land was restored to the Abbey, *Wottingglayvile* being held by the Abbot in TE p. 184a.

37,4 ASH. DB *Aisse*, required by the Tax Return for Pimperne Hundred (xxvi), which states that the King did not have tax from 2½ hides David held from William of Braose.
1 PLOUGH THERE. The scribe wrote a capital *I* for the usual *i*; Farley corrects the error.
3 SLAVES. In the MS *iii serui*; Farley misprints *iiii serui*.

37,6 CREECH. Henry *de Glanvile* holds *Crugh* in Hasler Hundred (28) in FA ii p. 37 from William *de Breouse*.

37,7 AFFLINGTON. See 28,6-7 note.

37,9 RUSHTON. It probably lay in Bere Hundred in 1086, see the Appendix. One of the several holdings here was at, or included, *Bennegere* [Binnegar GR SY 8787], FA ii p. 42.
W(ILLIAM) ALSO HOLDS. *Idem W. ten'* . Or perhaps "W(alter) also holds", referring to the sub-tenant of 37,6-8, although one would expect 'from William' to be added (but see DB Glos. 48,3 note). Cf. 37,6 *Idem W. ten'* where the meaning is obviously 'William also holds'.
BURDE HELD IT. Entered in the right margin of the MS with no transposition signs to indicate its correct position in the entry. *Burde* is perhaps from OFr *Burdel* (Latin *burdo* 'a mule') with AN loss of final *l*; PNDB p. 211.
SESTERS. See 12,12 note.

37,10 WORGRET ... ½ MILL. See 11,9 note. Henry *de Glanvill* holds in Barrow Hundred (22) in FA ii p. 42. One of the Worgret holdings (see 11,9 and 57,7) included Westport in Wareham (GR SY 9287), *Westeporte* in FA ii p. 42.

37,11 HETHFELTON. See 49,14 note.

37,12 SMEDMORE. DB *Metmore*; see EPNS i p. 86.

37,13 IN PURBECK HUNDRED. Written in the same size capitals as the other place-names, and lined through in red, not in large capitals as Farley prints. Cf. 1,30. It was apparently an alternative name for Ailwood Hundred (Tax Return xix) now Rowbarrow; see 1,8 note. It is perhaps significant only that the 7 hides less ½ virgate of this land, combined with the 17 hides ½ virgate of Worth (47,9;11), the 3 virgates of Worth (55,43) and the odd 1 virgate of Renscombe (11,16), make a 25-hide unit. This would locate the land near Worth Matravers; see next note.

WIFE OF HUGH SON OF GRIP HOLDS PART OF THIS LAND. The wife of Hugh held two places called Langton: Langton Herring (55,31) in her own fief and another 'Langton' in Purbeck. The salt from the salt-pans on this land was given by a descendant to Holme priory (Ch. 55 note). This 'Langton' lay in Langton Matravers (GR SY 9978) and was itself given to Ingram *le Waleys* whence it was called 'Langton Wallis' (FA ii p. 24). It is possibly the land mentioned in the present entry or less likely a part of Worth Matravers (55,43) or of Acton in Langton Matravers (55,41); see VCH iii p. 56 note 10, EPNS i pp. 33-34 and Hutchins i p. 630 and iv p. lxxvii.

5 SMALLHOLDERS. In the MS *v bord'* corrected from *ii bord'*.

Ch. 38 WILLIAM OF ÉCOUIS. DB *Scohies*. Écouis is in the département of Eure, France; see OEB p. 114.

38,1 (WEST) KNIGHTON. This land occurs in the Tax Return for Cullifordtree Hundred (xxxvii). DB *Chenistetone* means 'Farm of the thegns or retainers of a high personage' (EPNS i p. 207) and probably refers to the holding by 2 thanes before 1066. East Knighton is in Winfrith Newburgh parish, Winfrith Hundred (27).

5 VILLAGERS AND 5 SMALLHOLDERS. In the MS there is a small gap after *bord'* due to the erasure of a couple of letters; Farley does not show it, as is frequently his practice with erasures. It is unlikely that the scribe intended to add *coscez* 'Cottagers' or *cotarii* 'cottagers', as VCH iii p. 5 seems to think.

38,2 (STOURTON) CAUNDLE. See 26,70-71 note. The land is identifiable in the Tax Return for Brownshall Hundred (xxviii), and the 5 hides are probably represented in Fees p. 89 by 2½ hides held by Henry of Haddon from Robert *Malherbe* and 2½ hides by Thomas son of Thomas son of Brian both at Stourton Caundle; see RBE ii pp. 547-8.

Ch. 39 WALSCIN OF DOUAI. He is sometimes referred to by his name Walter (OG *Walt(h)er*, Forssner 243), as in DB Surrey and in some entries in Devon and Somerset (see Somerset General Notes L 24), and sometimes, as here and in DB Wiltshire and some entries in Devon and Somerset, by the nickname variant of it (not discussed by PNDB, OEB or Ellis; Searle is misleading). This *Walscin* appears to be the Norman French version of an OG *Walzin* (*sc* etc. for *z*; see Zachrissen 37-8; PNDB pp. 110-111; Forssner 39 and compare his spelling for *Azelin*) which would be a double-diminutive pet-form of *Walter* (an *-in* suffix derivative — see Forssner 278-9 — of the recorded *-z* suffix form *Walz(e)*, see Bach 1, i para. 97,1; 100,2).

Douai (*Dwai, Duai, Douuai* in DB; *duaco* in Exon. for Somerset and Devon) is in the département of Nord in France; OEB p. 87.

39,1 'WINTERBORNE'. Neither the river nor the Hundred has been identified.

ALWARD AND ALWIN HELD. The scribe originally wrote *Aluuard tenuit*, and then added 7 *Aluuin* above and corrected the verb to the plural *tenuer̄*. For a similar omission and consequent correction, see 57,1 note. Alwin and Alward may have been brothers, or father and son, or close relatives, with common prototheme in their personal name, *Aethel-* or *Aelf-*.

39,2 WIMER. OE *Wigmaer*.

(STOURTON) CAUNDLE. This land has not been identified in later records; see 26,70-71 note.

Ch. 40 WALERAN. Waleran Hunter, as in the Landholders' List. His lands later form the Barony of Dean (40,3 note) and descendants, Walter *Walerand* and William *de Sancto Martino*, are found holding some of his lands *passim* in FA ii.

40,1 WALERAN. In the MS and Farley *WALERAN*'; the facsimile fails to reproduce the abbreviation sign. Cf. 34,1 note.

MANSTON. A fee of the heir of Waleran in Fees p. 753; held in Gillingham Hundred (4) from William *de Sancto Martino* in FA ii p. 22. See Fees p. 425; FA ii pp. 33, 52.

40,2 KINGTON. Probably in both Great and Little Kington. Little Kington farm (Kington Parva) in West Stour parish is a fee held from the heir of *Waleran'* in Fees p. 753; see FA ii pp. 22, 33, 52 and the notes to 32,1 and 56,2. In Cal. Inq. PM vol. ii (Ed. I) no. 7, Maud late wife of Robert *Waleraund* holds one-third of Kington manor, *Little Kyngton*, and one-third of *Mangirston* [Madjeston in Gillingham, GR ST 8025, probably a part of Gillingham (1,4) in 1086].

40,3 SUTTON (WALDRON). The secondary name is derived from Waleran, the 1086 holder, or from the early 13th century *Walerand*. The land is held in Fees (p. 91) of the heirs of Walter *Walerant*, and in FA ii p. 21 is held by William *de Sancto Martino* from the Barony of *Dene* (now East and West Dean on the Hampshire/Wiltshire border). The land occurs in the Tax Return for Farrington Hundred (xxxv).

40,4 'WINTERBORNE'. Probably Winterborne Muston or Tomson, or both, held in 1242-3 as Winterborne *Turbervill'* and Winterborne *Thom'*, a fee of the heir of Waleran, Fees p. 753; see Fees p. 426, FA ii pp. 39, 43, 48 and VCH iii p. 135 note 82. Winterborne Tomson has remained in Combsditch Hundred (16); Winterborne Muston is later in Bere Hundred (22), but a tithing of Combsditch.

40.6 FIFEHEAD (NEVILLE). 'Five Hides' held at *Vyfhyde Nevyle* in Pimperne Hundred (9) in FA ii p. 27 from Reginald *de Sancto Martino*; see Fees p. 425. It seems required to make up the Tax Return total for *Hunesberga* (xxv), whereas Fifehead St. Quintin (19,9) is in (Sturminster) Newton Tax Return Hundred (xxi).

40,7 (CHURCH) KNOWLE. So identified by VCH and DG. There are a number of other places called Knowle or Knoll in Dorset and no evidence has been found to confirm Waleran's holding here; see Hutchins i p. 578.
HE WAS FREE WITH THIS LAND. He was free to choose any lord; see 1,29 note.
EARL WILLIAM. William son of Osbern (William Fitz Osbern), brother of Bishop Osbern of Exeter, palatine earl of Hereford from 1067 to his death in battle abroad in 1071. He was most probably also palatine earl of Glos., and wielded extra powers in Worcs.; see W. E. Wightman 'The Palatine Earldom of William Fitz Osbern in Gloucestershire and Worcestershire (1066-1071)' in EHR lxxvii (1962). William was joint 'regent' with Bishop Odo of Bayeux during King William's absence in 1067 and was responsible (with Walter of Lacy and others) for defending the Welsh border. See DB Herefords. Introductory Note 2. He was married to Adeline, sister of Ralph of Tosny. Like Ralph of Limesy (see 34,6 note), Earl William may have held much land in Dorset, but this is the only hint of it in DB Dorset.

40,8 (MAIDEN) NEWTON. This holding seems to be required to make up the total of the Tax Return for Tollerford Hundred (xiv). It is held as *Mayden Nywton* in FA ii p. 35 from John *de Engham* who holds other lands (Kington and Winterborne Tomson 40,2;4) from William *de Sancto Martino*; see Ch. 40 note and Hutchins ii p. 682.

40,9 TOLLER. Probably in Tollerford Hundred (13) like the previous entry and thus distinct from Toller Whelme (26,66). There are later two distinct settlements, Toller Porcorum and Toller Fratrum or Great and Little Toller, one of which, and possibly both, represents the DB entry; see Hutchins ii p. 696, Eyton *Dorset* pp. 139-140 and Fägersten p. 235. Walter *Walerand* holds *Tore* in Fees p. 426; possibly the same land that is held from Richard *de Tolre* as *Swyne Tolre* [Toller Porcorum] in FA ii pp. 35, 55 in Tollerford Hundred (13). In Cal. Inq. PM vol. ix (Ed. III) no. 118, *Swyntolre* is held by the heir of Oliver *de Hyngram*; in a separate entry it is associated with *Mayden Nywton* (40,8).

Ch. 41 WALTER OF CLAVILLE. *De Clavile* here and in the Landholders' List, *de Clayilla* in Exon. and *de Clavilla* in the Tax Returns. It is either Claville-sur-Cany or Claville-Motteville, both in the département of Eure, France; OEB p. 82. See 41,1 note. Walter's descendants became tenants of the Honour of Gloucester, Holme and West Morden (41,3;5) being held by them in 1285 (FA ii p. 24); see Fees p. 750.

41,1 WALTER OF GLANVILLE OR CLAVILLE. In the MS *t Clavile* is interlined, probably in correction, although *Glanvile* has not been underlined for deletion. The *t* is not well written (probably because of lack of space, having been written after the rubricated heading) and could abbreviate *id est* rather than *vel* 'or'. It does not appear in Exon. A Robert of Glanville (*de Glanuill'*, *de Glauilla*; département of Calvados, France) appears frequently in DB, but only in Suffolk and, to a lesser extent, in Norfolk, whereas Walter of Claville is a tenant-in-chief in Devon and Dorset and sub-tenant in Cornwall. A Robert of Claville occurs in DB Suffolk. Glanville and Claville are far apart in different départements in France. It is likely, therefore, that we are dealing not with a double name here, but with a simple error. *C* and *G* are similar in the script used in DB and an abbreviation sign could easily have been added: thus *Clavile* → *Glavile* → *Glāvile* → *Glanvile*. This fief becomes part of the Honour of Gloucester, the *Clavile* family continuing as tenants.
AFFLINGTON. See 28,6-7 note.
BRICTRIC. Most probably Brictric son of Algar (1,17 note): he was Walter's predecessor in DB Devon 24,21 and Cornwall 1,19.

41,2 HE ALSO HOLDS. Repeated at the beginning of 41,2-5.
(CHURCH) KNOWLE. See the Tax Return for Hasler Hundred (xxix). The 1066 holder Beorn seems to have given his name to Barnston farm (GR SY 9381); see Fägersten p. 132 and EPNS i p. 88.

41,3 (EAST) HOLME. Both his holding and that of 56,43 can be identified in the Tax Return for Hasler Hundred (xxix). East Holme has remained there; West Holme is in East Stoke parish, Winfrith Hundred (27), although a tithing of Hasler Hundred (28) (see Tithings note in the Appendix). In FA ii p. 24 *Holne* is held from the Honour of Gloucester by William *de Clavile* in Hasler Hundred; see Fees p. 750.

41,4   COOMBE (KEYNES). Required by the Tax Return for Winfrith Hundred (xxx); see 6,4 note.

41,5   MORDEN. The land can be identified in the Tax Return for Charborough (Loosebarrow) Hundred (xviii). It is probable that it covered both East and West Morden, the former a part of Loosebarrow Hundred (23), the latter a tithing in Rushmore Hundred (see the Appendix). In FA ii p. 24 West Morden in Rushmore Hundred is held by John *de Clavyle* from the Earl of Gloucester (see FA ii pp. 37, 56); while in FA ii p. 44 John *de Glaunvile* holds from the Earl of Gloucester in Loosebarrow Hundred (23).

Ch. 42   THIS ENTRY is written on the other side of the scrap of parchment (folio 81a,b) to 36,4-11. See 1,31 note. It is written in 2½ lines with heading and is rubricated. In this edition each Latin line is set as 2 lines, an indentation marking the break thus introduced. BALDWIN. Baldwin of Moeles (now Meulles in the département of Calvados, France) or Baldwin of Clare was the younger son of Count Gilbert of Brionne; his elder brother Richard was a landholder in DB Wilts., Devon, Beds. etc. He was delegated with other leading men-at-arms to help build a castle at Exeter after the revolt of 1068 and to remain there as part of the garrison (Orderic Vitalis ii p. 181) and the custody of the castle remained in his family. He also had his own castle at Okehampton (DB Devon 16,3) and became a great landholder in that county. He was Sheriff of Devon by 1070 (*Regesta* i no. 58) and no doubt held the office until his death some time before 1096 when his son William is addressed in a charter together with Bishop Osbern and Warin the Sheriff of Cornwall (Mon. Ang. ii p. 497). Baldwin was married to a cousin of King William. His heirs are the Courtenay family.

42,1   IWERNE (COURTNEY). This manor can be deduced from the Tax Return for Farrington Hundred (xxxv), and is held in Fees p. 91 (*Ywern'*) and in FA ii p. 21 (*Iwerne Cortenai*) from the Honour of Okehampton. It is also called Shroton 'Sheriff's *tun*' from Baldwin the Sheriff; see Fägersten p. 10 and Fees p. 260, FA ii pp. 32, 40, 52. In FA ii p. 33, land at *Childakford* [Child Okeford 1,7 note] is held from Hugh *de Cortenay*, possibly a part of this holding; see 44,1 note. For the constituents of this estate, see Cal. Inq. PM vol. ii (Ed. I) no. 71.

43,1   BREDY. In Burton Bradstock parish. It can be deduced from the Tax Return for Godderthorn Hundred (x); see FA ii pp. 11, 34, 54. HARDING. According to the Tax Return for Godderthorn Hundred (x), Berengar's predecessor holds of him at a revenue (*tenet ... ad firmam*); Berengar's lordship is there given as 1½ hides and the third part of 1 virgate. VALUE £3. Almost certainly *ualet* is a scribal error for *ualuit* 'the value was'.

44,1   (GOLD) HILL. This 'Hill', DB *Hille*, is identified by DG, Eyton *Dorset* pp. 125–126, Fägersten and VCH with Hill farm (GR ST 8814) in Iwerne Minster. Despite the arguments of C. D. Drew in his 1947 article and although Hill in Iwerne Minster is said by Hutchins iii p. 540 to have belonged to the Courtenays, Earls of Devon (which suggests that it was part of Iwerne Courtney 42,1), the Hill in Iwerne Minster probably lay in Sixpenny Hundred (xxiv) in 1086 and would have been surveyed as an unspecified part of Iwerne Minster (19,7). Osbern Giffard's 'Hill' is clearly identifiable in the Tax Return for Farrington Hundred (xxxv) which later merged with Gillingham (4); Osbern is called *Osbertus* there (see DB Devon Exon. Notes to Ch. 43 for other examples of Osbern/ Osbert). In FA ii p. 33 Ralph *de Hulle* holds in Gillingham Hundred Child Okeford from the Count of Mortain, and *Hulle* from the heirs of John *Giffard*. 'Hill' is thus likely to be near Child Okeford and has been tentatively identified with Gold Hill. The same holding is called Hill *Parva* in FA ii p. 52. See Cal. Inq. PM vol. vii (Ed. III) no. 78.

Ch. 45   ALFRED OF 'SPAIN'. Omitted in error from the list of landholders on col. 75a, Ch. 45 there being Matthew of Mortagne (Ch. 46 in the text). The numbering of the text thus continues one ahead of the landholders' list until Ch. 56 where the numbering tallies because the text gives no chapter number to the Land of Isolde (55 in the landholders' list). Alfred came from Épaignes in the département of Eure, France (OEB pp. 92, 134); *Hispaniensis* (in the Chapter heading the second *i* was probably omitted in error), also *de Hispania* elsewhere in DB, is a kind of word-play. He also held land in Devon, Somerset, Wiltshire, Gloucestershire and Herefordshire.

45,1   ALWY. DB *Aluui* represents OE *Aelfwig* or *Aethelwig*; see PNDB pp. 157-8. As with *Aluuardus* (see 3,1 note) safety indicates keeping to the base form. This Alwy was undoubtedly the same as Alfred's predecessor *Aluui* in his lands in Somerset, Devon and

Wiltshire, and who on several occasions in DB Somerset is called Al(f)wy son of Banna and may also have been Al(f)wy the King's reeve; see Somerset General Notes 35,1 and Somerset Exon. Notes to 35,24.
PASTURE ... 4 IN WIDTH. In the MS *IN* is interlined, the *I* extending down after *iiii* and the *N* being attached to the *l* of *lat̄*. Farley prints *In* interlined.

Ch. 46 MATTHEW OF MORTAGNE. Mortagne is in the département of Manche, France.

46,1 MILBORNE (ST. ANDREW). The two Milborne parishes lay adjacent to each other, but in different Hundreds, mainly divided from each other by a tributary of the river Piddle, but Milborne St. Andrew parish in its northern part extended both sides of the stream. Milborne St. Andrew was in Puddletown Hundred (21), Milborne Stileham in Bere (22); see 54,12 and 56,53 notes. Since 1933 Milborne Stileham has been incorporated in Milborne St. Andrew. The present Milborne is identifiable in the Tax Return for Puddletown Hundred (viii) and is held there from William *Le Moyne* in FA ii p. 16. The same man names Owermoigne (46,2). The northern part of Milborne St. Andrew parish was called Milborne Deverel. Although included by EPNS (i p. 306) and Fägersten (p. 173) in Puddletown Hundred, it lay in Barrow Hundred (a later sub-division of Bere) in the Middle Ages and may represent the holding at 54,12. Elias *de Deverel* holds *Muleborn* in FA ii pp. 37, 42, 56. The land included Deverel farm (GR SY 8098) and perhaps a part of Winterborne Whitechurch, FA ii p. 44.

46,1-2 JOHN. Probably John the Dane, one of the predecessors of Matthew of Mortagne in Somerset and probably also in Gloucestershire.

46,2 OWERMOIGNE. DB *Ogre*. The holding can be identified in the Tax Return for 'Chilbury' Hundred (xxxi). Ralph *Monachus* holds *Oweres* in Winfrith Hundred (27) in Fees p. 89; see RBE ii p. 547 and Fees pp. 260, 1387. William *le Moinne* holds in FA ii p. 6.

Ch. 47 ROGER ARUNDEL. *Arundel* in DB, *Arundellus* in Exon., from OFr *arondel* 'little swallow' (Mod.Fr *hirondelle* 'swallow'), ultimately from Latin *hirundo* (OEB p. 359); no connection with the Sussex place-name nor the Earls of Arundel. Roger's lands later form the Honour of Powerstock, being then held by the Newburgh or Fitzpaine families.

47,1 WYNDLAM. DB *Windelham*, which seems to be needed to complete the total for the Tax Return of Gillingham Hundred (xxvii). *Winesham* is a fee of Robert *de Novo Burgo* in Fees p. 751.
ROGER *DE MARGELLA*. It has not proved possible to identify this place-name. A descendant, William *de Margellis*, is a tenant in Dorset in RBE i p. 217.

47,2 MELBURY. The land was at Melbury Bubb held in Fees p. 94 by William *Bubbe* from Robert of Newburgh. It can be identified in the Tax Return for Yetminster Hundred (i); see 26,35 note. From FA ii p. 36 it seems that the land may have included *Batecumbe* [Batcombe GR ST 6104].

47,3 CHELBOROUGH. See 36,8 note. This land can be deduced from the Tax Return for Tollerford Hundred (xiv) and is probably East Chelborough. Robert *filius Pagani* holds *Chawberge* in FA ii pp. 35, 55; see Hutchins ii p. 652.
UNBROKEN MARES. Exon. *indomitas equas* (accusative), probably the same as the *siluestres equae* 'wild mares' or forest ponies which occur elsewhere in Exon.

47,3 -4;9 AETHELFRITH. *Aluert, Aieluert, Ailuert* in DB; *Ailuert* and *Agelferdus* in Exon.; see PNDB p. 183. Identified by Round in VCH *Somerset* i p. 419 as the *Æilferth minister* who witnessed King Edward's grant of Ashwick (DB Som. 7,15) to Bath Abbey in 1061. See also Eyton *Somerset* i p. 156.

47,4 ROBERT TILLY. In the Exon. MS *atilet* here (or possibly *attlet*, as Ellis prints) and *atillet* for 47,10. Perhaps this is an unexplained surname of local type, from the OE preposition *aet* 'at' with some such word as, say, OE *hlet* 'a share, a portion, an allotment, an estate', or *(ge)laet(e)* 'a mill-leat or conduit, a crossroads'. However, the manor is later in the hands of the Tilly family, so it is possible that *atil(l)et* is a variant of that surname. Tilly, OFr *de Tilie, de Tilli*, is derived from either Tilly-sur-Seulles, dép. Calvados, or Tilly, dép. Eure. The place-name *Tilly* belongs to a type derived from Latin *tilius* (feminine) 'a lime-tree'. The form *atil(l)et* represents OFr *à tillet* (Latin *ad tiletum*) meaning '(place) at a grove of lime-trees'. A Ralph of Tilly (*de Tilio*; see OEB p. 115 and Reaney s.n.) is found as a sub-tenant of Tavistock Abbey in the Exon. for Devon; see Devon Details Table under 5,1.
(LANGTON LONG) BLANDFORD. This is held as *Langeblaneford' Tilly* from Margery *Paganus* in Fees p. 752; see Fees p. 88, FA ii p. 43 and RBE ii p. 548. She also holds Worth (Matravers) 47,9 and Rollington 47,10. See 26,29 note and Hutchins i p. 282.
TAX FOR 5 HIDES. Only the lordship land (4 hides) is detailed, the villagers' land holding being omitted; see Exon. Notes 1,18.

47,5 BEXINGTON. *Bexinton'* is a fee of Robert *de Novo Burgo* in Fees p. 751 and is held in Uggescombe Hundred (25) from Matilda *de Arundel* in FA ii p. 7. From Fees p. 94 it would appear to have included *Luk'* [Look farm in Puncknowle, GR SY 5488] and *Notinton'* [identified by Fägersten p. 153 and EPNS i p. 200 as Nottington in Broadwey, GR SY 6682, far distant from Bexington].
9½ HIDES. The details in Exon. add up to 9 hides, less ½ virgate. See 1,19 note.

47,6 POWERSTOCK. The land can be identified in the Tax Return for Eggardon Hundred (iv) and is held in the same Hundred by Robert *de Novo Burgo* from Roger *de Arundel* in FA ii p. 2. It included *Wytherstone* [Wytherston farm GR SY 5397]; see Fees p. 93, RH i p. 97 and FA ii pp. 33, 53.

47,7 RALPH HOLDS WRAXALL ... 10 HIDES. DB implies that Ralph holds all of Wraxall at 10 hides from Roger and that William's 3 hides and the man-at-arms' hide are separate; however, Exon. (see note) makes it clear that Roger had 3 sub-tenants in Wraxall.
WRAXALL. In Eggardon Hundred (Tax Return iv). *Wroxhale* is a fee of Roger of Arundel in FA ii p. 3. Subdivisions of the holding (possibly the lands of William or the man-at-arms) were at *Stapelford* ['Stapleford', lost in Hooke, Fägersten p. 240] and *Nether Keinecumb* [Lower Kingcombe GR SY 5599, now in Toller Porcorum parish, Tollerford Hundred (13), formerly in Eggardon]; see Fees pp. 94, 751, FA ii pp. 2, 33, 53, Cal. Inq. PM vol. v (Ed. II) no. 607 and 6th note under 1,2 and notes to 32,3 and 40,9.
4 SLAVES. In the MS only the top half of the first *i* of the *iiii* is there, perhaps added to an original *iii*. It is unlikely to be an enlarged dot, as the scribe does not usually have a dot before a number when it succeeds an *7*. Farley reads it as *iiii*.
WILLIAM HOLDS 3 HIDES. Perhaps William Cheever (*capra*, not *capru* as Ellis prints) who in the Tax Return for Eggardon Hundred (iv) did not pay the King tax on 3½ hides (not 3 hides as here) that he held from Roger Arundel.
3 HIDES ... 4 VILLAGERS. VALUE £3. From the Exon. rendering '4 villagers have these 3 hides for £3 in tribute' it would seem likely that the villagers held the 3 hides at a revenue, i.e. for a money rent. Cf. 56,39 where 6 men hold 1 hide in Ringstead 'at a revenue'. See 1,7 note on 'value' and cf. next note and notes to 57,2;17. For clear examples of land being 'farmed' by the villagers, see the Exon. addition to DB Devon 25,28 and 26,1, Middlesex 3,17, Kent 5,141 and probably Surrey 8,29. See also DB Devon General Notes to 21,11. 25,28 and 34,14. See R. S. Hoyt 'Farm of the Manor and Community of the Vill in Domesday Book' in Speculum xxx (1955).
MAN-AT-ARMS ... 20s. From Exon. it would seem that the 20s was a money rent; see preceding note.
IN TOTAL, VALUE ... £9. That is the sum of the values of the 3½ hides lordship, 2½ hides held by the villagers, William's 3 hides and the man-at-arms' hide.
WHEN HE ACQUIRED IT. Although *Q'do recep* (DB and Exon.) could be extended to *quando recepta (est)* 'when (the manor; *mansio*) was acquired', a translation favoured elsewhere in this series, it is more likely to abbreviate *quando recepit* referring to Roger (as also in 28,2). The phrase is very common in Exon. and on a great many occasions is written in full as *quando recepit*. See 1,9 Exon. Notes and cf. 28,2 note above.

47,8 POORTON. Identifiable in the Tax Return for 'Redhone' (Beaminster) Hundred (xiii), see 13,7 note.
ALWIN AND ULF HELD IT AS (....) 2 HIDES. Almost certainly 'two manors' or 'TRE; it paid tax for' has been omitted after 'held it (as)'. Exon. shows that there were two manors, one held by Alwin, the other by Ulf.

47,9 WORTH (MATRAVERS). Required by the Tax Return for Ailwood (Rowbarrow) Hundred (xix). *Wurthe* or *Worzthe* is a Fitzpaine fee in Hasler Hundred (28), together with Rollington (47,10), in Fees p. 752 and FA ii pp. 37, 44, 56.
AETHELFRITH. See 47,3-4;9 note.
WOODLAND, 7 FURLONGS IN BOTH LENGTH AND WIDTH. Exon. indicates that the woodland measured 7 furlongs in length and as many in width, the furlong here being used in a linear sense and the phrase apparently being equivalent to 'woodland, 7 furlongs'. See 1,1 note.

47,10 ROLLINGTON. In Hasler Hundred (28); see 47,9 note.
TAX FOR 2½ HIDES, LESS THE FOURTH PART OF 1 VIRGATE. In the MS *min'* (= *minus* 'less') is added in the margin; at first the scribe obviously took the meaning to be 'it paid tax for 2½ hides and the fourth part of 1 virgate' and then, when he added the *min'*, he presumably omitted to delete the *7* after *dimid'*. However, Exon. also has an *&* in error when it states that 'these thanes still have in lordship these 2½ hides (and) less the

fourth part of 1 virgate' (see Exon. Notes), though not when it gives the tax earlier in the entry; the *minus* is not an addition but begins a new line in the Exon. MS and could have been overlooked. This appears to be a clear example of the Exchequer scribe copying directly from Exon. as we have it now, mistakes and all. See 56,56 note.

47,12 HERSTON. The land appears as *Suanewik'* [Swanage] in the list of Arundel fees in Fees p. 94; see Fees p. 751.
HER. It is possible that Herston is named after *Her*, standing for OE *Here*, a shortened form of names such as *Herefrith, Heremod* etc. (although PNDB p. 289 considers this unsatisfactory); see EPNS i p. 55.

Ch. 48 SERLO OF BURCY. Burcy is in the département of Calvados, France. His lands pass to a daughter Geva, then to the children of her first husband, Martin.

48,1 WATERSTON. DB *Pidere*. Identifiable in Puddletown Hundred (Tax Return viii). It is held as *Pidela Walteri* in Fees p. 93 by William *filius Martini*; and as *Pudele Walterreston* in FA ii p. 15; see Fees p. 379, FA ii pp. 35, 54, 61 and Taylor pp. 212-213.

48,2 WHITECLIFF. Required by the Tax Return for Ailwood (Rowbarrow) Hundred (xix).

Ch. 49 AIULF THE CHAMBERLAIN. He was the brother of Humphrey the Chamberlain; VCH (Som.) i p. 416. He had succeeded Hugh son of Grip as Sheriff of Dorset by 1082/84 (*Regesta* i no. 204; Round CDF no. 1206 p. 435, see 26,20 second note) and was Sheriff of Somerset by 1091 (*Regesta* i no. 315), holding both offices in the reign of Henry I and perhaps until 1120. He was probably also at court a deputy to Robert Malet the King's great Chamberlain; W. A. Morris 'The Office of Sheriff in the Early Norman Period' in EHR xxxiii (1918) p. 151 note 48. Aiulf also held land in Wiltshire. Some of his Dorset lands are later held by the *Gouiz* family, which also holds those of Hugh son of Grip (Ch. 55). For the form *Aiulf*, see last note under 1,8.

49,1 BLANDFORD ST. MARY. Identifiable in the Tax Return for Combsditch Hundred (xvi); see 26,29 note.

49,3 HAMPRESTON. DB *Hame*. This land can be identified in the Tax Return for *Canendona* Hundred (vii). In FA ii p. 27 (Cranborne Hundred 6), John *de Gouyz* and Alice *de Lucy* hold in *Hamme* from the Earl of Gloucester; see FA ii pp. 39, 46.
6 HIDES. In the MS the *vi* appears to be a correction, possibly from *iii*, with an odd mark over the *v*. The parchment is scraped here.

49,4 *SELAVESTUNE*. The place can be deduced from the Tax Return for Badbury Hundred (vi), but has not been precisely identified; see EPNS ii p. 189.

49,5 'TARRANT'. The association of this place with Stubhampton, Chettle and Farnham (the last in *Langeberga* Hundred Tax Return xxii) suggests a place on the upper reaches of the river, in *Langeberga* Hundred; possibly Tarrant Gunville, Hutchins iii pp. 451, 459; see Introductory Note 2 on 'Rivers').

49,7 AETHELHARD. This OE personal name is represented in DB by *Aelard* (Sussex 11,8), *Ailardus* (Devon 34,53) and with AN interchange of *l, r* by *Airard* here. See PNDB p. 184.

49,8 FARNHAM. In *Langeberga* Hundred (as 49,17) in 1086 (49,5 note), later in Cranborne (6) where Robert *de Lucy* and John *de Gouiz* hold from the Earl of Gloucester in FA ii p. 26.
IT PAID TAX FOR 2 HIDES, WHICH ARE THERE. It looks as though the scribe has omitted the phrase *Terra est ... car̄* which normally precedes the phrase *qui ibi sunt (cum)* (see 49,6. 50,3 etc.). It is not possible to tell how many ploughs were there.

49,9 BRADLE. A fee of Alfred of Lincoln in Fees p. 750; held in Hasler Hundred (28) from the heirs of William *de Gouiz* and Roger *de Haselden* in FA ii p. 37; see FA ii pp. 44, 56.

49,10 TATTON. The entries here and at 55,23 can be identified in the Tax Return for Uggescombe Hundred (iii). Tatton is now in Cullifordtree (26), as the result of a later change in the Uggescombe/Cullifordtree boundary. In FA ii p. 7 Brian *de Govis* and Andrew *de Tattun* hold in Uggescombe Hundred (2) from the Earl of Gloucester.
CERNE CHURCH. It had also lost 2 hides in Tatton to Hugh son of Grip (55,23). Cf. 49,17 and 55,21, other alienations of church land (this time from Shaftesbury) by Aiulf and Hugh's wife. However, there is no reference under the holding of Cerne Abbey (Ch. 11) to these alienations, as there is under Shaftesbury Abbey (19,11) for 49,17 and 55,21.

49,11 DURWESTON. In *Hunesberga* Hundred in 1086 (Tax Return xxv). Bryan *de Gouiz* holds in Pimperne Hundred (9) from the Honour of Gloucester in FA ii pp. 27, 43, 46; see Fees p. 750.

49,11 VINEYARD. Aiulf also had a vineyard on one of his estates in Wiltshire (DB Wilts.
-12 55,1).

49,12 WOOTTON (FITZPAINE). It can be identified in the Tax Return for Whitchurch
      Hundred (ii). See 26,63 note.
      4 CARUCATES ARE IN LORDSHIP. *carucatae* is probably an error for *hidae*, which is
      usual in this phrase (e.g. 1,7): carucates were used of land not hidated (see 2,6 note) and
      this holding paid tax for 12 hides.
      ARPENTS. An *arpent* was a French measure of uncertain and probably variable size,
      usually applied in DB to vineyards, but occasionally to meadow and woodland (see DB
      Wilts. 12,4 note). The vineyard in 49,11 is measured in acres, unusually.
49,13 BRIDGE. DB *Brige* here, *Briga* in 55,18, the most likely identification being with Bridge
      farm in Wyke Regis; EPNS i p. 268.
      LAND FOR 2 OXEN. The number of oxen appear quite frequently in place of 'y ploughs'
      in this phrase in Dorset (e.g. 55,12;18. 56,25;41 etc.). There were normally reckoned to
      be 8 oxen to a plough-team, but there is evidence for smaller teams in the south-west;
      see R. Lennard in EHR lx (1945) p. 217 ff. and in EHR lxxxi (1966) p. 770 ff. and
      H. P. R. Finberg in EHR lxvi (1951) p. 67 ff. In Herefordshire there is evidence that, at
      least on the King's lordship land, a plough-team of 6 oxen was the norm; see DB Herefords.
      1,50 note. See also DB Devon 3,36 General Notes where '6 oxen in a plough' are recorded
      and examples given of '3 oxen' in Exon. corresponding to DB's '½ plough'. In the latter
      case, however, the Exchequer scribe may merely have rounded up Exon.'s odd oxen to a
      ½ plough: on a number of occasions the DB scribe seems to have discounted odd oxen,
      as the 2 oxen in 55,40 (see also Devon Exon. Notes 15,33).
      2 FISHERMEN; THEY PAY 5s. Or perhaps, reading *redd'* as abbreviating *reddit* rather
      than *reddunt*, "2 fishermen. It (the virgate) pays 5s". See notes to 2,5. 47,7 and 57,2.
49,14 HETHFELTON. This entry is required by the Tax Return for Bere Hundred (xv). Since
      Worgret was similarly in Bere Hundred in 1086, it seems probable that the southern
      boundary of the Hundred was the river Frome. Hethfelton is later in Winfrith Hundred
      (27); Worgret was later in Hasler Hundred (28); see 11,9 note.
      VALUE WAS 5s; NOW 40s. A large increase; see 56,12 note.
49,15 LULWORTH. It can be identified in the Tax Return for Winfrith Hundred (xxx).
      ALFRED THE SHERIFF. Of Dorset before 1066; see Harmer no. 1 and p. 557.
49,16 (LONG) CRICHEL. *Lang Kyrchil* is held in FA ii p. 28 (1303) in Knowlton Hundred
      (10) by John *de Gouyz*; the same man holds Farnham (49,8) and Hampreston (49,3); see
      1,3 and 34,11 notes and Hutchins iii p. 482.
      AIULF HOLDS ... FOR AS LONG ... SHERIFF. Cf. DB Herts. 1,13 where the Sheriff
      Ilbert gave land to a man-at-arms of his while (*dum* i.e. 'for as long as') he was Sheriff.
49,17 FARNHAM. See 49,8 note.
      FARNHAM ... SHAFTESBURY CHURCH. See 19,11 and note. See 55,21 for another
      part of Farnham, similarly held before 1066 by Shaftesbury. See also 49,10 note. Aiulf
      restored this ½ hide to Shaftesbury when his daughter became a nun there; see the
      confirmation charter dated 1121–2 in *Regesta* ii pp. 346–347 no. clv (Calendar no. 1347).
Ch. 50 HUMPHREY THE CHAMBERLAIN. Brother of Aiulf the Sheriff (see Ch. 49 note). He
      was probably of the household of Queen Matilda: he held land in Surrey (DB Ch. 31)
      from her holding and she gave him two manors in Gloucestershire (DB Glos. 69,6-7) and
      she herself held the rest of Edmondsham (1,18). His estates became part of the Honour
      of Gloucester; some of his heirs and tenants from the Gloucester Honour are a branch of
      the De Gurnay family.
50,1-2 EDMONDSHAM. See 1,18 note. The land seems to have lain in *Albretesberga* Hundred
      (v) in 1086 and was later in Cranborne Hundred (6) where Bartholomew *Payn* (who holds
      50,4 Stourpaine) holds in *Emodesham* from John *de Badeham* in FA ii p. 27 and see
      pp. 39, 40.
50,1 DODA. See 1,18 note.
50,2 EDEVA. Perhaps the widow who in the Tax Return for *Albretesberga* Hundred (v) held
      1 hide at a revenue from Humphrey the Chamberlain and from which the King had no tax
      "because Aiulf states that the Queen had remitted it for the soul of her son Richard".
      The name represents OE *Eadgifu.*
50,3 HEMSWORTH. Probably in Badbury Hundred in 1086 (Tax Return vi).
50,4 STOURPAINE. DB *Sture.* The place can be identified in the Tax Return for Pimperne
      Hundred (xxvi) which states that of the 5 hides Humphrey the Chamberlain holds in
      lordship he gave ½ hide to the church with the King's consent. In Fees p. 753 *Stures Paen*
      is held from Robert *Gurnay* and in FA ii p. 28 has the same holders as Edmondsham
      (50,1-2); see Fees p. 87, FA ii pp. 43, 46, 47, Cal. Inq. PM vol. vii (Ed. III) no. 416 and
      Hutchins i p. 304. See 57,19 note.

Ch. 51   THIS ENTRY is squeezed in at the bottom of col. 83b, extending a couple of letters into the central margin, the last line being below the bottom marginal ruling which was done so firmly that it cut the parchment.
HUGH OF PORT. From Port-en-Bassin near Bayeux in the département of Calvados, France; OEB p. 108. He was Sheriff of Notts. and Derbys. 1081–1087, and also Sheriff of Hants. *c.* 1070–1096 where most of his lands lay.

51,1   COMPTON (VALENCE). The 10 hides are divided between two Tax Returns; 6 hides 1 virgate are in Tollerford Hundred (xiv) and 3 hides 3 virgates in Frampton Hundred (xxxviii), although all 10 hides actually pay tax in Tollerford. In Fees p. 94 William *de Pont del Arch* holds *Cumton'* (also Compton *Pundelarche*, Fägersten p. 230) from Adam *de Port*, perhaps a descendant of Hugh of Port.
IN LORDSHIP 3 PLOUGHS. In the MS *iii car̄*; the first minim stroke is slightly smaller, possibly the reason why Farley missed it. The cut in the parchment comes here (see Ch. 51 note).

Ch. 52   HUGH OF ST. QUENTIN. Probably Saint-Quentin in the département of Manche, France; OEB p. 113. He also held land in Hampshire.

52,1   STINSFORD. In Fees p. 425 Philip *Quentin* holds in *Stinteford*. The holding can be identified in the Tax Return for Dorchester Hundred (xxxii).

52,2   THE SECOND LINE of this entry is written below the bottom margin ruling of col. 83a. Both 52,1 and the first two lines of 52,2 are compressed.
RINGSTEAD. This holding is required by the Tax Return for 'Chilbury' Hundred (xxxi) which was later absorbed by Winfrith Hundred (27). Ringstead is now in Osmington parish, and so in Cullifordtree Hundred (26) although it was long a tithing in Winfrith Hundred and was a separate parish until the 15th century. There were four holdings in DB (see also 55,34;36 and 56,39) and several villages in the Middle Ages. 'West Ringstead' is still on the OS maps, represented by the remains of a church and the earthworks of a deserted village. 'Up Ringstead' (perhaps a part of West Ringstead, 55,34 note) is probably represented by Upton (GR SY 7483); East Ringstead survived as a field name on the 1839 Tithe map, while Middle Ringstead is lost; see EPNS i p. 212 and RCHM ii p. 179 ff. The present holding is perhaps 'Up Ringstead', the ½ mill at 4s answering that at Watercombe (1,29). The natural site for the mill would be on the small brook that runs east–west between Upton and Watercombe, then reaches the sea at Osmington.
FOUR THANES. The *Q̄ttuȯ* (*Quattuor*) is written over an erasure in the MS, hence the unusual abbreviation and cramping.

Ch. 53   [LAND OF HUGH OF BOSCHERBERT]. The chapter heading has been omitted through lack of space. He is *de boscherberti* in the Landholders' List and *de boschherberti* in 53,1; in Exon. he occurs as *de bosco herberti* for 36,3 and as *de nemore herberti* for 55,46 and in the Tax Returns for Uggescombe Hundred (iii) and Dorchester Hundred (xxxii). The French place-name cannot be identified; OEB p. 74.

53,1   'CERNE'. One of the Lower Cernes (Forston, Herrison or Pulston) in St. George Hundred (20). It can be identified in the Tax Return for Dorchester Hundred (xxxii) and is stated, without evidence, to be Wolfeton in Charminster parish (1,4 second note) by Eyton *Dorset* pp. 123–4.

53,2   THE UNNAMED LAND lay in Uggescombe Hundred (Tax Return iii), where Hugh of Boscherbert is stated as holding 5 hides in lordship (the hidage of 53,1 'Cerne', Hugh's only other holding, being too small to account for it). This major holding has not been identified, but might possibly be Litton Cheney (GR SY 5590), lying in this Hundred, an important land in Fees pp. 93, 425 and in FA ii pp. 6, 34, 53, stated to have been in the King's hand since the time of William I. It included *Gorewull* [Gorewell farm in Long Bredy, GR SY 5787] and *Ekerdun* [Eggardon, the Hundred moot, GR SY 5393]. Further evidence is needed to clinch this identification. See 1,2 note.

Ch. 54   [LAND OF HUGH OF IVRY AND OTHER FRENCHMEN]. The chapter heading is supplied from the Landholders' List (no. 53 there; see Ch. 45 note), having been omitted in the text through lack of space.

54,1   HUGH OF IVRY. In the MS *Hugo de lVRI* (or perhaps *IVRI* but not *LVRI* as Farley) here, but *Hugo de Luri* in the Landholders' List (col. 75a). The form *Luri, luri*, which also occurs in DB Northants. 24,1 and in 23,16 with Roger of Ivry, is probably due to scribal confusion of *I* and *L*, as the byname occurs regularly in DB as *Iuri* and *Ivri* and is Ivry-la-Bataille in the département of Eure, France (OEB p. 93). Hugh of Ivry was Butler (*pincerna*) in the Norman household before 1066 (see Round CDF nos. 1167, 73) and was still called *pincerna* in 1082 (*Regesta* i no. 150); he was a tenant-in-chief in Northants.,

Oxfords. and probably Beds. (see Round KS p. 141). He was probably the brother (or perhaps the nephew) of Roger of Ivry who was also styled *pincerna* and was a tenant-in-chief in several DB counties (see notes to DB Glos. W 1 and Ch. 41). See Round KS pp. 140-141 and G. H. White 'The Household of the Norman Kings' in TRHS 4th ser. vol. xxx (1948) p. 141.
PLACES. In the MS *locis*; Farley misprints *Locis*.

54,2 (STOURTON) CAUNDLE. The land can be identified in the Brownshall Hundred Tax Return (xxviii); see 26,70-71 note.
[VALUE ...]. Probably omitted in error, as also in 54,14 and 57,16; see also 56,61 and note. Cf. 55,45 which has a value and for which Exon. states that the 1086 holder has a plough and 'nothing more'. See also notes to 2,5. 12,13. 49,13 and 57,2 on other possible reasons for omitted value statements.

54,3 'WEY'. It lay in Cullifordtree Hundred (Tax Return xxxvii), see Introductory Note 2 on 'Rivers'.

54,4 MOORBATH. The land lay in Whitchurch Hundred (Tax Return ii).

54,5 RICHARD OF REVIERS. Reviers in the département of Calvados, France; OEB p. 109.
MOSTERTON. The land can be located in the Tax Return for Beaminster Hundred (xii).

54,6 SHILLINGSTONE, earlier Shilling Okeford, *Acforde Eskelin*, named from the 1086 holder Azelin (*Schelin*), EPNS ii pp. 238-9. The land seems to have been parcelled out of Child Okeford (1,7), both being held by Earl Harold before 1066. Shillingstone is later a detached part of Cranborne Hundred (6), held of the Honour of Gloucester, Fees p. 750; FA ii pp. 26, 39, 45.

54,7 POORTON. See 13,7 note.

54,8 ANSKETEL SON OF AMELINA. He appears to be the same as Ansketel of Cherbourg (*de Carisburgo* from *Caesaris burgum*; not Charborough as OEB p. 39 which is *Cereberie* in Dorset 1,9; nor Carisbrook as VCH iii p. 123; cf. Osbern of Cherbourg, *de Keresburg* in DB Glos. 71,1); see the Tax Return for Hasler Hundred (xxix) where he holds 2 hides 1½ virgates lordship land.
BRICTRIC. Probably Brictric son of Algar; see 1,17 note.
DID NOT PETITION THE KING (FOR IT). *regem non requisiuit*. At Queen Matilda's death in 1083 the land would have fallen to the King and it would have been natural for Ansketel to have requested renewal of his sub-tenancy, but he did not do so, and seems therefore to have been holding the land illegally in 1086.

54,9 RALPH. Probably Ralph of Cranborne who is recorded as holding 1 hide and 1 virgate in lordship in the Tax Return for *Langeberga* Hundred (xxii).
'TARRANT'. This land was in *Langeberga* Hundred (xxii). It is possible that this Ralph, or the man of 55,29, named Tarrant Rawston; Fägersten p. 61; EPNS ii p. 127; Eyton *Dorset* pp. 131-2.

54,10 (WEST) PARLEY. Can be identified in *Canendona* Hundred (Tax Return vii). East Parley is in the adjacent Hurn parish just over the Hampshire border. West Parley is held from the Earl of Gloucester in Cranborne Hundred (6) in FA ii pp. 27, 46, 59.

54,11 FARNHAM. The land lay in *Langeberga* Hundred (xxii) in 1086 (Tax Return xxii).

54,12 MILBORNE (STILEHAM). The land can be identified in the Tax Return for Bere Hundred (xv); see 46,1 note. The sub-tenant Doda may have named Dodding's farm in Bere Regis; see 55,15 note.

54,13 THE SON OF EVERBOLD. Most probably Odo (54,11) rather than a different son.

54,14 PETERSHAM. Held as *Pitrichesham* in two portions from the Honour of Gloucester, Fees p. 750; in Cranborne Hundred (6) in FA ii pp. 26, 39, 46. See Ch. 55a note. It lay in *Canendona* Hundred in 1086 (Tax Return vii).
[VALUE ...]. Omitted in error; see 54,2 note.

Ch. 55 LAND OF THE WIFE OF HUGH SON OF GRIP. In the MS *Hugonis filii G(rip)* is written over an erasure. She was called Hawise; see 23,1 note. See B 1 note on her husband the Sheriff of Dorset before Aiulf. She appears to have remarried, this time to Alfred of Lincoln; see T. Bond 'On the Barony of the Wife of Hugh Fitz Grip' in PDNHAS xiv (1893) pp. 116-118. Certainly her lands are later in the possession of Alfred of Lincoln and his heirs. A frequent holder in the feodaries is William *de Gouiz*. Alfred of Lincoln's son Robert founded the priory of East Holme, a cell of Montacute, and endowed it with lands, tithes and churches from his holdings (see VCH iii p. 80). The list in MC pp. 160-161, nos. 118-119, contains 3 virgates in *Wrde* [Worth Matravers 55,43], the land of *Plys* [Plush, see 8,3 note], salt from the salt-pans at *Langeton* in *Purbike* [Langton Matravers, see 37,13 note], the tithes of *Acforde* [Okeford Fitzpaine 8,2], *Winterburne Gurewambe* [see 55,1 note], *Langeton* near *Abotesbire* [Langton Herring 55,31], *Corfton* [Corton in Portesham, 13,4 note], a garden near *Bradle* [probably Orchard, 55,47 note, near Bradle 49,9], *Cheselbumeforde* ['Little Cheselbourne' 55,3], *Watercumbe* [part of Ringstead (?), see 55,36], and the church of *Wermewelle* [Warmwell 55,35]. In the *Inquisition post mortem* of Alfred of Lincoln (1264, Cal. Inq. PM vol. i (Henry III) no. 580) and that of William *de Gouyz* (Cal. Inq. PM vol. iii (Ed. I) no. 541) many of the lands held by the wife of Hugh, both in chief and as sub-tenant, reappear.

55,1   MARTINSTOWN. DB *Wintreburne*; the fuller modern form, Winterborne St. Martin, survives as the parish name. This entry can be identified in the Tax Return for Dorchester (St. George) Hundred (xxxii) and the land later became *caput* of the Barony of Robert Fitzpaine, see FA ii pp. 17, 31, 50 and Cal. Inq. PM vol. i (Henry III) no. 580.

Of the eight holdings named 'Winterborne' in the lands of the wife of Hugh, two — Winterborne Houghton (55,17 see note) and the present entry — can be positively identified. Of the remainder, 55,9 can be deduced from the Tax Return for Cullifordtree Hundred (xxxvii) and 55,11-12 from that for Combsditch (xvi), while 55,27-28 are to be located in the Tax Return for *Hunesberga* Hundred (xxv). This places the 'Winterbornes' in particular Hundreds, but does not individually identify them. The only other 'Winterborne', 55,7, while it cannot be found in a Tax Return, lies in a group of Cullifordtree Hundred (26) places that begins with Buckland Ripers (55,4) and ends with 'Winterborne' (55,9).

Later evidence sometimes identifies more precisely the land of the wife of Hugh. Thus in Cullifordtree Hundred (26) lay *Winterborne Esse*, now Ashton in Winterborne St. Martin, St. George Hundred (20), (but formerly in Cullifordtree); see EPNS i p. 375 and Hutchins ii p. 573. It is held from Alfred of Lincoln in Fees p. 750 and from William *de Gouiz* in FA ii p. 19, Cal. Inq. PM vol. iii (Ed. I) no. 541. This probably represents the land of 55,9.

In Combsditch Hundred (16) Winterborne *Rocheford* [now Winterborne Whitechurch] was held from the Barony of Alfred of Lincoln in Fees p. 751. In FA ii pp. 29, 44, 48, the same land appears as *Wynterbum Blaumuster* held by Ralph *de Rocheford* and in Cal. Inq. PM vol. iii (Ed. I) no. 541 it is *Wynterbum Whitchurch*. Furthermore, in the grant by Robert of Lincoln to Montacute Priory (Ch. 55 note above) there appears a *Winterburne Gurewambe*. This form is not noted in the EPNS volume, but might be the same as *Winterbum' Guah(e)bon*, noted but without decisive evidence of identity, under Whatcombe in Winterborne Whitechurch (EPNS ii p. 84; see 55,34;36 note). These lands will probably correspond to one of 55,11-12.

Adjacent to Winterborne Whitechurch but in Bere Hundred (22), William *de Gouyz* held half of *Kyngeswynterbom* [Winterborne Kingston] in FA ii p. 12. This holding may well have been in Combsditch Hundred in 1086 and account for one of 55,11-12.

Also held from the Barony of Alfred of Lincoln was Winterborne *Quarel* (Fees p. 751) [now Quarleston farm in Winterborne Stickland, see FA ii pp. 28, 43, 47]; this will probably have lain in *Hunesberga* Hundred (xxv) in 1086 and will correspond to the entries at 55,27-28.

55,2   FROME (WHITFIELD). The land is held as *Frome Vitefell* of the Barony of Winterborne St. Martin (55,1 note) in FA ii p. 17; see FA ii pp. 31, 50 and VCH iii p. 144. It is a fee of the Barony of Alfred of Lincoln in Fees p. 751 and in the Inq. PM of 1264 (see Ch. 55 note above).

55,3   ROGER BUSHELL. Exon. *boisellus* here and *bissellus* for 11,6 (other spellings being *buissel, boiscellus* etc.; OEB pp. 373-4). See 11,6 second note.

'(LITTLE) CHESELBOURNE'. In Puddletown Hundred (21), alternatively *Cheselbornford* ['Cheselbourne Ford'], held by William *de Gouiz* in FA ii pp. 16, 35, 54. For the location of the place see EPNS i p. 316, Taylor p. 211 and RCHM vol. iii p. 230. The heirs of William *de Gouiz* also seem to have had some interest in Dewlish, which is adjacent; FA ii pp. 38, 57. On the possession by Abbotsbury Abbey, see Hutchins iv p. 348.

55,4   BUCKLAND (RIPERS). The holding can be identified in the Tax Return for Cullifordtree Hundred (xxxvii). In Fees p. 750 *Boclande* is a fee of Alfred of Lincoln and is held by John *de Ripirs* (of Rivers) from Robert Fitzpaine (the latter holds 55,1-2) in FA ii pp. 19, 38, 57.

55,5-6   'WEY'. *Brodewaye* [Broadwey] and *Waye Pigace* [Upwey, see Fägersten p. 159 and EPNS i p. 245], are held from the Barony of Alfred of Lincoln in Fees p. 750; in FA ii pp. 19, 38 and Cal. Inq. PM vol. v (Ed. II) no. 457 *Brodeweye* [Broadwey] is held from William *de Gouiz*. *Rowaldeswey* ['Rowaldsway', lost in Broadwey] was held by William *de Gouiz* in

Cal. Inq. PM vol. iii (Ed. I) no. 541. Another settlement may have been 'Wayhoughton' a lost place in Broadwey, the name being derived from a Hugh, possibly Hugh son of Grip; EPNS i p. 201; see EPNS ii p. 129.

55,6 THANES. In the MS there is an ink blot over the *t* of *taini*, but the meaning is clear.

55,7 'WINTERBORNE'. Among Cullifordtree Hundred (26) places in the order of the text; see 55,1 note.

55,8 STAFFORD. The land was at West Stafford in Cullifordtree Hundred (26), held in FA ii pp. 20, 38 by William *de Gouiz* and Robert Fitzpaine, the split tenure reflecting the 1086 division. In Fees p. 750 it is held from the Barony of Alfred of Lincoln as *Stafford Turberevil'*. See 26,7 note.

MEADOW ... PASTURE. There is an erasure of about 9 letters in the MS after *p̃ti* with a line drawn to link up *p̃ti* and *7 xvi* ... to show that the scribe did not intend to add anything there. Farley does not print the link line here (nor in 57,1), though he does occasionally, e.g. DB Herefords. 29,16 (see note) and Worcs. 15,11.

PASTURE, 16 FURLONGS AND 8 ACRES. It is possible that *siluae* 'woodland' has been omitted after *āc* (see VCH iii p. 4 and p. 104 note 45), although there is a full-stop after *āc* in the MS. Exon., which gives details of Hugh's and William's holdings separately (see Details Table), has '8 furlongs of pasture and 4 acres' for each tenant, and again *nemoris* 'woodland' may have been omitted, though there is no sign of this in the MS and it would be out of the normal sequence; see Exon. Notes 36,3. There are several examples of furlongs and acres being mixed in a measurement; see 5,1 note with special reference to 19,4. It may be that there were 16 furlongs of pasture in one place and 8 acres in another (cf. 36,2. 55,29 and Exon. Notes to 1,8).

55,9 'WINTERBORNE'. One of the Winterbornes on the South Winterborne river in Cullifordtree Hundred (26); see 55,1 note and the Appendix.

55,10; 13-14 WILLIAM CHERNET. The forms of this byname which appear in Exon. are *chernet, de creneto* and *chernaet* respectively. It might be a Breton place-name surname from one of the group: Kernay, Kerné, Kernéac(h), Kernec'h, Kernerc'h, indexed on p. 202 of F. Falchun and B. Tanguy *Les Noms de Lieux Celtiques*, 2nd series, Rennes 1970. More precise identification is impossible at present.

55,10 MORDEN. The land was later called Morden *Roberti*, a fee of Alfred of Lincoln, Fees p. 751; see 26,24 note.

LAND FOR 1 PLOUGH. A gap suitable for about 22 letters follows this statement, possibly left for such details as Exon. gives, although the Exchequer scribe does not always give the amount of land in lordship and never the villagers' land holding in Dorset. It is more likely that the space was left for the ploughs in lordship and the number of villagers and their ploughs and the resources, information similarly omitted by Exon.; see fourth note to 1,1 and 1,2 note ('Woodland ... wide') on gaps left by the Exchequer scribe.

55,11 -12 'WINTERBORNE'. One of the eastern 'Winterbornes' in Combsditch Hundred (xvi): see 55,1 note and the Appendix.

55,11 5 HIDES ... 3 HIDES ... 1½ HIDES. It is likely that Exon.'s 3 hides lordship is a mistake for '3½ hides', which is the figure given for Hugh's wife's lordship in the Tax Return for Combsditch Hundred (xvi), and which would then add up with the villagers' land to the 5 hides. See 1,19 note on other discrepancies between the details and tax total.

55,12 'WINTERBORNE'. See 26,13 note.

55,13 WIMBORNE (ST. GILES). The identification is not certain, but the order of the text suggests a place in *Albretesberga* Hundred (v) rather than in Badbury Hundred (which would imply Wimborne Minster). The part mill may be associated with that of 57,9.

THE THIRD PART OF A MILL WHICH PAYS 15d. The Latin is ambiguous: the *redd'* could refer either to the third part or to the whole mill. Exon., however, makes it clear that it is the third part of the mill which pays 15d (see Exon. Notes). Cf. 56,12 note.

55,14 AETHELWARD. DB and Exon. *Ageluuardus*; see 36,2 note.

55,15 BERE (REGIS). Identified by EPNS i p. 274 (after Eyton *Dorset* pp. 115-116) and by VCH as Dodding's farm in Bere Regis, but no evidence is cited. See 54,12 note.

LEOFMER. DB *Leomer*, Exon. *Leōmaer'*; perhaps OE *Leodmaer* (PNDB p. 319).

LAND FOR ½ PLOUGH. In the MS there is a pale orange blot of ink (or perhaps a water blot), probably contemporary, partially obscuring the *ē* of *T̃ra ē* ... . See 1,24 note for a similar blot.

55,15a WILLIAM ... 20s. Recent close study of the MS of the size of the *W* of *Will's* and the amount of red ink applied to it, and comparison with the similar Devon 3,32;71 (see General Notes to these) suggests that this is not a subdivision of 55,15 (as first thought), but a separate entry (as it is in Exon.). There is no evidence there that William is William of Moutiers or that the 1½ virgates were in Bere Regis.

55,16 (TURNERS) PUDDLE. The land can be identified in the Tax Return for Bere Hundred (xv). The affixed name is from the surname of Walter found in the Tax Return and in Exon.: *tonitrus* and *tonitruum* respectively, from Latin *tonare*, OFr *toner* 'to thunder'; see EPNS i p. 295 and OEB p. 382. In FA ii p. 37 the land is held by Henry *Tonere* from the heirs of William *de Gouiz*, and is named *Pydele Tunere* in the 1264 Inq. PM (see Ch. 55 note above).
GERLING. In Exon. *Ierlincus* (not *Lerlincus* as Ellis prints); PNDB p. 260.
TAX FOR 6 HIDES. The details amount to 5 hides; see 1,19 note.

55,17 HUGH. Hugh of Boscherbert; see 36,3 Exon. addition. He may also be the sub-tenant Hugh in 55,18.
WINTERBORNE (HOUGHTON). This 'Winterborne' is identified by the fact that the disputed 1 virgate is part of William of Mohun's manor of Winterborne Houghton (36,3). The added name *Houghton* may be derived from Hugh of Boscherbert or Hugh son of Grip (EPNS ii p. 129).

55,18 HUGH. See 55,17 note.
BRIDGE. See 49,13 note.

55,19 WILLIAM OF DAUMERAY. Exon. *de almereio* here; DB *de Dalmari* for 57,4;11; Daumeray in the département of Maine-et-Loire, France (OEB p. 85). In Fees p. 93 Jordan *de Stertel* holds ½ fee in Sturthill and the other half in Walditch (57,11) which is likewise held in 1086 by William of Daumeray.

55,20 GRASTON. In Godderthorn Hundred (18), held by the Abbot of Abbotsbury from William *de Gouiz* in FA ii p. 11.

55,21 FARNHAM ... SHAFTESBURY CHURCH. See 19,11 and 49,17 notes.
55,21 WHEN HUGH ACQUIRED IT. Hugh son of Grip. Likewise for 55,25; 27; 36.

55,22 PUNCKNOWLE. In Uggescombe Hundred (25) held by William *de Wytefeuld* from Robert *filius Pagani* in FA ii pp. 5, 34, 53.

55,23 TATTON. In Fees p. 93, in Uggescombe Hundred (25), Avicia *de Tatton'* holds in *Tatton'* from Alfred of Lincoln. It can be identified in the Tax Return for Uggescombe Hundred (iii).
BEFORE 1066 TWO THANES ... Or perhaps the *TRE* belongs with the preceding phrase: "... which were (part) of the lordship of the Abbey of Cerne before 1066. Two thanes held ...". Exon. favours this alternative (see Exon. Notes for this entry).
DESPITE THE ABBOT. *super abbatem. super* 'over, against', is difficult to render in this sense. The primary notion is that of a battle or contest, fair or unfair, in which Hugh 'wins' and the Abbot 'loses'; cf. DB Cambs. 3,5. The reality, however, could be that the land was taken against the Abbot's wish or without his knowledge.

55,24 LODERS. The land held by Walter (perhaps Walter Thunder; see 55,16 note) is probably *Lodres Luttone* (now Matravers) held by *Egidius Tonere* in FA ii p. 11 in Godderthorn Hundred (18) from William *de Gouiz*; see notes to 1,13 and 26,41–42.
PASTURE. The scribe originally wrote *pti* (= *prati* 'meadow') and then changed it to *p̂stě* for *pasture*, genitive. *Pastura* is not normally abbreviated in DB.

55,25 ½ HIDE. Only the lordship land (1 virgate) is detailed, the villagers' land holding being omitted; see Exon. Notes 1,18.
'TARRANT'. This holding can be identified in the Tax Return for *Langeberga* Hundred (xxii), but no Hundred can be assigned to the 'Tarrants' of 55,29–30. One of the three holdings was probably Tarrant Rawston held as Tarrant *Antioch* (EPNS ii p. 127) by Nicholas *Antioche* in FA ii p. 43 and in Fees p. 751 where he holds from Alfred of Lincoln. The wife of Hugh also seems to have held land in Tarrant Gunville, since 'Higher and Lower Barn Down', lost places in that parish, were earlier *Barndedon' Gouytz*, EPNS ii p. 243.

55,26 [WIDTH]. As Exon.; DB has *l̄g* in error.
55,27 'WINTERBORNE'. On the upper reaches of the eastern Winterborne river, perhaps
 -28 Quarleston in Winterborne Stickland; see 55,1 note and the Appendix.
55,28 1 HIDE AND 1 VIRGATE OF LAND. There is a gap in the MS after this, extending to the end of the line, perhaps intended for the plough estimate. Exon. does not give one either; see fourth note under 1,1.
KING WILLIAM ... 1 VIRGATE. This information also appears in the Tax Return for *Hunesberga* Hundred (xxv).

55,29 'TARRANT'. The 1086 Hundred is unknown, though the place may be Tarrant Rawston from the name of the sub-tenant; see 54,9 and 55,25 notes.

55,30 'TARRANT'. See 55,25 note.

55,31 LANGTON (HERRING). The land can be identified in the Tax Return for Uggescombe Hundred (iii). In Fees p. 93 it is held from Alfred of Lincoln in Uggescombe Hundred (25) and in FA ii p. 6 half the village is held of the fee of William *de Gouiz*, the other half no doubt representing the King's land 1,23. For the gift of Langton Herring to the priory of Holme, a cell of Montacute, see Ch. 55 note. The wife of Hugh held land in another Langton, 'Langton Wallis', see 37,13 note.

55,32 RUSHTON. See 55,35 note.

55,33 CHALDON. Probably West Chaldon, held as *Chauedon Boys* by William *de Gouiz* in FA ii p. 1; see Fees p. 750, Cal. Inq. PM vol. iii (Ed. I) no. 541, Hutchins i p. 339 and 1,12 note above. The affixed name *Boys*, ML *boscus*, Fr. *bois* 'wood' may be from the surname of the 1086 tenant, Hugh (of Boscherbert), or a descendant, see 55,46.

NINE THANES. In the MS and Farley *Nouē*; the facsimile fails to reproduce the abbreviation sign.

IN HUGH'S LIFE-TIME. The exact date of Hugh son of Grip's death is not known; see notes to B 1 and Ch. 49. Cf. DB Devon Exon. Notes 1,30 for probably another example of the value of a manor being given for three dates.

55,34; RINGSTEAD. Possibly 'East' and 'West' Ringstead, both held in FA ii pp. 9, 29 by
36 William *de Gouiz*. A comparison of the two surveys in FA suggests that 'Up Ringstead' may have been a part of 'West Ringstead', the holding of Milton Abbey from Nicholas *Antyoch* (who holds from William *de Gouiz*) being called 'West Ringstead' in one and 'Up Ringstead' in the other. See 52,2 note. The wife of Hugh may have held another part of Ringstead from Cerne Abbey (11,6 note). The holder of 'East Ringstead' in FA ii p. 9, Roger *de Bosco*, may be a descendant of Hugh (of Boscherbert), see 55,46) the 1086 holder. In Fees p. 750 and in the grant to East Holme Priory (Ch. 55 note above), Alfred of Lincoln holds a place called *Watercombe*. This is probably Watercombe adjacent to Ringstead (see 1,29), rather than Whatcombe farm (GR ST 8301) in Winterborne Whitechurch which the wife of Hugh also held (55,1 note; see Hutchins i p. 199).

55,34 2 SMALLHOLDERS. In the MS and Farley *ii bord'*; the facsimile fails to reproduce most of the first minim which is rather faint in the MS, making the number appear '*i*. .

55,35 WARMWELL. *Wermewull'* is a fee of Alfred of Lincoln in Fees p. 750; it is held from William *de Gouiz* in Winfrith Hundred (27) in FA ii p. 9 and coupled with *Rysston* [Rushton 55,32] in FA ii p. 30.

1½ HIDES. Perhaps a mistake for '1½ hides and 1 virgate'; see Exon. Notes here.

55,36 RALPH THE STEWARD. Exon. *dapifer*. He was Ralph of Montpinçon (in the département of Calvados, France); see Orderic Vitalis ii p. 435.

HUNWINE. DB *Onouuin'*, Exon. *Honowin'*; see PNDB p. 296.

55,37 ROBERT THE CORN-DEALER. In Exon. *Frumtinus*, a garbled form of Latin *frumentarius* due to the loss of the second contraction mark and confusion of *-rius* and *-inus*. Not as OEB p. 219.

BOLLE. DB *Boln*, Exon. *Bolo*; from OE *Bolla*. See PNDB pp. 205–6 s.nn. *Bolla* and *Boln*.

55,38 ROBERT BOY. *Puer*, similar to *cilt* 'Young', was probably used as 'younger' to distinguish from a senior Robert. Cf. Gruffydd Boy in DB Herefords. 1,34–35.

A BURGESS. Probably in Wareham which is the closest borough to Hurpston.

55,40 WILKSWOOD. It lay in Ailwood (Rowbarrow) Hundred (Tax Return xix).

TAX FOR 3½ HIDES AND 2 PARTS OF 1 VIRGATE. The detail amounts to only 3½ hides; see 1,19 note.

55,41 ACTON. In Langton Matravers parish and perhaps standing for it, DB *Tacatone*, see EPNS i p. 34. It is required by the Tax Return for Ailwood (Rowbarrow) Hundred (xix); see 37,13 note.

55,42 SWANAGE. *Swaneswich* is held as a fee of Alfred of Lincoln in Fees p. 750; see 8,3 note.

55,43 WORTH (MATRAVERS). Falls in a group of Rowbarrow Hundred (29) places in the order of the text of DB. See 37,13 note.

55,44 LAND FOR 1 PLOUGH. There is a gap of about 12 letters' width in the MS after this, probably left for details of population and resources, but see 1,2 note 'Woodland ... wide'.

55,44 'THORNE'. DB *Torne* identified by Eyton (*Dorset* pp. 111–112) with Durnford and by
-45 DG with Thornford in Church Knowle. EPNS i pp. 5, 35, 42 identifies it with the field name *La Thorne* at Court Pound, one-third of a mile west of Durnford House. In the order of the text, it falls naturally in a group of Rowbarrow Hundred (29) places.

55,45 ROBERT, HUGH'S NEPHEW. It is not clear from Exon. which Hugh this is; whether Hugh son of Grip, or Hugh of Boscherbert who is the sub-tenant of the next entry, or even the Hugh who according to Exon. was a man-at-arms of Hugh son of Grip's wife (55,33–34).

55,46   HUGH OF BOSCHERBERT. Other occurrences of Hugh in this chapter may be the same man: see notes to 55,33 and 55,34;36. For the name, see Ch. 53 note.

55,47   ORCHARD. The place can be identified in the Hasler Hundred Tax Return (xxix). This may be the same holding as *Gardinum* (French *jardin* 'a garden'), held in Fees p. 750 as a fee of Alfred of Lincoln and identical with the 'garden near Bradle' (Ch. 55 note); it is *Gardins* in Cal. Inq. PM vol. iii (Ed. I) no. 541. Another gift of Hugh to Cranborne Church is Gillingham 10,1.

AN ORCHARD. *uirgultum* (in DB and Exon.), usually in classical Latin 'a thicket' or 'shrubbery', but a ML extension of the meaning is 'orchard', the word being glossed by Ducange as *viridarium, pomarium*. The English place-name is probably due to the presence here of a notable orchard. See EPNS i p. 90. *Uirgultum* also occurs in DB Devon 15,1 (see note) where the Count of Mortain has one in Exeter, together with a church and a house.

HUGH'S WIFE ... ½ HIDE; VALUE 20s. Exon. makes it clear that the interlined *Valet .xx. sol'* belongs with the line below (that is the value of the ½ hide), rather than with the line above (the orchard being valued at 20s), as the interlineation *xv solid'* in 55,43 does. The value of the 1½ hides is thus 40s.

55,48   DURAND CARPENTER HOLDS ½ HIDE. Exon. here *carpĕtari'*, in the Tax Return *carpentari'*; it is not clear whether he was a carpenter by trade or the word had become a surname in his case by 1086. According to the Tax Return for Ailwood (Rowbarrow) Hundred (xix) the King did not have tax from ½ hide held by Durand Carpenter from Hugh's wife.

ALL THE THANES ... COULD GO TO WHICH LORD THEY WOULD. A rather sweeping statement: in 55,21 the 1066 holder Alwin is specifically said not to have been able to separate from Shaftesbury Church; also Exon. gives this information for little more than a third of the entries (see Exon. Notes here). See also the Exon. Notes for 1,29 and 58,3.

Ch.[55a]   [LAND OF ISOLDE]. In the MS there is a gap of 2 lines after 55,48 which Farley does not show. The space was not sufficient, however, for the rubricator to insert the chapter heading and he omitted the chapter number too. See Ch. 45 note. This manor is the only holding of Isolde's given in DB; it may have passed to the Honour of Gloucester with the other portion of Petersham (see 54,14 note). It lay in *Canendona* Hundred in 1086 (Tax Return vii).

56,1   MILTON (ON STOUR). DB *Mideltone* can be identified in the Tax Return for Gillingham Hundred (xxvii). It is probably the land held of the Honour of Chewton (56,14 note) in Gillingham Hundred (4), Fees p. 753; FA ii pp. 22, 32, 52.

56,2   KINGTON. Probably Kington Magna, *Mangna Kyngtone* held by Herbert *de Sancto Quintino* from the Earl of Gloucester, FA ii p. 22 in Gillingham Hundred (4). It can also be identified in the Tax Return for Gillingham Hundred (xxvii). See notes to 32,1 and 40,2.

56,4   GODRIC. Probably Godric Hunter who holds 1 virgate in lordship in the Tax Return for Gillingham Hundred (xxvii).

56,6   AELFRIC. Perhaps Aelfric Hunter who is recorded in the Tax Return for Bere Hundred (xv) as holding 2 hides in lordship; the other hide is probably at 56,60.

'WINTERBORNE'. The location in Bere Hundred (Tax Return xv) suggests Winterborne Kingston (see VCH iii p. 134), which was in this Hundred in 1285 (FA ii p. 12); see 55,11-12 note. In Fees p. 1387 Richard *de Wytewell'* holds in *Kingeswynterborn'*; William *de Wytewille* holds a half of the same village in FA ii p. 12 in Barrow Hundred. The other half is probably 55,11-12. In Cal. Inq. PM vol. v (Ed. II) no. 346, the same man holds *Wynterborn Regis, Craweford* (56,12) and *Bovyngton* (56,59) all held by Aelfric in 1086.

56,7   MAPPOWDER. It lay in Buckland Hundred in 1086 (Tax Return xxxvi) and is probably the land held in Buckland Newton Hundred (8) by Edward *de Mortuo Mari* in FA ii p. 30. See Fees p. 425 and 56,9-11 note.

HE HELD IT HIMSELF. *Ipse tenuit* in the MS with a very faint *li* (no doubt the beginning of *libere*) above the *te-* of *tenuit*. Farley prints the *li*, although it was probably erased. See next note.

7 FREE THANES. *Liberis* interlined to agree with thanes; perhaps a mistake for *libere* 'freely' which should have been written earlier, where Farley mistakenly began the *li*. See 1,30 fifth note.

MEADOW, 16 [ACRES?]. After *Ibi* in the MS *aliq' tū* (= *aliquantum* 'a little') is written, but underlined for deletion, and *xvi* interlined above, though with no indication as to the measure; however, with only three exceptions (13,2. 24,4 and 55,5) meadow is measured in acres in DB Dorset.

56,8   BOLLE. Probably Bolle the priest who holds 2½ hides ½ virgate in lordship in the Tax Return for Cullifordtree Hundred (xxxvii).
CHICKERELL. In Cullifordtree Hundred (26). It is West Chickerell, held as *Westchikerel* in Fees p. 753 from Margery *de Revers* (of Redvers) who also holds 'Great Crawford' 56,12. This land passed to the Courcy family, like 35,1, and then to Matilda *de Revers*; see Fees p. 425, FA ii pp. 19, 38, 57.

56,9   BRICTWIN. Perhaps Brictwin the reeve who holds 3 hides, less ½ virgate, in lordship in
-11   Cullifordtree Hundred (Tax Return xxxvii). Many of Brictwin's lands are later found in the hands of the *de Mortuo Mari* (Mortimer) family.

56,9   'WEY'. Deduced from the Tax Return for Cullifordtree Hundred (xxxvii); see 1,22 note and Introductory Note 2 on 'Rivers'. The land appears to have been at 'Stottingway' in Upwey [a name in local use, GR SY 6684, EPNS i p. 247]. John *de Baiocis* holds a fee of Ralph of Mortimer in *Stokingway* in Fees p. 426; it is *Stottynways* in FA ii p. 20.

56,10   'WINTERBORNE'. One of the south 'Winterbornes' in Cullifordtree Hundred (Tax Return xxxvii); see Introductory Note 2 on 'Rivers' and the Appendix. Descent from Brictwin was to the Mortimers; in Fees p. 425 Ralph *Belet* and Philip *de Mortimer* hold an unidentified Winterborne, perhaps 'Winterborne Belet', see 57,3 note; in FA ii p. 6 and Cal. Inq. PM vol. iv (Ed. I) no. 235 *Wyntrebom Stupelton* is held from Edmund *de Mortuo Mari*. Winterborne Steepleton is, however, in Uggescombe Hundred (25) and this cannot be reconciled with the evidence of the Tax Return.

56,11   LEWELL. See 57,2 note. It lay in Cullifordtree Hundred in 1086 (Tax Return xxxvii).

56,12   '(GREAT) CRAWFORD'. In Spetisbury parish, Loosebarrow Hundred, the other side of the Stour river from Tarrant (Crawford), the latter sometimes called Little Crawford (6,1 note). In the order of the text it falls in the right place for a Loosebarrow Hundred (23) place coming before Morden, which is included in the Tax Return for Charborough (Loosebarrow) Hundred (xviii). This lost place formed the south-east end of the village of Spetisbury; see Taylor p. 208; RCHM vol. iii p. 242 ff.; EPNS ii p. 64; Hutchins iii p. 521. It is recorded on the first edition one-inch OS map (No. 15 of 1811, reprint sheet 85 of 1969). See Fees p. 753, FA ii pp. 28, 44, 47 and notes to 56,6;8 and 1,5 third note.
FOURTH PART OF A MILL WHICH PAYS 30d. The rest of the mill is probably to be found at 57,4. It is not clear from the Latin whether the 30d is the payment of the whole mill or only of the quarter (see 55,13 note). 30d is one of the common payments from mills (e.g. 2,6. 55,3;29), but if the payment of ¾ of the same mill is 9s, then 30d is more likely to be the payment of the quarter. There is no reason for parts of the same mill to have paid equal renders, although they often did, as in DB Wilts. 24,20. 67,22-23;25 where each of the parts of a mill at Somerford rendered 15d (see also 1,29 note above). VALUE WAS 30d; VALUE 40s. The sixteen-fold increase in value between 1066 and 1086 is unusual and may well be due to a scribal error ('40s' being a mistake for '40d'). Cf. the lesser, though still large, increase in value in 49,14.

56,13   WULFRIC. Probably Wulfric Hunter who holds 1½ hides in lordship in the Tax Return for Charborough (Loosebarrow) Hundred (xviii).
MORDEN. In Fees pp. 88, 260 Geoffrey *de Pourton'* holds *Mordun'* in Loosebarrow Hundred (23). This same man holds Thorn Hill (56,18) which was also Wulfric's in 1086. The land appears in Fees p. 1182 as *Estmordon'*, held from the Barony of *Tyderleg'* (Tytherley, Hampshire); see 56,30 note.
WIFE OF WULFRIC'S BROTHER. Perhaps the Wulfeva who is recorded in the Tax Return for Charborough Hundred (xviii) as holding 3 virgates in lordship.

56,14   EDWIN. His lands descend to the Sifrewast family and form part of the Honour of Chewton; see 56,31-33 note.

56,14   BLANDFORD (ST. MARY). DB *Bleneforde*, see 26,29 note. Identifiable in the Tax Return for Combsditch Hundred (xvi). Edwin Hunter is there recorded as having 3 hides and ½ virgate in lordship. He also holds a 'Blandford' at 56,31, but this present land is most probably the Combsditch Blandford because of the odd ½ virgate and because in the order of DB entries it is followed by another Combsditch place, Thornicombe (see 56,15 note).
(1)½ VIRGATES. See 12,16 note.

56,15   THORNICOMBE. Deduced from the Tax Return for Combsditch Hundred (xvi), where Alward Colling holds 1 hide in lordship.

56,16   WULFGEAT. Probably Wulfgeat Hunter who holds 1 hide in lordship in the Tax Return for *Albretesberga* Hundred (v).
WIMBORNE (ST. GILES). This *Winburne* lay up the river Allen (see Introductory Note 2 on 'Rivers') in *Albretesberga* Hundred (v).

56,17 BRICTWIN. Probably Brictwin the reeve who had 3 hides in lordship in Yetminster
Hundred (Tax Return i).
MELBURY. See 26,35 note. Ralph *de Mortimer* holds *Melebur'* in Fees p. 426; see
56,9 note.

56,18 THORN HILL. The land can be identified in the Tax Return for *Canendona* Hundred
(vii), where Wulfric is Wulfric Hunter with 1 virgate lordship. In Fees p. 88, ½ hide in
Thornhill' in *Canendon'* Hundred is held by Geoffrey *de Pourton'*, and in Fees p. 1182
from the manor of Tytherley; see 56,13 note.

56,19 QUEEN GAVE THIS LAND TO AZELIN. Queen Matilda; Azelin (*Schelin* in the MS;
Farley misprints *Schelm*) is probably the same person as the Azelin who according to
Exon. was her sub-tenant in 1,18;20.
NOW THE KING HAS IT IN LORDSHIP. He also had in lordship another part of
Hampreston which had belonged to Queen Matilda (1,19).

56,20; THESE UNNAMED PLACES fall in a *Canendona* (vii) Hundred group (56,18–24); that
22 at 56,22 is required by the reconstruction of the Tax Return for that Hundred; the odd
one-third virgate may be connected with the 3 and one-third virgates of Hampreston 56,19.

56,20 QUEEN GAVE THIS LAND TO DODA IN ALMS. Perhaps Doda the monk (57,8).

56,21; WILKSWORTH; WALFORD. These places seem to have lain in *Canendona* Hundred
23–24 (Tax Return vii) in 1086.

56,21 WITH ... 2 SMALLHOLDERS WHO HAVE. Unless *habentes* is a mistake for *habentibus*
(to agree with *uill(an)is* after the *cum*), which is likely, the smallholders alone have the
½ plough. Cf. 11,3 last note.

56,26 'WINTERBORNE'. This 'Winterborne' can be identified in the Tax Return for Combsditch Hundred (xvi).

56,27 THE UNNAMED LAND is to be found in the Tax Return for Badbury Hundred (vi).
MEADOW, 9 ACRES. *Acras*, accusative after *habet*.

56,28 WINTERBORNE (HOUGHTON). This land, like Plumber (56,29), was held by Swein in
1086 and by the Earl of Salisbury in Fees p. 753 as *Winterborn' Moyun*; see 36,3 note.
VALUE WAS 100s. In the MS the *c* has been corrected from another figure, perhaps *v* '5'.

56,29 PLUMBER. *Plumber'* is a Salisbury fee in Fees p. 753, and is held by Roger *de Plombier*
from the Honour of Canford (see 31,1 note) in FA ii pp. 27, 47.

56,30 WULFRIC HUNTER ... 1 HIDE. Wulfric's lands later form part of the manor or sergeanty
of Tytherley, named from the holding of Tytherley mentioned in DB Wilts. 67,66, although
it actually lay in Hampshire. The present land, lying in Woodlands parish in Knowlton
Hundred (10), is variously named. In Fees p. 88 it is *Cnolle* [Knowle Hill GR SU 0309],
held by Geoffrey *de Pourton'* (56,13 note); in Fees p. 1182 it is *Chnoldon* [Knowlton
GR SU 0210], held of the Barony of Tytherley, and in Fees p. 1268 and FA ii p. 13 it is
1 hide in *Baggeriggestrete* ['Baggeridge', lost in Woodlands, probably near Bagmans Copse
and farm, GR SU 032091; see EPNS ii pp. 284-285 and Taylor pp. 209-210].

56,31 EDWIN. Probably Edwin Hunter whose lordship land is recorded in the Tax Return for
-33 *Langeberga* (xxii), Pimperne (xxvi) and Uggescombe (iii) Hundreds. His lands form the
Honour of Chewton (56,14 note).

56,31 (LANGTON LONG) BLANDFORD. The *Langeberga* Hundred Tax Return (xxii) records
Edwin Hunter as holding 2 hides 3 virgates of lordship land, no doubt part of his 5 hides at
Bleneford; see notes to 26,29 and 56,14. This land is found in Fees p. 753 as *Blaneford
Philippi de Tylly* (EPNS ii p. 107), held from the Honour of Chewton (see 56,14 note).
A MILL. In the MS *molin*; Farley misprints *moin*.

56,32 LAZERTON. DB *Werne*, named from the river Iwerne; see the Tax Return for Pimperne
Hundred (xxvi) and 30,3 note. Lazerton was held in Fees p. 753 from the Honour of
Chewton as *Latherton'*. Lazerton farm lies in Stourpaine parish, but close to the boundary
of Iwerne Stepleton; see 26,3 note.

56,33 SHILVINGHAMPTON. Held by Richard *de Sifrewast* in Fees p. 92 from the Honour of
Chewton; see FA ii pp. 6, 34, 53, and next note.

56,34 BRYANSTON. There is no Tax Return evidence to locate this place. In the order of DB
entries, it falls after Shilvinghampton which is in the Tax Return for Uggescombe Hundred
(iii). Since other *Hunesberga* Hundred lands are grouped with Uggescombe, it is possible
that this 'Blandford' is Bryanston, see 26,29 note. This is given some support by Fees
p. 87 which records a grant of Bryanston in *Hundesburg'* Hundred by William I; see FA ii
pp. 1, 43. None of the other 'Blandfords' in Ch. 56 could have been in this Hundred; see
Hutchins i p. 248.

56,35 BRICTWIN. HE ALSO. Probably Brictwin the reeve who holds 2½ hides in lordship in
-36 Eggardon Hundred (Tax Return iv) and 1 hide 3½ virgates in lordship in Uggescombe
Hundred (Tax Return iii).

56,35 CHILCOMBE. This lay in Eggardon Hundred in 1086 (Tax Return iv; see FA ii p. 3); it was later in Uggescombe (25). *Chiltecumbe* in Eggardon Hundred (19) is held from Edmund *de Mortuo Mari* (Mortimer) in FA ii p. 3; see 56,9-11 note.
56,36 WADDON. The place is accounted for in the Tax Return for Uggescombe Hundred (iii). The land probably lay at Waddon *Krey* [Little Waddon, see Fägersten p. 250], held in FA ii p. 34 from Edmund of Mortimer; see Fees pp. 93, 426, FA ii p. 53 and Cal. Inq. PM vol. iv (Ed. I) no. 235.
THE COUNT OF MORTAIN NOW HOLDS IT. *Quod* presumably refers to *manerium* understood. The other land exchanged does not seem to be mentioned in DB. The Mortain interest in Waddon is recalled in FA ii p. 7.
56,37 BRICTWIN ALSO HOLDS. Repeated at the beginning of 56,37-40. The Brictwin of 56,37-38 would appear to be Brictwin the reeve who is stated in the Tax Return for 'Chilbury' Hundred (xxxi) as holding 3 hides 1 virgate in lordship. Presumably Brictwin of 56,39-40 was also the reeve.
56,37 MORETON; GALTON. Lay in 'Chilbury' Hundred (Tax Return xxxi) in 1086, Moreton
-38 being held in Winfrith Hundred (27) by Reginald son of Peter (a Mortimer tenant, see 56,9-11 note) in FA ii p. 30.
56,39 RINGSTEAD. See 52,2 note.
LAND FOR. Before *Tra* in the MS is written an 7 no doubt a mistake: part of the *T* of *Tra* covers most of it. Farley does not show it. The same thing happens in 36,10 and 57,7; 15; see notes to these.
SIX MEN HOLD IT AT A REVENUE. That is, they paid rent for it; DGSW p. 92 note 5. See 47,7 note.
56,40 STINSFORD. Most of this village lay in St. George Hundred (20) in 1086 (52,1 note). But in the order of this chapter, Brictwin's Stinsford falls between two places in Culliford-tree Hundred (26). Moreover, Brictwin has no lordship land in the Tax Return for Dorchester (St. George) Hundred (xxxii) but 3 hides less ½ virgate in that for Cullifordtree (xxxvii).
56,41 BRIDGE. See 49,13 note.
THESE LANDS. That is, 56,40-41.
56,43 HE ALSO HOLDS. Repeated at the beginning of 56,43-47. As the Edric of 56,43;49 is probably Edric the reeve who is recorded as holding 1 hide in lordship in the Tax Return for Hasler Hundred (xxix), all these references here are probably to Edric the reeve. (EAST) HOLME. See 41,3 note.
56,44 'STOKE (WALLIS)'. DB *Stoche*. If 'Studley' (56,45;47) has been correctly identified, 56,44-47 would form a natural Whitchurch Hundred grouping, thus helping to identify this 'Stoke'. See 33,5 note.
56,45; 'STUDLEY'. DB *Slitlege, Stodlege* may well be different renderings of the same lost
47 place-name, see Fägersten p. 298 note 1. At least one of these holdings is required to make up the total of Edric's lordship in Whitchurch Hundred Tax Return (ii).
56,46 PILSDON. In Whitchurch Hundred (Tax Return ii). This land had belonged to Glastonbury Abbey, GF p. 48. Although DB does not record the alienation, it is held in FA ii p. 38 from Glastonbury.
56,48 BRIANTSPUDDLE. It is required by the Tax Return for Bere Hundred (xv), where Godric is Godric the priest holding 4 hides, less 10 acres, in lordship. Briantspuddle is also called *Prestes Puddle* (EPNS i pp. 289-290) possibly from Godric the priest. As *Prestpiddle* it was confirmed on Christchurch, Twynham, by William Rufus and in the grant said to be near Affpuddle, *Regesta* i no. 361.
56,49 EDRIC. See 56,43 note.
TYNEHAM. In Hasler Hundred in 1086 (Tax Return xxix).
56,50 WOOLCOMBE. Now in Toller Porcorum, Tollerford Hundred (13). This entry and that at 57,8 are, however, required by the Tax Return for Eggardon Hundred (iv).
56,51 LODERS. See 1,13 note. This holding is probably to be identified in the Tax Return for Eggardon Hundred (iv).
56,52 BLACKMANSTON. The entry seems to be duplicated in 56,65; see Tax Return xxix for Hasler Hundred, which states that Aelfric Hunter holds ½ hide in lordship.
LAND FOR 1 PLOUGH ... The rest of the line has been left blank after this, presumably for further details, which were never added because of the repetition of the entry in 56,65.
56,53 MILBORNE (STILEHAM). The holding can be identified in the Tax Return for Bere Hundred (xv); see 46,1 note. The hidage appears to have been omitted in error, but must have been at least 1½ hides because in the above Tax Return the King did not have tax from 1½ hides held by Osmund from Swein. In FA ii p. 12 (Barrow Hundred (22)) the

land is measured in carucates, one each being held by the Abbot of Bec and John *de la Strode* from the heirs of the Earl Marshall.

56,54 (STOURTON) CAUNDLE. See 26,70–71 note. Godric's land can be identified in the Tax Return for Brownshall Hundred (xxviii) and may be the land held in Fees p. 89 by Henry *Toneir'*, a grant made *de conquestu*.

56,55 (PURSE) CAUNDLE. See notes to 26,70–71 and 15,1. The 2½ virgates of this land appear in the Tax Return for Sherborne Hundred (xxxiv). With the 4 hides and 1½ virgates of Purse Caundle held by Athelney Abbey (15,1) they form a 5-hide unit. RH i p. 103b records Athelney Abbey as holding *Prus Candel* except for ½ hide held by John *filius Alani* for nursing the King's dogs injured in Blackmore Forest. This ½ hide is probably the 2½ virgates of the present entry and the same piece of land found in FA ii p. 5, Fees p. 90, Cal. Inq. PM vol. iii (Ed. I) no. 111 and vol. viii (Ed. III) no. 241; see Hutchins iv p. 144.

56,56 THE FOURTH PART OF 1 VIRGATE. This land lay in Ailwood (Rowbarrow) Hundred (Tax Return xix) and the odd fraction may answer to the 2½ hides less ¼ virgate of Rollington, 47,10.

56,57 AELFRIC HOLDS COOMBE. DB *Come*. In Ailwood (Rowbarrow) Hundred (Tax Return xix), where Aelfric Hunter is recorded as holding 4 hides, less 1 virgate, in lordship. 1 VILLAGER AND 4 SMALLHOLDERS ... There is a gap of about 8 letters' width in the MS after *bord'*, probably for the villagers' ploughs to be added. See 1,26 note.

56,59 BOVINGTON. See 56,6 note.
56,60 AELFRIC. Probably Aelfric Hunter; see 56,6 note.
'WINTERBORNE'. The place can be located in Bere Hundred (Tax Return xv) and could therefore be Winterborne Kingston; see 56,6 note.

56,61 THERE IS A GAP of about 1½ lines in the MS after this entry, no doubt left for the scribe to enter details of population, resources and value, when available.

56,62 ALWARD. Probably Alward the reeve who holds 1 hide in lordship in the Tax Return for Winfrith Hundred (xxx).
WOOL. See 57,17 note.

56,63 AELMER. Perhaps the beadle who is recorded in the Tax Return for Winfrith Hundred (xxx) as holding 1 virgate in lordship.
WOOL. In FA ii p. 24, 1 virgate in *Wolle* in Hasler Hundred (28) is recorded as held from the Earl of Gloucester. It is odd for it to be included in Hasler, as it was and is in Winfrith Hundred (27).

56,65 BLACKMANSTON. See 56,52 note.
Ch. 57 LANDS OF THE KING'S SERVANTS. In the MS and Farley *SERVIENT'*; the facsimile fails to reproduce the clear abbreviation sign over the *T*. Dorset is unusual in placing the King's Servants after, instead of before, the King's Thanes.

57,1 WILLIAM BELLETT. A descendant of William Bellett, Robert *Belet*, holds his lands in Fees and in FA these same lands are found in the hands of Edmund *Everard*, which enables more precise identification of some places. The William of 57,3;12–14;19 appears to be or is said to be William Bellett.
'FROME (BILLET)'. Named from the DB holder or his descendants. It is now represented by Stafford House (GR SY 724899) in West Stafford parish and may have included the land called 'Everard's farm', Hutchins ii p. 511 and EPNS i p. 243. The parish lies in Cullifordtree Hundred (26) but 'Frome Billet' itself was a tithing of St. George Hundred (20) and can be identified in the Tax Return for Dorchester (St. George) Hundred (xxxii), see EPNS i p. 195. It is held by Robert *Belet* in St. George Hundred in Fees p. 88 (see RBE ii p. 545) and as *Frome Belet* by Edmund *Everard* in FA ii p. 17.
HELD. In the MS *tenuit* corrected to *teneb'* (= *tenebant*, imperfect plural), probably when 7 *Bricfrid* was interlined. Farley misprints *tenuit*. For a similar correction by the scribe, see 39,1 note.
3 HIDES. LAND FOR ... In the MS there is an erasure from under the *iii* of *iii hid'* to the *ē* of *Tra ē*; the scribe drew a line to join up the two phrases to indicate that nothing was to be added in the gap left. Farley does not print this link line; see also 55,8 and note.

57,2 HUGH. Probably Hugh Gosbert who holds 3 virgates in lordship in the Tax Return for Cullifordtree Hundred (xxxvii).
LEWELL. In FA ii p. 20 the Prior of St. John of Jerusalem holds 1 hide in *Lywolle* from Hugh *Poyntz* in Cullifordtree Hundred (26). This may well account for the 3 virgates of the present holding, plus the 1 virgate of 56,11. The holding can be deduced from the Tax Return for Cullifordtree Hundred (xxxvii).

2 SMALLHOLDERS WHO PAY 20d. The lack of a value statement for this entry suggests that the 20d might be a rent paid by the smallholders for 'farming' the land (see 47,7 note and cf. notes to 12,13. 49,13 and 57,17). However, see 54,2 note on other examples of no value statement, and 1,23 where a smallholder pays 30d and a value is given to the holding.

57,3   WILLIAM ... TWO THANES HELD IT. William is William Bellett who holds 1 hide in lordship in the Tax Return for Cullifordtree Hundred (xxxvii). This Tax Return also states that the King did not have tax from 5 virgates which 1 thane, whose land it had been, holds at a revenue from William Bellett.

'WINTERBORNE (BELET)'. Identifiable in the Tax Return for Cullifordtree Hundred (xxxvii). Like 'Frome Billet' (57,1) the place is named from William *Belet* or his descendant Robert *Belet* who holds a Winterborne in Fees p. 88; see RBE ii p. 545 and FA ii p. 18. 'Winterborne Belet' lies in Winterborne Came and is now probably represented by Cripton (EPNS i pp. 261–2). Winterborne Came is in Frampton Liberty and so perhaps was regarded as part of St. George Hundred (20), but Cripton was a tithing in Cullifordtree (26). The holding is probably the *Wynterburn Hundynton* [Winterborne Huntingdon], that is in Winterborne Came (EPNS i p. 263), held in 1303 from Edmund *Everard* in FA ii pp. 30, 49, coupled with Woodsford (57,13); see 17,1 note.

57,4–5   THE UNNAMED LANDS can be located in the Tax Return for Charborough Hundred (xviii) and the first may have been a part of 'Great Crawford', the ¾ of a mill at 9s answering to a ¼ mill at 30d in 56,12 (see note).

57,4   WILLIAM. In the MS a *ten*ᵗ 'holds' has been erased, though still partially visible, after *Will's*, the scribe momentarily not having realised that the man had a surname. Farley does not show it.

57,5   HUGH GOSBERT. In the MS *gosbert* is interlined above *Hugo*; Farley misprints *Gosbert* with a capital.

57,6;   'WINTERBORNE'. Both places can be identified in the Tax Return for Combsditch
10   Hundred (xvi) and are therefore on the eastern Winterborne river; Winterbornes Anderson, Clenston, Tomson, Muston, and possibly Houghton.

57,7   WORGRET. In the Tax Return for Bere Hundred (xv), later in Hasler (28) geographically, though a tithing of Barrow Hundred (a later sub-division of Bere). See 49,14. 37,10 and 11,9 notes.

LAND FOR. In the MS an *7* is written before the *Tra*, no doubt by mistake. Farley does not print it. Cf. notes to 36,10. 56,39 and 57,15.

57,8   WOOLCOMBE. See 56,50 note.

57,9   HERVEY THE CHAMBERLAIN. *Cubicularius* in DB; *camerarius* in the Tax Return for *Albretesberga* Hundred (v). He is Hervey of Wilton who is one of the King's Servants in DB Wilts. (68,1); Eyton *Somerset* i pp. 149-150.

WIMBORNE (ST. GILES). This 'Wimborne' is identifiable in the Tax Return for *Albretesberga* Hundred (v).

MILL 22½ ... In the MS there is a gap of about 6 letters' width after *xxii 7 dim̄*; the *7* was added later as it covers the dot at the end of *xxii*. It is difficult to know what should have been added here — possibly *sol'* 'shillings' or *den*ᵗ 'pence', the mill paying either 22s 6d or 22½d. The phrase *in molino uillę* is unusual with renders. The mill may be related to the third of a mill paying 15d in 55,13.

57,10   JOHN. Probably John the Usher who holds 1 hide 1½ virgates in lordship in the Tax Return for Combsditch Hundred (xvi). He also held land in DB Somerset and Wiltshire as one of the King's Servants.

'WINTERBORNE'. See notes to 26,13 and 57,6. With the 'Winterbornes' of 26,48 and 55,12, this would form a 5-hide unit.

ALWOLD. See 33,1 note.

57,11   WILLIAM OF DAUMERAY. See 55,19 note.

57,12   WALDITCH. This land can be identified in the Tax Return for Godderthorn Hundred (x).

WILLIAM BELLETT. In the MS the interlined surname looks more like *belot* than *belet*, although *belet* is the more usual form and occurs in the interlineation in 57,19. Farley prints *belet*.

NUTFORD. A fee of Robert *Belet* in Fees p. 753. See 1,28 note.

57,13   WOODSFORD. The land was at West Woodsford in Winfrith Hundred (27), held in 1285 from Edmund *Everard*, FA ii p. 9. See 11,7 note, Fees p. 88, RBE ii p. 545 and FA ii pp. 30, 49. It lay in 'Chilbury' Hundred in 1086 (Tax Return xxxi).

57,14   LYME REGIS. In Fees p. 88 *Lim'* is held by Robert *Belet*; see RBE ii p. 545.

57,15   BROADWINDSOR. Now a parish in Beaminster Hundred, including the village of Little
-16   Windsor. In 1086, only 1 hide, perhaps 57,16 Little Windsor, lay in Beaminster Hundred

(Tax Return xii), the rest of the land lying in Whitchurch Hundred (ii). The holding can be found in the Book of Fees where in 1212 Thomas of Windsor held *Windesor'* ... *de conquestu et de dono Willelmi Bastardi* [*regis*] *Anglie per seriantiam* (Fees p. 94); see VCH iii p. 54.

57,15 HUNDGER SON OF ODIN. Hundger (DB and Tax Returns *Hungerus*) is a 12th-century form of OScand *Hundigeirr*; see Fellows-Jensen p. 144. Odin (DB *Odinus*; Tax Returns *Audoenus*) is OScand *Authunn*; see Fellows-Jensen p. 41 and OEB p. 192.
WOODLAND ... IN LENGTH AND 8 ... In the MS two 7's are in error after *lḡ*, the second one being partially covered by the *v* of *viii*. Farley prints only one 7. See notes to 36,10. 56,39 and 57,7 for similar cases of 7's which should not be there.

57,16 [VALUE ...]. See 54,2 note.

57,17 OSMUND THE BAKER. The evidence of RBE and Fees (see next note) suggests that in this case Osmund's byname *pistor* does describe his own occupation, rather than that of one of his ancestors.
GALTON. From OE *gafol* and *tūn* 'farm subject to tax or rent', perhaps referring to the render of 12s 4d by four men in 1086; see EPNS i p. 140 and VCH iii pp. 34, 114. The land was in 'Chilbury' Hundred in 1086 (Tax Return xxxi). This holding of Galton by Osmund the Baker in 1086 develops into a serjeanty involving land at Wool (56,62) as well. In RBE ii p. 547 Robert *de Welles* holds 2 hides in Wool and one in Galton *per servicium pistoris*, see Fees pp. 89, 1387 (*per serianteriam faciendi panem domini regis*) and Round (KS) pp. 232-233.
4 MEN. Perhaps the same as the 'four free men' who held in 1066. As no 1086 value is given for the land, it may be that these men held it at a revenue ('farmed' it); VCH iii p. 12. Cf. 47,7 and note.

57,18 WOODSTREET. It lay in Winfrith Hundred in 1086 (Tax Return xxx).

57,19 STOURPAINE. DB *Sture*. The odd hidage, 1 hide 2½ virgates, added to that of 50,4 (6 hides 1½ virgates) makes a round figure of 8 hides.
EDWARD LIP. *Lipe*; OE *lippa, lippe* 'lip'; OEB pp. 320-321.

57,20 AFFLINGTON. See 28,6-7 note.

57,21 'MOULHAM'. A lost place in Swanage. The name, also spelt 'Mowlem', survives in local use; see EPNS i p. 55. It can be identified in the Tax Return for Ailwood (Rowbarrow) Hundred (xix).

57,22 GODFREY SCULLION. *Scutularius*; see OEB pp. 268-9.
THESE ... The MS breaks off abruptly here, with no note for the scribe in the margin reminding him to finish the sentence, and with the rest of folio 85 blank. The *has* could perhaps be the beginning of the phrase, common in Exon. but rare in DB (but see Wilts. 13,2 and cf. 8,1 above): *Has possunt arare ... caṝ* '... ploughs can plough these', although *hanc*, referring to the 1 virgate, would have been expected here.

Ch. 58 COUNTESS OF BOULOGNE. Ida (DB Som. 17,7) of Lorraine, second wife of Count Eustace. Her lands pass to the Cluniac priory of Le Wast (near Boulogne in the département of Pas-de-Calais, France). Her holding here appears to have been added later, as one would normally expect it to occur either with the lands of other nobles (as it does in DB Surrey) or with other female tenants-in-chief (as does the land of Countess Judith in DB Beds.); moreover, as she was of higher standing than the wife of Hugh son of Grip (Ch. 55), her fief should have been written first. In Exon. her holding appears on folio 33a, the rest of which is blank, as also most of the preceding folio and the 2 succeeding ones, which end a gathering (or 'booklet') that commences with lands held by and from Queen Matilda: this may be the reason for the Exchequer scribe overlooking the fief, if, as seems likely, he was copying from Exon.

58,1 BOCKHAMPTON. Held in Fees p. 88 and FA ii p. 17 by the Abbot of Le Wast. It lay in Dorchester Hundred in 1086 (Tax Return xxxii).

58,2 WINTERBORNE (MONKTON). Held in 1212 from Eustace *le Moigne* who holds from the Abbey of Le Wast, Fees p. 88; see FA ii pp. 19-20. It is also known as Winterborne *Wast*, see EPNS i p. 266 and VCH iii pp. 114, 147. It can be identified in the Tax Return for Cullifordtree Hundred (xxxvii).
6 HIDES. Originally written *v hid'* in the MS and corrected to *vi*.

58,3 SWANAGE. In the Tax Return for Ailwood (Rowbarrow) Hundred (xix) Count Eustace holds 1 hide and one-third virgate in lordship which must be this holding in Swanage. He was a major landholder in his own right; see DB Somerset, Oxfords., Surrey (where his wife also has a fief), Herts., Hunts., Beds., etc., but according to Ellis *Introduction* i pp. 416-7 this Eustace may be Countess Ida's son, not husband. This parcel of land is said by Hutchins i p. 660 to have formed a narrow strip at the eastern end of Swanage called Eight Holds or Eight Holes; see EPNS i p. 60.

WULFEVA. DB *Vlueua* represents OE *Wulfgifu*. She was probably Wulfeva Beteslau (of Beslow, Shrops., ? see DB Wilts. 68,24 note), who was dead by the time of the DB survey (Hants. 6,12) and was probably also the Countess' predecessor in Somerset.

LAND FOR 1 PLOUGH. 1 VILLAGER HAS IT THERE. The villager has the plough (not the whole manor, as VCH iii pp. 16, 137), which is made clear by the Exon. "1 plough can plough it, which 1 villager has on that land". See fourth note under 3,14.

PLACES ELSEWHERE

A distinction is here made between places that were in the County in 1086, but entered in the folios of adjacent counties (prefixed E), and those in adjacent counties in 1086, but later transferred to Dorset (ED for Devon places, ES for Somerset places). In the Somerset entries referred to here, the bracketed figure in the right-hand margin is the folio and section number for the corresponding entry in the Exon. Book. Fuller notes are to be found in the relevant county volumes.

Holdings in Dorset in 1086

E 1   'BISHOPSTONE'. Lay and lies in Somerset; the exchanged land lay in Dorset. The name of the Count's castle, Montacute, has now displaced the earlier name, although 'Bishopstone' survived as a tithing of Montacute into the 19th century.

THE MANOR CALLED (PURSE CAUNDLE). The exchange is not mentioned in the description of Purse Caundle (15,1 above). The Count succeeded in gaining both a site for his castle and a manor of greater extent and value.

E 2   EARL AUBREY. Probably Aubrey of Coucy, created Earl of Northumbria in 1080. As he was 'of little use in difficult circumstances' he resigned and went home to Normandy. His lands were in the King's hands in 1086 and had not yet been granted afresh.

GUSSAGE. The land was in Dorset in 1086 and evidently included in the Wiltshire folios in error. It may be that in the Exon. which has not survived a heading for Earl Aubrey's land in Dorset was omitted in error or was unclear (as the marginal 'heading' for Glastonbury's lands in Somerset; see Devon Exon. Notes Ch. 4) and the Exchequer scribe missed it. However, since some of the original Domesday returns seem to have been by fief and may have spanned several counties, places were sometimes included in the wrong county, as several times in Northamptonshire. This is especially so where a holder has only one or two lands in another county: here Gussage was Earl Aubrey's only Dorset holding. This Gussage is Gussage St. Michael, required in the Tax Return for Badbury Hundred (vi), in 1086 and later a detachment from the main body of the Hundred. See 26,44 note and FA ii p. 14.

THESE THREE MANORS. That is Elcombe, Stratford Tony and Gussage St. Michael (Wilts. 23,8-10), from which the 1066 holders had been omitted. The first two are and were in Wiltshire.

ALL THIS LAND. Referring to all the lands surveyed in the chapter.

E 3   GILLINGHAM. A second mistaken inclusion in the Wiltshire folios. This land is required by the Tax Return for Gillingham Hundred (xxvii).

A FURTHER DORSET PLACE may be mentioned in DB Somerset 1,27. Under an entry for Martock, it is recorded that 1 hide and 1 virgate of land in *Contone* have been taken away from the manor and are held by Ansger Cook. This 'Compton' has been tentatively identified with Compton Durville, the nearest Compton to Martock, in the Somerset volume of this series. In the Tax Return for Sherborne Hundred (xxxiv) 1 hide and 1 virgate held by Ansger Cook from the King are recorded as paying no tax. Since this holding is nowhere recorded in DB Dorset, it is possible that it represents an outlying part of Martock at Over or Nether Compton in Dorset; see VCH iii p. 145.

Holdings outside Dorset in 1086. For the dates of transfer to Dorset see Introductory Note 3 on the County Boundary. For the full text, translation and notes, see the relevant county volumes in this series.

ED 1   THORNCOMBE. In 1086 a detached part of Axminster Hundred, Devon.

ES 1   SEABOROUGH ... ANOTHER SEABOROUGH. 'Another Seaborough' is clearly part of the same village, which contained two manors held in 1066 by different people; the main Exon. entry 154 a 1-2 has 'Seaborough ... the manor of Seaborough', but the *Terrae Occupatae* entry (513 a 5) has 'Seaborough ... another manor called Seaborough'. There is no later trace of two villages. Examples of this use of *alia* are found elsewhere in DB; e.g. at Thistleton in Rutland and Courteenhall in Northamptonshire.

ES 4;   ADBER. The three holdings account for Over Adber in Horethorne Hundred and Nether
7;9   Adber in Stone Hundred.

EXON. EXTRA INFORMATION AND DISCREPANCIES WITH DB

Introduction
The Notes below incorporate material supplied by the Exon. Domesday for Dorset, which is not in DB and which it has not proved possible to include in small type in the translation nor in the Details Table following these Notes. Also mentioned are any differences between the two texts, other than simply of wording, and information given in DB that is not in Exon.

It may be noticed that, unlike in the Somerset, Devon and Cornwall editions in this series, there is no Lordship and Villagers' (land and ploughs) Table for Dorset. This is due to three factors. Firstly, Exchequer Dorset gives the lordship land in many more entries than do Somerset, Devon and Cornwall, ånd where it does not, this information can be fitted into the text in small type from Exon. after the lordship ploughs have been given. Secondly, details of ploughs and land, both in lordship and held by the 'villagers', are omitted altogether from several entries in Exon. for Dorset. Thirdly, there are only about nine occurrences in the part of Dorset Exchequer DB, for which Exon. survives, of the phrase "(Land for) y ploughs, which are there", referring both to the lordship and to the villagers' ploughs: in these cases the Notes below incorporate the details given in Exon. of the holder(s) of the ploughs, and which in Somerset, Devon and Cornwall merit a separate table.

Where the Tax Returns for Dorset (see the Appendix and the beginning of Introductory Note 1) provide evidence of bynames or of the identification of places and manors, this is usually given in the General Notes, though occasional reference is made in the Notes below.

The summaries of the fiefs of Glastonbury Abbey, Robert son of Gerald and the Count of Mortain provide very little useful information, much of which does not correspond either to the main Exon. entries or to Exchequer DB, probably because deriving from a different source and/or date; but see General Notes 8,1 and 1,2 on cottagers.

No section survives for Dorset in the *Terrae Occupatae*.

Scribal errors in the Exon. MS, of which there are a great many, are given only when they occur in a quotation.

It seems very likely that the compiler (and/or scribe) of the Exchequer DB had in front of him the Exon. MS in its present form, no doubt with the portions of Devon, Dorset and Wiltshire which have not survived. Many aspects of DB and Exon. suggest this. Firstly, though the policy throughout DB was to include Hundred headings, they are surprisingly absent from DB for the southwestern counties and from Exon.: it would seem that for some reason (on which see Galbraith pp. 114-5) they were not thought necessary in Exon. and by the time that volume reached Winchester it was too late to discover in which Hundred the thousands of places lay and so the Exchequer scribe had to follow his copy in not including them. Secondly, within a fief the order of entries in Exchequer DB frequently, especially in Somerset, Devon and Dorset, followed almost the exact order of those in Exon. But it is when one comes to study the two MSS closely that the immediate dependence of one on the other becomes obvious. There are a great many instances of the DB scribe's repeating unusual phrases from Exon., of copying obvious mistakes, of leaving spaces where there are spaces in Exon. (see fourth note under General Notes 1,1) or where he was unsure of a statement (as at 11,5). Moreover, there are several occasions where Exchequer DB preserves, rather than changes, the formulae of Exon., presumably by accident (see General Notes 28,2 and cf. the placing of slaves with the villagers — as in Exon. — not after the lordship in 8,1 and 49,5). Likewise, in many entries in Exon. an item of information has been initially omitted and then added out of place, and very often this item is similarly misplaced in DB (see Notes below to 16,1 and 55,15). In some cases a whole entry is added at the foot of a column in DB that is also postscriptal in Exon. (see Devon 3,19 and notes) and what is marginal in Exon. is often marginal in DB (see Devon General Notes 15,47-52). It may be thought that this indicates merely that late information was added to both Exon. and DB at the same time, but in a great many cases in Exon. the colour of the ink and the scribe of the addition are the same as for the main part of the entry, which would be unlikely if it were done much later, considering the number of scribes employed in writing Exon. Again, there are numerous examples of figures being corrected in Exon. (often not well done) and the DB scribe sometimes misunderstanding or missing altogether the alteration (see Notes below to 1,19). Though it is possible in some instances that the correction was done to the Exon. MS after the Exchequer scribe had used it, it is obvious that some of the later corrections and interlineations in Exon. were seen by the DB scribe, such as the interlineation in the fourth note under B 2. In some cases a figure is altered in Exchequer DB to agree with a correction in Exon. (see Devon Exon. Notes to 3,67).

All these instances make it impossible for Exon. to be unconnected with Exchequer DB (the view of Eyton *Somerset* pp. 4-5; Reichel in VCH *Devon* i p. 377ff; Salzman in VCH *Cornwall* i, viii, pp. 45-46 etc.; both Reichel and Salzman believed that the Dorset and Wiltshire sections in Exon. were taken from Exchequer DB, but that for Devon, Cornwall and Somerset, DB and Exon. were 'independent compilations'), or for Exon. to be a later compilation (so Vinogradoff p. 228). Moreover, they make it unlikely, considering also the lack of time, that a fair copy of Exon. was made which was used in the compilation of DB and then destroyed when it had served its purpose (so Finn LE pp. 28, 52-54 and his article 'The Immediate Sources of Exchequer Domesday' in BJRL xl (1957); Galbraith pp. 31-32 and Ch. VIII; see below).

There are, of course, discrepancies between Exon. and DB, but a study of the Exon. MS has explained many of these: in several cases interlineations or marginal additions in Exon. (though done at the same time as the main body of the entry, judging by the colour of the ink and with no change in scribe) were missed by the Exchequer scribe (see Notes below to 1,9. 12,16 and 36,4); values and measurements sometimes span two lines in Exon. and the DB scribe only noted the first part (as at 1,13 and 55,35); see also the Notes below to 55,14;29;37 and 47,8 on woodland and the General Notes to 47,10 and Ch. 58. Scribal error too must have played a part. Some of the differences, such as in the names of sub-tenants or the numbers of population, may be ascribed to information becoming available after Exon. had been compiled. The three instances of Exchequer DB for Dorset containing items that are not in the main Exon. (see last note under B 4 below) and the other instances in Devon, Cornwall and Somerset, can probably be explained by the DB scribe's having recourse to other sources of information (such as, perhaps, the Tax Returns or Hundred lists, local data or the results of lawsuits) or to simple deduction (as probably for 11,12), rather than to a copy of Exon.

According to Finn LE pp. 52-54 this copy, now lost, contained some extra information but perhaps did not include later additions to the surviving Exon., and the foliation was different (hence the original omission in DB of Dorset 36,4-11). However, it seems odd that if such a copy were made, so few new details were added to it and hardly any of the mistakes of the original corrected and the numerous spaces left for information unfilled, as DB shows. See F. H. Baring 'The Exeter Domesday' in EHR xxvii (1912) pp. 309-318. In this fair copy, which was sent to Winchester while the surviving Exon. MS remained at Exeter where it had been compiled, it is argued that some attempt was probably made to arrange the King's lands and those of his thanes and servants in an order closer to that adopted for the other counties in DB (e.g. see General Notes Ch. 1 and Devon General Notes Ch. 1 and Exon. Notes Ch. 22); Galbraith pp. 105-107, though Finn LE p. 54 disagrees. These rearrangements, however, were neither too extensive nor too complicated to have been done entirely by the compiler of DB at the time of writing. It is possible that some of the material relating to the Inquiry remained at Exeter for the hearing of claims and the sorting out of illegal tenure and occupation, while the Exon. we have was at Winchester being used for the compilation of Exchequer DB. This material, amplified or corrected at the hearings, may have produced the *Terrae Occupatae* which was later bound up with the Exon. Domesday.

In using the material in Exon. the DB scribe largely changed the formulae, writing, for example, TRE (*tempore regis Edwardi*) "in King Edward's time" for Exon.'s more elaborate *ea die qua rex Edwardus fuit vivus et mortuus* ("on the day on which King Edward was alive and dead", i.e. 5th Jan. 1066), and "Land for y ploughs" for Exon.'s "(z hides) which y ploughs can plough", etc. There is a list of equivalent formulae for DB and Exon. by Ellis in DB3 pp.xiii-xiv; see also the specimen at the front of this volume.

Exon. often omits nouns (as DB less often), as in "the King has 3 ploughs in lordship and the villagers 4", where "4 ploughs" are intended: where DB gives the expected noun no attention is drawn here to the Exon. omission. Exon. regularly abbreviates personal names to the first letter (e.g. *H.* for *Hugo*), generally when the name in full has already occurred in the entry. In these Notes the name thus abbreviated is always written e.g. "H(ugh)", except in the cases of *rex E.* and *rex W.* (usually in the phrase *tempore rex E./W.*) which are so common that there is no doubt about the full version of the names.

In the statement "the villagers have *y* hides ... *z* ploughs" Exon. regularly uses the term *villani* in the general sense of the inhabitants of a *villa*, covering smallholders, Cottagers (*coscez*), cottagers (*cotarii*) — and possibly also other classes of population such as pigmen, salt-workers, etc. — as well as villagers. Often no villagers are mentioned in the holding, just smallholders and slaves (e.g. for 12,5;11). However, for 12,16 and on a few other occasions in the Exon. for Dorset, where there are only smallholders and slaves on a manor, the term *bordarii* takes the place of *villani* in the statement of their land and ploughs.

In many cases the Exchequer scribe has cut out from Exon. material of a type that he elsewhere includes, such as the plough estimate for 18,2, the woodland details for 36,8. 47,8 and 55,29, the mill details for 55,16, the garden for 36,4, cottagers for 1,15. 11,5 and 36,6 (see Notes below to all these), as well as sub-tenants for 13,5 and 36,5 and TRE holders for 15,1 and 55,18;25;28. See also General Notes to 11,5. 12,3 and 55,10.

Ellis' edition of Exon. is not as accurate as Farley's one of the Exchequer DB. Apart from larger errors and omissions, there are numerous occasions when the transcriber Ralph Barnes leaves gaps where there are none in the MS and vice versa, omits underlining (indicating deletion) or puts it in wrongly, positions interlineations incorrectly, omits transposition signs, etc. It must be said, however, that many entries in the MS are untidy with much erasure, overwriting and correction; also, some of the letters are malformed and misled the Exchequer scribe as well as Mr. Barnes (e.g. see Devon Exon. Notes 25,20 on *Aisa/Disa* and cf. 55,29 note below). The scope of this edition prohibits mentioning all but the more important mistakes of Mr. Barnes and checking the transcription of all the place-names, though it is worth noting here that 3 of the 39 names of the Hundreds in the Tax Returns for Dorset are wrongly transcribed (see footnotes to the list in the Appendix). Ellis' edition has misled a number of people, especially in the case of the place-names: Reichel with his many articles on Devon place-names does not appear to have checked the MS and in his translation of Exon. for the Devon VCH he perpetuates the errors of Ellis' edition. The present editors hope in the near future to produce a full list of corrections to Ellis' printed text.

The Victoria County History for Dorset vol. iii translates the Exchequer DB text with the corresponding Exon. (where it survives) beneath each entry. A survey of the different scribes of Exon. is to be found in an article by R. Welldon Finn 'The Exeter Domesday and its Construction' in BJRL xli (1959).

Quotations are from, and references to, the Exon. folios given beside the translation, unless otherwise stated. When quoting from the text, the abbreviated forms of the Latin are extended only where there is no reasonable doubt. References to notes are to the Exon. Notes, unless otherwise stated.

B 1 THEY ANSWERED ... GUARDS ... "They paid tax in 1066 for 10 hides, that is, 1 silver mark for the guards' use, and for every service of the King they answered for 10 hides ...".
88 HOUSES THERE. "88 (houses) still standing".

B 2 THEY ANSWERED ... KING'S GUARDS ... "They paid tax in 1066 for 5 hides, that is, ½ silver mark for the guards' use, and for every service of the King they answered for 5 hides ...".
ONE NIGHT'S REVENUE. "the night's revenue".
100 HOUSES THERE. "100 (houses) still standing".
20 HAVE BEEN SO NEGLECTED THAT ... PAY TAX. "20 of these 100 houses have been so ruined that ... pay tax (*ita sunt adnichilate quod*, interlined in a paler ink; Ellis misprints *na* for *ita*). And 20 houses have been completely destroyed from the time of Hugh the Sheriff until now". It is not clear whether these are the same 20 houses as those "ruined".

B 3   143 HOUSES IN THE KING'S LORDSHIP. "143 houses in the King's lordship which pay tax".
THIS TOWN ... KING'S GUARDS ... "This town paid tax in 1066 for 10 hides, that is, 1 silver mark for the guards' use, and for every service of the King it answered for 10 hides ...".
ONE NIGHT'S REVENUE. "the night's revenue".
70 HOUSES THERE. "70 (houses) standing".
FROM THE TIME OF HUGH THE SHERIFF. "... until now".
ST. WANDRILLE'S. "The Abbot of St. Wandrille's".
DERELICT. "destroyed" (*destructae*).
OTHER BARONS. "other of the King's barons".

B 4   IN THE BOROUGH OF SHAFTESBURY. "In (the Borough of) St. Edward" (*in sancto eduuardo*). Shaftesbury was sometimes called after Edward the Martyr.
104 HOUSES IN THE KING'S LORDSHIP. "104 houses in the King's lordship which paid tax".
THIS TOWN ... KING'S GUARDS. "It paid tax in 1066 for 20 hides, that is, 2 silver marks for the guards' use, and it always answered for every service of the King for 20 hides".
66 HOUSES THERE. "66 (houses) standing solidly" (*stantes in uirtute*). Ellis misprints a gap after *stantes*.
111 HOUSES THERE. "111 houses standing".
THE ABBESS HAS 151 BURGESSES ... 65s. Omitted; for the two other major additions in Dorset by the Exchequer scribe, see notes to 11,12 and 36,2 (and cf. 36,3). There are only about twenty-five such additions in those parts of the five south-western counties for which Exon. survives.

1,1   THE KING HOLDS. "The King's lordship in Dorset" heads the entries corresponding to 1,1–14 (and also 18,1–2 and 24,1–3, see notes to these; as well as the odd Winterborne entry, see Ch. 49 note below).
THIS MANOR ... PAYS. "This manor ... pays ... a year"; *per annum* here and elsewhere with values of manors and, generally, with the payments of mills (e.g. 1,8).

1,2   BURTON ... CHIDEOCK. "The King has 1 manor called Burton ... Chideock". In the value paragraph, however, "These manors ... pay". It would appear that the scribe began the entry (and those corresponding to 1,3–6) in the normal manner, realising by the end of the entry that a group of manors was involved.
IT IS NOT KNOWN ... AND THEY DID NOT PAY TAX. "It is not known ... because they did not pay tax".
SCRUBLAND ... CAEN. "Scrubland at 'Hawcombe' belongs to the said manor, that is, Burton (Bradstock). In 1066 two parts of this scrubland were attached to the King's revenue in such a way that (*ita ut*) no one had any part of this scrubland except for Earl Godwin who had by reckoning (*per adnumerationem*) the third oak of this scrubland: this (third oak) now belongs to the manor of St. Stephen's, Caen, called Frampton".

1,3–5   THIS MANOR WITH ITS DEPENDENCIES PAYS ... "These manors with their dependencies and customary dues pay ..." for each entry. See 1,2 first note.

1,6   THIS MANOR ... PAYS. "These manors ... pay". See 1,2 first note.

1,7   8 SMALLHOLDERS. "9 smallholders".
2 MILLS WHICH PAY 20s. "... of which the King has half the value" *medietatem pretii*; Ellis misprints p̄tu for p̄tii − which led VCH iii p. 22 to put *partum* (*sic*) −), that is 10s, the Count of Mortain having the other 10s from the 2 mills there (see 26,4).
VALUE WAS AND IS £10. "Value of this manor £10 a year and when Fulcred acquired it at a revenue from the King (i.e. 'farmed' it; see 1,9 note) it paid as much". In the MS *valet* with *reddit* interlined above. In this case the *valet* is not underlined for deletion or erased, but it is in many others (e.g. for 11,1–2;4;7 etc.) and the *reddit* written in a darker ink by a different scribe. In Somerset and Devon, however, *valet* and *reddit* appear interchangeable in DB and Exon., so it may be that there was no real difference between the two words; see General Notes 1,7 and the Introduction to the Exon. Notes in the Somerset volume in this series.

1,8   WOODLAND. "Woodland, 1 league and 8 furlongs in length and 1 league in width; in another place woodland, 2 furlongs in length and as much in width".
LAND FOR 1½ PLOUGHS. 1 plough can plough the 1½ hides in 'Purbeck' and ½ plough can plough the ½ hide in Mappowder.
SHIRE. "County" (*comitatu*).

1,9   1 PLOUGH THERE. "1½ ploughs". The & *dim̄* is interlined, in the same colour ink and probably by the same scribe as the rest of the entry; this was perhaps the reason for its omission in DB.

VALUE WAS. "Value when he acquired it"; the *ille* perhaps refers to Fulcred who acquired the manor immediately preceding this one in Exon. (DB 1,14). *recepit* "acquired" may mean "acquired at a revenue" i.e. 'farmed' the land: it seems likely that Fulcred is the same man as he who acquired Child Okeford at a revenue (DB 1,7; see note). However, Exon. regularly, especially for Devon, has "value when he (1086 holder) acquired it" for DB's plain "value was" or when no past value is given in DB; see 11,8 note and cf. 1,18 last note and 47,7 General Notes. Lennard p. 148 agrees that the subject of *recepit* does not necessarily 'farm' the manor and that there is doubt as to whether Fulcred, who may have been a Sheriff at some stage, did 'farm' all the manors in Dorset that Exon. says he "acquired", but that he may have had charge of them and let out the 'farming' to someone else. With the exception of 56,39, Dorset Exchequer DB does not mention the practice of 'farming', whereby a *firmarius* acquired at a fixed rent a manor from the lord (— or perhaps the Sheriff; see Glos. 1,62 where the translation should read "... it was not at a revenue, but now the Sheriff has placed it out at 60s at face value"). Many DB counties refer to land being "held at a revenue", e.g. Herefords. 1,75, Glos. 1,36, Cambs. 1,18; see also 1,7;13 and 11,7 in these notes.

1,10   VALUE WAS. "Value when Fulcred acquired it". Similarly for the past values of 1,11–12;14.

1,13   VALUE. "It pays £34 and when Roger acquired it at a revenue it paid as much". In the MS the *xxx* is at the end of a line and the *iiii* at the beginning of the next and the first *i* is slightly apart from the others and rather smudged, so easily missed by the Exchequer scribe.

1,14   VALUE. See 1,10 note.

1,15   QUEEN MATILDA HELD ... "Land of Queen Matilda in Dorset" head the entries for 1,15-21.
SMALLHOLDERS. "8 cottagers" included after the smallholders. 'Cottagers' (*cotarii*) were often excluded by the Exchequer scribe for some reason: apart from the 5 for 11,5 and the 2 for 36,6, there are some 46 in Somerset and 17 in Devon who appear in Exon., but not in DB.
VALUE WAS. "Value when Aiulf acquired it"; probably Aiulf the Sheriff (see 1,21 note).

1,16   PASTURE 2 LEAGUES LONG. "Pasture 2½ leagues long". See General Notes here.
WOODLAND 2 LEAGUES LONG. "Woodland 2½ leagues long".
VALUE WAS £24. "This manor paid £24 while the Queen was alive". Similarly for the £15 past value of 1,17. She died in 1083.
THREE THANES ... "Three thanes held and still hold 3 hides of these 10 hides from Brictric; they could not be separated from him. Each of them pays 20s a year apart from service". See General Notes here.

1,18   DODA ... 1066. "... and he could go with his land to whichever lord he would".
TAX FOR 2 HIDES ... 1 HIDE ... IN LORDSHIP. There is no mention in Exon. of any land (or ploughs) held by the smallholders. Similarly for 47,4 and 55,25. This omission of villagers' land holding, when the lordship land is nevertheless given, is very common for some reason in the Exon. sections relating to Devon. The reason may have been lack of information for the villagers' holding or lack of a holding altogether or scribal error (the last being less likely because of the regularity of the omission). See General Notes 1,19.
VALUE. "Value 60s a year; value when Azelin acquired it, as many (shillings); he held this manor from the Queen". This may mean that Azelin 'farmed' the land for the Queen (an Azelin held Foddington in Somerset at a revenue from the King; see DB Som. Exon. Notes 45,15), though in the Tax Return for *Albretesberga* Hundred (v) Azelin holds 1 hide in lordship, which, with the evidence of 1,20 and 56,19, suggests that he was simply a sub-tenant of the Queen. However, it is possible that Azelin was both a sub-tenant and a 'farmer' (so Lennard p. 125 note 2). See 1,9 note on 'farming'.

1,19   HAMPRESTON. "... which William Bellett held from the Queen and Saul held it before 1066 and he could go with his land to whichever lord he would". The Latin does not make it clear whether the "he" is William Bellett or Saul.
LAND FOR 2 PLOUGHS. Ellis prints *potest arare ii d̦icar̄*. In the Exon. MS the , is below the *di* (? the beginning of *dimidia*, making the land ploughable by 2½ ploughs) and is probably a deletion mark.
1 HIDE ... LORDSHIP. "1½ hides, less 6 acres, in lordship".
5 VILLAGERS. "2 villagers". In the Exon. MS *iii* or *iiii* was originally written and the last *i*, or *ii*, erased and an attempt possibly made to join the remaining *ii* together to form a *v*. The villagers, smallholders and slaves are interlined.

1,20   TWO THANES ... 1066. "... and they could go with their land to whichever lord they would".

5 VILLAGERS. So Exon. MS; Ellis misprints *vi*.
VALUE WAS. "Value before when Azelin acquired it, as much (100s). He held it from the Queen and never paid tax to the King on the 2 parts of 1 hide which we have mentioned above in this manor" (*nominauimus*). A rare occurrence of the first person in Exon. (but see the Exon. Notes to DB Somerset 36,7 and 40,2 and to Devon 23,5; the scribe of this Dorset entry may also have written the Devon entry, but is definitely not the same as the scribe of the Somerset entries). Ellis misprints '*&icelin*' for the Exon. MS '*ᵃᵉscelin*' (for *aescelinus* or *etscelinus*, OG Azelin). The Tax Return for Badbury Hundred (vi) also mentions the fact that the King had no tax from the 2 parts of 1 hide which Azelin (*Eschelin*') holds.

1,21   WIMBORNE. "The King has 1 manor which lies in (*adiacet*) Wimborne".
IN LORDSHIP. *In dominio* omitted, perhaps in error.
WOODLAND. Not written in its usual place before the meadow, but after the value statement: "To this manor belongs woodland ...".
VALUE WAS. "Value when the Sheriff acquired it".
DOES NOT BELONG TO THE REVENUE OF ... "does not belong at all to the night's revenue of ...". See 1,3 for the payment of one night's revenue by the Wimborne Minster group of manors.

1,22   HUGH SON OF GRIP ... QUEEN. "Lands which men-at-arms held from the Queen in Dorset" heads the entries corresponding to 1,22-29. All the eight manors, however, were held by plain Hugh (no doubt Hugh son of Grip).
'WEY'. "Now the King holds this land in lordship".

1,24   VALUE WAS. "Value when Hugh acquired it". Similarly for 1,26-28.

1,28   1 VIRGATE ... AELFRIC. "Aelfric, Hugh's predecessor ...".
2½ HIDES. "... of these the King has in lordship 2½ hides and 1 plough, less 8 acres which 2 Cottagers hold".
3 COTTAGERS. "2 Cottagers" (*duo coceti*) hold the 8 acres (see preceding note), but immediately after this in the account of the people and resources: "The King has 3 Cottagers" (*ii* with *i* interlined). The scribe may have omitted to correct the first number because it was written in full rather than in the more usual figures.

1,29   THE HOLDERS ... WOULD. Entered for every section except for the one corresponding to 1,22.

1,30   DETAILS OF THESE TWO MANORS do not appear in the surviving portion of the King's
-31   lands in Exon.; perhaps, as they had been held by Countess Goda in 1066, they were in a separate gathering from the King's lordship lands and those held by and from Queen Matilda. Or, in the case of 1,30, the problem of its wrongful removal from Shaftesbury Abbey by Earl Harold may have caused information on it to be delayed.

Chs. 2   NO CORRESPONDING ENTRIES in Exon. survive for these chapters. A summary of the
-10   Glastonbury Abbey fief in Dorset appears in the incomplete folios at the end of Exon. (527 b 4-6). It corresponds fairly closely to DB Ch. 8; see General Notes to 8,1 and to 1,2 on cottagers.

11,1   ST. PETER'S CHURCH ... HOLDS. "The Abbot has", here and elsewhere in Ch. 11. The Church is only mentioned in Exon. in the heading for this DB chapter.
BRICTWIN HOLDS 4 HIDES. "A thane called Brictwin holds 4 hides of thaneland".
VALUE OF THE CHURCH'S LORDSHIP ... "This manor pays £21 for the Church's use; value when the Abbot acquired it, as much".
(VALUE) OF BRICTWIN'S, 100s. "This land (of Brictwin's) pays 100s a year. And this thane pays 30s a year to the church apart from service". The Latin for the second sentence reads *Et iste tegnus reddit per annum xxx solidos ecclesiae quo minus excepto seruitio*, which is untranslatable as it stands (the VCH translation "And this thegn renders 30s a year to the church by which (it is) the less except service" does not make sense). *Quominus* is a conjunction restricted to use after verbs of hindering and preventing. It looks as if the scribe intended to write *quominus seruitium faciat* (or some such), the clause *reddit...xxx solidos ecclesiae* having the force of a 'preventing' clause, the whole meaning being "this thane pays 30s a year to the church to avoid (or to discharge his obligation of doing) service". The scribe may have been unable to manage the construction after *quominus* (rare in ML) and fallen back on the usual phrase in these circumstances *excepto seruitio* "apart from service" (see DB and Exon. for 1,16), which is ambiguous, and then failed to delete the *quominus*. Apart from this, the entry is clear and neat and there is no change of scribe, either within the entry or immediately after it, to account for this lapse in grammar.

11,2 LITTLE PUDDLE. "It is (part) of the church's own land".
IN LORDSHIP 1 PLOUGH. "In lordship 1½ ploughs".
VALUE WAS. "Value when W(illiam) acquired it".

11,4 9 SMALLHOLDERS. So Exon. MS; Ellis misprints *viii*.
17 PIGS; 26 [SHEEP?]. *x 7 vii porcos 7 xx 7 vi porcos*; one of the *porcos* is a scribal error, probably the second as pigs are normally entered after cobs, with sheep succeeding them. However, "17 cattle; 26 pigs" could be the intended meaning.

11,5 4 SMALLHOLDERS. "5 cottagers" included after them; see 1,15 note.
WHEN ... GRIP. *& quando abbas recepit valebant c. solidos plus predictae due mansiones quia pro h. filio grip fuerunt depredati*; (*depredati* is a scribal error for the feminine *depredatae* to agree with *mansiones*). A confused sentence with *predictae due mansiones* out of place. It would seem by the use of *pro* that Hugh son of Grip got his henchmen to do the plundering for him. In the Exon. MS there is an erasure of about 14 letters before this statement, part of an erasure which began after *vii lib'* in the preceding line. The Exon. scribe definitely changes with this last sentence (but possibly as early as after the *vii lib'*) and it might be that this sentence was added after the Exchequer scribe had used the MS, though this would not explain the omission in DB of the *in lat* 'in width' in the woodland measurement, nor of the value of the manor.

11,6 4 VILLAGERS ... SHEEP. These details follow the statement about the wife of Hugh son of Grip and it is not clear whether the *habet* refers to Roger Bushell (see next note and General Notes 55,3) or to the Abbot.
3 HIDES ... 1 PLOUGH THERE. Roger Bushell holds the 3 hides from Hugh's wife and he has 1 plough there.
THIS LAND WAS. "... in 1066".
VALUE 40s ... £7. "Value of this village for the Abbot's use £7; for Roger Bushell's use, 40s".

11,7 WOODSFORD. Brictwin has it from the Abbot at a revenue; he has 2 ploughs there. *Bristuin'* in the Exon. MS; Ellis misprints *Bristuan'*.

11,8 IN HETHFELTON 3 VIRGATES. "3 virgates of land called Hethfelton".
VALUE WAS. "Value when the Abbot acquired them". Similarly for the past values in 11,11;15-17.

11,9 IN WORGRET 1 HIDE. "1 hide called Worgret".

11,10 VALUE WAS. "Value in the time of Abbot E.". Abbot Edward; see *Heads of Religious Houses, England and Wales, 940-1216* (eds. D. Knowles, C.N.L. Brooke, V.C.M. London; Cambridge 1972) p. 37.

11,11 LAND FOR 10 PLOUGHS. "10 ploughs can plough them (the 10 hides) a year"; the inclusion of *per annum* is rare in this phrase.

11,12 LAND FOR 9 PLOUGHS. Omitted in Exon. and perhaps obtained by the Exchequer scribe by adding the lordship, villagers' and thane's ploughs (though this was not a reliable method because of the discrepancies elsewhere between the plough estimate and the actual ploughs; see 1,2 General Notes). A similar addition by the Exchequer scribe occurs in Devon 3,50 and 23,1; see Exon. Notes to these. It is interesting that the DB scribe does not give a plough estimate for the next entry (11,13) where it is similarly missing in Exon., though he could have 'deduced' one from the 3 (or 5½) ploughs actually recorded; see also the first General Note under 55,28 and cf. 19,14 General Notes. It is of course possible that the Exchequer scribe had additional information for 11,12, but not for 11,13. For the other additions by the DB scribe, see the last note under B 4.
7 VILLAGERS AND 9 COTTAGERS. Classed as *rustici* ("countrymen") when their ploughs are mentioned, but as the usual *villani* when their land is stated. Cf. 55,24 note.
A THANE. "An English thane"; he has the plough.
VALUE. "This manor pays £18 for the Abbot's use and £3 for the thanes' use" (*tagnorum*, genitive plural, a scribal error for the singular *tagni*).

11,13 LAND FOR ... The plough estimate is totally absent. See fourth note under 1,1 General Notes for omissions by both Exchequer and Exon. scribes. Cf. 11,12 note.
2 PLOUGHS. "2½ ploughs".
WOODLAND. After the dimensions: "This woodland bears no fruit". In other words, it did not provide beechmast and acorns for pigs; cf. 11,16 *silua infructuosa*.
MAN-AT-ARMS HOLDS 2 HIDES. "A man-at-arms, a Frenchman, has 2 hides of thaneland, which could not be separated from the church, and 2 ploughs".
VALUE WAS £12. "Value when the Abbot acquired it, 20s more", thus making the whole TRE value £11 15s.

11,14 5 PLOUGHS. "3 ploughs".
VALUE WAS. "Value when he acquired it", presumably referring to the Abbot.
11,16 VALUE WAS. "Value when Abbot W. acquired it". Perhaps the William Abbot of Cerne who was present at the council of Gloucester in 1085 according to the compiler of the Chronicle of Lanercost; MS Cotton Claud. D vii f.53v (55v new foliation).
Ch. 12 MILTON ABBEY. "St. Peter's Church, Milton".
12,1 CHURCH ... HOLDS. "The Abbot has", here and elsewhere in this chapter.
12,3 VILLAGERS ... 2 PLOUGHS. See General Notes here for this and other similar omissions by the Exchequer scribe.
12,5 SMALLHOLDERS (HAVE) ½ HIDE. "The villagers (have) ½ hide The Abbot has 5 smallholders ...". An example of 'villagers' being used in a general sense. The same happens for 12,11 and 36,7, but see 12,16 note.
12,7 127 SHEEP. *c oues 7 xx 7 vii.* Numbers are often written like this in Exon., especially with *c, cc, ccc* etc.
12,13 NO PLOUGH IS RECORDED THERE. "There is no plough on these (3 hides) and none (*nec*) can plough (them)".
12,14 THIS MANOR ... CLOTHING. "This manor was always for the monks' supplies and clothing and it was always before 1066 (part) of the lordship revenue of the Abbot".
12,15 1 PLOUGH ... THERE. "The Abbot has 1 plough there"; *in dominio* omitted, perhaps in error.
12,16 5 SMALLHOLDERS (HAVE). "7 smallholders", the *vii* corrected early on from *iii*. *Bordarii*, instead of the usual *villani*, in the statement of their land; likewise for 55,5. See 12,5 note.
MILL ... 20d. "... 25d"; the *v.* is interlined and for that reason probably missed by the Exchequer scribe; the scribe and the colour of the ink is the same as for the rest of the entry, implying that the interlineation was not done later on. The fact that the other interlineation in the entry – the 'less 5 acres' of the lordship land – was originally missed by the DB scribe and then added at the end of the line (see General Notes here), does not prove that these interlineations in Exon. were done after the Exchequer scribe had seen the entry, because the omitted words were obviously added almost immediately, before the scribe wrote the next line with the population etc.
VALUE WAS 10s. "Value when Aiulf acquired it, 10s".
THE HOLDER ... CHURCH. "Edric held before 1066; he could not be separated from the church's service".
Ch. 13 ABBOTSBURY ABBEY. "St. Peter's Church, Abbotsbury".
13,1 ABBOTSBURY CHURCH HOLDS. "The Abbot has", here and elsewhere in this chapter.
TO THIS MANOR ... BY FORCE. Written in the left margin.
13,7 2 VILLAGERS HAVE IT THERE. "2 villagers, who hold this land and have 1 plough there".
13,8 BOLLE ... WIDOW. Bolle holds 1 hide and the widow the other hide.
2 PLOUGHS ... THERE. Bolle has 1 plough and the widow the other plough; *in dominio* omitted, perhaps in error, here – as also for the land.
1 VILLAGER. The widow has the villager.
3 SMALLHOLDERS ... SHEEP. Bolle has them.
Ch. 14 NO ACCOUNT of the lands of Horton Abbey in Dorset survives in Exon.
Ch. 15 LAND OF ATHELNEY ABBEY. "Land of the Abbot of Athelney" and "The Abbot has" for DB's "Athelney Church holds".
15,1 OF THIS LAND ALFRED ... 1½ VIRGATES. "Alfred the Butler who holds from the Abbot 1½ virgates of these 4 hides". See General Notes here.
VALUE. "Value for the Abbot's use, 60s; for Alfred the Butler's use ... 7s 6d".
Ch. 16 LAND OF TAVISTOCK ABBEY. "Land of the Abbot of Tavistock, named Geoffrey".
16,1 TAVISTOCK CHURCH HOLDS. "Abbot Geoffrey has"; so also for 16,2.
2 TRIBUTARIES. *gablatores*; "people who pay in tribute"; see General Notes here. As in the Exchequer DB, they are added in Exon. after the other classes of 'villagers', just before the Value statement.
16,2 WOODLAND. "underwood" (*nemusculi*), as on some dozen occasions in Devon and some five occasions in Somerset; the reverse (DB *silua minuta* 'underwood' for Exon.'s *nemus* 'woodland') also occurs.
VALUE WAS. "Value when the Abbot acquired it".
Ch. 17 NO ACCOUNT of the lands of St. Stephen's of Caen in Dorset survives in Exon.
Ch. 18 THIS CHAPTER appears in Exon. as part of the King's lordship land in Dorset; see Ch. 24 note.

18,1 ST. WANDRILLE'S CHURCH HOLDS. "The Abbot of St. Wandrille's has"; so also for 18,2.

18,2 1 HIDE BELONGS; 1 PLOUGH THERE. "1 hide of land belongs, which can be ploughed (with) 1 plough, which is on this land". There is no obvious reason (such as in 47,8 note on woodland and 36,4 on the garden) why the Exchequer scribe failed to record the plough estimate.

Chs. 19-23 NO EXON. survives for these chapters.

Ch. 24 THE FIRST 3 entries of this chapter appear in Exon. as part of the King's lordship land in Dorset. No doubt they were originally recorded separately as well (together with 24,4-5, for which no Exon. at all survives, and probably 18,1-2) under the heading "Lands given in alms in Dorset", like the entries for DB Somerset Ch. 16, and these entries in the King's land are merely cross-references.

24,2 ½ PLOUGH THERE. Bolle has it; *in dominio* omitted, perhaps in error.

Chs. 25 NO EXON. survives for these chapters. Summaries of the total holding of Robert son
-35 of Gerald in Dorset, Somerset and Wiltshire are given in 530 b 3-5, but the figures and values given do not relate very closely to his lands in these counties. A summary of the Count of Mortain's fief in Wiltshire, Dorset, Devon and Cornwall appears in 531 a 2.

36,1 FROM THE KING. Omitted; Exon. very rarely notes that a manor is held "from the King" and no further references to these omissions are made in these notes.
2 PLOUGHS ... THERE, IN LORDSHIP. "Geoffrey has 2 ploughs"; *in dominio* perhaps omitted in error.
VALUE WAS. "Value when W(illiam) acquired it". Similarly for the past values in 36,3-5;9.

36,2 SPETISBURY. "... which a thane, Alward (*Alwardus*; see General Notes here), held in 1066. It paid tax for 5 hides, 1 virgate and 6 acres. 4½ ploughs can plough these. In the same village William has a manor which Godric held in 1066, which paid tax for 2 hides. 1½ ploughs can plough these. William holds these two manors as one".
OVERLOOKING THE WATER. Omitted in Exon.; see last note under B 4.
VALUE WAS. "Value when he acquired it", presumably referring to William (but see 55,29-30 notes). Likewise for the past values in 36,7-8.

36,3 ALWARD HELD. "Alward held jointly" (*pariter*).
LAND FOR 2 PLOUGHS. The 1 virgate held by Hugh of Boscherbert "can be ploughed with 2 ploughs". No mention is made of a plough estimate for the rest of the land.
MEADOW, 2 ACRES; PASTURE, 6 FURLONGS; UNDERWOOD, 13 ACRES. *xiii agros nemusculi & vi quadragenarias pascuae & ii agros*. The DB scribe, if copying directly from Exon., has supplied *prati* after *ii agros*, assuming that the Exon. scribe had omitted it as he or his fellow scribes did on a number of occasions (possibly thinking it unnecessary in a list with a standard sequence of woodland — or underwood —, meadow, pasture; see DB Devon Exon. Notes 1,46). However, as *prati* would thus be out of sequence and as acres are in Dorset several times linked with furlongs in measurements (see General Notes 5,1), it is possible that the Exon. scribe intended the pasture to measure 6 furlongs and 2 acres, but wrote the word *pascuae* too early in error. See also General Notes 55,8 for a similar case.
OF THESE ... WILLIAM. There is no apparent reason for the omission of this statement from DB: it was not added in Exon., the entry is neat and the scribe does not change.

36,4 TWENTY-ONE THANES HELD. "... jointly; they could go to whichever lord they would".
A GARDEN ... 3d. Interlined in Exon. on 2 lines mostly in the right margin, perhaps the reason for its omission in Exchequer DB. The scribe is the same as, and the ink only slightly different in colour to, the rest of the entry, and nothing indicates that the addition was a late one, after the MS had been used by the DB scribe. See Devon Exon. Notes 3,44 and 10,1 where details of two gardens are also added later and cf. B 4 above where a garden features in the information added by the DB scribe.

36,5 GODRIC. "A thane called Godric".

36,6 4 VILLAGERS AND 7 SMALLHOLDERS. 2 cottagers are also recorded; see Details Table and 1,15 note.
A MILL. Two mills may be recorded: it is not clear whether the 18d Dodman and Nigel each get from a mill is from the same mill. See Details Table.
PASTURE 17 FURLONGS LONG AND AS WIDE. The two holdings of 8½ furlongs in length and width in the Details Table amount to half the Exchequer measurement, as is also the case in 55,8 (see General Notes here).
TWO MEN. Dodman and Nigel; see Details Table.

36,8 WOODLAND ... WIDE. There is no obvious reason why the Exchequer scribe omitted the woodland details: the Exon. entry is fairly neat and written by just one scribe and the woodland appears in its usual place; it is possible, however, that as the detail occupies exactly one line, the DB scribe merely skipped a line in error. Similar omissions for no apparent reasons occur for 55,16;29. Cf. General Notes 12,3 and also 36,3 and 36,4 notes above.

THE KING ... RIGHT. *Rex vero iussit ut inde rectum habeat.*

36,10 ALWARD HELD. "... and he could go to which lord he wished".

36,11 AELMER HELD. "... and he could go to whichever lord he would".

Chs. 37–40 NO EXON. survives for these chapters.

Ch. 41 WALTER OF CLAVILLE. *de Clayilla.* The alternative byname (or correction) given in 41,1 (see General Notes there) is not mentioned in Exon.

41,1 IN LORDSHIP 2 PLOUGHS. "Walter has 2 ploughs"; *in dominio* perhaps omitted in error or implied.

PASTURE, 4 FURLONGS IN LENGTH AND WIDTH. "Pasture, 4 furlongs in both length and width".

VALUE WAS. "Value when W(alter) acquired it". Likewise for the past values in 41,2-5.

41,2 BEORN. "A thane, Beorn".

41,3 ALDRED. "Aldred, a thane".

41,4 TWO THANES HELD. "... jointly".

41,5 FOUR THANES HELD. "... jointly".

Chs. 42–46 NO EXON. survives for these chapters.

Ch. 47 LAND OF ROGER ARUNDEL. Entered in Exon. under the heading of "Land of Roger Arundel of (*de*) Dorset"; *de* is similarly used, presumably in error for the usual *in*, in the heading for Ch. 48.

47,1 ALNOTH HELD. "... and he could go to whichever lord he would".

VALUE WAS. "Value when R(oger) acquired it". Likewise for the past value in 47,2.

47,2 ROGER ... VIRGATE. *In dominio* probably omitted in error or implied.

47,3 MEADOW, 2 ACRES. So Exon. MS; Ellis misprints *vi.*

VALUE WAS. "Value when he acquired it", presumably referring to Roger (but see 55,29-30 notes). Likewise for the past values in 47,4-7;9.

47,4 15 PIGS. In the Exon. MS *xii* written originally, but an attempt made to correct it to *xv.*

47,7 RALPH HOLDS. Ralph holds only 6 hides in Wraxall, William and the man-at-arms holding the remaining 4 hides of the 10 hides taxed. See the Exon. Notes to DB Somerset 36,7 and to Devon 34,27 for similar examples of the Exchequer scribe giving as 1086 holder of the whole of a manor someone who held only a part of it.

ALSO IN THIS VILLAGE. "In the same manor".

4 VILLAGERS. VALUE £3. "4 villagers have these 3 hides for £3 in tribute" (*de gablo*); see General Notes here.

A MAN-AT-ARMS ... VALUE 20s. "In the same village Roger gave 1 hide to a man-at-arms, from whom he has 20s".

47,8 POORTON. "Roger has ... Poorton, which Alwin held in 1066; it paid tax for 1½ hides. Roger has a further ½ hide there, which Ulf held. Now Guy holds these 2 hides from Roger".

IN LORDSHIP 1 PLOUGH. "Guy has 1 plough there". Unusually, it is written separately from the 1 hide and 1 virgate he has in lordship, though probably only in error (cf. the misplaced woodland in this entry). This also occurs in 55,2 (see note).

PASTURE. "... 15 furlongs in both (*inter*) length and width".

WOODLAND, 15 ACRES. Written in the middle of the list of livestock, hence, probably, its omission by the Exchequer scribe.

47,9 AETHELFRITH ... KING ... 1066. "Aethelfrith held it in 1066 and could not be separated from the King's service".

WOODLAND, 7 FURLONGS IN BOTH LENGTH AND WIDTH. "Woodland, 7 furlongs in length and as many in width".

47,10 NINE THANES ... FREELY. "Nine thanes held it in 1066 and could go to whichever lord they would [for "freely" being omitted, see 55,6 note] ... These thanes* still have in lordship these 2½ hides, less the fourth part of 1 virgate (Ellis misprints *quarta parte* both here and earlier in the entry for the Exon. MS's *quartā partē*; the correct grammar, however, is *quarta parte*)"; they also have the meadow and probably the pasture. In this manor the lordship appears to have remained unusually in the hands of the TRE holders, not passing to Robert with the rest of the land. Lower layers of sub-tenancy are not normally mentioned either in Exon. or in DB, though they are a feature of satellite documents such as Evesham A (see DB Worcs. App. IV). In this case the Exon. scribe considered the unusual information important, but the Exchequer scribe has ruthlessly omitted it. *In the Exon. MS *illi tagni* is interlined above *habent adhuc in dominio* to clarify further.

47,11 ALWARD HELD. "... and he could go to whichever lord he would".
½ PLOUGH ... THERE. "Roger has ½ plough there"; *in dominio* perhaps omitted in error.

47,12 HER HELD. "... and he could go to whichever lord he would".

Ch.48 LAND OF SERLO OF BURCY. "Land (*Terram*, accusative, in error) of Serlo of Burcy of (*de*) Dorset"; see Ch. 47 note.

48,1 12 VILLAGERS ... "There are on that land 12 villagers ...", rather than the usual formula "(the 1086 holder) has ...". This also occurs with the 'villagers' in 55,13-14;31 and five times in the Exon. for Devon (see Devon Exon. Notes 3,84).
MEADOW. "Meadows", *pratorum*, gen. plural, perhaps a scribal error for *prati*, gen. singular, though the plural occurs similarly in the Exon. for Devon 42,24, an entry written by a different scribe (see Exon. Notes there). Cf. General Notes 5,2.

48,2 ALWARD HELD. "... and he could go to which lord he wished".
VALUE WAS. "Value when he acquired it", presumably referring to Serlo.

Ch.49 AIULF THE CHAMBERLAIN. No Exon. survives for Aiulf's fief in Dorset, with the exception of one reference which has no corresponding DB entry. Under the heading of the King's lordship land in Dorset, between entries referring to DB 24,2 and 18,1 is found the following:
28 a 3: "Aiulf the Sheriff has 1 virgate of land in *Wintreborna* of reeveland. It pays 5s a year".
The entry was probably included under the King's lordship land in Exon. because it was reeveland (land that the Sheriff – 'shire-reeve' – has exclusively for his own use, all customs, services and payments belonging to him) which is often recorded under the King's land (see DB Herefords. 1,2). This 'Winterborne' is probably the same as the 'Winterborne' in the group of manors held by the King in 1,6 which is detailed in Exon. at 28 a 1; see General Notes 1,6.

Chs. 50-54 NO EXON. survives for these chapters.

55,1 NINE THANES HELD. "... from King Edward".
VALUE WAS. "Value when Hugh acquired it"; Hugh son of Grip is meant. Likewise for the past values in 55,2-6;9;12;16;18-22;24-28;31;33;35-36;38;40-42;45. For 55,8;17; 34 "value when Hugh son of Grip acquired it".

55,2 IN LORDSHIP 2 PLOUGHS. "William has 2 ploughs there", written after the statement of the 4 hides in lordship; no doubt the ploughs were also in lordship; see 47,8 note. *In dominio* is similarly omitted for 55,3.

55,4 LAND FOR 3 PLOUGHS. So Exon. MS; Ellis misprints *iiii*.

55,5 3 MILLS WHICH PAY 35s. "Hugh's wife has ... 1 mill which pays 10s a year ... 2 mills which pay 25s a year are attached to this manor".
9 PIGS. So Exon. MS; Ellis misprints *viii*.

55,6 FIVE THANES HELD IT FREELY. "freely" omitted, probably because implied in the phrase "they could go to whichever lord they would with their lands" which succeeds this statement (see 55,48 note). "freely" is also omitted for the same reasons for 47,10 and 55,32;34.

55,7 IT PAID TAX FOR 1 HIDE. "Hugh's wife has 1 hide of land in 'Winterborne' "; the tax is not mentioned separately. Similar omissions (by a different scribe) occur in the Exon. for Devon; see Devon Exon. Notes to 34,11 and 36,9 and cf. Devon General Notes 34,32. However, see 55,15 note below for an example of both the hidage and tax payment of a manor being given.

55,8 STAFFORD. "Hugh's wife has a manor called Stafford, which two thanes held jointly in 1066; they could go with their lands to whichever lord they would. It paid tax for 4 hides before 1066. 2 ploughs can plough them (*sunt arare* in error for *possunt arare*). In the same manor Hugh's wife has 2 hides of land, which Leofing held as one manor in 1066; he could go to whichever lord he would. 1 plough can plough these 2 hides. Hugh and William hold (*tenet* for *tenent*) the said two manors from the wife of Hugh son of Grip ...". See Details Table.
VALUE WAS. "Value of these two manors when Hugh son of Grip (*Grippi* with *ni* interlined (= *Grippini*, genitive), not *iii* interlined as Ellis prints) acquired them". See 55,1 note.

55,10 THE VILLAGERS. The number is not given, however.
VALUE WAS. "Value when he acquired it". The *ille* probably refers to Hugh, but it could refer to William Chernet: see 55,29-30 notes and also DB Devon Exon. Notes 16,88. Likewise for the past values in 55,13-14.

55,11 VALUE WAS. "Value when H(ugh)'s wife acquired it".
55,13 MILL. "He has there the third part of 1 mill, that is 15d"; *treciam paste*, a scribal error for *tertiam partem*.
55,14 1 VILLAGER AND 2 SMALLHOLDERS. "1 villager and 1 smallholder"; the 7 is close to the *i bord'* and was possibly mistaken for a second *i*.
55,15 ½ HIDE. "There is not now, nor was, more than ½ hide of land and it paid tax for as much before 1066".
LAND FOR ½ PLOUGH, WHICH IS THERE. "William has ½ plough there, because it can be ploughed by as much" (*pro tanto*). An unusual formula, like the statement of hidage in the preceding note. It looks as though the scribe carelessly adopted the phrase from the taxability which is in the line immediately above. The entry as a whole is neat and clear and the scribe wrote the entries before and after this one, and they do not contain unusual features.
A MILL WHICH PAYS 20s. "A mill at 20s". As in DB, the mill is written before the smallholder, meadow and pasture (another example of the DB scribe copying from Exon.); the livestock in Exon. are also written out of the usual order.
55,16 (TURNERS) PUDDLE. After the statement that Gerling held it TRE: "Hugh (son of Grip) held this manor for 6 hides and there is ½ hide, 4 acres and a garden; it has never paid tax, but (the tax on it) has been concealed". The Latin for the second half of this is *quae numquam gildavit sed celatum est*; *quae* is feminine singular and could refer to the *mansio* 'manor' (as in other similar instances) or to the ½ hide. The latter is proved to be the case in the Tax Return for Bere Hundred (xv) which states that the King never had tax from ½ hide which Walter Thunder held from Hugh's wife. *Celatum est* is neuter singular and is probably a *constructio ad sensum*, the scribe understanding *geldum* (neuter) out of *gildavit*: "the tax has been concealed", as in 27,10 (see General Notes to it).
IN LORDSHIP 2 PLOUGHS; 4½ HIDES. *In dominio* omitted, perhaps in error.
MILL ... YEAR. There is no apparent reason why the Exchequer scribe omitted the mill details: the Exon. entry is neat and clear and written by one scribe; however, the mill appears after the woodland, meadow and pasture, rather than in its usual place before them. Cf. 36,8 note.
55,17 TO WILLIAM OF MOHUN. "to William of Mohun's manor"; i.e. of Winterborne (Houghton), 36,3.
55,20 IN LORDSHIP 1 PLOUGH. "... 1½ ploughs".
15(?) CATTLE. In the Exon. MS $\overset{.x.}{v}$.; the x could either be intended to add to the v making xv, or as a replacement, making "10 cattle".
55,21 1 PLOUGH THERE. "Ilbert has 1 plough there"; *in dominio* not mentioned, either in error or because implied.
55,23 (PART) OF THE LORDSHIP OF THE ABBEY OF CERNE. "which in 1066 (*die obitus edwardi regis*, literally "on the day of King Edward's death", an unusual phrase in Exon.) were Cerne Abbey's own" (or "the Abbot of Cerne's own": *proprie abb' cerneliensis*, as *abb'* can abbreviate both *abbatia* and *abbas*; see General Notes 37,1).
HUGH ... ABBOT. "... and his wife still keeps them back".
55,24 1 VILLAGER. "1 countryman" (*rusticus*, a rare term in DB; see notes to DB Wilts. 67,66 and Worcs. 2,57 and cf. 11,12 note).
55,25 1 VILLAGER AND 1 SMALLHOLDER. "1 villager who lives there has the other virgate and ½ plough. Hugh's wife has 1 villager and 1 smallholder". There was probably only 1 villager there; but see the Exon. Notes to DB Somerset 5,21 and Devon 1,9 for the splitting of the 'villagers' into those with the land and ploughs and those presumably without them.
55,28 IN LORDSHIP ½ PLOUGH. "Robert has ½ plough there"; *in dominio* probably omitted in error.
VALUE. Reversed: the value is now 25s and was 20s when acquired. For other examples of this, see DB Somerset Exon. Notes to 8,5. 26,4 and 45,12.
55,29 MEADOW, 16 ACRES. In the Exon. MS "17 acres": xvi changed to xvii with *agros* interlined. Ellis (who prints *xvi,*), and probably the Exchequer scribe, mistook the added *i* as an omission mark (for *agros*), but it is quite clearly the lengthened *i* usually written to emphasise a corrected figure.
PASTURE, 8 FURLONGS. "pasture, 8 furlongs in both length and width", which would appear from 47,9 (see note) to mean that the pasture measured 8 furlongs by 8 furlongs. See also for 55,36;38;40. See General Notes 1,1 on furlongs.
WOODLAND ... WIDTH. See 36,8 note.

VALUE WAS. "Value when R(alph) acquired it". See next note and DB Devon Exon. Notes 16,88 for other examples of the past value of a manor being when it was acquired by the sub-tenant, rather than by the tenant-in-chief (as is usually the case). See also the last note under Devon Exon. Notes 3,22.

55,30 VALUE WAS. "Value when B(erold) acquired it"; see note above.

55,32 TWO MEN-AT-ARMS HOLD ½ HIDE ... MEADOW ... PASTURE. "Two men-at-arms hold it (½ hide) from Hugh's wife — except for 16 acres of meadow which she holds herself in lordship (Ellis omits the superscript *s* above *agri* and *quô* in this interlined clause). One of them, Thorold, has 10 cattle, 20 goats, 2 acres of meadow and 100 acres of pasture. The other man-at-arms (has) as much in acres (*agrarum*; or possibly *agrorum* 'fields') and pastures and no livestock (*nihil pecuniae*)". This unnamed man-at-arms may be Hugh, the sub-tenant of 55,33–34. See DB Devon Exon. Notes 3,91 for another example of the lordship of a manor remaining with the tenant-in-chief and not passing to the sub-tenant with the rest of the manor; and cf. Devon 19,36 where the lordship is held by the villager, and 47,10 note above where it is held by the TRE tenants.

THREE THANES HELD IT FREELY. "Three thanes held before 1066 and they could go with their land to whichever lord they would"; see 55,6 note.

55,33 HUGH. "A man-at-arms of hers", with "Hugh" interlined. Likewise for 55,34.

55,34 WULFNOTH HELD IT FREELY. "A thane, Wulfnoth, held it; he could go to whichever lord he would"; see 55,6 note.

55,35 THOROLD. "A man-at-arms of hers, Thorold". Perhaps the same man as one of the sub-tenants of 55,32 (see note).

TAX FOR 1½ HIDES. "It paid tax for 1½ hides and 1 virgate", which agrees with the details of lordship and villagers' land held. As the *i virg* is on a new line it could easily have been missed by the Exchequer scribe.

55,36 PASTURE, 4 FURLONGS. "Pasture, 4 furlongs in both length and width"; see 55,29 note.

55,37 ½ PLOUGH ... THERE. "Robert has ½ plough"; *in dominio* perhaps omitted in error.

PASTURE ... 3 FURLONGS IN WIDTH. "Pasture ... 4 furlongs in width", the last *i* of the *iiii* being badly written and slightly apart from the rest (probably the reason why the Exchequer scribe missed it). Both meadow and pasture are interlined by a different scribe to the rest of the entry, suggesting some sort of correction of the text here, though at an early stage, before the MS went to Winchester.

55,38 WOODLAND, 1 FURLONG. "Woodland, 1 furlong in length and as much in width"; see 55,29 note.

55,39 ½ HIDE. "a manor ... it paid tax for ½ hide".

VALUE 12s 6d. "This land has been completely laid waste (*omnino deuastata est*); however (*tamen*) the value is 12s 6d". The Latin implies that the land had been devastated (reason unknown), not merely that it had lain untilled, which is a possible meaning for *wasta* (see DB Worcs. 8,8 and note), especially in an entry where population and resources are mentioned and which has a value, despite being 'waste'. See also DB Herefords. 6,1 note.

55,40 WOODLAND, 4 FURLONGS. "Woodland, 4 furlongs in length and width"; see 55,29 note.

55,42 1 PLOUGH ... THERE. "Walter has 1 plough there"; *in dominio* omitted, perhaps in error.

55,43 RALPH. "A man-at-arms of hers", with "Ralph" interlined.

½ PLOUGH ... THERE. "Ralph has ½ plough there"; *in dominio* perhaps omitted in error.

55,45 1 PLOUGH ... THERE. "Robert has 1 plough and nothing more"; *in dominio* probably omitted in error or implied.

55,47 FOUR THANES HELD ... "Four thanes held jointly ...".

AN ORCHARD. "1 orchard".

CHURCH OF CRANBORNE. "Abbey of Cranborne".

HUGH'S WIFE HOLDS THE ½ HIDE. She also holds the smallholders and orchard.

55,48 ALL THE THANES ... WOULD. Mentioned, with the addition of "with their land(s)", for 55,1;3-9;11;25;30;32;36-37. Given as in DB for 55,34-35;48. Not mentioned at all for 55,2;10;12-24;26-29;31;33;38;40-47, although the 1066 holders are called "thanes" for 55,40-42;44-46. The 1066 holders are not described as "thanes" for 55,7;9;25;37.

Chs. 55a-57 NO EXON. survives for these chapters.

58,1 THE COUNTESS OF BOULOGNE. "The wife of Count Eustace". She is called "The Countess of Boulogne" in the heading in Exon., as well as for 58,2, and "Countess" for 58,3.

58,3 SHE COULD ... WOULD. Only mentioned for 58,3.

D

DETAILS OF HOLDINGS OMITTED IN DB AND GIVEN IN EXON.

ac. = acre   f. = furlong   v. = virgate   h. = hide

DB ref.	PLACE	Sub-tenant	Holding	Land for ploughs	LORDSHIP land	LORDSHIP ploughs	VILLAGERS HAVE land	VILLAGERS HAVE ploughs	Villagers	Small-holders	Cottagers (cotarii)	Slaves
36,6	Chilfrome	Dodman	5 h.	—*	5 h. less 1 v. and 4 ac.	2	—	—	2	1	2	2
		Nigel	5 h.	3	5 h. less 1 v.	2	1 v.	—	2	6	—	2
55,8	Stafford	Hugh	3 h.	—	—	—	—	—	—	3	—	—
		William	3 h.	—	—	2†	—	—	—	5	—	1

* Presumably the plough estimate for Dodman's holding was 3, as for Nigel's, because 6 ploughs is given at the beginning of the Exon. entry as the estimate for the whole 10 hides.

† *in dominio* omitted, perhaps in error.

DB ref.	PLACE	Sub-tenant	Cobs	Cattle	Cows	Pigs	Sheep	Goats	Mills	Wood	Meadow	Pasture (*length by width*)	VALUE 1086	when acquired
36,6	Chilfrome	Dodman	—	—	—	7	60	7	1 at 18d.	4½ ac.	10 ac.	8½ f. by 8½ f.	60s.	60s.
		Nigel	—	5	—	7	140	7	1 at 18d.	4½ ac.	10 ac.	8½ f. by 8½ f.	£3	£3
55,8	Stafford	Hugh	—	—	1	—	300	—	—	—	12 ac.	8 f. and 4 ac.‡	30s.)	
		William	3	—	12	37	400	—	—	—	12 ac.	8 f. and 4 ac.‡	40s.)	£4

‡ See General Notes here.

APPENDIX

THE DORSET HUNDREDS

Although two Hundreds are named incidentally in the text of DB Dorset — Buckland Hundred at 1,30 and Purbeck Hundred (probably Ailwood i.e. Rowbarrow Hundred, see 1,8 note) at 37,13 — the schedule of lands completely lacks hundredal rubrication, in common with the other four south-western counties.

The Exon. Book, however, contains Tax Returns for Dorset covering 39 Hundreds and from these valuable evidence for the identification of places can be obtained when the names of landholders and the sizes of estates are compared with DB entries, even though the Tax Returns do not themselves contain a single place-name (see the second and third paragraphs of Introductory Note 1). Set out below are the names of these Tax Return Hundreds (in the nominative; in the Exon. MS they occur in the genitive, ending in -e or -ę (for -ae), in phrases such as 'In the Hundred of Yetminster') with the modern equivalent name in brackets where it exists, their hidage totals and the Exon. column reference. The names in the last column refer to the later Hundred or Hundreds in which they were incorporated. The numbering of the Tax Return Hundreds is that adopted by the VCH volume (iii) following their order in Exon.; of the 'modern' Hundreds the numbering is that of the Maps and Map Keys in this edition.

h. = hides   v. = virgates   c. = carucates

Exon. column		Tax Return name and modern form	Hidage	'Modern' Hundred
17 a 1	i	*Etheministra* (Yetminster)	47 h.	7 Yetminster
17 a 2	ii	*Witchirca* (Whitchurch)	84½ h. 1 v.	11 Whitchurch Canonicorum
17 b 1	iii	*Oglescoma* (Uggescombe)	104 h.	25 Uggescombe
18 a 1	iv	*Glochresdona* (Eggardon)†	66½ h.	19 Eggardon
18 a 2	v	*Albretesberga* (—)	47 h.	6 Cranborne (part)
18 a 3	vi	*Bedeberia* (Badbury)	32 h. 1 v.	17 Badbury (part); 6 Cranborne (part)
18 b 1	vii	*Canendona* (—)	48 h. 3 v.	17 Badbury (part); 6 Cranborne (part)
19 a 1	viii	*Pideletona* (Puddletown)	91 h.	21 Puddletown
19 a 2	ix	*Stana* ('Stone')	63½ h.	14 Cerne, Totcombe and Modbury (part)
19 a 3	x	*Goderonestona* (Godderthorn)	28½ h.	18 Godderthorn (part)
19 b 1	xi	*Haltona* (Hilton)	86 h. 1 v.	15 Whiteway
19 b 2	xii	*Beieministra* (Beaminster)	106 h. less 1 v.	12 Beaminster (part)
19 b 3	xiii	*Redehana* ('Redhone')	7 h.	12 Beaminster (part)
20 a 1	xiv	*Tolreforda* (Tollerford)	59 h.	13 Tollerford (part)
20 a 2	xv	*Bera* (Bere)	49 h. 1 v.	22 Bere and Barrow 27 Winfrith (part)
20 a 3	xvi	*Concresdic* (Combsditch)‡	77 h.	16 Combsditch

† So Exon. MS, with the *l* interlined above and between the *g* and *o*; Ellis misprints *ǵo-chresdonę*.
‡ So Exon. MS, with *Con* interlined above and to the right of *cresdic* which is written right up against the *In*; commas indicate the position of the interlineation. Ellis misprints *cresdie* and separates the *In* from it.

Exon. column		Tax Return name and modern form	Hidage	'Modern' Hundred
20 b 1	xvii	*Cocdena* (Cogdean)	86 h.	24 Cogdean
20 b 2	xviii	*Celeberga* (Charborough)	41½ h.	23 Loosebarrow
21 a 1	xix	*Aileuesuuoda* (Ailwood)	73 h.	29 Rowbarrow
21 a 2	xx	*Hanlega* (Handley)*	20 h.	5 Sixpenny Handley (part)
21 a 3	xxi	*Neuuentona* (Newton)	47 h.	3 Sturminster Newton
21 a 4	xxii	*Langeberga* (–)	84 h.	9 Pimperne (part); 6 Cranborne (part)
21 b 1	xxiii	*Chenoltuna* (Knowlton)	36½ h.	10 Knowlton
21 b 2	xxiv	*Sexpena* (Sixpenny)	50 h.	5 Sixpenny Handley (part)
21 b 3	xxv	*Hunesberga* (–)	79 h.	9 Pimperne (part)
22 a 1	xxvi	*Pinpra* (Pimperne)	34½ h.	9 Pimperne (part)
22 a 2	xxvii	*Gelingeham* (Gillingham)	79 h. less ½ v.	4 Gillingham and Redlane (part)
22 b 1	xxviii	*Brunesella* (Brownshall)	52½ h.	2 Brownshall
22 b 2	xxix	*Haselora* (Hasler)	64 h. 1 v.	28 Hasler
23 a 1	xxx	*Winfroda* (Winfrith)	49 h. 1 v.	27 Winfrith (part)
23 a 2	xxxi	*Celberga* ('Chilbury')	51½ h.	27 Winfrith (part)
23 a 3	xxxii	*Dorecestra* (Dorchester)	73 h. 1 v.	20 St. George (part)
23 b 1	xxxiii	*Morberga* (Modbury)	63 h.	14 Cerne, Totcombe and Modbury (part)
23 b 2	xxxiv	*Sireburna* (Sherborne)	75½ h. 25 c.	1 Sherborne
23 b 3	xxxv	*Ferendona* (Farrington)	37 h.	4 Gillingham and Redlane (part)
23 b 4	xxxvi	*Bochena* (Buckland)	39 h. less 1 v.	8 Buckland Newton
24 a 1	xxxvii	*Cuferdestroua* (Cullifordtree)	109 h.	26 Cullifordtree
24 a 2	xxxviii	*Frontona* (Frampton)	35 h.	20 St. George (part); 13 Tollerford (part)
24 a 3	xxxix	*Lodra* (Loders)	20 h.	18 Godderthorn (part)
(24 a 4		Tax total for Dorset).		

* So Exon. MS; Ellis misprints *hanglege*.

It will be noted that very few of these 'Hundreds' contain a figure close to 100 hides (if that was the original total); several, such as Pimperne (xxvi) and Buckland (xxxvi), are much smaller while others, for instance Loders (xxxix) and Handley (xx), are merely individual manors which for some reason returned their tax separately. Some of these 'Hundreds' may well have been temporary, artificial creations for the needs of a particular survey. It is probable that the 'Hundreds' which supplied the Tax Returns and the 'Hundreds' which contributed to the compilation of DB differed from each other (such is the Somerset evidence) and may well have differed again from the Hundreds which under the Saxon kings had particular administrative and judicial functions.

The villages that formed each Hundred in the Tax Returns can be identified with differing degrees of completeness: the list below includes those where the identity seems reasonably certain;

Appendix

it largely agrees with the VCH reconstruction and is less total than the work of Eyton (*Dorset*) which has heavily influenced Anderson's otherwise excellent work on the Hundreds. The present editors hope to publish their analysis separately at a later date.

The relation of these Tax Return Hundreds to the later Hundreds is given above.

YETMINSTER HUNDRED (i) certainly contained Yetminster itself and all the holdings called Melbury; it is likely that the total is made up by Woolcombe and Clifton Maybank.

WHITCHURCH HUNDRED (ii) contained Symondsbury, Pilsdon, 'Studley', Lyme Regis, Abbots Wootton, Moorbath, Catherston Leweston, Wootton Fitzpaine, Atrim and 'Stoke Wallis'. Most of Broadwindsor was also here in 1086, but later transferred to Beaminster Hundred (12); see 57,15-16 note.

UGGESCOMBE HUNDRED (iii) certainly contained Abbotsbury, Portesham, Littlebredy, Waddon, Langton Herring, Tatton (now in Cullifordtree Hundred, 26), Shilvinghampton and Fleet. Elworth, Puncknowle, Corton and Bexington were also probably here in 1086.

EGGARDON HUNDRED (iv) certainly contained Winterborne Abbas, Long Bredy, Nettlecombe, West Milton, Powerstock, Wraxall, Chilcombe (this last subsequently in Uggescombe Hundred, 25), Woolcombe, later in Tollerford (13) and the Loders holdings of 26,58 and 56,51, later in Godderthorn (18). Askerswell lay in 'Redhone' Hundred (xiii) in 1086, but paid tax in Eggardon and was later transferred here. Kingcombe, later in Tollerford Hundred (13), was here in 1303 (FA ii p. 33) and probably earlier; see LSR p. 72 and 32,3 and 47,7 notes.

ALBRETESBERGA HUNDRED (v) contributed Cranborne, Boveridge, Edmondsham and Pentridge to Cranborne Hundred (6); Brockington to Knowlton Hundred (10) and Wimborne St. Giles (see Fees p. 92 and 10,3 note) to the later Hundred of that name, here mapped in Cranborne (see 'Later Hundreds' note below).

BADBURY HUNDRED (vi) was later divided between Badbury (17) and Cranborne (6). To Badbury it contributed *Selavestune*, 'Odenham', part of Hinton Martell (see vii below), Wimborne Minster, and Tarrant Crawford. To Cranborne it gave Witchampton, Preston and Hemsworth. Gussage St. Michael also lay here in 1086 and was later a detached part of Badbury Hundred (mapped in Knowlton Hundred in this edition). Preston is included in both Badbury and Pimperne Hundreds in LSR pp. 76-77; see FA ii p. 43.

CANENDONA HUNDRED (vii) was similarly divided. From it Badbury Hundred (17) acquired Horton, Didlington, part of Hinton Martell (see vi above), Petersham, Thorn Hill (see Fees p. 88), Wilksworth, Walford and Mannington; Cranborne Hundred (6) gained Hampreston and West Parley. In the Middle Ages, Petersham (now in Holt parish) was a part of Cranborne Hundred; see LSR p. 75 and FA ii p. 39.

PUDDLETOWN HUNDRED (viii) contained Puddletown itself, Little Puddle, Tolpuddle, Piddlehinton, Waterston, Milborne St. Andrew and Dewlish. The Hundred total is probably completed by Athelhampton, 'Bardolfeston', 'Little Cheselbourne', Ilsington and Tincleton. Dewlish was sometimes counted in Whiteway Hundred (15) in later times (see 25,1 note).

'STONE' HUNDRED (ix) contained Piddletrenthide and Cerne Abbas, and probably Alton Pancras (2,2 note), Up Cerne (2,3 note) and the *Cernel* (possibly Godmanstone) of 24,5. Up Cerne is later in Sherborne Hundred (1) and Alton Pancras is included there in LSR p. 70.

GODDERTHORN HUNDRED (x) had Bredy, Walditch and part of Loders (26,41, see 1,13 note), and probably Swyre as well, although this was later in Uggescombe Hundred (25).

HILTON HUNDRED (xi) certainly contained Melcombe Horsey, Ibberton, Cheselbourne, Stoke Wake, Hilton itself, Milton Abbas, Woolland and Lyscombe.

BEAMINSTER HUNDRED (xii) combined with 'Redhone' (xiii) to form the enlarged Hundred of Beaminster. The 1086 Hundred included Beaminster itself, Corscombe, Mosterton, Toller Whelme, Catsley and a part of Broadwindsor (see ii above). Chardstock was a detached portion to the west (see 3,13 note and FA ii pp. 7, 8, 41). Stoke Abbott (3,9) and Wellwood (3,18) also probably lay here in 1086.

'REDHONE' HUNDRED (xiii) contained several holdings at Poorton, as well as a detached portion, Askerswell (see iv above).

TOLLERFORD HUNDRED (xiv) certainly comprised Wyford Eagle, Chelborough, Rampisham and a part of Compton Valence (see xxxviii below). It probably contained also Chilfrome, Cruxton, Maiden Newton, Toller Fratrum and Toller Porcorum and Frome Vauchurch.

BERE HUNDRED (xv) covered an area larger than the later Bere and Barrow Hundreds (22). To these it contributed Winterborne Kingston, Briantspuddle, Turners Puddle, Affpuddle and Milborne Stileham. It is likely that the southern boundary of the Hundred was the river Frome (49,14 note); thus Worgret, later in Hasler Hundred (28), though a tithing of Barrow Hundred, was here in 1086 as were Hethfelton and Bestwall, later in Winfrith Hundred (27). The Hundred will no doubt have contained Bere Regis itself, as well as Rushton, Holton and Bovington, three places more recently in Winfrith Hundred. Clyffe (12,6 note), later in Puddletown Hundred (21), may have been here in 1086. Worgret, Bestwall and Rushton were in Barrow Hundred in the 14th century, FA ii pp. 20, 42; LSR p. 69.

COMBSDITCH HUNDRED (xvi) contained Bloxworth, Thornicombe, Blandford St. Mary and Littleton (26,28 note), also several places called Winterborne. Among them will have been Anderson, Winterborne Clenston (26,13 note), Winterborne Tomson (40,4 note) and Winterborne Whitechurch (12,11 and 55,1 notes). Winterborne Muston, later in Winterborne Kingston (Bere Hundred), although a tithing of Combsditch Hundred, was probably here in 1086 (40,4 note). Part of Winterborne Kingston may also have been here (55,1 note).

COGDEAN HUNDRED (xvii) contained Canford Magna, Kinson, Corfe Mullen and Sturminster Marshall and probably Lytchett Matravers.

CHARBOROUGH HUNDRED (xviii) included Charborough itself, Spetisbury, Mapperton, Morden and probably 'Great Crawford' (56,12 note).

AILWOOD HUNDRED (xix), also apparently known as Purbeck Hundred, incorporated Worth Matravers, part of Kingston (19,10 note), part of Afflington (28,6-7), Ower, Whitecliff, Swanage, Coombe, Wilkswood, Acton and 'Moulham'. It is likely that Ailwood itself, Studland, Rollington and Herston were also here.

HANDLEY HUNDRED (xx) contained only the manor of (Sixpenny) Handley.

NEWTON HUNDRED (xxi) included Hinton St. Mary and Fifehead St. Quintin. The latter has since 1920 been part of Fifehead Neville parish and so in Pimperne Hundred (9), but actually was a tithing in Cranborne Hundred (6) (see 19,9 note and 'Tithings' note below).

LANGEBERGA HUNDRED (xxii) contributed to the later Hundreds of Pimperne (9) and Cranborne (6). To Pimperne it gave Langton Long Blandford and Tarrant Keyneston (see Fees p. 87), as well as Tarrant Hinton, Tarrant Launceston and perhaps Tarrant Rawston (see 54,9 note and Introductory Note 2). To Cranborne it gave Farnham, Ashmore and possibly Tarrants Rushton and Gunville (1,24 note). Tarrant Monkton was also here in 1086 and possibly Chettle, both being later parts of Monkton Up Wimborne Hundred (here mapped in Pimperne and Cranborne Hundreds respectively, see below). Tarrant Monkton was sometimes included in Cranborne Hundred (LSR p. 75).

KNOWLTON HUNDRED (xxiii) contained Long and Moor Crichel, Gussage All Saints, Knowlton and 'Philipston' (20,2 note). Of these, Moor Crichel is later in Badbury Hundred (17) and 'Philipston' is a tithing of Knowlton Hundred (10) in Wimborne St. Giles parish and Hundred (see below).

SIXPENNY HUNDRED (xxiv) contained Compton Abbas, Fontmell Magna, Iwerne Minster and Melbury Abbas, all belonging to Shaftesbury Abbey.

HUNESBERGA HUNDRED (xxv) was almost completely redistributed after Domesday. Some places, including certainly Quarleston (55,1 note), Durweston, Bryanston (Knicteton' and Blaneford' in Fees p. 87) and Winterborne Stickland went to Pimperne Hundred (9). Pulham (36,4) went to Buckland Newton Hundred where another part is recorded in the Tax Return (xxxvi). Hammoon, probably here in 1086, also went to Pimperne and is still in that Hundred but is separated from it by Okeford Fitzpaine (certainly in Hunesberga in 1086, now in Sturminster Newton Hundred (3)) and Shillingstone (probably here in 1086, now a detached part of Cranborne Hundred, mapped in Sturminster Newton Hundred). Plumber, Turnworth and Fifehead Neville were also probable constituents of the Hundred in 1086; Plumber is now in Sherborne Hundred (1), Turnworth a detachment of Cranborne (6) here mapped in Pimperne.

PIMPERNE HUNDRED (xxvi) itself contained Nutford, Stourpaine, Ash and Ranston and Lazerton (30,3 and 56,32 notes).

Appendix

GILLINGHAM HUNDRED (xxvii) included Silton, Milton on Stour, Gillingham, Kington, Stour and Nyland and it is likely that Buckhorn Weston, Wyndlam, Fifehead Magdalen, Todber and Thornton (now in Sturminster Newton (3)) were here in 1086.

BROWNSHALL HUNDRED (xxviii) had Stalbridge and Stalbridge Weston, Stourton Caundle and part of Purse Caundle (26,70-71 note). Stock Gaylard, now in Sherborne Hundred (1), may well have been here.

HASLER HUNDRED (xxix) contained Orchard, Church Knowle, East Holme, Steeple, Creech, Kimmeridge, Blackmanston, Tyneham, Povington and Stoborough as well as two places later in Rowbarrow Hundred (29): part of Afflington (28,6-7 note), part of Kingston (19,10 note) and possibly Renscombe (11,16 note).

WINFRITH HUNDRED (xxx) formed half of the later Hundred of the same name, contributing Chaldon, Coombe Keynes, Lulworth, Woodstreet and Wool to it.

'CHILBURY' HUNDRED (xxxi) formed the other half of Winfrith Hundred (27) and contained Watercombe, Poxwell, Woodsford, Owermoigne, Moreton, Galton and Holworth. Ringstead was here also (as it was in FA and LSR), but was later a tithing of Winfrith Hundred in Osmington parish, Cullifordtree Hundred (26). The two holdings at Mayne (27,4-5) may also have been in 'Chilbury', Broadmayne now being in St. George (20) and Little Mayne in Cullifordtree (26).

DORCHESTER HUNDRED (xxxii) had Martinstown (Winterborne St. Martin, 55,1 note), part of Stinsford (56,40 note), Bockhampton, Bradford Peverell and a number of 'Cerne' holdings, probably Forston, Pulston and Herrison (see 26,5 note and Introductory Note 2). 'Frome Billet' was also here; it was later a tithing of this Hundred in West Stafford parish, Cullifordtree Hundred (26). West Stafford may also have been here in 1086 (26,7 note). Ashton, later in Martinstown, was in Cullifordtree Hundred in the Middle Ages.

MODBURY HUNDRED (xxxiii) included Sydling St. Nicholas, Cattistock, Frome St. Quintin, this last now in Tollerford Hundred (13), and an outlying part at West Compton (mapped in Tollerford).

SHERBORNE HUNDRED (xxxiv) contained Sherborne, Oborne, Thornford, Bradford Abbas, Compton and part of Purse Caundle (56,55 note).

FARRINGTON HUNDRED (xxxv) comprised Child Okeford, Hanford, Gold Hill, Iwerne Courtney, Sutton Waldron and probably Manston.

BUCKLAND HUNDRED (xxxvi) contained part of Pulham (see 24,4 note), Glanvilles Wootton, Mappowder and no doubt Buckland Newton itself.

CULLIFORDTREE HUNDRED (xxxvii) included all the holdings named from the river Wey (see Introductory Note 2), and a number of 'Winterbornes': Winterborne Monkton and 'Winterborne Belet' certainly, and probably Ashton (55,1 note), Winterborne Herringston and Winterborne Farringdon, part of Winterborne Came (26,13 note). Other places definitely in this Hundred were Buckland Ripers, Lewell, Radipole, Chickerell, Bincombe, Osmington, Whitcombe, West Knighton and the 2 hides of Frampton not accounted for in the next Tax Return (see 17,1 note). Part of Stinsford may have been here (56,40 note).

FRAMPTON HUNDRED (xxxviii) contained the major portion of Frampton (later in St. George Hundred (20)) and part of Compton Valence (the rest lay in Tollerford Hundred (xiv) in 1086, see 51,1 note).

LODERS HUNDRED (xxxix) at 20 hides was a return from the royal manor of Loders (1,13).

The smaller Hundreds of the above list were amalgamated to form larger units soon after 1086 and individual manors which had given separate returns were absorbed into adjacent larger Hundreds, while at the eastern end of the County, a fuller re-organisation took place. These changes yielded the medieval Hundreds found in the Feudal Aids and the Book of Fees, which largely survived into modern times.

Because these later Hundreds provide fuller detail about boundaries and the location of villages than the information that can be recovered from the Tax Returns, they have been used as the basis for the maps and indices of this edition. Certain features of these later Hundreds have, however, been ignored as follows:

Detachments

The medieval Hundreds sometimes include detached portions, often geographically remote, attached to the Hundred later than 1086 for particular reasons by the lord of the Hundred. These have been mapped in geographically appropriate Hundreds. Thus in STURMINSTER NEWTON HUNDRED (3) Hammoon is in fact a detachment of Pimperne Hundred (9), and Shillingstone of Cranborne Hundred (6). Mapped in PIMPERNE HUNDRED (9) is Turnworth, another detachment of Cranborne Hundred (6), and in TOLLERFORD HUNDRED (13) is included West Compton, a detachment of Modbury Hundred (xxxiii) in 1086 and of Cerne, Totcombe and Modbury Hundred (14) later. Charlton Marshall, a detached part of Cogdean Hundred (24), is here mapped in COMBSDITCH HUNDRED (16). Broadmayne is mapped in CULLIFORDTREE HUNDRED (26) with Little Mayne, although the former is a detachment of St. George Hundred (20). Gussage St. Michael is mapped in KNOWLTON HUNDRED (10) with Gussage All Saints', although the former is a detached part of Badbury Hundred (17). Finally, Chardstock is included in WHITCHURCH CANONICORUM HUNDRED (11), although it was an outlier of Beaminster (12).

Many detachments are, however, close to their Hundreds and have become separated only by the creation of a Liberty (see below) or of another detachment. These (e.g. Up Cerne) have been placed in their original Hundreds.

Hundreds of late medieval or later creation are similarly ignored.
BARROW (or HUNDREDSBARROW) HUNDRED is treated as a part of Bere Hundred out of which it was formed. It included the DB places of Affpuddle, Briantspuddle and Turners Puddle. Winterborne Zelston, the sole member of RUSHMORE HUNDRED, apart from West Morden tithing (see below), is included in Combsditch Hundred (16).
MONKTON UP WIMBORNE HUNDRED, formed from manors belonging to Cranborne and Tewkesbury Abbeys, included Chettle and Boveridge tithing, both mapped in Cranborne Hundred (6), and Tarrant Monkton, here mapped in Pimperne Hundred (9), as well as Monkton Up Wimborne itself (10,3 note) in Wimborne St. Giles parish.
WIMBORNE ST. GILES HUNDRED, a post-medieval Hundred (EPNS ii p. 263), incorporated Woodyates (but East Woodyates is a tithing of Cranborne Hundred) and Wimborne St. Giles itself, both here mapped in Cranborne Hundred (6). Most places in these two Wimborne Hundreds were in Cranborne Hundred as late as 1327 (see EPNS ii p. 194).

Tithings

A number of places are locally in one Hundred but tithings of another. These are of various origins, but a list of the major places is given here since in many cases the 'tithing' recalls the Hundred where the place lay in 1086.

Place	Tithing in	Actually in
East Woodyates (8,4)	Cranborne Hundred (6)	Pentridge parish in Wimborne St. Giles Hundred (−)
Boveridge (10,2)	Monkton Up Wimborne Hundred (−)	Cranborne parish and Hundred (6)
Worgret (11,9 etc.)	Barrow Hundred (−)	Arne parish in Hasler Hundred (28)
Fifehead St. Quintin (19,9)	Cranborne Hundred (6)	Fifehead Neville parish in in Pimperne Hundred (9)
'Philipston' (20,2 note)	Knowlton Hundred (10)	Wimborne St. Giles parish and Hundred (−)
Winterborne Muston (26,13 and 40,4 notes)	Combsditch Hundred (16)	Winterborne Kingston parish in Bere Hundred (22)
West Morden (26,24 etc.)	Rushmore Hundred (−)	Morden parish in Loosebarrow Hundred (23)

Appendix

Place	Tithing in	Actually in
Thornton (34,1)	Redlane Hundred (4)	Marnhull parish in Sturminster Newton Hundred (3)
West Holme (41,3 note)	Hasler Hundred (28)	East Stoke parish in Winfrith Hundred (27)
Ringstead (52,2)	Winfrith Hundred (27)	Osmington parish in Cullifordtree Hundred (26)
Ashton (55,1 note)	Cullifordtree Hundred (26)	Winterborne St. Martin parish in St. George Hundred (20)
'Frome Billet' (57,1)	St. George Hundred (20)	West Stafford parish in Cullifordtree Hundred (26)

For Hawkchurch, a tithing of Cerne, Totcombe and Modbury Hundred, see 11,1 note.

Liberties are similarly ignored and the places located in their original Hundreds. The Dorset Liberties were Frampton (including Bincombe, Benville in Corscombe, part of Winterborne Came, Compton Valence, Bettiscombe and Burton Bradstock); Loders (including Lyme Regis); Powerstock; Broadwindsor; Fordington; Piddlehinton; Portland Island; Dewlish; Sutton Poyntz and Preston; Upwey; Gillingham; Halstock; Alton Pancras; Piddletrenthide (including Minterne Magna); Sydling St. Nicholas; Stour Provost; Owermoigne and Bindon (including Chaldon Herring, West Lulworth and Wool).

The Hundred Names
Many of the names both of the Tax Return Hundreds and of the later Hundreds, mapped and indexed in this edition, are those of major settlements forming DB holdings and they present no problems of identification and location. A few, however, require brief discussion.

A number of the Tax Return Hundreds have remained of about the same extent since 1086, but have changed their names. Thus *Haltona* (xi) has been replaced by Whiteway (15), but Hilton, a parish within it, preserves the name. Whiteway itself is apparently named from a site on the road from Binghams Melcombe to Hilton (Hutchins iv p. 347; Fägersten p. 188; Anderson p. 116).

Celeberga (xviii), Charborough in Morden parish, has been succeeded by Loosebarrow (23), the name of a barrow, now flattened, near the western end of Charborough Down (Hutchins iii p. 494; Anderson p. 125; EPNS ii p. 55). Although the name has changed, the site of the Hundred moot may well have remained the same as is the case with *Aileuesuuoda* (xix), Ailwood in Corfe Castle parish, now Rowbarrow Hundred (29). Rowbarrow is said to be represented by Rowbarrow Lane, not on OS maps, south of Tabbits Hill farm (GR SY 986809) in Woolgarston parish (Hutchins i p. 629; Anderson p. 123; EPNS i p. 4).

Dorchester (xxxii) has been followed by St. George, named from the dedication of the church in Fordington in Dorchester (Hutchins ii pp. 533, 791; Anderson p. 118; EPNS i p. 334).

Finally in this group, Farrington (xxxv), a hamlet in Iwerne Courtney (*alias* Shroton) parish (GR ST 8415; Anderson p. 137), has been replaced by Redlane (4), a part of Gillingham and Redlane Hundred, now represented on OS six-inch maps by Red Lane which leads from the village of Todber towards Hayes farm (GR ST 798197; Anderson p. 139; Hutchins iv p. 56).

Some of the Tax Return Hundred names are unidentified, uncertain or have barely survived. Thus *Albretesberga* (v) and *Hunesberga* (xxv), though both found in Fees (pp. 92, 87), are named from barrows that have not been identified (Anderson pp. 131, 133; EPNS ii pp. 194, 86). *Langeberga* (xxii), a similar name, is possibly named from Pimperne Long Barrow (GR ST 907115; Hutchins i p. 214; Fägersten p. 50; Anderson p. 133; EPNS ii p. 87). The site of *Canendona* (vii) is lost, but the name is to be associated with Canford and may be connected with Cannon Hill in Hampreston parish (GR SU 0401; Anderson p. 129; EPNS ii p. 133; see Fees pp. 88, 260).

'Stone' (ix) has not been located (Anderson p. 115), although it could be connected with Godmanstone. There is also some difficulty about the position of 'Redhone' or 'Redhove' (xiii);

it is placed by Hutchins (ii p. 153) in North Poorton parish, but a 'Redhove' is found at GR SY 4797, south of Beaminster, on the first edition one-inch OS map (sheet 18 of 1811, reprint sheet 84 of 1969; Fägersten p. 261; Anderson p. 108).

Celberga (xxxi) is probably represented by Chilbury Plantation just to the west of Owermoigne (GR SY 765851; Eyton *Dorset* p. 58; Anderson p. 120; EPNS i p. 107).

Among the names of later Hundreds, some of them the same as Tax Return Hundreds, Brownshall (2) is represented by Brunsells farm (GR ST 715152) and Brunsells Knap, a lane name (GR ST 725147) in Stourton Caundle parish on OS six-inch maps, and by 'Browns Wheel' (GR ST 719152 on the first edition one-inch OS map, sheet 18 of 1811, reprint sheet 84 of 1969; see Fägersten p. 33 and Anderson p. 135). Tollerford (13) is a ford on the river Toller (now called the Hooke) on the boundary of Toller Fratrum and Maiden Newton parishes (GR SY 5897; Anderson p. 112). Totcombe, in Cerne, Totcombe and Modbury Hundred (14), is now represented by Tatcombe Wood (GR SY 6799) near Bramble Bottom on the boundary of Cerne and Nether Cerne parishes. Likewise Modbury, OE *(ge)mōt beorg* 'meeting barrow', is said by Hutchins to be north-east of Cattistock (Hutchins iv p. 1; Fägersten p. 193; Anderson p. 116).

Combsditch (16) is named from the prominent Iron Age or Romano-British fortification running north-west to south-east that forms a boundary of the Hundred (most clearly seen at GR ST 8502 and ST 8800; Anderson p. 127; EPNS ii p. 71). The meeting place of Badbury was no doubt the notable camp of Badbury Rings (GR ST 9603) in Shapwick parish (Anderson p. 129; EPNS ii p. 133). The site of Godderthorn (18) is unknown, but Eggardon (19) is preserved in Eggardon Hill (GR SY 5494) and Eggardon farms (SY 5393) in Askerswell (Anderson p. 110).

The barrow that named Barrow or Hundredsbarrow Hundred (22) lay in the south of Bere Regis parish (GR SY 8493; Anderson p. 124; EPNS i p. 288). Cogdean (24) survives as Cogdean Elms in Corfe Mullen parish (GR SY 992980; Anderson p. 128; EPNS ii p. 1). Uggescombe (25) is a name now lost, said by Hutchins to be 'Mystecombe', north-east of Portesham, marked on the first edition one-inch OS map (sheet 17 of 1811, reprint sheet 92 of 1969; GR SY 614867; Hutchins ii pp. 714, 763; Fägersten p. 244; Anderson p. 111). Cullifordtree (26) is a barrow lying in Whitcombe parish, marked on the same OS first edition one-inch sheet (GR SY 700854; Anderson p. 119; EPNS i p. 195). Finally, Hasler (28) is the name of a wood in Steeple parish (GR SY 905815; Hutchins i p. 550; Anderson p. 121; EPNS i pp. 70, 98).

INDEX OF PERSONS

Familiar modern spellings are given when they exist. Unfamiliar names are usually given in an approximate late 11th century form, avoiding variants that were already obsolescent or pedantic. Spellings that mislead the modern eye are avoided where possible. Two, however, cannot be avoided: they are combined in the name of 'Leofgeat', pronounced 'Leffyet' or 'Levyet'. It should be noted that in the Dorset volume certain personal names have been treated differently: thus the Alfward of previous volumes in this series has become Alward; Alfwold, Alwold; Alfsi, Alsi and Alfwy, Alwy; attention is drawn to the notes at the first occurrence of these names. The definite article is omitted before bynames, except where there is reason to suppose that they described the individual's occupation (as at 57,17; see note). The chapter numbers of listed tenants-in-chief are printed in bold type at the beginning of the list of references and are the numbers of the text, not the Landholders' List. Names in italics indicate that persons or bynames occur only in Exon.; likewise references in italics indicate that the name, or a fuller form of it, is to be found only in Exon. In this edition these names are found either in small type in the translation or in the Exon. Notes. It should be emphasised that this is essentially an index of personal names, not of persons; it is probable that in the case of some entries of simple names more than one person bearing the same name has been included. Likewise, a person who bears a title or byname may be represented under the single name, e.g. in Dorset many of the references to plain Hugh are undoubtedly to Hugh son of Grip (see Exon. Notes 55,1). Where there is a cross-head in the translation (e.g. 'William also holds') referring to several succeeding entries, the reference in this Index is to the first entry only, above which the cross-head appears, so that an individual might hold more manors than would appear from the Index. Similarly when a phrase such as 'Brictric held all these lands before 1066' occurs, usually exdented in the translation and referring to several preceding entries, the reference here is to the last entry only, before which the statement occurs.

Walkhere	39,1
Walscin of Douai	39
Walter *Thunder*	55,16;42;44
Walter of Claville/Glanville	41
Walter the deacon	24,5
Walter	3,13;18. 37,6-8;9(?)-10. 55,24
Warengar	40,1
Warmund	8,3
White, see Wulfgar, Wulfward	
Wihtnoth	35,1
Abbot W(illiam?)	*11,16*
Earl William	40,7
William Bellett	1,*19*;30. 57,1;12–14;19
William Chernet	55,10;13–14
William of Braose	37. 19,10
William of Daumeray	*55,19.* 57,4;11
William of Écouis	38
William of Eu	34
William of Falaise	35
William of Mohun	36. 55,17
William *of Moutiers*	11,2. 55,15;22
William, the King's son	3,6
William	2,4. 3,11;13. 26,6;45;59;64–65. 27,2-11. 34,1–3;6;8;12. 47,7. 55,2;8;15a;20. 57,3
Wimer	39,2
Wulfeva	58,3
Wulfgar White	1,30
Wulfgar	55,17
Wulfgeat	1,27. 8,6. 26,28;41. 33,5. 54,11. 56,16;34
Wulfnoth	55,34
Wulfred	26,69
Wulfric Hunter	56,30
Wulfric Hunter's father	56,30
Wulfric	1,31. 56,13;18
Wulfric's father	56,13;18
wife of Wulfric's brother	56,13
Wulfward White	35,1
Wulfward	6,1. 8,5. 26,14. 34,4. 57,1
Wulfwen	31,1–2
Wulfwin	56,5

CHURCHES AND CLERGY

Abbess of:	(Shaftesbury)	B 4
Abbeys of:	Abbotsbury	13
	Athelney	15. E 1
	Cerne	55,23
	Cranborne	*55,47*
	Horton	14
	Marmoutier	26,20
	Milton	12
	Shaftesbury	19
	Tavistock	16
	Wilton	20
	St. Peter, Winchester	9
Abbots of:	*Athelney*	*15. E 1*
	St. Peter's, Abbotsbury	*13. 55,3*

SECULAR TITLES AND OCCUPATIONAL NAMES

Baker (*pistor*) ... Osmund
Boy (*puer*) ... Robert
Butler (*pincerna*) ... Alfred
Carpenter (*carpentarius*) ... Durand
Chamberlain (*camerarius*) ... Aiulf, Hervey, Humphrey, Odo
Clerk (*clericus*) ... Edward
Cook (*cocus*) ... Gotshelm
Corn-dealer (*frumtinus,* see 55, 37 note) ... Robert
Count (*comes*) ... Alan, Eustace, of Mortain
Countess (*comitissa*) ... of Boulogne, Goda
Earl (*comes*) ... Aubrey, Edwin, Godwin, Harold, Hugh, William
Hunter (*venator*) ... Edward, Godwin, Waleran, Wulfric
Interpreter (*interpres*) ... David
Queen (*regina*) ... *1,16–20.* 54,8. 56,19–20. Edith, Matilda
Reeve (*prepositus*) ... Godwin
Scullion (*scutularius*) ... Godfrey
Sheriff (*vicecomes*) ... Aiulf, Alfred, Baldwin, Hugh
Steward (*dapifer*) ... Ralph
Treasurer (*thesaurarius*) ... Odo

INDICES OF PLACES

The name of each place is followed by (i) the number of its Hundred and its numbered location on the Maps in this volume; (ii) its National Grid Reference; (iii) chapter and section reference in DB. Bracketed figures here denote mention in sections dealing with a different place. Unless otherwise stated in the notes, the identifications of VCH and DG and the spellings of the Ordnance Survey are followed for places in England, of OEB for places abroad. Places that occur only in the Exon. Book are indexed Exon. with the folio references. Other Exon. references and those to the Tax Returns are given beside the translation and in the notes. Inverted commas mark lost places with known modern spelling, some no longer on modern maps, others now represented not by a building but by a wood, field or road name; unidentifiable places are given in DB spelling, in italics. The National Grid reference system is explained on all Ordnance Survey maps, and in the Automobile Association Handbooks: the figures reading from left to right are given before those reading from bottom to top of the map. Dorset lies partly in four 100-kilometre Grid squares; Grid References beginning with t are in square ST, with u in SU, with y in SY and with z in SZ. Places with bracketed Grid References are not found on modern 1:50,000 maps. A few places that were in Dorset in 1086 are now in adjacent (pre-1974) counties, whose names are given after them in Index 1. The Dorset Hundreds are numbered from west to east working southwards on the Maps, and their names and numbers are listed at the head of the Map Keys. Within each Hundred places are numbered alphabetically. Places in Somerset and Devon in 1086 but later transferred into Dorset are prefixed S and D respectively in place of the Hundred number in the Map Keys. Because there is insufficient evidence to reconstruct the 1086 Hundreds fully, the 'modern' Hundreds are followed, but ignoring certain later changes that are detailed in the Appendix. Places named after the principal rivers (Cerne, Frome, Winterborne, etc.) are grouped together in the Index; the problems of their identification are discussed in Introductory Note 2 at the head of the General Notes (see also Index 5 below). A name in brackets following a place-name is that of a parish or adjacent major settlement, given to distinguish this place from others of the same name in Indices 1 and 4. A star beside a place-name in Index 1 indicates that there is a further entry in Index 4 below.

1. PLACES NAMED IN DB

	Map	Grid	Text
Abbotsbury	25-1	y57 85	13,1
Acton	29-1	y98 78	55,41
Adber	S-1	t59 20	ES 4;7;9
Afflington	29-2	y97 80	28,6–7. 37,7. 41,1. 57,20
Affpuddle, see River Piddle			
Ailwood	29-3	y99 81	56,58
Allington	18-1	y46 93	33,4
Alton Pancras	14-1	t69 02	2,2
Anderson, see River Winterborne (Eastern)			
Ash (in Stourpaine)	9-1	t86 10	37,4
Ashmore	6a-1	t91 17	1,17
Ashton, see River South Winterborne			
Askerswell	19-1	y52 92	16,1
Athelhampton, see River Piddle			
Atrim	11-1	y44 95	13,8
'Bardolfeston', see River Piddle			
Beaminster	12-1	t47 01	3,10
Bere Regis	22-2	y84 94	1,2. 24,1. 55,15
Bestwall	27-1	(y92 87)	26,49
Bexington	25-2	y53 86	47,5
Bhompston, see River Frome			
Bincombe	26-1	y68 84	17,2
Blackmanston	28-1	y91 80	56,52;65

	Map	Grid	Text
'Blandford':			
Langton Long Blandford	9-2	t89 05	26,37. 47,4. 56,31
Blandford St. Mary	16-2	t88 05	26,29. 34,6. 49,1. 56,14
Bryanston	9-3	t87 06	26,46. 56,34
Bloxworth	16-3	y88 94	11,4
Bockhampton	20-3	y72 92	58,1
Boveridge	6b-1	u06 14	10,2
Bovington	27-2	y82 88	56,59
Bowood	12-2	y44 99	3,17
Bradford Abbas	1-1	t58 14	3,4
Bradford Peverell	20-4	y65 93	34,2
Bradle	28-2	y93 80	49,9
Bradpole	12-3	y48 94	1,2
Little Bredy, see Littlebredy			
Long Bredy	19-2	y56 90	11,12
Bredy	18-2	y50 89	43,1
Brenscombe	29-4	y97 82	55,46
Briantspuddle, see River Piddle			
Bridge	26-2	(y65 77)	49,13. 55,18. 56,41
Bridport	11-2	y46 92	B 2. 3,12. 18,1
Broadmayne, see Mayne			
Broadwey, see 'Wey'			
Broadwindsor	12-4	t43 02	57,15–16
Brockington	10-1	u01 10	26,47
Bryanston, see 'Blandford'			
Buckham	12-5	t47 03	3,18
Buckhorn Weston, see Weston			
Buckland Newton	8-1	t69 05	8,3
Buckland Ripers	26-4	y65 82	55,4
Burleston, see River Piddle			
Burstock	11-3	t42 02	27,11
Burton Bradstock	18-3	y48 89	1,2. 18,1
Canford Magna	24-1	z03 98	31,1
Catherston Leweston, see River Cerne (now River Char)			
Catsley	12-6	t52 03	27,10
Cattistock	14-2	y59 99	12,4
Purse Caundle	1-2	t69 17	15,1. 56,55. E 1
Stourton Caundle	2-1	t71 15	26,70–71. 34,15. 38,2. 39,2. 54,2. 56,54
River Cerne			3,14. 12,16. 24,5. (26,64)
*'Cerne':			
Forston	20-8	y66 95)	
Herrison	20-11	(y67 94))	26,5;8–11. 53,1
Pulston	20-13	(y66 95))	
Cerne Abbas	14-3	t66 01	11,1
Up Cerne	1-3	t65 02	2,3
Charminster	20-5	y67 92	2,1
River Cerne (now River Char)			
Catherston Leweston	11-4	y36 94	26,64
Charmouth	11-6	y36 93	26,67
Chaldon	27-3	y79 83	1,12. 24,3. 55,33
Charborough	23-1	y92 97	1,9
Chardstock (DEVON)	11-5	t30 04	3,13
Charlton Marshall	16-4	t90 03	1,5
Charminster, see River Cerne			
Charmouth, see River Cerne (now River Char)			
Chelborough	13-1	t54 05	36,8. 47,3
Cheselbourne	15-1	y76 99	19,14
'Little Cheselbourne'	21-4	(y77 96)	55,3
Chettle	6a-2	t95 13	49,7

Places 1

	Map	Grid	Text
Mayne	26-10	y72 86	27,4–5
Melbury Abbas	5-5	t88 20	19,6
Melbury:			
Melbury Bubb	7-2	t59 06	} 26,35. 32,2. 47,2. 56,17
Melbury Osmond	7-3	t57 07	}
Melcombe Horsey	15-5	t76 02	1,30. (19,14)
Milborne Port (SOMERSET)	S-3	t67 18	(2,6)
Milborne St. Andrew	21-8	y80 97	46,1
Milborne Stileham	22-4	(y80 97)	54,12. 56,53
Milton Abbas	15-6	t80 01	12,2
Milton on Stour	4-8	t80 28	35,1. 56,1
West Milton	19-4	y50 96	11,14
Moorbath	11-9	y43 95	54,4
Morden	23-4	y91 95	26,24. 41,5. 49,2. 55,10. 56,13
Moreton	27-11	y80 89	26,56. 56,37
Mosterton	12-10	t45 05	54,5
'Moulham'	29-8	(z01 80)	57,21
Netherbury	12-11	y47 99	3,11
Nettlecombe	19-5	y51 95	11,13
Buckland Newton, see Buckland			
Maiden Newton	13-9	y59 97	40,8
Sturminster Newton	3-4	t78 13	8,1
Nutford	9-10	t87 08	1,28. 57,12
*Nyland	4-9	t73 22	26,2. 33,2–3
Oborne	1-5	t65 18	3,2
'Odenham'	17- –	– – –	7,1
Okeford:			
*Child Okeford	4-10	t83 12	1,7. 26,4
Okeford Fitzpaine	3-5	t80 10	8,2
Shillingstone	3-6	t82 11	54,6
Orchard	28-8	y94 80	55,47
Osmington	26-11	y72 82	12,7
Ower	29-9	y99 85	12,13
Owermoigne	27-12	y76 85	46,2
West Parley	6b-7	z09 97	54,10
Pentridge	6b-8	u03 17	8,5
South Perrott	12-12	t47 06	27,9
Petersham	17-7	u02 04	54,14. 55a,1
River Piddle			
Affpuddle	22-1	y80 93	11,5
Athelhampton	21-1	y77 94	3,16
'Bardolfeston'	21-2	(y76 94)	3,15
Briantspuddle	22-3	y81 93	56,48
Burleston	21-3	y77 94	12,5
'Piddle'	21- –	– – –	(19,14). 26,21–22
Piddlehinton	21-9	y71 97	26,20
Piddletrenthide	14-4	y70 99	9,1
*Little Puddle	21-10	(y71 96)	1,14. 11,2. 12,15
Turners Puddle	22-5	y83 93	55,16
Puddletown	21-11	y75 94	1,8. 24,3
Tolpuddle	21-13	y79 94	13,2
*Waterston	21-14	y73 95	48,1
Piddlehinton, Piddletrenthide, see River Piddle			
Pilsdon	11-10	y41 99	56,46
Pimperne	9-11	t90 09	1,5
Plumber	1-6	t77 11	56,29
Poorton	12-13	y51 98	13,7. 16,2. 32,4. 47,8. 54,7
Portesham	25-9	y60 85	13,4
Portland	26-12	y69 72	1,1

Places 1

	Map	Grid	Text
*Sydling	14-5	y63 99	12,1. 26,26–27
Symondsbury	11-15	y44 93	11,17
River Tarrant			
'Tarrant':	– –	– – –	1,24–26;(31). 34,12. 49,5. 54,9. 55,25;29–30
Tarrant Gunville	6a-5	t92 12	
Tarrant Rawston	9-18	t93 06	
Tarrant Rushton	6c-3	t93 05	
Tarrant Crawford	17-9	t92 03	6,1
Tarrant Hinton	9-14	t93 11	19,8
Tarrant Keyneston	9-15	t92 04	6,3
Tarrant Launceston	9-16	t94 09	21,1
Tarrant Monkton	9-17	t94 08	10,6
Tatton	26-17	y63 82	49,10. 55,23
Thorncombe	D-1	t37 03	ED 1
'Thorne'	29-14	(y99 78)	55,44–45
Thornford	1-9	t60 13	3,3
Thorn Hill	17-10	(u03 04)	56,18
Thornicombe	16-5	t87 03	56,15
Thornton	3-7	t80 18	34,1
Tincleton	21-12	y77 91	27,3
Todber	4-14	t79 20	36,1
Toller:			
Toller Fratrum	13-11	y57 97	40,9
Toller Porcorum	13-12	y56 97	
Toller Whelme	12-15	t51 01	26,66
Tolpuddle, see River Piddle			
Trent	S-7	t59 18	ES 5
Trill	1-10	t59 12	(27,6)
Turnworth	9-19	t82 07	45,1
Tyneham	28-13	y88 80	26,55. 27,8. 54,8. 56,49
Upwey, see 'Wey'			
Up Wimborne, see Wimborne St. Giles			
Waddon	25-13	y61 85	23,1. 56,36
Walditch	18-9	y48 92	57,11
Walford	17-11	(u00 00)	56,24
Wareham	27-16	y92 87	B 3. (2,1. 14,1). 18,2. (26,54. 27,4. 30,4. 34,5). Exon 48 a 1 (= 36,4)
Wareham Castle (i.e. Corfe Castle)	– –	– – –	(19,10)
Warmwell	27-17	y75 85	26,57. 27,7. 55,35
*Watercombe	27-18	y75 84	1,29
*Waterston, see River Piddle			
Weathergrove	S-8	t61 21	ES 2
Wellwood	12-16	t47 03	3,18
Buckhorn Weston	4-15	t75 24	26,1
Stalbridge Weston	2-3	t71 16	3,7
River Wey			
'Wey':	26- –	– – –	1,22. 26,14–16. 54,3. 55,5–6. 56,9
Broadwey	26-3	y66 83	
Upwey	26-18	y66 85	
Weymouth	26-19	y67 79	
Whitchurch Canonicorum	11-16	y39 95	18,1
Whitcombe	26-20	y71 88	12,8
Whitecliff	29-15	z03 80	48,2
Wilkswood	29-16	y99 79	55,40;48
Wilksworth	17-12	u00 01	56,21;23
Wimborne Forest	– –	– – –	(14,1)

	Map	Grid	Text
*Wimborne':	– –	– – –	26,32
Wimborne Minster	17-13	z00 99	1,3;21;(31. 14,1. 31,1)
Wimborne St. Giles	6b-9	u03 12	1,3. 10,3. 20,2. 55,13.
(i.e. Up Wimborne)			56,16. 57,9
Windsor, see Broadwindsor, Littlewindsor			
Winfrith Newburgh	27-19	y80 84	1,6. 24,2
Rivers Winterborne (Eastern or South Winterborne)			
'Winterborne'	– –	– – –	1,6. 5,1–2. 39,1. Exon 28 a 3
			(1,6 note)
River Winterborne (Eastern)			
'Winterborne':	– –	– – –	26,30–31;33–34;36;48.
			40,4. 55,11–12;27–28.
			56,6;26;60. 57,6;10
Anderson	16-1	y88 97	
Quarleston	9-12	t83 03	
Winterborne Clenston	16-6	t83 03	
Winterborne Kingston	22-6	y86 97	
Winterborne Muston	22-7	y87 97	
Winterborne Tomson	16-7	(y88 97)	
Winterborne Zelston	16-9	y89 97	
Winterborne Houghton	9-20	t82 04	36,3. 55,17. 56,28
Winterborne Stickland	9-21	t83 04	22,1
Winterborne Whitechurch	16-8	t83 00	12,11
River South Winterborne			
'Winterborne':	– –	– – –	26,13;18–19. 55,7;9. 56,10
Ashton (in Winterborne	20-1	y66 87	
St. Martin)			
Winterborne Came	26-22	y70 88	
Winterborne Farringdon	26-23	(y69 88)	
Winterborne Herringston	26-24	y68 88	
Winterborne Steepleton	25-14	y62 89	
Martinstown	20-12	y64 88	55,1
Winterborne Abbas	19-7	y61 90	11,11
'Winterborne Belet'	26-21	(y70 86)	57,3
Winterborne Monkton	26-25	y67 87	58,2
Witchampton	6c-4	t98 06	1,20. 26,40
Woodsford	27-20	y76 90	11,7. 57,13
Woodstreet	27-21	y85 85	57,18
Woodyates	6b-10	u02 19	8,4
Wool	27-22	y84 86	26,60. 56,62–63
Woolcombe (in Melbury Bubb)	7-4	t60 05	34,7
Woolcombe (in Toller Porcorum)	13-13	y55 95	56,50. 57,8
Woolgarston	29-17	y98 81	37,14
Woolland	15-8	t77 06	12,10
Abbotts Wootton	11-17	y37 96	13,6
Glanvilles Wootton	8-4	t67 08	37,1–2
Wootton Fitzpaine	11-18	y37 95	26,63;69. 49,12
Worgret	28-14	y90 86	11,9. 37,10. 57,7
Worth Matravers	29-18	y97 77	47,9;11. 55,43
Wraxall	19-8	t56 01	47,7
Wyndlam	4-16	(t78 29)	47,1
Wynford Eagle	13-14	y58 95	34,9
Yetminster	7-5	t59 10	2,4

2. PLACES NOT NAMED IN DB

(Main entries only are included, not subdivisions of a named holding)

37,13	Richard from William of Braose, 7 hides less ½ virgate in Purbeck Hundred.
53,2	Hugh of Boscherbert, 10 hides.
54,1	Hugh of Ivry, 5 hides in 3 places.
55,15a	William from the wife of Hugh, 1½ virgates.
56,20	Doda, ½ hide.
56,22	Alward, the third part of 1 virgate.

56,27	Godwin Hunter, 1 virgate 4 acres.
56,30	Wulfric Hunter, 1 hide.
56,56	Two smallholders, the fourth part of 1 virgate.
57,4	William of Daumeray, 3 hides 2½ virgates.
57,5	Hugh Gosbert, 1 virgate.

3. PLACES NOT IN DORSET

Names starred are in Index 1 above; others are in the indices of Persons or of Churches and Clergy.
Words in italics refer to people found only in Exon.

Elsewhere in Britain

DEVONSHIRE	Chardstock*; Exeter ... Bishop; Stockland*; Tavistock ... Abbey, *Abbot Geoffrey*; Church.
HAMPSHIRE	Kinson*; Winchester ... Abbey, Church, Monks(?).
MIDDLESEX	London ... Bishop, Bishop Maurice.
SOMERSET	Athelney ... Abbey, *Abbot*, Church; Glastonbury ... Church; Milborne Port*.
WILTSHIRE	Salisbury ... Bishop, Edward; Wilton ... Abbey, Church.

Outside Britain

The départements to which French places belong are given under the first occurrence of the name
in the General Notes.

Bayeux ... Bishop
Beaumont ... Roger
Boscherbert ... Hugh
Boulogne ... Countess
Braose ... William
Burcy ... Serlo
Caen ... Churches
Carteret ... Humphrey
Chernet ... *William*
Claville (Glanville) ... Walter
Courseulles ... Roger
Coutances ... Bishop, Canons
Daumeray ... William
Douai ... Walscin
Écouis ... William
Épaignes, see 'Spain'
Eu ... William
Falaise ... William

Glanville, see Claville
Hesdin ... Arnulf
Ivry ... Hugh
Limesy ... Ralph
Lisieux ... Bishop
Marmoutier ... Abbey
Mohun ... William
Mortagne ... Matthew
Mortain ... Count
Moutiers ... *William*
Port ... Hugh
Reviers ... Richard
St. Quentin ... Hugh
St. Wandrille ... *Abbot*, Church
'Spain' (Épaignes) ... Alfred
Villars ... Church, Monastery

Country unknown
Margella ... *Roger*

4. IDENTITIES OF UNNAMED DB HOLDINGS OR OF UNNAMED SUBDIVISIONS OF NAMED DB HOLDINGS

Index 1 lists the identifications of DB places as printed in the Translation. The present index
contains two categories of place-name found in the Notes: (a) the identification of holdings that
DB does not name (e.g. 56,30 1 hide which can be deduced from later evidence to be 'Baggeridge'
in Woodlands); (b) the names of subdivisions of DB holdings. Many DB entries refer to a large
number of hides by a single place-name (e.g. 2,1 Charminster 10 hides) although these hides must
have contained many separate named settlements: this index lists the place-names that later
evidence shows were included in the DB holding. In both cases the evidence is of varying certainty.

Omitted from this index are the conjectural identification of places merely called 'Winterborne'
in the Translation. These are given in Index 5 below.

Places starred are also found in Places Index 1 above since a named main DB holding also lay
there in 1086.

5. IDENTIFICATION OF PLACES NAMED FROM THE WINTERBORNE RIVERS

Listed here are both certain identifications (printed in the Translation) and conjectures (included in the Notes). As explained in Introductory Note 2, Index 1 also lists those parish names that are derived from the Rivers and which probably represent DB holdings. Where there is no certainty, no chapter and section reference is given in Index 1. This index includes all Winterborne names, parish names and others, found in the Translation or the Notes or Index 1.

Anderson	26,13 note
Ashton	55,1 note
Martinstown	26,13. 55,1 notes
Quarleston	55,1 note
Winterborne Abbas	11,11 note
'Winterborne Belet'	56,10. 57,3 notes
Winterborne Came	17,1 note
Winterborne Clenston	5,1-2. 26,13 notes
Winterborne Farringdon	26,13 note
Winterborne Herringston	26,13 note
Winterborne Houghton	36,3. 55,17. 56,28 notes
'Winterborne Huntingdon'	17,1. 57,3 notes
Winterborne Kingston	55,1. 56,6;60 notes
Winterborne Monkton	58,2 note
Winterborne Muston	26,13. 40,4 notes
'Winterborne Nicholston'	26,13 note
'Winterborne Phelpston'	26,13 note
Winterborne Steepleton	56,10 note
Winterborne Stickland	22,1 note
Winterborne Tomson	40,4 note
Winterborne Whitechurch	12,11. 26,13. 46,1. 55,1 notes
Winterborne Zelston	1,6 note

MAPS AND MAP KEYS

For reasons explained at the end of the Appendix, Dorset places are mapped in the 'modern' Hundreds that survived into the 19th century. On the maps and in the map keys detached parts of Hundreds are distinguished by letters (a, b, c, etc.) after the figure for the Hundred. Where possible, single detached places are directed by an arrow to the main body of their Hundred and numbered with it.

The Dorset Hundreds, with the modern name and the number of the corresponding Tax Return Hundreds (see the Appendix) are as follows:

1 Sherborne (xxxiv Sherborne)
2 Brownshall (xxviii Brownshall)
3 Sturminster Newton (xxi Newton)
4 Gillingham and Redlane (xxvii Gillingham and xxxv Farrington)
5 Sixpenny Handley (xx Handley and xxiv Sixpenny)
6 Cranborne (v *Albretesberga* and vi Badbury (part) and vii *Canendona* (part) and xxii *Langeberga* (part))
7 Yetminster (i Yetminster)
8 Buckland Newton (xxxvi Buckland)
9 Pimperne (xxii *Langeberga* (part) and xxv *Hunesberga* and xxvi Pimperne)
10 Knowlton (xxiii Knowlton)
11 Whitchurch Canonicorum (ii Whitchurch)
12 Beaminster (xxii Beaminster and xiii 'Redhone')
13 Tollerford (xiv Tollerford and xxxviii Frampton (part))
14 Cerne, Totcombe and Modbury (ix 'Stone' and xxxiii Modbury)
15 Whiteway (xi Hilton)
16 Combsditch (xvi Combsditch)
17 Badbury (vi Badbury (part) and vii *Canendona* (part))
18 Godderthorn (x Godderthorn and xxxix Loders)
19 Eggardon (iv Eggardon)
20 St. George (xxxii Dorchester and xxxviii Frampton (part))
21 Puddletown (viii Puddletown)
22 Bere and Barrow (xv Bere (part))
23 Loosebarrow (xviii Charborough)
24 Cogdean (xvii Cogdean)
25 Uggescombe (iii Uggescombe)
26 Cullifordtree (xxxvii Cullifordtree)
27 Winfrith (xv Bere (part) and xxx Winfrith and xxxi 'Chilbury')
28 Hasler (xxix Hasler)
29 Rowbarrow (xix Ailwood)

Apart from dots, the following symbols indicate places on the maps:

o A place in another county in 1086, all except Milborne Port (S 3) being later transferred to Dorset (see Introductory Note 3 on the County Boundary).

+ Places that are detachments of distant Hundreds or members of a Hundred of recent creation. They are mapped here for convenience in a geographically appropriate Hundred. Such places are marked with a cross in the Map Keys and are discussed in the Appendix. Places starred in the Map Keys are tithings of another Hundred (see Tithings note in the Appendix). In both cases, the bracketed figure or letter is that of their actual Hundred. Hundreds of recent creation are Barrow (B), Monkton Up Wimborne (M), Rushmore (R) and Wimborne St. Giles (W).

County names in brackets after a place-name in the Map Keys are those of the modern (pre-April 1974) counties to which places that were in Dorset in 1086 were subsequently transferred.

The Dorset Hundreds are numbered from west to east working southwards on the Maps and within each Hundred places are numbered alphabetically.

The County Boundary is marked on the maps by thick lines, continuous for 1086, broken where uncertain, dotted for the modern pre-1974 boundary. Hundred boundaries are marked by thin lines, broken where uncertain.

In 1086 Dorset contained an outlying part of Somerset (Holwell) and itself had an outlying portion (Stockland). The former was transferred to Dorset and the latter to Devon in the last century.

National Grid 10-kilometre squares are shown on the map borders. Each four-figure square covers 1 square kilometre or 247 acres, approximately 2 hides at 120 acres to the hide.

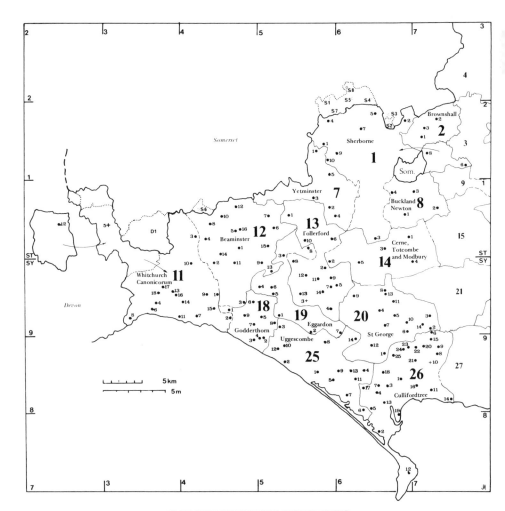

DORSET WESTERN HUNDREDS

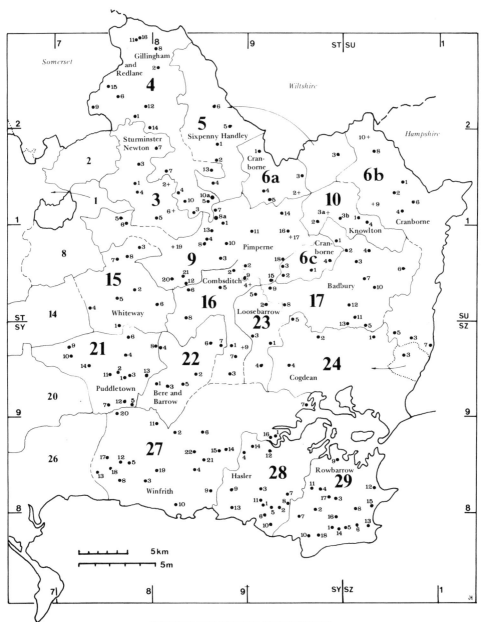

DORSET EASTERN HUNDREDS

TECHNICAL TERMS

Many words meaning measurements have to be transliterated. But translation may not dodge other problems by the use of obsolete or made-up words which do not exist in modern English. The translations here used are given in italics. They cannot be exact; they aim at the nearest modern equivalent.

ARPENT. A French measure of uncertain size, usually applied to vineyards in DB (see 49,12 General Notes). *arpent*

BORDARIUS. Cultivator of inferior status, usually with a little land; see 1,1 General Notes. *smallholder*

CARUCA. A plough, with the oxen that pulled it, usually reckoned as 8; see 49,13 General Notes. *plough*

CARUCATA. Normally the equivalent of a *hide* in former Danish areas, but elsewhere, especially in the south-west counties, the equivalent of 'land for *y* ploughs'; see 2,6 General Notes. *carucate*

CENSORES. People who pay in tribute, rent-payers; see 16,1 General Notes. *tributaries*

COLIBERTUS. A continental term, rendering OE *(ge)bur*; a former slave, sometimes holding land and ploughs and rendering dues; see 1,2 General Notes. *freedman*

COSCET, COSCEZ. A cultivator who lived in a cottage; see 1,8 General Notes. *Cottager*

COTARIUS. Inhabitant of a *cote*, cottage, often without land; see 1,2 General Notes. *cottager*

DOMINICUS. Belonging to a lord or lordship. *lordship* or *household* (adjs.)

DOMINIUM. The mastery or dominion of a lord (*dominus*), including ploughs, land, men, villages, etc., reserved for the lord's use; often concentrated in a *home farm* or demesne, a 'Manor Farm' or 'Lordship Farm'. *lordship*

FEUDUM. Continental variant of *feuum*, not used in England before 1086; either a landholder's holding or land held by a special grant. *Holding*

FIRMA. Old English *feorm*, provisions due to the King or lord (see 1,2 General Notes); a fixed sum paid in place of these and of other miscellaneous dues. See 1,9 Exon. Notes. *revenue*

GABLUM. Old English *gafol*, tribute or tax to the King or lord. *tribute*

GELDUM. The principal royal tax, originally levied during the Danish wars, normally at an equal number of pence on each *hide* of land. *tax*

HIDA. A unit of land measurement, generally reckoned at 120 acres, but often different in practice; a measure of tax liability, often differing in number from the hides actually cultivated; see B 1 General Notes. *hide*

HONOR. Equivalent to *feudum*, Holding. *Honour*

HUNDREDUM. A district within a Shire, whose assembly of notables and village representatives usually met about once a month. *Hundred*

LEUGA. A measure of length, usually of woodland and pasture, generally reckoned at a mile and a half, possibly shorter; see 1,2 General Notes. *league*

PERTICA. A measure of length 5½ yards, a 40th of a furlong; see 11,6 General Notes. *perch*

PREPOSITUS. Old English *gerefa*, a royal officer. *reeve*

QUARENTINA, QUADRAGENARIA. A subdivision of the league; see 1,1 General Notes. *furlong*

r. Marginal abbreviation for *require*, 'enquire', occurring when the scribe has omitted some information.

RUSTICUS. Probably a less prosperous villager; see Exon. Notes to 11,12 and 55,24. *countryman*

SEXTARIUM. A liquid or dry measure of uncertain size, reckoned at 32 oz. for honey; see 12,12 General Notes. *sester*

TAINUS, TEGNUS. Person holding land from the King by special grant; formerly used of the King's ministers and military companions. *thane*

T.R.E. *tempore regis Edwardi*, in King Edward's time. *before 1066*

T.R.W. *tempore regis Willelmi*, in King William's time. *after 1066*

VILLA. Translating Old English *tun*, 'town'. The later distinction between a small *village* and a large *town* was not yet in use in 1086. *village* or *town*

VILLANUS. Member of a *villa*, usually with more land than a *bordarius*. See the Introduction to the Exon. Notes on Exon.'s use of *villani* as a comprehensive term to cover most classes of population in a village. *villager*

VIRGA. A measure of uncertain length; see 11,6 General Notes. *'rod'*

VIRGATA. An areal measure, a fraction of a hide, usually a quarter, notionally 30 acres. *virgate*